THE ART OF READING ART

This book is dedicated to my Dad:
the man who taught me how to fight for
my dreams. The first person in my corner
every time, and the last to leave it.

MATTHEW OLIVIER

THE ART OF READING ART

UNDERSTANDING WHAT MAKES GREAT ART GREAT

Smith Street Books

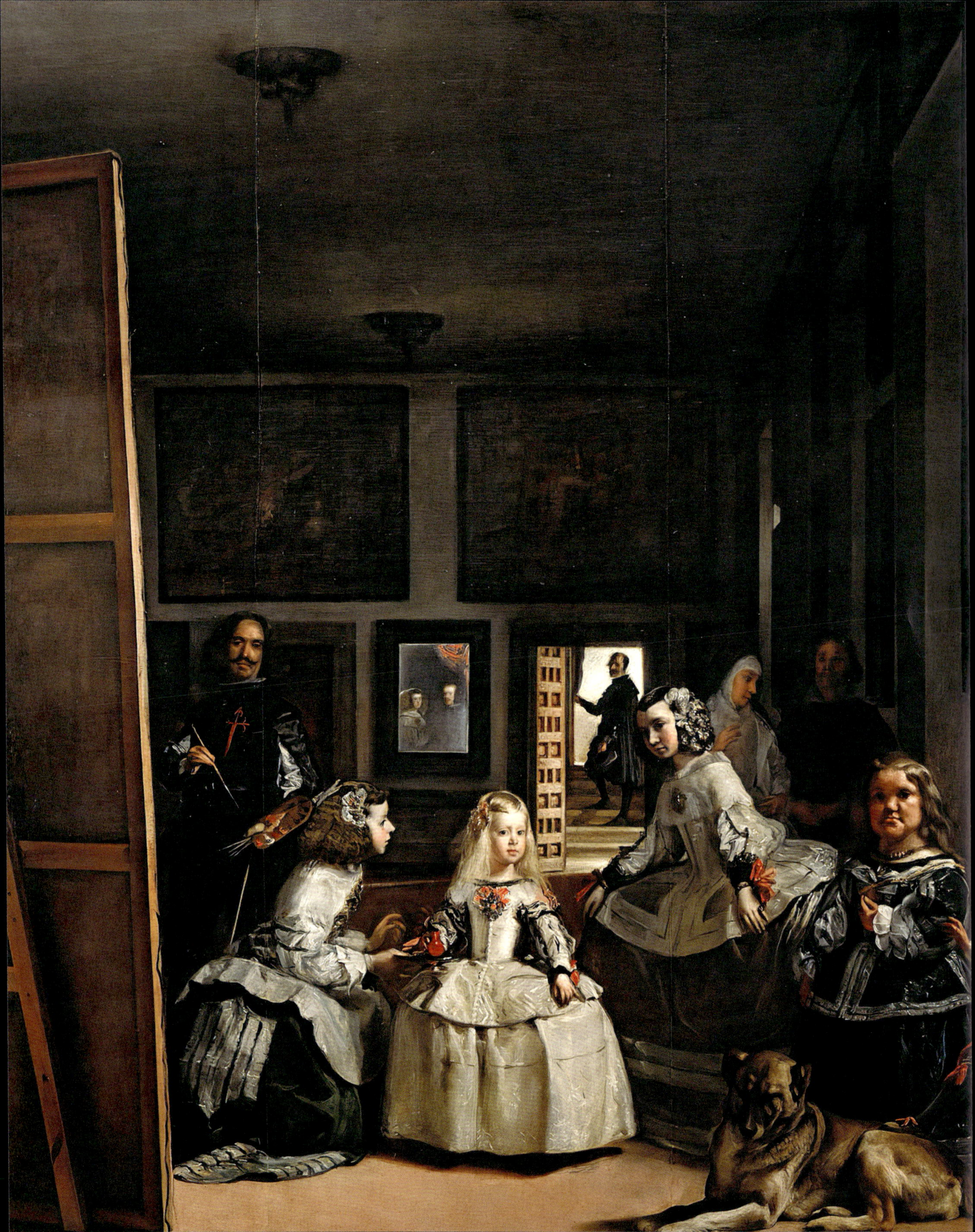

CONTENTS

Introduction 6

Revenge 12

The Art of Tension 24

Love Letters 34

Portraits 62

Insane Details 96

More than Meets the Eye 132

Politics and Propaganda 162

The Lonely World of Edward Hopper 202

Masters of Genre 210

Composition 226

Great Ideas 248

Visual Index 266

About the Author 278

INTRODUCTION

"Matthew, how do I read a painting?"

It is a question that I have spent the better part of the last decade thinking about, and in truth, there isn't a correct answer. People look at art for entirely different reasons. Some people like a pretty image, others enjoy the complex life of an artwork. Some people have a general interest in the process of painting, and others just enjoy a good story. For my part, I approach art as a language.

I remember the first time that I ever visited an art museum, long before I had decided that I wanted to be a painter. I didn't know what the hell to do, as I walked around. I remember thinking to myself, *Am I supposed to cry?* as I looked at one of Warhol's *Campbell's Soup Cans*. I didn't know what it meant, let alone what I was looking at. The gravity of Warhol's artistic contributions was completely lost on the teenager who had decided to visit a museum that day to see what happened. I remember "reading" all the little plaques beside the paintings, but I don't think I retained a single word. I was *pretending* to be interested. At this point, art was just this thing. It was kind of boring, and the cursory information on the plaques didn't help.

It would be years until I'd ever step back into a museum, and even longer until I'd pick up a paintbrush, which is when my journey into art actually started. Not in a European museum, and not online, not in a classroom, but in a warehouse on a cold winter night, all on my own, with a box of cheap acrylic paints and a tiny canvas. I will never forget the feeling of spattering colors onto the fabric. It was an unorganized, uncontrolled mess, and it was the single greatest feeling I had ever had, like opening my eyes for the very first time. In that moment, nothing else mattered.

I went back to the warehouse every single night after that. I sucked, but I didn't give a damn. It was my little secret that consumed me. I wanted to get back and try something new, try something bigger. Canvas after canvas, painting after painting, and I was free from this mediocre life that I had carved out for myself. Actually, it made that life kind of great. I was starting to find a voice, and starting to find the something that was uniquely my own instead of just blurring in with the rest of the world.

After many nights and many attempts, I started to run out of room in the warehouse. As it turns out, canvases take up a lot of space. What the hell was I going to do now? I didn't want to destroy the paintings, and I didn't really want to give them away, but eventually, they would need to go *somewhere* because I wanted to keep making more. So, after much deliberation, I figured, *let me share one on social media and see what happens*. What a terrifying thing to do—up until this point, outside of my parents, nobody knew that I was painting. But space was running out, so I posted one online.

Sold. I couldn't believe it. The very first painting that I ever shared, and somebody wanted it. $250 for my miniature mess of colors, a smiley face carved into the middle—the sky opened. It was, quite possibly, the best feeling I'd ever had. So, I did it again. SOLD. And the next one, SOLD. And the next, SOLD! *I am invincible*. This nightly hobby, my little secret, turned into a money-making machine (a small one, albeit) and I had a newfound validation from others that, at the very least, there was something about my work that was good enough for them to want it—imagine if I put more time into improving? *But, my god, what does that even look like?*

I'd never gone to art school. I didn't know any artists. I didn't know what to search, or what books to read, or what I should study, until a friend invited me to tag along to a gallery he'd helped build for an art collector. While wandering past the hundreds of paintings, I found myself staring at a work by Helen Frankenthaler. "You know Matthew, she was one of the most technically gifted artists in the world, but you wouldn't know it by looking at her work."

I didn't understand what my gallery chaperone meant. "When you say technical, what do you mean?"

"In order for an abstract artist to bend the rules, they need to know the rules. The very best of them, know all of them. The artists in this building were probably some of the most knowledgeable artists in the history of art, and that's why they are all so great."

It clicked, right there in that room, right in front of that painting, thanks to my chaperone passing an idea down as casually as holding a door open. I knew exactly what I had to do. If I was going to be good, and I mean really good, I needed to know everything there was to know about art. This wasn't a matter of what to study—I needed to study everything, right now.

I went home, ordered my first art book, and spent the rest of the night looking at works by Picasso, and Monet, and everyone under the sun. I had a blank slate, and I needed to fill it as fast as possible. Every day, I'd explore another bit of art history until my brain turned to mush. Once that happened, I'd go to bed and repeat.

So what did all that research teach me about how to read a painting?

Well, "how" is the wrong starting place. Instead, your first question should be, Why should I read a painting? And to that, I have an answer. Painting is a puzzle, and the artist's job is to solve it. Studying art is a way to see how an artist approaches getting his or her answer, and when you understand how they went about it, it will almost certainly inform how you might.

Imagine, for instance, that an artist wants to convey a moment of deep inner thought. Well, how could they achieve that? Is the transmission of the mind, from artist to audience, achieved through facial expression? Is it a cause and effect of how a scene is lit? Is inner thought expressed more easily through cropping a subject intensely? There are so many possibilities, and what an artist chooses is, in essence, how they solve the puzzle of art-making.

Now, you don't need to be a painter to learn to read a painting, but looking at art every day addressed a very real need for me. I asked questions like Why did Caravaggio use chiaroscuro? And that would open up an entire can of worms. It would lead me to study the history of the Church, and how Caravaggio fit into papal programming in the late 1500s. I'd ask, Who inspired Picasso to paint this way? And I'd go on to learn about his rivalry with Matisse, and that he was an admirer of Cézanne. The list really goes on. Every line of question would lead to an entire ocean of questions, and I needed to have an answer for everything, which meant I spent a lot of time looking at everything all at once. That is, until I saw a painting by Jan Steen.

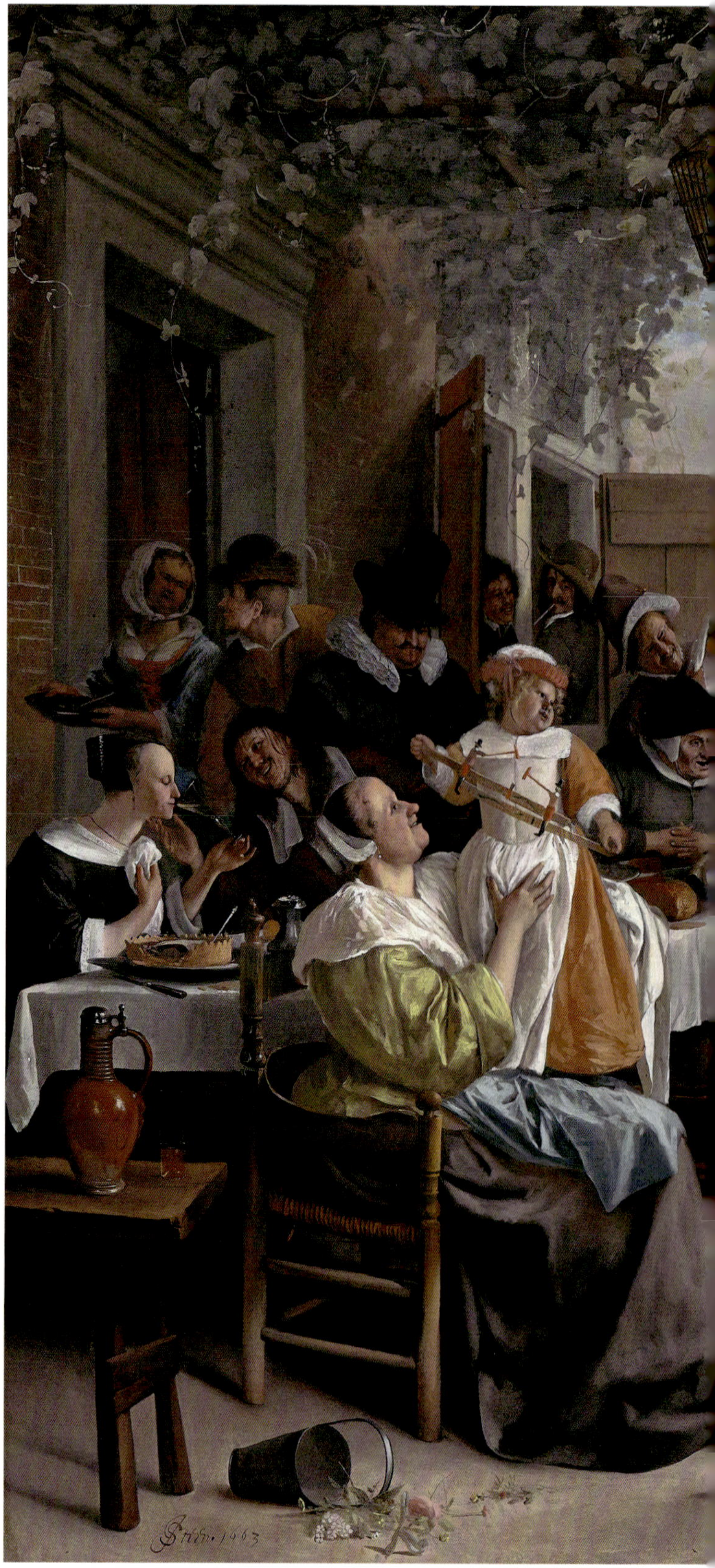

The Dancing Couple, Jan Steen, 1663

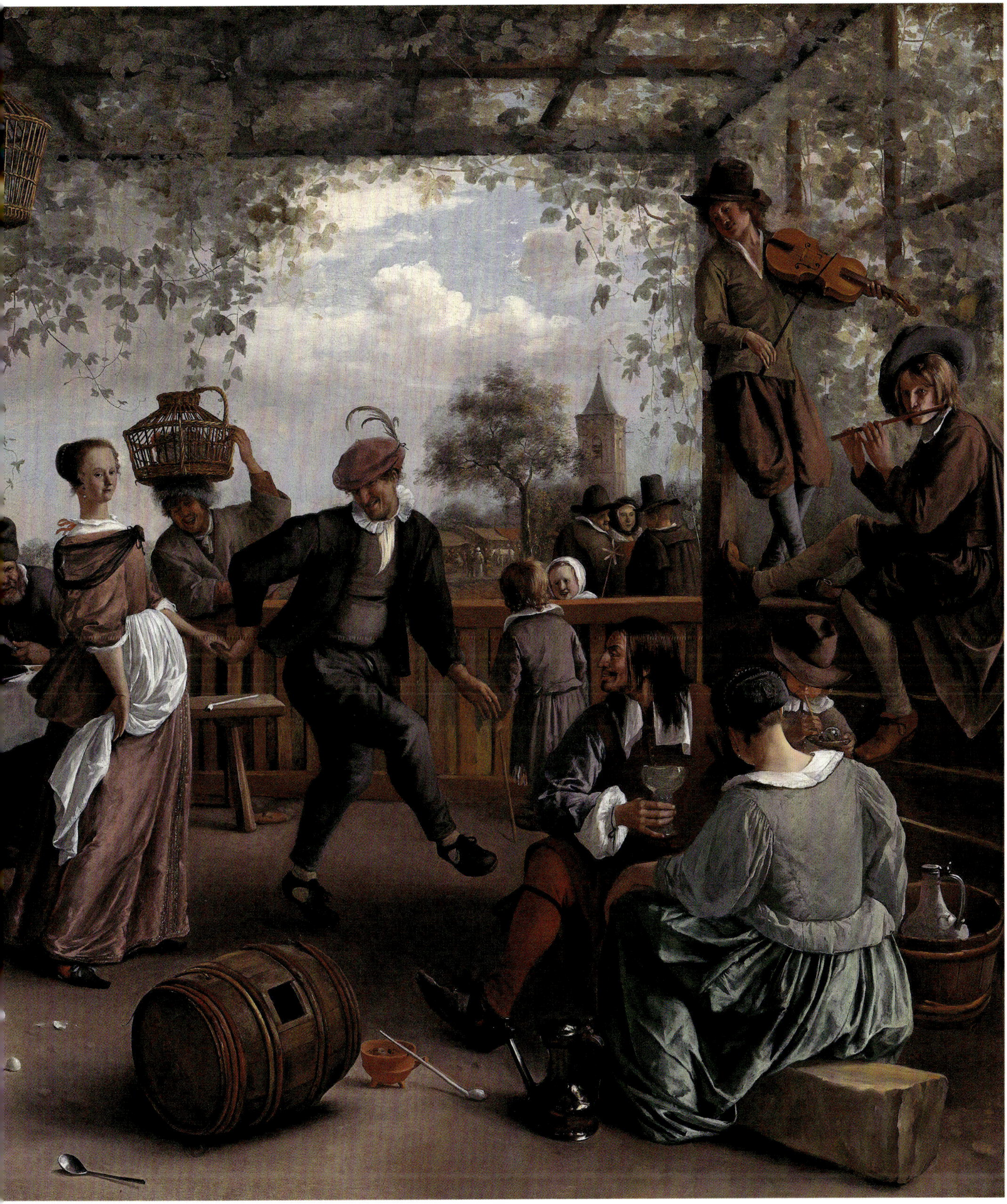

The Dancing Couple

Jan Steen, 1663

What a wonderful party this is. And in a painting filled with so many happy partygoers, it's no wonder that our plump friend in black isn't alone in the excitement. There are patrons enjoying wine and pie, and flirtatious gazes to go around. There is meat, and bread, and toys, and bubbles, new friends and old friends, and hours upon hours of conversation. Hell, there is even a guy with a chicken on his head. And at the center of it all is a couple dancing.

What a lovely place to enjoy good company and cheerful music, under the cover of pretty vines. And that, my friends, is exactly what makes this painting by Steen a triumph. Where most artists would lean into the raw fundamentals of painting (color, values, forms, perspectives, etc.) to capture normal people, the Dutch Master ingeniously leans into something else entirely: the five senses. Touch, smell, taste, sight, sound.

By strategically employing these across his composition, the artist transforms the seventeenth-century scene into something very relatable. Have a look at the painting again. Ask yourself, *What's happening here?* At the center of it all a couple dances to music that seems to flood the air, casting smiles from ear to ear; it's light and fun and *obvious*, right? While we don't know what the musicians are playing, you get the sense that it's cheerful and that everyone gathered is affected. You can also probably hear the bubbles being blown by the young boy in the right bottom corner, and the chattering of voices. And even though the people behind the fence are a little distant, and we can't make out exactly what it is that they're discussing, we feel inclined to *listen in* while we watch the picture's central action: the couple dancing.

Laughter: a reply to cheeky facial expressions and sly dance moves. It's exciting to see people excited, whether we're as young as the child standing on her mother's lap, or older and no longer capable. Steen feeds us with a bounty of food and wine, and we can almost taste it all. You're suddenly hungry and curious. You can smell it too: the drinks, the meat, the vines, the tobacco. A sensory explosion, and he reins it all in with the delicacy of a pair of dancers' hands, which serve as the focal point of the entire picture.

Touch: skin to skin. A hand on a chin and another on clothes. On a toy. On a flute, a bowl, a knife, a glass, and we get it. We just get it. A perfect painting of a perfect party. When I saw it for the first time, I never wanted to look away.

The Dancing Couple stuck with me, because every time I'd studied a painting, I'd tried to unpack it by searching for hundreds of details, picking apart every aspect of its fundamentals. But Steen solves the *messaging* of this artwork by simply playing with your senses. And that's just it. Painting doesn't need to be over complicated: It just needs to be focused. You, looking at a painting, also don't need to make it overly complicated. You just need to focus your observation. After viewing this work, my approach to considering art dramatically changed. Now, when I look at a painting, I focus on one thing and one thing alone. And while that *one thing* changes from painting to painting, the narrowness of my focus stays the same. Now back to your original question.

How do you read a painting?

My answer is, simple. We don't need to make a mess of a masterpiece. Pick one focus. Think about it from every possible angle, and then move on. And in the process of simplifying art, and looking at paintings as a series of stories, or motifs, or objects, or whatever it is that we pick as our lens, let's make the art that we're exploring fun. Reading art is supposed to be fun. If it's not, why the hell would we ever do it to begin with?

Throughout the course of this book, I'm going to show you exactly how it is that I see paintings. I want you to get the exact same joy that I get, every single time I walk into a museum, or an art gallery, or my studio, because for me, art is the best thing that has ever happened, and I want it to be that for you too.

Now, remember what I touched on earlier: Everyone sees art in their own way, because art has a unique role to play in everyone's life. Just because I have an opinion on something, it doesn't mean that it's the right opinion, and just because someone else sees it differently, it doesn't mean they're wrong. Our differences are the things that make us beautiful, and those differences make the world of art a spectacular place, so let's give every idea a fair shake.

I hope that you enjoy this book. I hope that it lights a flame in you. It has been the greatest pleasure of my life to tell these stories, and to share my love for art with you. Now let's dive into the good stuff, and I will see you on the other side.

REVENGE

What is the greatest act of revenge in the history of art? As you can probably imagine, in a timeline that spans from antiquity to the modern day, across the careers of millions of artists and the creation of tens of millions of artworks, there are a few options to pick from.

"But Matthew, what's the best one?"

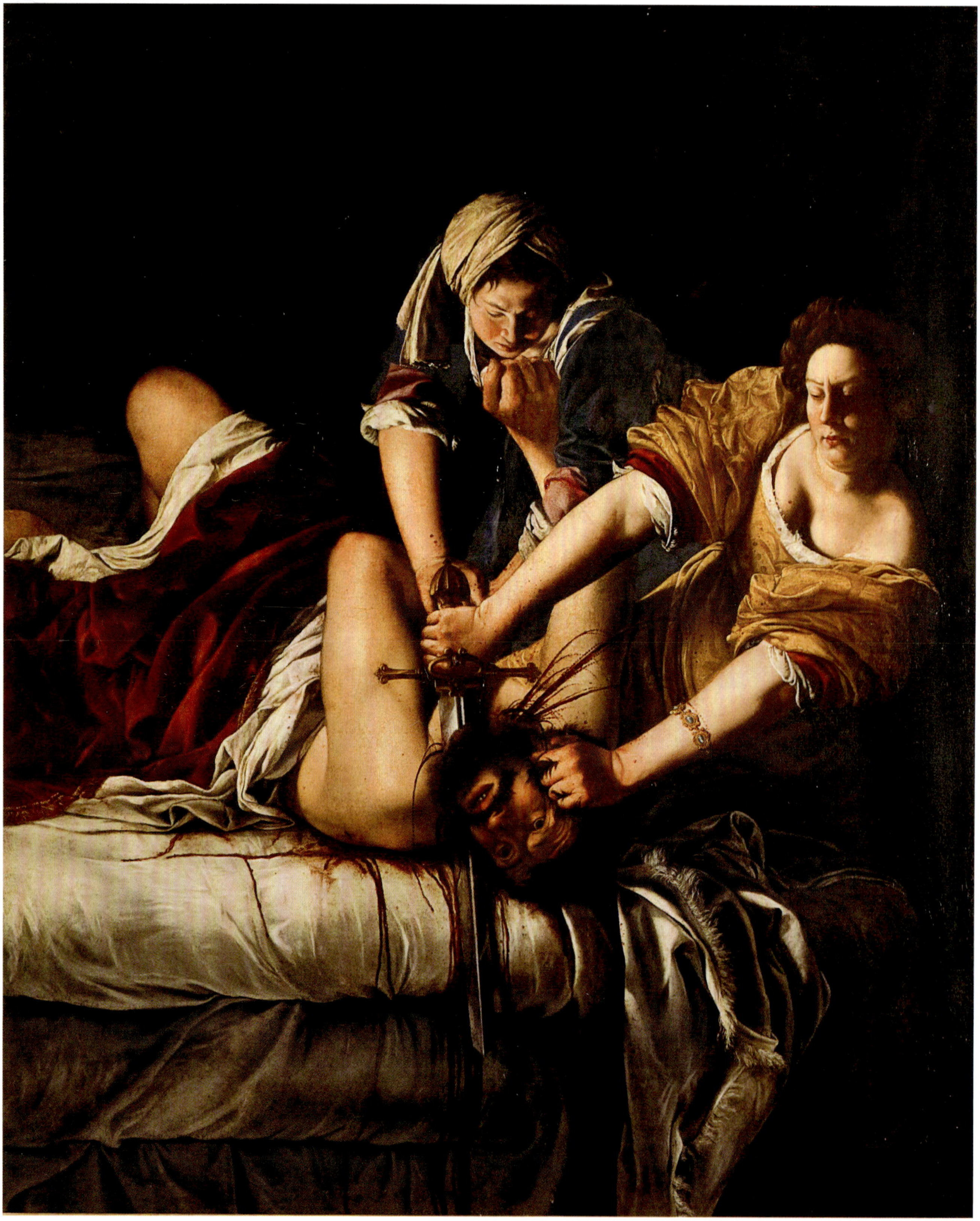

Judith Beheading Holofernes

Artemisia Gentileschi, 1620

I have always been drawn to the story of Artemisia Gentileschi and her painting of Judith slaying Holofernes. Oh yes, a masterpiece, no doubt, of classical revenge and redemption.

At the age of 17, in the comfort of her home, Gentileschi was assaulted by her art teacher, and father's friend, Agostino Tassi. And, if that isn't terrible enough, a friend who was present during the act did nothing at all to help. But the story of Gentileschi's humiliation doesn't end just yet, because upon discovering the rape, Gentileschi's father demanded that Tassi marry his daughter. This meant that the young painter, against her will, would be forced to live with and bed the man who assaulted her, at his own leisure. That is, of course, until Tassi decided that he was done with the arrangement, and backed out of the marriage entirely. Artemisia's father, who decided that *now* would be the right time to feel outraged, took Tassi to court and saw him sentenced to two years in prison for the assault. Justice served, right? Not yet. Because in what might be the century's most badass act of revenge, Artemisia Gentileschi canonized Tassi into the "Piece of Shit Hall of Fame" for the rest of time in this work, inspired by an earlier painting by Caravaggio.

Judith Beheading Holofernes

Caravaggio, c. 1598–1602

If you're familiar with the Baroque period, you'll recognize this painting. Compare it to Gentileschi's version and you'll see some major differences between the two.

The exact same biblical story, with the exact same characters, staged in two entirely different theaters. In one, we witness an execution in progress, and in the other, we witness the psychological repercussions of said execution. Gentileschi constructs a version of Judith and her maid who are fully committed to the act. Judith's sword is buried deep into the neck of Holofernes, and from here, there is no turning back. Gentileschi's version is a bloody mess as a byproduct of *intense* physical force, perfectly capturing the labor of violence.

In Caravaggio's, we see something else. Judith *hesitates*. She feels reluctant: tentative, as though she can't believe that she's about to commit a murder. There is something about this version that feels suspended, almost as if Judith lives on the edge between committing the act and running away. She quite literally leans back. Her expression, a cocktail of disgust and discomfort, is a far cry from Gentileschi's Judith, who is by all accounts an agent of death. She is a woman who is psychologically *invested* in the action. No revulsion, no recoil. She is stone cold, efficient, and focused on the task at hand. Her maid, too.

In Gentileschi's version, the maid is an accomplice, whereas in Caravaggio's, she is passive. Caravaggio theatrically puts the entire weight of the artwork's moral dilemma on the shoulders of Judith, while Gentileschi emphasizes a collective strength in numbers, which restrains Holofernes in his final moments of life. You can feel the weight of their bodies as the women overpower him, and I'm certain that Gentileschi wished she'd had the help of another in the moments when she felt completely powerless. Yet, here, in this painting, she's in control. In the place of Judith, Gentileschi paints herself, and in the place of Holofernes, she paints Tassi—and now the scene reads as a righteous vengeance. There are no questions as to who deserves power in the moment, and there is no question who will come out the victor. And the rest, my friends, is history.

"Wow, what a woman!"

She was. And while the tale of Artemesia's revenge is one of the great stories in the history of art, there is another that you might have never heard, even if you've witnessed its enduring legacy: one that lives in the most unsuspecting place, committed by an unsuspecting person, that thousands upon thousands of people bear witness to every single day.

For this story, we'll need to rewind all the way back to 1504, when the ceiling of the Sistine Chapel sustained a crack that rendered the building unusable. The then Pope Julius II hired Piero Rosselli, a friend of Michelangelo, to remove the ceiling's existing artwork, effectively setting in motion a sequence of events that would revolutionize the art world forever.

Known as the warrior pope, Julius undertook an aggressive campaign to unite Italy under the Church during his papacy. An advocate for propaganda, he decided to rebuild Saint Peter's Basilica to symbolize the potency of his power. The full truth, however, is that he also needed a grander place to house his own tomb. And who better to design his grandiose freestanding mausoleum, that was set to feature 40 life-sized marble statues, than Italy's greatest prodigy? So, as Popes do, he summoned Michelangelo from Florence in the early half of 1505, and for a time, it looked like he was going to get what he wanted. That is, of course, until he and Michelangelo got into a heated argument, probably over creative control, and the artist escaped back to Florence.

Now, if you've made it this far in the story, you've probably guessed that Julius II was pissed. But despite his ego, he didn't have time to stew. Shortly after Michelangelo's escape, the Pope had another clever idea.

"Why don't I have the ceiling of the Sistine Chapel repainted? To make it the greatest piece of art the world has ever seen?" I imagine him saying to himself. But our Pope had a very obvious problem, which was that the man he had in mind for the job was long gone. So, he asked Rosselli to write a letter on his behalf to coax Michelangelo back to Rome.

After some back and forth, and some careful negotiating, the artist was convinced to return on the condition that he would have complete creative control. And finally, in 1508, Michelangelo's most ambitious project ever was underway. Over the span of four years, from 1508 to 1512, he would create what many would argue is the most impressive series of artworks that the world had ever seen.

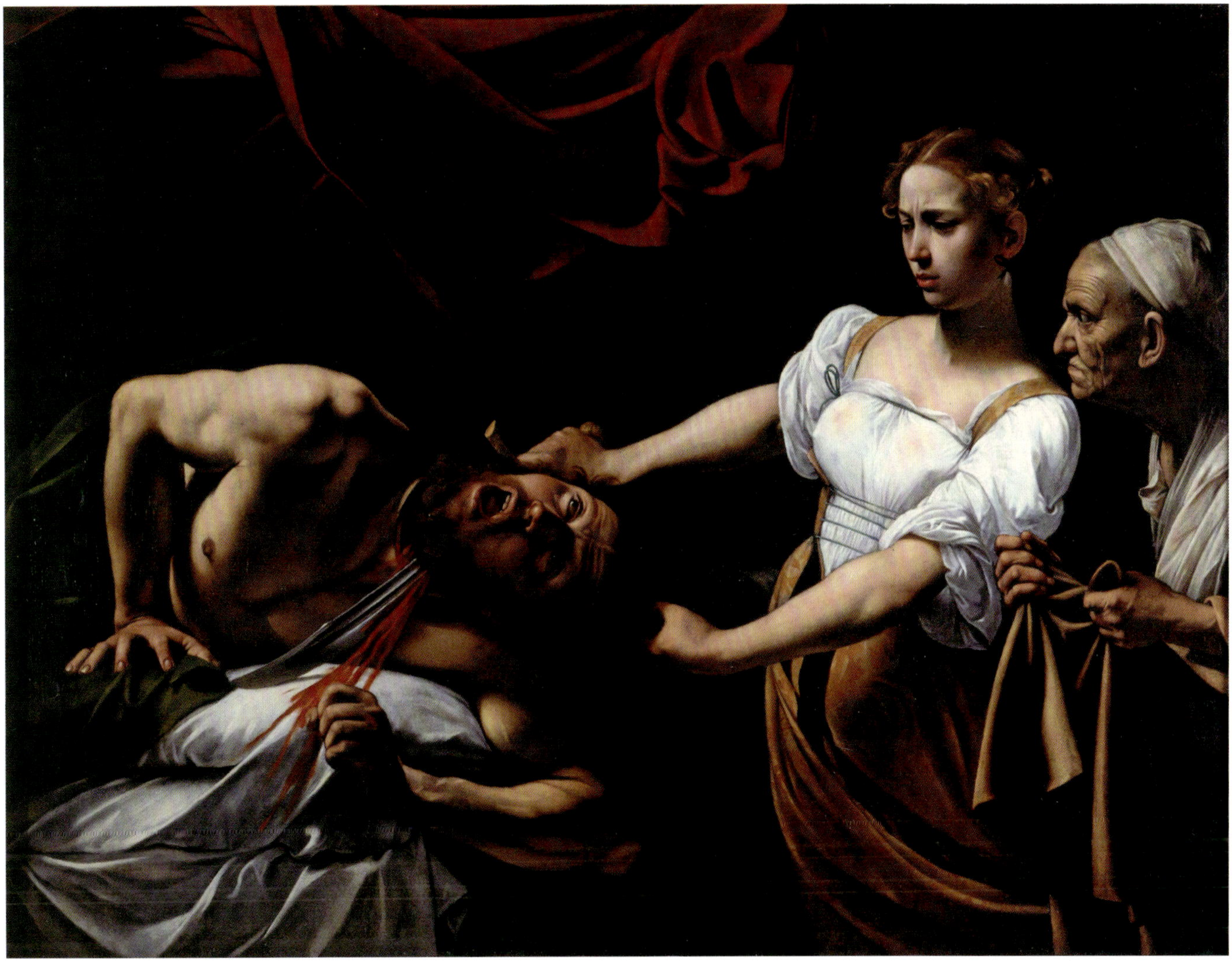

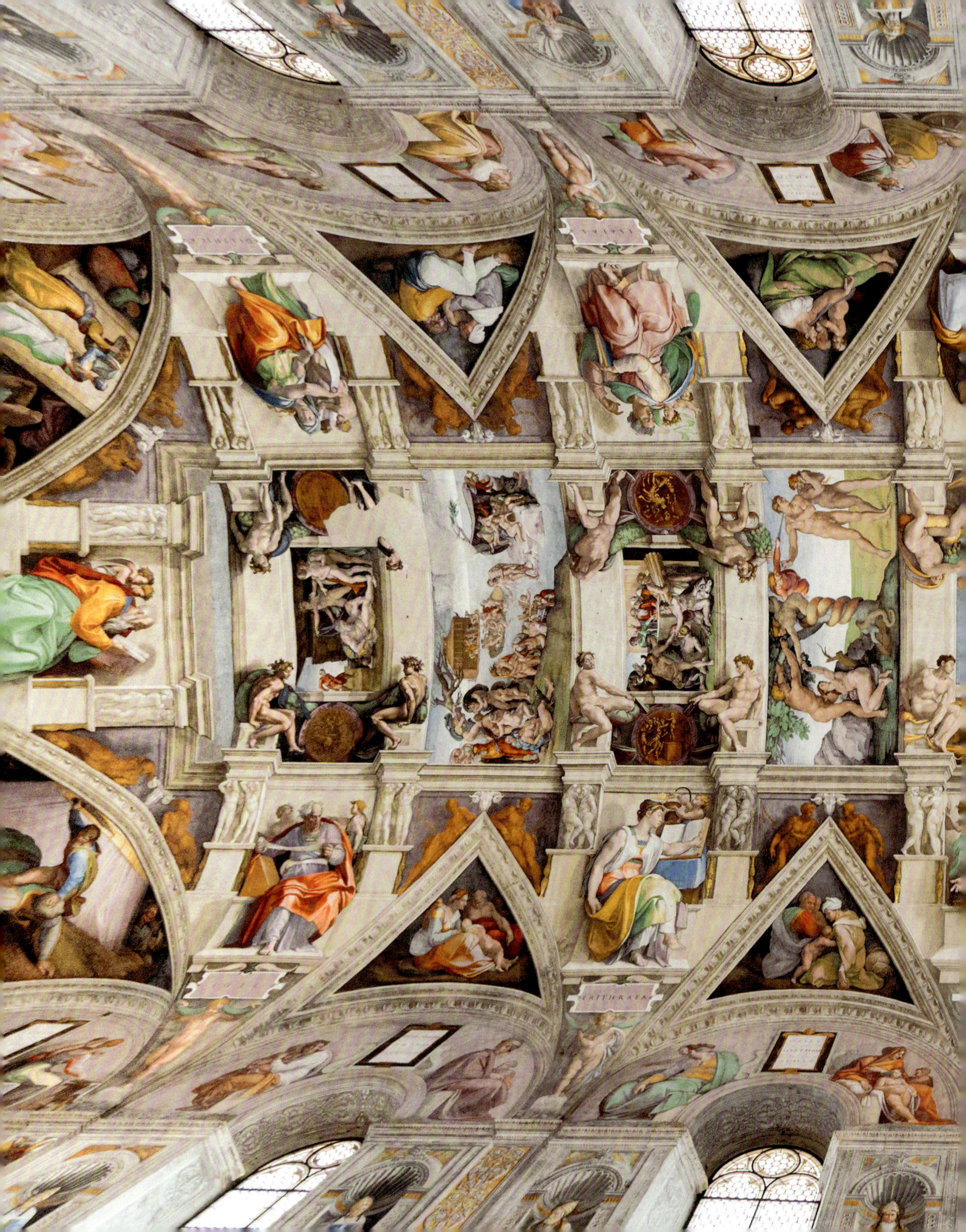
ERITHRAEA

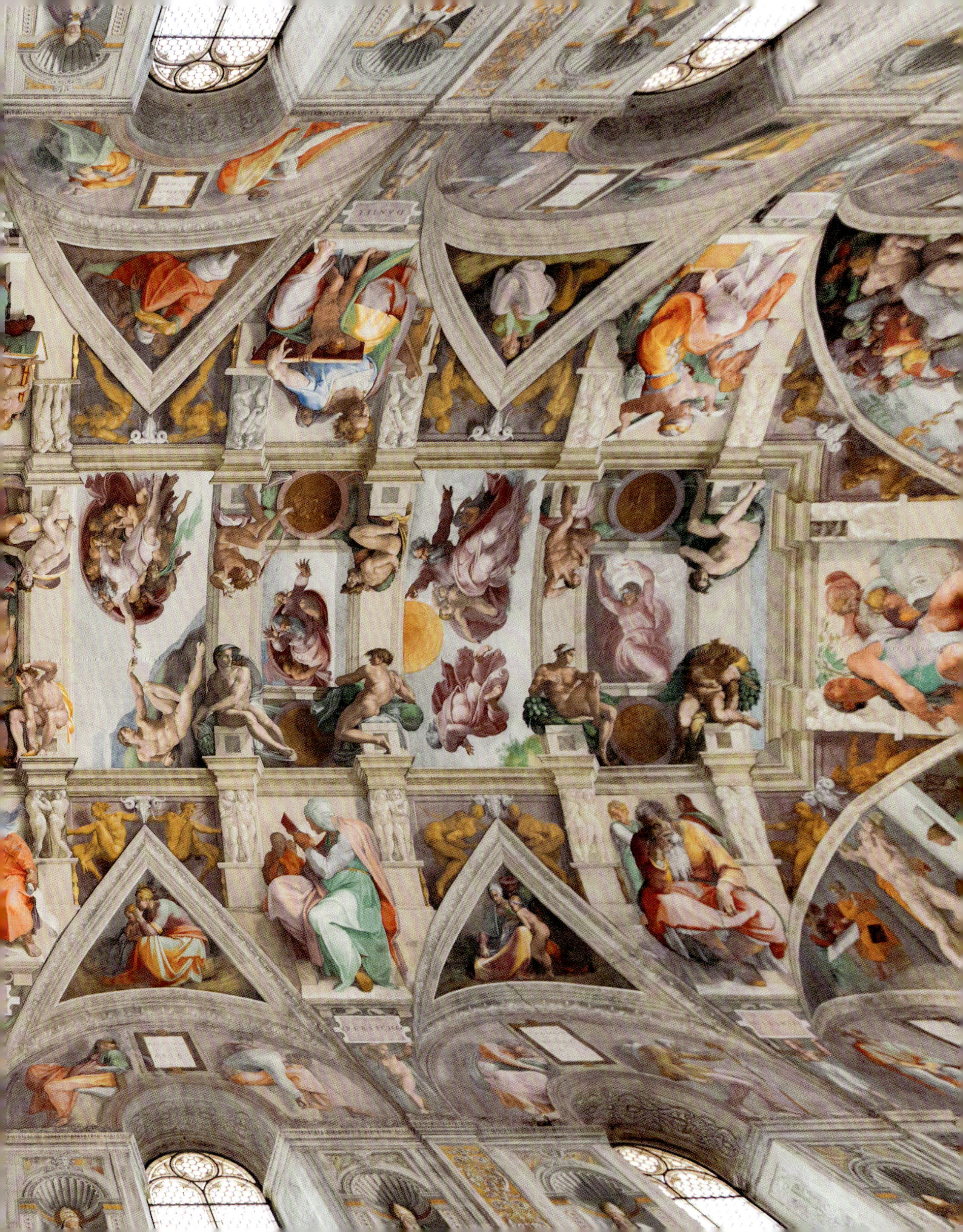

The Sistine Chapel ceiling and *The Creation of Adam*

Michelangelo, 1508–12

Nine giant panels depicting nine spectacular scenes from the Book of Genesis, surrounded by a range of other biblical figures and stories that break every notion of what is humanly possible at the highest levels of art-making. Michelangelo shows us perspective at a scale that we can hardly comprehend. He shows us composition and color and produces what is arguably one of the most recognizable pieces of art in history.

Neck flung back as you gaze toward the heavens in a room riddled with symbols and larger-than-life figures, a question often lingers: *Why aren't they touching?* Among the details the Italian master left us that are open to interpretation, including what looks to be a human brain around God, *The Creation of Adam*'s most poetic motif is at its center. God's finger is fully extended: perhaps a symbol of his omnipresence. Adam's hand, alternatively, is slightly coiled: a representation of choice, and one that tests the artwork's philosophical boundaries, because right before contact, Adam hesitates. Why?

Imagine for a second, what it would mean, to meet your maker. More so, what it would mean to swear an oath to him. Paradise in return for unwavering devotion, but at what cost?

Adam hesitates, while God doesn't. He's all powerful, but even still, there is something at stake for him too: the possibility of betrayal. This is a tension that can't possibly be represented outside of the split second before their oath is sealed. Michelangelo paints a finger extended by God, in contrast to a hand coiled by Adam, to show us that God has left us the option. He doesn't force us to accept him, but rather, bestows free will onto humanity, so that we might make the decision ourselves. A powerful idea, among many others … and Michelangelo paints it all in four years. Four tortuous years, after which he vowed to never paint again, which he followed through on until 1530, when he painted a small fresco.

"So basically he said, 'screw you' to the Pope. But how is that better than the Gentileschi story?"

Hang on, things are just about to get good. You see, 25 years after the ceiling was completed, Michelangelo was convinced to return to Rome by Pope Clement VII to paint one of the chapel's walls. And in a spectacular encore, he would create the staggeringly detailed 48 x 44 feet *The Last Judgment*.

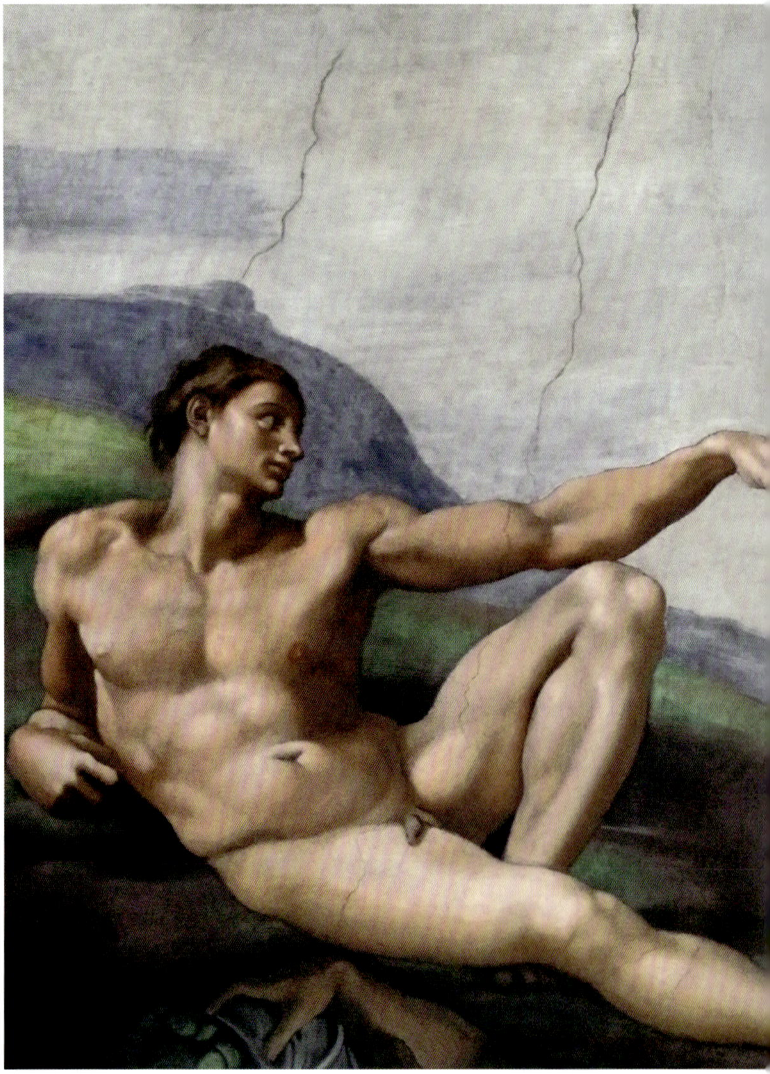

Pages 18–19: The Sistine Chapel ceiling

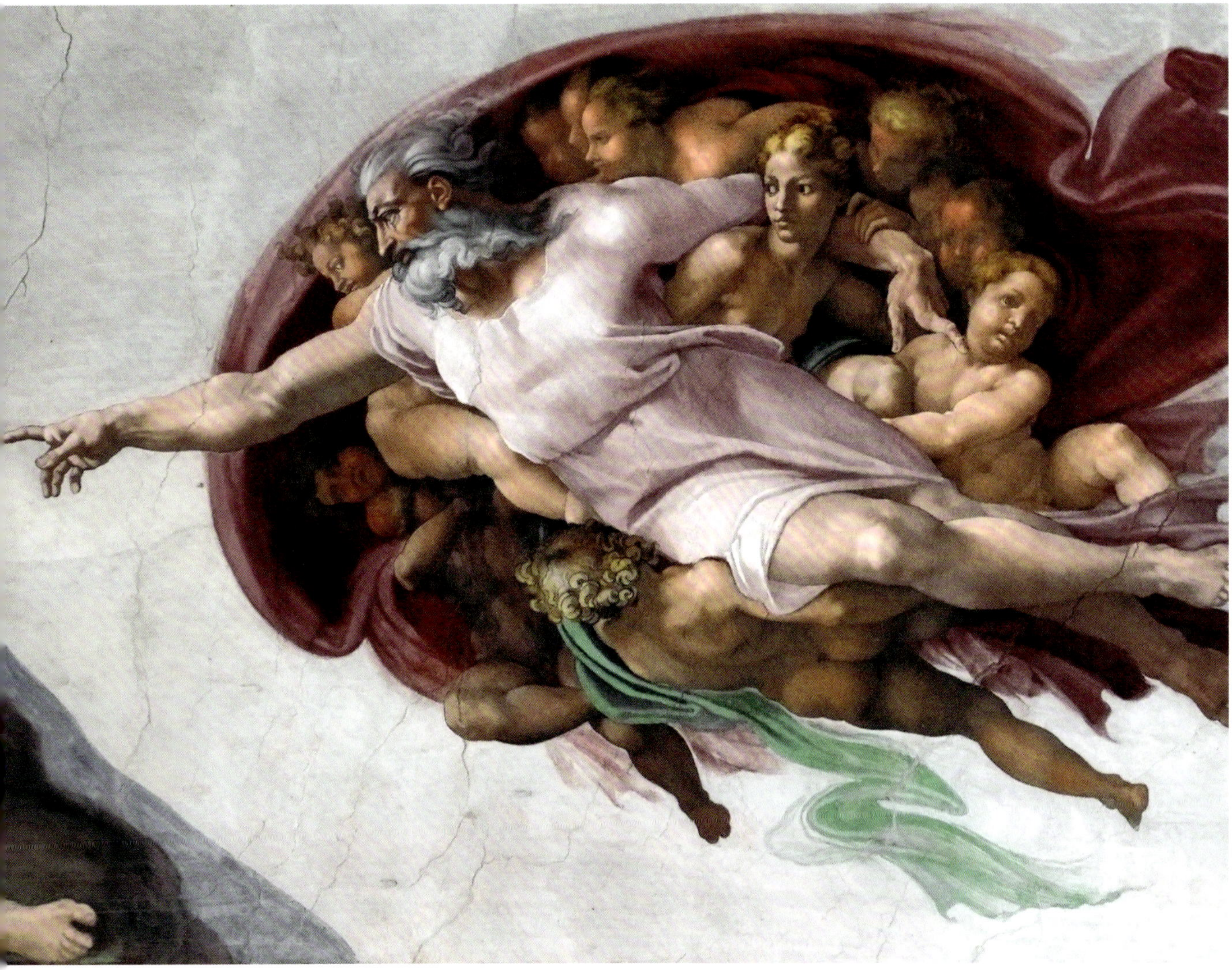

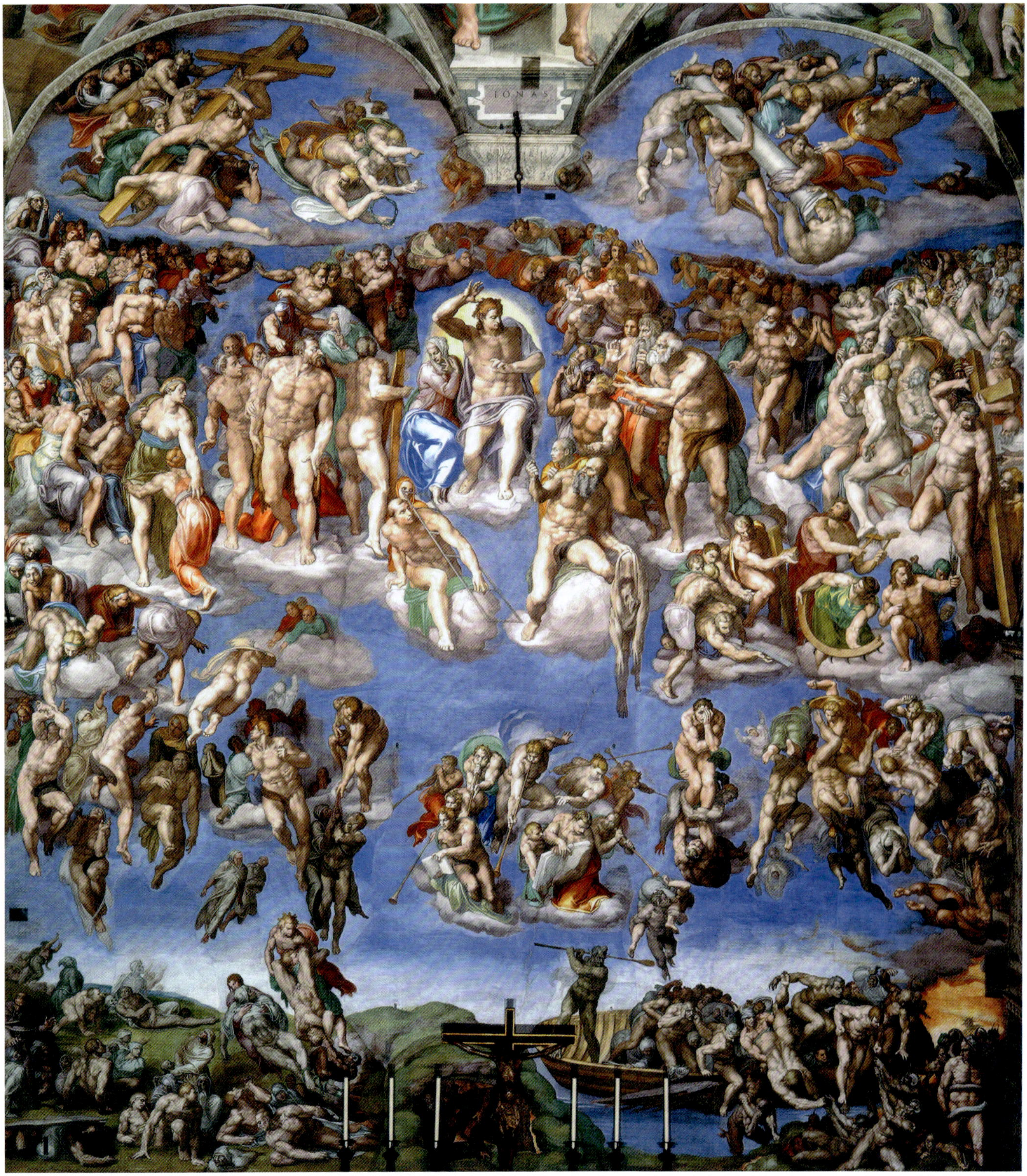

IONAS

The Last Judgment

Michelangelo, 1536–41

A giant fresco depicting the Second Coming of Christ and the final and eternal judgment of God on all of mankind. Three hundred anatomically extravagant nude characters, blending the worlds of the mythological and the mortal in a violent composition filled with biblical tales and cheeky Easter eggs, like Saint Bartholomew. He's just right of the center holding his flayed skin, which bears the face of Michelangelo, perhaps to suggest that his time with the Church left the artist as a shell of himself. On the left of the image, we have the ascension to heaven. In the center, we have Christ, the Virgin Mother, and the apostles, and on the right side, we have the descent to hell.

"Wow, this is incredible. Everyone must have loved it."

Well, not everyone. Nearing the fresco's completion, Biagio da Cesena, the papal master of ceremonies, popped into the chapel for a visit, and did the unthinkable. Not only did he throw a fit at the nudity on the wall, but he is said to have remarked that the artwork was both appalling and suited only for a brothel.

And that, my friends, was all it took.

It was the straw that finally broke the camel's back. In what would become arguably the most visible act of revenge in the history of art, Michelangelo would take out his rage like no artist ever really had. At the bottom-right corner of the fresco, guarding the portal to hell, is an image of Minos, the gatekeeper of the abyss, painted in the likeness of da Cesena, for everyone to see. And if that isn't humiliating enough, he sports a pair of donkey ears and is wrapped in the coil of a snake, who's biting the tip of his bit.

But wait, it gets even better. The papal master of ceremonies was so angry, he ran to the Pope and demanded that it be removed. And in a statement so gangster, it could be its own rap album, Pope Paul III is said to have told him, "My jurisdiction does not extend to hell, so the portrait must stay."

THE ART OF TENSION

What defines a masterpiece? It's a question I've yet to truly answer. The truth is, it's an impossible question, but there are many signs of an exceptional piece of art, in technique and in narrative. For my part, across all of the truly exceptional artworks that I've had the pleasure of reading, the ones that generate *tension* have always stood out from the rest, and there are few painters who achieve this more deftly than Sir John Everett Millais, through his arrangement of quiet acts. Context is certainly important to understanding his elaborate storytelling, but to better navigate his paintings' hallmark tension, it's often in the micro that we discover Millais's most potent propositions.

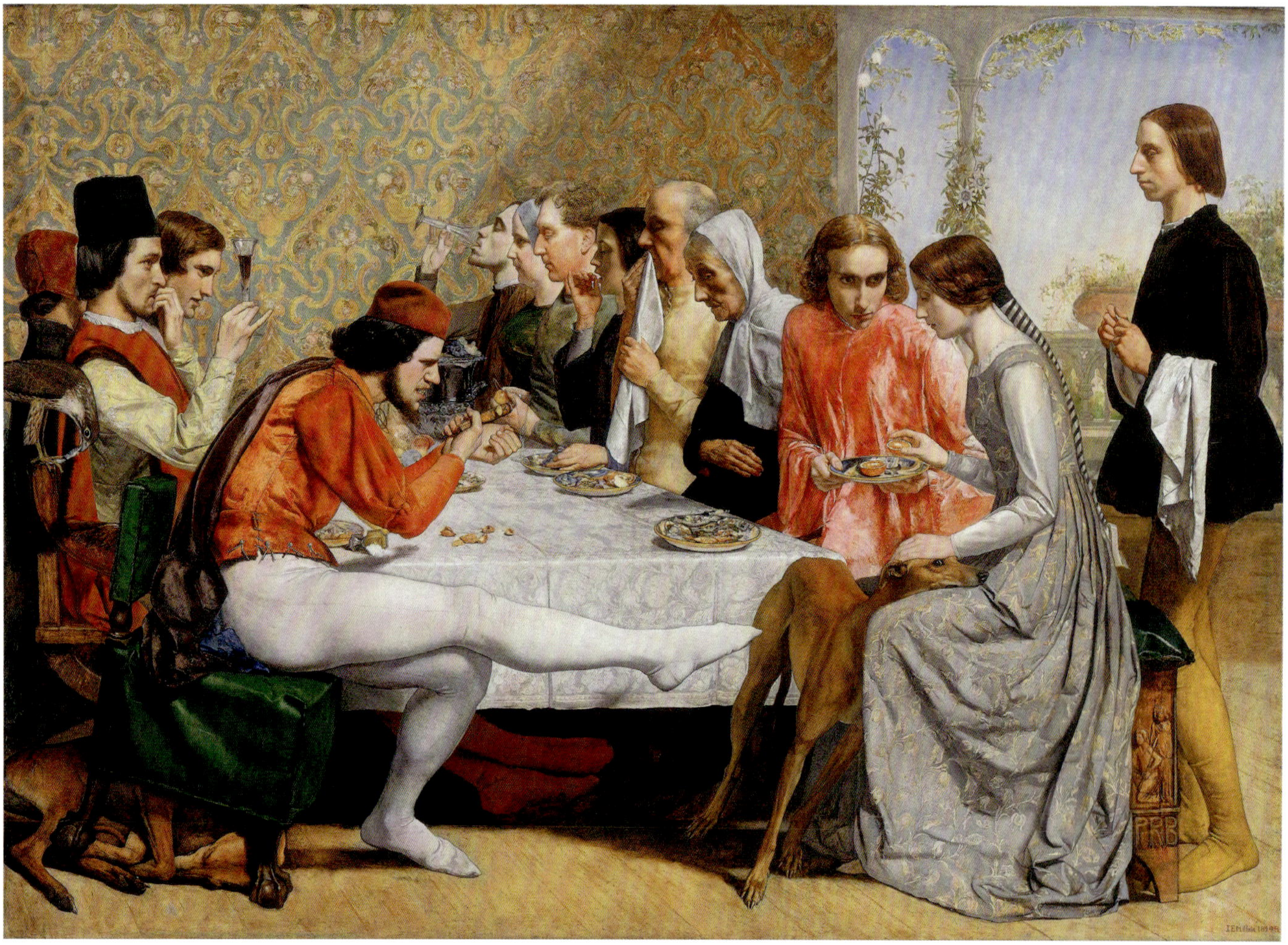

Isabella

John Everett Millais, 1849

Something odd is going on here, but I can't quite put my finger on it.

There's two dogs, a family having lunch, a server, food, wine or some sort of spirits, and a bird of prey, among a few other minor details. From the outside looking in, nothing seems out of place, right? But, you see, when considering that what we're looking at is, in fact, a painting by Millais, a founder of the Pre-Raphaelite Brotherhood (a group of painters known for their use of symbolism), you'll quickly realize that nothing is ever what it seems.

Have a close look at the woman in the foreground, on the right side of the table, dressed in grey. Her name is Isabella, and she is taking one half of a sliced blood orange from our second character, Lorenzo. And it is exactly at this point that Isabella's brothers, the gentlemen sitting on the opposite side of the table, catch on to the fact that there might be a little more happening than the sharing of an after-lunch snack.

"Well, what's the problem with that?"

Everything is the problem with that, because Isabella's brothers aren't just her brothers, but also, very wealthy medieval merchants who employ Lorenzo. And Lorenzo? Well, he's just… Lorenzo, who was invited to a casual family lunch. And while everyone else chomps away at their meals, her brothers, right there, are plotting to chomp off his head.

On the left of the image, on the side of murderous intentions, you'll notice a bird of prey playing with a feather. Is this a symbol, perhaps, for soothing one's predatory rage? It's awfully similar to one biting their nails, as they pretend to analyze a glass of digestive spirits. Or, pretending to smile, as they look out in disbelief. While some gestures of discomfort are subtle, not everyone can hold it in, as the brother in the foreground crushes a nut in a manner that can only be described as angry, kicking at the poor pup who had nothing to do with the sharing of a sliced orange at all. Oh, and the blood orange? A sweet after-lunch treat, yes, but also, a symbol in art for a decapitated head.

This painting is one of many examples of a great story inspiring another: a theme as old as time itself, and yet, there is nobody quite as good at it as Millais. In this example, he visually transcribes a story from Giovanni Boccaccio's fourteenth-century *Decameron*, capturing the entire tale through various symbols.

In the original story, Isabella's brothers plot to murder Lorenzo because they wish to marry her off to a wealthy nobleman. It's a plot in which they succeed, setting the tension needed for an outright tragedy. Upon discovering the body of her buried lover, Isabella spirals into madness, cuts off Lorenzo's head, and takes it with her. Millais foreshadows the event with the simple act of handing over an orange. Lorenzo is literally handing his own head to his lover: his life as the price of this subtle, yet affectionate, public gesture that symbolically and literally knocks Isabella's brothers out of their seats.

Speaking of whom, let's return to how Millais signals their distress with a variety of symbols and actions.

A bird of prey can be seen preening: a process in which birds pick their feathers to remove dirt and parasites. On its own, the choice to include this predator might seem meaningless, until you consider that a bird preening mirrors a man biting his nails. Suddenly, the connection between the two is unmistakable: two physical responses to stress, as a metaphor for ridding oneself of unwanted baggage. Furthermore, a bird that plucks its feathers in excess is also a signal that something is wrong. It is a form of self-mutilation tied directly to sickness, anxiety, and disorder, which makes perfect sense within the context of this story. Lorenzo is an intruder. An agent of disorder in the eyes of Isabella's brothers, and he must be dealt with. And while they outwardly display discomfort as a response to the romantic tension between their sister and Lorenzo, there is yet another detail, hidden in plain sight, that is so brilliantly discreet, you would have certainly missed it on multiple passes over the painting.

Isabella's brother, who sits on a tilted chair in the foreground, kicking out at the dog in anger and frustration, crushes walnuts in a nutcracker. Crushing nuts is as blunt as symbolism could possibly get, but there's something else. Have a very close look at the shadow of the nutcracker, and pay even closer attention to where that shadow is cast. Mind-blowing, right?

In a 2012 article about sexual symbols in art, British art curator Carol Jacobi highlights that "The imagery of masturbation and the anxieties around it and being unable to control yourself sexually would have been well known." Millais, with a single shadow, highlights a lack of control and the anxiety that comes with it, making for one of the most spectacular stories ever told on a canvas.

A Huguenot, on St. Bartholomew's Day

John Everett Millais, 1852

The context for this pair of lovers sharing a tender embrace is the Saint Bartholomew's Day massacre. The bloody event began in Paris on the eve of the Feast of Saint Bartholomew in 1572, and lasted for several weeks, with an estimated death toll of up to 70,000 Huguenots across France.

During the massacre, Catholics were instructed to wear white armbands to distinguish themselves from the Protestants, and that's exactly what the woman in the painting is trying to force onto her lover: a white armband, to disguise him. To save his life, because he is a Protestant, and she is a Catholic, and the only chance that they have to live out their love is a deception that stands in the face of faith.

But he denies her. He loves her, beyond a shadow of a doubt, but he chooses his faith because it is the honorable thing to do. It's this single, simple idea that holds the entire picture together, and it takes the form of a white cloth.

Imagine for a second that his hand represents a faith in God, and hers represents the faithfulness of love. Both ideas can exist together, but here, on this day, he must choose. He looks his lover in the eyes, embraces her with one hand, and with the other, he denies her. He knows the consequences of his choice, and yet, he is willing to risk everything for his beliefs, refusing to bend the knee and concede as a matter of principle. His convictions take precedence over the preservation of his love, because to compromise when faced with trying times, even at the potential cost of his life, risks the destruction of his faith toward both God and his beloved. He is firm in his stance—as firm as the tension on the surface of that cloth—and she is left bereft.

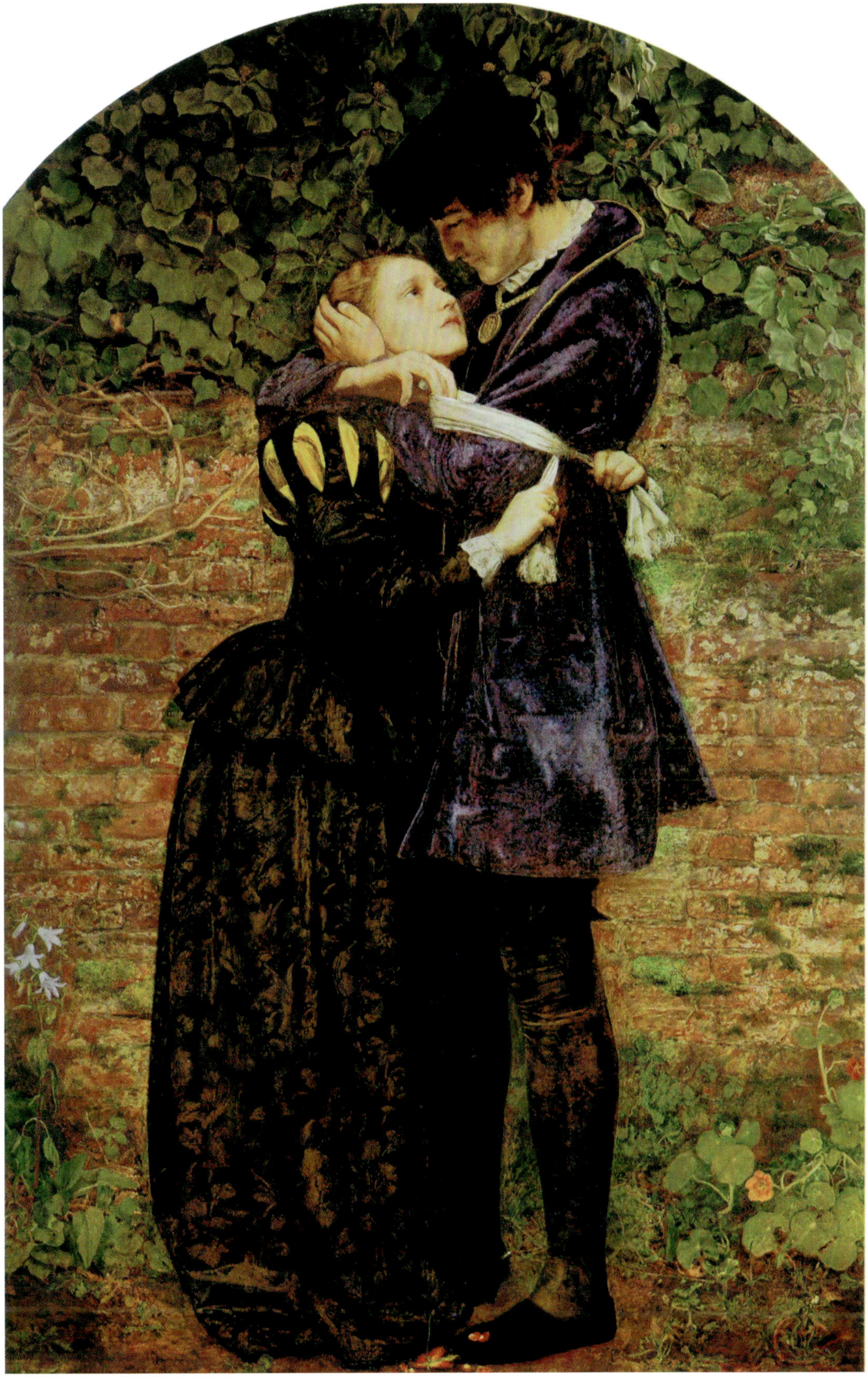

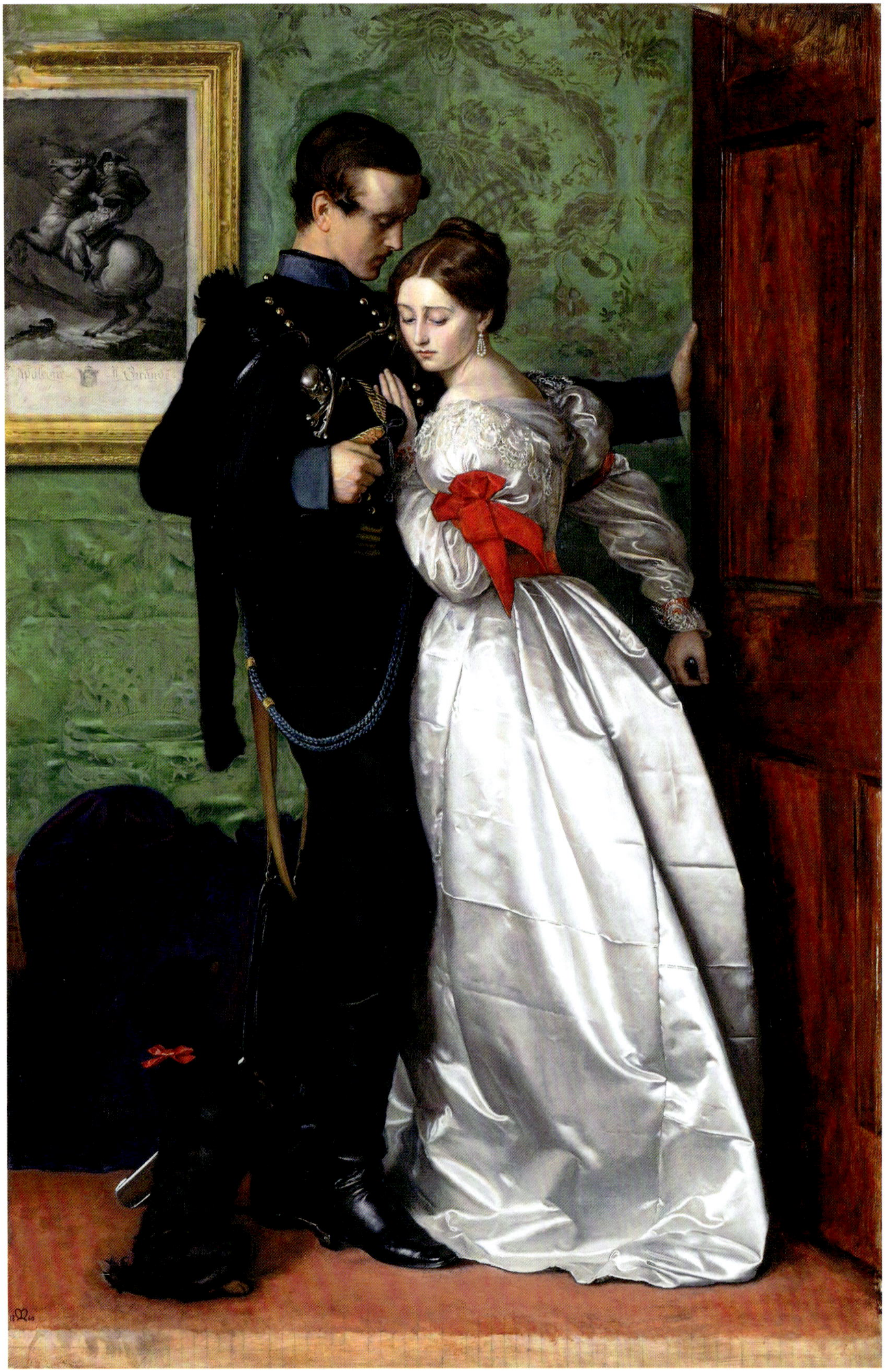

The Black Brunswicker

John Everett Millais, 1860

Millais plays on physical tension once again in his 1860 classic, *The Black Brunswicker*, but in a slightly different way. A soldier bids his lover a farewell before marching off to battle, but she appears to deny him a quick escape. As he tries to pull the door open to leave his home, she pushes it shut, and with her other hand, pushes his chest to hold him back. He's a Black Brunswicker, as made clear by his distinctive black uniform and the skull and bones badge on his hat: a soldier in a volunteer military unit formed to resist Napoleon's occupation of German territory.

Unlike *A Huguenot*, which displays a tension between faith in God and faith in love, this is a tension rooted in duty. It is also a tension formed through direction. Where the figures in *The Huguenot* are tightly bound together and feel inseparable, here, the hastiness to leave is undeniable.

Our female figure is a resisting force between two elements that seem to close in on her: the door and the man. She is the last barrier between him leaving and them staying together, preserving their union. Even more interesting still is how Millais uses contrasting colors in this painting to reinforce his concept and highlight conflicting ideals. Where in *A Huguenot* both characters are defined by their faith in God, and moreover unified by that faith, the couple in *The Black Brunswicker* are, as far as a centralized belief system goes, opposites. He's a soldier following orders, and she is asking him to abandon them. The only obvious connection between them is that they are A) in love, and B) alive. Plain and simple.

But those two connections are strong enough motifs to carry the painting. Our desires to preserve life and love are at the heart of being human. Even when we might not have anything in common beyond the fact that we exist, we all have a need to live, and often, a greater need to live together. It's not shiny, and it's not glittering, but an idea doesn't need to be to create a powerful painting.

"But Matthew, does tension in a painting always need to show itself as a physical resistance of some sort? Crushing walnuts, pushing and pulling on a door?"

Not exactly. Because unlike with *Isabella*, *A Huguenot*, and *The Blackwater Brunswicker*, Millais removes physical tension entirely in *Ophelia*.

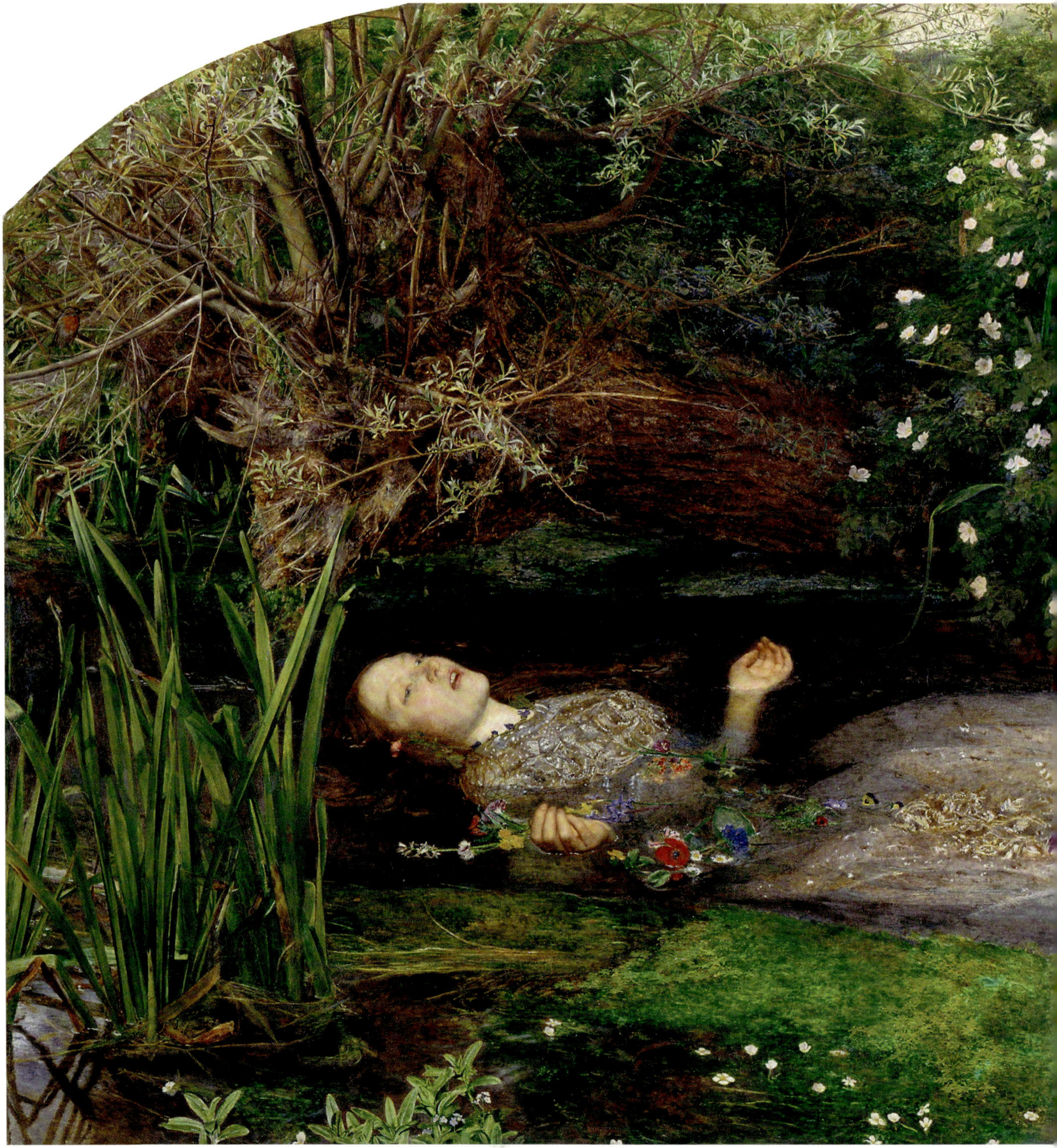

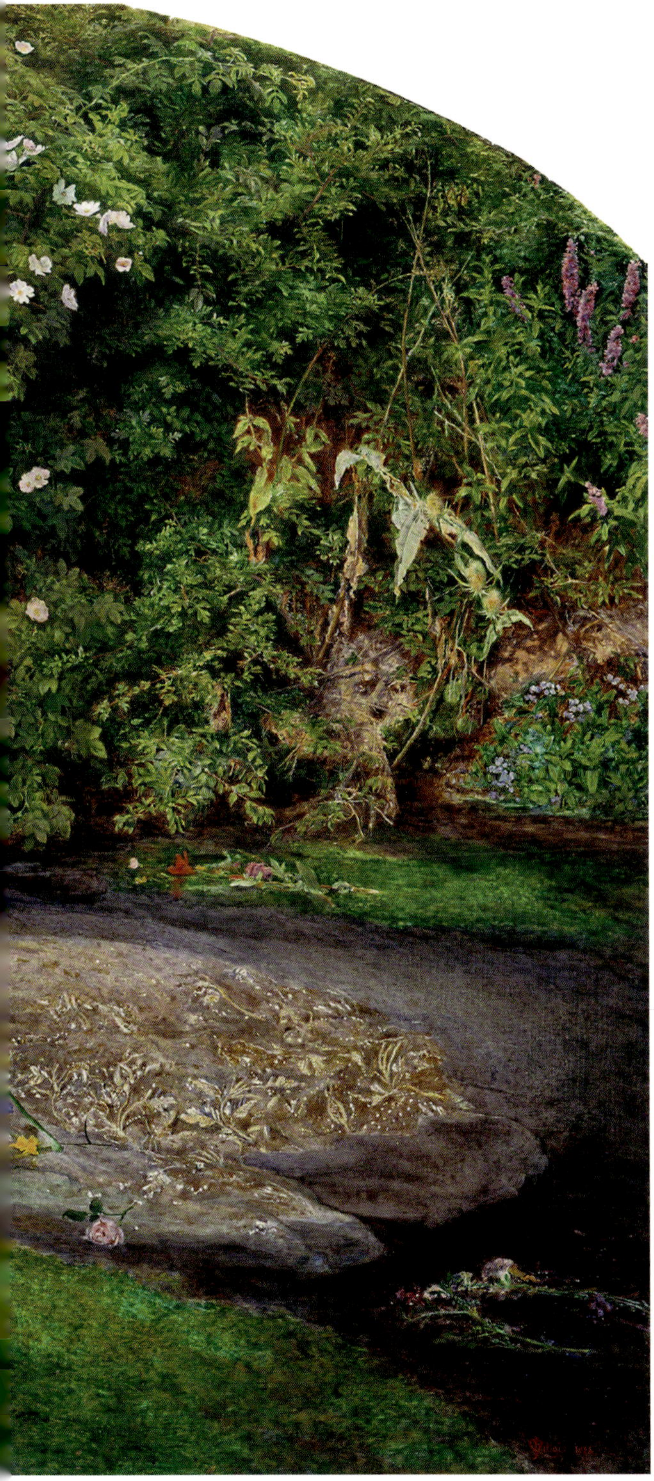

Ophelia

John Everett Millais, 1851–52

This is *not* a love story.

Ophelia: a daughter, a sister, and a potential suitor who, over the course of a series of subtle gestures and unprecedented circumstances, unravels into utter madness and meets her end drowned in a river. Shakespeare's heroine has been played over, and over, and over again, on stage and on the tip of a paintbrush, but it is only in Millais's 1852 depiction that we get anything nearing the brilliance of the Bard himself.

While asleep in his garden, a king is poisoned by his brother and suffers an excruciating death. At least, this is the story that Prince Hamlet is told by the ghost of his father after Claudius, Hamlet's uncle, marries the widowed queen, becoming the King of Denmark. Hamlet, by way of this fateful vision, realizes that something beyond love is at play.

As the prince's sanity deteriorates, another story of equal importance unfolds. Ophelia, a noble daughter of a noble servant to the king, begins the play in love with Hamlet. She is made to believe that he is above her station, yet she knows that this love is true.

But on the fateful night that Hamlet confronts his mother about her marriage to his uncle, her panic sets the central figure of our painting on a path of no return. With a thrust of his blade, Hamlet stabs the curtain. It's not his uncle hiding, though. The prince accidentally kills Ophelia's father, and metaphorically, so too kills Ophelia. His own insanity is the very cause of hers, because she loves him, but she also loves her father. And here, Millais shows us his genius: a snapshot of a person torn in two.

Ophelia lies in a river on the cusp of her own death, teetering on the edges of sanity before she is swallowed by the riverbed. She sings a song in her final moments, and Millais perfectly captures her madness, contrasting it all with a vibrant scene of beautiful things. There is something to be said about her form. An erotic posture? Or one of martyrdom? Surrounded by flowers that take on so many different meanings: violets for faithfulness and daisies for innocence. Pansies for thought and love in vain. Poppies for sleep and roses for youth. Willows for forsaken love, and nettles for pain.

Ophelia is helpless. She is consumed by her own insanity, akin to being consumed by the river, and we can't do anything about it. If she doesn't get up, if she doesn't swim away, she will drown. But with a lack of physical tension to hoist her up and preserve her life, we are left tormented, mirroring the way that she undoubtably was.

LOVE
LETTERS

Now, Millais wasn't the only one who could tell a great story. In fact, for as long as we've been making art, the themes of love and heartbreak have been central. We are creatures who seek immense purpose, and we often find it through our relationships.

"Some might even say that the purpose of life is love."

Exactly. Or perhaps, it is even better said that *how we find purpose* is through love. What are we willing to do for it? How does it change us? How does it shape our views of the world?

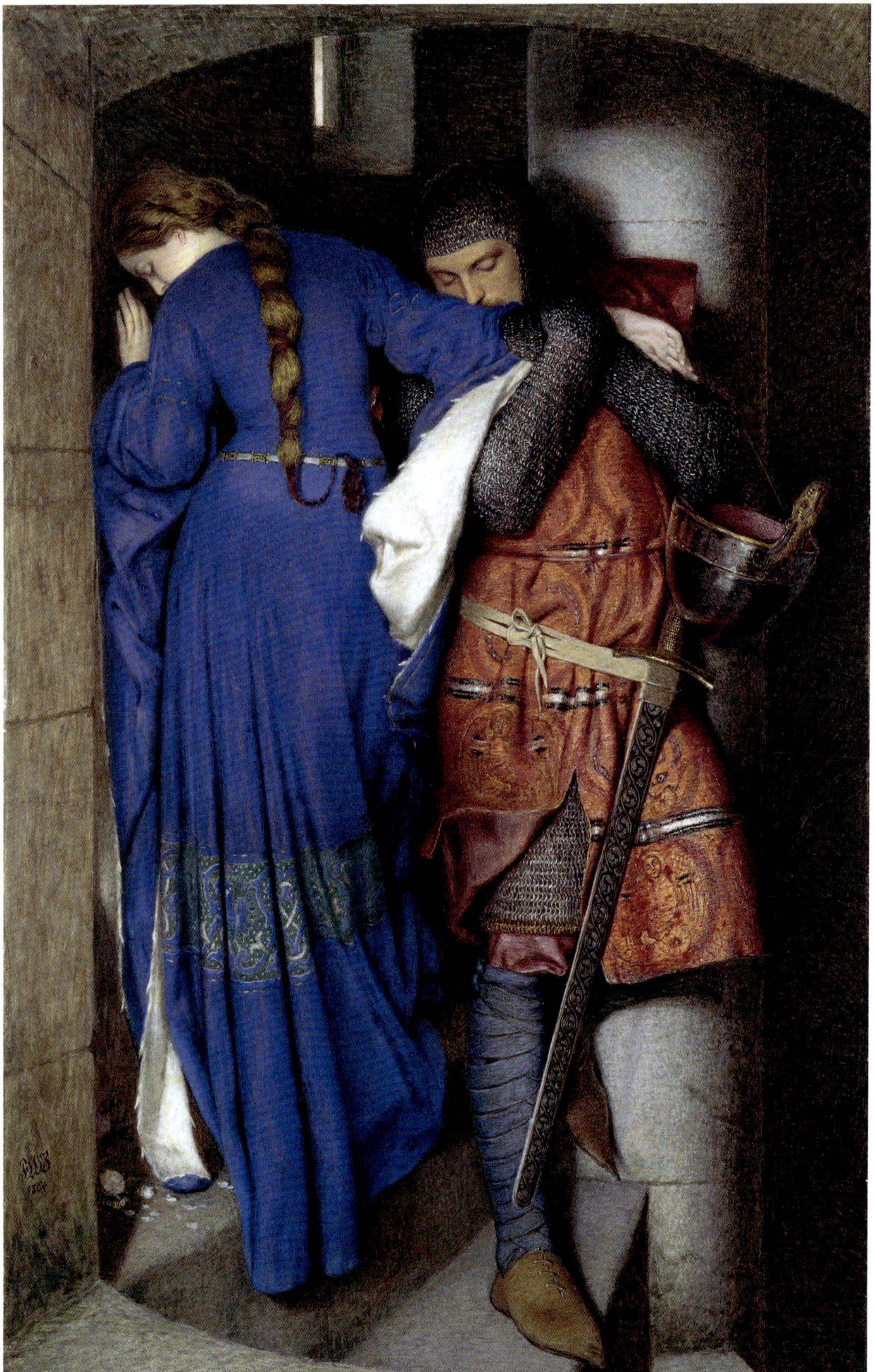

The Meeting on the Turret Stairs

Frederic William Burton, 1864

Frederic William Burton's painting is a love story for the ages. In a final fleeting moment, a pair of lovers desperately embrace in a last-ditch act of devotion toward one another. Neither know for certain yet, but this will be the last loving embrace they ever share, because Hellelil, a princess who fell in love with her bodyguard Hildebrand, against her father's will, is going to watch her "prince" as he walks out of the castle tower to face off against her brothers in a duel for her heart.

It is a motif that the Irish master captures in a genius manner. He serves us this final chapter of their romance in five different ways, and we feel every single push and pull when reading the painting in its entirety.

What you might have noticed first is direction. Hellelil is walking up the stairs of the tower while Hildebrand is headed downward, and on that alone, you can cut the scene with a knife. But Burton is far more clever than simple ideas.

He paints Hellelil in a vibrant blue and Hildebrand in a potent orangey red. For the color theorists, this is a nearly perfectly split complementary color set, implemented to maximal effect. Hildebrand is also dressed in a rugged chainmail: the perfect counterbalance to Hellelil's much softer exterior. But we can dive even deeper, because Burton holds, once again, another trick up his sleeve.

The brave bodyguard pins the delicate arm of Hellelil against his armor, to his heart, and here we witness a meeting between soft and hard. Hellelil, in disbelief at it all, clings on to the only thing that she can as he leaves: the tower wall, in a fusion of warmth and cold. And as the story goes, Hildebrand will walk off to face Hellelil's seven brothers and her father, taking the lives of each one.

That is, except for her youngest brother, who Hellelil will ask Hildebrand to spare. But unbeknownst to her, that same brother will take the chance to fatally wound her beloved, and she will ultimately lose Hildebrand too. And it is right there that Burton injects his final motif, which reveals itself once you know the full story.

In this fleeting moment on those tower stairs, had both Hellelil and Hildebrand known the fate of the day, would they have maybe gone about it differently? Perhaps instead of clinging to a wall, she would have clung on to her lover? And maybe he would have stayed in that tower and saved her heart, and his life.

The Shadow

Edmund Blair Leighton, 1909

Love shows its face in many forms, but perhaps it never holds more power than in the moments before it is lost forever.

In one of the most romantic gestures you will ever see, this woman traces her lover shadow's onto a wall.

The truth is, she doesn't know if she will ever see him again, because this brave soldier, covered head to toe in chainmail and war garments, sword strapped to his waist, helmet in hand, is about to head off to battle. And where a kiss and warm embrace may seem like the human thing to do, there is just something so incredibly fleeting about physical contact. This is the last time they will ever touch—a singularity in a romance that feels as though it's lasted an eternity—and it's in danger of being lost to time because that is the very nature of memory.

"I love you." Her soft words caress the face of her brave soldier for the very last time, and all she can do is trace his shadow on the wall. Because at least this will last a little longer.

And it is that right there—how she hangs on in desperation—that makes Edmund Blair Leighton a conductor for broken hearts. In the original story, derived from a Greek myth, the daughter of Butades traces the shadow of her lover on the walls of her bedchamber, where it is protected from the elements. However, on this battlement overlooking the sea, the lines of this silhouette will undoubtedly suffer the wind, the rain, and the sun. He will fade away.

While in the most desperate of times, we cling on to every ounce of hope that we can wrap our hands around, the fact is, we are all subject to fate. No matter how romantic the gesture, and no matter how badly she wishes she wasn't.

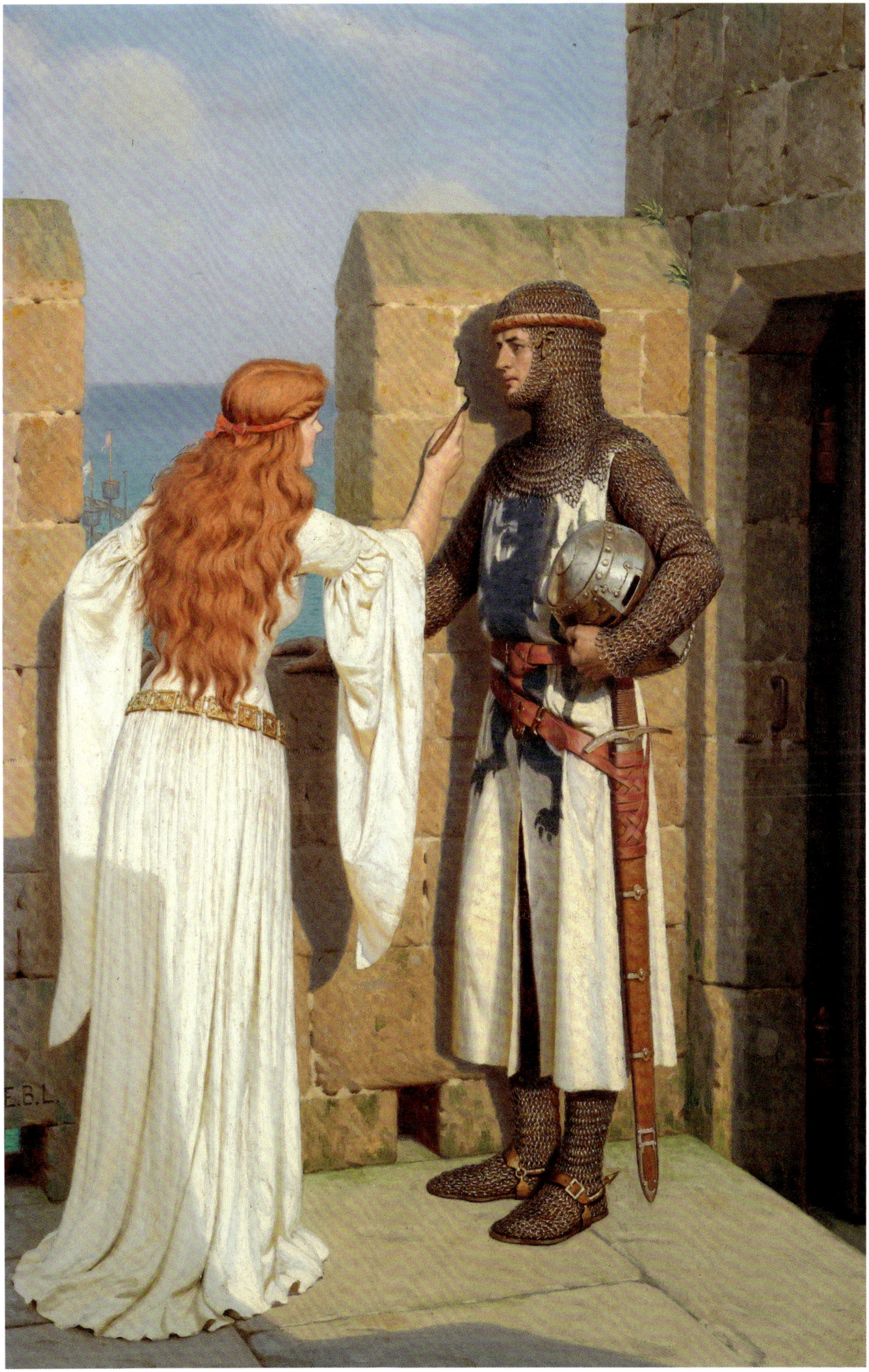
E.B.L.

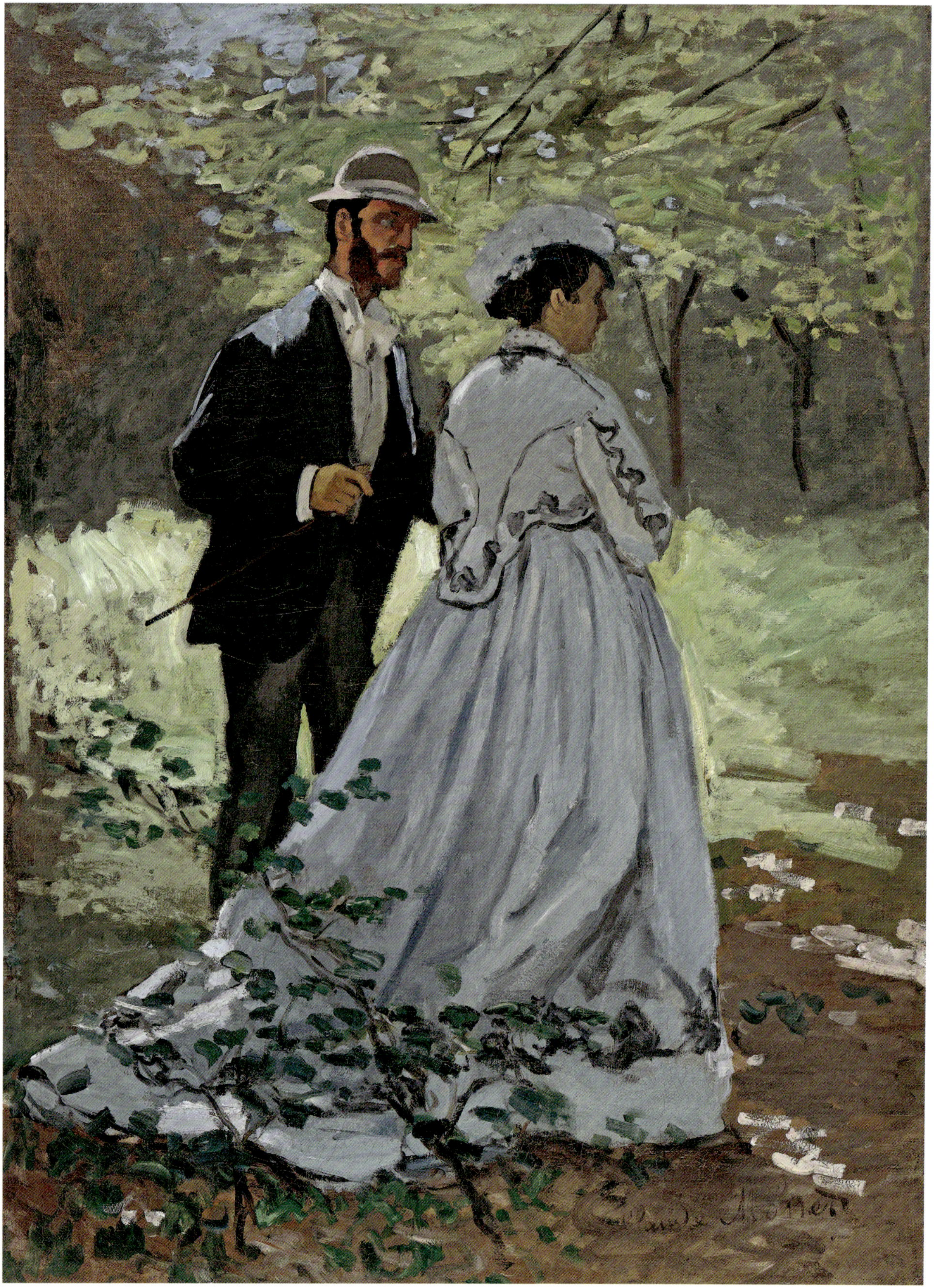

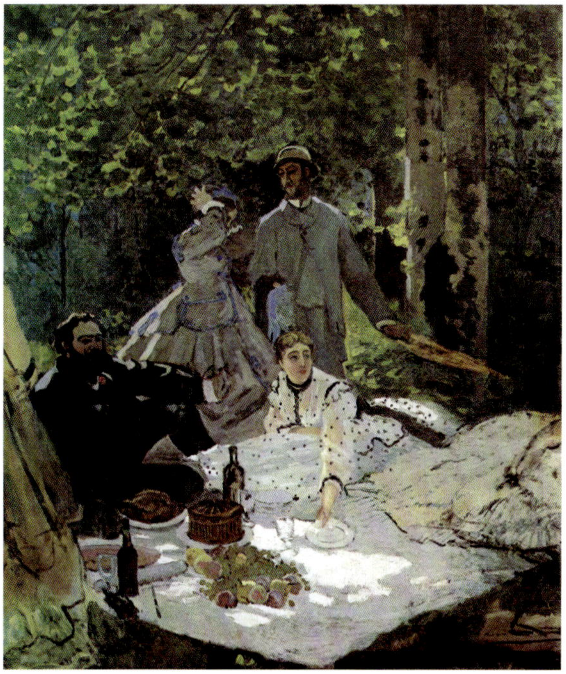

Le Déjeuner sur l'Herbe, Claude Monet, 1866

Bazille and Camille

Claude Monet, 1865

Love doesn't occur as a flash in a pan. It's drawn out. Love is an arc, not a point in time.

A great artist can capture a romance's most critical moments, but some might propose that it would be better to see love for what it is—an evolution.

A series of events and moments that, as individual units, fail to paint the picture. And yet as they compound, and as we connect the dots, love in its fullest form becomes visible. We start to see the arc of the greatest story that a person on Earth might ever experience, because love is the soul's great driver.

While it is impossible to truly understand the complexities of relationships outside of our own, there is one case in art that gives us a glimpse into another's romance, unlike any we've ever had.

It is the love story of Claude Monet and his wife Camille, and a catalog of paintings that evolved over the course of 15 years, which give us a unique insight into the true power of love itself. And it starts with a study named *Bazille and Camille*, or as some call it, *The Strollers*: a study for Monet's response to Édouard Manet's *Le Déjeuner sur l'Herbe* (1863).

There isn't anything about the artwork that screams love at first sight. It's *professional* in every sense: an artist painting models in preparation for another work.

Here, we have Frédéric Bazille and Camille Doncieux, perfectly framed in a vertical composition, in a style that is so undeniably Monet. Loose brushwork, vibrant colors, and while the painter is still early in his career, we can see the formulation of the ideas that would later define him. Every mark on the canvas is used to maximal effect to explore how light interacts with forms, with materials, and so on. The image doesn't *pretend* to represent reality through calculated proportions and perfect line work, but instead, focuses on capturing the essence of the scene itself: a warm day in a park, where a man and a woman are out on a walk.

This painting is nothing more and nothing less. Simply a professional engagement that gave Monet the tools to finish his version of *Le Déjeuner sur l'Herbe* (1866): a depiction of 12 individuals having a picnic in a park. However, it was never fully completed, and therefore, never entered the Salon that year.

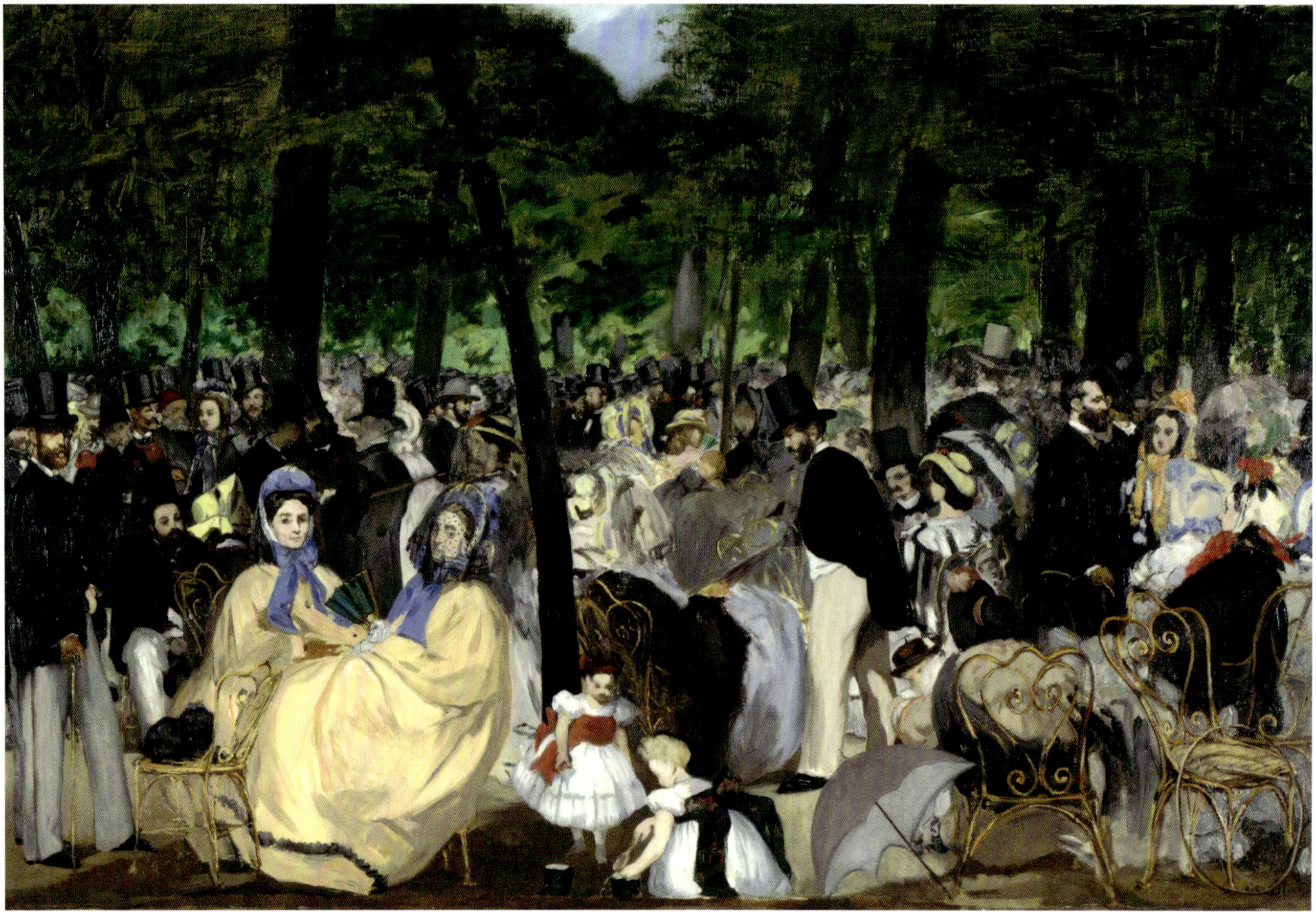

Music in the Tuileries Gardens, Édouard Manet, 1862

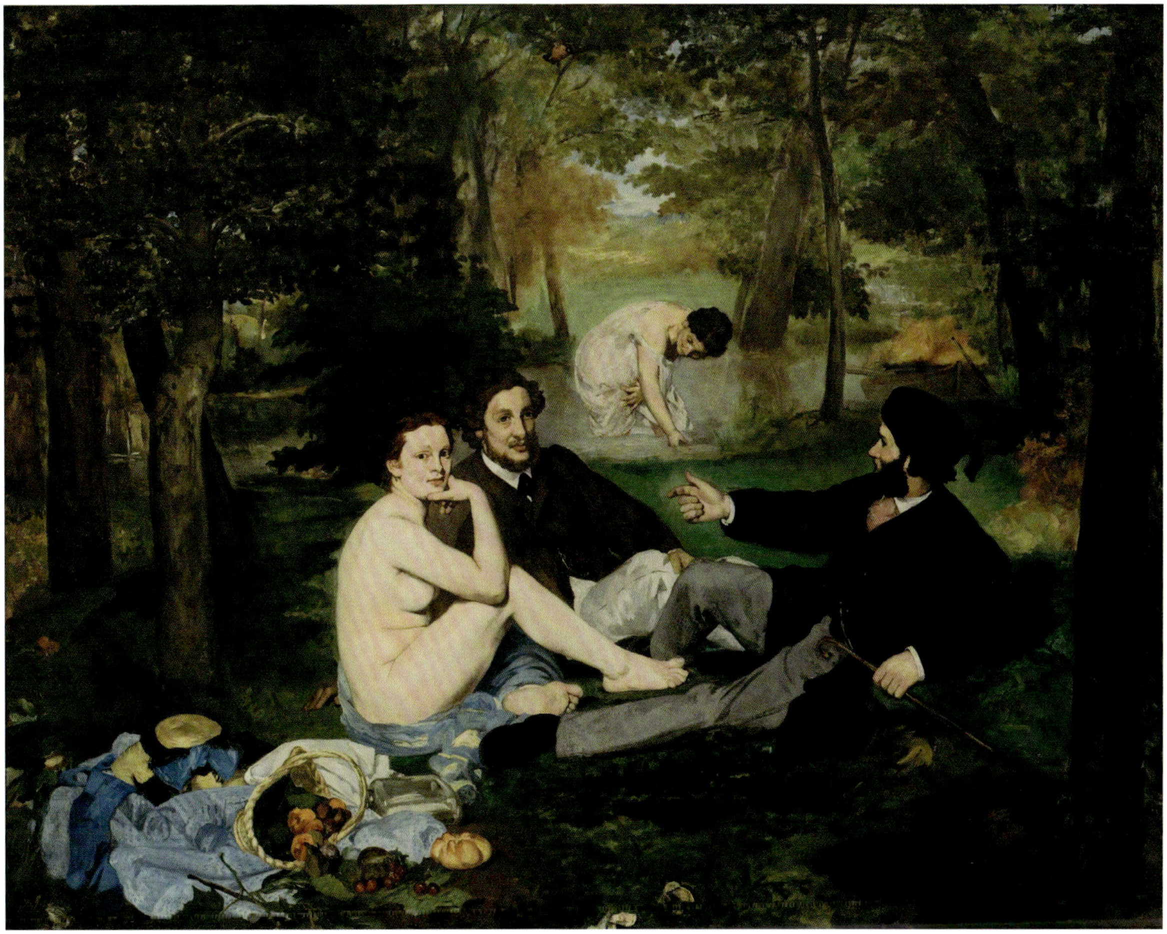

Le Déjeuner sur l'Herbe, Édouard Manet, 1863

"Um. There are only four individuals, Matthew."

Right. In the surviving "central panel." But in the gigantic original artwork, in which Monet had hoped to display life-sized people, there were 12. But while offering the painting to his landlord in exchange for rent, *Le Déjeuner sur l'Herbe* was badly damaged, and to preserve the unspoiled parts, Monet had to divide the painting into three separate panels. Only *two* of which survived: the left panel and the central panel.

What a shame, because the artwork, even though unfinished, is a sight to behold. Monet captures the reality of the space by playing with light and shadows. He brilliantly creates an atmosphere by depicting life caught in direct sunlight, and life caught in the shade of the trees, and it has the effect of immediacy. We aren't caught looking at a painting that tells us how to feel; *we simply feel*, instead, through a clever use of contrasting elements. And while exposed to the genius of Monet and his unique approach to painting, we're also exposed to his work ethic, because Monet was a student of great art. Not only does he use Manet's original version as the basis for his own, but he studies other great paintings that inform his decisions. Have a close look at Édouard Manet's *Music in the Tuileries Gardens* (1862), and compare it with Monet's own artwork. Can you spot the similarities?

I digress. While we can clearly see the characteristics of an artistic style that would cement Monet as one of art history's greatest craftsmen, what we don't see immediately is a love story that would define his personal life, here or in his other early pieces that feature his most potent muse and future wife, Camille.

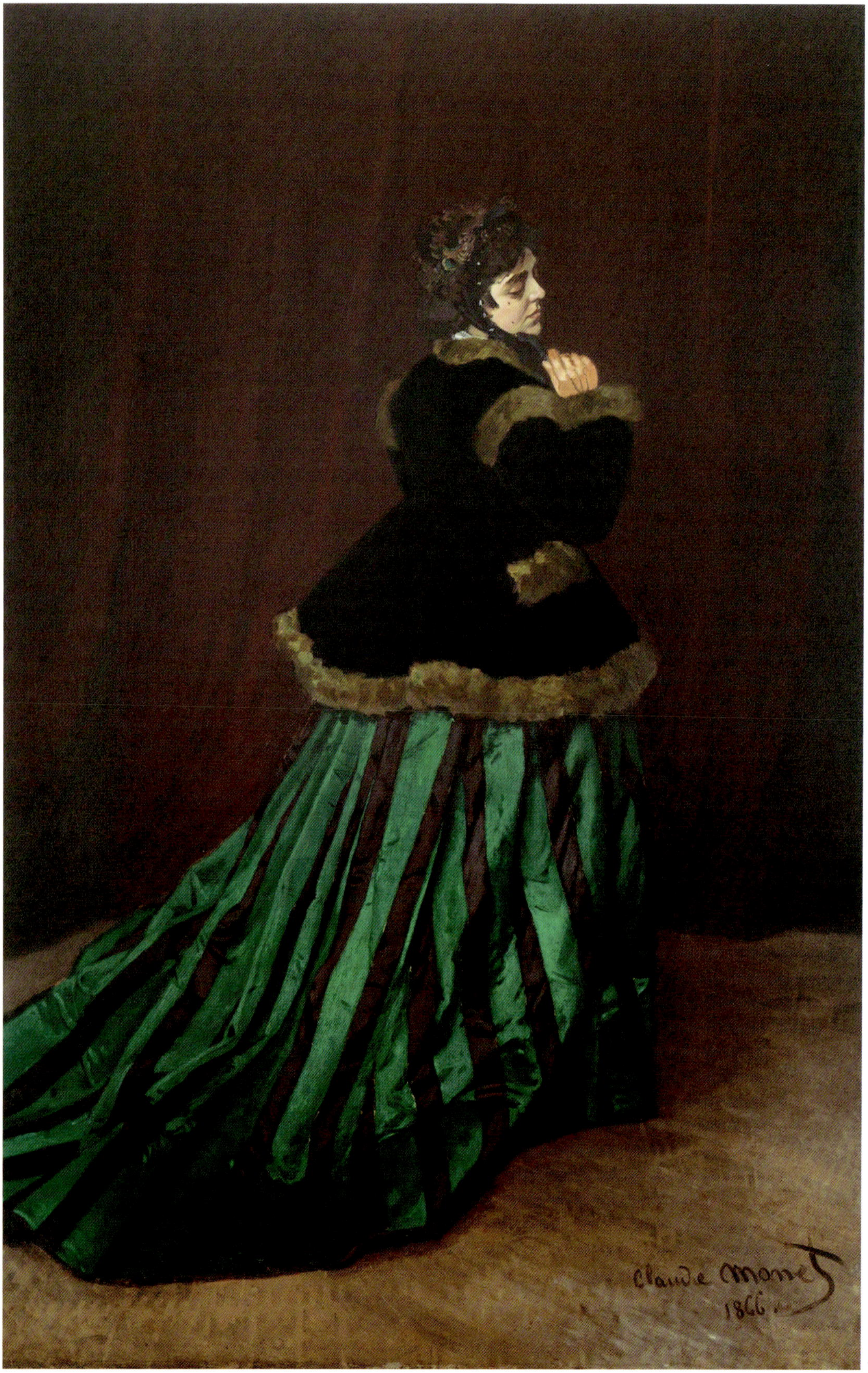
Claude Monet
1866.

The Woman in a Green Dress and *Camille with a Small Dog*

Claude Monet, 1866

Both of these paintings depict a woman who Monet certainly loved, but in a style that feels "professional." At the time that they were painted, the couple were, no doubt, a couple. However, this was meant to stay under wraps, because Monet's family did not approve. After all, she was an impoverished *artist's* model, and the Monets were a wealthy bourgeois family. Within this context, we glimpse some very interesting insights.

Looking at both paintings, we find portraits that feel rather subdued compared to Monet's wider canon. They are no doubt *technically* sound—the works of an incredibly talented artist—but they seem to lack the emotional framework we see in his later masterpieces.

In both portraits, Monet utilizes the space of a vertical composition and highlights the intensity of a vibrant garment against a dull backdrop. In one, it is a brilliant red shawl, and in the other, a striped green dress. He also chooses to frame each painting in interesting ways. In *Camille with a Small Dog*, he captures his muse in a three-quarter frame, and in doing so, highlights her more personal characteristics. What she's thinking about, we couldn't possibly say, but this is irrelevant, because the feeling we get is that this is an exploration of technique, rather than a painting intended to highlight the interpersonal. Monet is using the composition to harness more control over lighting and form to occupy space in a way that feels voluminous and atmospheric.

That same feeling is present in *The Woman in a Green Dress*, but this time we have a full-length portrait. Here, motion is the dynamic instrument Monet uses to capture our attentions. The beautiful green dress takes on a life of its own, almost hovering, breathing life into a space that lacks it. The posture of his muse injects personality: a juxtaposition against the brown drapery. Monet, again, studies the effects of his tools. In a style traditionally used to document the rich, the royal, and the famous, he captures the inner life of a regular person.

Key word: regular. We don't identify her as a lover. She is simply a model: a feature of the composition, and nothing more. But this is about to radically change, as Camille would soon become pregnant. Upon discovering this, Monet's father recommended that his son break off the engagement. In fact, to continue to access familial funds, Monet needed to pretend that he had. But the couple's course was set. On 8 August, 1867, Camille gave birth to Jean, their first child.

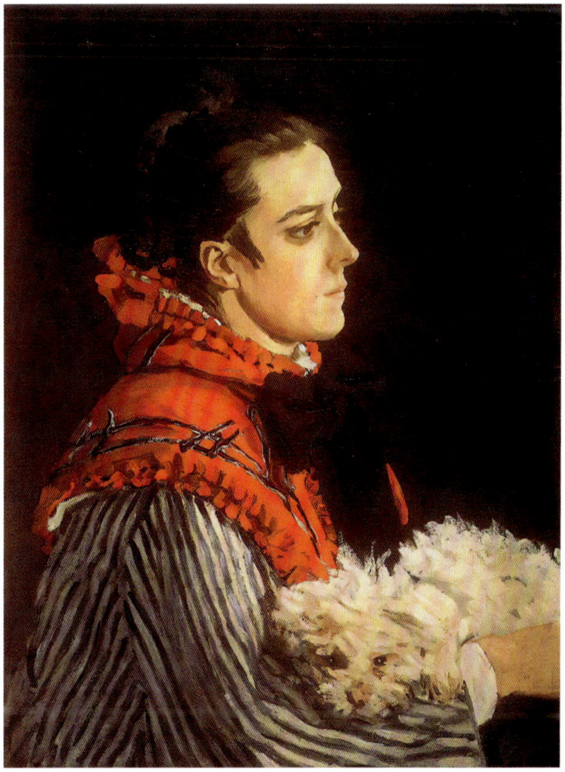

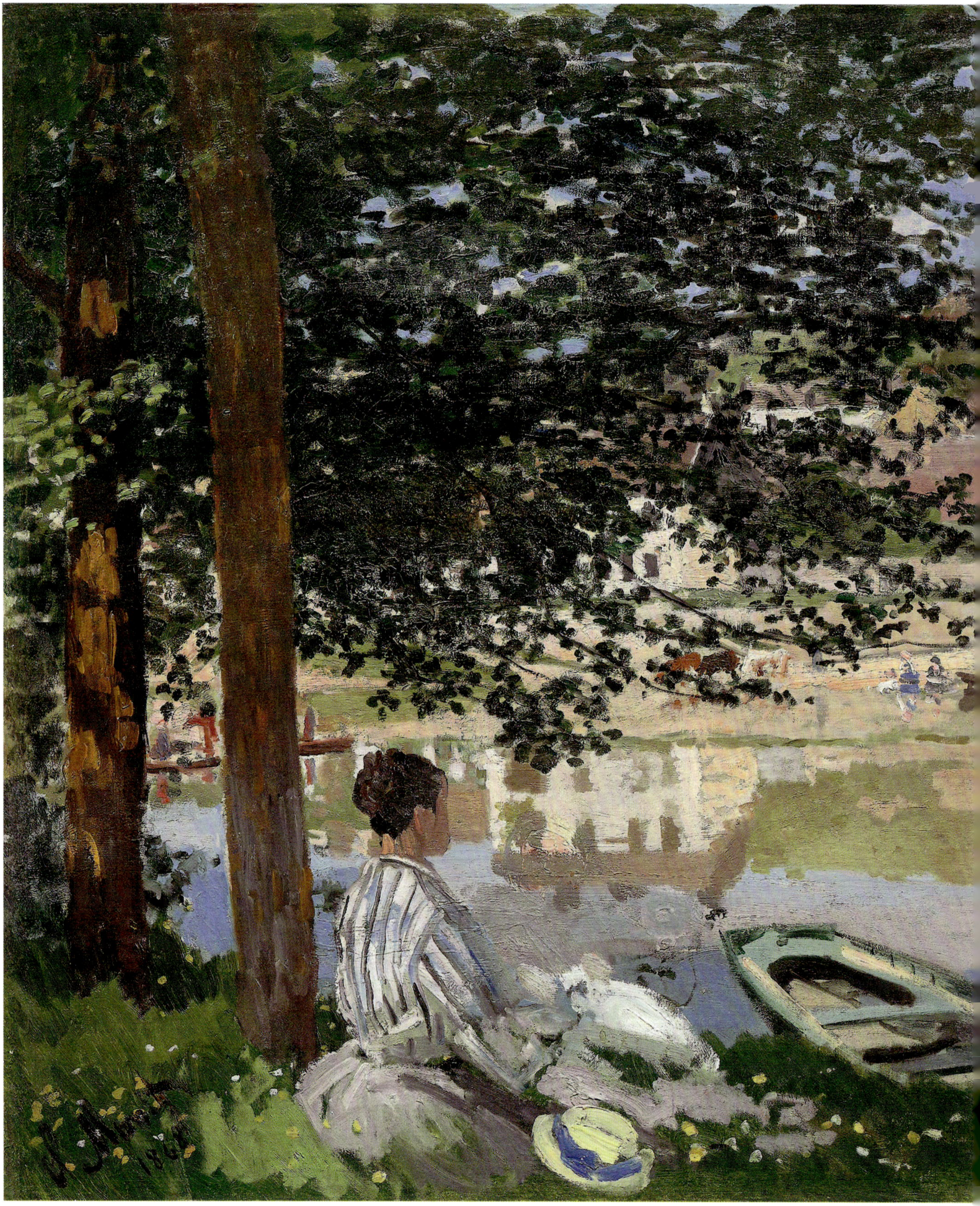

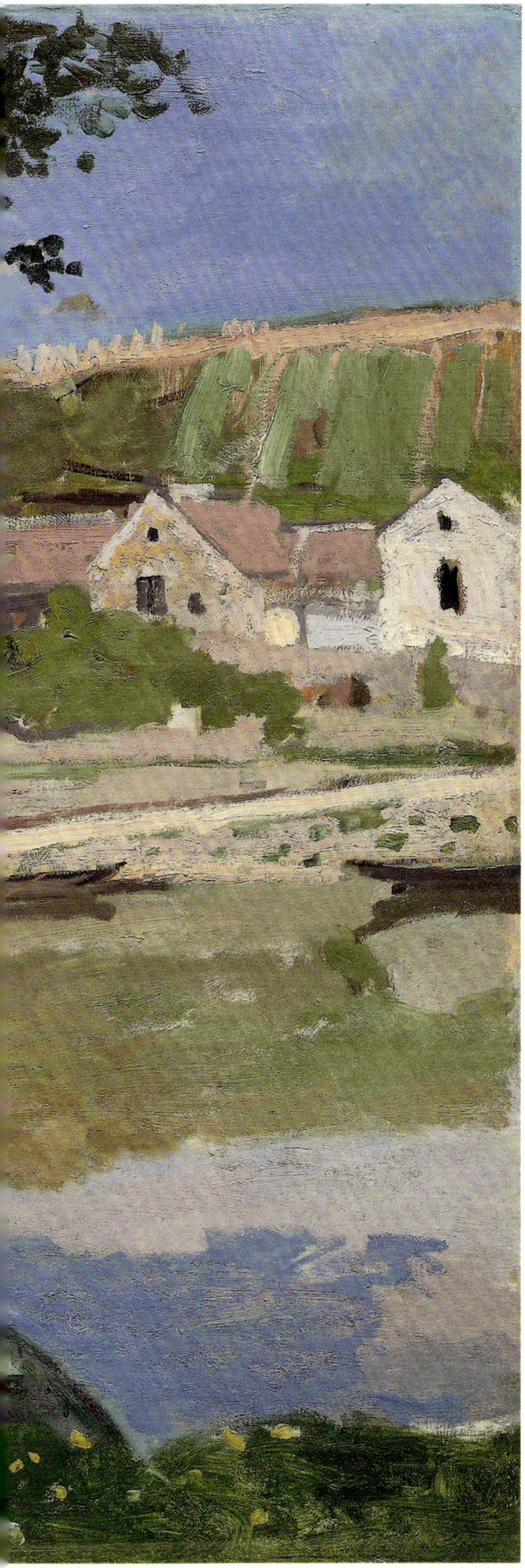

On the Bank of the Seine, Bennecourt

Claude Monet, 1868

In 1868, Monet captures his lover looking toward the village of Gloton on the outskirts of Bennecourt. This year marked a low point for the artist, who was on the brink of financial ruin, seemingly "on the run" with his lover and child. Yet Monet gives us an inkling that at least one thing in his life feels right: the family that he made, with the woman he chose.

Stylistically, there are similarities between this painting and *Bazille and Camille*. Both artworks eschew perfect proportions and accurate academic styling, instead representing reality by capturing the essence of real life. Again, we experience an atmosphere of light and shadow, captured through loose brushwork and vibrant patterns of color. Yet, this painting feels wildly different to his 1865 work. Monet doesn't explicitly state "I love her," but Camille is no longer a model posing for a job. She is now a very real person: one who he knows intimately in his heart and head.

Camille inhabits so much less of the physical space in this composition than she did in the study, and yet *here* she is so much larger. We are consumed by the possibilities of who she might be. What is she doing there? What is she looking at? How does she feel?

We imagine what it might be like to trade places: to sit in the warmth of that sun. To listen to the lapping water as it touches the riverbank and the wind caressing the leaves. We can smell it, we can taste the air: elements that are impossible to capture unless you were really there, and a person impossible to capture, unless you really knew her. This is an artwork that introduces us to a new side of Camille that we can begin to understand, because we all know what it feels like to love someone or something. We can imagine that object in such fantastical ways, because they exceed every expectation, even in trying times. It didn't matter that Monet's world was caving in on him, or whether he could see beyond the slump. All that mattered was this moment and this woman, captured for us on a canvas.

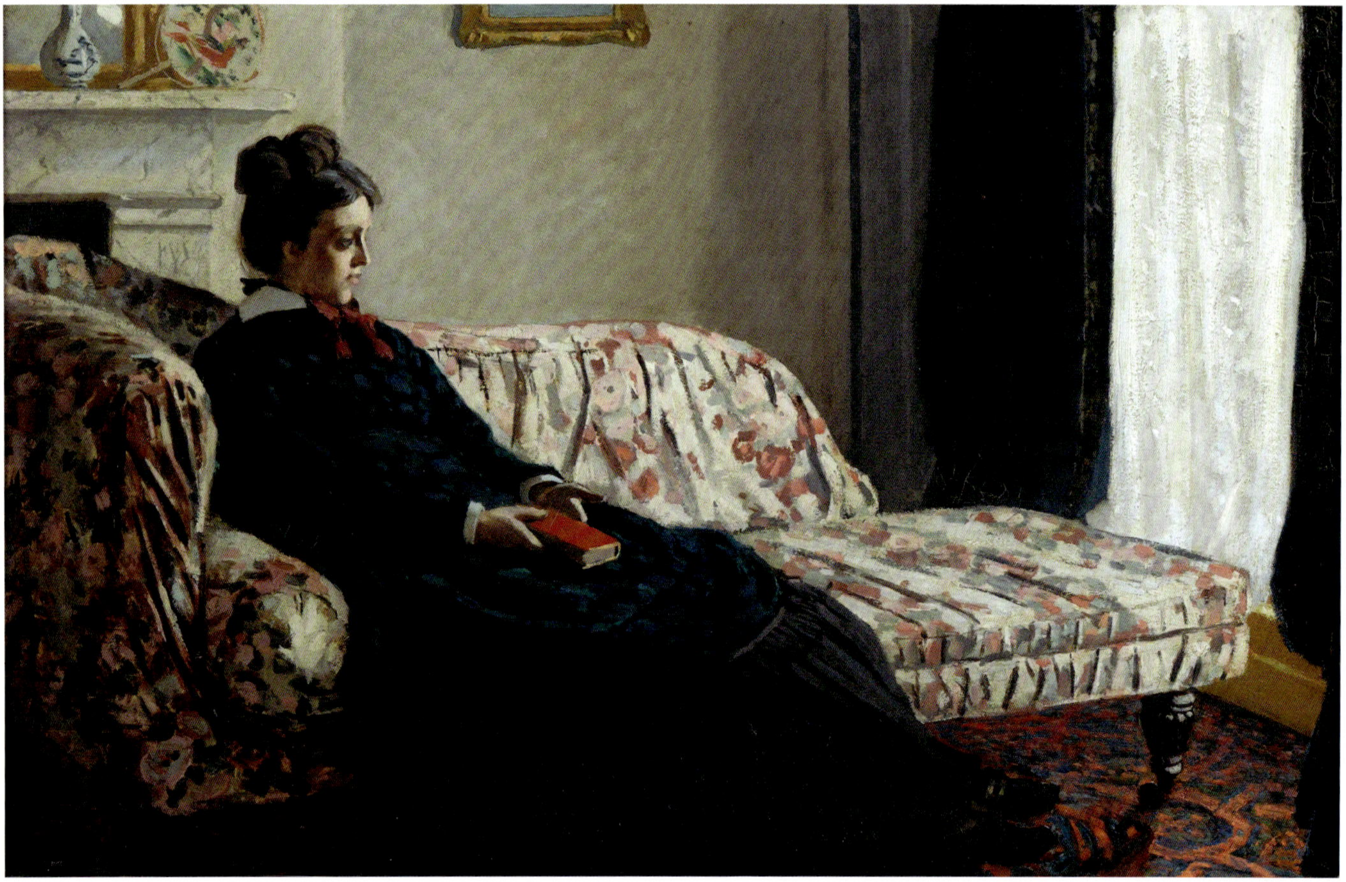

Meditation, Madame Monet on the Sofa
Claude Monet, 1871

On 28 June, 1870, Claude Monet and Camille Doncieux finally marry. To preserve his own life and the well-being of his loved ones, and to secure his future, Monet moves his family to London: a form of self-inflicted exile from France to avoid conscription into the Franco–Prussian War. His bond with Camille would take another step forward, and again, we can see it in his work.

This is the only painting of his wife created during their stay in the United Kingdom. In the light of the window, Camille quietly leans back into the comfort of a chaise lounge, book in hand, contemplating, once again, only God knows what, but it doesn't even matter. Whatever it might be that flies across the spaces of her mind, it is quickly forgotten under a cascade of tender light that wraps around the front of her body and her beautiful face. Monet catches his wife in meditation, not only in the way that he sees her, but in the way that he feels her presence. This is the mother of his child, and the woman of his greatest desires.

There is a stillness to this painting—a quiet reflection. To close your eyes and see it in your mind is to hear the faint squeaking sounds of a wooden floor and her garments rubbing against the sofa's cloth cover in an all-consuming whisper. You hear the smacking sound of lips separating moments before a word is cast out. True silence is death, but this is life, at its *fullest*. Real life, and all the little moments that make it real.

Springtime
Claude Monet, 1872

We see a slow transition in Monet's work, and a gradual improvement in his craft: an air of confidence that shows its face through what feels like loose, more expressive brushwork. There is a sense of experimentation in this period of his practice. This is, of course, not all a consequence of romance; our proficiency in any language increases as we master more of its words, which shape how we think and the clarity of what we express. If a strong technical foundation in art allows us to master the complex language of the soul, then Monet takes his leap into fluency in the 1870s.

A return to France spells a return to familiarity, and a new beginning for his young family. In the spring of 1872, in his garden in Argenteuil, Monet once again captivates our hearts.

Springtime is as delicate as a painting could get. Camille is seated under a canopy of lilacs. Sunlight chases sunlight through the cracks of the canopy, pooling in puddles on the grass and on her blushing muslin dress: real-life reimagined as fantasy, because at this precise moment, it was.

As we scan across the painting, every detail is formless, except for the only one that matters: Camille's precious face. Monet creates depth through a brilliant contrast of values, and so too, the atmosphere of a moment that exists only for a fleeting second. Considering his intentional brushstrokes, we can deduce that Monet was truly observing his wife. She doesn't blend into the scene but serves as her own individual element that contrasts it all. On this beautiful spring day, with the perfume of flowers to go around, our eyes are drawn to her face: the central axis of our desires, and the central axis of Monet's, in a painting that sets the tone for what might be his greatest work.

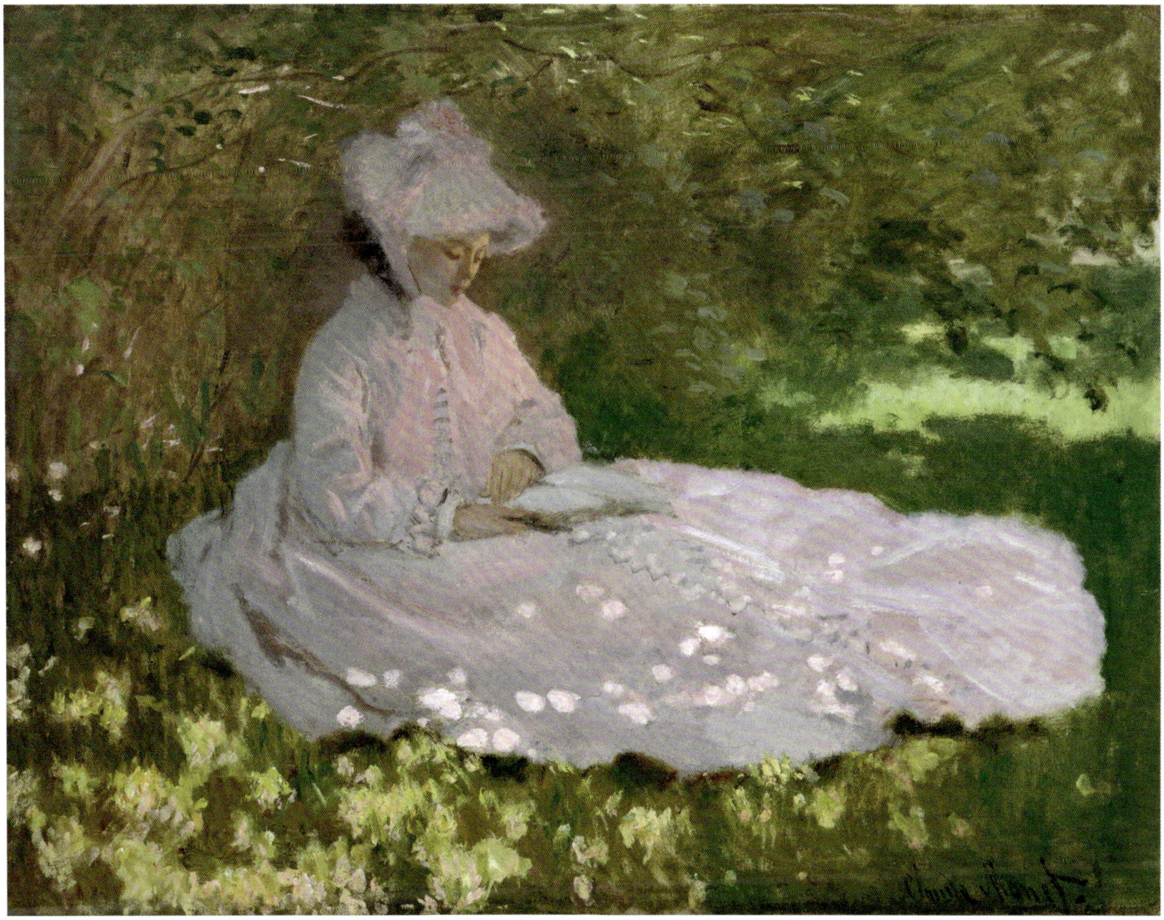

Woman with a Parasol — Madame Monet and Her Son

Claude Monet, 1875

When asked to pick Monet's greatest contribution to the arts, many might point to his landscapes. His paintings of Giverny have the capacity to transform how we feel about centuries of paintings: the hay and grain stacks that capture light in impossible ways. The flower gardens and lily ponds that swallow us whole.

But my personal feeling is that there is one painting in his collection, and one alone, that truly pushes the boundaries of what is possible in art. Through the eyes of many, it may be one of the most spectacular examples of love that has ever been displayed.

In it, Monet captures a love so pure, it is beyond even the fantasy of what love could be. A flash in a romantic arc full of heartbreak and happiness—of cries of sorrow and tears of joy. Every single little moment that led to his full heart, immortalized for all to see. *Woman with a Parasol* is the climactic peak in a love story that has endured it all: the apex of what is humanly possible to feel, captured on a surface no larger than a small child in a single sitting.

It is a painting of Camille and her son, caught in the wind on a sunny day. The swell of her billowing white dress is a force of motion that swirls around the picture, enchanting us with its mystical properties. The pair are captured from below in a fantasy of waving grass, suspended against a sky of bright blue and dream-like clouds. Monet captivates our imaginations with a control only possible through an exquisite understanding of art. Remember what I said about fluency?

He doesn't paint his son directly beside his wife, but instead, captures him at a distance, skewed toward the left side of the canvas. By choosing to paint Jean in this way, Monet gives the image a sense of depth. A depth, I might add, that is reinforced even further by painting Camille's shadow so it breaks into the foreground, effectively pinning his wife to the center of the three-dimensional space of the artwork. Monet delivers an anchor of stability and a sense of control in an environment where we feel that we could be swept away at any moment, and in fact, the moment you understand how Monet utilizes three-dimensional space to harmonize the artwork, you'll notice that everything about this painting is focused on balance. The weight of the colorful lower third doesn't for a second outweigh the bright blue sky. The chaotic flurry of elements is held in check by the steadiness of his muses. Monet equalizes *everywhere*.

Even the parasol that blocks the sun from Camille's eyes holds her comfortably in place by mirroring her shadow as a tool for symmetry. This painting is, by all accounts, a fundamentally perfect piece of art that captures a flash in the emotional life of three people who are bound together by love.

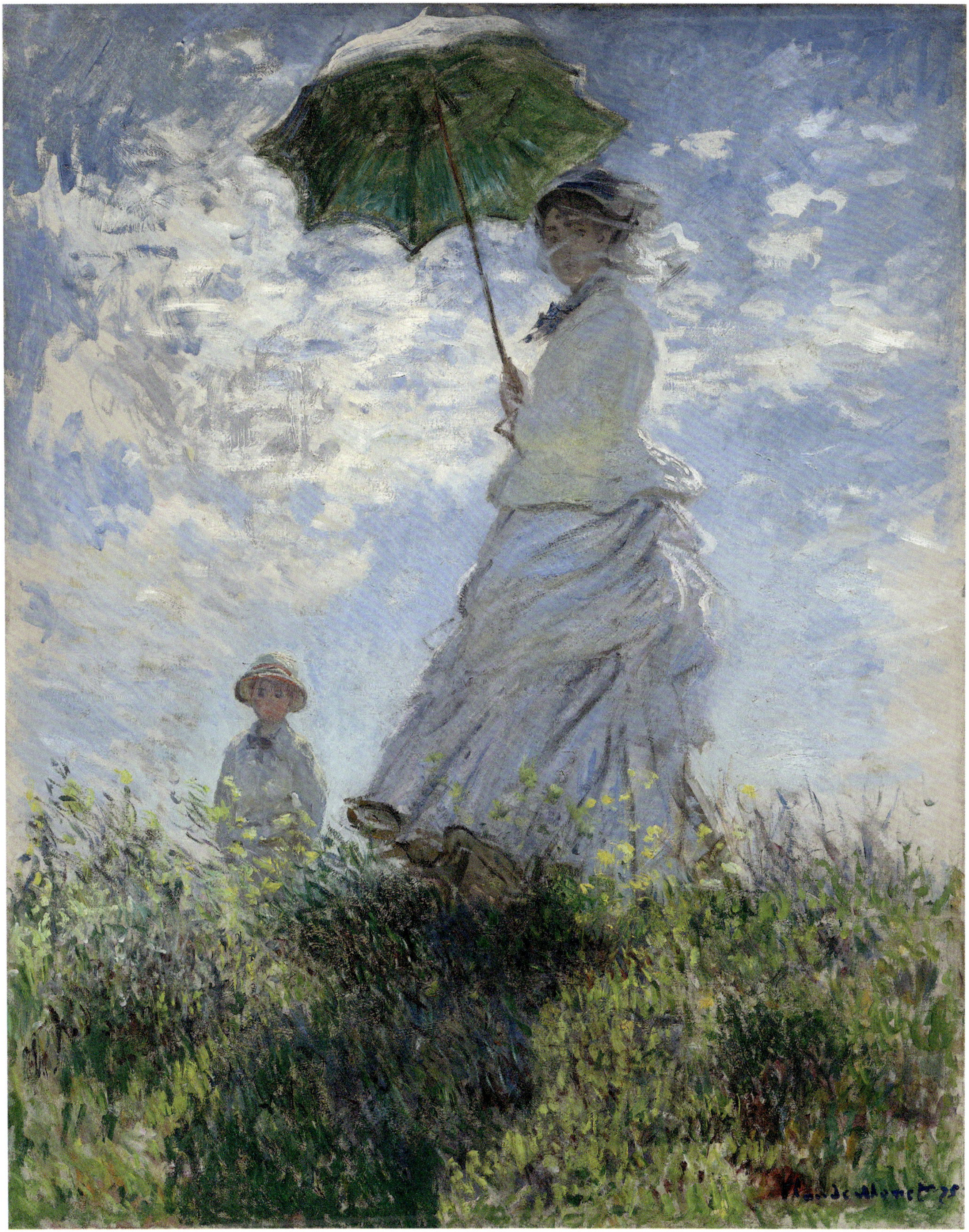

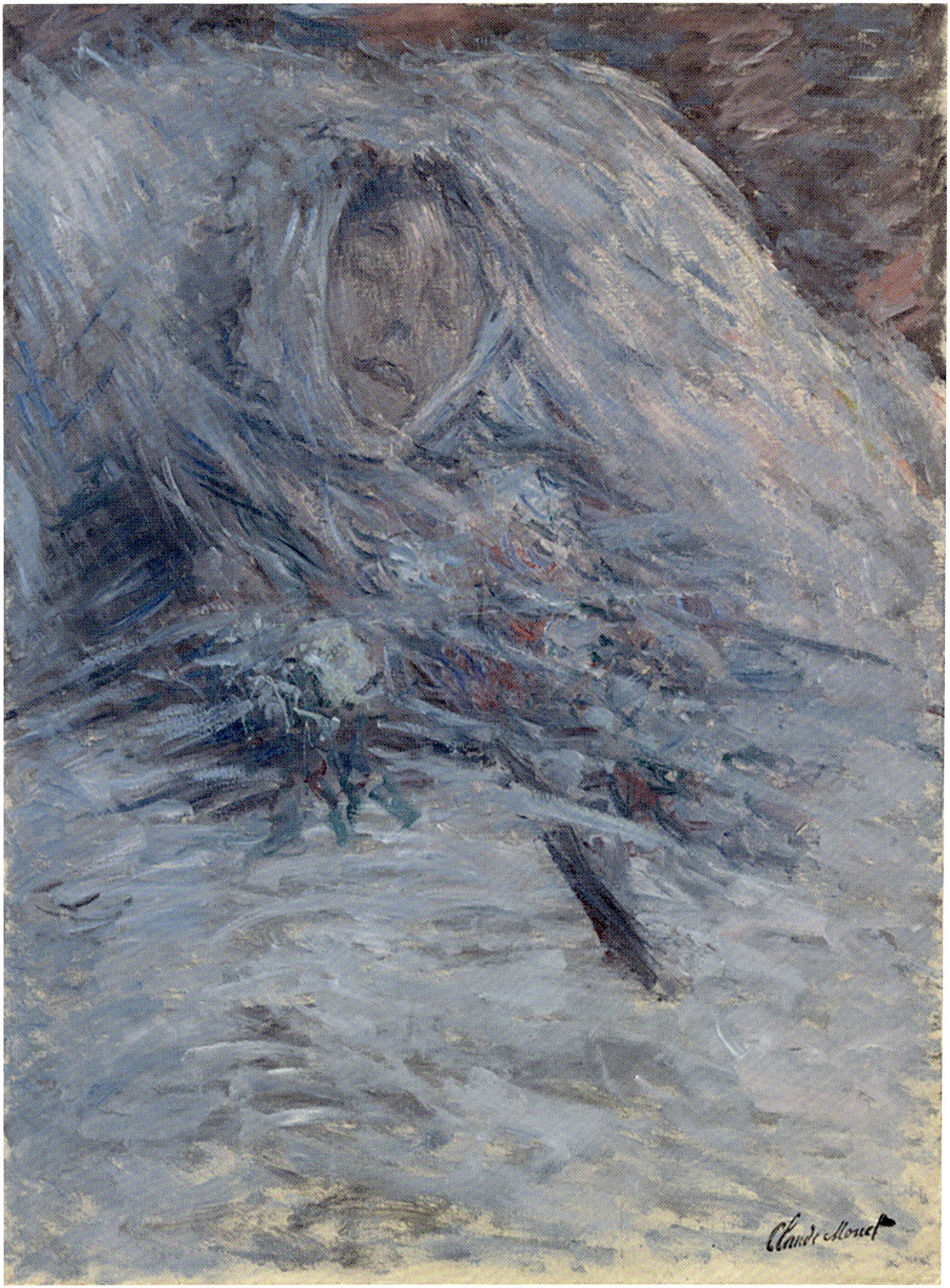
Claude Monet

Camille Monet on Her Deathbed

Claude Monet, 1879

Tragedy can befall even the loneliest of people, which poses a question: *for whom* is the event tragic? As an observer of tragedy, I must weigh the outcomes to determine how I feel about it. If I've only ever known the weight of a great burden, then what is the weight of yours? To some, your burden is heavy. To others, your life is a privilege. The nature of life, and more specifically, the nature of *observation*, is a matter of perspective.

Love is too. You must understand what it means to be completely alone to appreciate the full embrace of another. And it is that truth that makes Claude and Camille's story one of the greatest artistic records of love that has ever existed.

On 31 August, 1879, Camille Monet was read her last rites. She was 32 years old, a mother of two sons, and dying. She was the muse of Claude Monet's heart and soul, and this is where the arc of their lives together ends. As she lies on her deathbed, moments away from meeting God, Monet captures her for the very last time.

It is the single darkest painting in his entire body of work. A litany of lines anxiously move from left to right, up and down, and loosely make the bed and body of his most precious possession. A gift from God, now returning to God, and there was nothing he could do but capture one last moment.

Where other great works of art hold onto the hope that life might be preserved, it is here that Monet could only hold onto memories. Of moments in a park, or at a picnic. In a dull room in a green dress or with a dog. On the riverbank of the Seine. On a sofa in the light of a window. Under lilacs on a sea of green or caught in the wind on a sunny day. Memories that will fade into the abyss, because that is their nature.

This Kiss

Francesco Hayez, 1859

Now that we've explored art's tragic side and the powerful effect of heartbreak, I think it's time to explore some of the more "lighthearted" ways that artists have recounted love as a motif.

"Thank God."

The world of art, and the practice of art-making, is full of symbols: abstract ideas disguised in rich details that may feel impenetrable until the context is revealed. It's one of the most enjoyable areas of analysis to devour. Parsing these details can provide a viewer with many interpretations and dramatically affect how we feel when we walk away from a painting. Take, for instance, *The Kiss* by Francesco Hayez.

It captures the final moment between a couple who share a kiss of such intensity and romance, it still reverberates through the halls of art history. But no matter how observant your eyes are, or how many times you've looked at this painting, there is a very good chance that you might have missed its secret message. And by unlocking it, you can unseal a series of historical events that makes this one of the most spectacular political artworks ever made.

The painting projects urgency, but you'd need to look at it very carefully to spot it. The bent knee of the male figure, whose foot rests on the staircase, suggests motion and a need for a quick getaway. His sheathed knife, which hides in the shadows, is a symbol of imminent threat. Hayez *suspends* tension through the subtle contrast of the physical and metaphysical—through the soft dress, which is painted within the rigidity of dangerous circumstances. The desperate need for a moment longer, as seen through the intensity of the woman's embrace, tugs against the psychological imperative of needing to flee quickly.

"It's a brilliant use of the physical. So, what does it have to do with a secret message?"

Well, this painting's lovers have less to do with romance and more to do with Hayez disguising his real message to avoid censorship from the authorities.

The Seventh Coalition, a group led by Britain, Russia, Prussia, and Austria, would decisively defeat Napoleon at the Battle of Waterloo in 1815. This victory would be followed by one of the most historically significant diplomatic events in history called The Congress of Vienna, chaired by Austrian statesman Klemens von Metternich, which would effectively redraw the map of Europe. As part of this reorganization, Napoleon's "Kingdom of Italy" was divided into seven states and left under the control of the Austrian Empire, meaning that a unification, or Risorgimento, under one flag was impossible. That was, of course, unless Italy made an agreement in secret to support the successful rebellion its people so desperately wanted. And who would that be with? Napoleon II of France. Do you see it now? Still, no?

Look at their clothes: green, white and red, for the flag of the Kingdom of Italy. (Look under her hand to spot the green.) Blue, white and red: the flag of the French Empire.

The Plombières Agreement was sealed in secret between Napoleon III and Camillo Benso, Count of Cavour, and Hayez visually seals the alliance in the form of a kiss, hidden from the sight of all who lurk in the shadows. Discovery would undoubtedly mean a gruesome and untimely death, and now their postures make perfect sense; the man's foot, posed to flee, represents the imminent threat to Italian patriots, his knife, the dangerous nature of rebellion. The woman grips him tightly, in desperate need of an alliance that will determine the fate of the rebellion. And if none of that is convincing, consider that the painting is said to have been inspired by Robin Hood, the champion of the oppressed, who was a symbol of redemption and a hero for the Italian people when they needed one.

Love can be political: a love for your country and for your freedom, which Hayez disguises here as a love between people. The stakes are so similar, because to relinquish sovereignty is to give up the power over your life.

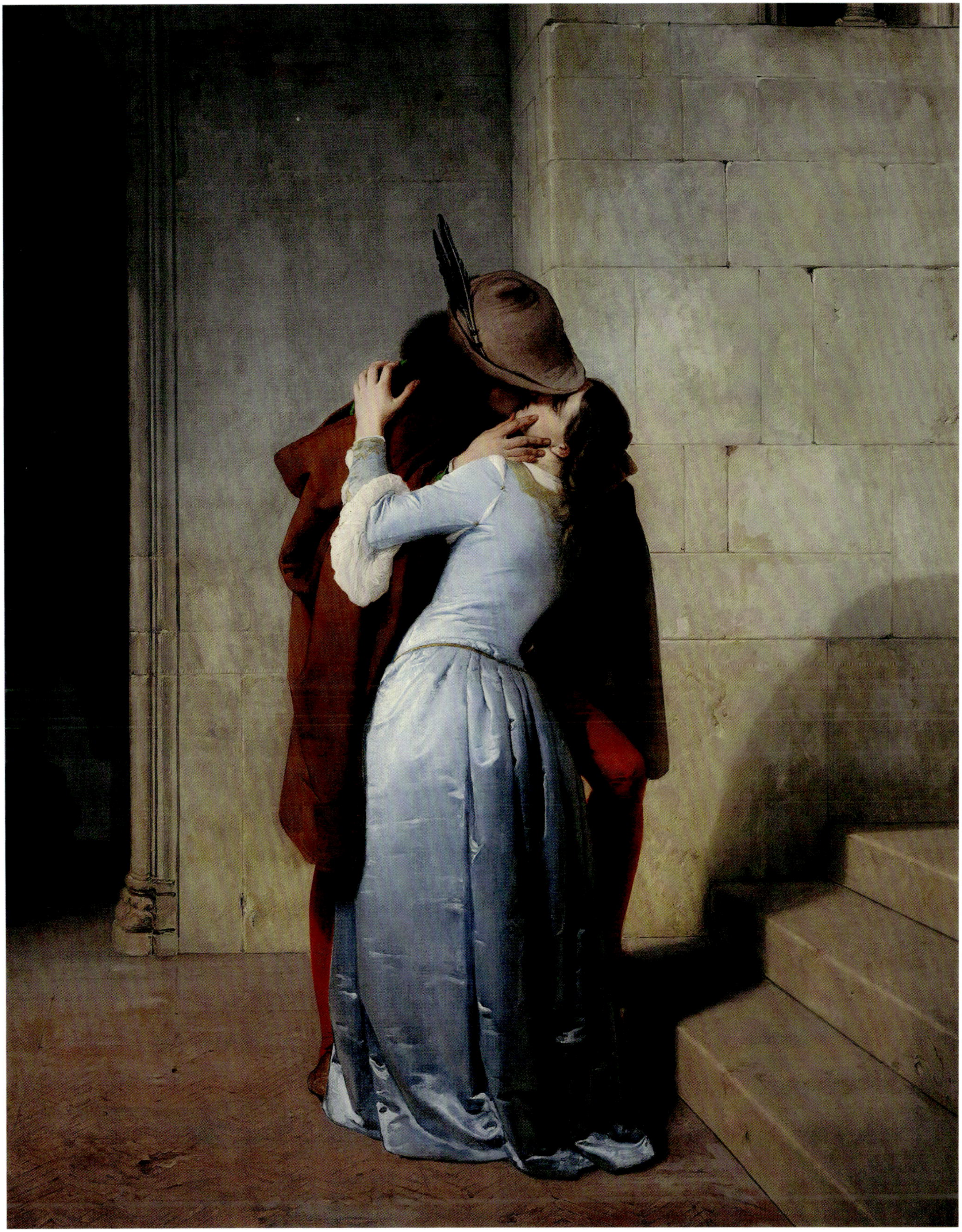

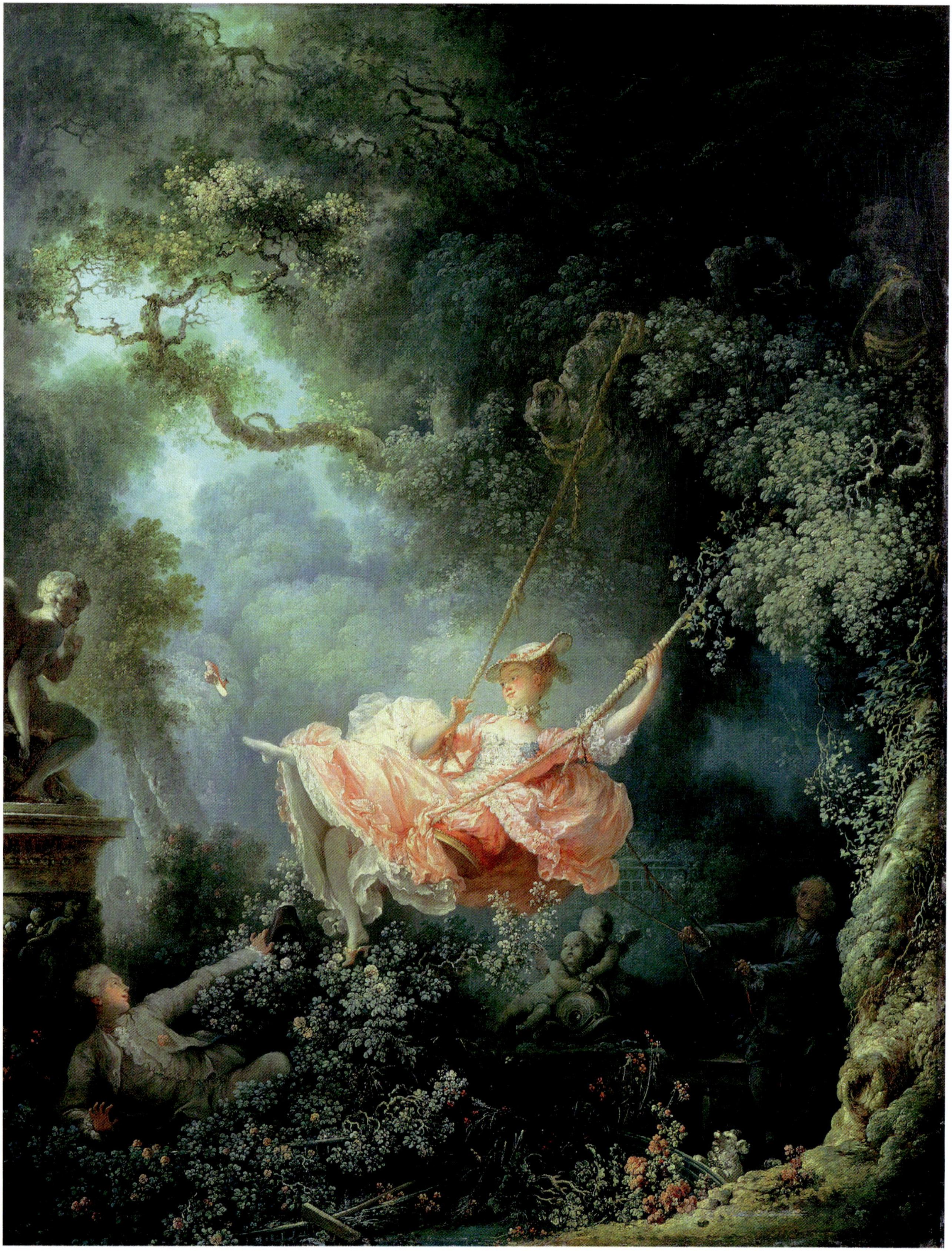

The Swing

Jean-Honoré Fragonard, c. 1767–68

Love in a painting can also be scandalous—a play on mischievous deeds.

The poor fellow to the right is in love with the lady on the swing, who can't get her eyes off the guy on the left, hiding in the bushes. And the only one who seems to notice what's going on is the dog down there, in the bottom-right corner. He's a character that you probably missed: a slip-up you can be forgiven for, because this painting by Jean-Honoré Fragonard is intentionally overflowing with detail.

Fragonard's first trick is to inject the feeling of motion, and to do this, he bombards you with what feels like an endless number of shiny trinkets, and your eyes do the work: back and forth, up and down, and it's a little overwhelming. That is, until the moment that you learn to see what Fragonard intended. Have a close look at her dress. While it's undoubtedly flung open to suggest promiscuous intentions, it's an understated secret from the artist's brush that ties the lovers together.

The layers on layers of her thin, silky garment seem to blossom like a rose, visually connected only to the picture's other roses: those in the bushes surrounding the young man on the left, and the single rose pinned onto his jacket. Fragonard makes their connection undeniable, but its secrecy is of the utmost importance.

If you guessed that the statue was Cupid, on the far-left side of the picture, you're right. And he's here to do a lot more than keep this affair under wraps, with a finger to his lips. Because while he is certainly a symbol for erotic desires and love, he's also likely the culprit behind this fellow's infatuation.

Struck with an arrow and drunk with desires, eyes wide open and arm outstretched: the man in the bushes can't help himself. All of which is reinforced by the dancing maenads beneath Cupid, which are symbols of the untamed, primal forces of nature. Yes: *untamed nature*. A painting overflowing with it, juxtaposed by unnatural, man-made elements that seem to serve as the last bastion for order. The wild, primitive nature of people kept in check by the construction of societal expectations, but only barely.

And when we take a step back and inspect the painting in its entirety, you might have noticed that Cupid is at it again, but in an entirely different way. Have a look again at the finger over his lips: He becomes the perfect counterbalance to the dog that just can't keep his mouth shut. And while the putti can't seem to make up their minds on how it is that they feel, the older man beside them has no clue what's happening. We can't definitively say if he's the woman's husband or not, but he certainly feels like he could be. He tugs on the ropes that swing his suspected wife back and forth, giving her the energy required to whimsically launch her shoe off into the open air—the maker of his own fate, so to speak, and he doesn't even know it. And just like the young man who's been caught in the corner of a love triangle for the ages, this man is caught too. And it's all happening literally right underneath his nose.

It's a shame he doesn't speak dog.

Jupiter and Io

Antonio da Correggio, c. 1530

Love is imperfect. Life is quirky. Stories can take an odd turn, and it's all part of the fun. We've highlighted love through the lens of heartbreak, tragedy, secret symbols, and scandalous intentions, but what about love as an abstract? Romance with mythical properties that are unrelatable yet *transcendent* when captured by the eyes of a talented practitioner?

Some paintings are plain weird—and I mean *really* weird.

Once in a generation, a talented artist will come along and, with a single flick of their brush, create a painting that captures it all. Take, for instance, this masterpiece by Antonio da Correggio that depicts the Roman god Jupiter, disguised as a cloud as he embarks on a scandalous affair.

The radiant skin of Io contrasts perfectly against the granular darkness of a storm cloud. The immaterial form of the god is counterbalanced by the smooth skin of the woman whose toe touches the ground, connecting her to the natural world. The wisp of cloud fades off into the sky, binding its fate to the heavens. Their embrace is a push and pull, balanced by the waning clutch of neediness and a kiss.

It's not a painting that is particularly complicated, or moreover, particularly relatable, but thanks to the hand of Correggio, *we get it*: the natural, the supernatural, and a meeting in the middle, under the guise of an affair. Io doesn't feel threatened, but rather swept away, even in an encounter with a lustful Jupiter. The cloud, though dark and omnipotent, still bears a softness equal to that of her skin—flush, silky, and delicate.

The painting is almost equally divided into two parts, in which the natural world occupies half the space, and the supernatural inhabits the rest. In framing the couple this way, Correggio equalizes. We are not overwhelmed by either side but are instead welcomed to witness the synergy of two very different worlds meeting. We aren't threatened by the interaction, nor do we feel inclined to protect Io. Instead, we watch the scene in complete silence, so as to not disturb, or better still, to not give away that we're watching at all.

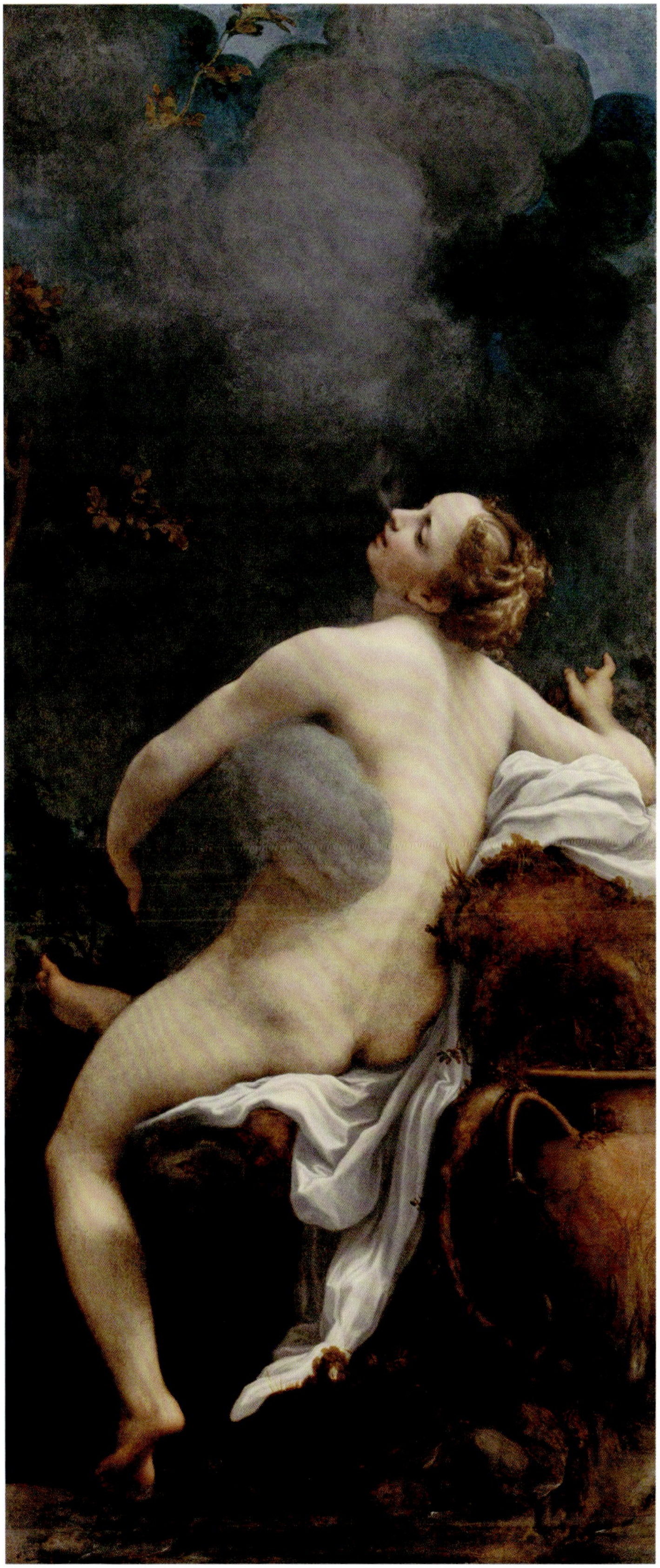

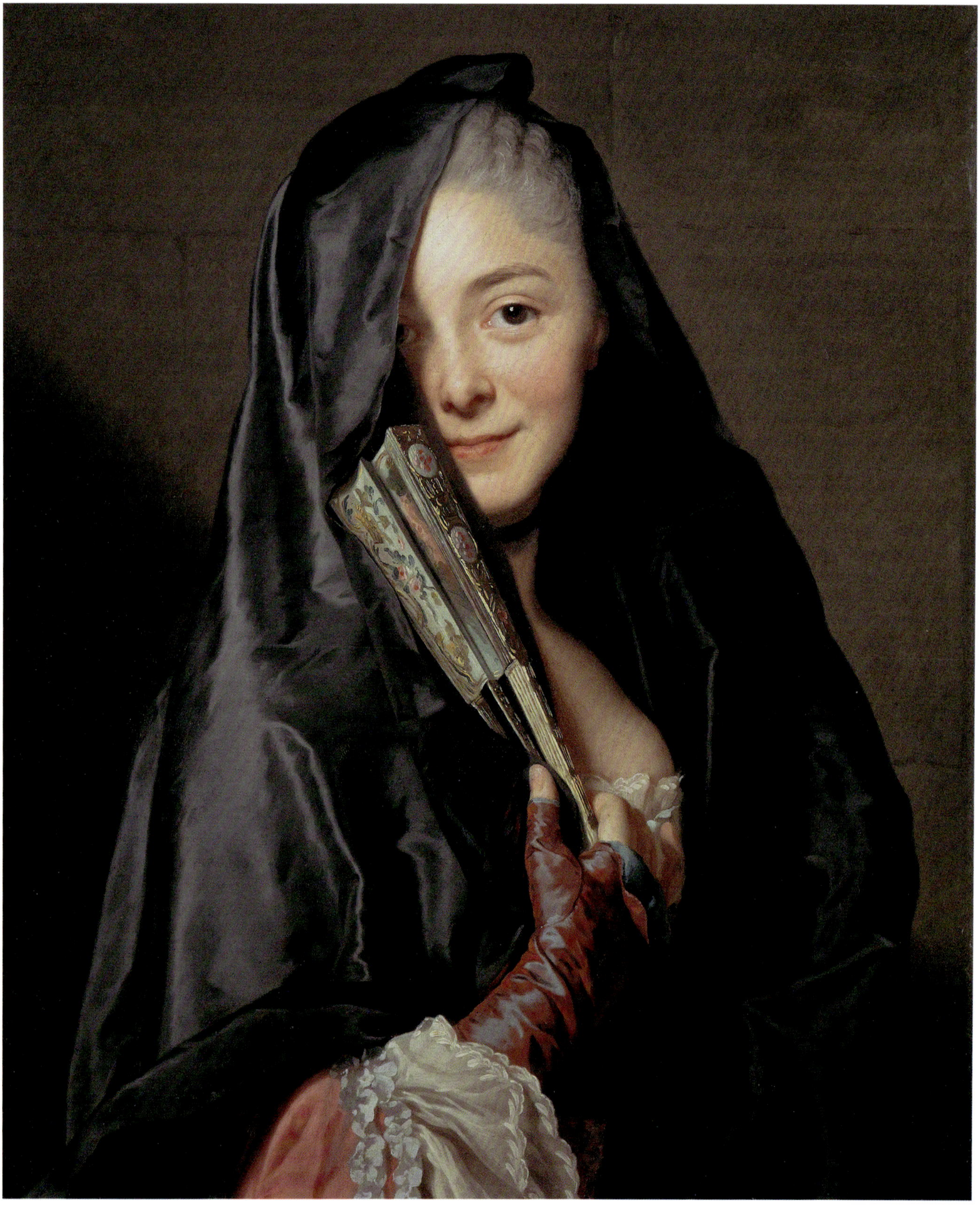

The Lady with the Veil

Alexander Roslin, 1768

A sure way to distinguish a mastery of one's craft is through a considered injection of subtlety and simplicity: the basics executed so precisely that we take them for granted. While many might lean on complex formulas to express abstractions, sometimes, the greatest ideas stare us plainly in the eye.

Now, what I'm about to show you could very well be some of the most spectacular uses of technique that you have ever seen in a painting. But first: Who is she?

Her name is Marie-Suzanne Giroust, and she's the wife of the renowned Swedish artist Alexander Roslin, who, it so happens, painted this picture. It makes perfect sense, because the portrait is so *unbelievably* flattering, with each element executed to tell us a little more about the artist's connection with his muse. To start, everything feels so soft, doesn't it? From the shadow's edge on the back wall to the garments that cover her head and shoulders, there's an unmistakable air of delicacy that hovers over the entire picture. Even an element like the fan, which, in contrast with the satin black veil, is clearly made of a rigid, hard material, *and yet* it is somehow gesturally soft and sensuous. The way that she holds it in her hand, hiding a small portion of her face, is so flirty and so playful.

We ignore every characteristic about her physicality in exchange for something else entirely: a feeling, equally as soft as her perfectly captured skin, not a blemish in sight. It's rosy and exquisite, and framed by the silky hair on her head and on her brow. All of which leads to the main event of this incredible portrait—her eyes. Or in this case, her *eye*. One big, beautiful eye as deep as the night sky itself, and it keeps you coming back, over and over. And the fact that we can only see one is all it takes to have us wanting more in an irresistible push and pull.

You're probably wondering why you can't simply look away. Every part of you wants to stare for a little longer, because Roslin gives us exactly what we need to keep us attentive, and all of it under the disguise of her mysterious intentions. I don't blame you for staring. Only if you've ever been in love could you possibly understand this look. A soul mate's gaze. Unconditional attraction.

And that's the genius of Roslin's brush. He captures what is impossible to convey in words. And where our own attempts at flattering a lover with a fraction of the pedigree seen here risks a trip to the proverbial doghouse, we can say with the utmost certainty that Roslin slept inside.

PORTRAITS

While we can be certain Alexander Roslin
painted a portrait that his wife was happy with,
the same can't be said for Henri Matisse, who
likely spent weeks in the doghouse in 1905.
To tell you the tale of one of history's "ugliest"
portraits, first I'll need to set the scene.

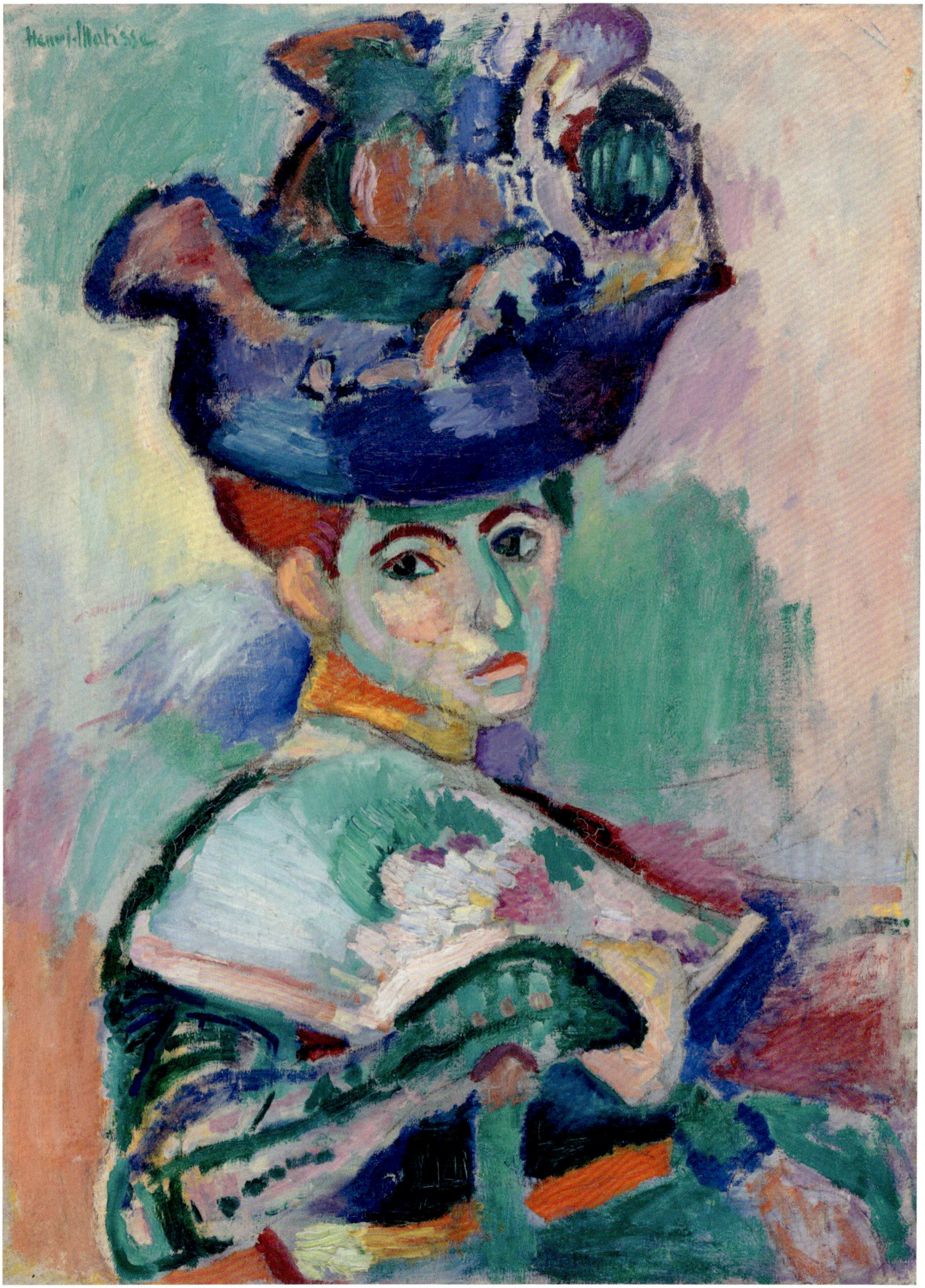
Henri-Matisse

Woman with a Hat

Henri Matisse, 1905

You are a beautiful woman and today is your *lucky* day because you've been asked to pose for a portrait by one of the greatest artists in Paris. You style your hair to perfection. You put on your very best dress, you're radiant, you're beautiful, and "hello world," you have arrived. Your grand debut. Your *big break*.

Well, in the case of Madame M, when she finally laid her eyes on a *Woman with a Hat*, it was anything but the debut that she had hoped for.

The Impressionists and Post-Impressionists were all for paintings that invoked a mood, but surely even they would have drawn a line when painting a portrait of a woman, let alone their own wife. Matisse, however, rarely conformed to drawing lines at all, and *Woman with a Hat* took the spirit of nonconformity to brand-new heights. As one might imagine, for many of its first-time viewers, it was categorically shocking. Even its eventual collector, Leo Stein, called it "the nastiest smear of paint" he had ever seen in his life.

Had Matisse painted a landscape in this style, it certainly would have caused a fuss amongst critics and socialites, but to portray a woman dressed to absolute perfection as a loose doodle of color was a tall order of madness. Can you imagine how his wife must have felt about it? But, for all the people that the painting bothered, the least affected by the entire ordeal was Matisse himself. When asked about what his wife was wearing on the day, in a statement, as cool as ice, he is said to have answered, "Well, black, of course."

Portrait of Henry VIII and *Portrait of Anne of Cleves*

Hans Holbein the Younger, c. 1537 and 1539

The art of portraiture is a tall task, regardless of whether you're painting your spouse or a queen. Think about it: In most cases, an artist is hired to capture the ins and outs of a person, focusing on each and every aspect of their character, to be framed and displayed for the rest of time.

Portraiture, by design, is a form of projection, due to the fact that, more often than not, someone paid for it. Someone with the intention of projecting themselves, and their ego-driven self-image, out into the world in what was historically largely a form of propaganda. At a time void of photography, when portraits were the ultimate flex, the noble, the rich, and the famous would pay large sums of money for their chance at immortality.

So how skilled does an artist need to be to get it exactly right? It's a tough job, often given to a person of immense ability. Someone, say, like the German Hans Holbein the Younger.

Now, if you know who the man in the painting to the right is, then you know that the story that I'm about to tell you is one of history's most ridiculous. And if you don't know him, he's the English king who was married six times, beheaded two of his wives, had some number of mistresses, and was apparently the pickiest person of the 1500s. He's Henry VIII.

"But Matthew, there were no dating apps back then. How did he even find the time to meet all these women?"

Funny you ask, because in the early 1500s, while there weren't dating apps, per se, there *were* portraits: a very common way of seeking out a monarch's potential suitors.

"Smart!"

Yes, and Henry was even smarter, because he knew portraits could be a little bit deceiving. The artist could make you a little thinner here, a little *bigger* where it counted—you get the point. Well, when Henry caught a glimpse of Anne of Cleves in one of these *deceiving* portraits, he had to be sure. So, he sent his personal royal court painter, Hans, all the way to Düren to paint her: a trip we have to thank for the portrait of Anne against a striking blue background from 1539.

Great painting, right? I'm sure Hans thought so too, so he delivered it to the king, who was so delighted that he proposed marriage and … got catfished. At least, according to Henry. He was so disgusted with Anne's true appearance that he refused to consummate the marriage. Within six short months he annulled it, accused Thomas Cromwell (who had organized the union, among other things) of treason, and off to the next portrait he went.

Happily, Anne kept her head, and in truth, even though Henry wanted out of the marriage, he quite liked his fourth wife. So much so that, upon agreeing to the annulment, she was granted the honorary title of "The King's Beloved Sister," along with a generous allowance, which ensured a high status in England. She went on to a mostly peaceful, albeit short, life, passing on at the age of 42 in 1557. Despite her young age, this meant that she outlived all of Henry's other wives. Now, had she looked anything like the Ugly Duchess, on the other hand … she'd likely have visited the Tower of London.

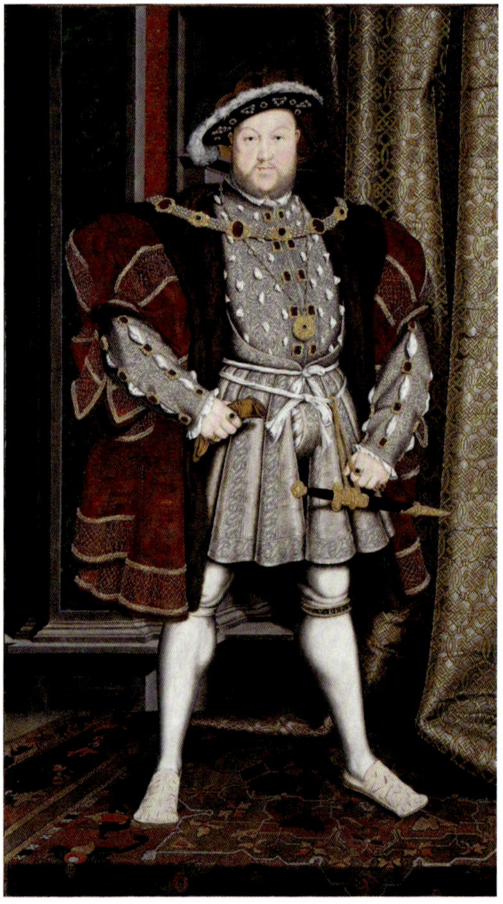

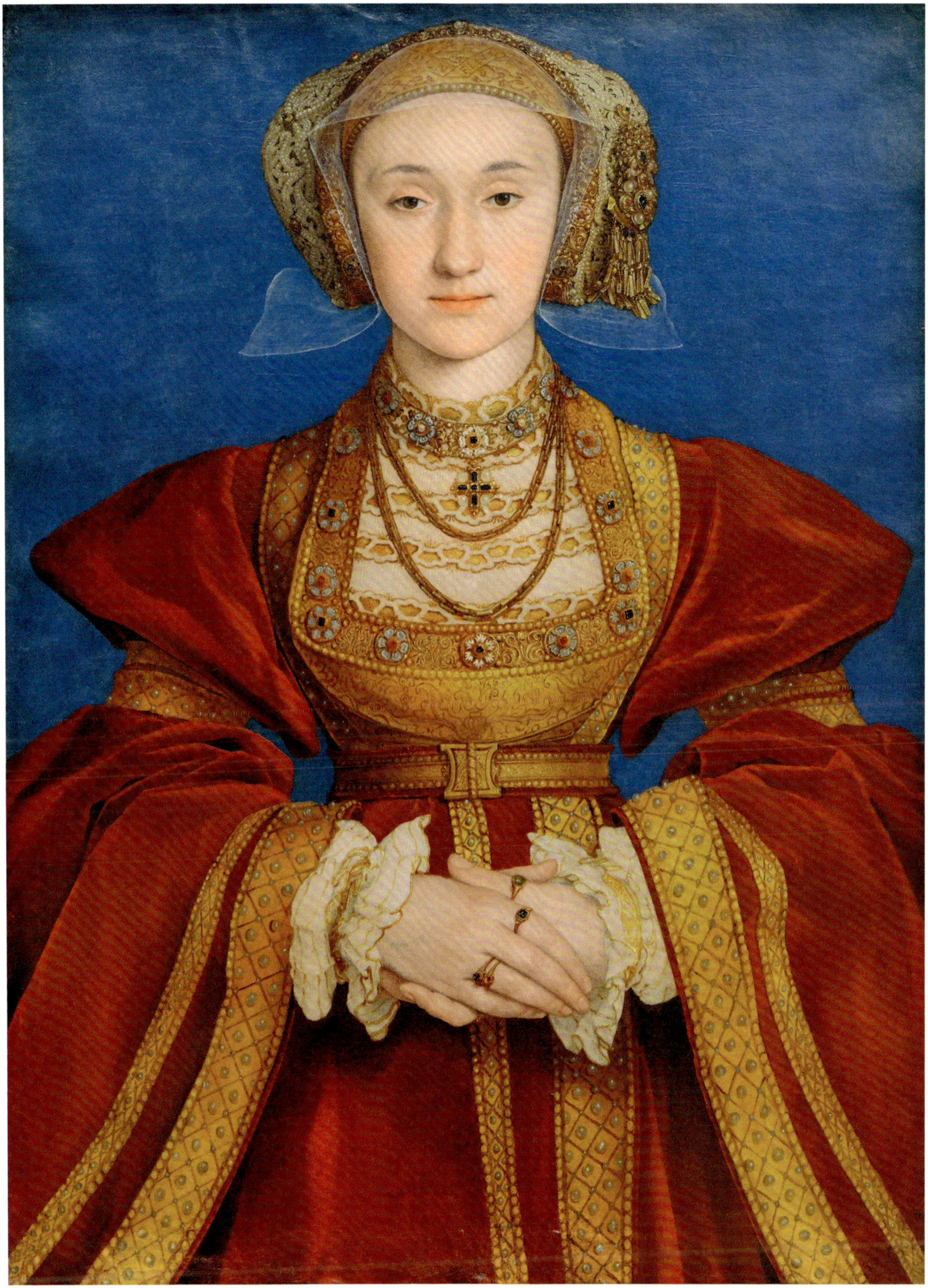

The Ugly Duchess

Quentin Matsys, c. 1513

A budding red flower. A bustling bosom bursting from a skintight corset. Manicured fingers and handcrafted jewelry. Only the best, of course: pearls, a silk veil, a hand-stitched headdress. However, no kings were likely to ask their advisors to arrange a marriage to this duchess.

So why all this effort for a painting that is clearly some sort of prank? Why go through the trouble of detailing it so vibrantly? The Flemish master Quentin Matsys was so precise, you can feel each individual detail: the fuzziness on her mole, the microscopic whitecaps of her pimples. Just look at the orange glimmer of her nasal cavity where light barely passes through. It's a level of attention that's usually reserved for portraits of royalty. And while the easy answer is probably that the Flemish master was so skilled that he simply painted this portrait because he *could*, one tiny piece of context draws a very cool conclusion. Because this painting might not be Matsys's original idea; this recreation of a lost sketch by Leonardo da Vinci, likely by Francesco Melzi, suggests that Matsys's entire painting is actually a nod to da Vinci.

While we can't be sure that the careful composition and exquisite workflow would have made the Italian proud, the satirical nature of the artwork would likely have made him laugh, carrying on the humor of the original. Matsys isn't the end of this sketch's lineage, however. His sixteenth-century work is rumored to be the inspiration for John Tenniel's illustration of the Duchess in Lewis Carroll's 1865 *Alice's Adventures in Wonderland*.

Speaking of Leonardo …

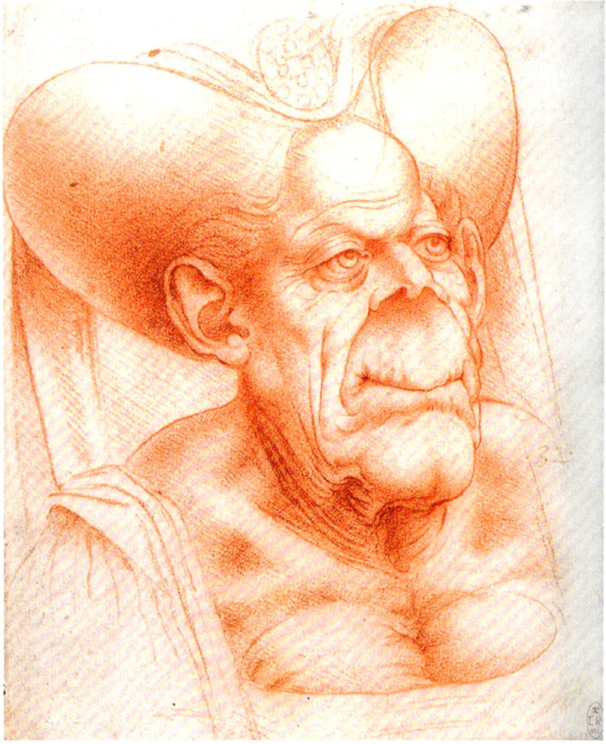

The Bust of a Grotesque Old Woman, After Leonardo da Vinci, c. 1510–20

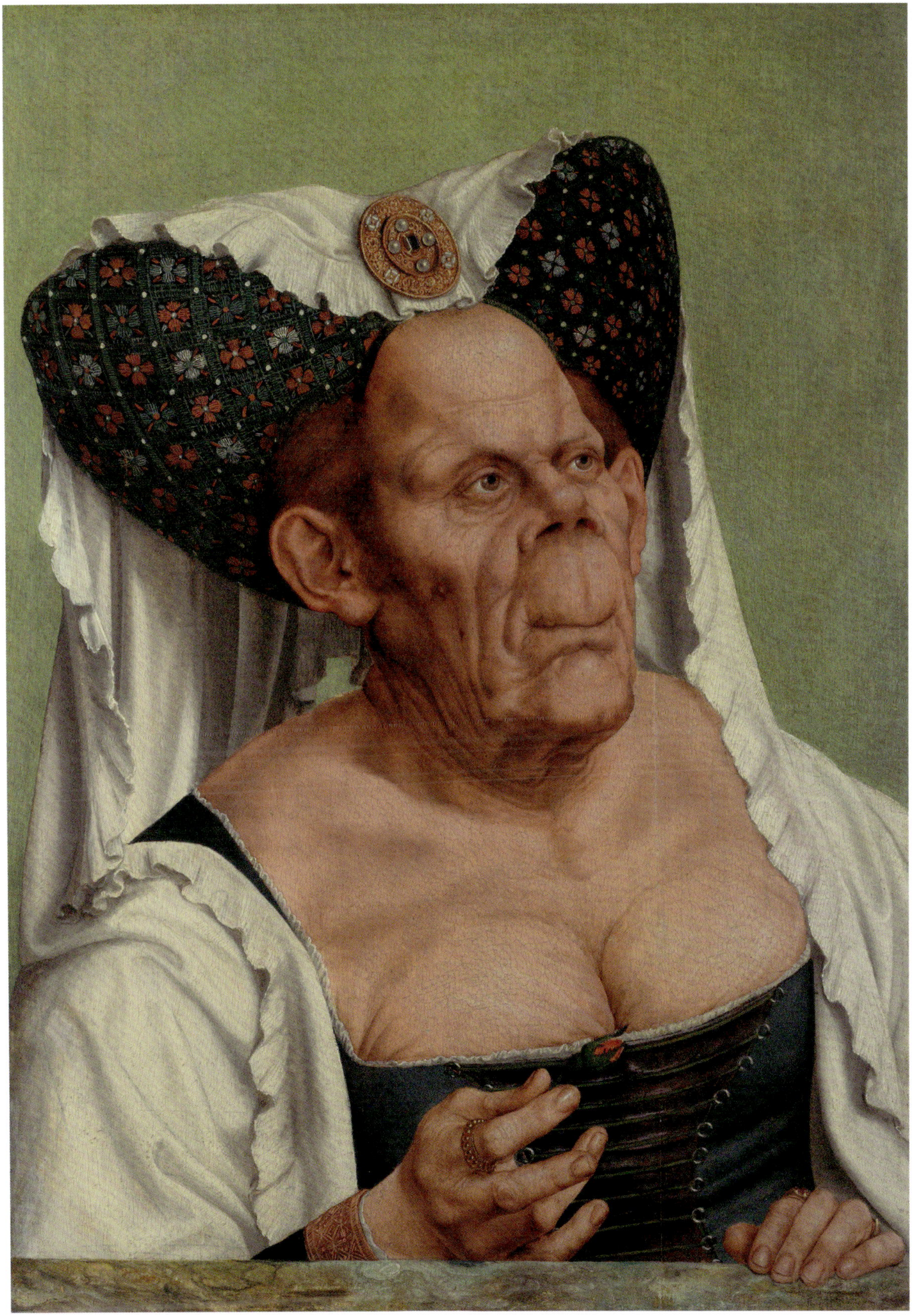

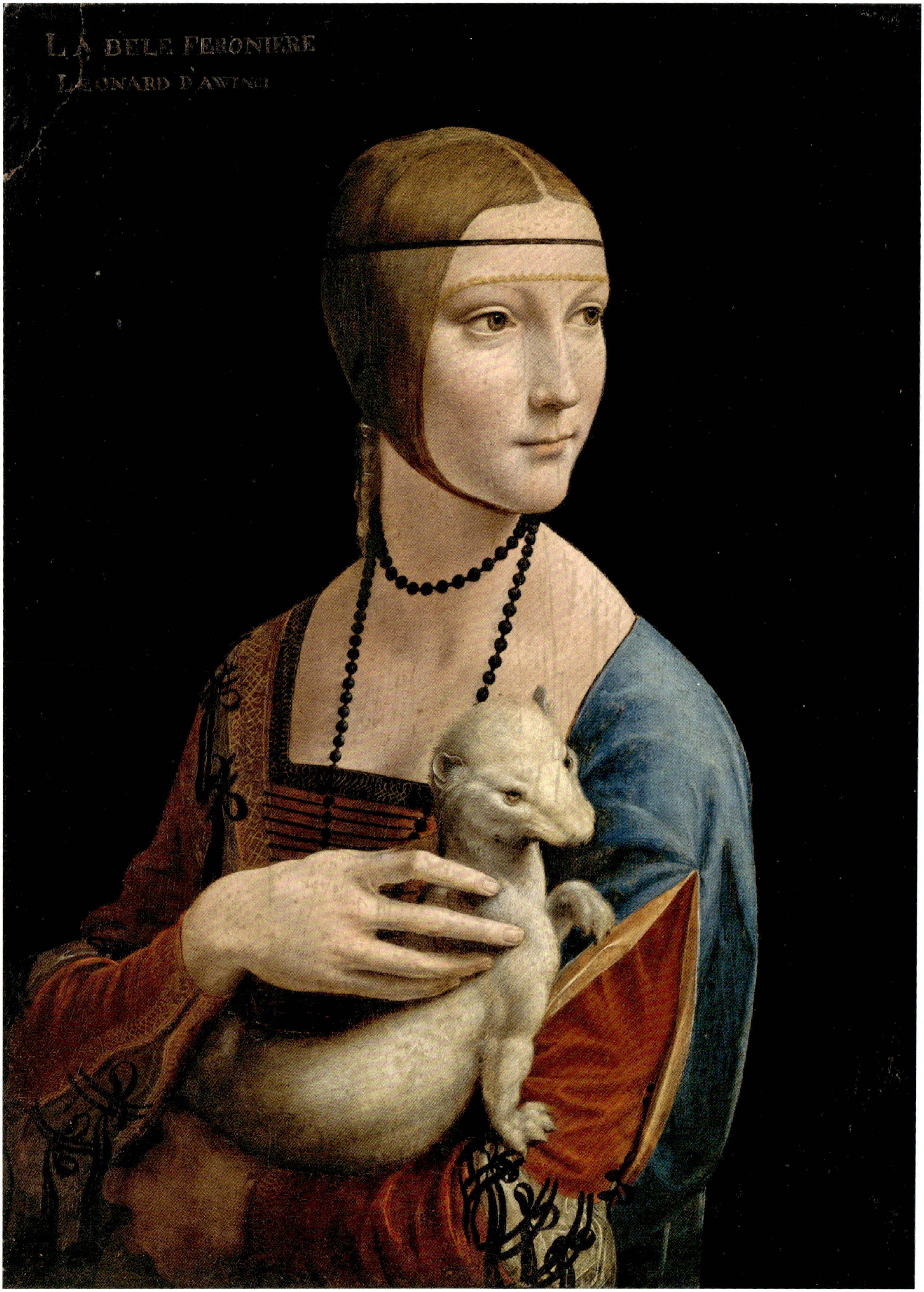
LA BELE FERONIERE
LEONARD D'AWINCI

Lady With an Ermine

Leonardo da Vinci, c. 1489–90

Why is this woman holding a weasel? And who *is* she?

Because while you might recognize her only as the lady with an ermine, the central figure of da Vinci's revolutionary painting—one of the first modern portraits in history—there is actually a backstory to her life, the weasel, and the picture that unlocks an entire segment of art history. And by understanding this story and all its clever little ideas, we peer into the brilliance of Leonardo, and come to understand that in a world of grand artistic personalities, we all stand on the shoulders of his genius.

So, who was Cecilia Gallerani? For starters, she was born into a non-noble family, but that didn't mean she wasn't an exquisite personality. Only a short time after entering the royal court as a lady-in-waiting, she became one of the Duke of Milan's most favorite companions.

She was young, beautiful, educated, and of a keen mind. She could write in both Latin and Italian and discuss literature at length. How could Ludovico Sforza not fall in love? The Duke may have been engaged, but the very same year that Ludovico married Beatrice d'Este, our beloved Cecilia would give birth to his son.

No. The weasel is *not* his son.

But knowing what we now know, we might presume there is more to this portrait than meets the eye. There is a brilliant use of light and shadow, and the subtlety of a master's brush, but we also might look at this portrait and see it for exactly what it is: a painting commissioned by a man in love.

Da Vinci paints Cecilia as an ideal beauty in non-noble clothes gazing off into the unknown. Her form and figure are subtle and sensuous. Her skin, delicate. And her little friend? The glue that can tie this story together, because while in da Vinci's own words, the ermine was a symbol of purity, on the fringes of art analysis, there are other fascinating ideas.

For one, Ludovico Sforza was known by the nickname The White Ermine, due to the King of Naples granting him the Order of the Ermine. Then there's Cecilia's surname: at the beginning of Gallerani, we can hear the word "Gale," which invokes both the Greek word for ermine and a minor character in myth who is turned into a weasel by Hecate for her abnormal sexual desires. The animal also might be a nod to Galinthias, a servant who helps with the birth of Hercules, and as a punishment, is turned into the animal by Hera. In Italian Renaissance culture, the ermine was also thought to protect pregnant women. Was this Leonardo's way of suggesting that Ludovico was protecting Cecilia? We will never really know.

However, what we do know is that da Vinci accomplished something incredible: a feat never before seen in an artwork, or at least a portrait. Cecilia Gallerani is alive. She isn't captured stiffly facing forward, as other portrait subjects were at the time, but is instead caught in motion. She turns her head mid-gesture, eyes teeming with life, as though reacting to something in the room, creating an immense sense of movement and thought. Her gaze is active: a living mind. Her portrait has a sense of psychological immediacy and cinema, centuries before movies were even a thought. Da Vinci shows us a woman who he knew to be intelligent, composed, and at that precise moment, slightly amused, and we can really sense it. How would you feel if you were posing with an ermine? It might be fun, right?

This portrait marks a pivotal point in art where a man or a woman could be regarded as an individual, capable of inner depth. People are no longer depicted as a mask, but as a mirror of consciousness. And by precisely integrating gesture, lighting, and space into his masterpieces, da Vinci suggests a real environment.

Have a look at the portrait on the page 73 by Piero della Francesca. Fantastic, no doubt, but so wildly different. When looking at *Lady with an Ermine* in comparison, you experience the environment of the painting in ways that shouldn't be possible, and yet, here we are. Cecilia Gallerani twists her torso, and we can suddenly breathe the same air. Real air, implied by observing a person who inhabits a *real* world, because she is *not* a symbol frozen in time.

A truly unbelievable achievement that highlights how art, at its absolute highest levels, can transcend the boundaries of a surface. It is a conduit for impossible experiences: a gift that Leonardo da Vinci would give us throughout his life, and isn't that the point? Art that transcends. Art that builds on what's come before it. Art that elevates the craft for future generations while marking your own little contribution to history in the process. An evolution.

It's easier said than done.

But time and time again, once in a generation, an artist comes along to break the mold. And where *Lady with an Ermine* marks the beginnings of a theoretical and philosophical bloodline that would give us *Mona Lisa*, it is Johannes Vermeer alone who gives us its equal.

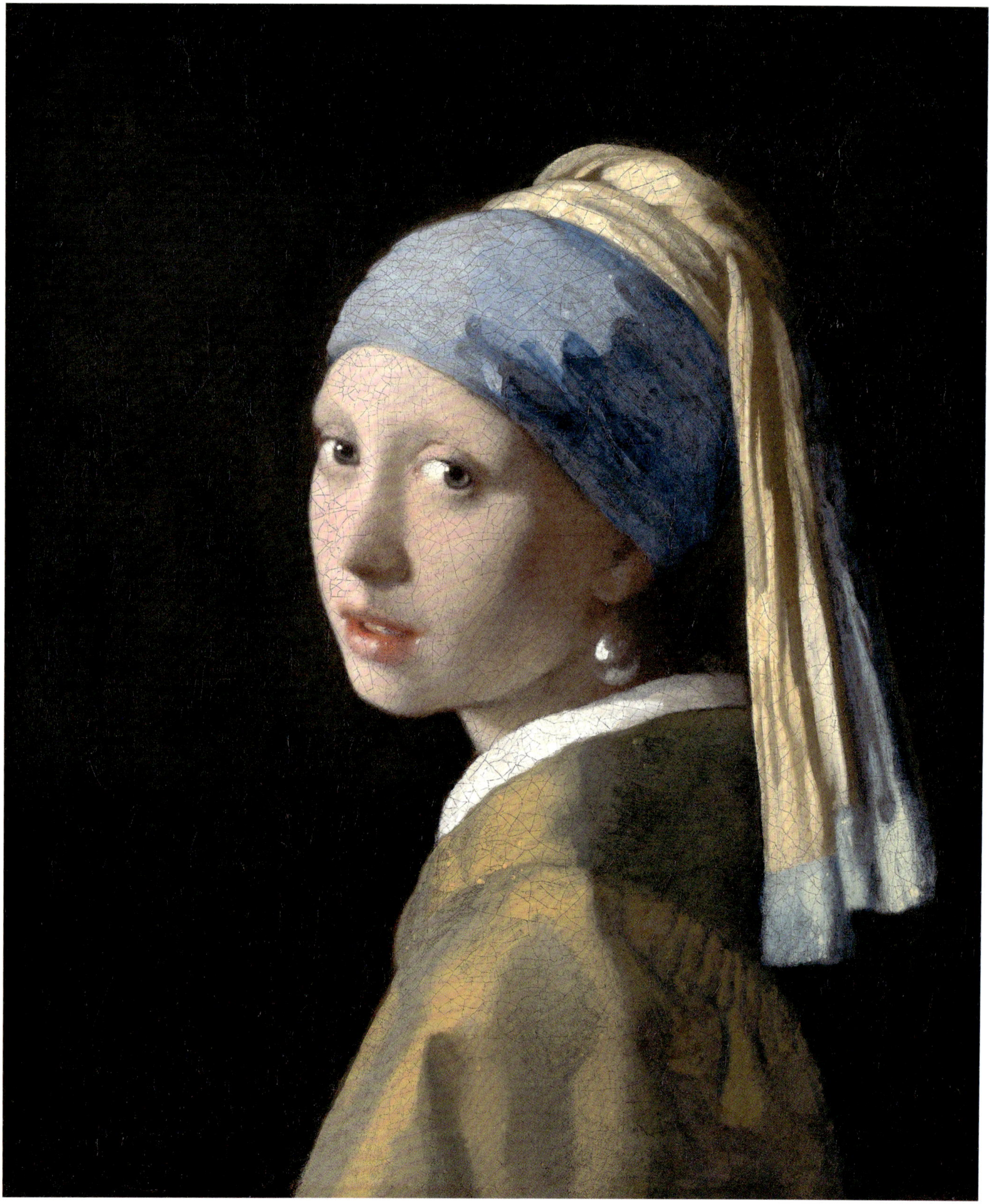

Girl with a Pearl Earring

Johannes Vermeer, c. 1665

It's not quite clear who Vermeer painted in the portrait to the left. Throughout history, this has been a hotly debated subject, some claiming it was his daughter, some an unknown model. Others insist she was a figment of his imagination: an idealized, exaggerated beauty. But what isn't up for debate is whether or not this is one of history's most remarkable artworks, because the answer around the room, regardless of the company you keep, seems to be a resounding "yes."

Girl with a Pearl Earring is a dance between realism of the highest order and an artistic vision—one that creates a lasting first impression beyond expression. And it's not as if you're fooled into seeing a photograph or something that feels real. In fact, quite the contrary. The moment you see her piercing eyes and her delicate features, you know *immediately* that what you're looking at isn't possible, and yet *every cell in your body* kind of wishes, if only for a moment, that she was.

Vermeer's masterpiece lives somewhere in the balance between both possibilities: This is why it works so well. It doesn't play tricks on your senses, but instead plays with the mind's fantasies. *What if?* The details aren't so rich that you gasp at the unimaginable time taken to execute them. Instead, they sort of hover somewhere between your emotions and your thoughts, and you can't look away from those perfect dots of paint. You've become fixated.

"But why?"

I'd like to think that it's because she *catches you looking*. To fully appreciate the potency of her gaze, however, it's worth analyzing other works by Vermeer, because the Dutch Master, over a very limited body of work, famously employs a very clever technique that profoundly affects how we experience his craft.

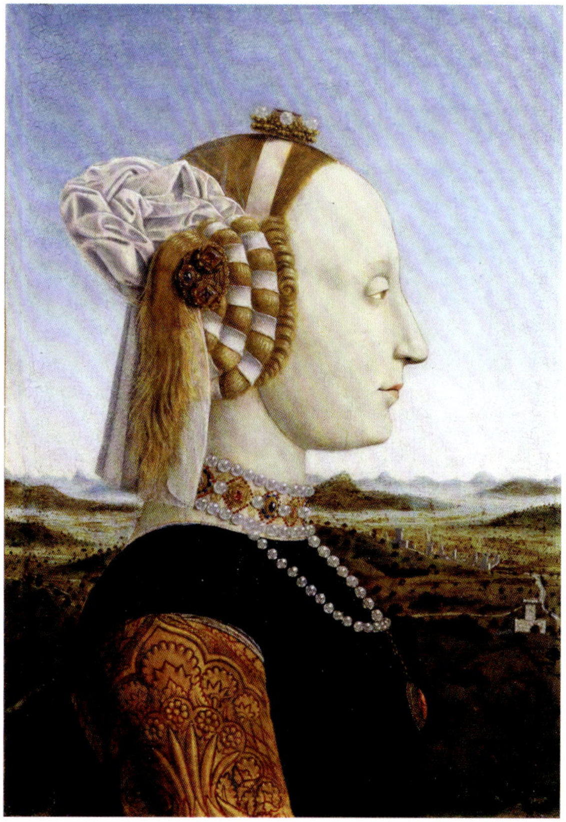

Detail of *The Duke and Duchess of Urbino Federico da Montefeltro and Battista Sforza*, Piero della Francesca, c. 1473–75

Various works by Vermeer

1657–68

The man was obsessed with textiles. I mean *really* obsessed with them. There are many reasons given to explain why Vermeer was a genius, including his exquisite use of lighting, relatable subject matter, or his unforgettable use of blue, but the actual brilliance of Vermeer comfortably lies in his love for a great pattern. And, it has nothing to do with the fact that they are among the most detailed examples of fabrics ever painted. Instead, it's all to do with their s*trategic* placement.

By placing a fabric in between us and the subjects of his artworks, Vermeer creates the illusion of privacy. We are not simply *observing a scene*, but instead, peeking around the corner of an object to witness a private encounter from a distance. We're not quite privy to entering the space and can only look inward.

Turn the page and you'll find *Officer and Laughing Girl* (c. 1657), in which a man in an all-consuming red uniform cuts us off from a conversation with his back turned to us. We wouldn't dare interrupt. In *The Glass of Wine* (1658–60), a couple chat at a table where an extra chair is pulled out from underneath, but it's piled with objects. It isn't an invitation to sit, and asking to join in would be an intrusion. Even in a picture like *The Girl with the Wine Glass* (c. 1658–69), where a young lady stares you right in the face, her large red dress makes approaching intimidating. It feels as though she catches you passing by as opposed to walking in, and you wouldn't for a second consider changing direction because it risks an unwanted confrontation. You wouldn't want to be rude.

This is why *A Girl with a Pearl Earring* works so well. There is nowhere to hide. No obstruction, no shelter, and by the time you make eye contact, it's too late. You've been caught staring: You're a trespasser in *her* space. You can't change direction because she's so intimately close and you're frozen in your tracks. What do you say to her? What do you do, locked into what feels like an eternity with one of the greatest portraits in existence?

"The eyes are such a powerful tool. They really say it all."

They do. But the eyes aren't the *only* windows to the soul. In fact, one of the greatest portrait painters in history found an even more revealing form of bodily expression, and frankly, it's unexpected.

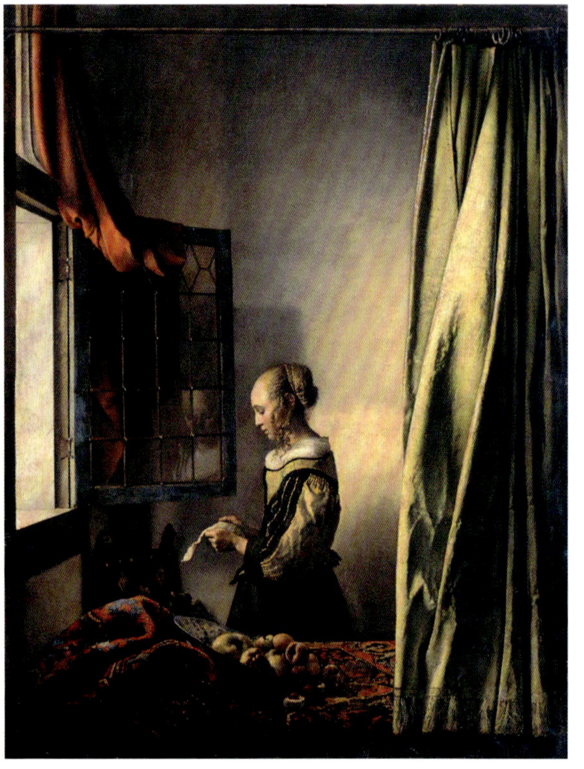

Girl Reading a Letter at an Open Window, c. 1657–59

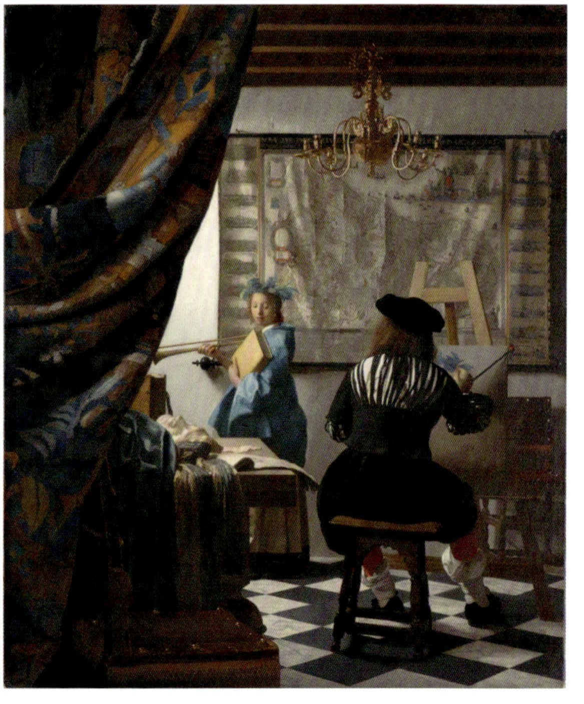

The Art of Painting, c. 1666–68

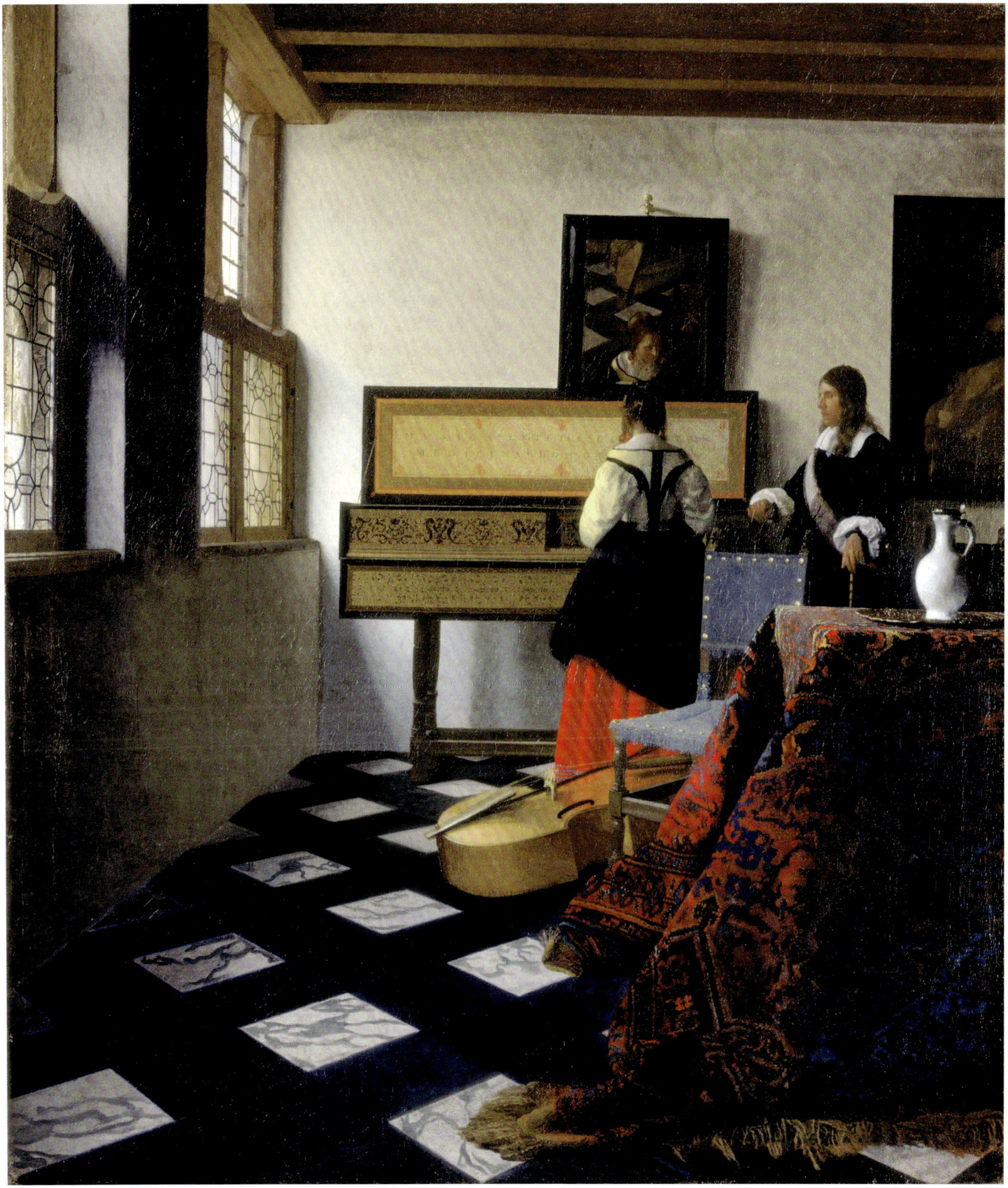

The Music Lessson, c. 1662–65

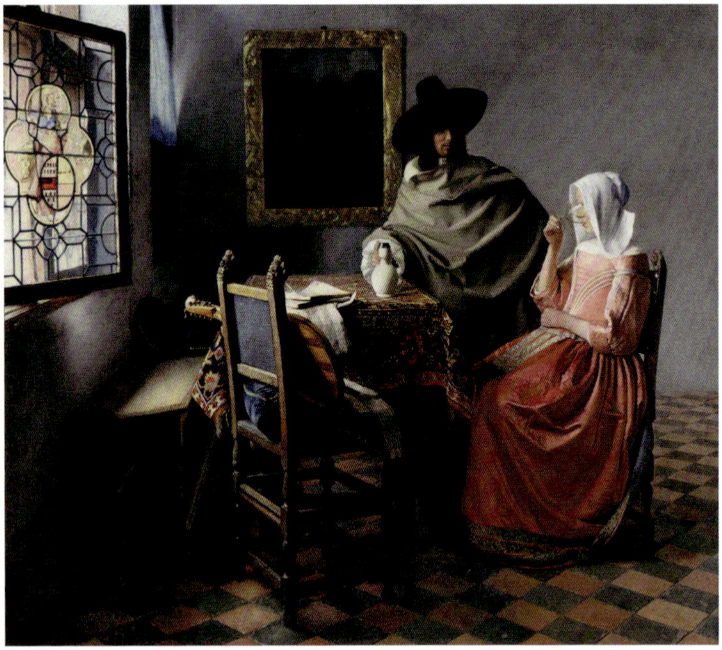

The Glass of Wine, c. 1658–60

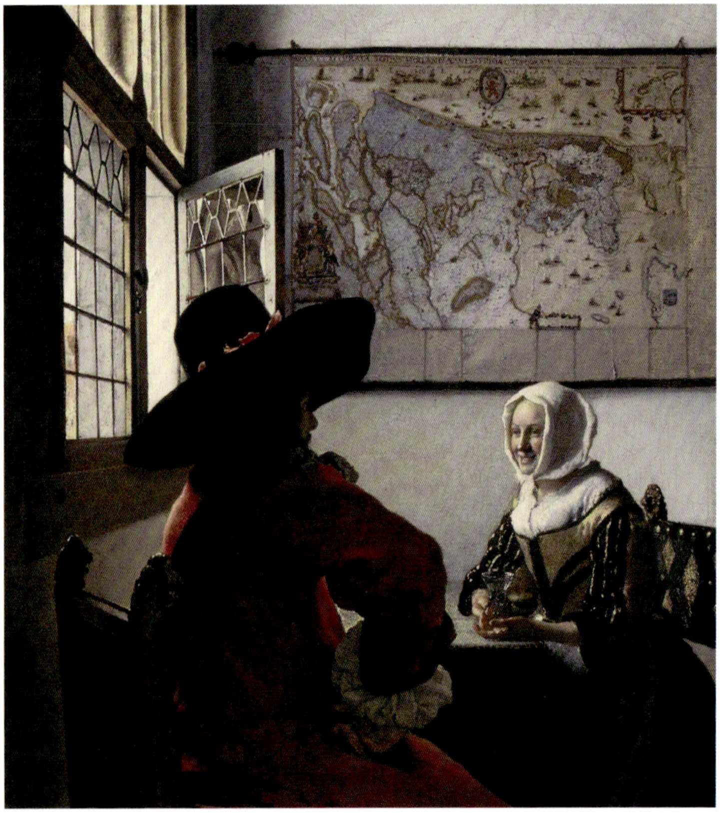

Officer and Laughing Girl, c. 1657

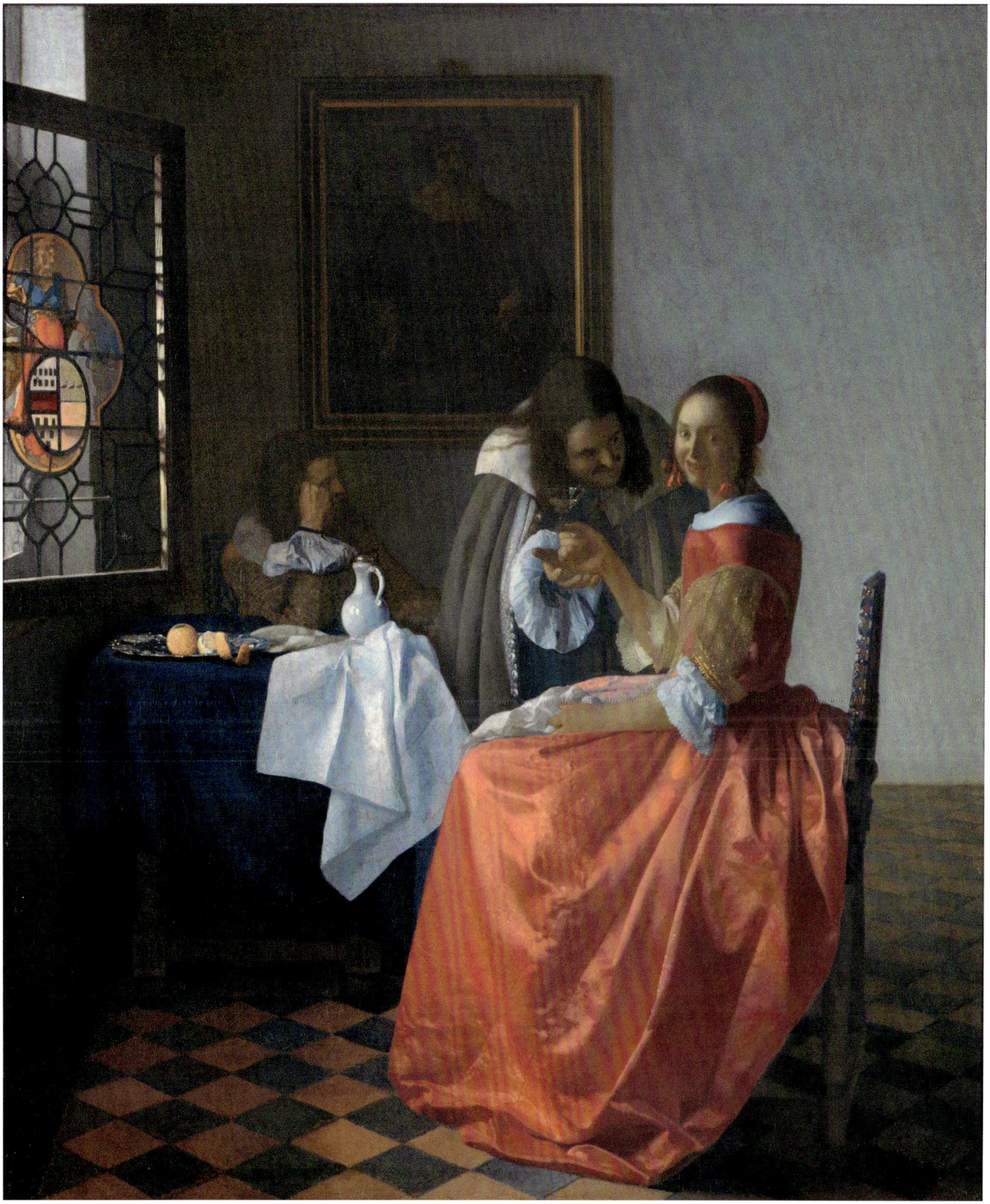

The Girl with the Wine Glass, c. 1658–59

El Jaleo

John Singer Sargent, 1882

The hands: an extremity that, when examined closely enough, can tell you everything you could ever want to know about a person. In John Singer Sargent's 1882 masterpiece, *El Jaleo*, they are the glue.

A Spanish dancer clacks her heels on the wooden floor, harmonized with the clacking of her castanets, and a line of musicians strum their guitars with a vibrant ferocity. An intense sense of motion is reassured by the axis of her posture. Sargent shows us form through sound, physicality, and theater in a way that is completely unique. Now have another look at the hands—not just the ones belonging to the dancer, but *all* of them.

On the left side of the painting, in the line of musicians, we can see a man clapping his hands, mirroring the snapping pitch of the central figure's castanets: an injection of sound and musicality that suits the vibrant strumming of guitars in the dramatically lit room. On the right, a woman in red reacts, hand raised above her head, all consumed by the frequency. She is responding to an audible experience, yes, but a visual one too, reflecting the dancer's movement. That very same dancer who, with one hand, holds her dress, and with the other, holds our eyes. We are watching a professional at work. Truly a master of her craft, her suspenseful pose enveloped by the crowd.

Three separate expressions to echo the marriage between three separate art forms, which *El Jaleo* nods to equally: music, dance, and the visual arts. Sound, form, and a visual stimulus. And Sargent doesn't do it with an intense, thought-provoking gaze, or micro facial expressions, but with an appendage, and it leaves an indelible mark.

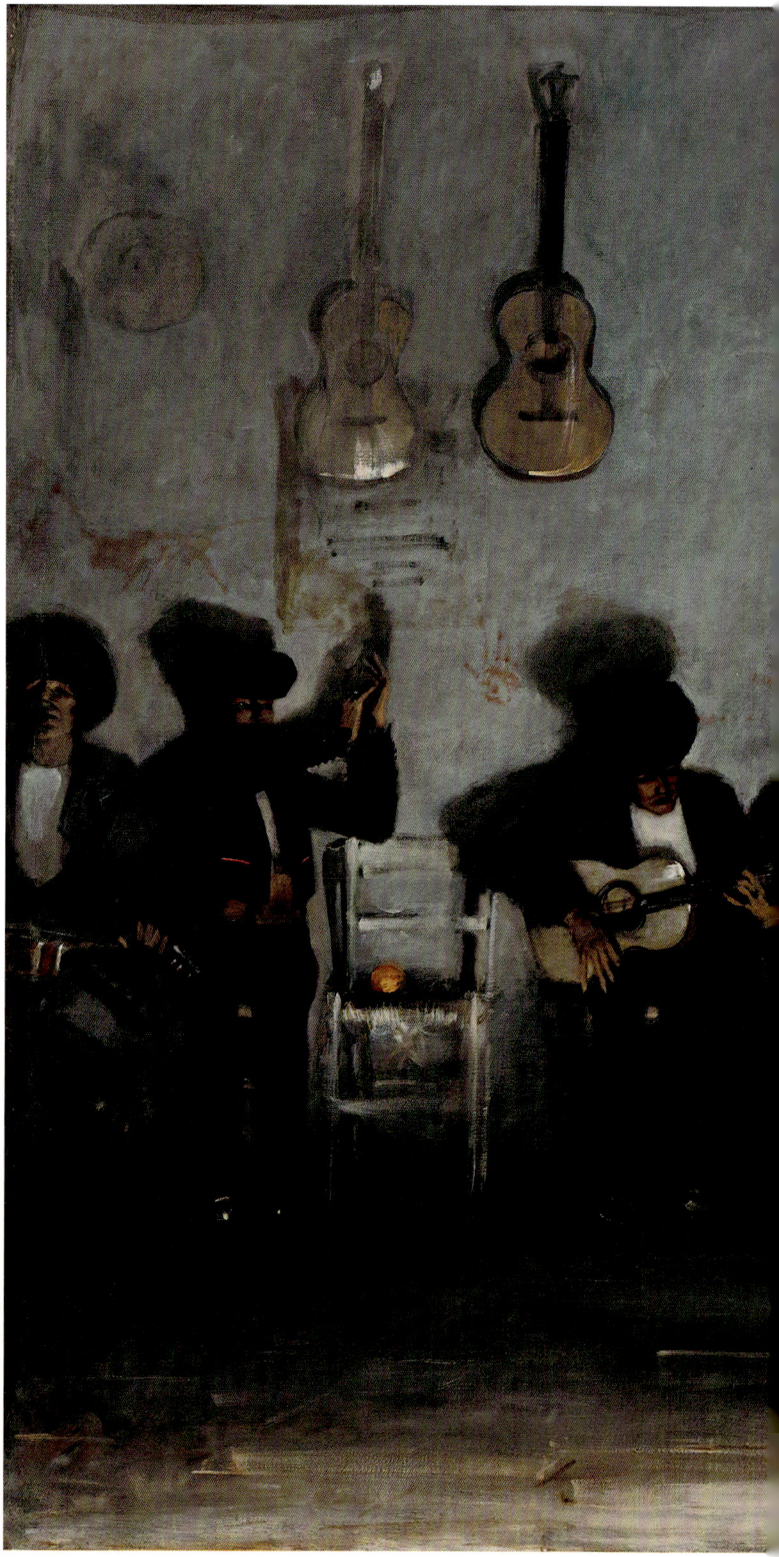

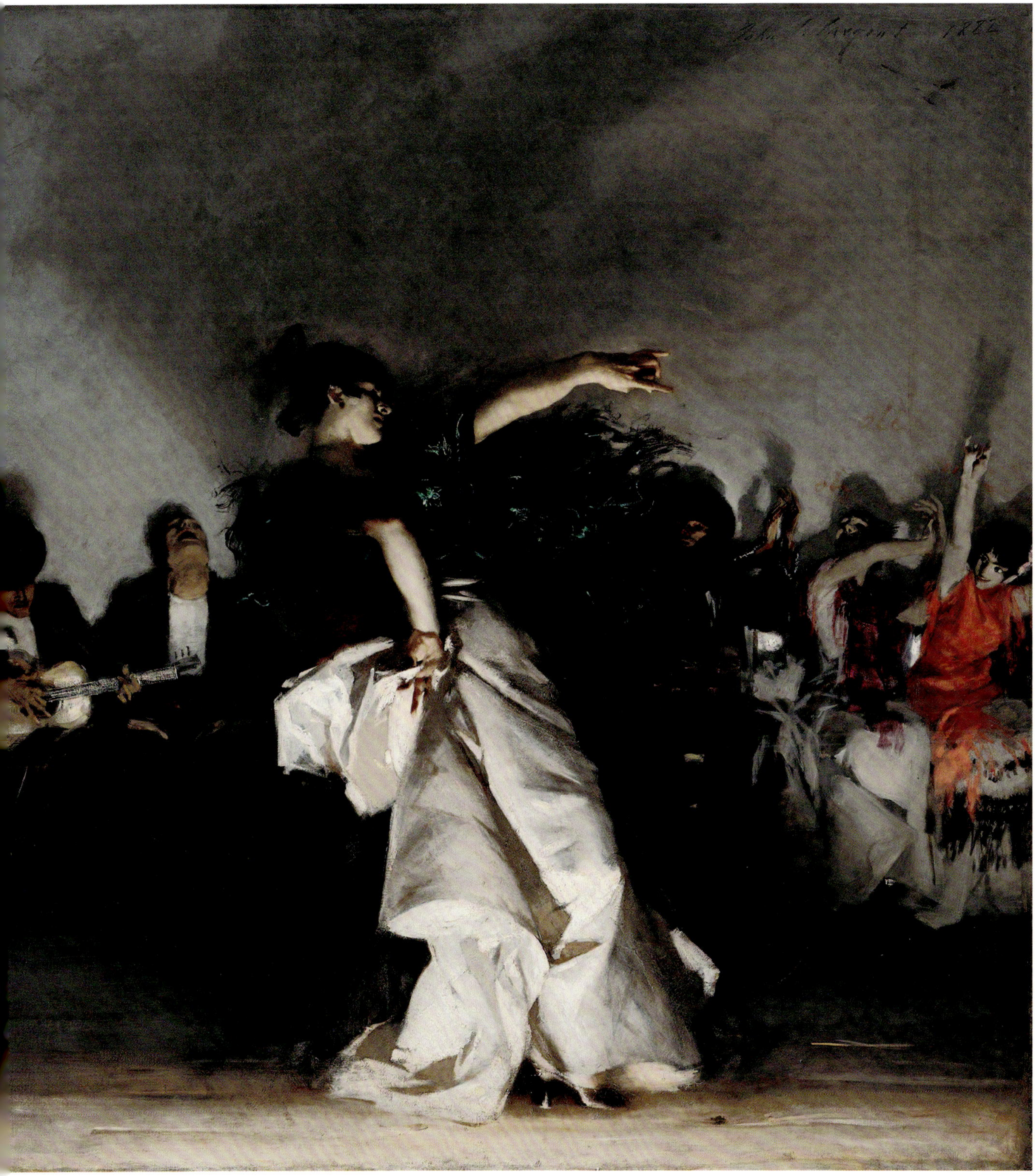

Carnation, Lily, Lily, Rose

John Singer Sargent, 1885–86

El Jaleo, at first glance, bears little connection to Sargent's 1885 masterpiece beyond its ability to sweep you off your feet. But while this colorful painting is so gesturally full—spectacular in every sense of the word—it is once again hands that serve as the glue in this garden strewn with roses, carnations, and lilies. Among the flowers, the delicate fingers of Dolly and Polly Barnard, daughters of illustrator Frederick Barnard, carefully handle wax tapers to light lanterns.

The composition is dominated by a fading evening light, capturing the garden's exact transition between the setting sun and the light of the paper lanterns. Its atmosphere *perfectly* catches a fleeting twilight glow that only exists for a few minutes each evening. It is a painting that embodies innocence, transience, and ritual. And while we might first observe it as a sensory experience evoked by all these elements, its heart of youthful bliss and the fragility of a moment can be reduced to the delicate nature of Sargent's figures, and to their hands specifically. The two girls handle their lanterns with the utmost sensitivity, and in this moment, we get the feeling nothing else exists for the pair.

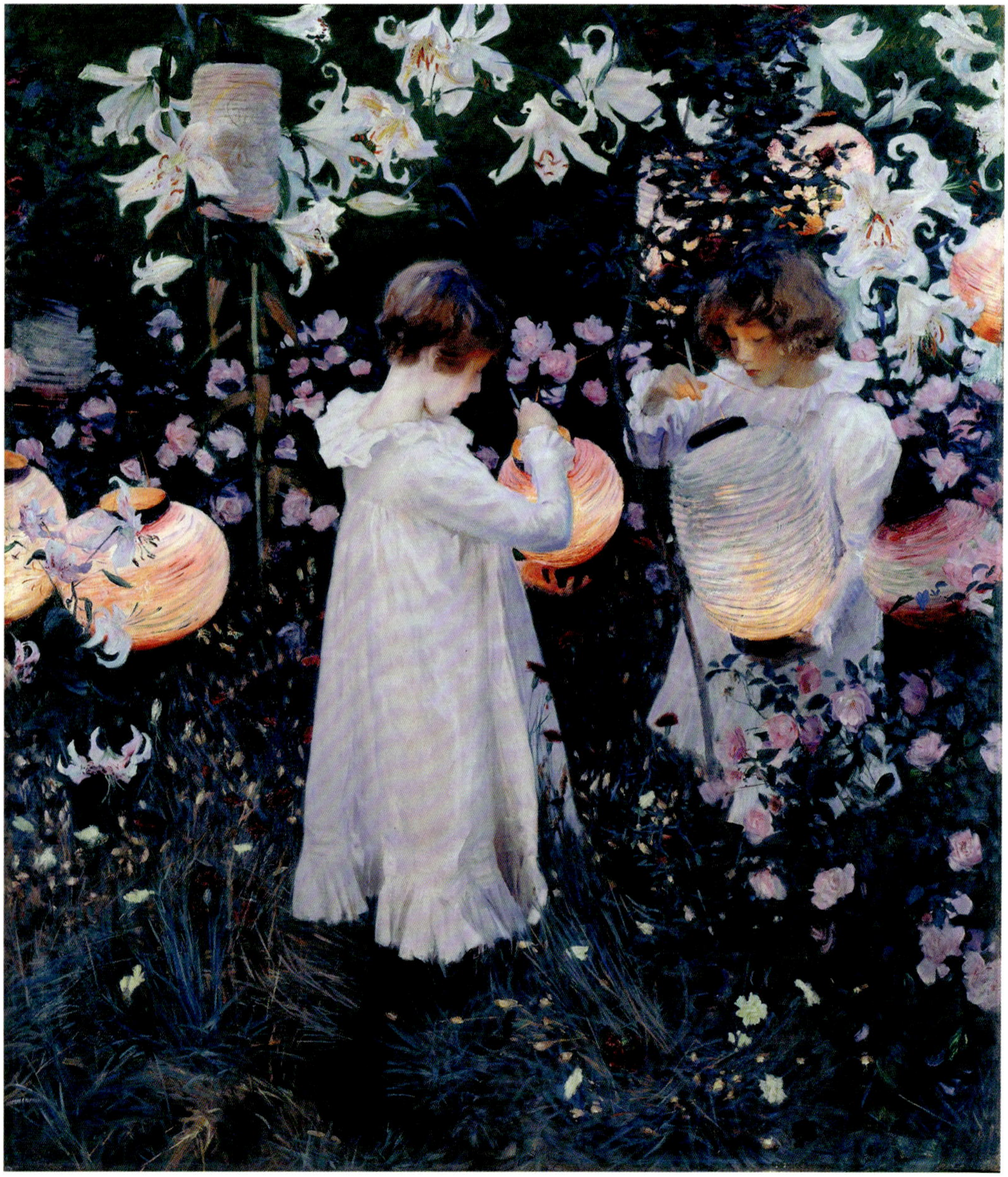

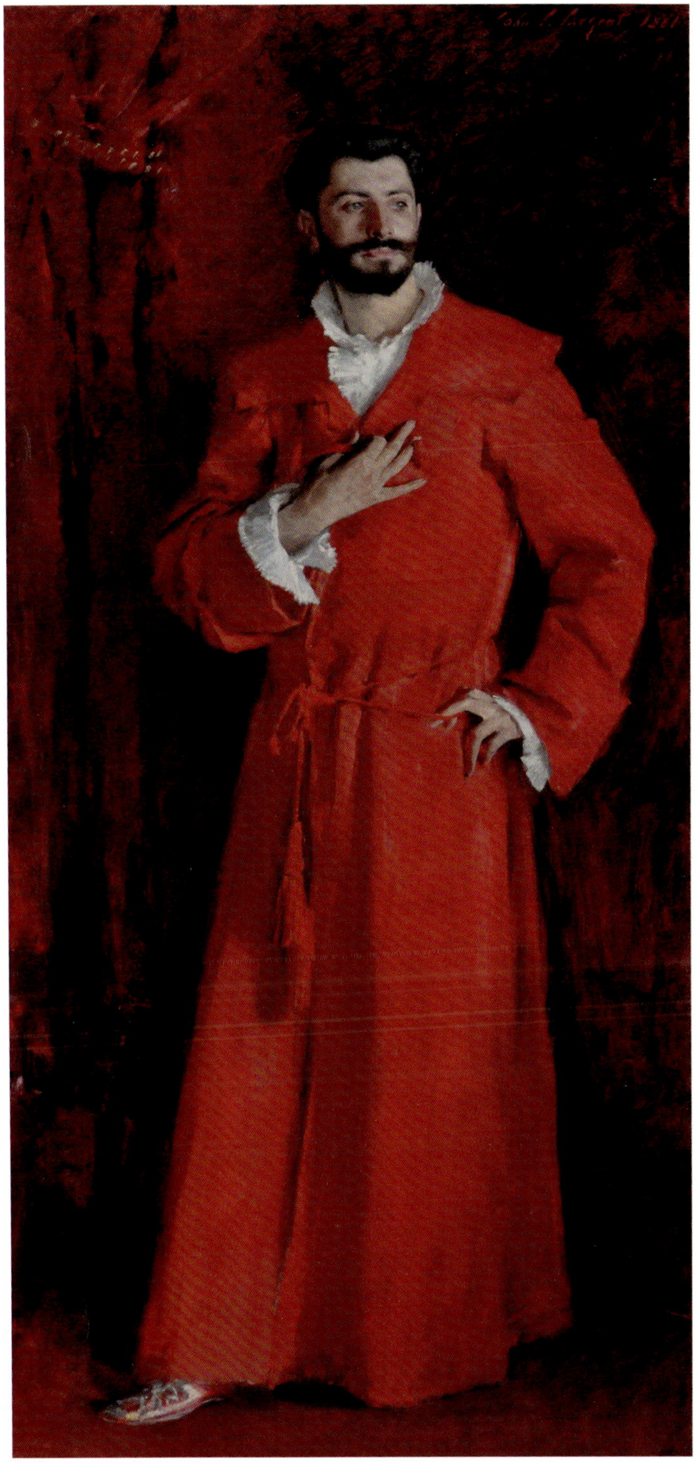

Dr. Pozzi at Home

John Singer Sargent, 1881

Sargent's portrait of this esteemed medical man in his home is rife with sexual innuendos. Just look at his vibrant red robe floating on a sea of an equally commanding red. He is undeniably handsome, and I'm not the only one who thought so. Dr. Pozzi was a famed gynecologist and art collector in the daytime, and an equally famous adulterer at night. This lends to the choice of color: a red to match a highly public and prolific love life.

But what of his hands? In this portrait, Pozzi is shown to be carefully holding together the front of his robe, assisted only by a thin string of silk on his waistline. Is this a gesture to reinforce his sensuous nature? Or is it a nod to his profession? Or, maybe it's both? In the wider canon of John Singer Sargent, it may even be the first domino that set in motion one of the greatest scandals in art's history, as we'll see on the next page.

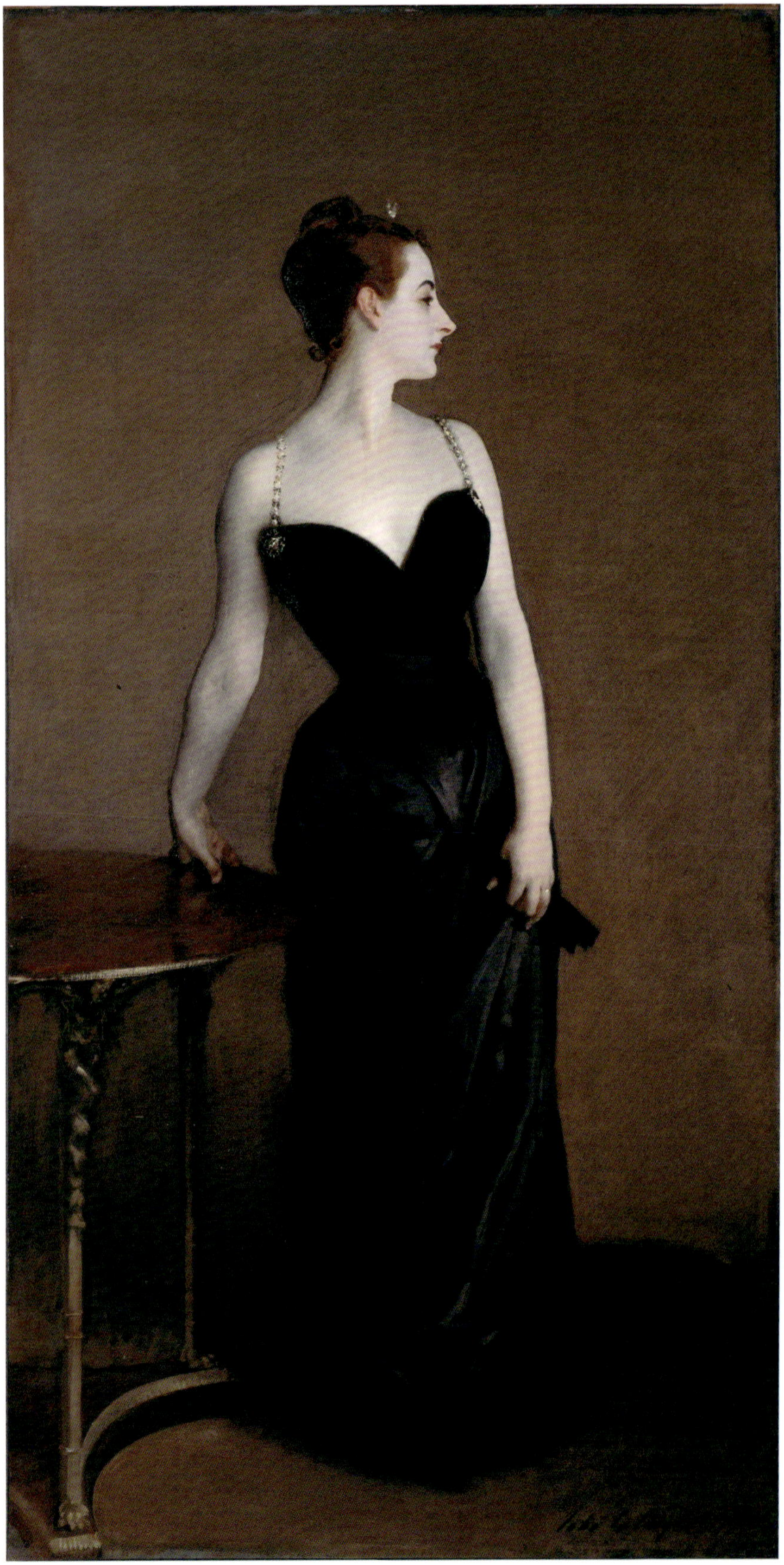

Madame X

John Singer Sargent, 1883–84

The scandal in question involves a hand, a dress, and a strap that ruined a woman's life. Viewed through modern eyes, the entire ordeal is kind of nuts. That is, of course, until you realize that everything in 1800s Paris was also kind of nuts.

The woman in this portrait is Virginie Amélie Avegno Gautreau, and she was the nineteenth-century equivalent of an influencer. She was exotic, beautiful, desirable, fashionable, easy to adore, and a frequent figure in the tabloids. Everyone wanted a piece of her, which is why, when Sargent had a chance to paint her, he knew it could be career defining moment.

He was a rising star in a Western art world that was changing: the embodiment of painters who refused to create idealized images, instead capturing exactly what they saw. And that's what he did with Virginie.

Over a sea of muted earth tones, she is painted in a stunning black evening dress with sparkling golden straps and a V-shaped plunging neckline, exposing all her sensuous features. Her pale skin and pretty face, her tiara for status, her hand planted on the table, where it takes the form of an exotic dancer and echoes her entire figure; here we have the motif of hands used again to subtly expose the nature of her personality. Her hand doesn't scream for your attention, and neither does she. Rather, she just commands it. A curvature to meet her body's own, and a simple elegance to meet her extraordinary presence.

Madame X is one of the greatest portraits ever made. But why was it so scandalous? Well as I mentioned, 1800s Parisian society was nuts. And as it so happens, the version of this portrait that you're familiar with isn't the one that was shown at the Salon on opening day, because as Gautreau modeled for Sargent, the strap on her right shoulder slipped. In the original, it was painted like you see to the right.

People were outraged. So much so that Virginie was cast out of mainstream circles, and Sargent, in large part due to the negative reception, was forced out of Paris.

That was, of course, *after* he fixed the strap.

And the rest, my friends, is history.

All scandals aside, some might rightfully consider Sargent to be history's best when it comes to portraits. Others might point to certain Dutch Masters, like Rembrandt or Frans Hals. A case could be made for the great Flemish painters like Peter Paul Rubens, Anthony van Dyck, or Jan van Eyck. But a definitive answer? That's impossible. For a time it was Goya, but there is also Velázquez. Or maybe it's da Vinci, or Ingres, maybe Albrecht Dürer. The list goes on. But, on a list of the all-time greats, a name that constantly repeats is Élisabeth Louise Vigée Le Brun—"The Queen of the Portrait," and in my personal view, one of the genre's most important artists.

She was a visionary, who in her long and illustrious 86-year life, created around an astounding 660 portraits, and 200 landscapes. More than a painter who transformed her own craft, she elevated the entire craft of painting to new heights. A master of her form, Vigée Le Brun was also a master student with a keen eye: not only for the fundamentals, but for how and where one could improve.

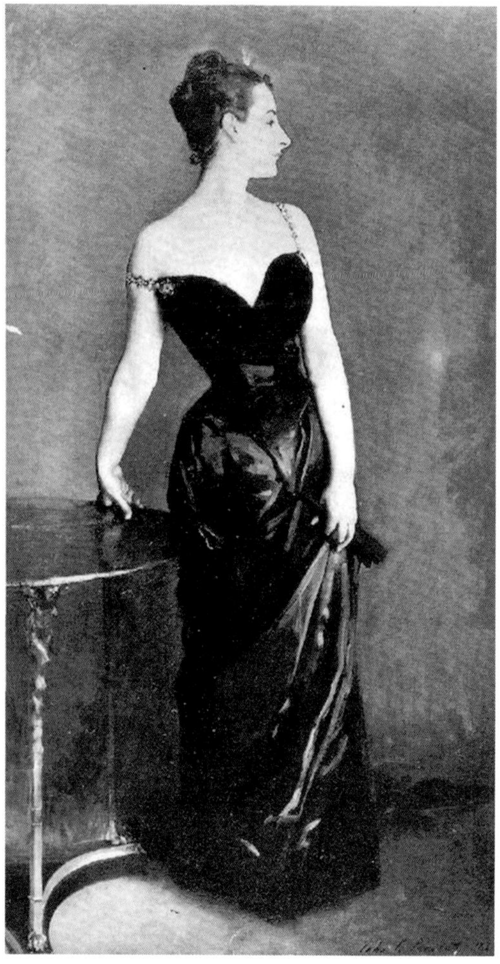

Madame X before repainting, 1883

Self-Portrait With a Straw Hat

Élisabeth Vigée Le Brun, 1782

On a tour of the Netherlands, Flanders, and Brussels in 1781, a 26-year-old Vigée Le Brun became infatuated with the Flemish Masters and their unique, stylized approach to painting. Her insights on this trip would directly impact one of her most significant artworks, *Self-Portrait With a Straw Hat*: a brilliant execution of ideas and an homage to Peter Paul Rubens's *Portrait of Susanna Lunden* (1622–25).

Making use of a vertical composition, both artists depict figures turned slightly in a three-quarter frame, looking directly toward the viewer with a wide-brimmed hat crowning their heads. Rubens, in his own right, was a master of chiaroscuro, a term referring to the use of strong contrasts between light and shadow to create a sense of drama and volume; his portrait employs aspects of the technique, though not to their full effect, to accentuate the inner life and dimensionality of its muse. Vigée Le Brun echoes his work, highlighting her own features and hat to convey vitality and immediacy.

Both paintings are vivid, lively, and with respect to the times, modern. The figures are dressed informally. They're fresh, spontaneous, and smiling, rejecting the artificiality of formal court portraiture in favor of something that feels natural. Both also portray agency and intellect; though nothing remarkable to modern viewers, in the male-dominated world of the 1600s and 1700s, this was a radical idea.

Of course, their most obvious shared element is the inclusion of a hat. It's funny to think of this as true their binding agent, until you recognize the accessories as symbols. The hats represent Independence: in Rubens's portrait, a bourgeois elegance; in Vigée Le Brun's, artistic freedom and enlightened ideals. Hers is a rejection of courtly ornaments in exchange for an item worn by real, everyday people.

This is a motif that would set Vigée Le Brun apart from the rest: her ability to humanize a subject, no matter who that person was.

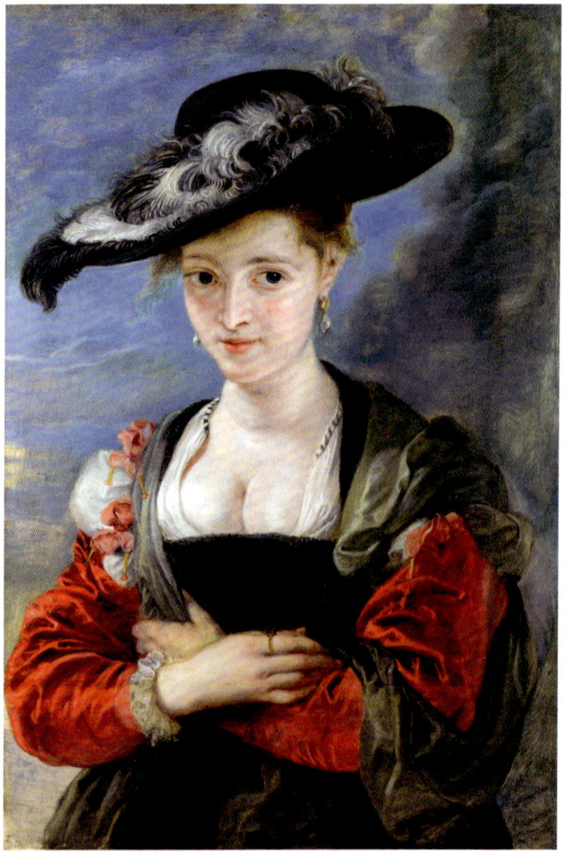

Portrait of Susanna Lunden, Peter Paul Rubens, c. 1622–25

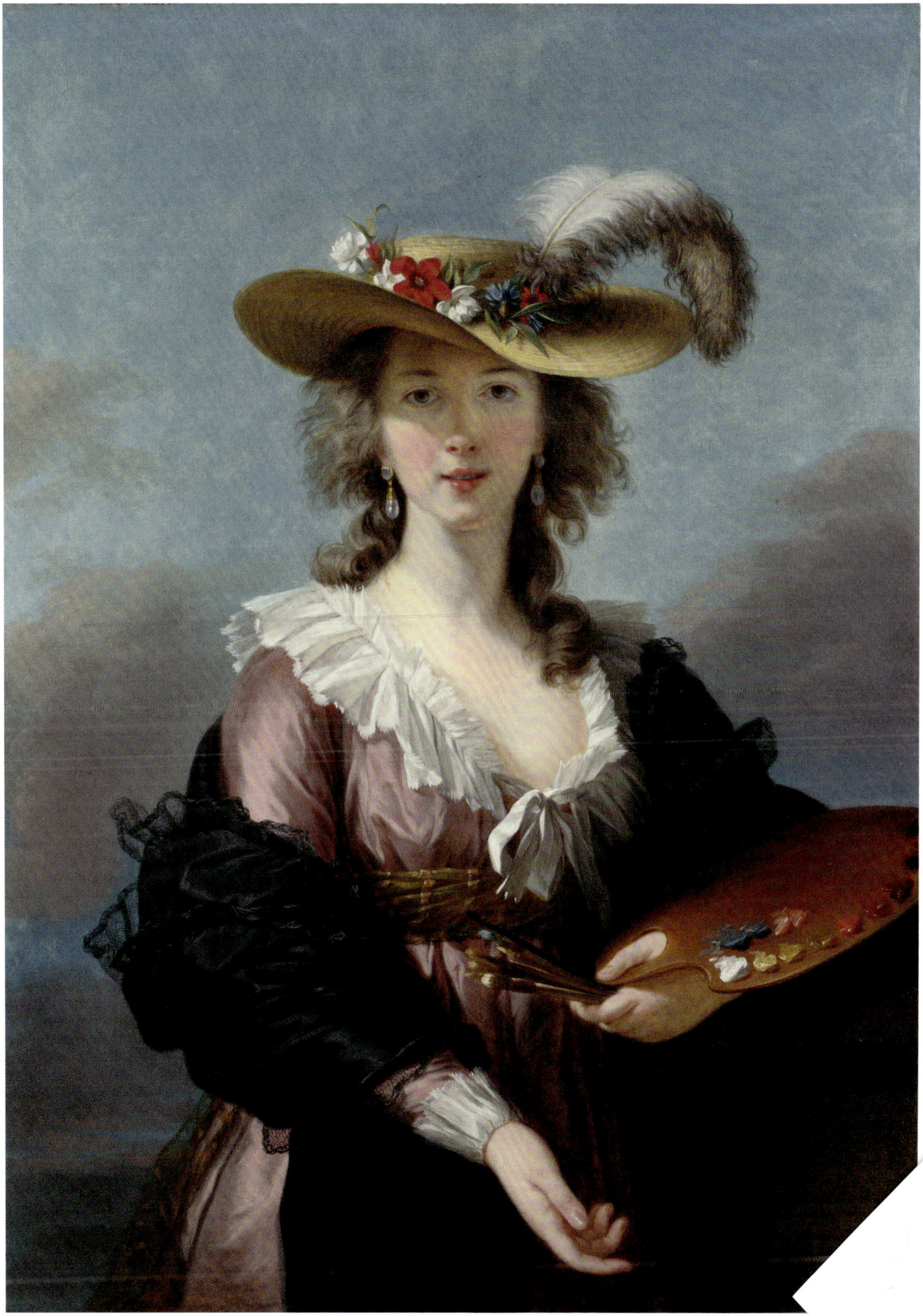

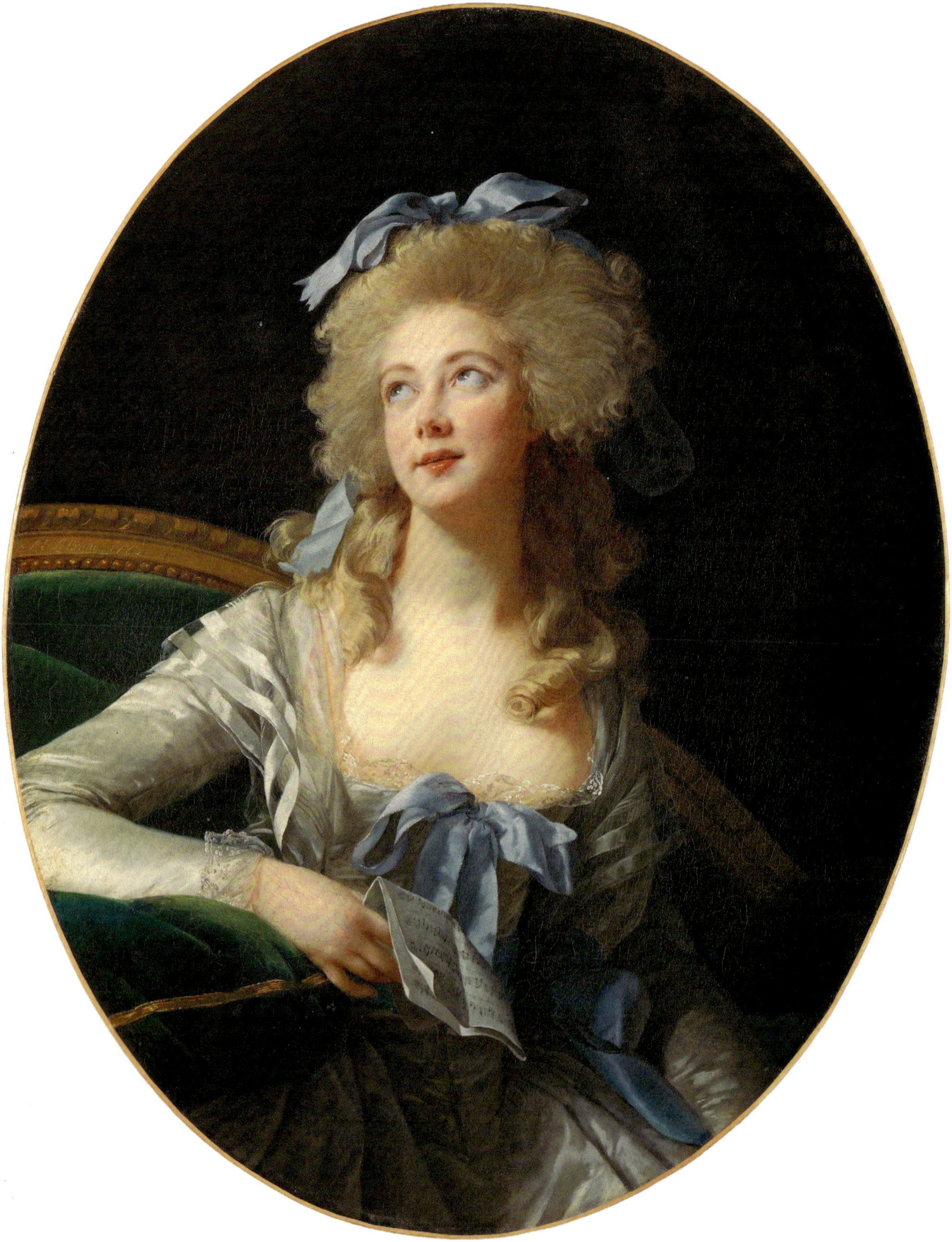

Madame Grand (Noël Catherine Vorlée, 1761–1835)

Élisabeth Vigée Le Brun, 1738

Noël Catherine Vorlée, later known as Catherine Grand, was born on 21 November, 1761, in Tranquebar, Danish India, to a French colonial officer and French mother. She was given a private education, learning to read and write, and showed immense talent at an early age in dance and art. In 1777, she married George François Grand (hence the name change), an officer in the English East India Company, and shortly after, became involved in a scandalous affair with a member of the Supreme Council of Bengal named Philip Francis.

She was in love but married to the wrong man—at least, that's how it seemed. Even after being sent back to live with her family in the hope of the affair ending, Catherine and her lover persisted. Which takes us to December of 1780, when the pair decided to leave India on separate ships, one to London and one to Paris, with the plan of meeting on the continent.

"Right…"

As it happens, Catherine would fall in love again before she left the ship: this time with a gentleman named Thomas Lewin, a colonial official from Madras. Her ship was actually diverted to London, where Francis was bound, but Catherine did not follow through on their planned reunion. She stayed with Lewin instead, and in 1782, the couple would move to Paris before their own relationship ended.

Are you getting the pattern?

This was a woman *beyond* conventional beauty. She was both exotic and familiar: intelligent, talented, a social butterfly, and as it appears, the desire of every man who ever crossed her path. *She was a flirt*. These are important details when understanding why her portrait by Vigée Le Brun is an incredible example of an artist capturing a person.

It was titled *Madame Grand*, because by this point in her life, Catherine had famously become a courtesan who kept elite company. And Vigée Le Brun, in an oval painting, shows us everything we could ever need to know about her.

Vigée Le Brun doesn't overcomplicate the image with sets and overzealous props, but instead, distils the rawest aspects of her subject so that we can see what makes her a *real* human. Catherine playfully rolls her eyes away from us, exposing her neckline, which is highlighted further still by a nearly black backdrop. She is of the most delicate qualities: her hair, the materials of her dress, the blue ribbons on her head and breast. She'll as likely forget us as she forgot Francis, but we don't care. Vigée Le Brun paints a portrait so commanding, we bend the knee. Think of what it was like to meet her. Really think about it. From the day she was married to the day she sat for this portrait, what spells were cast? That's the motif. That's the *genius*.

Vigée Le Brun doesn't simply catalog a person's appearance, but instead captures the feeling of encountering them in real life: an elevated heartbeat just to be noticed. The hope for one second of eye contact and acknowledgement. By positioning Catherine with her eyes rolled away from ours, Vigée Le Brun achieves exactly that effect. We chase her while wondering how many others have done the same.

A great painting isn't about first impressions. It's about the pulse of the experience long after you walk away. It's about how, with your eyes closed, you can picture the work with the clarity of someone who had taken it home. And, in ways, you have taken it with you. A great painting becomes a part of your fabric.

That was Élisabeth Louise Vigée Le Brun's talent. She was someone who painted unforgettable images; an artist of such profound qualities that, in the same year that she covers the inner life of a courtesan, she infamously paints one of the most important portraits of Marie Antoinette, the Queen of France, in one of her career's most politically charged works.

Marie Antoinette in a Chemise Dress

Élisabeth Vigée Le Brun, 1783

Marie Antoinette wanted to be portrayed as a natural, modern woman. She wanted to show a side of herself that celebrated simplicity and sincerity as opposed to being viewed as a distant monarch. That doesn't seem so bad, right? Letting the people of France see her for what she was, which was, indeed, a real person. Well…

In her portrait by Vigée Le Brun, Marie Antoinette is captured as a soft fixture against a warm backdrop. She wears a loose chemise dress made of a fine white muslin, flowing and unstructured, with no corset or heavy brocade. On her head she wears a straw hat, and, in her hands, she holds a brilliant pink rose to symbolize grace, femininity, and purity. Nothing overly complicated for the master painter, and Vigée Le Brun renders the textural elements of the picture to feel intimate and unpolished. Translucent fabric, warm skin tones: It's really unlike anything seen in a royal portrait, and especially one that would be entered into the Salon. This is a painting that broke almost every rule of royal representation, but so what? It was what the Queen wanted, and who was Vigée Le Brun to deny her?

Oh, what a disaster.

When the painting was finally exhibited at the Salon of 1783, the public outcry was explosive to say the least. It was a scandal on every front and confirmed to a public, who were already disgusted with the monarchy, that the Queen was frivolous and disconnected from her responsibilities. What was meant to be a dress that showed a casual and approachable side to Marie Antoinette was instead interpreted as an undergarment, and completely indecent. The muslin made matters even worse, because it was an item imported from the colonies, which was interpreted as an unpatriotic rejection of French silk, a major national industry.

The backlash was so severe, the painting was immediately withdrawn from the Salon. A career-ending outcome, unless you're Vigée Le Brun, because to save her reputation, and in attempt to do the same for the Queen, she quickly painted another portrait, to be re-entered into the Salon before the event ended.

Marie Antoinette with a Rose

Élisabeth Vigée Le Brun, 1783

The single most famous portrait of the monarch was painted with the sole aim of redemption. Vigée Le Brun paints her in nearly the exact same pose, with many of the same core attributes, but this time, with some major upgrades. In the place of a casual chemise dress, she covers the Queen in an elegant classic blue–grey silk. A large, stripped ribbon is tied underneath a tastefully exposed neckline adorned with rich pearl jewelry fit only for a woman of elite status. This was a Queen: one who not only looked the part, but did her part to support her people. Her expression is calm, maternal, and dignified, and against the background of the trees and sky, Marie Antoinette embodies the roles of grace and serenity. And Vigée Le Brun is still able to capture a little bit of what the Queen had initially hoped to project: a natural, modern woman, but this time she strikes a balance. Marie Antoinette is both queenly and approachable. She is of enormous status yet still human.

This time it works.

The portrait helped restore Marie Antoinette's dignity in the public eye, temporarily reestablishing her image as a benevolent, cultured monarch (at least to some), with a tremendous effect on the trajectory of Vigée Le Brun's career, who saw the prices of her paintings soar.

Today, the impact of the portrait still stands true. It is regarded as one of the great masterpieces of Late Rococo painting, a case study for how portraiture functioned as a form of political messaging, and a testament to Vigée Le Brun's artistry and determination. In a moment of great public outcry, the painter blended flattery, diplomacy, and psychological depth to set herself on a path for a legendary career.

A career that highlights, above all else, that the true function of portraiture at the highest levels is the art of capturing an actual person as they are. This doesn't require a hyper-calculated realism, or an explicit citation of the subject's characteristics through "on the nose" inclusions, but, instead, honesty. Which is exactly what the Dutch Master Rembrandt Harmenszoon van Rijn also manages in his 1641 portrait, *Agatha Bas*.

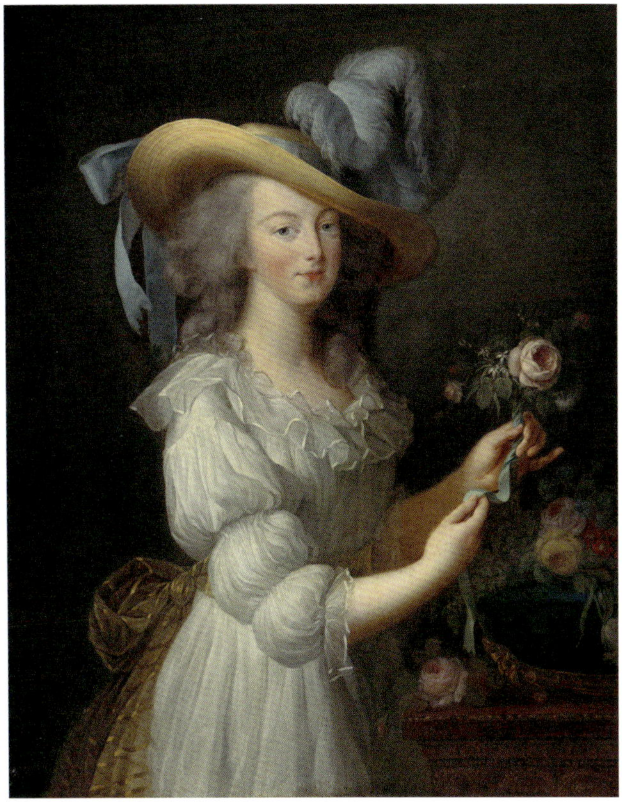

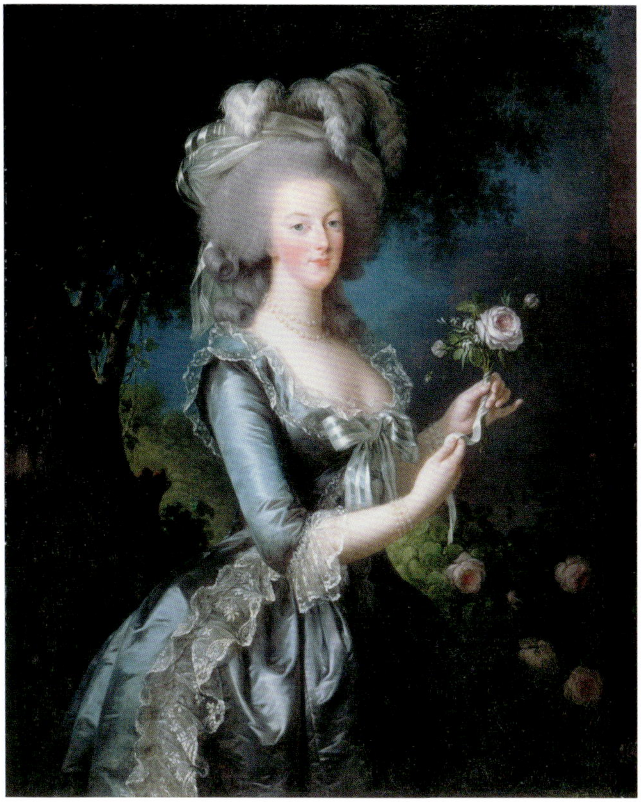

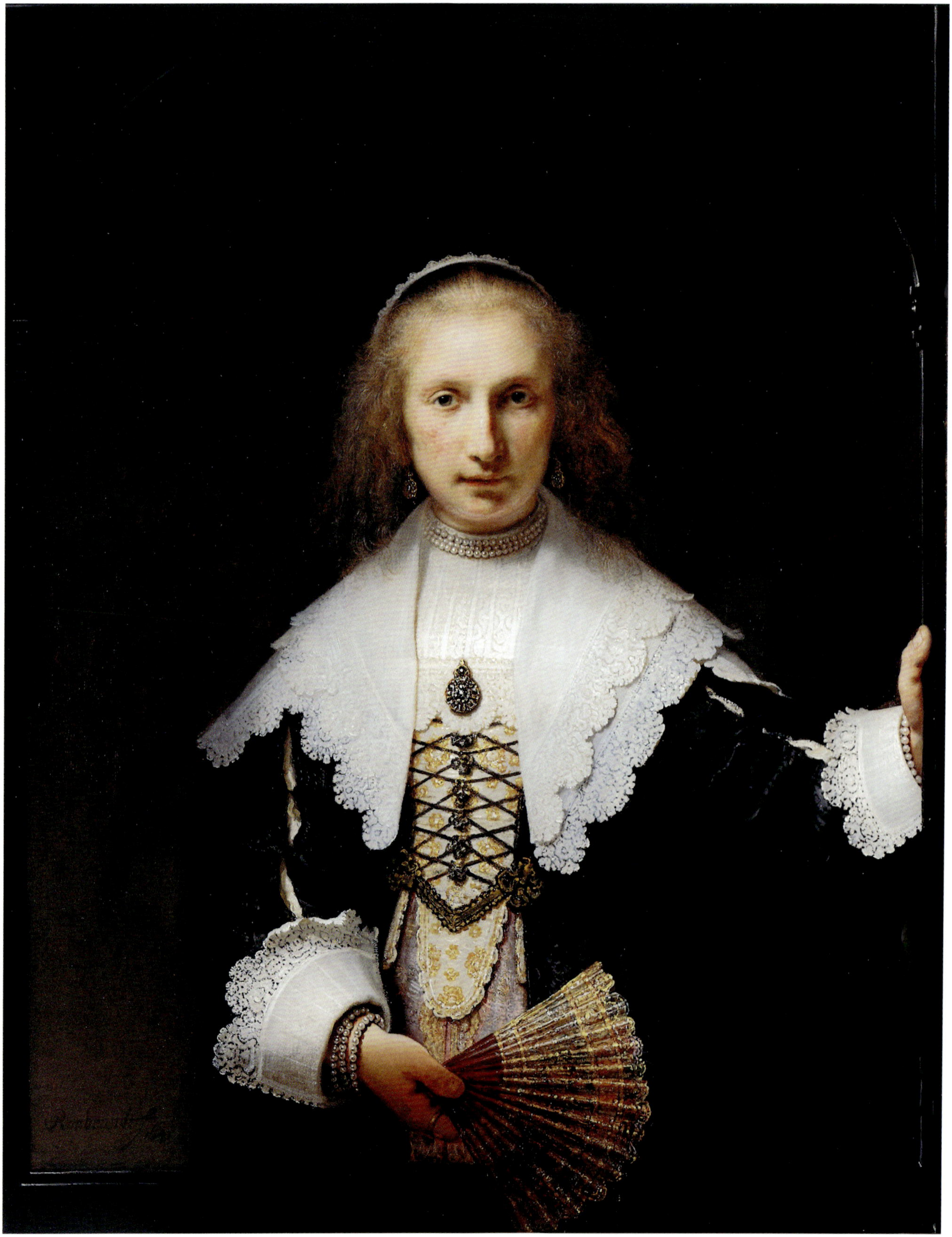

Agatha Bas

Rembrandt, 1641

Agatha was the daughter of a prominent Amsterdam family with ties to the Dutch East India Company. In her portrait, we see a delicate dance between thick globs of paint, spattered across the ribs of the folding fan, and thin layers of pigment delicately scattered across her exposed skin. Imperfect skin albeit, but portrayed truthfully and softly, akin to the real thing. Rembrandt provides us with dimension, with elements that pop off the canvas and break into real life. Look to the right side of the painting and notice the edge of her hand breaking the fourth wall as she grips the edge of a post, as if she's gripping the edge of a frame.

We no longer see, but instead feel the textures of each decorative detail: the silky quality of her coat, her cuff, the roundness of every pearl glimmering in the light, as if we were getting dressed for a portrait ourselves.

And as we comb through every little mark made by the master's brush, what is perhaps most impressive is that we've not only gathered a sense of this day's materiality, but we can feel the psychological properties of presence. A Rembrandt is often appreciated as a series of elements that bounce out of the foreground, but that ignores the painter's ability to draw us in, trapping us inside the work itself with this woman, on her special day with the master.

That same master employs this portrait's arrangement of details to extraordinary effect to create a unique experience. We aren't looking at the artwork convinced that it's more than a portrait, but rather, we accept that even though it is a painting, it contains properties beyond the mediums that made it.

The same, however, can't be said about a series of images created by Italian painter Giuseppe Arcimboldo, who over the course of his entire career, and more specifically, across a few very peculiar paintings, fully convinces you that you're seeing something that really isn't there.

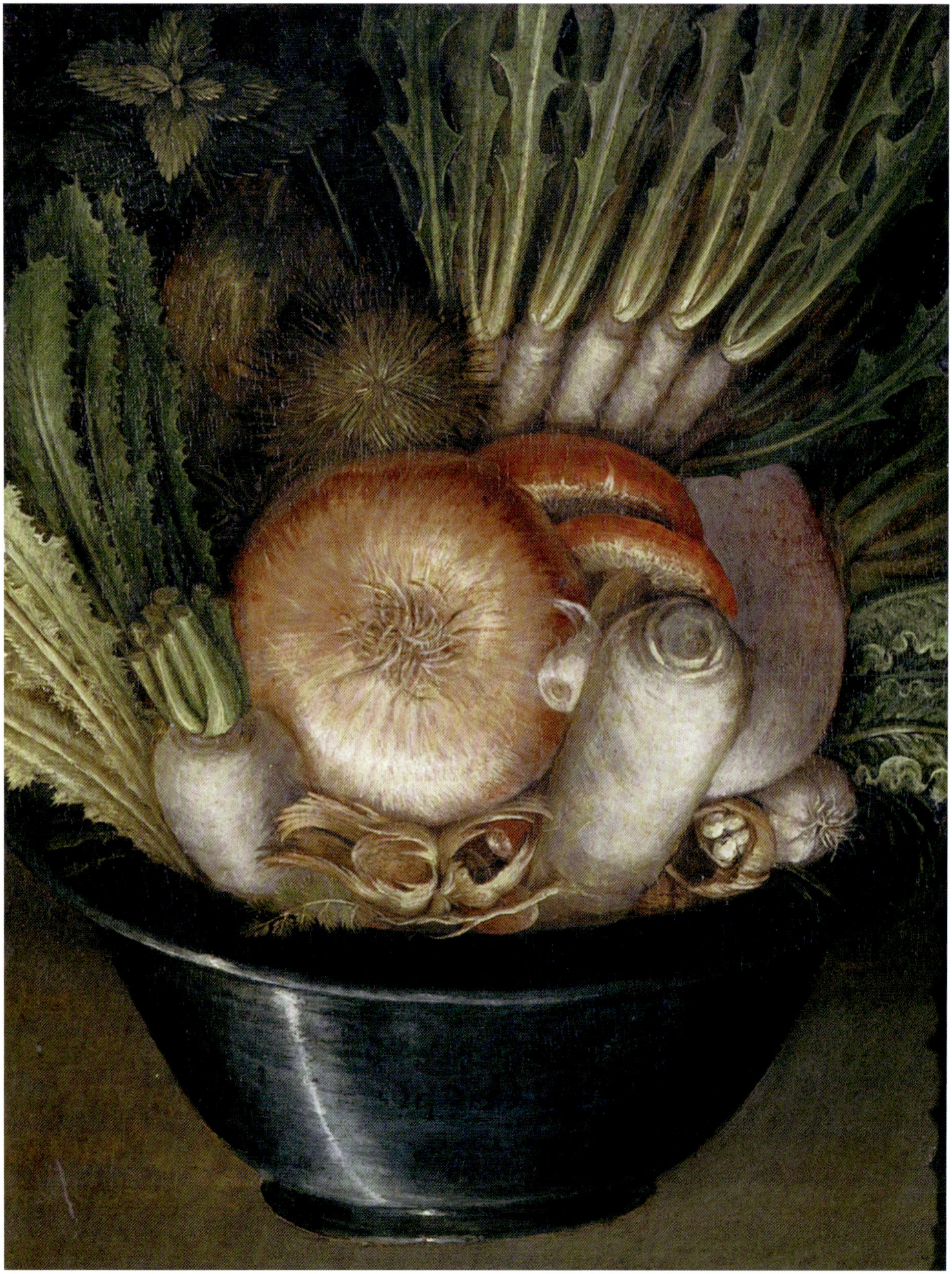

The Gardener, Giuseppe Arcimboldo, c. 1587–90

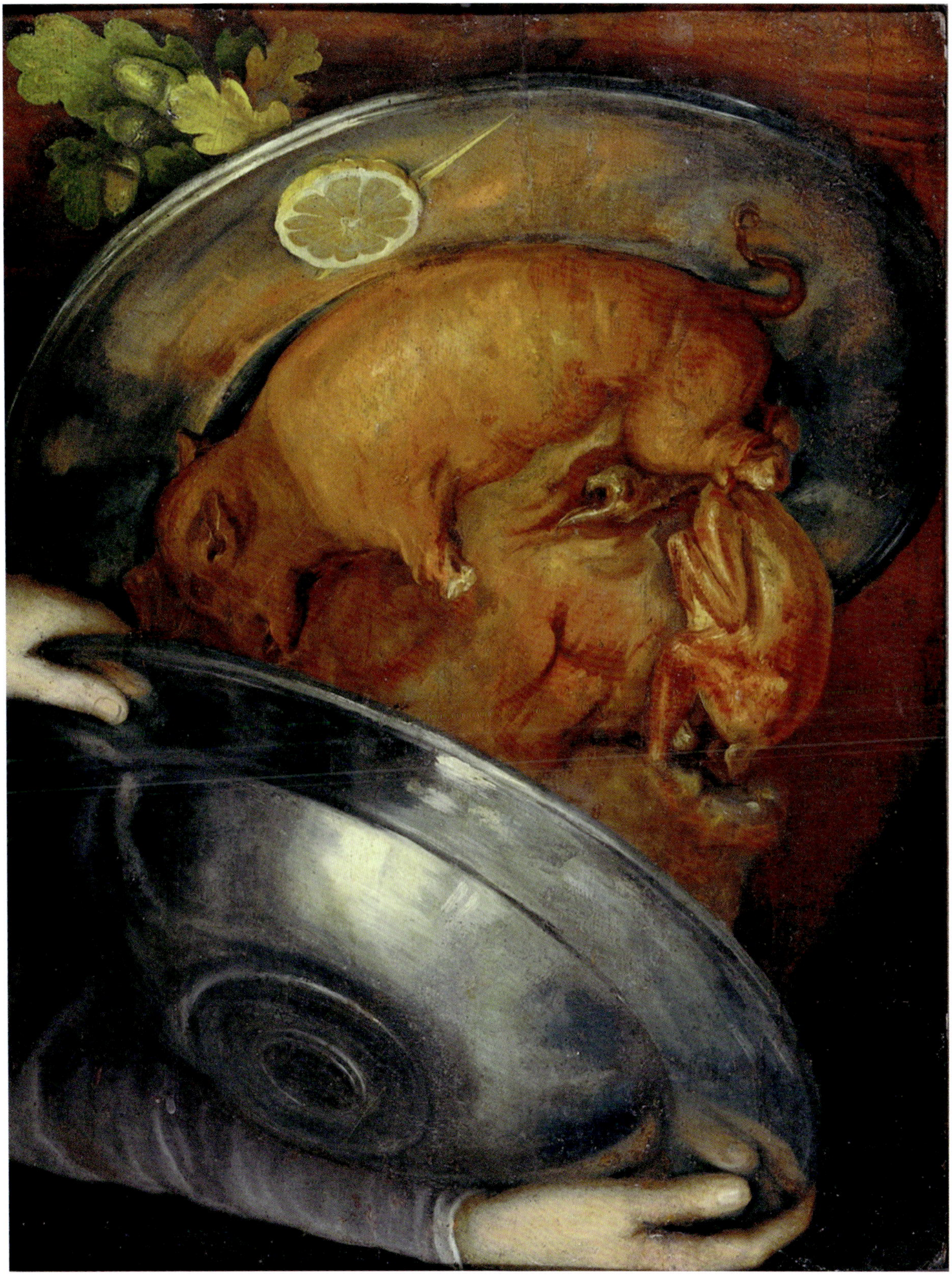

The Cook, Giuseppe Arcimboldo, c. 1570

Various works by Giuseppe Arcimboldo

1563–90

I want you to have a look at the paintings on the previous two pages. Give it a minute or two, and in your head (or on paper) mark out exactly what it is that you see.

Is one a bowl of vegetables? Good.

But when you flip it upside down, do you see a face? The eyes, the nose, the mouth, the cheeks, and even the beard and hair.

Flip the book upside down again and look at the painting on the right. What do you see? A lovely meal? Some pigs on a silver platter? Some lemon for seasoning? A pair of hands exposing the feast?

There's more. Flip the painting the right way up and, well, you guessed it: some eyes, a nose, mouth, a cheek, and now a fancy hat with a feather.

But why? Why is it that we see faces?

Near the end of the High Renaissance, a period earmarked by artworks that emphasized proportion, balance, and ideal beauty, came the exploration of Mannerism, a movement that exaggerated these qualities, often resulting in compositions and figures that were asymmetrical or unnaturally elegant.

And though Giuseppe Arcimboldo is not the founder of the movement, with many crediting that title to Rosso Fiorentino and Jacopo Pontormo, his unique approach to portraiture walks the line of elegance and the unnatural through optical illusions, in a way that no art ever had before. He plays on a biological phenomenon called pareidolia, or the tendency for people to impose a meaningful interpretation (say, for example, a face) onto a nebulous stimulus. In this case, plates and vegetables.

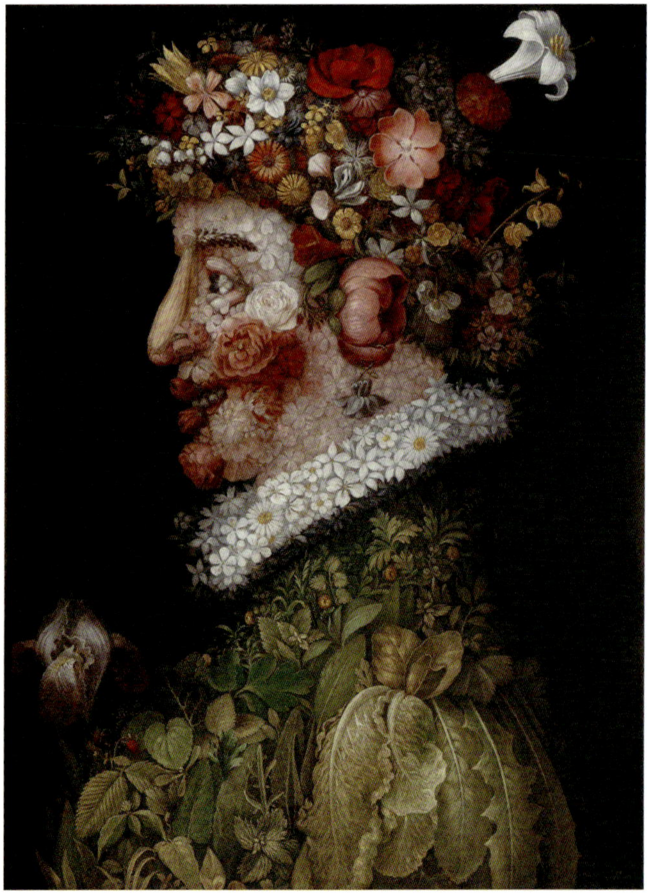

Spring, 1563

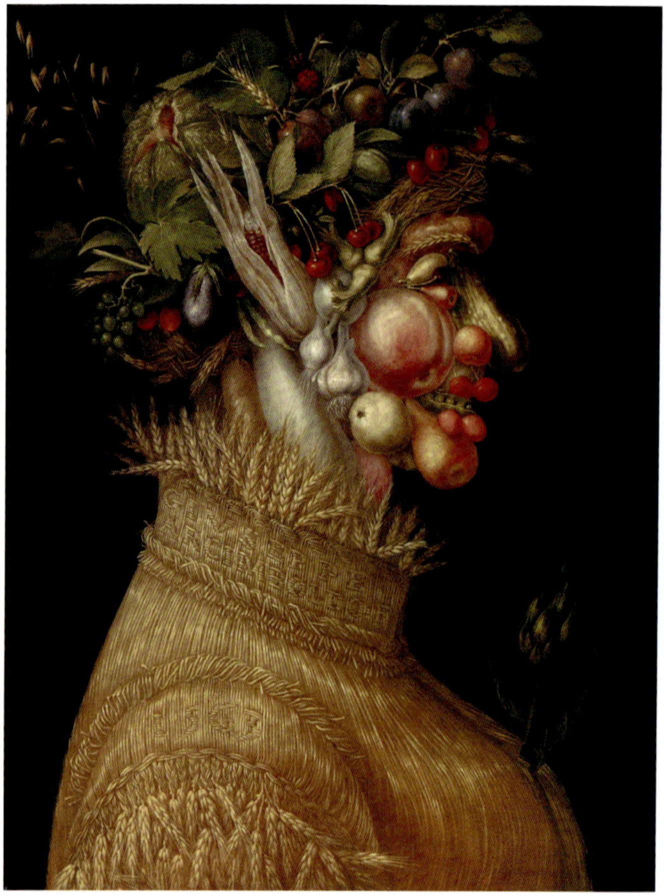

Summer, 1563

You can test this concept by viewing his work at a distance. Try it out! Have a look at any of the four paintings below from his interpretation of the seasons.

From further away, we can't distinguish between the finer details that make the objects, and instead blend the larger shapes to expose the "person." These faces are not as defined as the Mona Lisa's from a distance, but even still, you don't see the individual lines of the rose petals in the place of a cheek or the bumps on the pickle that makes a nose. Instead, you just see the cheek or the nose.

What takes it a step further is that these piles of produce are framed like traditional portraiture, the elements stylized to convince you that you're looking at someone in profile. Arcimboldo plays on the programming of the human mind, providing us with a level of familiarity to further convince us of a human presence, even if we're only looking at fruit on a canvas.

Like Rembrandt, and Vigée le Brun, and so many so others, Arcimboldo shows us the magical peculiarity of portraiture, and of art as a whole. We may be looking at an illusion, but in the hands of a skilled tactician, paintings, and the people in them, take on a life of their own.

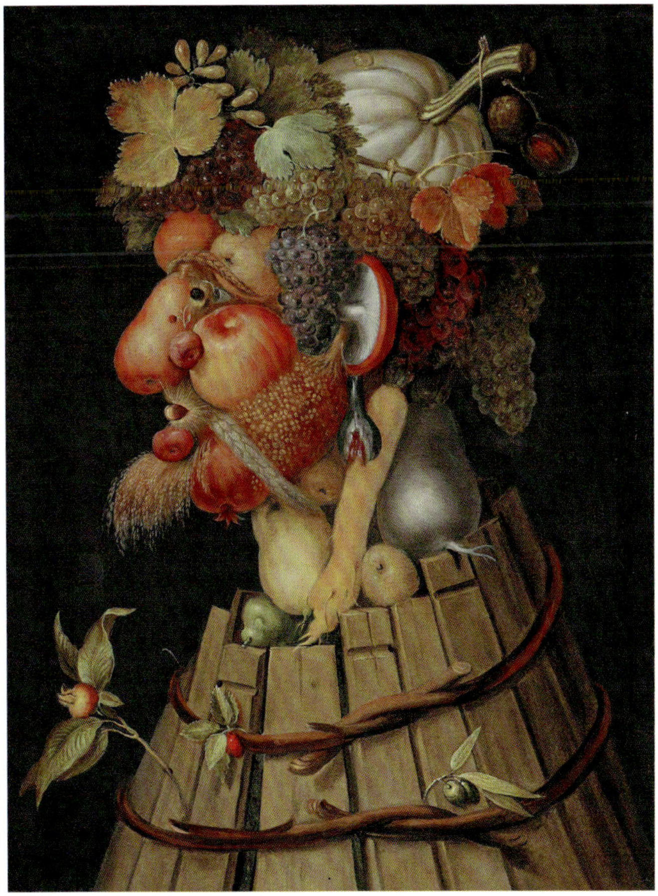

Autumn, 1573

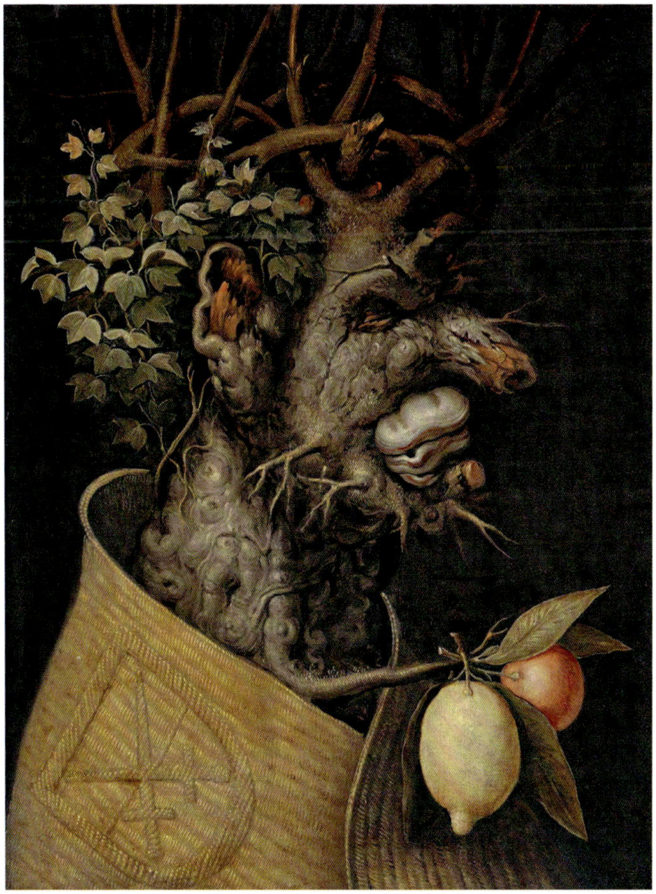

Winter, 1563

INSANE DETAILS

Intentionality is one feature of mastery. When exploring paintings that feel as though they are anchored by an endless bounty of impossibly detailed trinkets, the most intentional are often the ones we remember.

"But isn't all art intentional?"

Of course. Every single brushstroke, in theory, is intentional, and how an artist uses each tool matters. It's no different than a boxer throwing punches; a fighter who unleashes a fury of strikes simply trying to hit an opponent will tire faster than a fighter with precise tactics. The same applies to painting. Two artists could attempt to cover the same story, on a surface of equal proportions, and more often than not, it's the artist who's the most tacit in their approach that makes the largest impact. And while the amateur painter ferociously slugs away to meet the target, in the ring, there is only one Floyd Mayweather.

In the artworld, his name is Jan van Eyck.

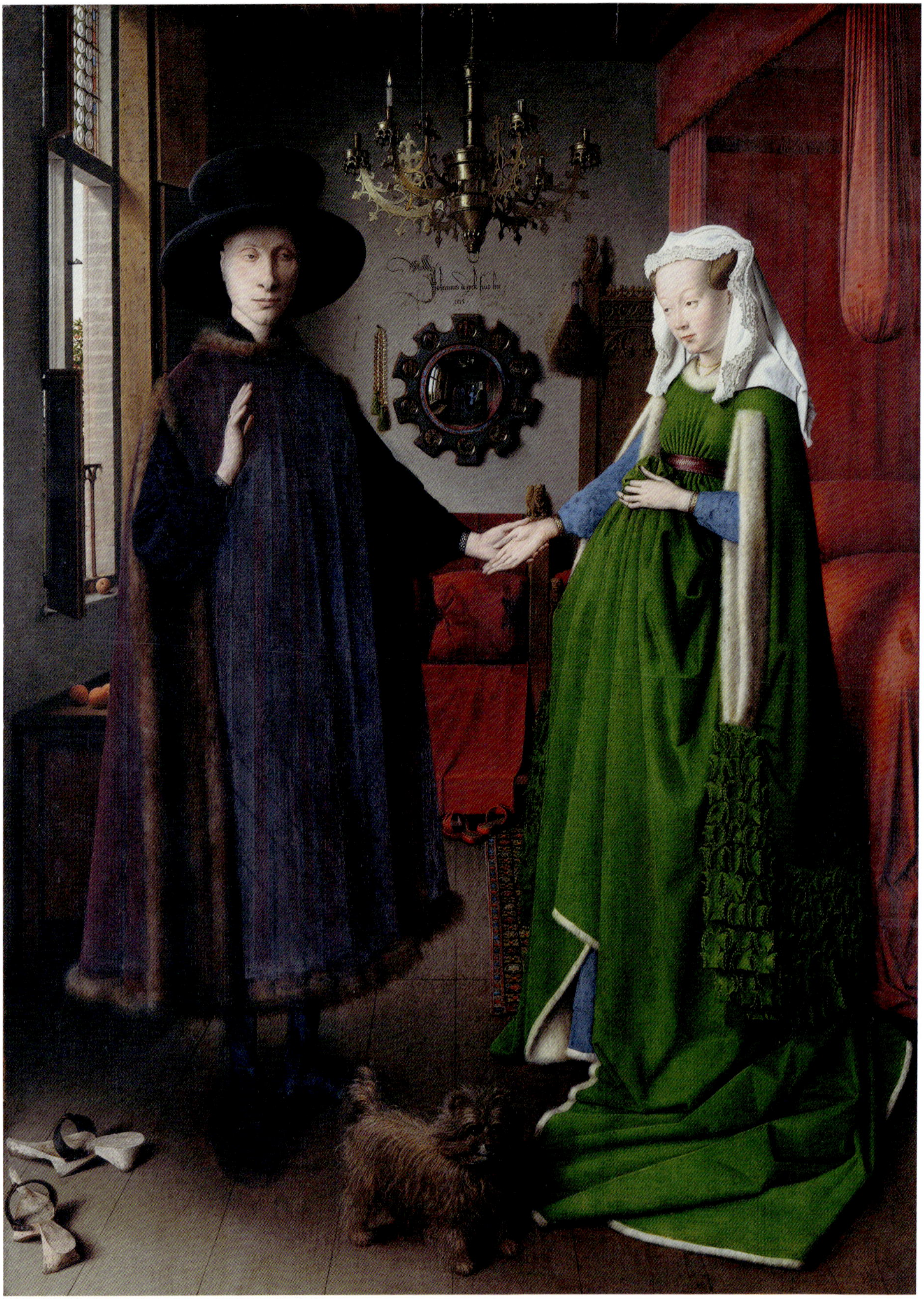

The Arnolfini Portrait

Jan van Eyck, 1434

A man, a woman, a dog, and whoever those other people in the mirror's reflection are. The Stations of the Cross around that mirror, the fancy chandelier, the oranges, the gargoyle above her hand, and that weird carving of a praying lady resting on the bed's headboard. From the outside looking in, nothing seems *that* out of the ordinary, right? But when you consider that we're looking at a painting by van Eyck, you'll quickly realize that nothing is *ever* what it seems.

Because that lady is probably dead.

"What?"

I mean, they're *technically* all dead. Every person in the artwork, including our furry friend and the mysterious figures in the reflection, have long moved on, but did you know that there's a very real possibility that even at the time this famous portrait was painted, the woman in the green dress was no longer with us? Have a closer look at the chandelier.

Notice anything off about it? On the left side of it, hovering over the shoulder of Mr. Arnolfini, we have what appears to be a candle and flame. However, pan over to the right and the motif seems to have taken a turn for the worse: no candle, only the remnants of wax. A full life ahead on one side and one that has perished on the other. Very curious.

And what about that mirror with the crazy reflection? Notice anything about it? Scenes from the Passion of Jesus frame it. On the left, Christ as he lived. On the right, Christ in death. And if you're thinking, "Matthew, this is a wedding portrait," you might be right. But consider for a moment that Jan van Eyck was a perfectionist, and that everything he ever put into a painting was intentional.

This was a man who could paint with such precision that particles of light bounce around inside crystal prayer beads before they're cast onto the wall. Have a look at the reflection of the oranges on the left, or each individual grain on the wooden pattens. And we haven't even gotten to her dress: a combination of elaborate textures met with soft furs and a silky headdress. Every single addition is a finely calculated premeditation, which lends to the possibility that, yes, the color of her dress *might* mean hope, and that their bed *might* symbolize a consummation. The mirror, in the shape of an eye, might be the eye of God who watches over their union. Is she pregnant? Probably, yes. But why, then, the symbols of death?

A depiction of Saint Martha, patron saint of the housewife, sits on a dragon overlooking two gargoyles strategically placed to ward off evil spirits. And we are left pondering why she'd need so much protection. Perhaps for safe passage to the other side? And if none of this has convinced you at all, what about Mr. Arnolfini himself? A keen sense of fashion? Or maybe, he was in mourning.

The Agony in the Garden with the Donor Louis I of Orléans* and *Madonna of Chancellor Rolin

Colart de Laon, 1405–1408, and
Jan van Eyck, c. 1430–35

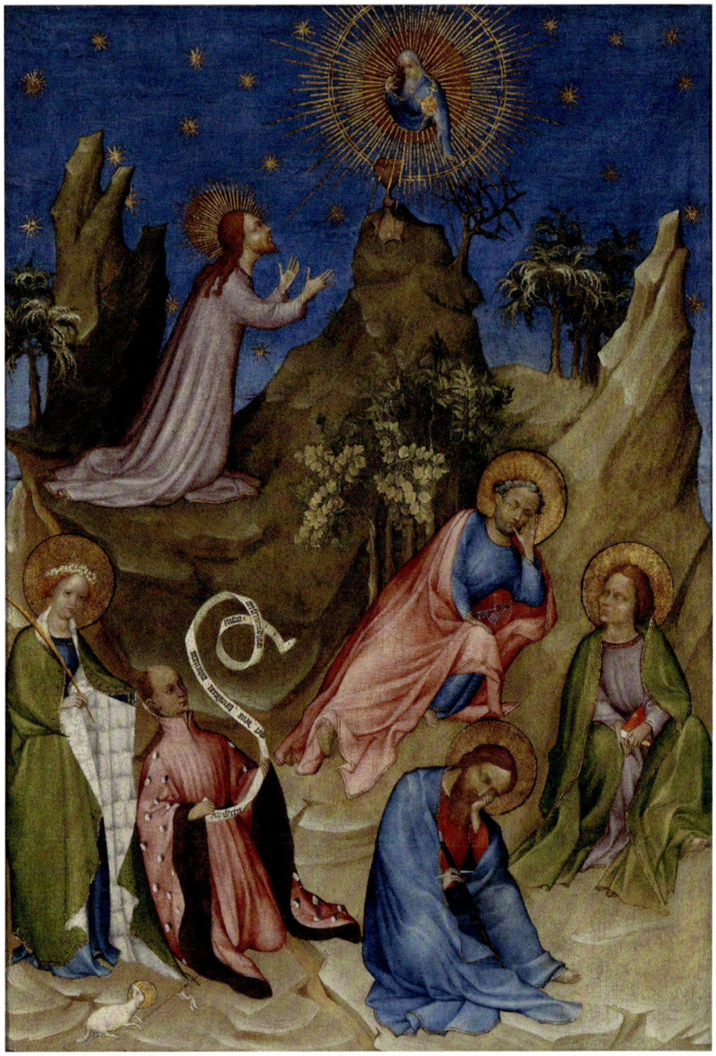

Van Eyck is so talented, it is nearly impossible to spot every detail of his paintings on a single pass. We're talking about a man considered by many to be the father of oil painting, and who, through a practice that delivered many of history's most revolutionary artworks, would redefine exactly what it meant to be a master.

To fully understand his talent, have a look at *The Agony in the Garden* immediately to the right, a painting by Colart de Laon that perfectly embodies the best that International Gothic has to offer.

Beautifully detailed and narrative driven, this genre's pictures had a major influence across western Europe from around 1370 to 1450, unifying nationalistic styles. Blending northern European elegance and precision with the naturalism and spatial awareness of Italian works, the artists who crafted this style created a new visual language that transcended local traditions.

International Gothic universalized the courtly aesthetic. It is an artistic style that is sophisticated and sensational, rather than strictly theological. And most importantly, during its creation, it considered how we perceive the world in a brand-new way: elements like plants, people, textiles, and light, arranged in three-dimensional spaces that, while still not scientifically accurate, are believable. These works are idealized and decorative, made from materials like gold and jewel-colored pigments, which turned paintings into status symbols as well as religious objects. In the process, they lent to the rise of the court artist. Powerful rulers like the Dukes of Burgundy and Visconti of Milan commissioned these paintings to reflect their own wealth and prestige, and in doing so, elevated the status of the artist, laying the groundwork for the Renaissance and for the idea of the artist as genius.

Just imagine, then, what patrons might have thought when they laid their eyes on *Madonna of Chancellor Rolin*. If artists of the era were celebrated for their innovations, then van Eyck would have earned himself a sainthood with this masterpiece.

If we put ourselves into the shoes of one of those dukes and compare this artwork to *anything* prior, we're left with the feeling that we've been duped. Van Eyck shows us the actual boundaries of what is possible in painting, and we question everything we've ever known about art. This isn't a "decorative" three-dimensional space, but an actual place filled with physically consequential objects, and as we take them in, our fifteenth-century jaws smash to the ground.

In a scene that depicts the Virgin Mary, who is crowned by a hovering angel as she presents an infant Jesus to Chancellor Rolin, van Eyck overloads us with a catalog of impossible features. He sets the scene inside a spacious loggia with richly decorated columns and bas-relief overlooking a city on a river, with mountains further off in the distance. The master painter thought of it all.

And I mean, every *single* thing, from how the fabric folds over Mary's shoulders to how the jewels on the crown hold light at different angles. Van Eyck paints patterned marble floors with such precision, we can *feel* the inlay, in the same way that we can feel the details of the bas-reliefs, and he's only just begun. A church thousands of meters away is given the same care, and he even accounts for the haze in the atmosphere: Details are slowly lost to the eye due to distance, but also, due to dense air. A blue hovers over the mountains, which matches the blue of the river that splits the composition down the middle.

All of these elements, when seen together, are overwhelming and impressive, and yet they pale in comparison to a cameo he hides in another painting.

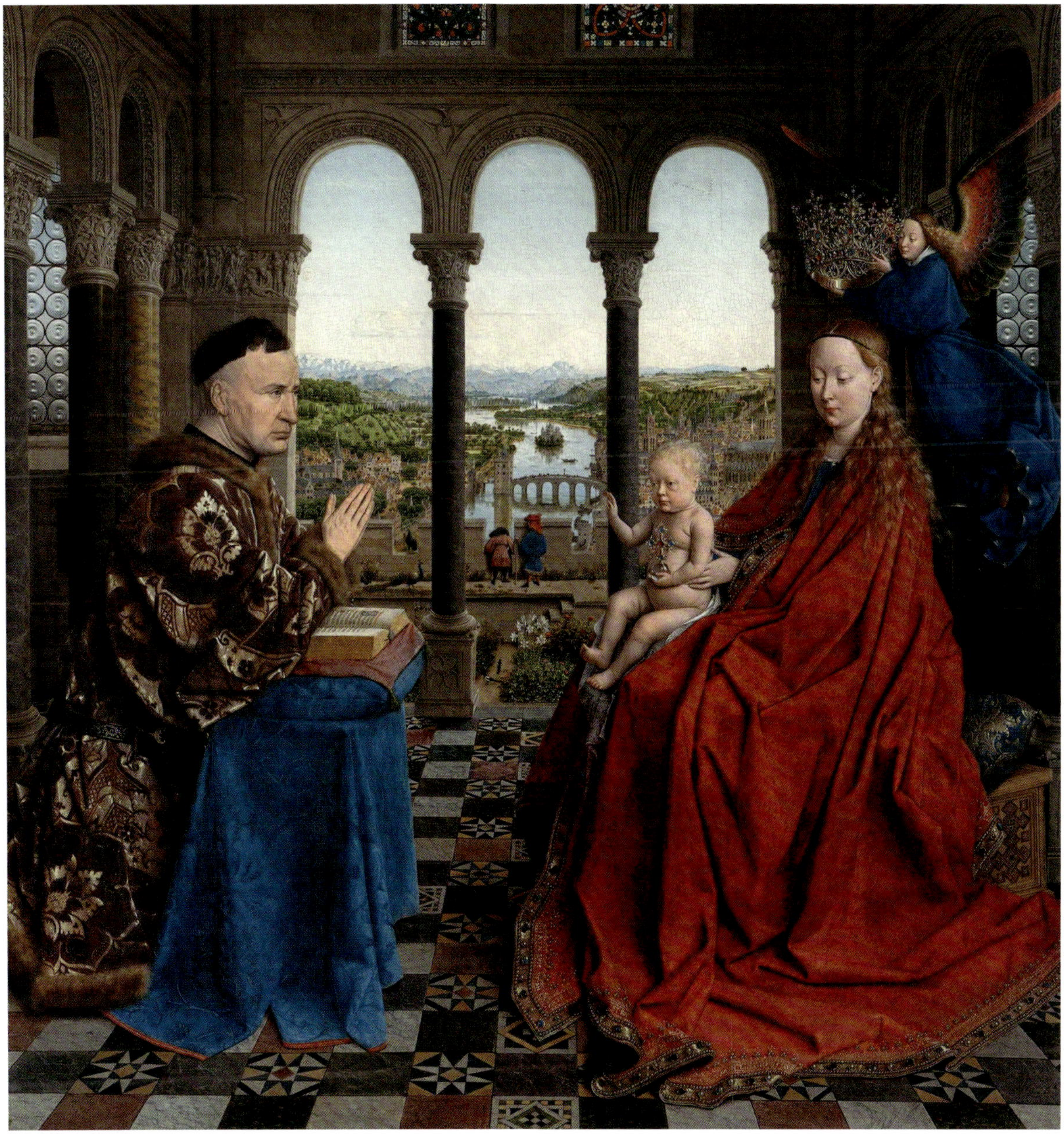

Virgin and Child with Canon Joris van der Paele

Jan van Eyck, 1434–36

This painting was commissioned by Joris van der Paele, a wealthy ecclesiastic from Bruges. Suffering from illness by the early 1430s, he hired Jan van Eyck to create a memorial piece in an attempt to reflect on his own morality. Van Eyck was at the height of his craft, painting at a level that meant he had complete control over his abilities, displaying technical mastery and deeply symbolic realism across his creative endeavors. In other words, it was the perfect moment for him to create a boundary-breaking artwork.

He gives us the Virgin Mary, seated on a large, elevated throne situated beneath an exceptionally decorated brocade baldachin decorated with white rose patterns symbolizing her purity. In one hand, she holds the Christ Child, and in the other, a small bouquet of red, white, and blue flowers. Sandwiched in between them is what appears to be a parrot. Symbols can take on many different meanings, but here, the bird perhaps further reinforces the Virgin's purity, Christ's Passion, and his resurrection. Mary too is represented as a symbol. Given the painting's setting in a church, she occupies the altarpiece position in the pictorial space, emphasizing a mediation between the donor and divinity.

The donor, Joris van der Paele, can be seen on the right side of the image, on his knees, dressed in a brilliant white canonical surplice. Over his shoulder stands Saint George, his name saint, and in his hands is a prayer book and his spectacles. Van Eyck paints this donor with his illness and frailty intact, and in doing so enhances the man's need for the spiritual. Saint George, and his brilliant suit of armor, strengthens the message. The saint presents van der Paele to the Virgin Mother as a lifelong servant to God, accentuating the length of that service through his own youthful appearance: a young face to play on the wrinkled face of a man nearing the end of his life, who has devoted that very life to the divine.

To the left of Mary, van Eyck gives us an image of Saint Donatian, and by putting him in that particular spot, the artist points us toward his significance. He is the dedicatee of the cathedral the painting was made for, and should therefore occupy the most important space in the picture.

"So what does it all mean?"

Jan van Eyck paints the donor, the saints, and the sacred figures in a way that highlights an interaction between them, in a space that blends the realms of Earth and Heaven. In doing so, he creates tension between the donor's morality and a divine eternity. Van Eyck does this all in the gap between realism and idealism: The textures and details are extraordinarily real, while the space itself remains fictive and symbolic. We feel the impact of the artist's extraordinary attention to detail, but know a meeting between the divine and the mortal is beyond our reality.

All of this, of course, has all been brought up to highlight that cameo I mentioned.

Look carefully at Saint George's shield and you'll find a reflection, painted with the same brilliance and execution as the one in *The Arnolfini Portrait*. And not just any reflection either, I might add, but one believed to be of the artist.

It is deliberately placed to reflect van Eyck at a perfect distance from the center of the painting, which is the intended distance that one must stand away from the canvas for it to engulf your field of vision. As a device, this pushes forth the idea that something exists outside of the artwork's visible boundaries, subconsciously playing on the painting's spatial depth; as a motif, it says even more. Though it is not as dimensionally accurate as either *The Arnolfini Portrait* or *Madonna of Chancellor Ronin*, by putting his reflection in a place that virtually nobody would notice, van Eyck pushes art-making into new territories. His cameo isn't necessary to the work, but he can paint it, so he does. In doing so, van Eyck injects his personality in a way that had never been realized in art before, at a skill level the world had never seen. And right there, in Saint George's shield, we see a precursor to his greatest and most important contribution to art, *The Ghent Altarpiece*.

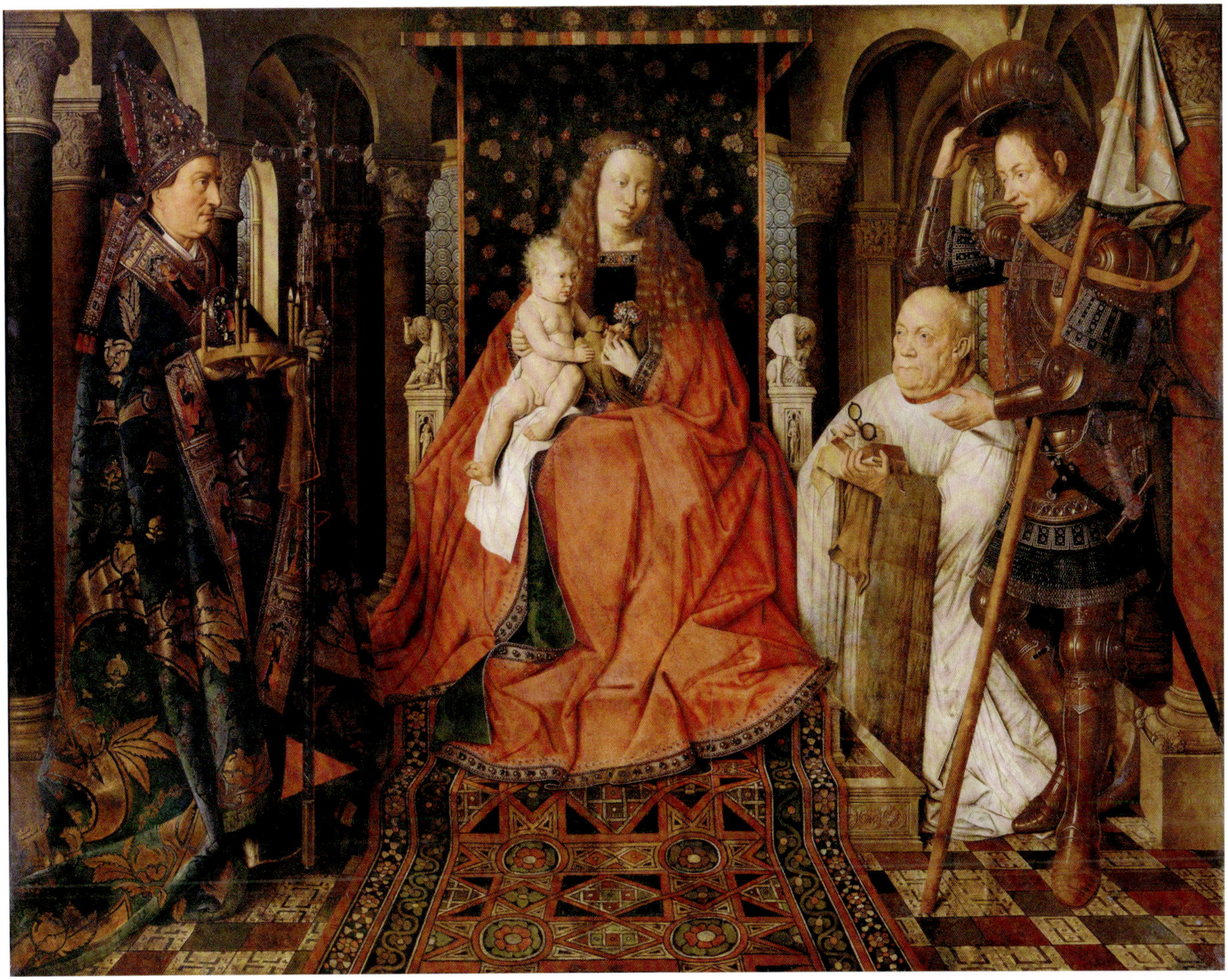

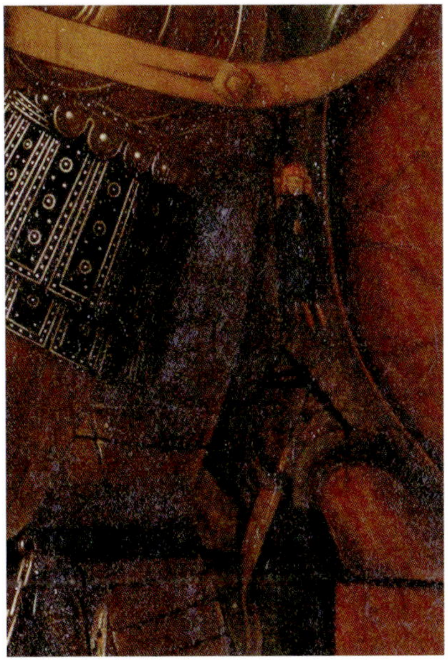

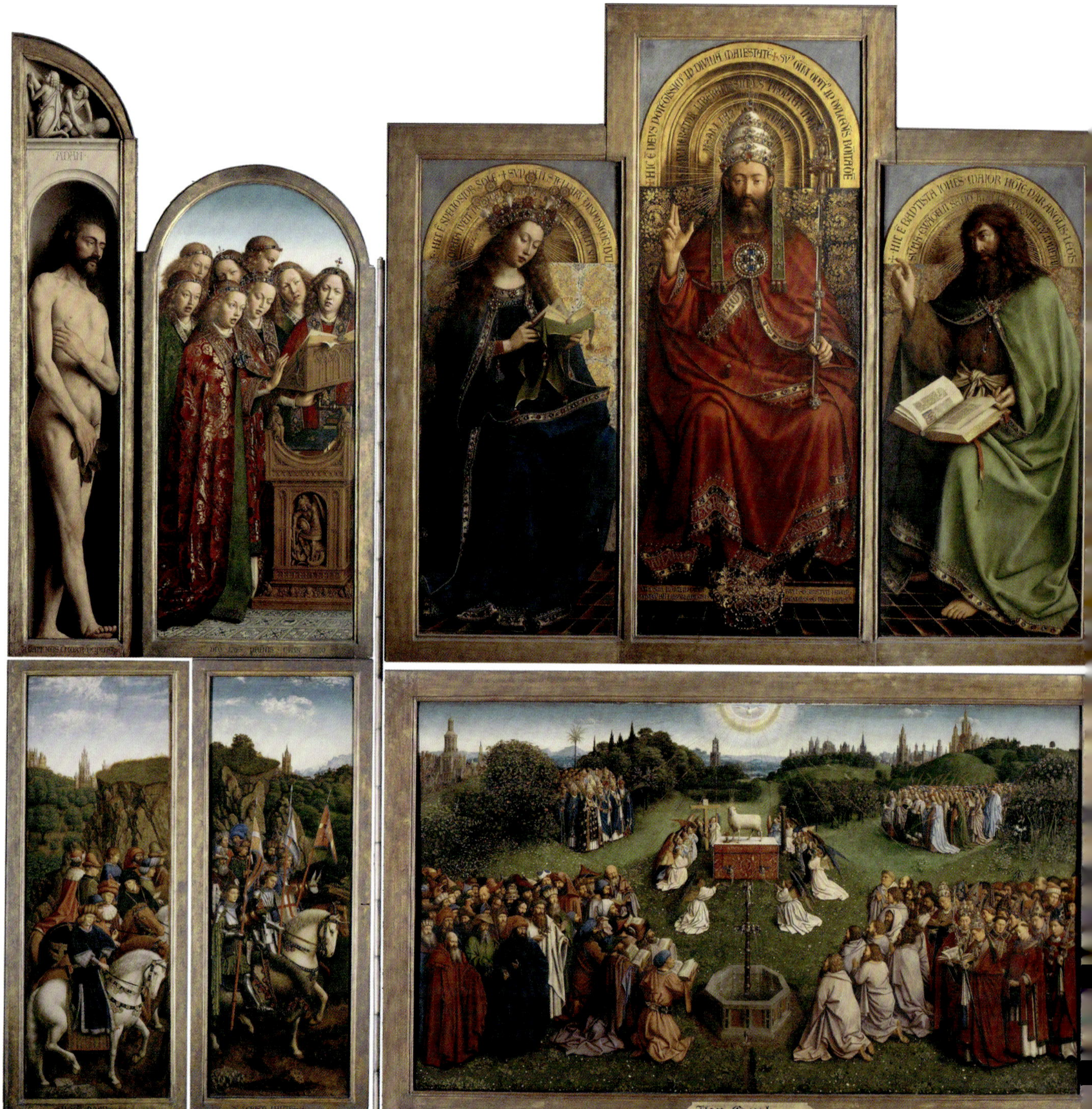

The Ghent Altarpiece front panels, 1432

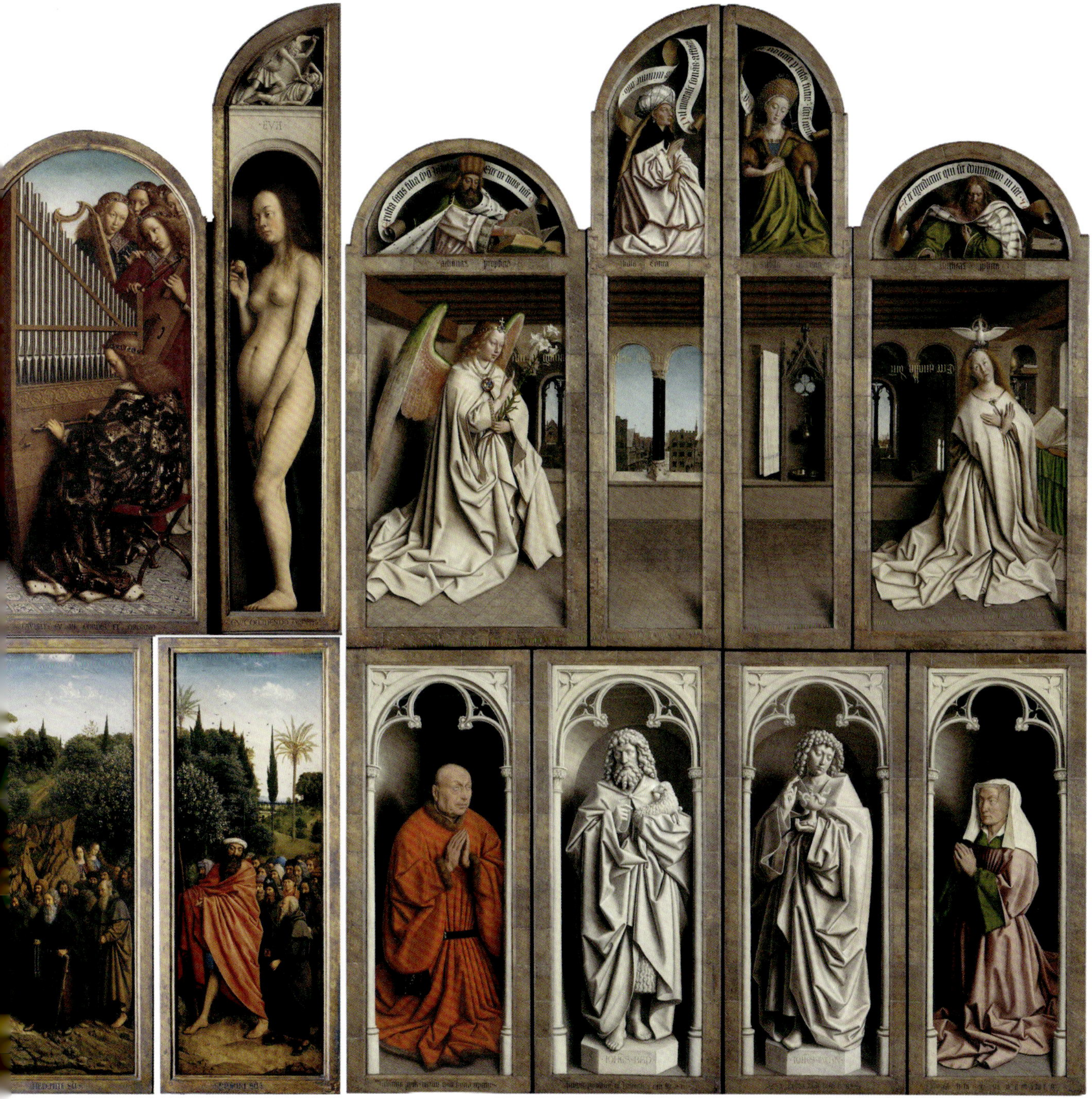

The Ghent Altarpiece back panels, 1432

The Ghent Altarpiece

Jan van Eyck, 1432

That lamb in the bottom row's middle panel has the eyes of a human, a punctured heart, and is spurting blood into a chalice. And that's not even the craziest part of this painting.

This is a van Eyck that we're talking about, of course. The Flemish master paints an exposed Adam and Eve, along with John the Baptist, and the Virgin Mary, who can also be seen in the rear center panels, standing with a watermelon-winged archangel Gabriel. There's Christ as king in the center, and below him Saint Livinus, Saint Stephen, angels, knights, and priests. Heck, there are even the patrons of the artwork itself on the bottom left and right, and on the back panels.

Hundreds upon hundreds of individually detailed characters, painted to perfection on 24 wooden framed sections of Jan van Eyck's largest ever artwork, *The Ghent Altarpiece*: a masterpiece that depicts man's original sin and Christ's sacrifice to redeem us all. And yet, while the immense scale is mind boggling at 11.5 x 15 feet, and the narrative is rich and spectacular in every possible way, there is nothing, and I mean nothing, that compares to zooming in on Adam's leg and seeing *each and every* individual hair. Or his hands, which the Flemish master paints with such an attention to detail, you can clearly make out his bluish colored veins.

Van Eyck paints a choir with such mastery you can almost tell which of the figures is the alto, soprano, tenor, and bass. You can see exactly which notes the angel is playing on the piano, and just look at her garment: a blend of sparkling gold and deep, velvety brown. And wait until you inspect the floor … to the average viewer, a bit of information that's lost to the eye, but to Jan van Eyck, it's a painting within a painting. And can we talk about the woodwork for a second?

Or the perfectly lit building outside the middle rear panel's window, which casts a perfect beam of light onto the wall behind Mary, tucked behind a pillar. Which has nothing to do with the foreground's scene of the Annunciation.

Arguably the greatest technician in painting's entire history, van Eyck was perhaps a man possessed, to have painstakingly detailed these gems, but he understood that atmosphere matters. If you're not willing to consider how the light of the church the painting was going to be placed in would interact with the light bouncing off your heavenly choir, and if you're not going to hide secret symbols about sacrifice and salvation in a tapestry no taller than one centimeter behind Christ, why even bother?

Jan van Eyck would leave such a powerful lasting impression that he would go on to shape Western art's culture and techniques forever. The father of oil painting, or at least, the father of many of its most influential techniques and concepts, his work would serve as the rocket fuel for the art form.

He refined the processes of how pigments were mixed with oils, and how they were layered to achieve a form of hyperrealism and detail. He was so precise, he made viewers feel as though they were looking into another world, and through his careful observations about light, perspective, and composition, he marked a turning point toward a more scientific approach to art, influencing a transition between the Gothic era and the Renaissance. Van Eyck defined the modern portrait, capturing the psychological and social identities of his subjects, and was instrumental in shifting art toward the realization of human-centered themes. He was an artist that paved the way for legendary painters like Rogier van der Weyden, Hans Memling, Albrecht Dürer, Leonardo da Vinci, Johannes Vermeer, Titian, Rembrandt, Hans Holbein the Younger, and many more.

Jan van Eyck is the progenitor for many of the greatest ideas in art, and by chasing the bloodline of his influence, we uncover what might be the ancestor of the modern "meme."

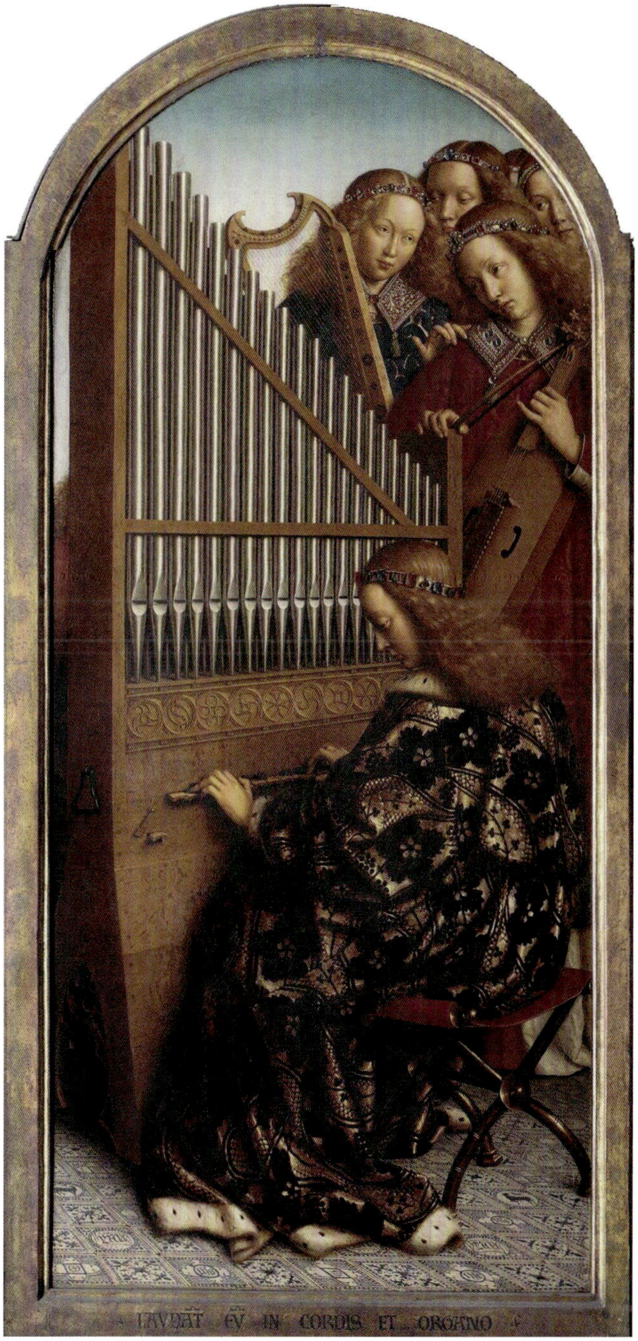
LAVDAT EV IN CORDIS ET ORGANO

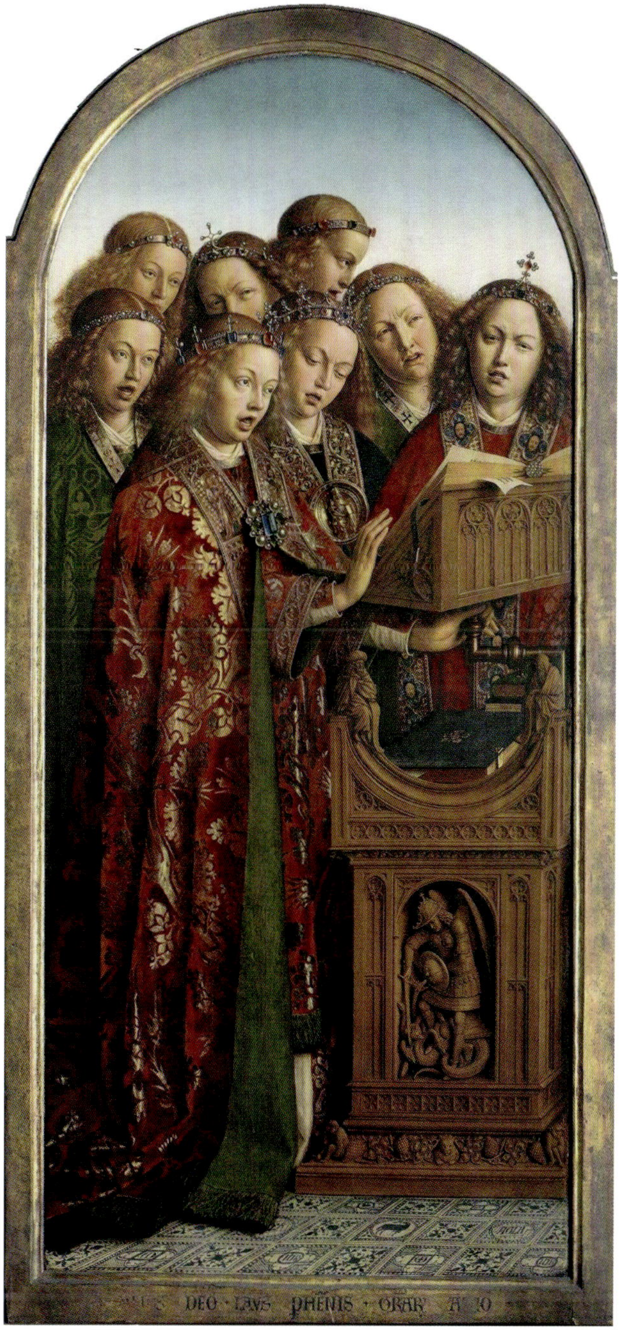

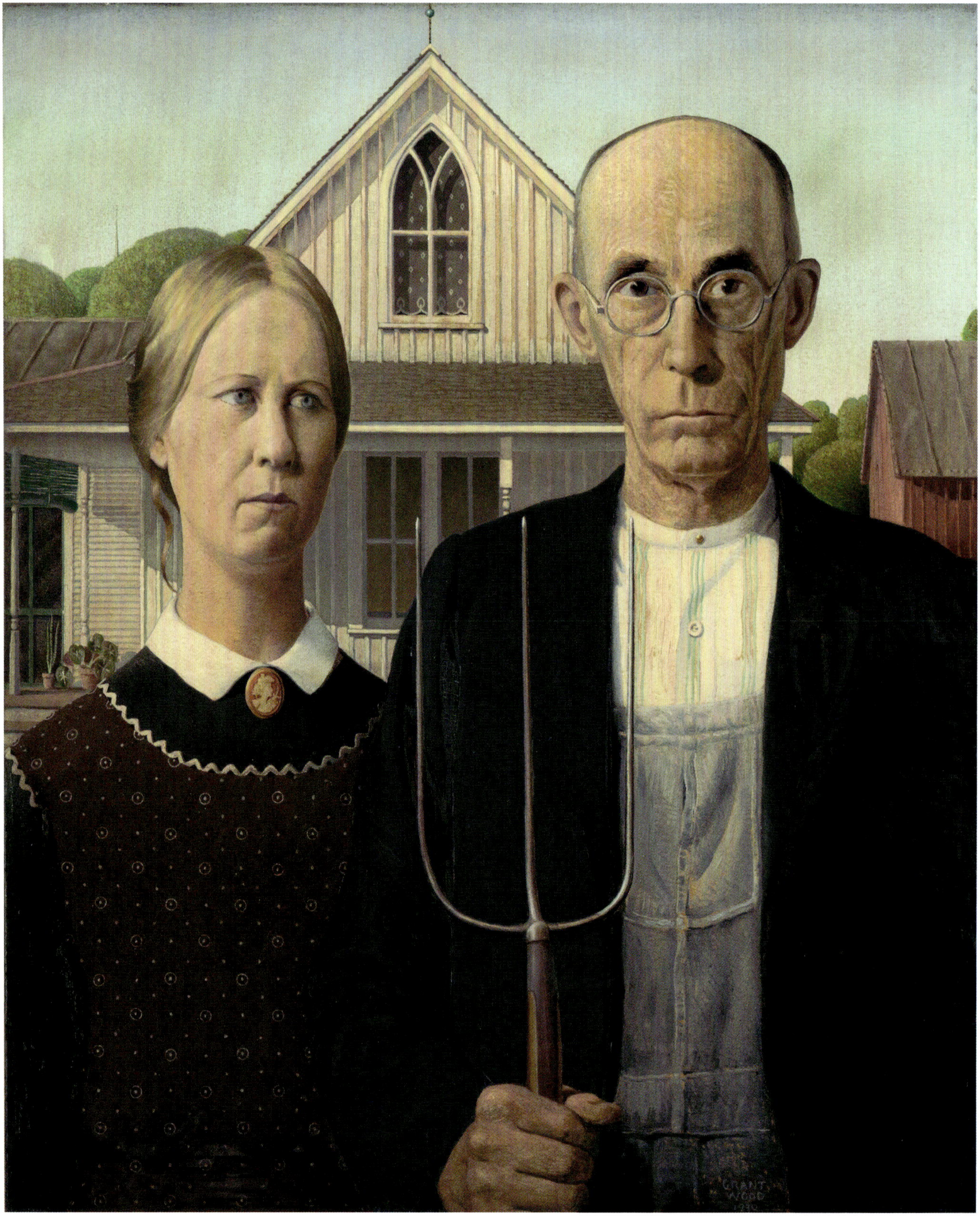
GRANT
WOOD

American Gothic

Grant Wood, 1930

It's late summer. Grant Wood, out and about in Iowa looking for inspiration, stumbles upon a small white house with a peculiar Gothic window and thinks to himself, "This is very paintable." After asking for permission from the homeowners to paint their house, he recruits his sister and his dentist to model for him and gets to work.

The medium-sized oil painting depicting a rural American family is anything but a simple portrait. In fact, to a careful eye, it is a perfectly harmonized composition with a range of fascinating symbols. The central figures are positioned frontally, filling the vertical frame. They mirror the vertical lines of the Gothic window and pitchfork, which underpin a sense of rigidity and moral seriousness: one that juxtaposes the "structural absurdity" and "borrowed pretentiousness"— Wood's own words as recounted by his biographer, Darrell Garwood— of a Gothic-style window set within the flimsy frame of a country farmhouse.

Muted earth tones dominate the picture: browns, greys, and greens, evoking simplicity and austerity. They balance the impact of the sharp crisp lines that make up the detailed motifs: the pitchfork, a symbol for hard labor and rural discipline, echoed in its shape by the farmer's overalls and the house, all emphasizing a moral uptightness and puritanical ethic. The Gothic window references European architecture, but transplanted onto this humble home, it is a blend of high European style and rural simplicity that underscores Wood's fascination with the dignities of his ordinary countrymen.

The farmer represents American values: resilience, self-reliance, and an unshakable work ethic. The woman, with a subdued expression and colonial-styled apron, suggests domestic virtue and quiet endurance. All fitting ideals to accurately represent rural American life, captured in a way that is both satirical and stoic.

"So where are you seeing van Eyck?"

It's all to do with the *subtler* aspects of the painting. Grant Wood became a great admirer of Northern Renaissance art after a trip to Europe and brought back many ideas that would inform his own paintings. He works in detail with a careful attention, highlighting a crispness and sharpness across the composition that recalls van Eyck's own fastidiousness. We look to the elongated faces and forms of our two central figures and are reminded of the figures in *The Arnolfini Portrait*, all radiating an aura of solemn virtue and inner order. Wood, like van Eyck, injects layers of meaning into ordinary objects that have been meticulously rendered to invite us into reflection. The pitchfork, the window, and the clothing are all modern equivalents of van Eyck–like symbols, representing labor, faith, and virtue.

But more important than any one detail painted in the scene is the philosophical connection between the two artists. Their treatment of realism and its effects represents a bond between both masters in the form of a spiritual discipline. Van Eyck uses realism and exquisite detail to reveal God's presence in matter. His twentieth-century counterpart does something similar, but not for God; Wood's organized approach emphasizes normal objects to ennoble rural America. In his art, even a humble home in Iowa and its occupants can be rendered with the same dignity as a fifteenth-century Flemish interior. Wood uses van Eyck's approach to sacred realism to elevate the American heartland into something beyond its own simplicity. A mythic moral space, suspended in a composition grounded in a formal symmetry that balances geometry and human presence.

Now, you would think that a painting as thoughtful and detailed as *American Gothic* would have been an instant artistic marvel, but it wasn't. The painting was entered into a competition held by the Art Institute of Chicago in 1930 to only win a bronze medal and $300.

It would then erupt into a hotly debated cultural proto-meme, reproduced in countless different ways thanks to the newspapers for all of the wrong reasons. The rise of the metropolitan lifestyle and a dismissive view of rural America would split audiences across the country as to whether or not Grant's masterpiece was a comedic mockery of America's agricultural backbone, or a tribute to an idyllic Arcadian lifestyle.

The Arcadian lifestyle: an idealized way of living that can be characterized by its simplicity, rural tranquility, and harmony with nature. It's a subject that doesn't need to be tied to sanctimonious ideas or the divine to make for great art. The Arcadian lifestyle can simply be covered "as is"; a truly gifted artist understands that the story of existence is enough to keep an audience engaged, and there is nobody better than Pieter Bruegel the Elder to tell that story. Or, as he is also known, "Peasant Bruegel," thanks to the Flemish icon's mastery of capturing the intricacies of peasant life.

As we'll soon see, he was a pioneer in genre painting, who, with a pass of his hand, could vividly depict the inner lives, manners, and rituals of entirely normal people in sixteenth–century Flanders.

The Harvesters

Pieter Bruegel the Elder, 1565

I want you to first have a look at the boat with two visible masts. This is a painting that has nothing to do with God or virtuosity, or any sort of deep philosophical exploration, and yet Bruegel paints it with a depth so intense, it's almost impossible to comprehend. The boat, as far as the entire painting goes, is completely insignificant. It's a detail that is so far off in the background, you hardly notice it. And why would you? There is so much happening up close. For example, underneath the tree in the foreground, so why look anywhere else?

It's not the only example of Bruegel's precision and attention to detail. In the right third of the painting, just over the crest of the hill, hidden behind the trees, is a church. Once again, doesn't serve much of a purpose outside of filling the landscape, but Bruegel paints it so convincingly, it feels as though the church *really is* behind that hill. He shows us people skinny dipping in a pond, rendered at the distance that our eyes would perceive it in real life. He paints a curious game and we, the viewers, upon noticing it, become curious. We spot mischievous activities in the shade of the tree line to the left and feel genuinely suspicious.

And while it's fun to spot the happy faces of the hungry congregation chowing down on bread and porridge, plucking apples from a tree, or napping underneath one, Bruegel's genius in this artwork has everything to do with perspective.

He gives us a glimpse into the everyday lives of people by highlighting the reality of everyday life—namely that things that don't concern us are always happening around us, and you might not catch it all. He understands the nature of curiosity, and the draw of observation from afar, and it adds to his universe. Yet, for all the eavesdropping we all do, our shared obliviousness means we're limited in our ability to focus on the things that are right outside of our peripheries.

Bruegel repeats his feat in five other surviving paintings, each depicting different seasons. They do no more and no less than capture life: simple art with a profound effect that reflects the essence of what observing art is all about. It doesn't need to be overcomplicated.

I want you to have a look at the other paintings in the series on the next two pages, but this time, without any "instruction" on where to look. Make a note on what you see, and how it makes you feel.

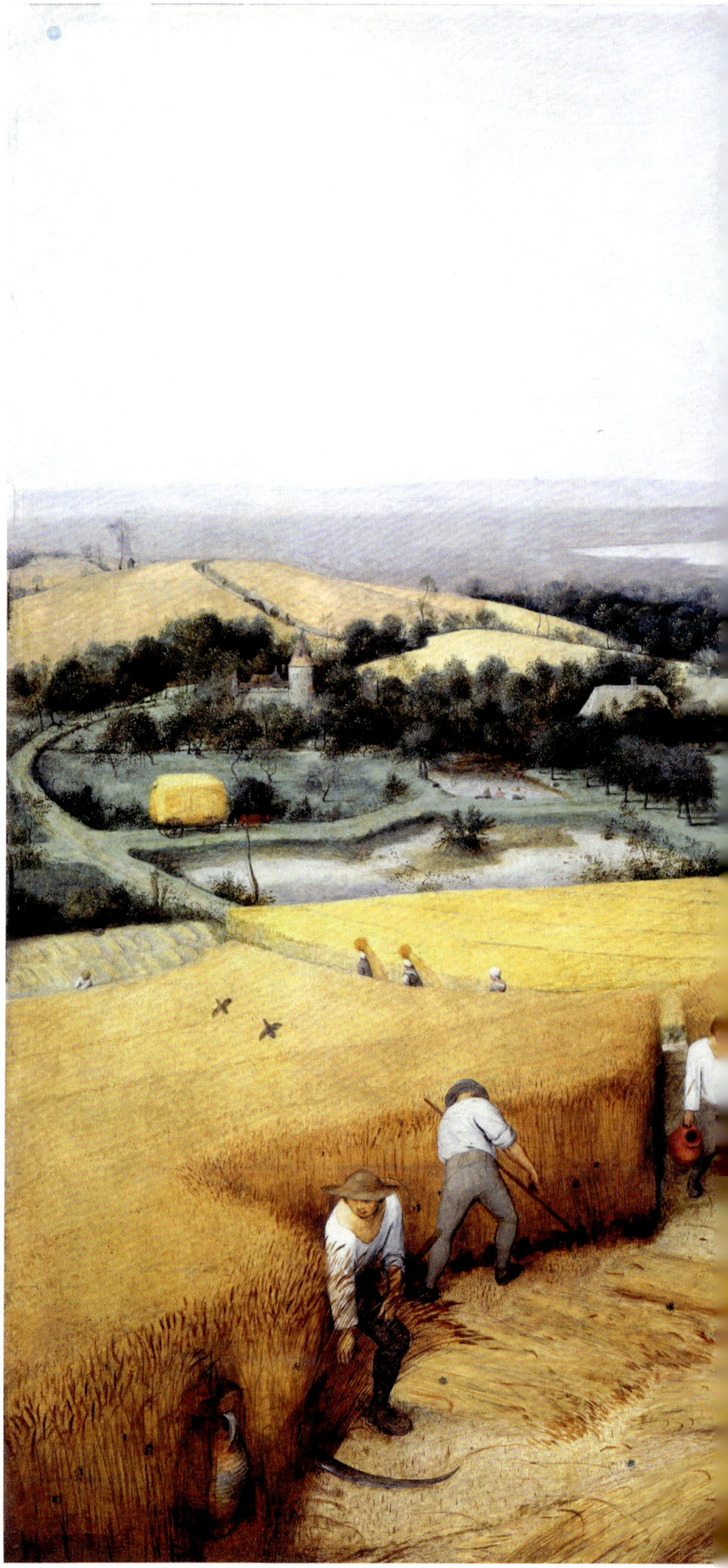

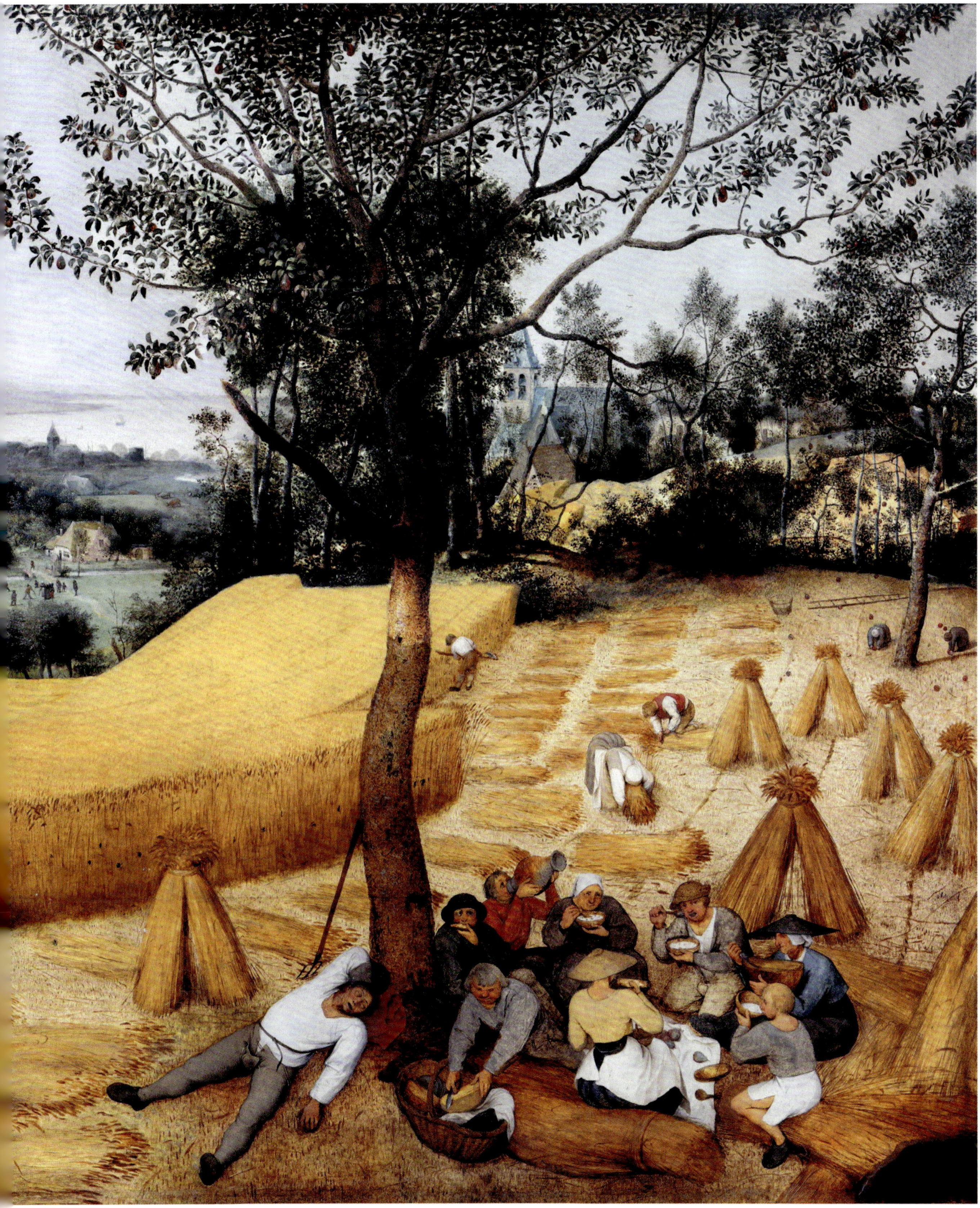

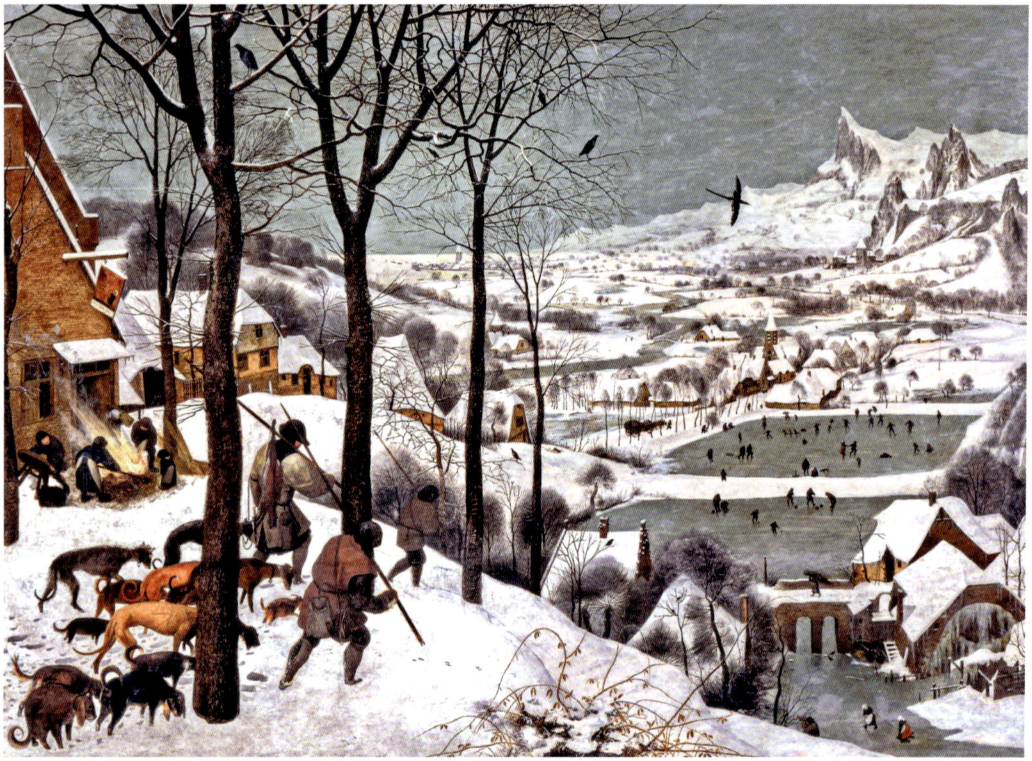

Hunters in the Snow, 1565

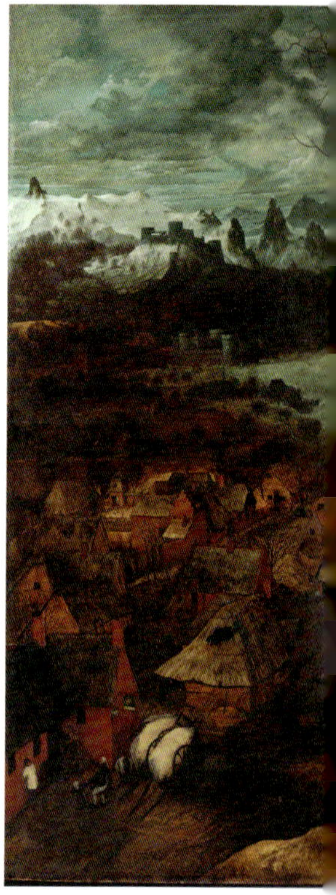

Gloomy Day, 1565

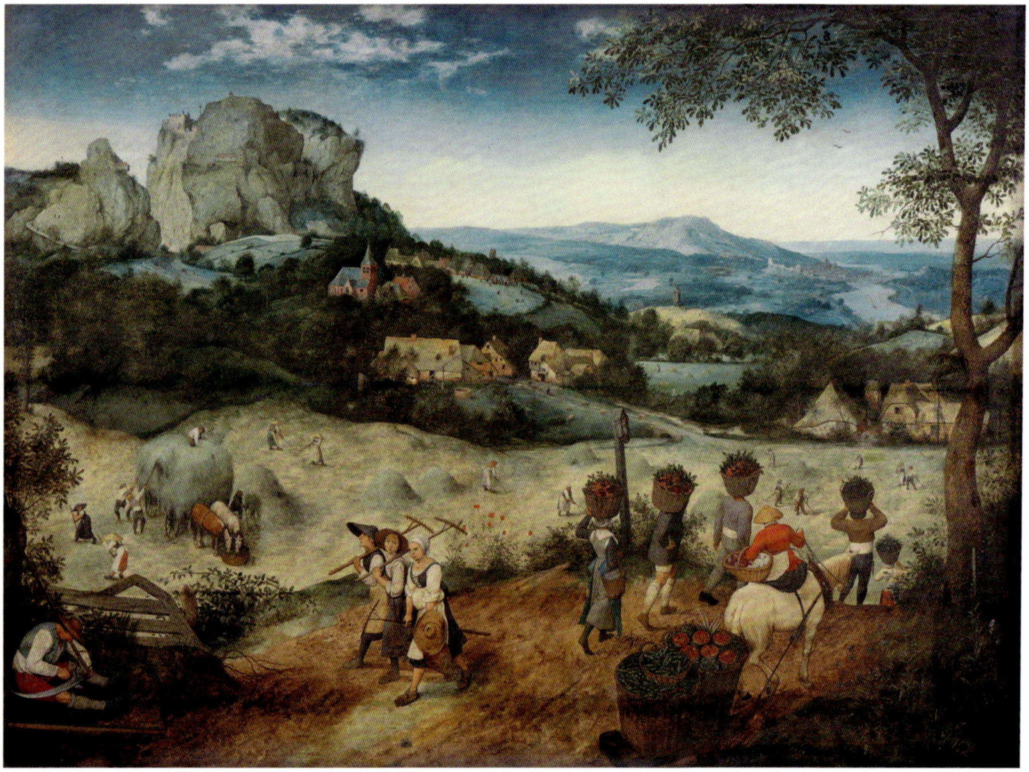

The Hay Harvest, 1565

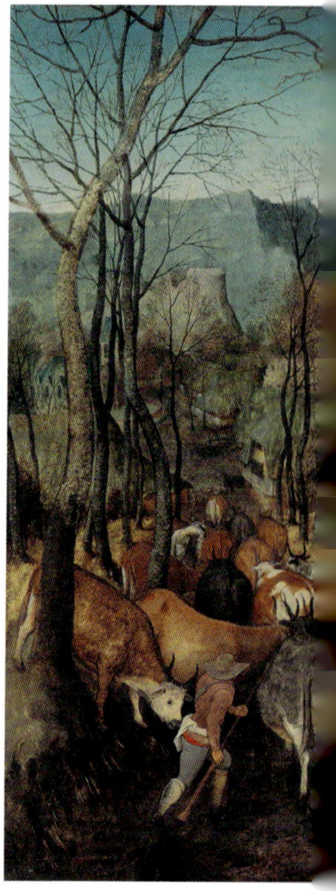

The Return of the Herd, 1565

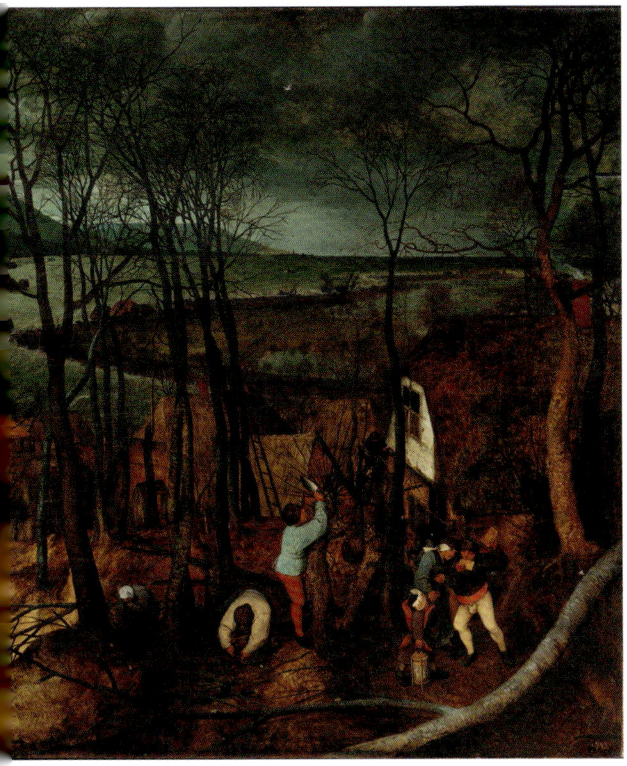

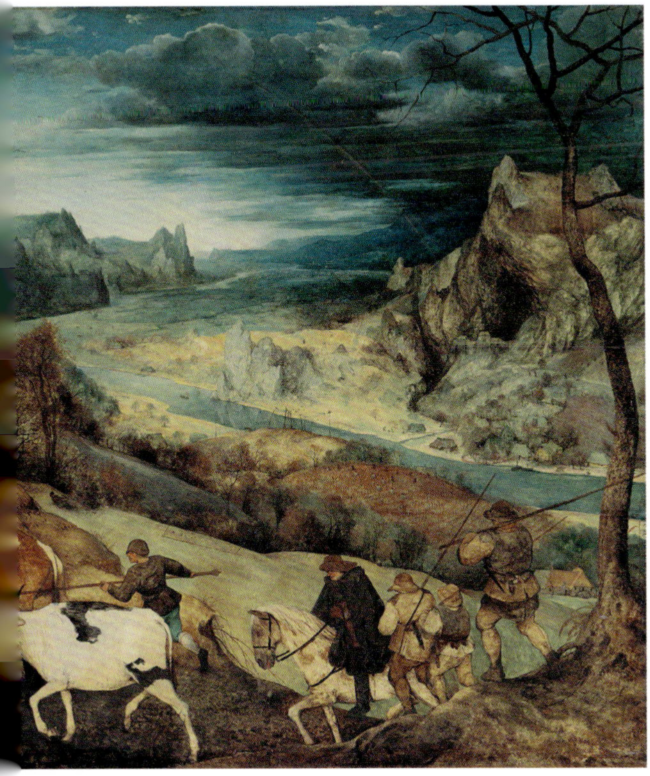

How was that experience? I hope, for some of you, it was wonderful. You might not have gotten the point of the exercise just yet, but don't worry, because now I'm going to ask you to go back and have another look, but this time with an objective.

In our reading of *The Harvesters*, which is set between the months of July and August, we touched on how Bruegel fills a canvas to highlight the everyday reality of normal people. He shows us that things are happening all around us, always, because in truth, they always are. We explored our inability to process information outside of a digestible sphere of influence, and our curiosity when an event is inserted on the edge of that sphere.

Look again at the artworks to the left, but this time with this single objective. Ask yourself, *if his intention is to highlight the lives of normal people, how is Bruegel achieving this?* Step into each with the understanding that a painting may not solve itself on its surface, but it can solve itself in your head. *If Bruegel is highlighting normal people, how does he achieve the effect of making me feel like one? How does he make it feel like real life is happening around me?*

Netherlandish Proverbs

Pieter Bruegel the Elder, 1559

Now just because Pieter Bruegel the Elder was renowned for painting simple themes in complex ways, it doesn't mean he didn't enjoy hyper-complex narratives. In fact, he was so talented, and possibly so insane, that in this painting, he blends over 100 Flemish proverbs in a wonderful sight to behold.

Let's play a game. Have a look through the painting and see if you can spot a devilish-looking baby getting tied to a pillow. It's a proverb that translates to "obstinacy overcomes everything." Now have a look for a person biting a pole: They're a religious hypocrite. A lady carrying a flaming coal in one hand and a bucket of water in the other? Well, according to Pieter, she's two faced and up to no good. Somewhere in the picture are some cards flailing about, meaning it's up to chance. And to the left of them is a globe turned upside down: Everything is opposite of what it should be. Which is probably true considering that there's a man taking a dump out of a window on said globe. The meaning? To despise everything. Two people under a hood? Stupidity loves company. A guy swatting two flies in one stroke? Two birds with one stone. To wipe your backside on a door is to treat something lightly, and to crap through the same hole means you're inseparable friends. Holding an eel by the tail is akin to holding a tiger by the tail, and falling through a basket is to have your deception uncovered.

Keeping the hen's egg and letting the goose egg go is probably a bad decision, and yawning against the oven is probably more than one can manage. If it's something useless, it's a hoe without a handle, and if you're finding an excuse, you're looking for a hatchet. If you find yourself carrying the day in a basket, you're bringing sand to the beach. And if you're sitting on hot coals—well, you get the point. But worry not, because beauty doesn't make up for a lack of substance and there's no sense crying over spilled milk.

I'll provide you with a list of the work's established proverbs on the following pages. See how many of these you can spot.

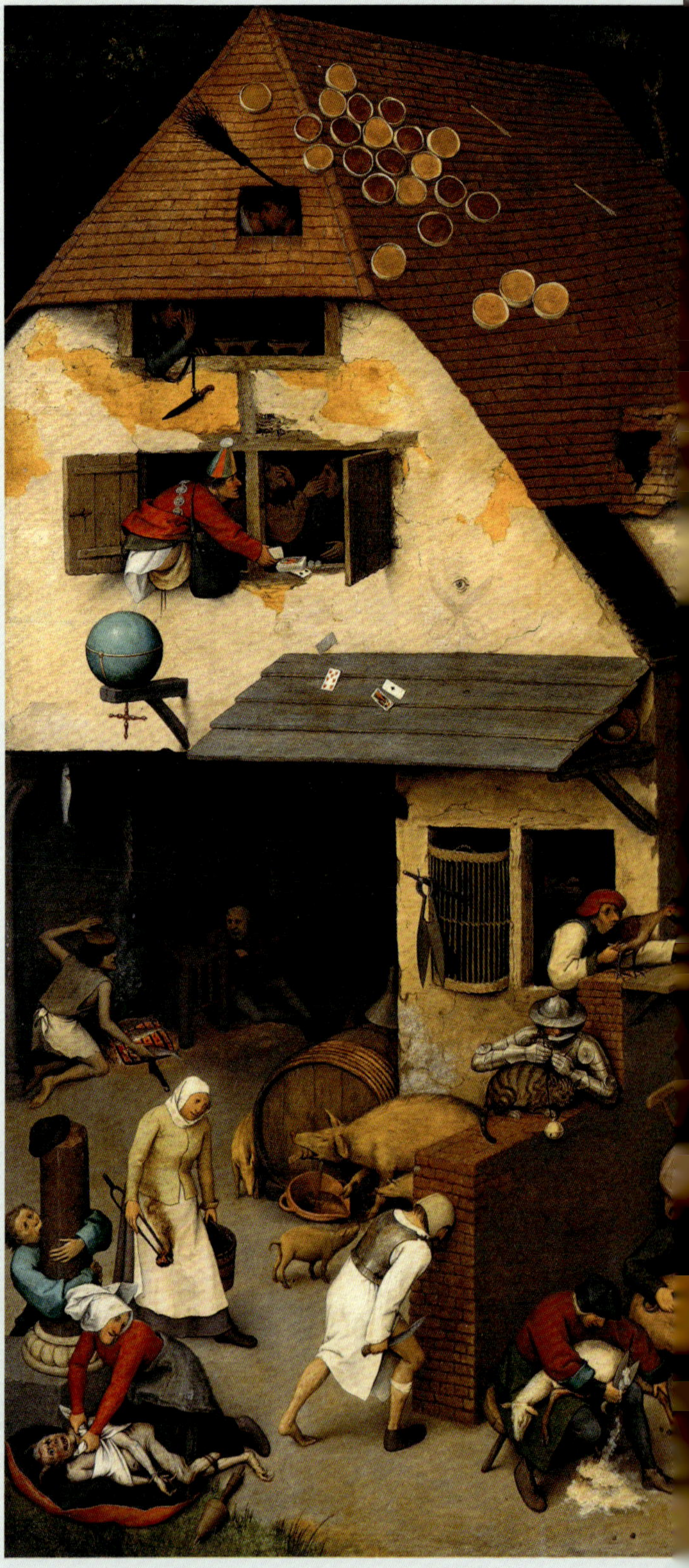

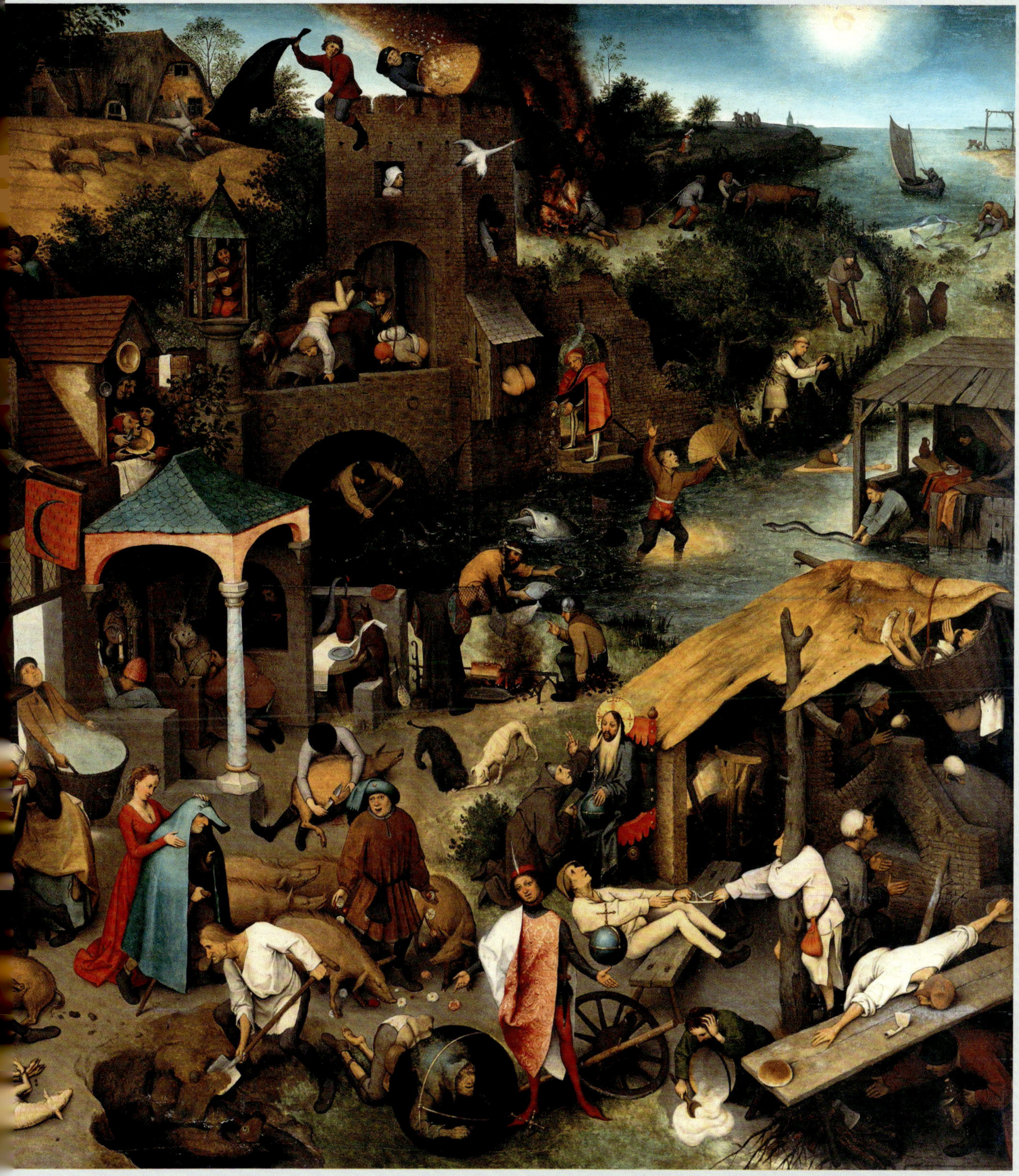

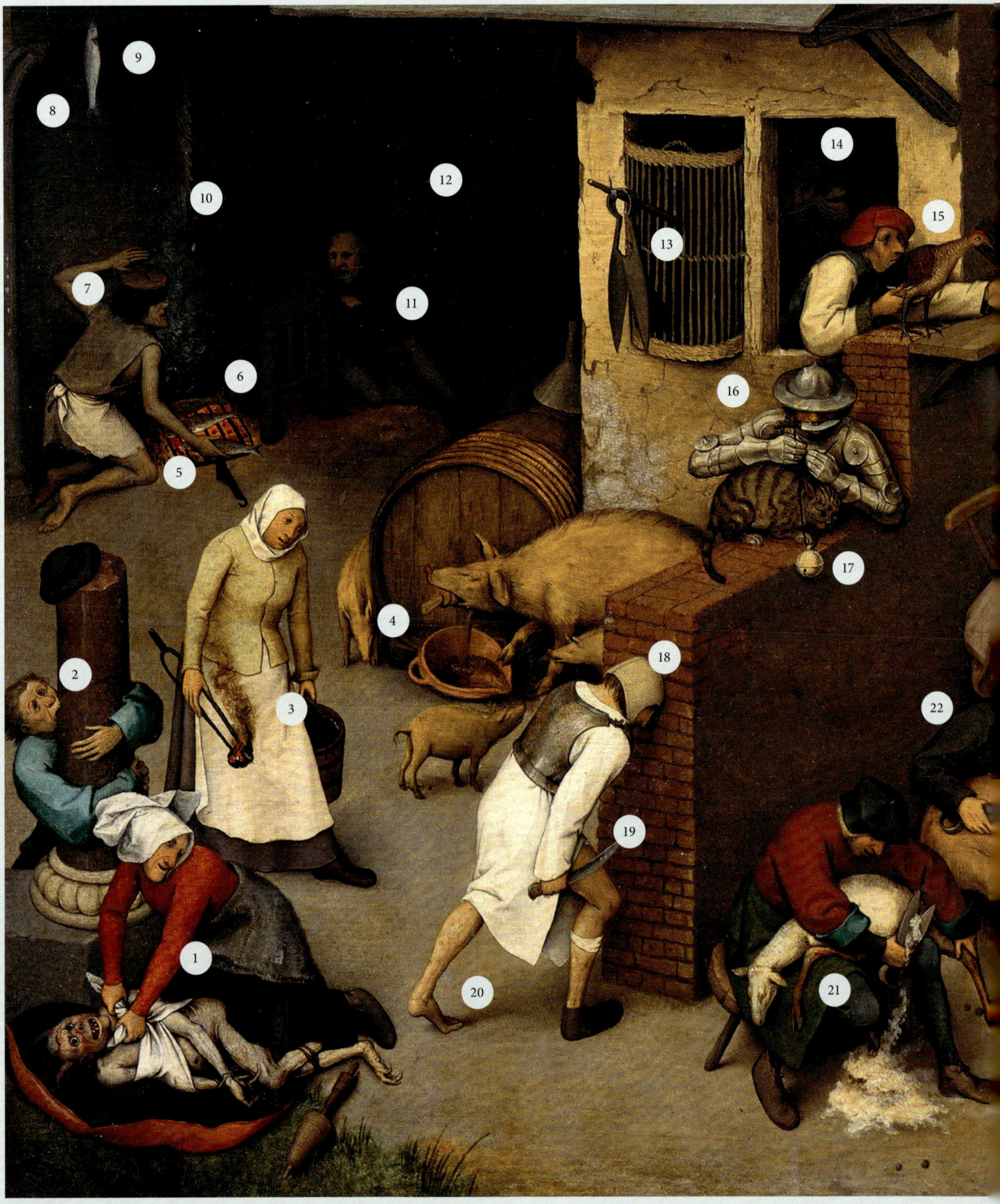
1
2
3
4
5
6
7
8
9
10
11
12
13
14
15
16
17
18
19
20
21
22

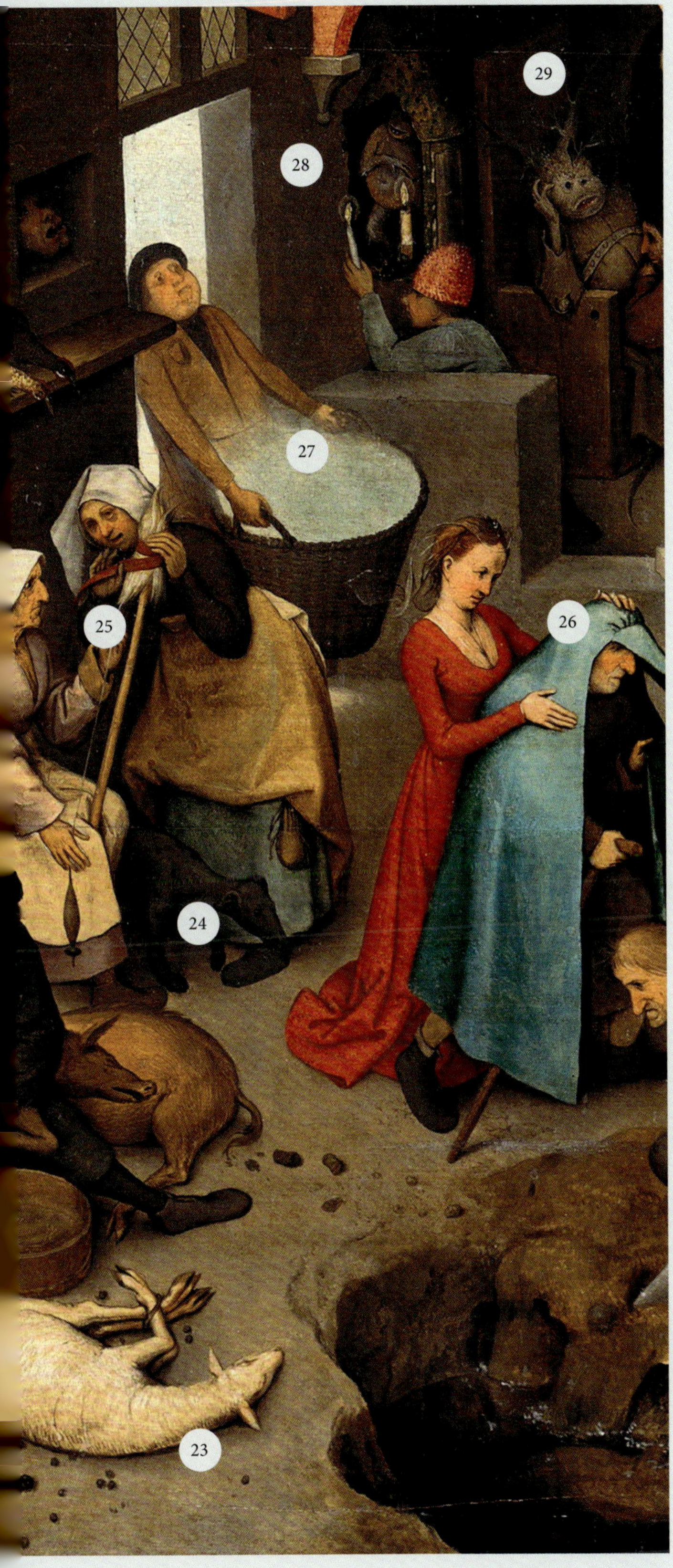

1 **To be able to tie even the devil to a pillow** Obstinacy overcomes everything

2 **To be a pillar biter** To be a religious hypocrite

3 **Never believe someone who carries fire in one hand and water in the other** They are two-faced and deceitful

4 **The sow pulls out the bung** Negligence will be punished

5 **The herring does not fry here** It's not going according to plan

6 **To fry the whole herring for the sake of the roe** To do too much to achieve a little

7 **To get the lid on the head** To end up taking responsibility

8 **The herring hangs by its own gills** You must accept responsibility for your actions

9 **There is more in them than an empty herring** There is more to it than meets the eye

10 **What can smoke do to iron?** There is no point in trying to change the unchangeable

11 **To sit between two stools in the ashes** To be indecisive

12 **To find the dog in the pot** To arrive too late for dinner and find all the food has been eaten

13 **The scissors hang out there** They are liable to cheat you there

14 **To always gnaw on a single bone** To always talk about the same subject

15 **To be a hen feeler** To be very miserly

16 **To be armed to the teeth**

17 **To bell the cat** To undertake a dangerous or impractical plan

18 **To bang your head against a brick wall** To try to achieve the impossible

19 **To put your armor on** To be up in arms

20 **One foot shod, the other bare** Balance is paramount

21 **Shear them but do not skin them** Do not press your advantage too far

22 **One shears sheep, the other shears pigs** One has all the advantages, the other none

23 **To be as gentle as a lamb**

24 **Watch out that a black dog does not come in between** Mind that things don't go wrong

25 **One winds on the distaff what the other spins** Both spread gossip

26 **She puts the blue cloak on her husband** She deceives him

27 **To carry the day out in baskets** To waste one's time

28 **To hold a candle to the Devil** To flatter and make friends indiscriminately

29 **To confess to the Devil** To reveal secrets to one's enemy

30 **The world is turned upside down** Everything is the opposite of what it should be

31 **It depends on the fall of the cards** It is up to chance

32 **The die is cast**

33 **Fools get the best cards** Luck can overcome intelligence

34 **To crap on the world** To despise everything

35 **To lead each other by the nose** To fool each other

36 **There hangs the knife** To issue a challenge

37 **There stand the wooden shoes** To wait in vain

38 **To look through one's fingers** To turn a blind eye

39 **To marry under the broomstick**
To live together without marrying

40 **To stick out the broom** To have fun while the master is away

41 **To have the roof tiled with tarts** To be very wealthy

42 **To shoot a second bolt to find the first**
To repeat a foolish action

43 **An old roof needs a lot more patching up**
Old things need more maintenance

44 **To have a hole in one's roof** To be unintelligent

45 **The roof has laths** The walls have ears

46 **Leave at least one egg in the nest**
Save something for a rainy day

47 **Here hangs the pot** It is the opposite of what it should be

48 **To be pissing against the moon**
To waste one's time on a futile endeavor

49 **To have toothache behind the ears** To be a malingerer

50 **To shave the fool without lather** To trick somebody

51 **It grows out of the window** It cannot be concealed

52 **Two fools under one hood** Stupidity loves company

53 **When the gate is open, the pigs will run into the corn**
Disaster ensues from carelessness

54 **When the corn decreases, the pig increases**
One person's loss is another's gain

55 **To run like one's backside is on fire** To be in great distress

56 **One who eats fire, craps sparks** Do not be surprised at the outcome if you attempt a dangerous venture

57 **To play on the pillory**
People who live in glass houses should not throw stones

58 **To hang one's cloak according to the wind**
To adapt one's viewpoint to the current opinion

59 **To toss feathers in the wind** To work fruitlessly

60 **To gaze at the stork** To waste one's time

61 **To kiss the ring of the door** To be obsequious

62 **One beggar pities the other standing in front of the door**
Being afraid of competition

63 **To go around shouldering a burden**
To imagine that things are worse than they are

64 **To wipe one's backside on the door** To treat something lightly

65 **To fall from the ox onto the rear end of an ass**
To fall on hard times

66 **To fish behind the net** To miss an opportunity

67 **Big fish eat little fish** The powerful prey on the weak

68 **To catch fish without a net** To profit from the work of others

69 **To be unable to see the sun shine on the water**
To be jealous of another's success

70 **A wall with cracks will soon collapse**
Anything poorly managed will soon fail

71 **To throw one's money into the water** To waste one's money

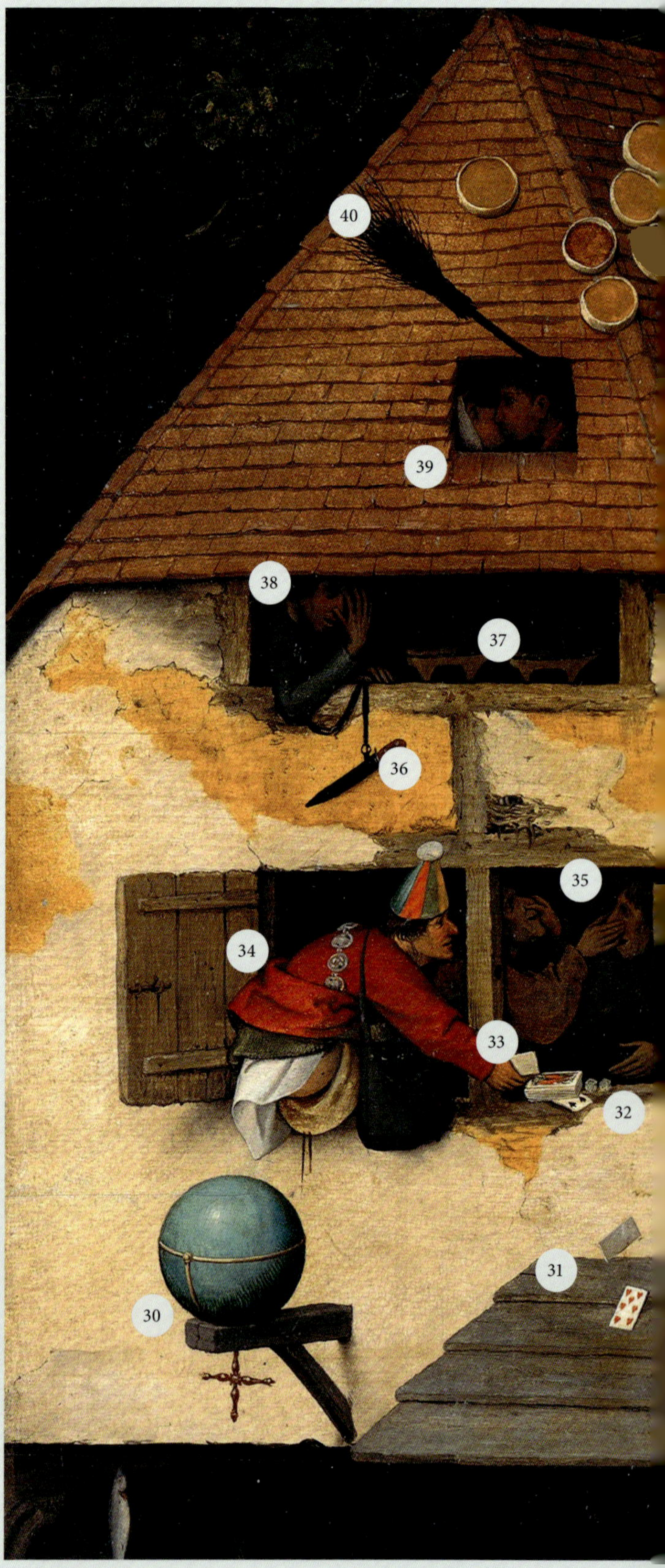

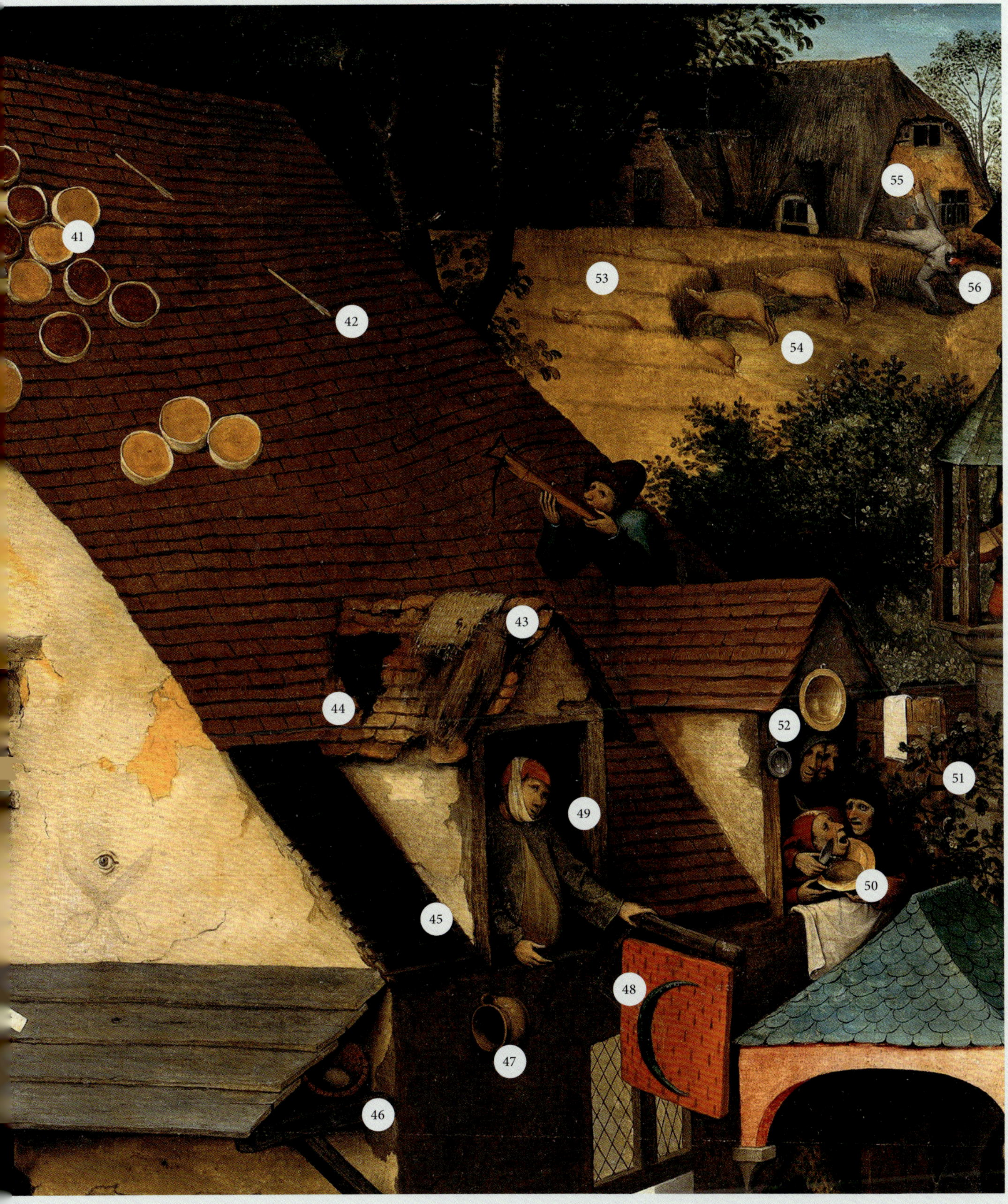
41
42
43
44
45
46
47
48
49
50
51
52
53
54
55
56

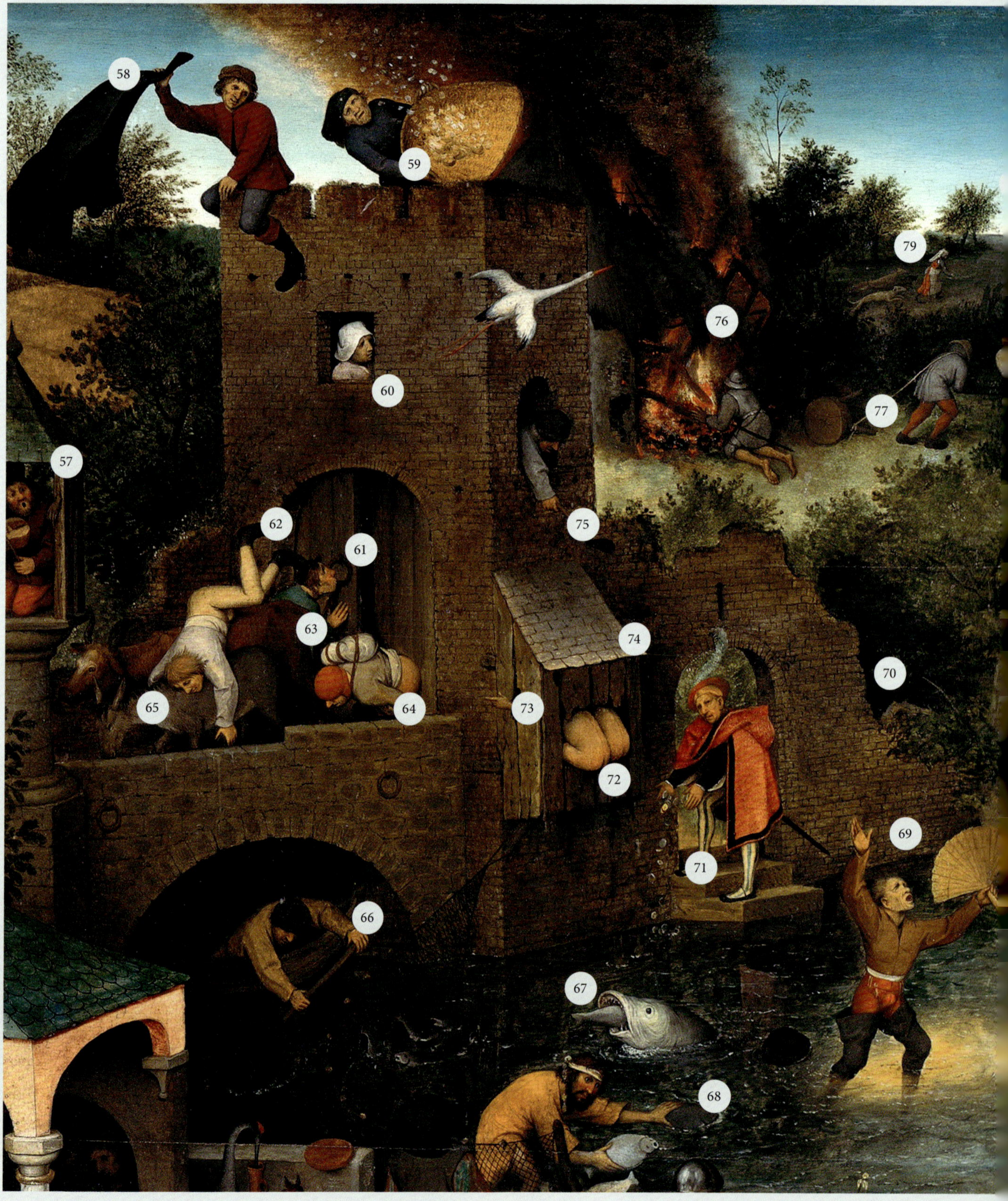
58
59
79
76
60
77
57
75
62
61
63
74
70
73
65
64
72
69
71
66
67
68

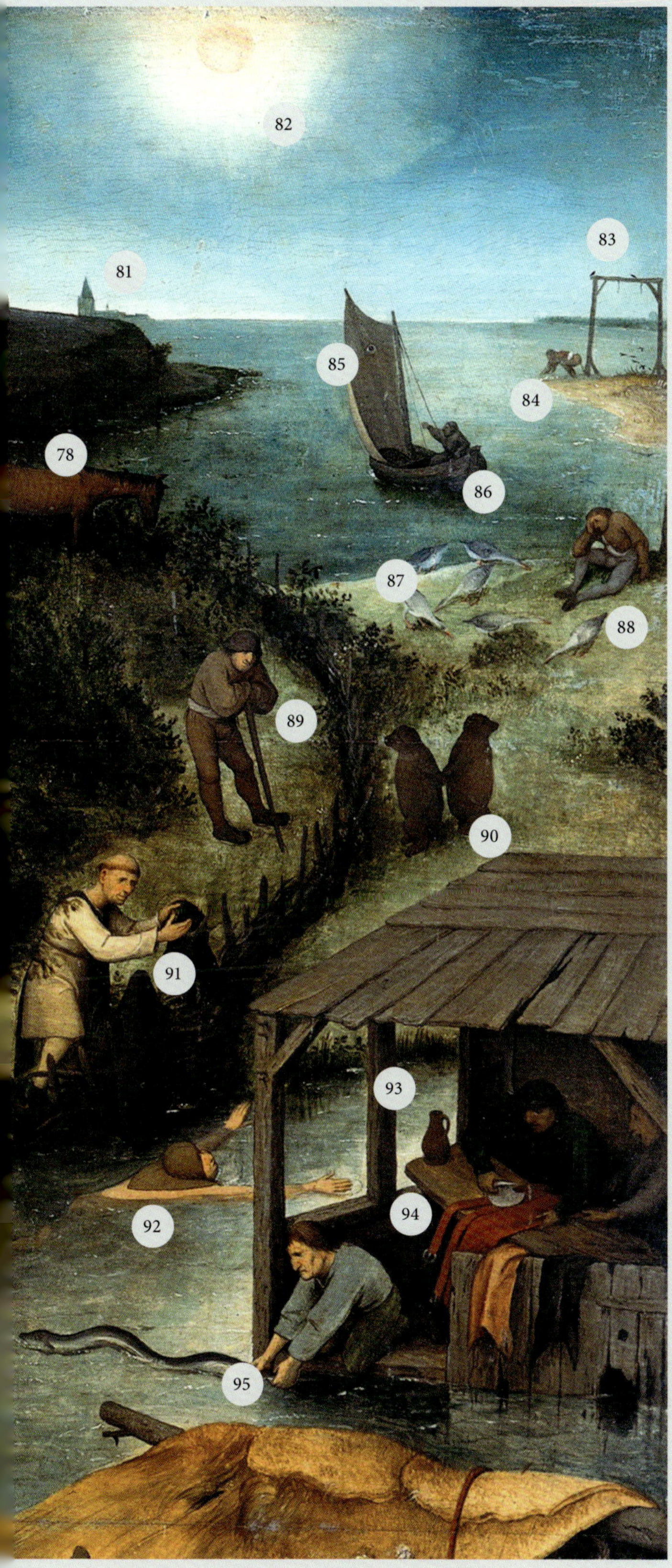

72 **They both crap through the same hole**
They are inseparable friends

73 **Anybody can see through an oak plank if there is a hole in it**
There is no point in stating the obvious

74 **It hangs like a privy over a ditch**
It is extremely obvious

75 **To try to kill two flies with one stroke**
To kill two birds with one stone

76 **To not care whose house is on fire as long as one can warm oneself at the blaze** To take every opportunity regardless of the consequences to others

77 **To drag the block**
To be deceived by a lover, or to work at a pointless task

78 **Horse droppings are not figs** Do not be fooled by appearances

79 **Fear makes the old woman trot**
The unexpected can reveal unknown qualities

80 **If the blind lead the blind, both will fall in the ditch**
The blind leading the blind

81 **The journey is not yet over when one can discern the church and steeple** Do not give up until the task is fully complete

82 **Everything, however finely spun, finally comes to the sun**
Nothing can be hidden forever

83 **Where the carcass is, there fly the crows**
If there's something to be gained, everyone rushes to be first

84 **To crap on the gallows** To be undeterred by any penalty

85 **It is easy to sail before the wind**
If conditions are favorable, it is not difficult to achieve one's goal

86 **To keep one's eye on the sail**
To watch which way the wind is blowing

87 **Who knows why geese go barefoot?**
There is a reason for everything, though it may not be obvious

88 **If I am not meant to be their keeper, I will let geese be geese**
Do not interfere in matters that are not your concern

89 **To see bears dancing** To be starving

90 **Wild bears prefer each other's company**
Birds of a feather flock together

91 **To throw one's cowl over the fence** To discard something without knowing whether it will be required later

92 **It is ill to swim against the current**
It is difficult to oppose the general opinion

93 **The pitcher goes to the water until it finally breaks**
Everything has its limits

94 **The broadest straps are cut from someone else's leather**
One is quick to another's money

95 **To hold an eel by the tail** To have a tiger by its tail

96 **To fall through the basket** To be found out

97 **To be suspended between heaven and earth**
To be in an awkward situation

98 **To keep the hen's egg and let the goose's egg go**
To make a bad decision

99 **To yawn against the oven**
To bite off more than one can chew

100 **To barely be able to reach from one loaf to another**
To have difficulty living within one's means

101 **A hoe without a handle** Something useless

102 **Here he is with his lantern**
To finally have your time to shine

103 **To look for the hatchet** To try to find an excuse

104 **One who has spilt their porridge cannot scrape it all up again**
No use crying over spilt milk

105 **To put a spoke through someone's wheel**
To throw a spanner in the works

106 **To have the world spinning on one's thumb**
To have the world in the palm of your hand

107 **To pull to get the longest end** To attempt to get an advantage

108 **Love is on the side where the money bag hangs**
Love can be bought

109 **No one looks for others in the oven who has not been in there himself** To imagine wickedness in others is a sign of wickedness in oneself

110 **To stand in one's own light**
To act against one's own happiness

111 **To tie a flaxen beard to the face of Christ**
To hide deceit under a veneer of Christian piety

112 **Two dogs over one bone seldom agree**
To argue over a single point

113 **To cast roses before swine** To waste effort on the unworthy

114 **To have to stoop to get on in the world**
To succeed, one must be willing to make sacrifices

115 **To fill the well after the calf has already drowned**
To take action only after a disaster

116 **The pig is stabbed through the belly**
A foregone conclusion, or what is done cannot be undone

117 **To be a skimming ladle** To be a leech

118 **What is the good of a beautiful plate when there is nothing on it?**
Beauty does not make up for a lack of substance

119 **To blow in the ear** To spread gossip

120 **The fox and the crane dine together**
If you trick someone, they might trick you back

121 **To chalk it up** To owe someone

122 **The meat on the spit must be basted**
Certain things need constant attention

123 **There is no turning the spit with him** He is uncooperative

124 **To sit on hot coals** To be impatient

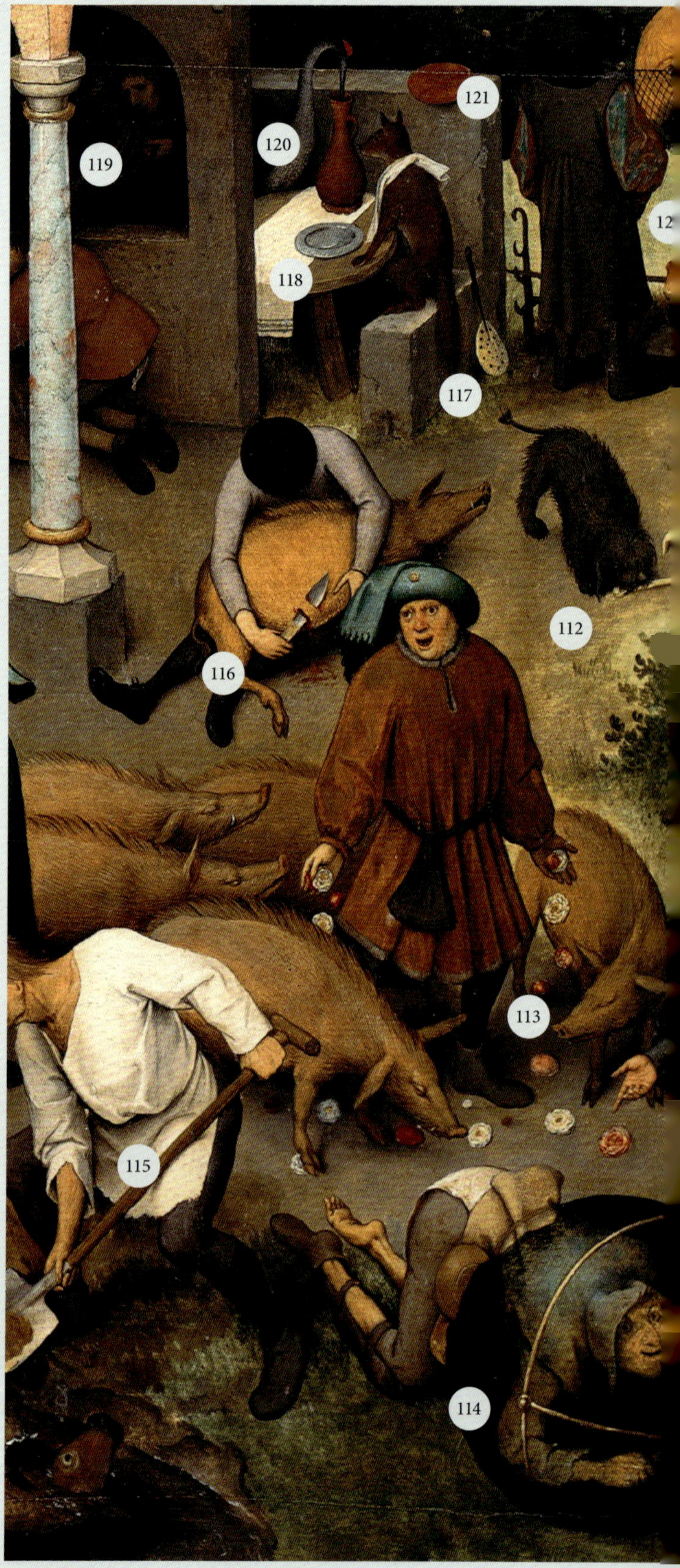

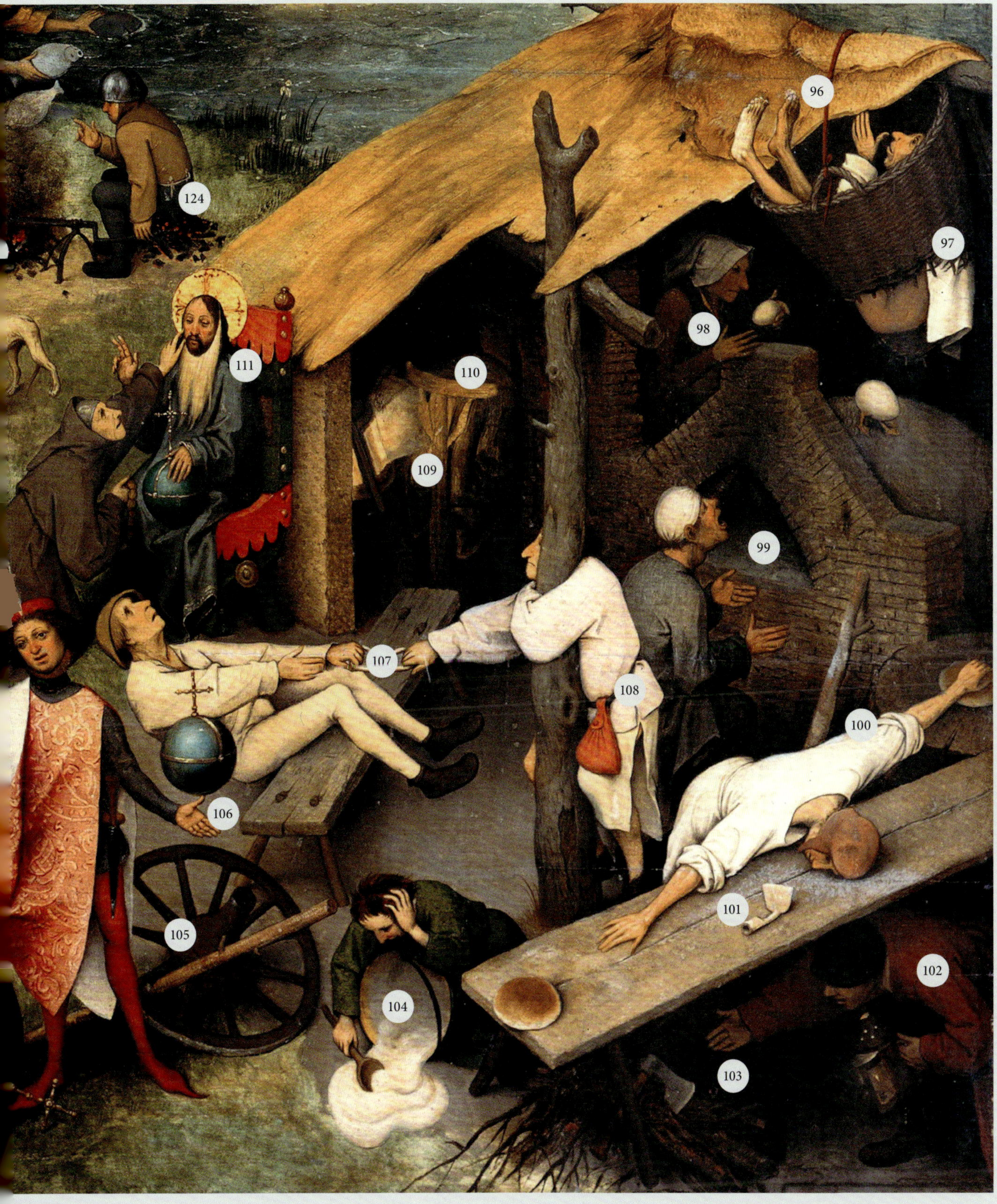
96
97
98
99
100
101
102
103
104
105
106
107
108
109
110
111
124

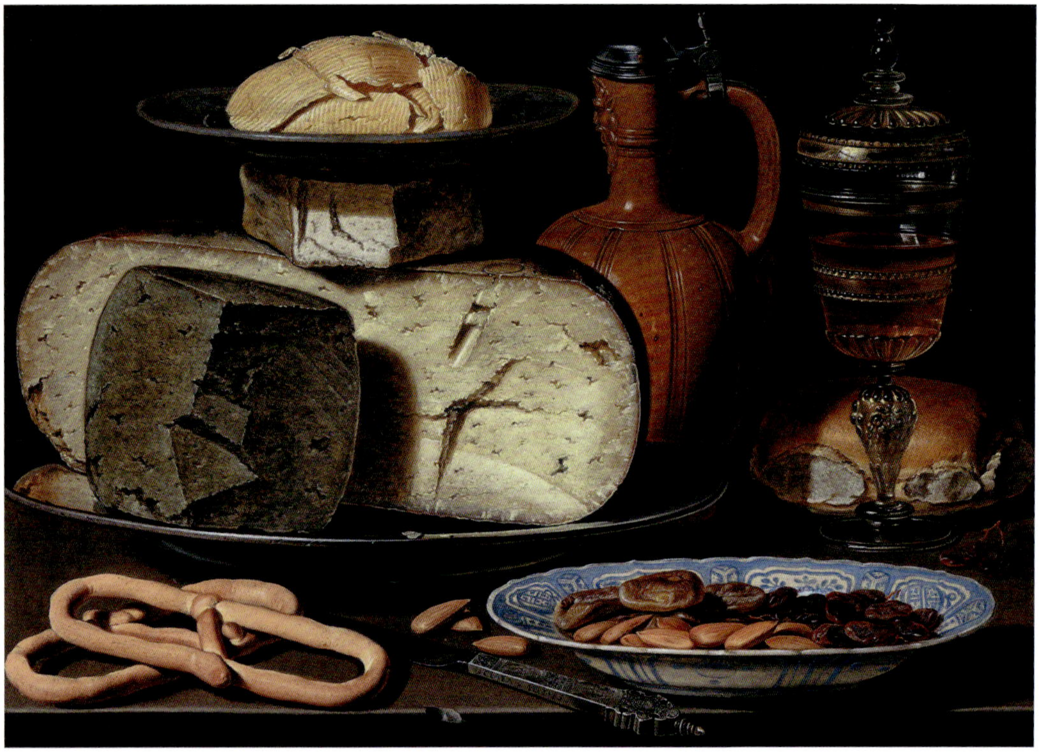

Still Life with Cheeses, Almonds and Pretzels, c. 1615

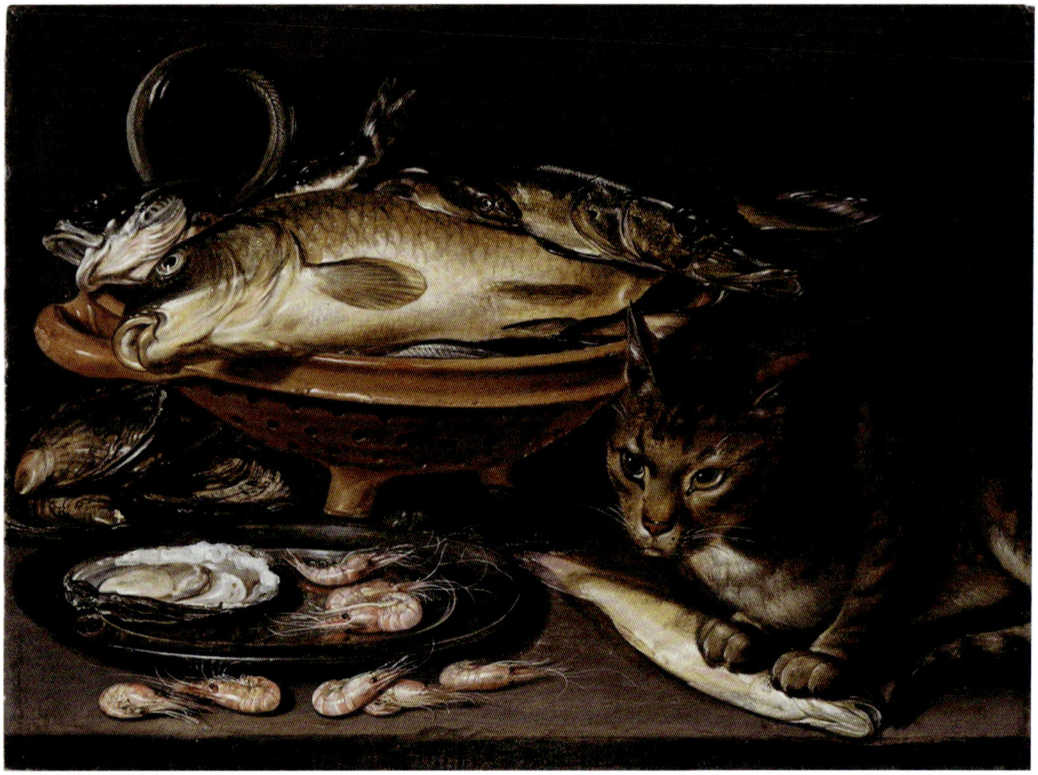

Still Life with Fish and Cat, after 1620

Various works by Clara Peeters

c. 1612–20

Still life. It is a genre of art that depicts inanimate subject matter—typically everyday objects that are either natural or man-made, arranged to study things like form and composition. At the highest level, a still life can explore the themes of beauty, morality, and the extraordinary in the ordinary, but sometimes, a still life goes beyond just that. *Sometimes*, it's a form where an artist can *truly* show off an exquisite understanding of the basics and boggle your mind in the process. Of course, it might be hard to imagine a genre that focuses on something as lifeless as a dead fish on a platter as a complex artform—that is, until you've been exposed to the Flemish Master Clara Peeters.

An artist who was so skilled, she could hide a reflection in a painting, and you wouldn't even know where to spot it. Do you see it? No? Well, it's on the lid of the jug in *Still Life with Cheeses, Almonds and Pretzels*. But Peeters is so much more than a reflection on the pewter lid of an earthenware jug, because in a body of work that consists exclusively of still-life paintings, and in a genre full of little symbols and hidden secrets, her talent for detail is commanding.

In the very same picture as the reflection, she paints a decorative glass with such precision, you can slide your finger across every single bump. She captures a piece of bread so thoroughly you can feel its hard exterior and soft, spongy insides. You can smell the cheese, taste the figs, and spread the butter with a knife. And speaking of a knife.

"Oh my."

Wielding a paintbrush like a surgeon with a scalpel, Peters shows us a knife hanging off the edge of the table with such mastery, we not only feel its weight, we see how light bounces out of every curve and off every notch. And if that hasn't blown your head off your shoulders, she signs the painting by engraving the knife's handle.

This is not a one hit wonder. Throughout her entire body of work, she does it again and again and again and again, with a never-ending supply of wine-filled glassware, dried fruits, birds and seashells, baked goods, and fragrant flowers. Reflection after reflection, and sometimes a cat, like the one over there sneaking a seafood snack.

He too, just like us, can probably smell the fish stacked into a bowl from a mile away. The moist scent of dense, fishy air shoots into your nose from a visual stimulation that only a true master can pull off. Slippery and wet, ice cold, and ready to eat: Peeters captures the fragile, transparent shells of those langoustines and the slimy insides of that oyster.

I don't blame the cat at all for wanting in on the action. And to tie it all together, Peeters, as only a person with a sense of humor could, says it all on the face of a fish on the cusp of becoming a meal:

"Holy crap."

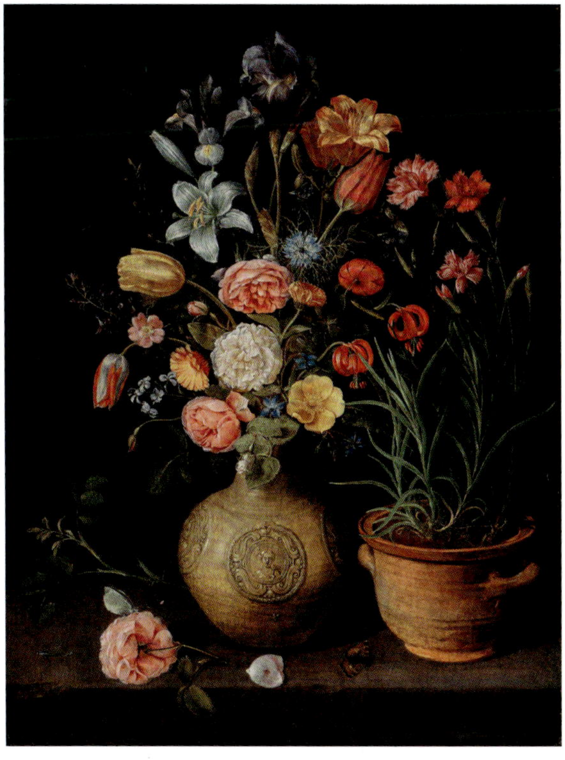

Roses, Lilies, an Iris and Other Flowers in an Earthenware Vase, With a Pot of Carnations and a Butterfly on a Ledge, 1612

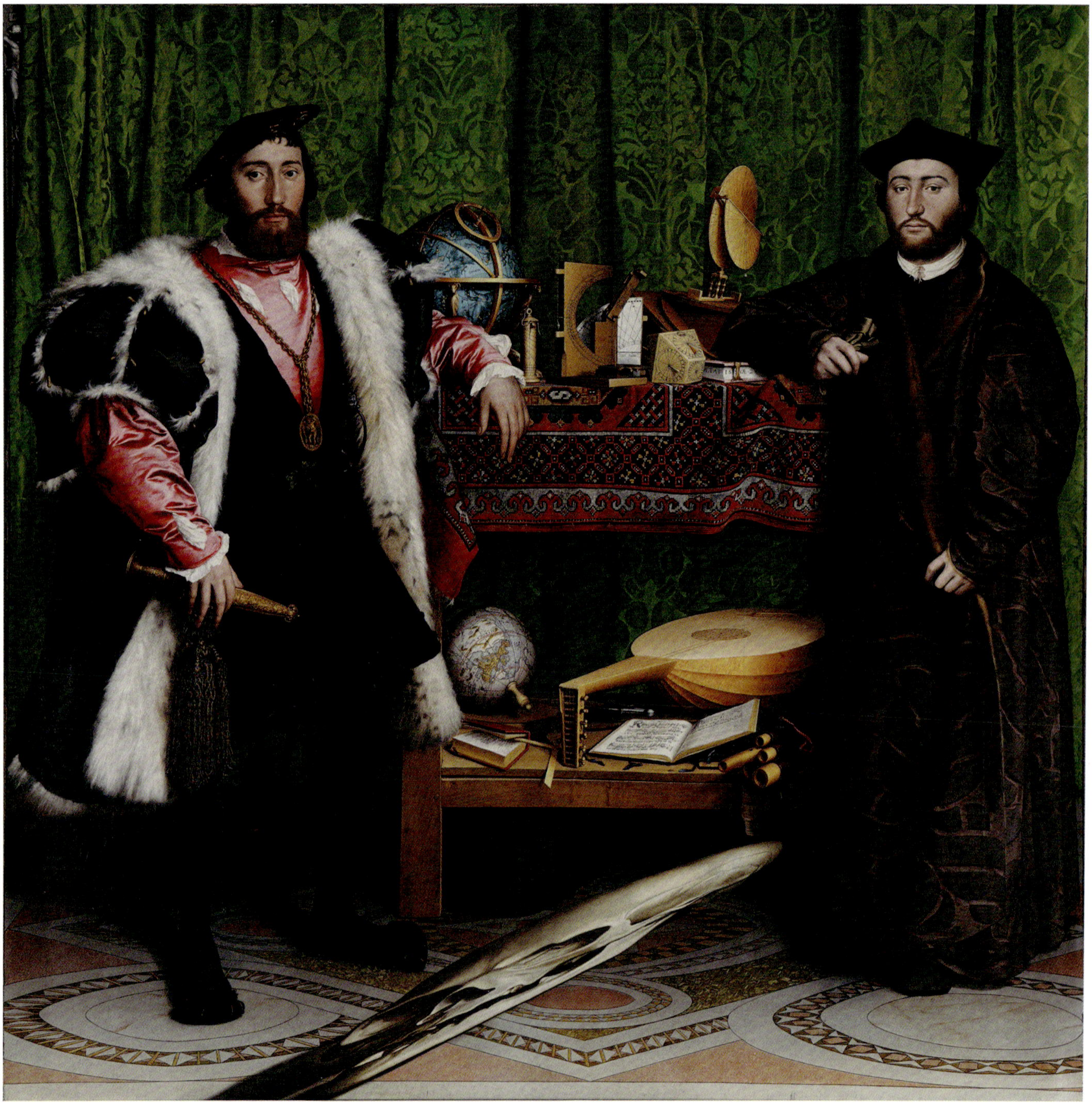

The Ambassadors

Hans Holbein the Younger, 1533

The fish in Peeters's painting isn't the only one shocked here. When it comes to the images I've studied, there is one clear example that stands out above the rest for its ability to surprise. It is an artwork that is so exceptional and perfectly executed, it feels like a fiction. It is the most insane painting that I've ever experienced in my life, and I'm confident that after I show you, it might be the most insane you've ever seen too.

That same court artist who painted Henry VIII and Anne of Cleves was so bloody meticulous in this masterpiece, you could zoom into either man's face and make out every single individual hair.

"Wow."

If you like that, look at the book open between them. It is so detailed, you can not only read it word for word, but can quite literally count out each and every individual page. What seems like just a globe from up close becomes an eye-soothing orb further away that Hans Holbein the Younger has painted with such precision you can *feel* its roundness with your eyeballs. And speaking of feeling things with your eyes, you can pass your hand through the fur of the men's coats, you can twist the knobs on the lute, pick each individual thread on the rug, and touch each individual groove on whatever the hell that flat, circular object is beside the man on the right. You can caress the details on each shiny object. Poke every knot and pluck every string, but be careful—you don't want to break another one. You can see the glitter of the gold specks on the floor, and the intricacies of the tedious marble inlay. And …

"What the hell is that?"

In a picture where every single feature is a perfect calculation, Holbein throws in a party trick so technically demanding, you'd forget that you were looking at a painting from the 1500s. What appears to be an out-of-place blob at the front of the canvas is, in actual fact, an optical illusion, and when approaching the artwork from the right, what you'll actually see is an anamorphic projection of a skull, which jumps right out of the canvas. Try it for yourself!

Insane, right? And it's no wonder that in a painting littered with optical tricks, you probably missed the entire point of the picture in the first place, and its four major characters.

"Hold on. There's only two?"

Well there's Jean de Dinteville, a French diplomat, and the Bishop of Lavaur, Georges de Selve, conducting a secret meeting to discuss the Protestant Reformation of the Church. However, what you've certainly missed is the cameo of Martin Luther in the form of a book.

Not just any book, I might add, but a hymn book translated by the man himself. On one page, a song of the Commandments, on the other a song on the Holy Spirit. A suggestion of consonance between the two, perhaps? Or, maybe not. Remember that broken lute string? A disruption in religious harmony? Or, a nod to the fact that you're watching a secret meeting, which has snapped the tension in the room—naughty. And a book on division reinforces the split.

"Fine. Three characters, but not a fourth."

Oh, yes, there is, because hidden in the top left corner of the masterpiece, tucked away in the shadows, a faint glimmer of silver catches our eyes: Christ poking his head around the corner. And even in a mysterious meeting between men, on a subject that requires the utmost secrecy, the omnipresence of God misses nothing.

"Jesus."

The Awakening Conscience

William Holman Hunt, 1853

Ew. He's definitely not her husband.

"How could you know that? "

Well, for starters, this room is a bloody mess, and by carefully combing over the bits strewn about, we reveal that she is *probably* his mistress. Have a look at her hands. Notice anything other than a slight agitation? She's got a ring on every single finger except for the one that counts: a sort of "I'm not married to this man" statement as far as symbolism goes. And we've only just scratched the surface, because if you pan over to the right, you might have noticed something else. No, not what appears to be the disease-ridden hand of the perverted gentleman—keep going a little more.

On the music rack of the piano is an arrangement titled "Oft in the Stilly Night," a real song by a very real person named Thomas Moore that speaks of missed opportunities and a happier past. And did you notice the cat playing with a poor, helpless bird?

I assure you, the bird isn't having fun, but it is intentionally placed to suggest a few intriguing ideas. A life destined for a poor outcome, for one thing: a detail to further enforce that *this* place is a mess. Or, is the man the predatory cat? And she the helpless bird, wings pinned down so that she might never fly off? We've got a clock concealed in glass, the strings of an unfinished tapestry scattered on the floor, and Alfred Tennyson's poem "Tears, Idle Tears" disposed like a piece of garbage. And remember the diseased hand? Well, it's not diseased, despite appearances, but is instead shielded by a glove: the partner glove to the one that's been tossed to the floor, suggesting wasteful intentions, or maybe even a wasted purpose. It's not politely put away, because *nothing* about this scene is polite to begin with. And while this bumbling fool sings away a song about wasted life, we pull away and realize that she, but a moment ago, was singing too. In fact, you can almost hear it: the final note that got away before she finally came to her senses.

While we've been uncovering the nature of this relationship and who it is that we're observing, we haven't really considered what's actually in front of us. *The Awakening Consciousness*: The title of the painting by William Holman Hunt is all the context we really need, because that's exactly what's going on inside her head. It's undeniable. She was just sitting in this man's lap. She was just singing this song. But the mirror in the background gives us a hint about her inner dialogue; as she realizes that her life isn't wasted, we too realize that there's a whole world out there, and everything inside this room can be forgotten. Something better is only a few steps away. And unlike the bird who's trapped inside this room, *this* cat can't keep her down any longer.

What a powerful thought. In the moment that the mind awakens and in the actions that follow, we are truly powerful. This woman is headed into the unknown, with her whole life ahead of her.

And behind her. Because what is life but a series of memories, with every choice we make a reference point on our roadmap as we head with her out of that room? All we have are the moments that led to this point, which leaves the question: Are we more than a collection of memories? And if so, what is our reality?

This is a subject Salvador Dalí is familiar with.

Adolescence

Salvador Dalí, 1941

I need to come clean about Dalí: I was never a fan. For all the time I spent studying art history, I didn't want to give the man a fair shake. Why? Well, in truth, I just didn't understand him. I felt that his work was "insufferable" and so "over the top"—a try-hard as far as details and symbols went, especially compared to some of the artists we've already discussed in this book. He wasn't for me, and I was convinced that he would never be. That was, until the day I stumbled upon *Adolescence*.

Flip the page and have a look at this painting. I want you to quickly make a mental note of the first thing that jumps out at you.

If you're 99 percent of people, it was a face, because, well, there's a mouth, a nose, a set of eyes. Right? Now let's back up and try again. Look carefully and say out loud exactly what you see.

Is it different this time? A woman sitting on a beach, perhaps? A young boy hiding behind her? Houses off in the background? Trees on a hill? The lines of a plowed field? Buildings and little islands? You wouldn't be wrong. Dalí created this painting in 1941, and you will need to remember this piece of information.

Now, did you notice the hidden words in the top left corner of the artwork? No? Not on the first viewing, maybe.

Tucked in the corner are the words *Pour Vous*, or "For You." This is the name of a popular weekly film magazine that ceased to exist after the German

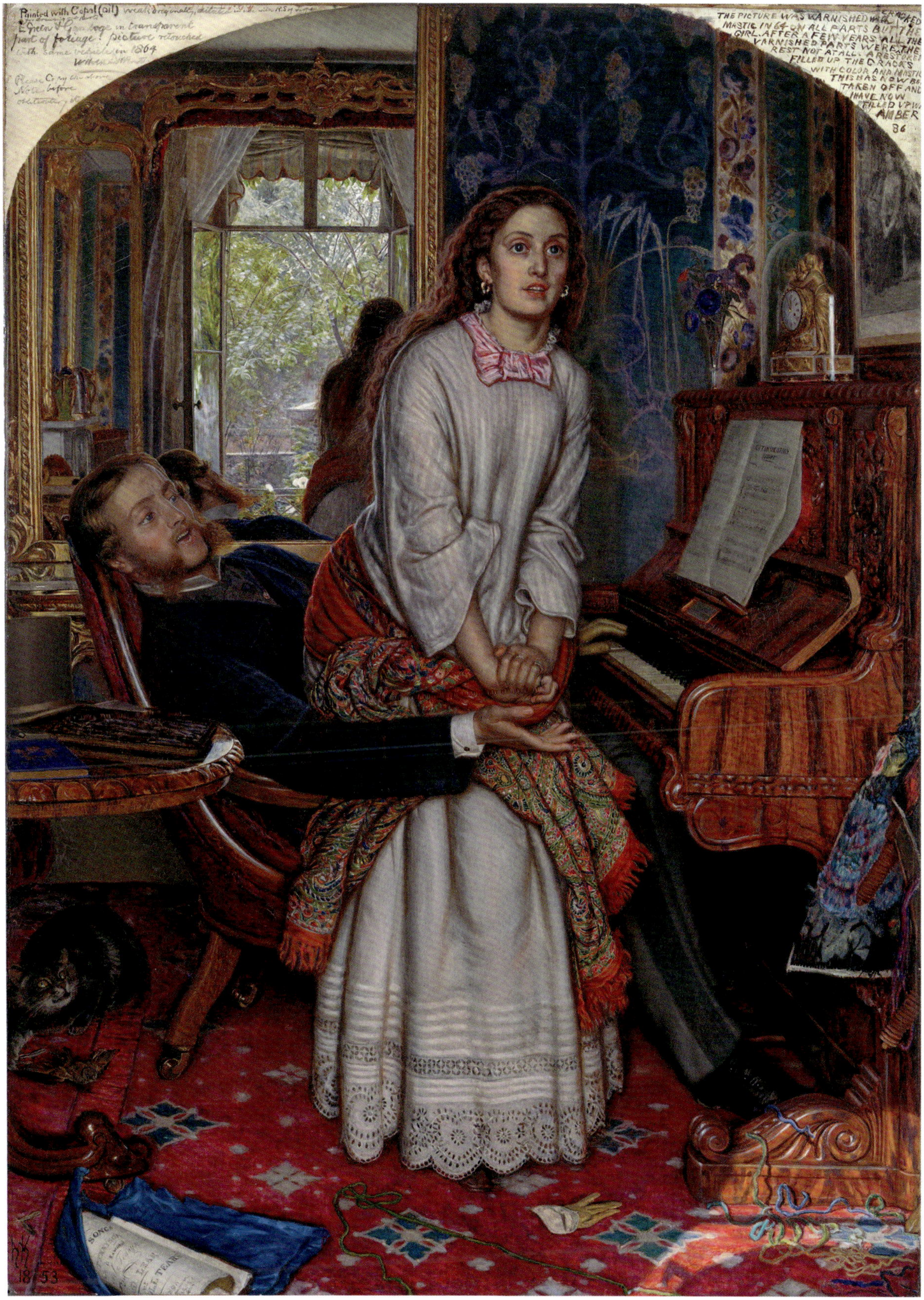
Painted with Copal (oil)
part of foliage! picture retouched
THE PICTURE WAS VARNISHED
MASTIC IN 64 ON ALL PARTS
GIRL. AFTER A FEW YEARS ALL
VARNISHED PARTS WERE
REST NOT AT ALL.
FILLED UP THE CRACKS
WITH COLOR AND
THIS HAS NOW
TAKEN OFF
I HAVE NOW
FILLED UP
AMBER
86
1853

occupation of France. And who's the woman whose face forms the lansdcape? She is none other than Australian actress Betty Stockfeld. But what does that have to do with anything? You're probably wondering "Why is he asking so many questions?"

Because, my friends, questions are exactly the point. And in what could be a painting about anything at all, Dalí gives us a form of controlled chaos that would become a signature of his style across his entire canon of work: a systematic confusion that contributes to the total discredit of the real world. The answer to any question is another question. That is, until we uncover a clue, like who this woman and this boy are at the painting's center.

They are a young Salvador Dalí and his beloved nursemaid, Llúcia, sitting on a beach at Cadaqués, where his family spent many summers. With this knowledge, the painting's secrets unravel. This is not an illusion, but a series of long-forgotten memories and sensations that reveal themselves one at a time, in the way memories of the distant past often do.

Dalí's *Adolescence* is a quintessential example of his "paranoiac–critical" method: the practice of using optical illusion and double imagery to probe the unstable boundary between memory, fantasy, and perception. The double image embodies Dalí's belief that "confusion can be systematized," as he writes in *The Conquest of the Irrational* (1935). His paranoiac–critical method encourages viewers to oscillate between competing readings of the same image, revealing the instability of the "real." In *Adolescence*, that instability mirrors the process of *remembering something*: the way childhood recollections mutate through desire, guilt, and nostalgia. Dalí transforms perception into a dream logic where meanings and interpretations shift every time the eye refocuses, resulting in a visual analogy for Freud's dream-work. Through confusion, displacement, and the fusion of incompatible scenes, Dalí's optical trickery becomes a mechanism for psychological revelation.

He executes *Adolescence* in gouache, ink, and pencil over a cover of *Pour Vous*. The decision to paint directly atop a mass-printed image of actress Betty Stockfeld's face collapses the line between popular culture and fine art, turning an ephemeral object into a site of transformation. Through subtle changes, Stockfeld's nose, lips, and chin become a woman sitting on a beach, while her eyes and brow morph into a hillside with trees and fields. This "metamorphic anatomy" converts a photographic face into an entire landscape and narrative, turning the primitive act of simply looking into a surreal act of perception.

The setting—the beach of Cadaqués—is charged with personal meaning. The seated woman represents Dalí's childhood nursemaid, a recurring maternal figure in his life who is protective yet monumental, and both sacred and fleshy. The boy with a hoop is young Dalí himself, and their presence transforms the painting into an eidetic reconstruction of a lost childhood, filtered through nostalgia and Freudian symbolism. The tender domestic memory collides with the erotic overtones of adolescence, marking the moment that youthful innocence and adult desires begin to intertwine.

Dalí explicitly connects this image to a formative episode described in his autobiography *La Vie secrète de Salvador Dalí* (1942), in which the young artist hides behind Llúcia to escape the gaze of "Galuchka," a girl who awakens his sexual awareness. In this moment, the feelings of shame, arousal, and maternal refuge become a psychic tableau of adolescence: the collision between Eros (the gaze of desire) and Thanatos (the retreat into protection and repression).

The woman's body and the landscape fuse: The maternal figure literally becomes the terrain of memory. Galuchka's eyes are transformed into hills and trees, but they still "watch" the viewer, despite the safety of Llúcia's maternal protection.

A memory turned into a timeless artwork that starts off by challenging the notion of what it is that we see, and in the end, transforms into the very feeling of what it is to be seen.

Adolescence distills the central tensions of Dalí's artistic practice between illusion and revelation, sexuality and sanctity, the subconscious and awareness. It stands as one of his most psychologically intricate works: an image that is deeply intimate and conceptually refined. Through minimal means, like a magazine cover and a few strokes of gouache, Dalí turns an everyday object into a mirror of the unconscious: a self-portrait and a psychoanalytic diagram, where memory, desire, and art all converge in a single metamorphosis.

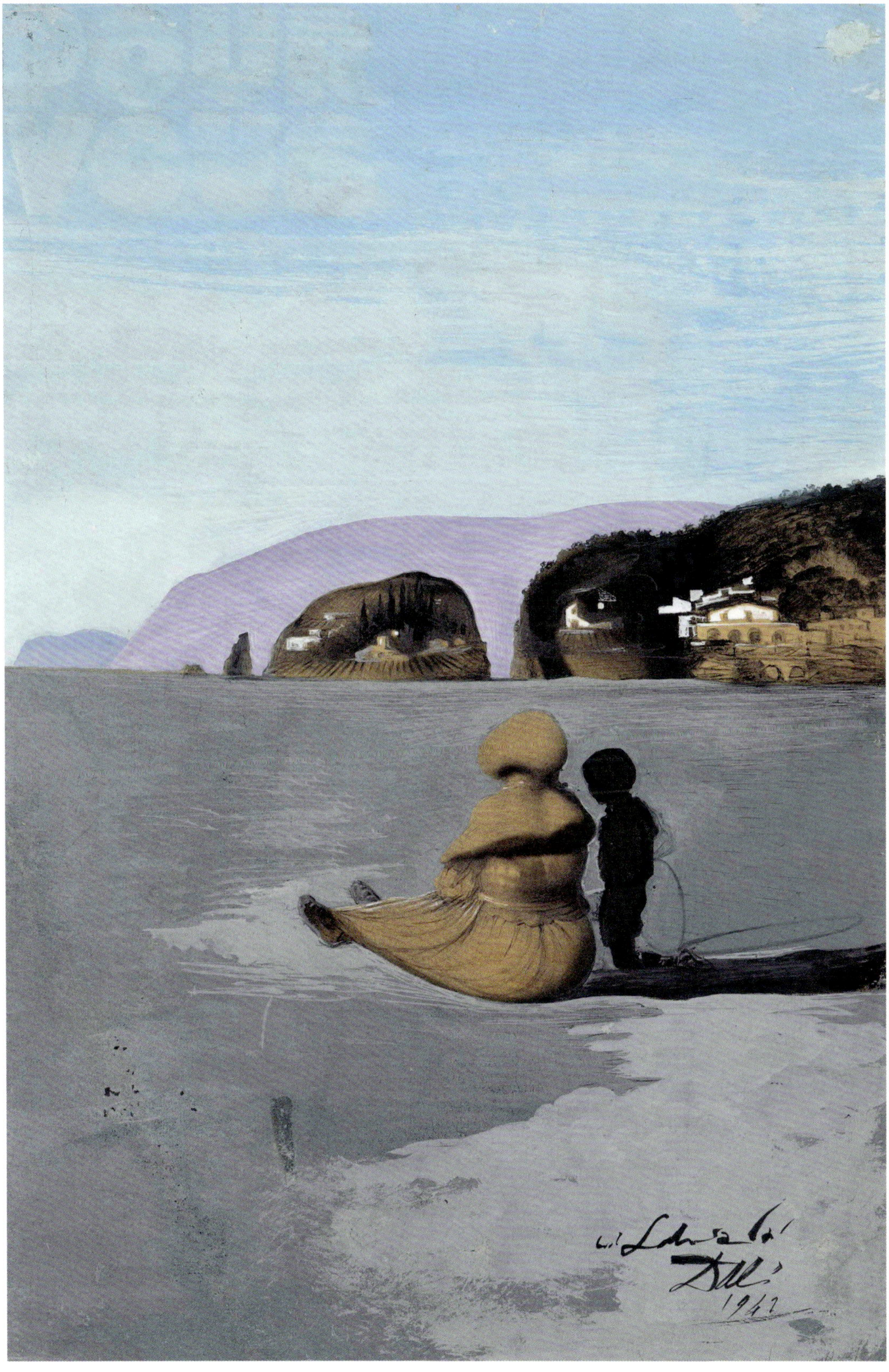

Adolescence, 1941, © Fundació Gala-Salvador Dali. VEGAP/Copyright Agency, 2026

MORE THAN MEETS THE EYE

The art of an understated idea: a motif that doesn't inherently reveal itself at the first opportunity, and yet, upon discovery, changes everything. Where a talented artist might flood the viewer with a barrage of complexly painted symbols and objects, there is much to be said about the injection of a curated *few* good things. Quiet motifs are one of the most powerful tools that an artist can wield, because at their best, they carry such possibility and impact.

A quiet motif can take the form of a single object, a question, a color, a posture, or so much more, and when executed perfectly, can make all the difference between viewing an artwork as great versus viewing an artwork as transformative.

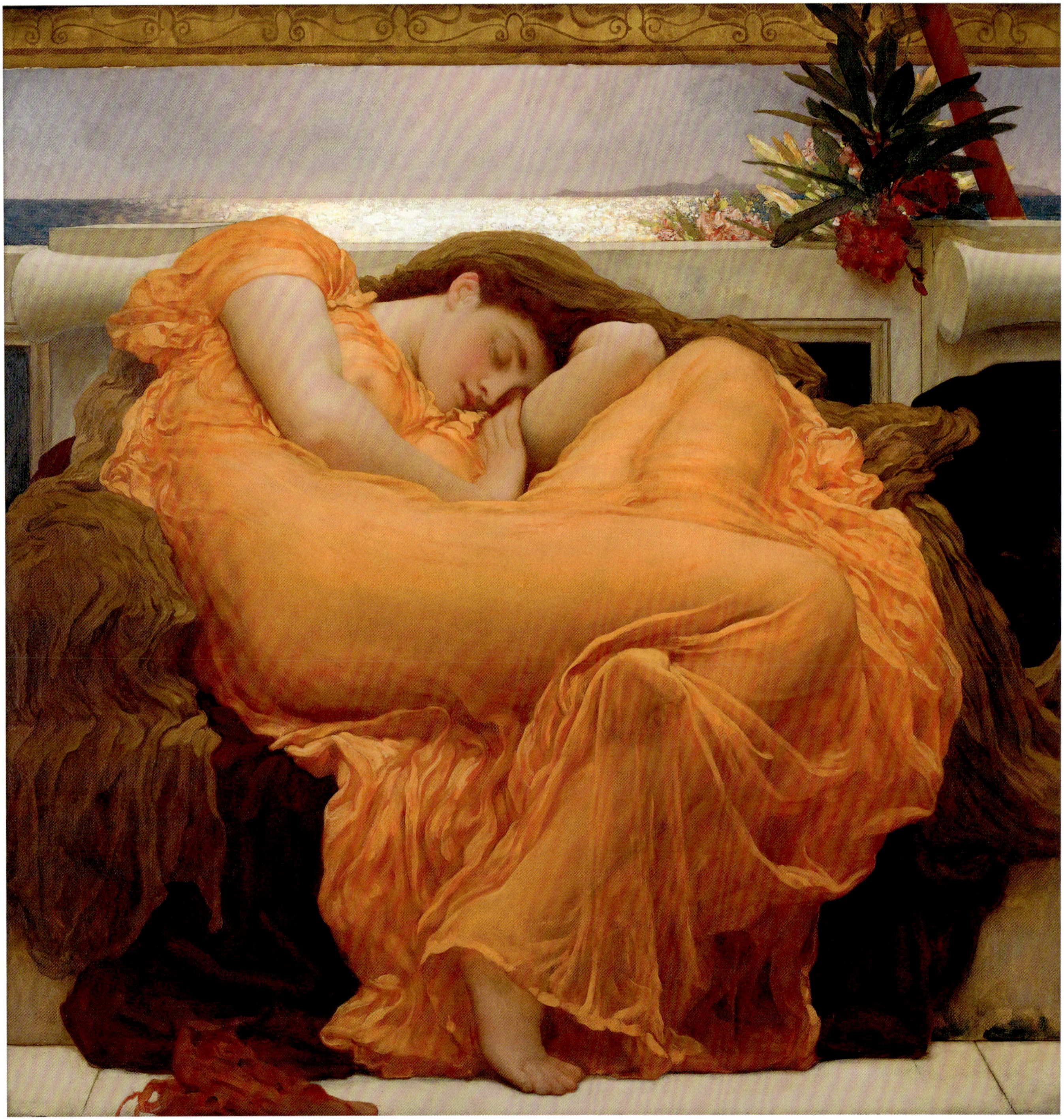

Flaming June

Frederic Leighton, 1895

Sleep and death are wildly different things. And yet when staring them in the face, one might not know the difference. And that, my friends, is because Sir Frederic Leighton is a master of disguises, and in his greatest painting, he uses a deceiving motif to obscure another, much more shocking one.

Our muse is an undeniable beauty: a radiant creature with perfect skin, muted features, rich tones, and sensuous form. Her brilliant bright orange dress is purposely placed to inject a feeling of immense warmth, and yet, when we look at the painting in its entirety, we're not overwhelmed. Leighton balances the feeling of warmth by countering it with the elements. He paints a light breeze shot off the sea, and we, the audience, experience it in real time—delicate and harmonious, just like the dress that it moves.

It's an item so perfectly painted it has its own breath. Every fiber of the silky orange cloth is a channel for a stream of crisp, cool air. And while we're distracted by a cocktail of elemental harmony, Leighton arouses our sensibilities with transparency. The vibrant garment doesn't simply cover the beautiful woman but rather hovers over her. Our curiosities run wild, and Leighton knows it. He plays this feeling to perfection, and all of it is a distraction. Because when you zoom out again, shaking off the drunken fantasy that is *Flaming June*, you might notice its secret.

The oleander is a poisonous plant that, if consumed, means a swift, eternal sleep. And there, above her shoulder, is a branch: a symbol of the fragile space between life and death. Between a blissful sleep and sleeping forever.

This reference to death isn't obvious, disguised underneath a disguise. We aren't guided where to look or what we should be looking for. Instead, the branch simply sits there. It quietly hovers on the ledge that divides the warmth of her dress and her flesh and the cool breeze of the sea. Further still, we need to have a knowledge of plants. Frederic Leighton doesn't paint a bottle labelled with a skull and bones so as to say, "Maybe she's dead," but instead allows us to view the painting twice over. Perhaps the first time, all we see is a woman peacefully asleep, and our attentions are guided to her form, but upon understanding the placement of the oleander, we see the painting again in an entirely different light.

A single detail that shifts our attentions with radical effect.

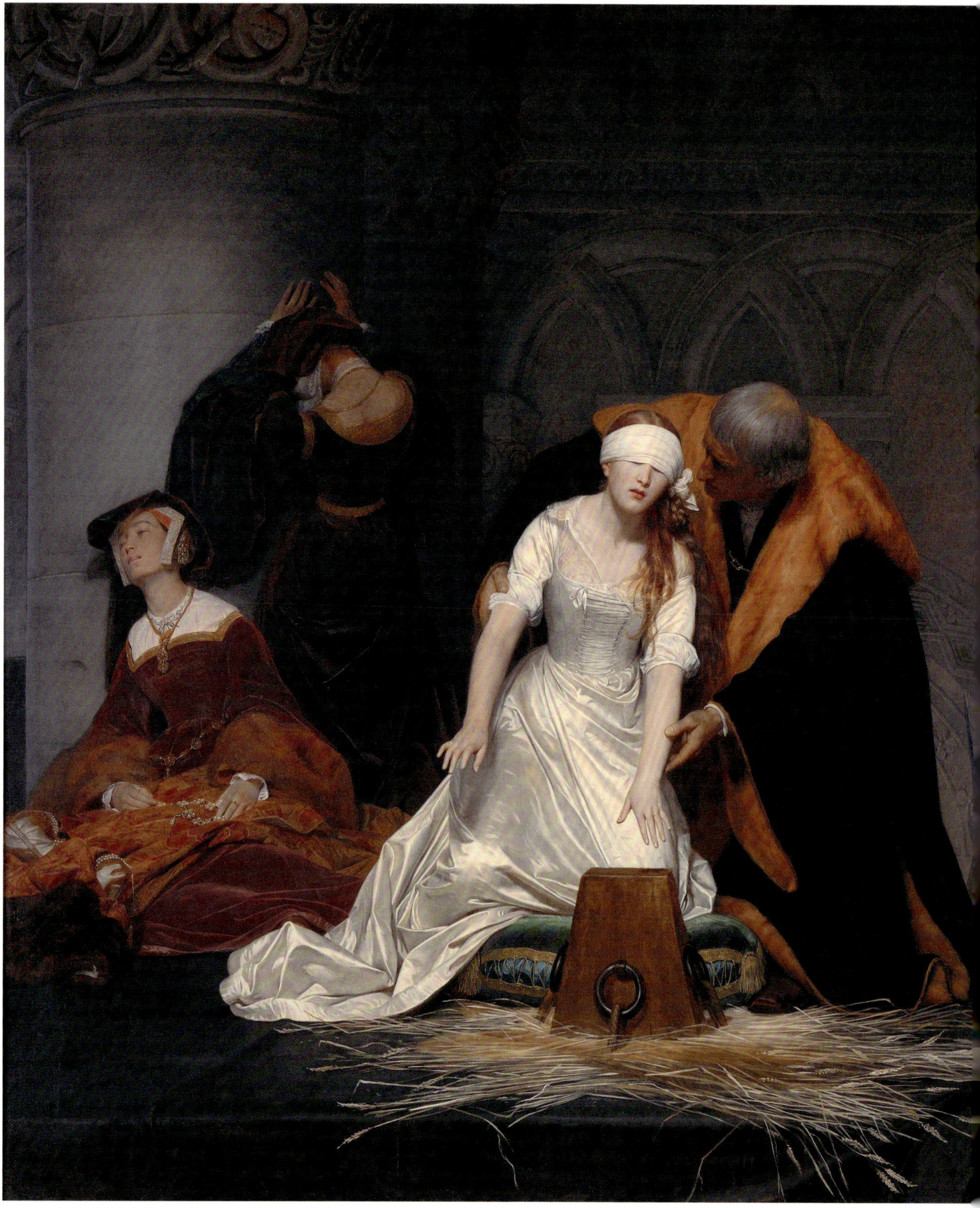

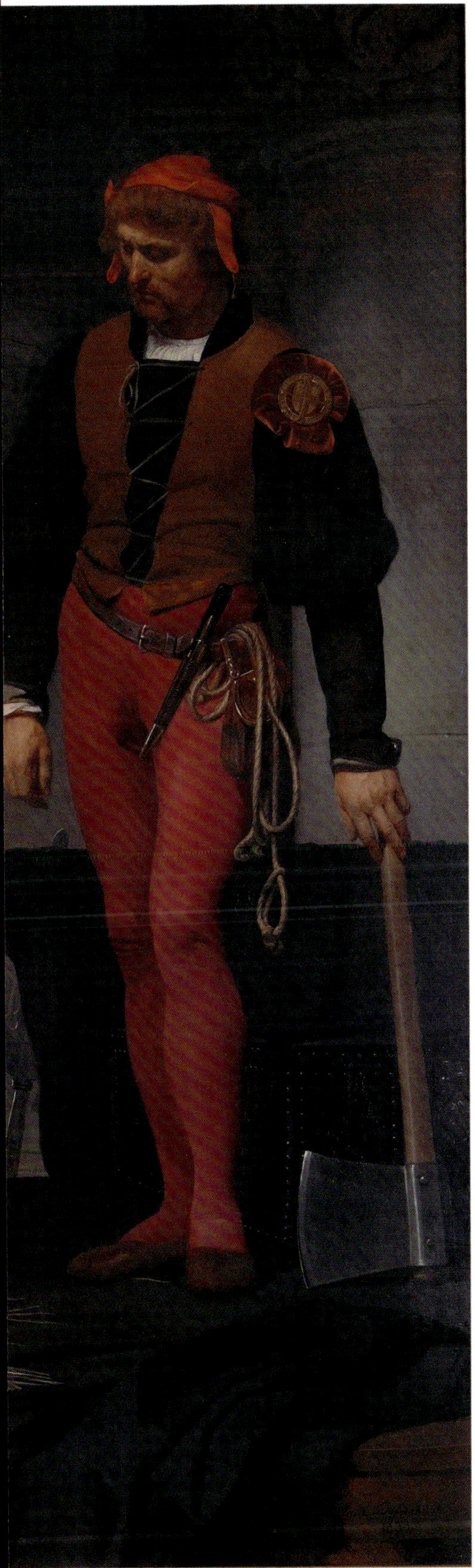

The Execution of Lady Jane Grey

Paul Delaroche, 1833

The same idea works in this painting by Paul Delaroche.

It is, as the title says, the story of Lady Jane Grey's execution, as ordered by her cousin Mary Tudor on the grounds of high treason, and within it, there are five characters. At center stage is the 17-year-old Jane Grey, who Delaroche paints in her final moments. "Where is the block," she thinks. "What must I do?" To her left are her ladies in waiting, who look devastated. One is on her knees, clutching the outer clothes and jewels of her mistress, while the other faces the wall, unable to bear the burden. Both of their necks are exposed, foreshadowing what is to come. To the right, the executioner waits casually, and at the center, next to Jane, is the Lieutenant of the Tower, guiding her hand, coaxing her forward toward her final moment on Earth with whispers.

A scene of heart-wrenching cruelty. And yet, the true genius of Delaroche only reveals itself when you realize that the event in question happened outdoors, on the grounds of the Tower of London. Because here, inside his greatest masterpiece, Delaroche chooses to paint the background as a monochromatic wall, while he paints the edges of the executioner's platform to create the illusion of a stage. He emphasizes a lighting that is so dramatic and ostentatious, you feel as though you're watching a performance.

We, the audience, are now transported inside into a theater, and it's a trick with enormous consequences, because now we are given a pass to stomach the atrocity without feeling inclined to intervene. Delaroche paints his figures to scale. Real people, from a real historical event, and we simply stand by and watch it happen, guilt free, because Delaroche said we could. And as far as painting goes, it's worth every ounce of drama.

The Roses of Heliogabalus

Lawrence Alma-Tadema, 1888

Speaking of drama …

While this might look like the best party you've ever seen, this work is one of the most sinister paintings from art's history.

On your first look around, you'll notice happy faces, beautiful music, wine, food, comfortable cushions, flowers …

Come to think of it, that's an awful lot of flowers. Enough to kill a man, perhaps? What about murdering everyone at a party? Well, in the case of Heliogabalus, the young prince of Rome, that's exactly what's going on. The debauched psycho thought it would be funny to host a lavish party and rig a false ceiling with thousands upon thousands of rose petals. When the time is just right, he will let them loose and smother his unsuspecting guests to death: The ultimate party prank, the ultimate Roman murder, and the ultimate story because it's so efficient.

Sir Lawrence doesn't need to drown you with hundreds of little secrets because he drowns you with a thousand roses.

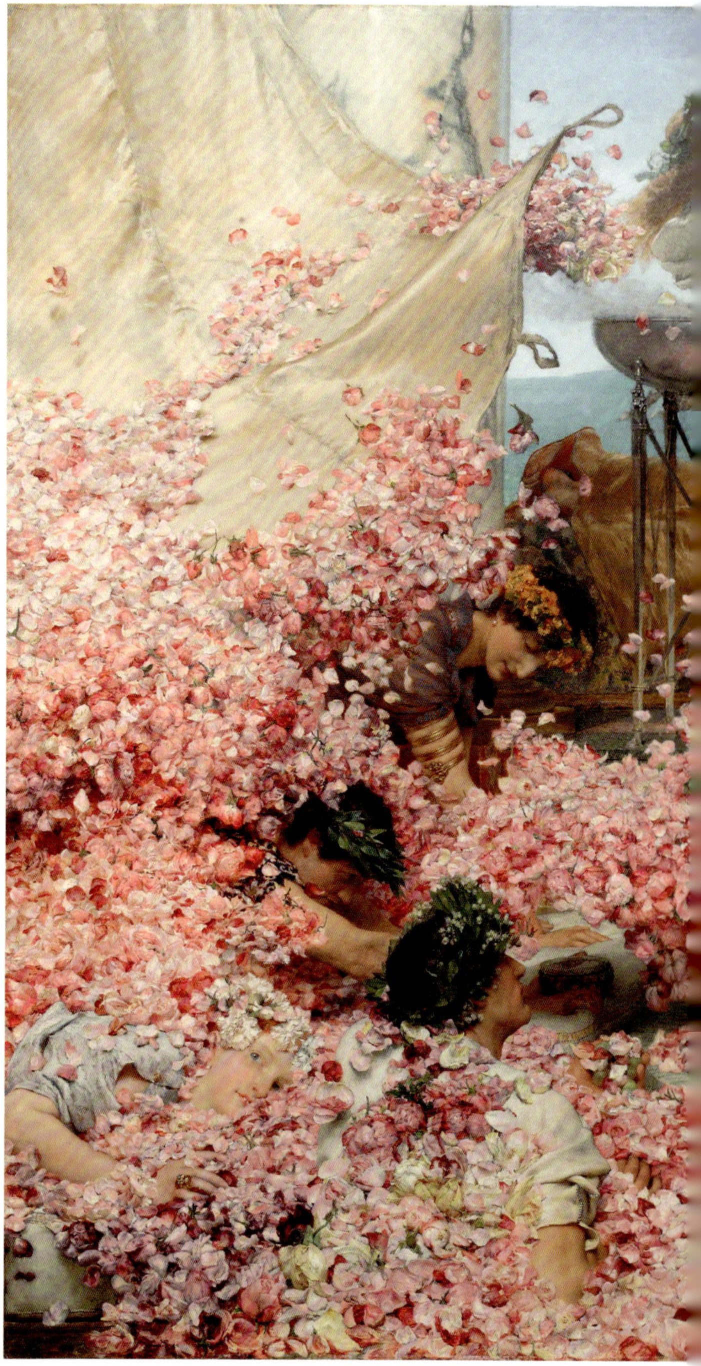

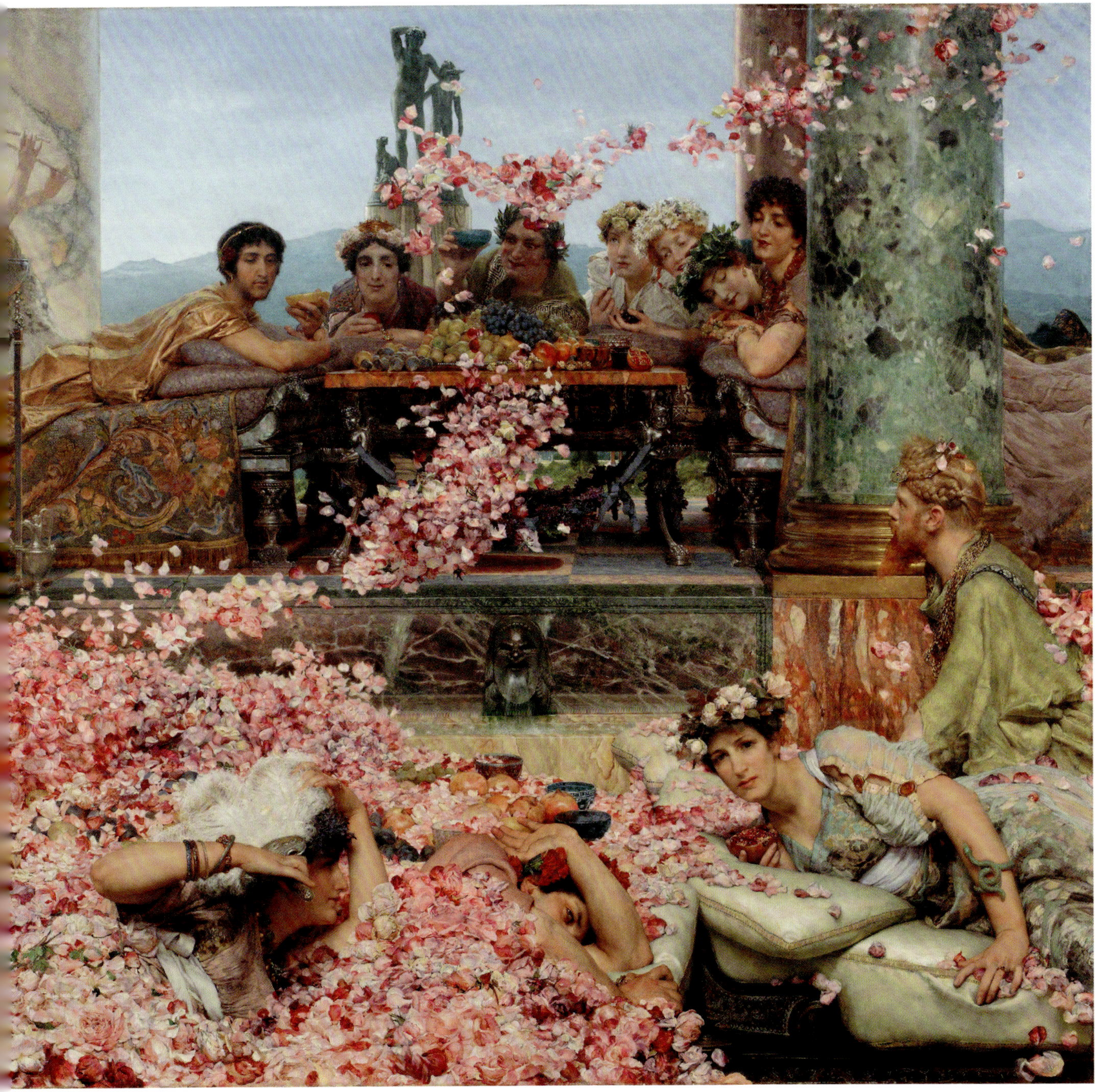

The Two Crowns

Frank Dicksee, 1900

Another painting riddled with flowers, but in an entirely different context. This is the story of a medieval prince returning from a great triumph, and what we notice first is the jubilation of the crowd.

"Long live the prince!" they shout from their balconies. We are consumed by the banners, the flowers, and the unshakable gaze of onlookers. And yet, our hero seems distracted, in his jeweled crown and opulent golden armor. Have a close look at his eyes and his expression.

Our prince has a vision. He has come face to face with the only king who truly sits above him.

You might not have noticed the crucifix at first, because Frank Dicksee distracts us with waves of color and motion. The controlled chaos of the crowd celebrating the return of their beloved prince blinds us: the brilliant bright horse, the flowers, and the excitement on every face. It's only when we focus on the prince himself that we notice his gaze, which directs us toward Christ.

This optical illusion painted in a dark hue feels as though it's been blended into the background, and that is the point. Dicksee dangles two very different worlds in front of us, where they patiently wait for us to notice them. The hyper-focused attention of onlookers in a celebration juxtaposed by the hyper-focused attention of a man who has been distracted. The prince is no longer surrounded by a crowd, but instead now occupies a space that exists between only him and God, and nobody else can see it.

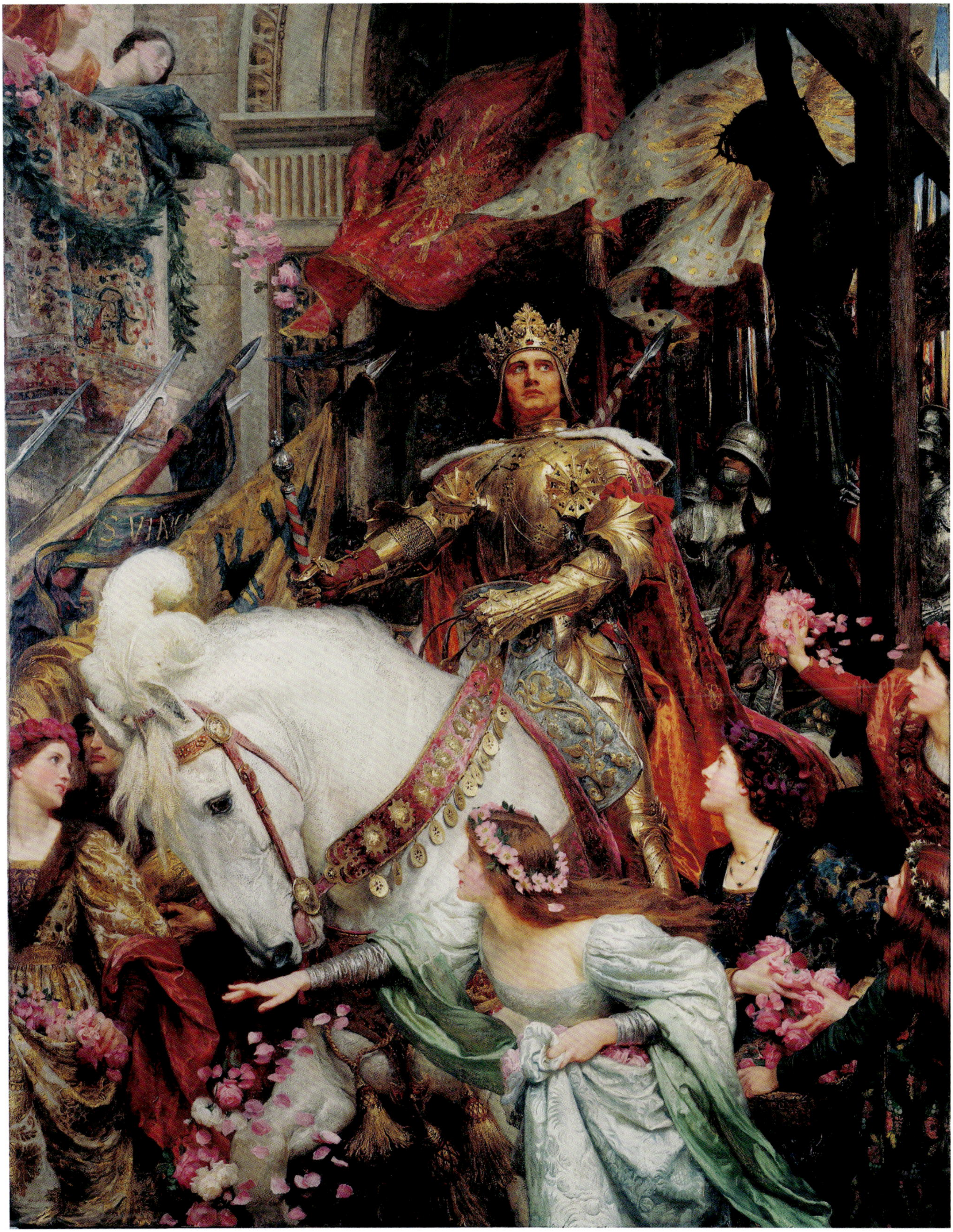

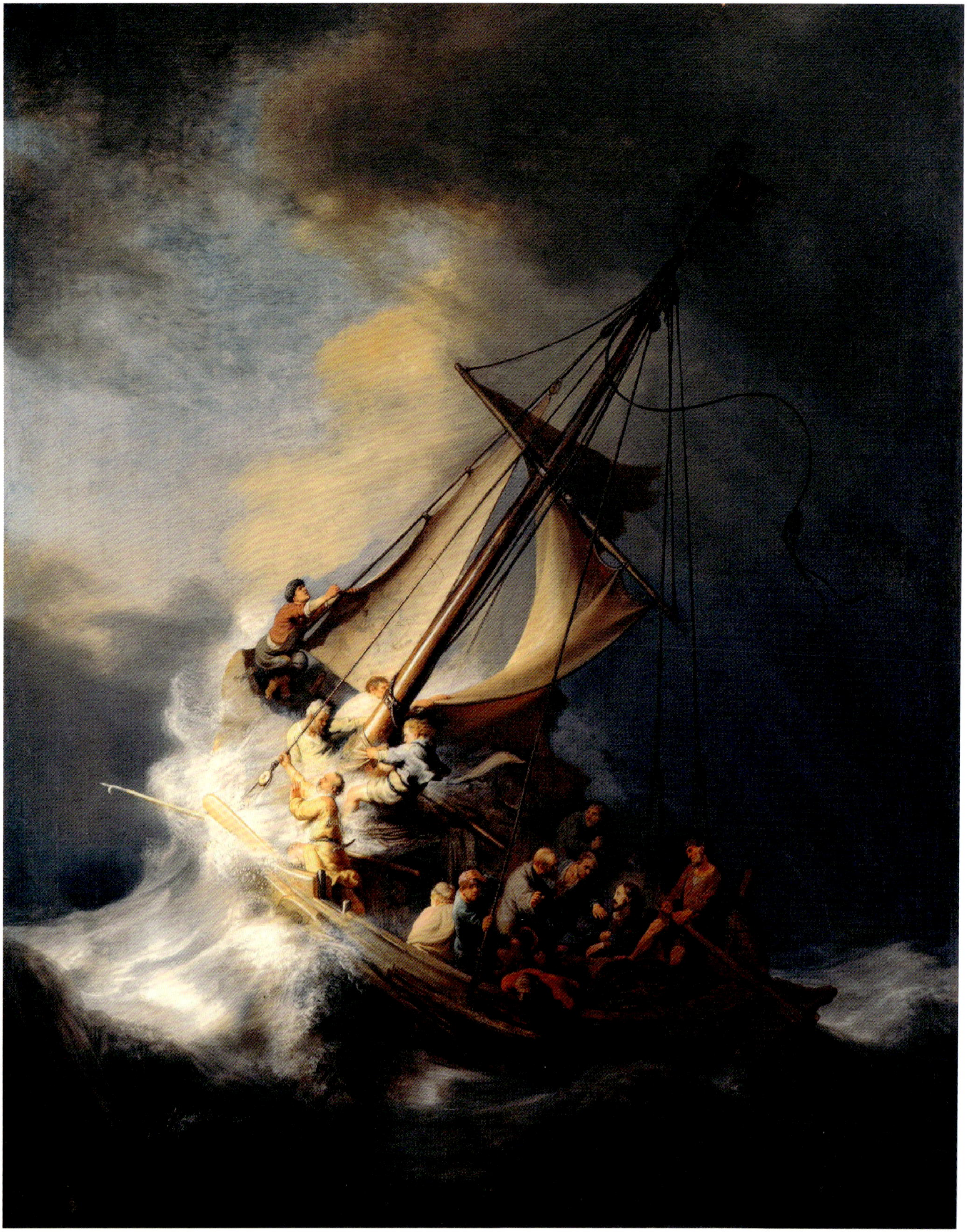

Christ in the Storm on the Sea of Galilee

Rembrandt, 1633

Speaking of gazes, do you see the guy looking out at you, breaking the fourth wall? He's the only person in the picture who seems to be doing so. And, as it so happens, that is a cameo of Rembrandt, right there on a ship that's on the verge of tipping over. At least that's how it feels, right?

Combing through the other characters, this may appear to be a straightforward depiction of Christ and his disciples navigating a storm. The truth is, however, that this work by the painter in their midst isn't so simple. In fact, this image has almost nothing to do with the biblical story at all, and almost everything to do with the psychological effects of faith.

Have a closer look at the horizon line. Do you notice anything curious about the temperament of the water in the lower quarter of the composition?

"Matthew, it's a storm ..."

Yes, but Rembrandt uses it to show us that in moments of great chaos, calmness is the victor.

He balances the violence of a catastrophe and the unrelenting rumble of hellish waves, bashing the sides of the unsteady ship, with the silence of the sky. In fact, if you cut the bottom of the painting away, the entire picture becomes quiet.

Pretty amazing, isn't it?

A beam of light breaks through the clouds, and we feel as though we have a moment to catch our breaths. These poor fellows certainly need it, hanging on for dear life as they try to right the ship. Every single one of them is ground down to their most primitive instincts to survive; that is, except for Jesus, who seems entirely unbothered by the whole ordeal. In the messiah's section of the painting, chaos heavily outweighs any calm, but Jesus simply gazes on. Rembrandt employs his presence to yet again balance out the composition's disorder, checking it with stillness.

So why is it, exactly, that Rembrandt injected himself into this maelstrom? Believe me when I tell you it's not some sort of seventeenth-century joke. It serves a very important purpose: By breaking the fourth wall, Rembrandt invites us to explore who we are.

Are we the madness in trying times? Are we the faithful? Or are we simply the observer caught somewhere in the middle, troubled by the waves of an unpredictable moment but finding faith when we need it the most?

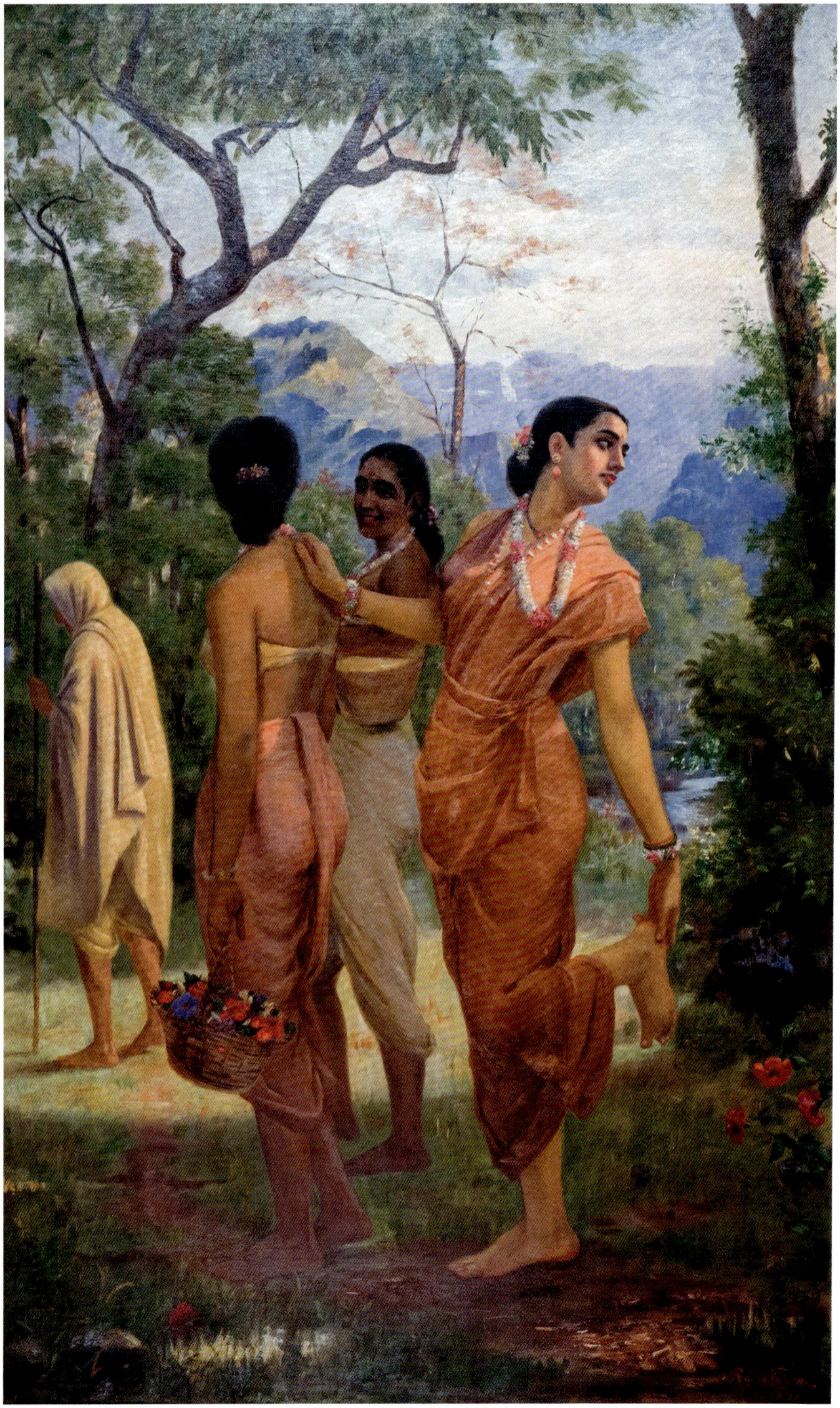

Shakuntala

Ravi Varma, 1898

Paintings, as you see, don't always solve themselves in obvious ways on the canvas. Sometimes, a painting requires us to allow a motif to take shape through context, whether that's the history of an execution or the pages of Indian epic.

Ravi Varma's extraordinary depiction of Shakuntala, from the ancient Indian epic the *Mahabharata*, is one of those paintings where a master's touch can sail right over your head. It is a work home to a detail so elusive, you've already missed it. The image is a scene of four figures walking through a forest, swallowed by breathtaking colors, whose singular purpose are to enforce Varma's grand idea.

We aren't looking at a picture of people. We are watching the seedling of a dilemma at the exact moment that it sprouts, and the tension created by it, as our main figure *pretends* to have injured her foot so that she can look for her lover, all the while acting as though what she really wants is to carry along with her friends.

She's playing a form of "hard to get" but can't contain it anymore, because to pretend that she doesn't care to her friends risks unwanted tension with her lover. Her heart can lie no further, and neither can her eyes or her face. We can see it: "Where is he?", "Is he coming?"

The jig is up.

And if that isn't interesting enough, just consider that this masterpiece is painted through the lens of the male perspective and, by design, entices us to fix our attentions on her. By itself, unsurprising, until you consider that maybe, just maybe, her entire ruse with her foot was so that she might lay her eyes on us.

What a dream come true for anyone, to be an object of desire, and to be sought out and thought about in such pleasant ways. Such a contrast to the hellish look of Auguste Toulmouche's reluctant bride.

The Reluctant Bride

Auguste Toulmouche, 1866

"Good God, she really doesn't want to be here."

Toulmouche was a genius, surrounding the central figure of this painting with such docile creatures. The soft kiss on her forehead, the comforting hands, the calming subtle pinks and warm vibrant reds are all devices used to contrast our main character and her wish to be anywhere but here. And yet the true brilliance of this artwork does not actually exist inside the painting, but instead in an extended knowledge of art: a knowledge that Auguste Toulmouche most definitely had.

Rückenfigur, which is German for "figure from the back," is a compositional device in painting used to convey a sense of longing, emotional isolation, and existential restlessness. In works that feature it, we are faced with the backside of a figure, who is often distracted or looking away: an invitation by an artist to identify with that figure and to reimagine the space they inhabit as if you were there yourself, experiencing it on your own.

Toulmouche, a dedicated student of his craft, flips this technique on its head: His bride is facing front and center. By pointing the gaze of this figure at us, we're isolated. He leaves us to feel naked, with nothing around for protection, and it is as if we're entirely to blame for the whole ordeal.

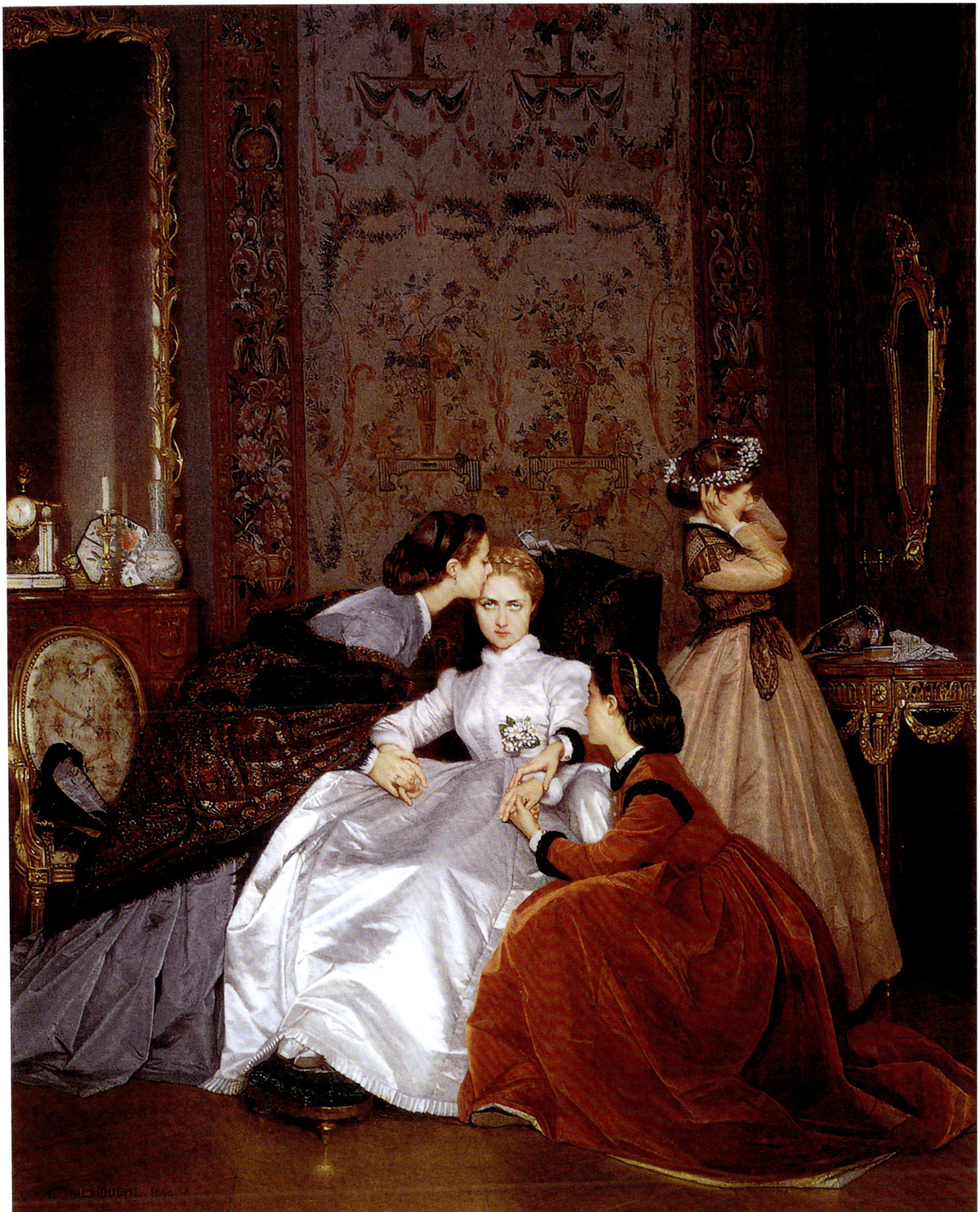

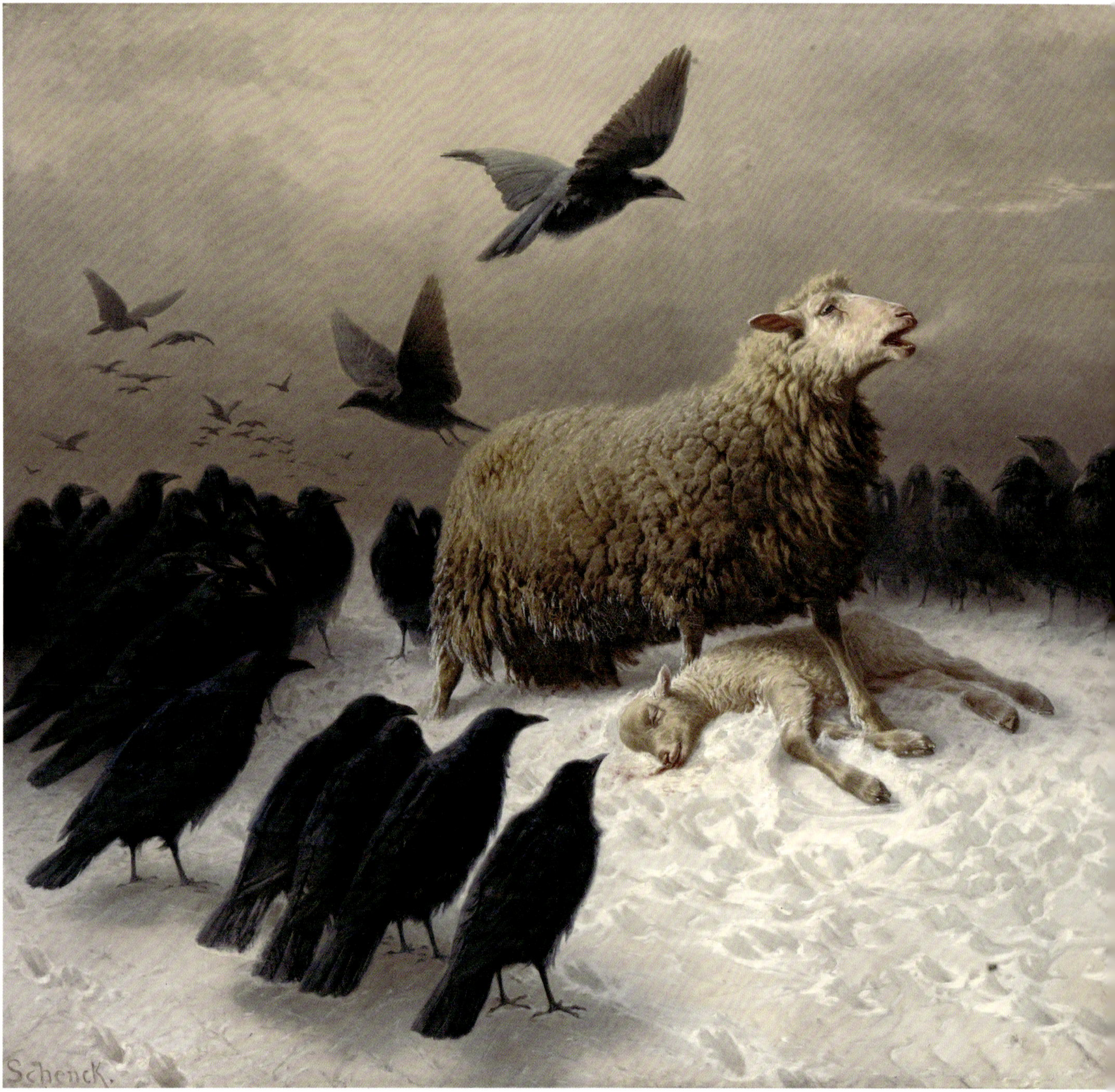
Schenck.

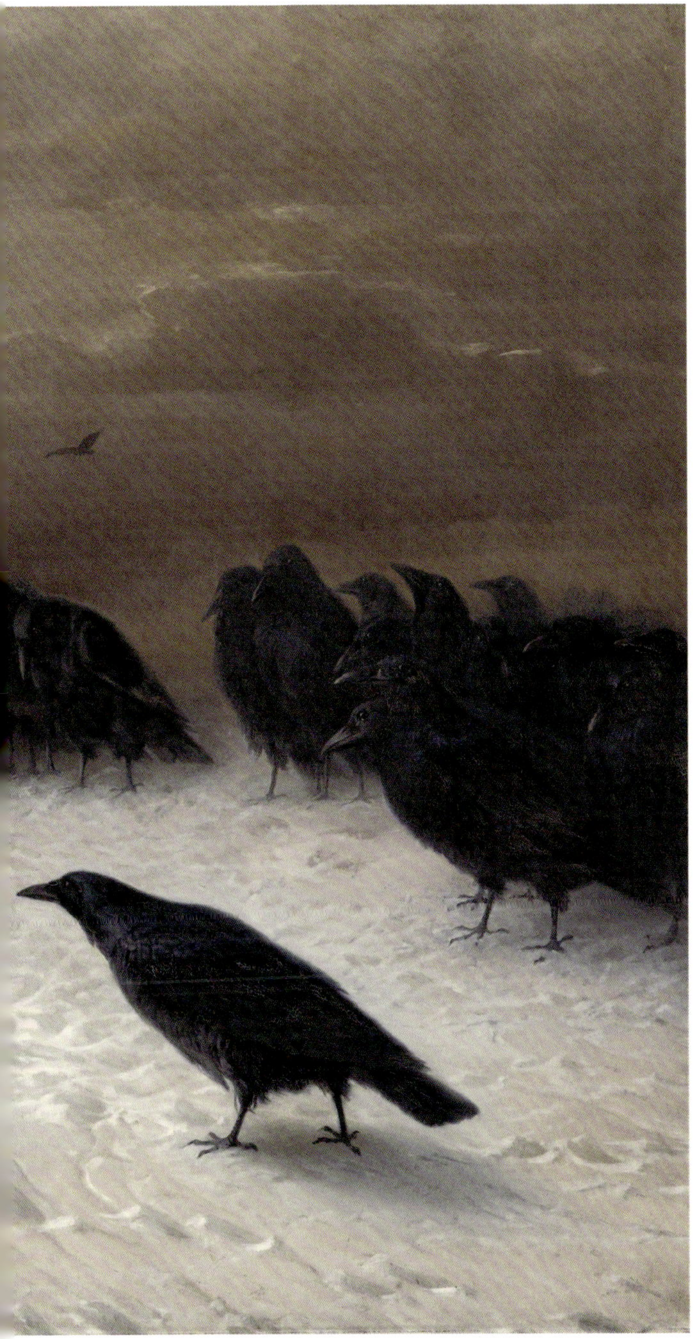

Anguish

August Friedrich Schenck, c. 1878

Rückenfigur isn't the only way to conjure isolation.

Art, as a language of sorts, is always a communication between the viewer and the object, but the nature of conversations is that they take many shapes—some loud and some quiet. Some blunt and some more subtle. The difference between the amateur and the excellent is almost always in the delivery: in the achievement of clarity, which is the challenge in any creative pursuit. When it comes to a message, an artist can paint it staring at you from the middle of a canvas, or they can capture it through an element that is abstract, but still stops you in your tracks, radically changing how you perceive art.

In this conversation, something terrible happened.

A ewe guards the corpse of her child on a mound of ice-cold snow. A frosted plume of air is squeezed from her lungs by the hand of the night as she cries out. Her child will feed the flowers, but first he will feed the crows: a sea of ominous black, strung across the plains of a painting that challenges our capacity for empathy. These predators are nature's cruelest aspects, cold and indifferent, preying on the weak in self-service.

For those who dare to observe *Anguish*, we feel acutely connected to this ewe and her helplessness. Despite the fact she isn't a person, we understand her as a mother.

But why? There is nothing about this picture that represents a human form of grief. And yet somehow, in some way, everything about it does. Within these troubling circumstances, there is something about her that is so unbelievably human.

This is the genius of it, in fact. We're not looking at a ewe, but at ourselves.

Life is ephemeral. It can flash by in an instant, and all we're left with are memories of those who once shared our reality. And here is a mother who, in hers, has outlived her child, and we can relate to her. We know exactly what it feels like to be swallowed by a space that once felt expansive as the walls close in. It's suffocating, and we find it harder to breathe.

She does her best. She guards this body with every bit of courage she can muster. But we, the audience, know it's too late. And as the blood of the lifeless lamb freezes over, and her howls are reduced into the whispers of the night, all we can do is watch.

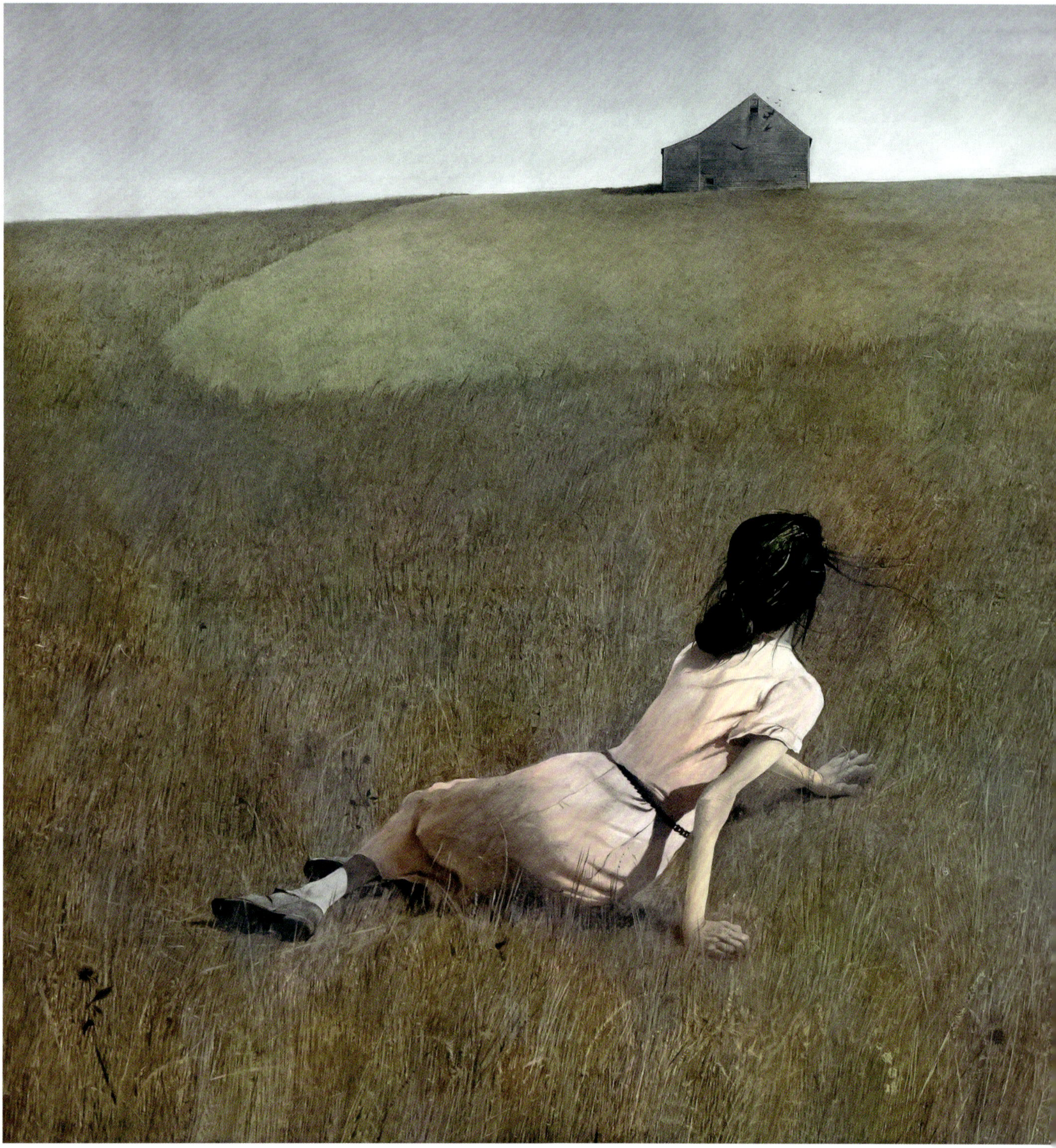

Christina's World

Andrew Wyeth, 1948

We don't need to experience everything in the same exact way to understand each other's struggles. One of the greatest qualities of our species is empathy. Regardless of whether the figure in a painting is a fellow human, or a simple shape, or a ewe, when we see another soul who suffers, we suffer with them.

In *Christina's World*, our suffering is physical.

What we see at first is a girl sitting in the grass. We see a house in the distance. We see a ladder, we see a barn, and tracks that appear to carve through the open field. It's a painting by Andrew Wyeth that, at first glance, is quite palatable.

"Okay Matthew, what am I missing?"

Well, that girl in the grass is Anna Christina Olson—Wyeth's real-life neighbor, who was no ordinary girl. You see, Christina suffered from polio and was crippled at a very young age. When given the opportunity to use a wheelchair, she refused, instead opting to drag herself around with her own hands.

You can see it now, can't you? She does seem a little *off*. She isn't *really* sitting in the grass per se, but is kind of *attached* to the ground, and her body does seem a little stiff. Now, I want you to have a closer look at her hands. You realize now that they aren't propping her up, but instead, *gripping the earth underneath her* as she drags herself forward, away from the artist and off toward her home.

We may not know exactly how it feels to suffer in the way that Anna Christina Olson would have, but we can all relate to the feelings that might have swirled around her head. A mixed bag of pride and shame, in varying degrees, depending on the day. Moments of bravery that at any second could trade place with a feeling of helplessness and uncertainty. We may not experience the same difficulty Olson did as she navigated through her obstacle-filled world, let alone the expanse of that field, and yet, when we realize that her hand is gripping the earth, in the flash of a second, we understand what Wyeth was painting perfectly.

Amazing, isn't it? The tiniest little surprises have such radical effects, exposing us to secrets while opening our eyes to the craft of painting. Through this lens, we can look for hidden messages on every canvas. For me, that's the best part of reading an artwork: understanding the intentionality of each decision and asking "why?". Why this look? Why this posture? Why this lighting? Why the red robe? Or, in the case of Gerrit van Honthorst's *Christ Before the High Priest*, why the candle?

Christ Before the High Priest

Gerrit van Honthorst, c. 1617

In a meeting between Christ and Caiaphas, life and death hangs on the edge of a string, and somehow Honthorst shows us the gravity of an entire moment with that candle at the center of the painting. But how?

Well, to understand the genius that is *Christ Before the High Priest*, we first need to understand what is going on. It's a trial of sorts. Jesus has been arrested and taken to the home of the High Priest of Israel for questioning. "Are you the Messiah, the Son of God?" A question designed to provoke a response that could be used to condemn Christ for blasphemy, a capital offense that is punishable by death. "I am," he responds, and in doing so guarantees his own execution.

And it is right there that Honthorst plays his first move. It is odd that the man in this room who holds all the power over Christ's life and death is the one who appears unstable. He's not quite falling out of his seat, but the slight tilt forward—especially in comparison to this composed version of Jesus—is jarring when the two are viewed together.

And speaking of Jesus, for a man who's willingly sentenced himself to his own gruesome death, he seems unbelievably calm. His posture, his face, his submissive hands are all an unexpected response to such a dire outcome.

"So, what does it have to do with the candle?"

Everything. Because where the composure of our figures was Honthorst's opening jab, the candle is the necessary ingredient for a swift knockout. Now, the obvious effect of a candle in a dark room is that it provides light, but how it lands upon these characters is where the magic lies. In the hands of the master painter, the lighting is no longer an effect of atmosphere, but one of inner dialog.

Have a closer look and see for yourself. Caiaphas, who's closest to the candle, is made up of the hard lines between light and dark, suggesting a man who is deeply at conflict. Contrast this with Jesus, who's much further away, and we see a soft transition between the light and shadows. This is a man who is at peace.

It's not just about the light, though. Take a step back to absorb the painting, and the candle serves another purpose: It drives a hard line between the two men. In fact, if you remove it entirely (try covering it with a finger), you might even agree that the conversation feels less intense, but with the wedge in between them, we know that they will never come to reasonable terms. Caiaphas's decision becomes an inevitability. Honthorst splits the painting along the two separate sides of a conflict, because a conflict, at the very least, requires two opposing views.

Makes perfect sense. Tension that takes on a form through contrast, and not just between the light and the dark, but between man and God, and in some eyes, between good and evil.

Another story as old as time itself: the classic motif of the moral versus the immoral, which has been the driving force of great storytelling for as long as we've had the capacity to tell stories, even if it sometimes appears more subtly.

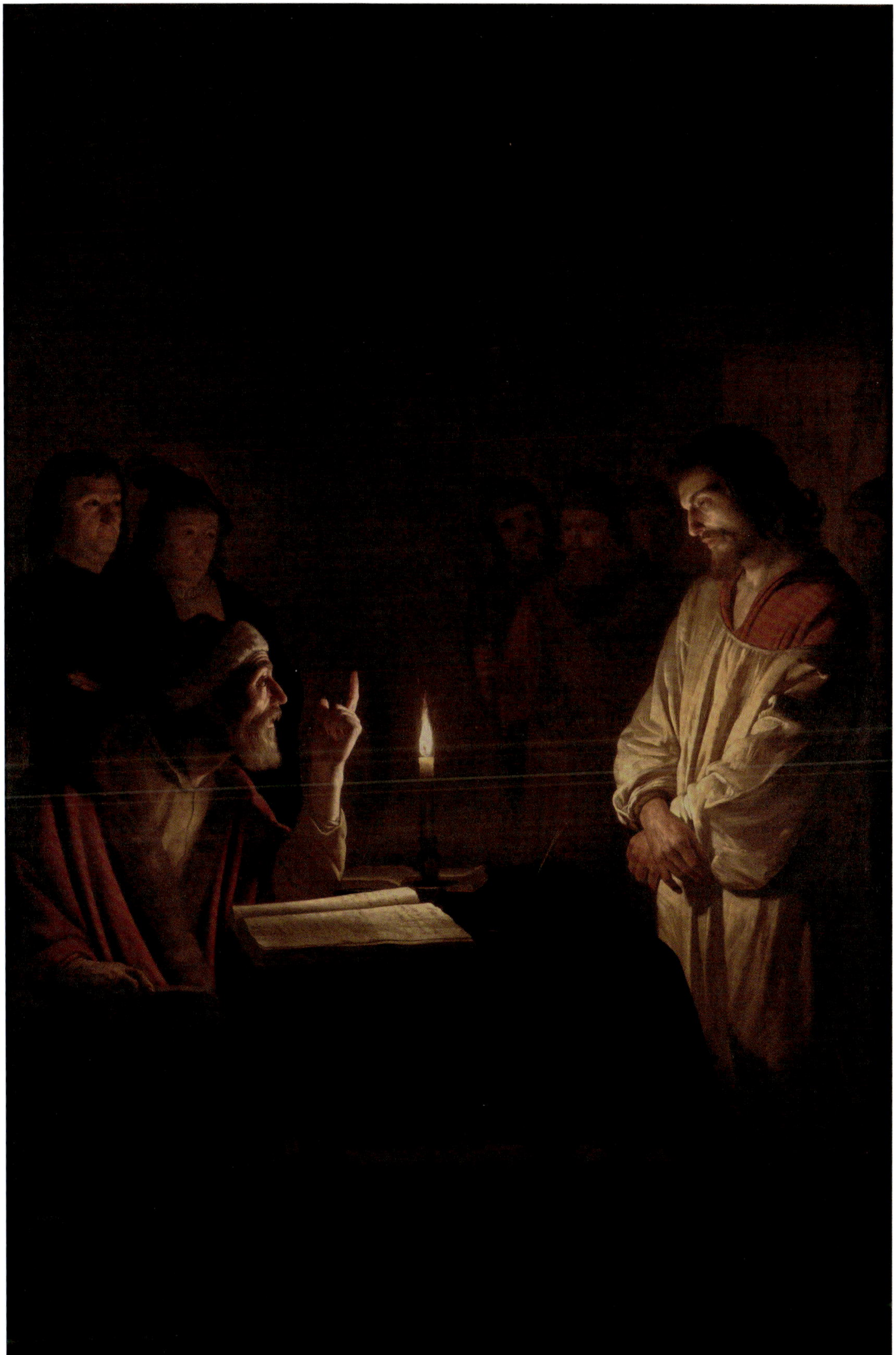

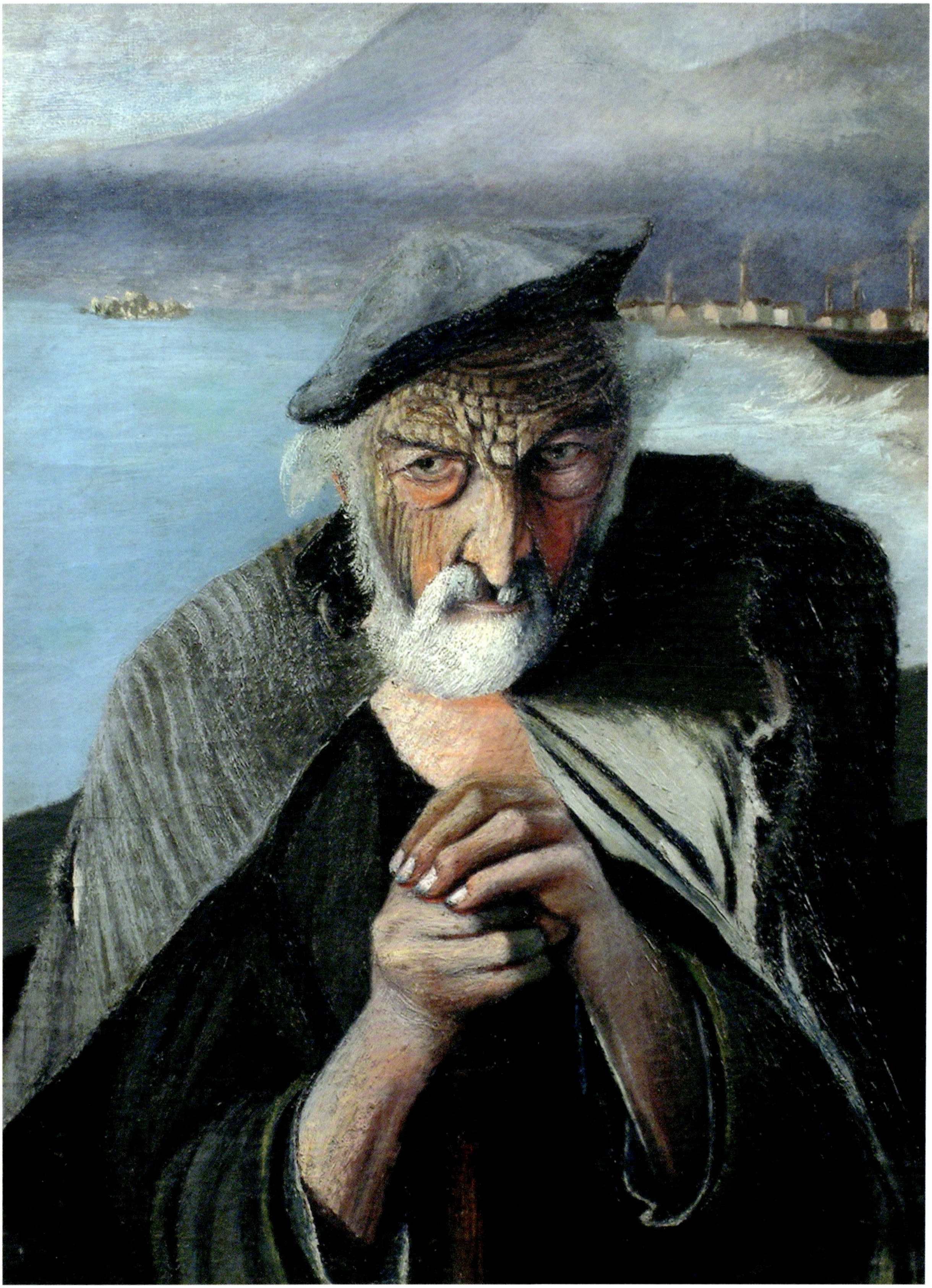

Old Fisherman

Tivadar Csontváry Kosztka, 1902

Have you ever seen this painting? If you have, then you are officially an art aficionado, and if you haven't, it's totally okay because this artwork is for very specific tastes. But did you notice the two other men?

"The other two men?"

No, I've not lost my mind. Try again and look very carefully. Still nothing? Alright, well, after I show you this fun detail, you'll have a very hard time not seeing it.

When looking directly at the painting, it's impossible to miss the scaly-looking old fisherman with the piercing gaze. But something seems a little off, doesn't it? Well, by placing a mirror in the center of the artwork, the true magic starts to unfold.

By reflecting the left side of the painting onto itself, you get what appears to be a man who's calm in nature, wonderfully reserved and pensive. You really feel it. Quite a contrast to the original, wouldn't you say?

Okay, so what happens if you reflect the other half? If you're not prepared for this, it may shock you …

Oh, yes, that just happened. It's a mood shift so startling, it feels like a cloud has blocked the sun. It is the face of pure evil, and it's terrifying to look at. Compared to the other gentleman who appears to be praying, this doppelgänger seems to be plotting. All of which begs a bigger question: Who are these other men? And did the artist mean to paint them? While it's hard to say whether or not the illusion was intentional, there is certainly some evidence that says it was.

Have a look at the left-hand fisherman again, but this time focus your attention on the background.

The water is calm, still, and completely silent, and it adds a tremendous effect to his demeanor. Now look back at the other fellow: do you see the difference? Waves crashing onto the shoreline, a little bit of chaos and commotion, and in the place of a serene fog, we have the smog of industrial plumes polluting the airways. Scary stuff. So, who are they then? We will probably never know. It could be God and the Devil. Good and evil. The natural world and the pitfalls of industry. Or maybe, it's us. The best and worst of both sides of the coin.

Or perhaps, just an old fisherman.

The Night Café

Vincent van Gogh, 1888

Of all the great secrets in art, and the amazing stories that have driven the pursuit forward, possibly the greatest of them all is the story of self. A moment of introspection, solace, and separation from the real world captured through the creation of something so pure, it surpasses the very act of creation in the process: It's a rare thing, as one might imagine. It takes a master to truly hide a heart on a canvas, on a wooden plank, or on a wall for all to see, so long as those who are looking know where to look, or better yet, how.

For generations, artists have attempted to truly capture their innermost feelings, but few have ever actually come close. That was, until Vincent van Gogh, the artist who painted himself. In the form of a portrait, a landscape, a still life, a room, a field, a night sky: Every single artwork is a clue into who the man was, every brushstroke a pulse. A record of agitation, longing for approval, anxiety, and brief moments of clarity, his paintings read like pages in a diary in which colors form long-winded confessions. Vincent van Gogh put every bit of ambition, instability, self-doubt and triumph into every one of his 900-plus paintings, and none of it feels as though it was done to celebrate the world that he lived in.

"I have tried to express the terrible passions of humanity by means of red and green … Everywhere there is a clash and contrast of the most alien reds and greens, in the figures of little sleeping hooligans, in the empty dreary room, in violet and blue. The blood-red and the yellow-green of the billiard table, for instance, contrast with the soft tender Louis XV green of the counter, on which there is a rose nosegay. The white clothes of the landlord, watchful in a corner of that furnace, turn lemon-yellow, or pale luminous green," Vincent van Gogh writes in a letter to his brother.

Van Gogh called *The Night Café* one of the "ugliest" paintings he had ever made, and he meant it as a triumph. Where most might look at the painting as a representation of what it was that van Gogh saw, through a careful observation of its concepts, and the weaponization of its individual components, we might conclude that the picture instead better represents how he felt. It is not a room, but in the most abstract sense, a "portrait." A projection of psychic unraveling, insomnia, loneliness, and volatility.

The room tilts forward, the lines converge aggressively, and the space is both claustrophobic and warped: an intentional distortion that lends to the feeling that you are falling into the painting, like the feeling of falling right before sleep. This is the nightmare of an insomniac who is trapped in a state of time that stretches for eternity.

Van Gogh rejects the use of color for creating beauty. In this café, he pits acidic green against a blood red, and in doing so turns old friends into mortal enemies: complementary colors that should appease the eyes, now set against one another to a nauseating effect. This battle further enhances the sense that you are now trapped in this psychological container, and the lamps make it even worse: four sources of light that cast the room into a sick yellow hell, bleaching the world of comfort.

Light that does not illuminate the room but interrogates all those who rest underneath it. The characters here have been reduced to props in a psychological theatre where the protagonist is the actual room itself. They do not represent individual souls, but the symptoms of the soul, slouched over, folded onto tables, dissolving into the background. They exist only to populate the void.

To understand *The Night Café*, one must forget the idea that this is a genre painting. This isn't a depiction of nightlife. This isn't a depiction of a place (it is, but not in this context). It's a confession, and van Gogh *is the motif, the subject, and the room.*

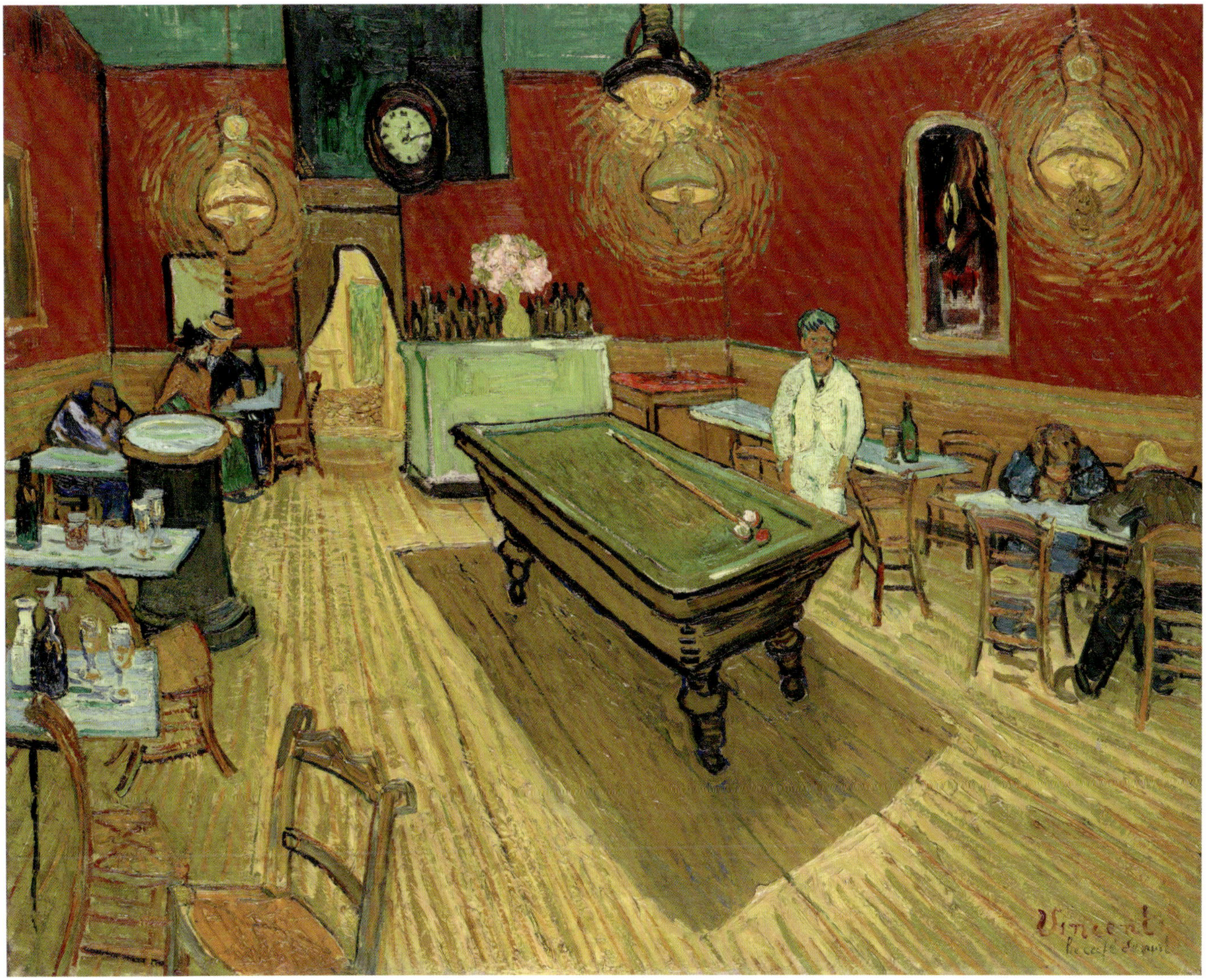
Vincent

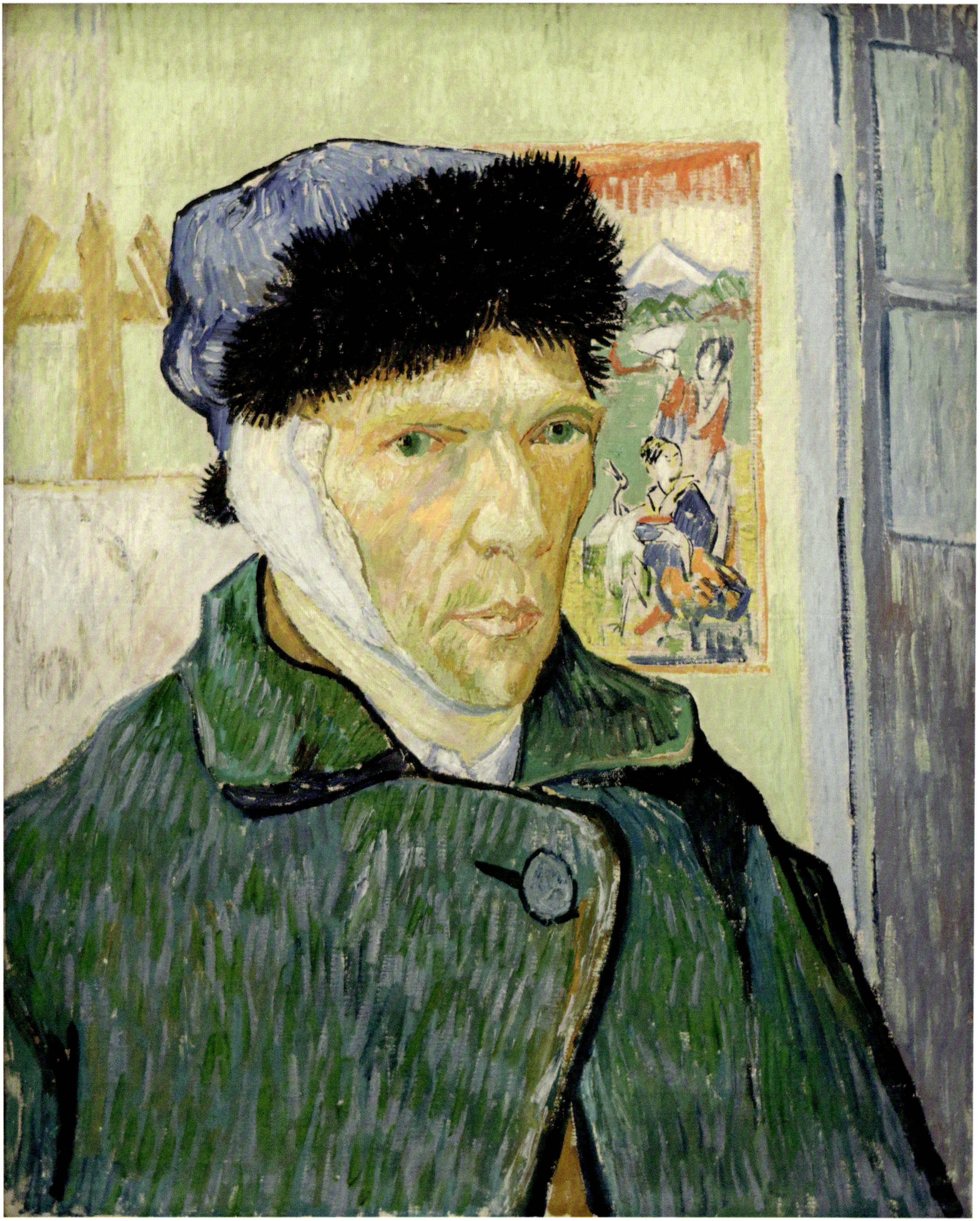

Self-Portrait With a Bandaged Ear
Vincent van Gogh, 1889

Brutally honest. This isn't self-portraiture as self-promotion or myth-building. It's van Gogh using the canvas as a mirror to stabilize himself in the aftermath of psychological catastrophe. And where most artists might conceal the nature of their crisis, van Gogh paints his. He's just mutilated himself, was admitted to the hospital for his mental state, and now tries to paint himself back to coherence. In the process, he documents his own fragility with a terrifying neutrality. He doesn't downplay the event by concealing the bandage but instead highlights it as the artwork's major feature.

A madman might not even know that he's mad, and we get a glimpse of that here. We don't get the sense that he's trying to project mania, but instead, is making a futile attempt at convincing us of his sanity. A ragtag version of "I'm back in control now," but we aren't buying it. Even in an image where everything is subdued, through color, texture, and more, we can sense the deception at play. He's hiding—behind a heavy, thick, oversized coat that swallows his body whole, accentuating the frailty of his figure.

And while I could point out the Japanese print, titled *Geishas in a Landscape* by Satō Torakiyo, and try to make some point about how Japanese art is meant to represent clarity and order, and it's the counterbalance to his instability, the truth is, it was likely just there in the room. He paints the print as honestly as he paints himself, and there is nothing more to it. It gives us a glimpse into his interests, but its inclusion doesn't carry any weight. Nothing here should. No single element matters, because all that matters is the fact that he paints himself, as he was at his worst. No attempt at sympathy. No romantic pose. No melodrama.

The Starry Night

Vincent van Gogh, 1889

Now, if you're following the pattern, you'll know that this is not a landscape. This is van Gogh's inner world, in the form of one of the most iconic nightscapes ever rendered, and none of it is real. It is a fiction, painted from the barred cell of an asylum room: a painting that blurs the boundaries between the tangible outer world and the mind that perceives it.

Van Gogh was obsessed with art. He was a man who gave his all to his craft, and wanted nothing more than the fruits of his efforts, and yet, I can't help feeling that him not being treated as a "serious artist" up until this point—at least in commercial and critical circles—would have played a major role in his mental degradation. On this night, however, we see a different van Gogh, because this is the version of the painter that is at peace. This is a version that hangs onto a glimmer of hope that maybe his world rights itself. *Maybe*, it stops caving in. This is a van Gogh that dreams.

He paints the sky as a series of swollen spirals and whirling bands of light that read like waves. Pulsating stars overstimulate the senses and rolling forms echo the nature of an active mind. He paints towering cypress trees that feel as though they possess a limitless reach. And while twisted and affected by the elements, they can be read as an element of stability, even in a world that might refuse it. All of this, pinned against the silence of the village below. A village that is entirely imagined.

This is an invention that's crucial. Van Gogh constructs a fantasy of calm at the bottom of the canvas as a counterbalance to the turbulence of the night sky. A world he craves versus the world he inhabits, and he blurs the line in the middle, because *the nature of existence is somewhere in the middle*. He collapses realism into a depiction of his own emotional truth and paints a night sky in the way he felt that night: a landscape transformed into a psychological metaphor, and a moment of great contemplation.

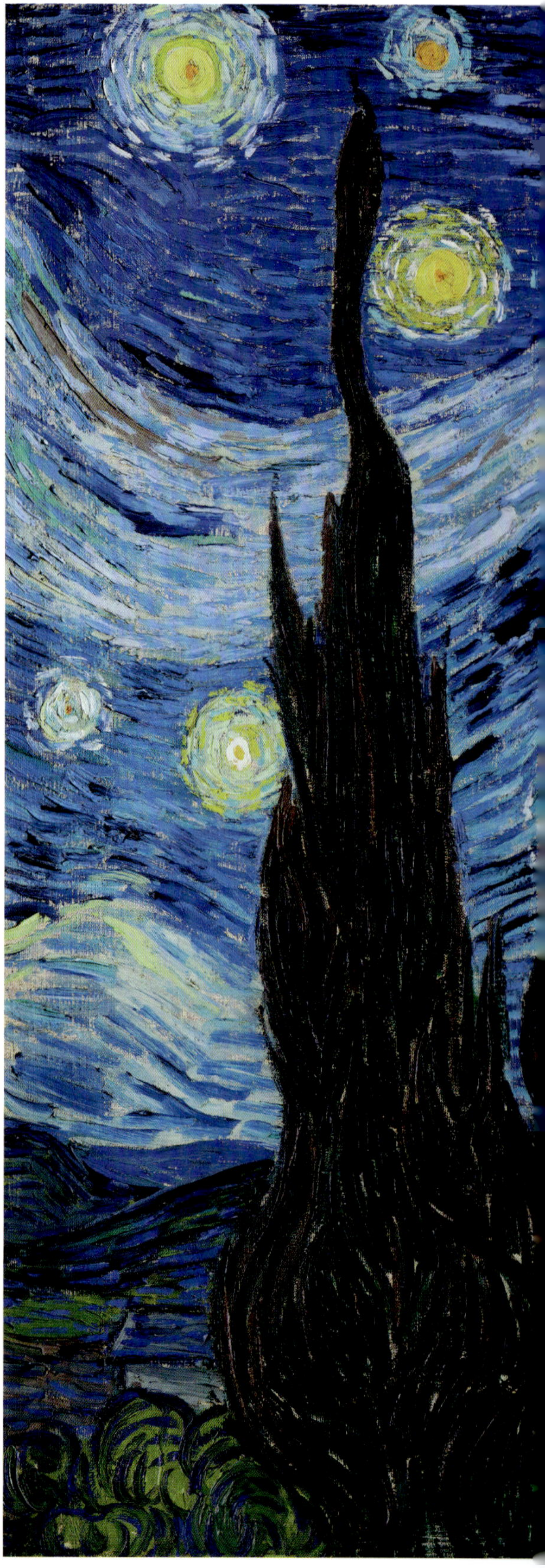

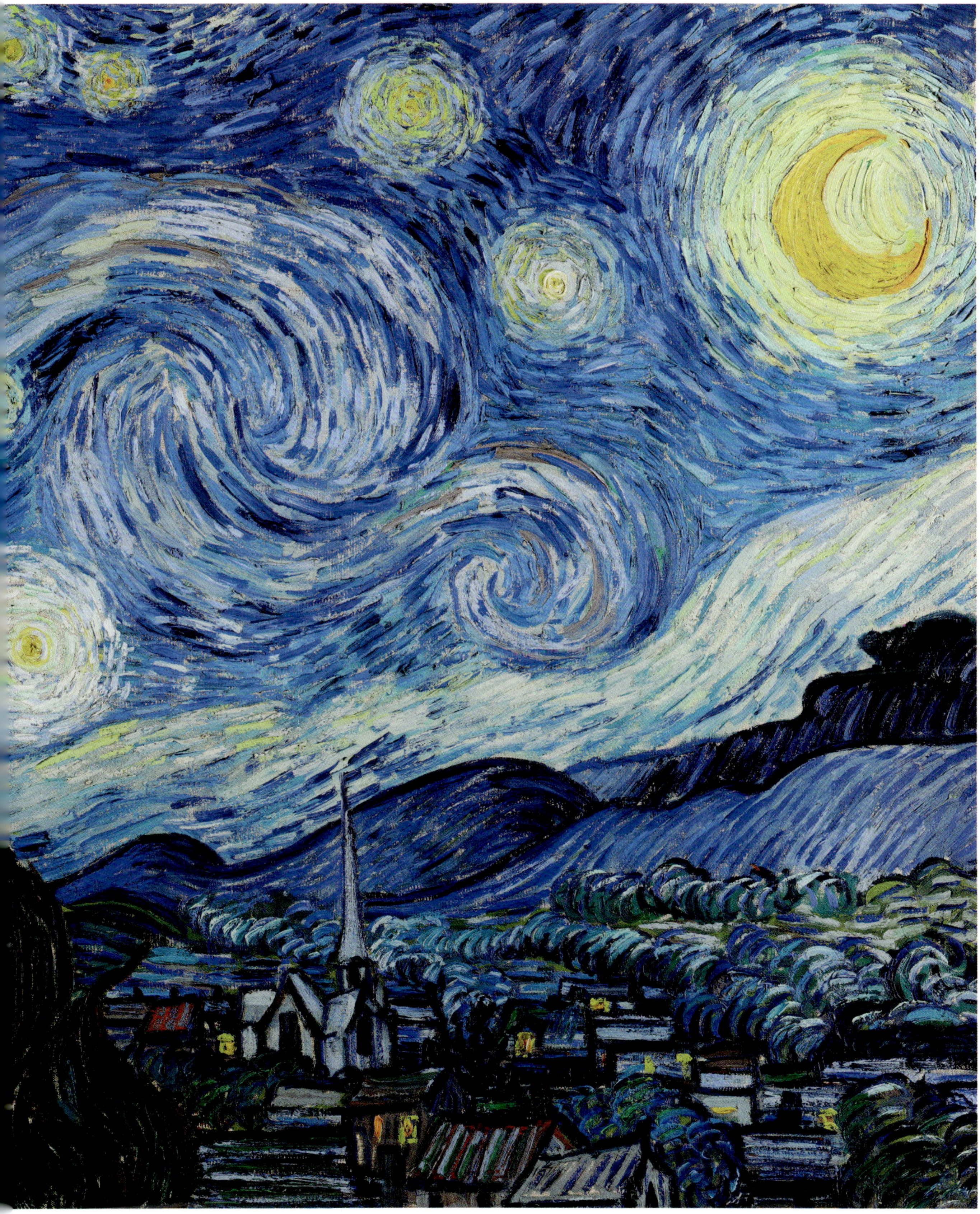

POLITICS AND PROPAGANDA

In 1746, in the tiny rural town of Fuendetodos, in Aragon, Spain, Francisco José de Goya y Lucientes, or as you would know him, Francisco Goya, was born. The posterchild of humble beginnings, he entered the world as a member of a family with little to no means and would go on to surpass every obstacle to achieve one of the most legendary careers in art's history. And yet, when all is said and done, upon a reading of his entire body of work, most might find themselves asking the question, *where did it all go wrong?*

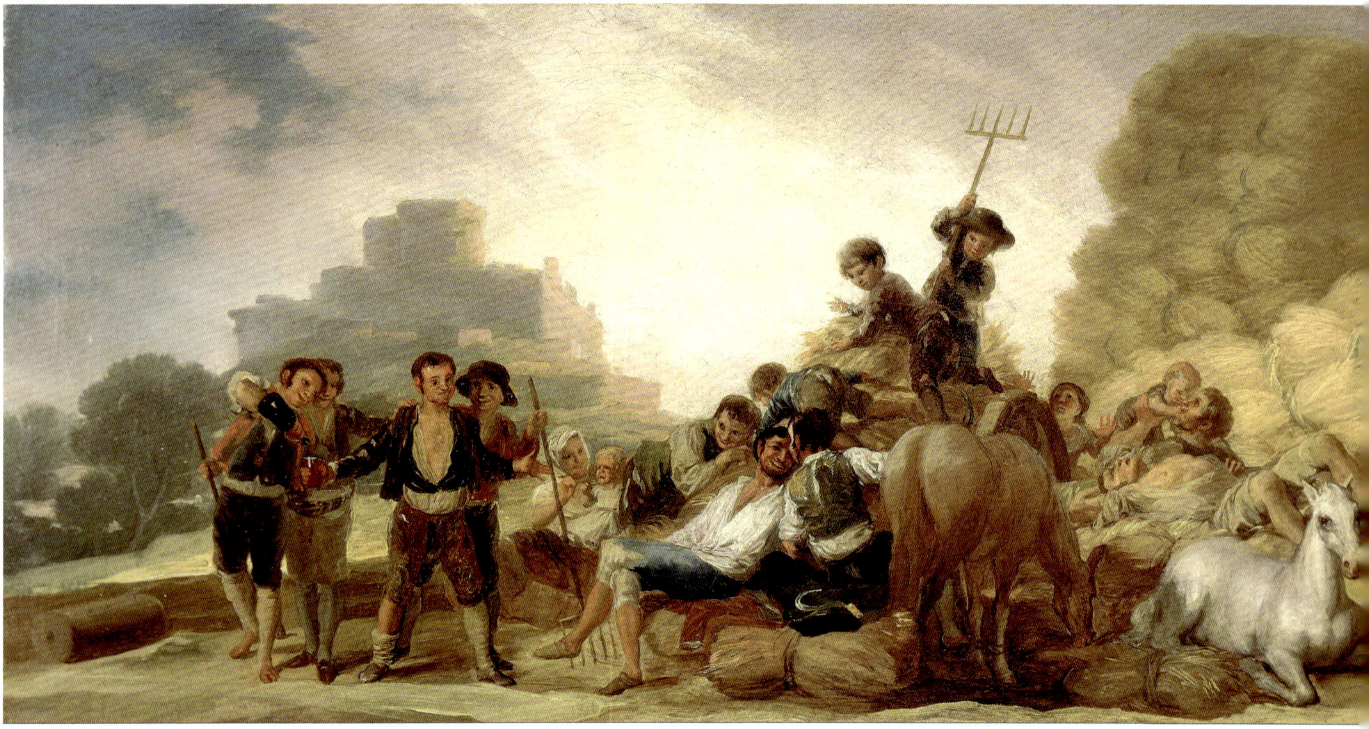

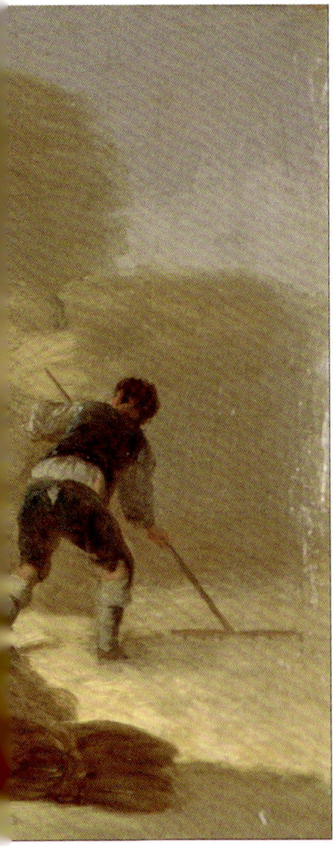

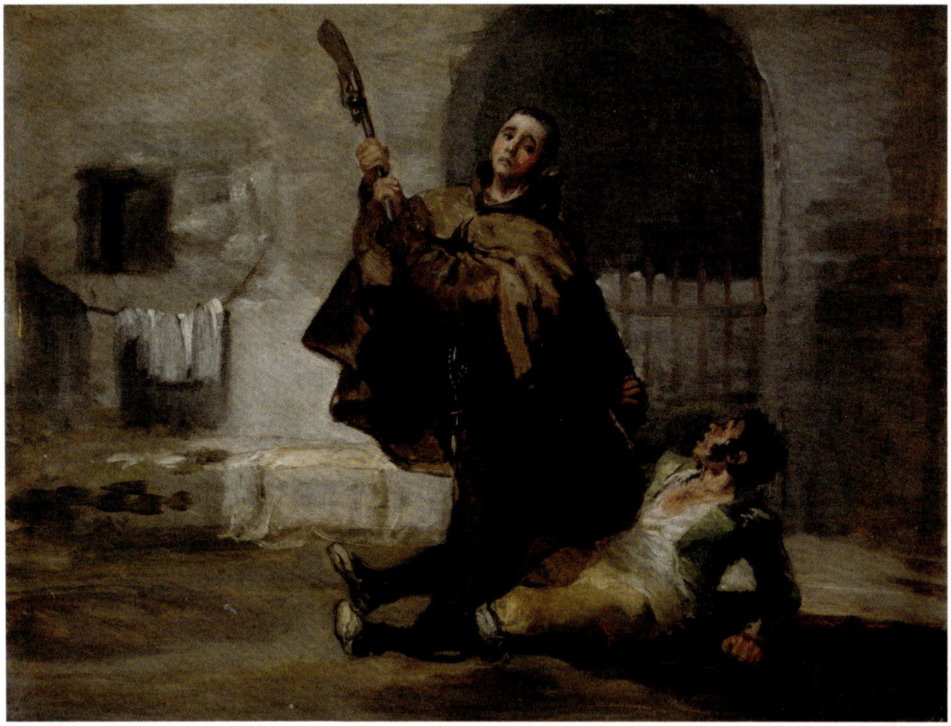

The Threshing Floor* and *Friar Pedro Clubs El Maragato with the Butt of the Gun

Francisco Goya, 1786 and c. 1806

How do we get from families gathered to celebrate the harvest to Friar Pedro beating a man with a gun?

Well as it turns out, in order to understand how Goya could have been driven toward the insanity of his Black Paintings, we need to understand his entire life. He is an artist whose work was not only an unstoppable force for the progression of art, but a study in how politics can shape and mold images. And all of this is because Goya grew up observing life from *within the struggle*. He wasn't a prodigy who was granted elite tutorship. He didn't have access to court circles. He wasn't born into an artistic lineage and didn't have financial backing. If he wanted to be a success, he would have to earn it all himself.

For Goya, every single day was an opportunity to improve, and every opportunity a stepping stone toward the next. Where most would have settled for fate after being rejected from the Royal Academy not once, but twice, Goya pushed on. He traveled to Italy in 1770 and studied the works of Raphael, Guido Reni, and Paolo Veronese, among other masters of the Renaissance and Baroque periods. He entered competitions and pitted himself against other artists to further test his abilities. And when all was said and done, he returned to Spain and moved to Madrid, where he finally secured his first real gig in the art world. Goya was going to design for the Royal Tapestry Factory.

The Parasol

Francisco Goya, 1777

Here's a version of Goya that most people never expect. We are so used to the darkness, the violence, and his great chronicles of madness, we forget that this was a man who once painted the sunlight.

A young woman sits, perfectly composed, while a boy lifts a parasol over her head to shield her from the sun. It's almost disarmingly charming. Goya creates a painting with *real* structure. Look for the triangle: Her body forms the base while the parasol rises like a pillar, forming one of the peaks. It locks the image in place, giving the figures a sense of quiet monumentality. The colors are bright, almost Rococo in their optimism, but they're grounded by a surprising weight. Goya doesn't float people in the way that Fragonard does.

You'll also have noticed the diagonal lines: the parasol. The top of the wall. Her arm and the boy's, splitting the composition into two registers that are countered only by the opposing line of the tree in the background, and here Goya gives us a sense of motion. He cleverly guides our eyes back and forth, in a way that doesn't feel staged, but rather natural and comfortable.

This is a version of Goya that is learning *how* to be an artist by working within a set of very rigid constraints, because this painting is not the final product: It's a template for a tapestry. Goya isn't free to take enormous risks and put every ounce of himself into the work. Rather, he needs to follow a careful set of rules and accept his role as a cog in the machine. He's learning to play the game—one that would take him to the next phase of his career in the royal courts.

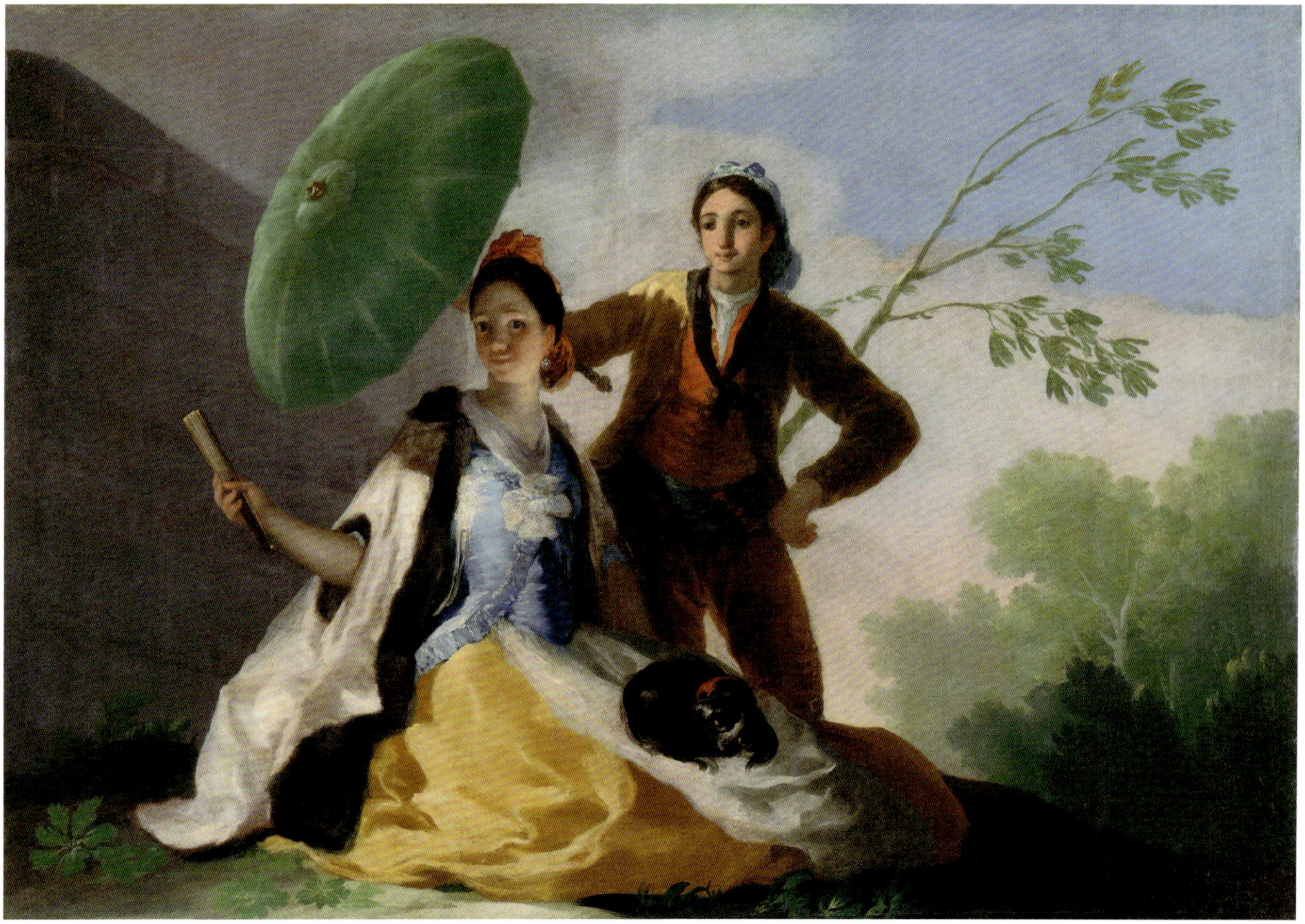

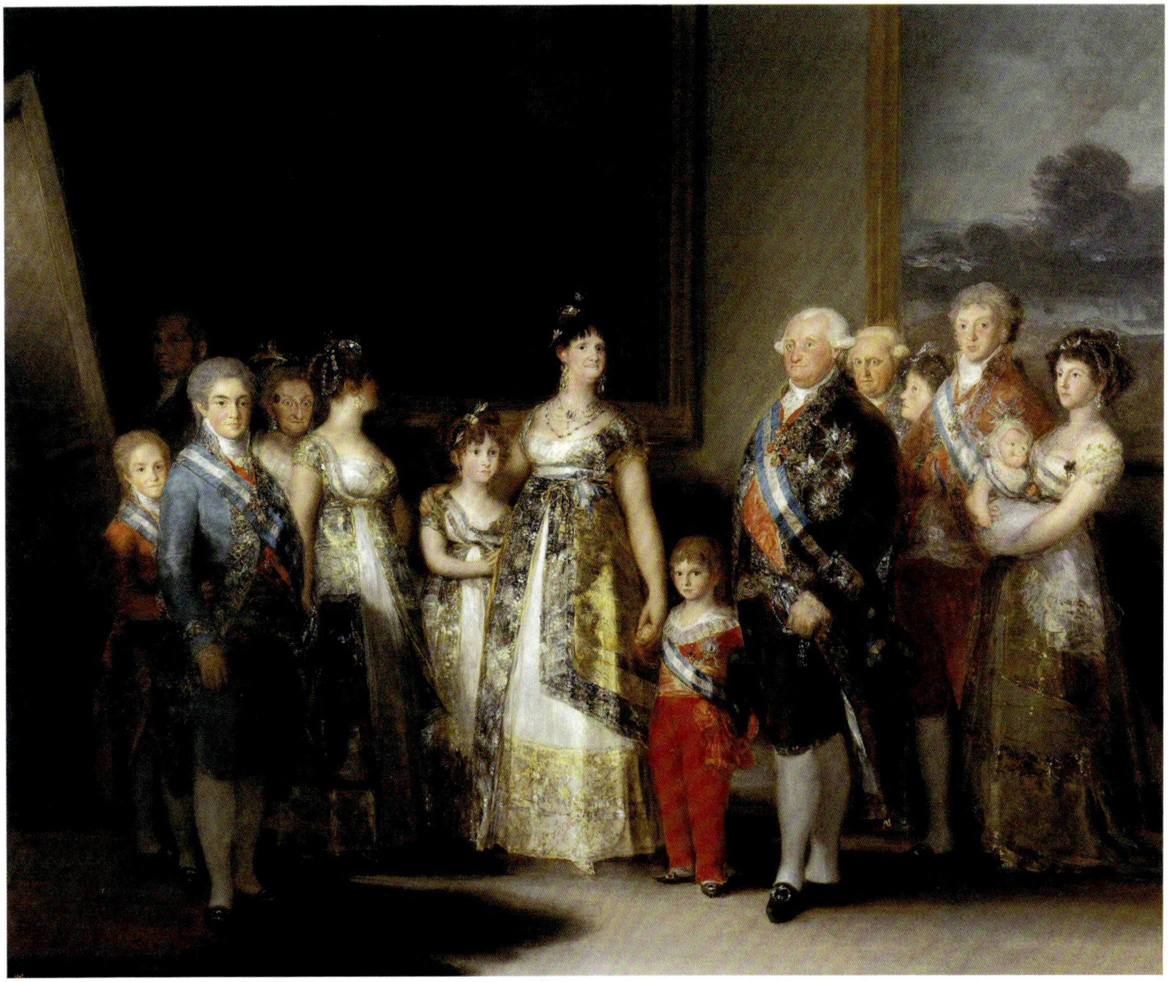

The Family of Carlos IV

Francisco Goya, 1800

A large, frontal, multifigure arrangement of 14 figures, 13 of whom form a loose semi-circle around the matriarch of the family, Queen Maria Luisa. And as would be expected in a painting for a royal family, the lighting is bright and intentionally directed to focus on the faces and the lavish clothing of its subjects: a truly lovely work of art.

Goya delivers harmony through so many different elements—a sign of a truly efficient master painter performing at his highest level—including the subtle pairings of contrasting themes. He highlights elegant clothing against a neutral background, and warm tones play with soft shadows. Nothing is overly dramatic or idealized, the family portrayed for what they are. Regal and elegant, but real. He even slips a cameo of himself into the artwork, but only in shadows, as seen on the left side, where he stands behind a large canvas. He doesn't overstate his presence or place within the order of things. Instead, he serves as a fixture in an immensely respectful way. From a small town into the house of the royal family: what a dream come true.

Right? That's one way to look at it.

There are many ways to read a painting, and while one might reasonably assume that this portrait shows the peaceful inner life of a peaceful family, we can reasonably point out more sinister intentions.

At the point this painting was made, Goya was deaf as a stump. About eight years deaf, to be more exact, thanks to an illness that nearly took his life. Now I don't know about you, but if I lost my hearing at 46 years old, I imagine my views of the world may radically change. It's understandable, I think, even for hopeless optimists.

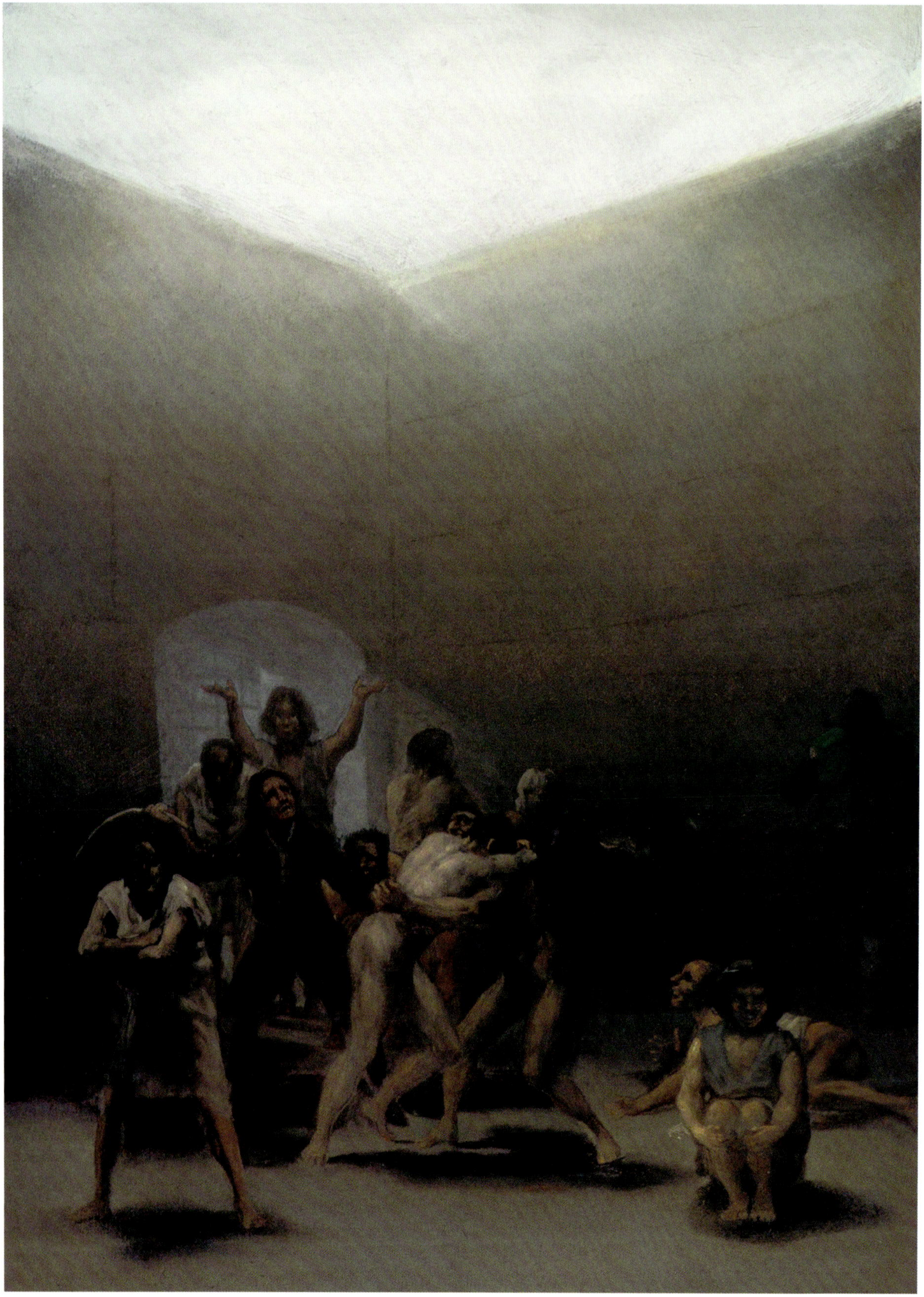

Yard with Lunatics

Francisco Goya, 1794

Goya most definitely changed. On a small tinplate, he paints this image in oil, and we see into the world of an entirely different man. I'd like to quickly point out, this is six years before the grand royal portrait, and right in the thick of him working in the royal courts, where he spent his time painting portraits and tapestries. This is Goya in his private time, exploring work in secret. Uncommissioned and unfiltered.

Art historian Arthur Danto puts it better than anyone I've ever heard: *Yard with Lunatic*s marks a point in Goya's career where he moves from "a world in which there are no shadows to one in which there is no light." This is a man who achieved every single one of his wildest dreams, playing at the highest level of society, and is now pinned back down to a perceived "bottom" for no reason other than the will of God. His health is in decline, his hearing is gone, and as his losses mount, his grip on his mind is slipping too.

In this small picture, Goya paints the underbelly of reality, where light is an afterthought. Cries of incomprehensible madness are all around as two nude men fight to the death, or for whatever semblance of life they have left, as a warden beats them down with a whip. This scene was informed by an actual place Goya had visited in his youth, while spending time in Zaragoza: one of a dozen small-scale images produced in tandem with his own degradation, in the silence of his own privacy, created to reflect his own self-doubt, anxiety, and fear.

This is the exact same guy who painted the royal family's portrait between 1800 and 1801, and we start to see how other conclusions could be made. A combination of his own ailments, social unrest due to war, a power shift across Europe, and a wave of revolution that would strike fear into the minds of the monarchy might have played a role in Goya's opinions shifting. I have a hunch he gave zero F–

"Matthew..."

Let's look at the painting again, but through a new set of eyes.

A large, frontal, multifigure arrangement of 14 people, 13 of whom form a loose semi-circle around the matriarch of the family, Queen Maria Luisa. But why is she in the middle? Was Goya suggesting that she was the dominating hand behind the King? Charles IV is present, of course, and right out in the front, but he is passive—submissive, almost. The family that surrounds them seem distracted and disengaged. They don't give the impression they care to be there. Goya doesn't give us an idealized version of royalty, but a somewhat subdued one, and while the case can be made that this is just a portrayal of real people, we might also make the case that Goya stopped giving a damn. He paints what he sees, and maybe, he paints what he thinks. Remember, this was a man who lived *in the struggle*, not above it, and now that he's here, maybe he sees them for what they are, and well, why not call it how it is? Why flatter them? He paints the royal family as ordinary beings and in doing so, he turns a luxurious outfit into a costume for a clown. A show with no monumental aura, no heroics—just a bit of theater. A family who inherited an empire that they could not maintain, and he's watching the disaster unfold from the shadows.

Conjecture? Maybe. Is it possible? Why not?

We have all the evidence to suggest that Goya was well on his way into his own decline, so why couldn't he be angry at the world? If you felt that jaded toward everything, would you care anymore?

Oh. And it gets even worse...

The Second of May 1808

Francisco Goya, 1814

King Charles IV was weak, his court was corrupt, and Spain was divided. Its prime minister, Manuel Godoy, was widely hated, with a government that was highly dysfunctional. And to make matters worse, Godoy, under the belief that Napoleon was unstoppable, secretly signed the 1807 Treaty of Fontainebleau, which allowed France to march its troops through Spain toward Portugal, with an understanding that both countries would split the territory once Portugal was taken. Wishful thinking.

The treaty was a trojan horse, and Napoleon was there to stay. His plan was to remove the Bourbon dynasty, install his brother as King, and keep everything to himself. It worked—at least for a time. Charles IV abdicated after a revolt against Godoy. He and his son were forced to renounce the throne, and Spain, which was effectively leaderless, was now fully under the control of the French. But not without a fight.

The 2nd of May, 1808, would go on to mark one of the most important events in the country's history, because it is the day that the people of Spain, and more specifically, the people of Madrid, fought back. Hundreds of poorly armed citizens took to the streets against heavily armed French troops, and chaos spread quickly throughout the city. These weren't soldiers fighting soldiers. This was a butcher, a barber, an artisan, a laborer, and whoever else could muster the strength to fight back, armed only with knives, chisels, hatchets, and whatever else they could get their hands on, embarking on an hours-long uprising that unfolded across city streets. Urban warfare of the most brutal type, because they really didn't stand a chance. Napoleon's horsemen were brutal, well-trained, and merciless. Citizens were trampled to death, cut down in the streets, crushed underneath the weight of horses, and the innocent would also suffer the consequences. Violence spread until the entirety of Madrid was under duress, and Goya captures it all perfectly.

Though only one of many rebellions that would take place during France's occupation of Spain, the Dos de Mayo Uprising marked the beginning of the Peninsular War and one of history's most violent days. Goya shows us the devastation of the violence: the Mameluke calvary slashing at civilians with scimitars, a sea of bodies and blood filling the streets. No clear order—only violence. He serves us confusion through the motif of extreme motion. Rearing horses, twisting bodies, blurred limbs: an uncontainable frenzy made up of the worst aspects of humanity. He doesn't idealize it either. This isn't a painting that celebrates the triumph of battle, but rather, one that highlights its costs. It isn't glorious—it's brutal and ugly and raw. Faces are contorted, enraged, and terrified, echoing the very nature of the Spanish desperation to fight. This was a memory for Goya: not the exact scene, perhaps, but the feeling of suppression. The artist experienced the occupation of his beloved Spain in real time, and the world kept falling in on him.

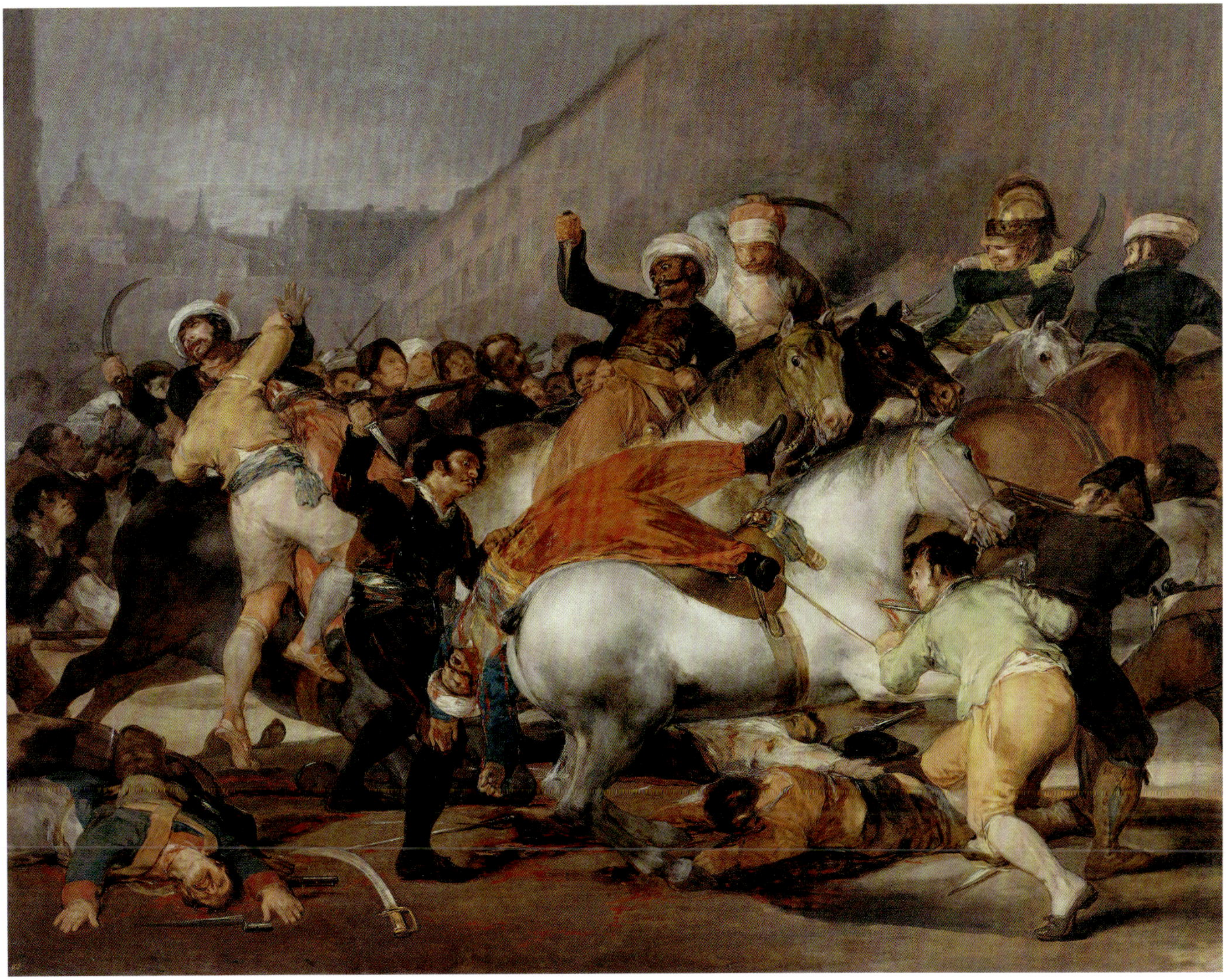

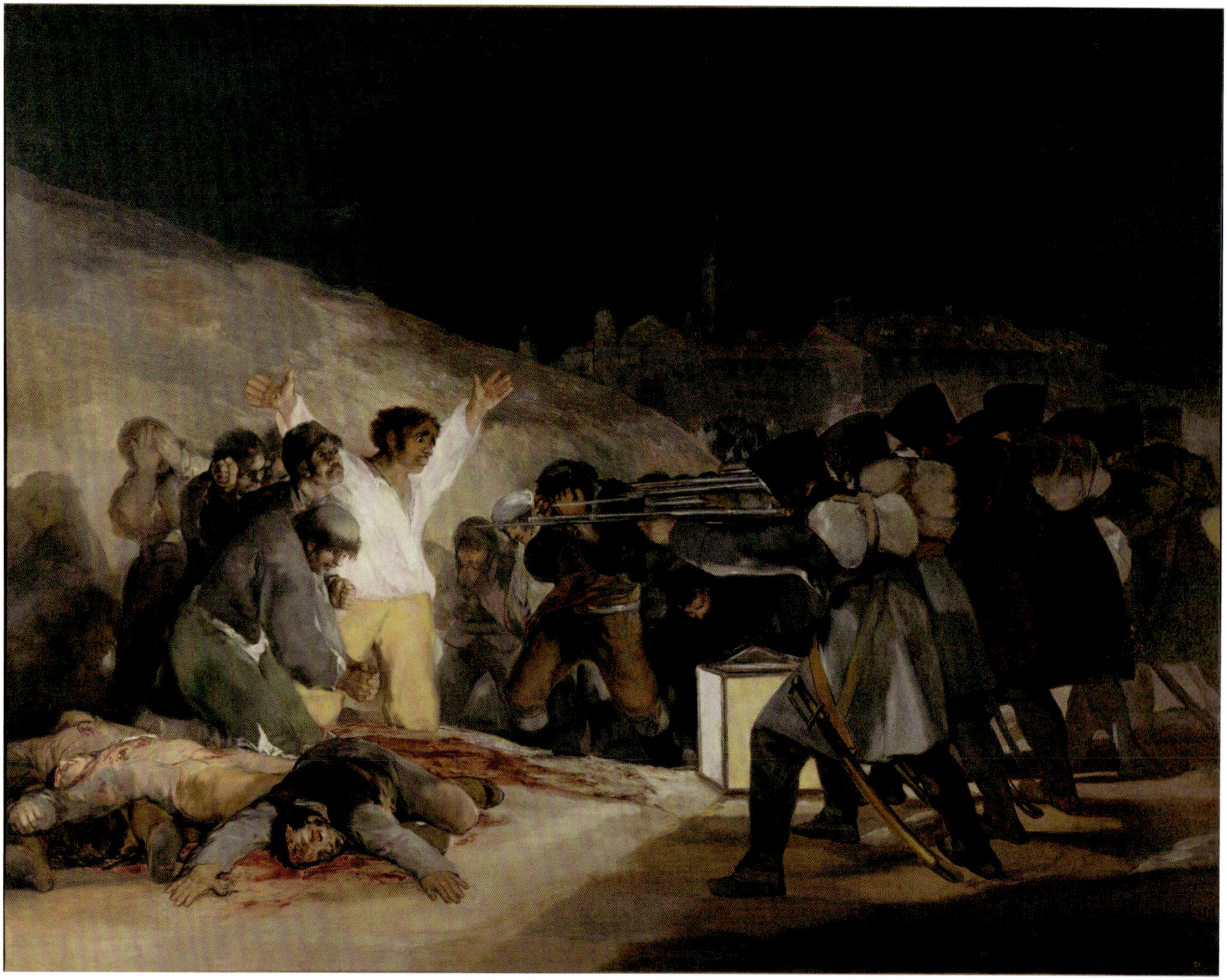

The Third of May 1808

Francisco Goya, 1814

The French answered the resistance with atrocity. The day after the uprising, they carried out a mass execution of hundreds of people: death by firing squad across the city.

Again, Goya doesn't idealize the trauma. Like its partner, this painting is not a wartime fantasy of heroics. It's ugly and heartbreaking in the worst ways possible, and in ways that Goya knew too well. How many deaths had he witnessed before he started sketching it? How many faces contorted with weeping? The stench of death everywhere, the taste of it as it slithers through the air.

This painting is of a real event, but not a real moment. This precise scene is fictional. What it shows us is not our world, but Goya's, and this makes the painting even worse, even lonelier. Louder. A man in a white shirt raises his arms, a visual echo of both Christ-like martyrdom and raw terror as he gives himself away in his last moments on Earth. To the left side of the composition is humanity and its plea for mercy. To the right side, the face of the soulless void. The cold black night sky is paralleled by a line of unknown soldiers, weapons ready and held just outside of the light of the lantern.

The lantern's placement is genius. By placing it at the center of the mess, Goya highlights the catastrophe even further. The light leads our eyes first to the picture's anchor—the man in the white shirt—and then down to his future. The fate of these people is sealed. In a second or so, they will join those bloodied bodies below.

This is a work that shocks you. It's not meant to be admired. It is an act of journalism and the first true modern depiction of war.

So when we ask where it all went wrong—well, where the hell do I even start? Goya might have been mad, but I ask, wouldn't you be?

Without any context, I understand how someone might look at an early painting by the Spanish master and doubt that it's even from him. Because to grasp how he arrived in the darkness of the Black Paintings, you need to understand everything that led from his birth in a small town to his final years, which he spent transforming the walls of a farmhouse with monstrous forms.

Fourteen depictions of figurative hell, painted as murals in his home between 1820 and 1823, some of which are on the next two pages. The Black Paintings are the contemplations of a man destroyed by life. I won't read them for you, because you don't need know to anything about art to understand what they're saying.

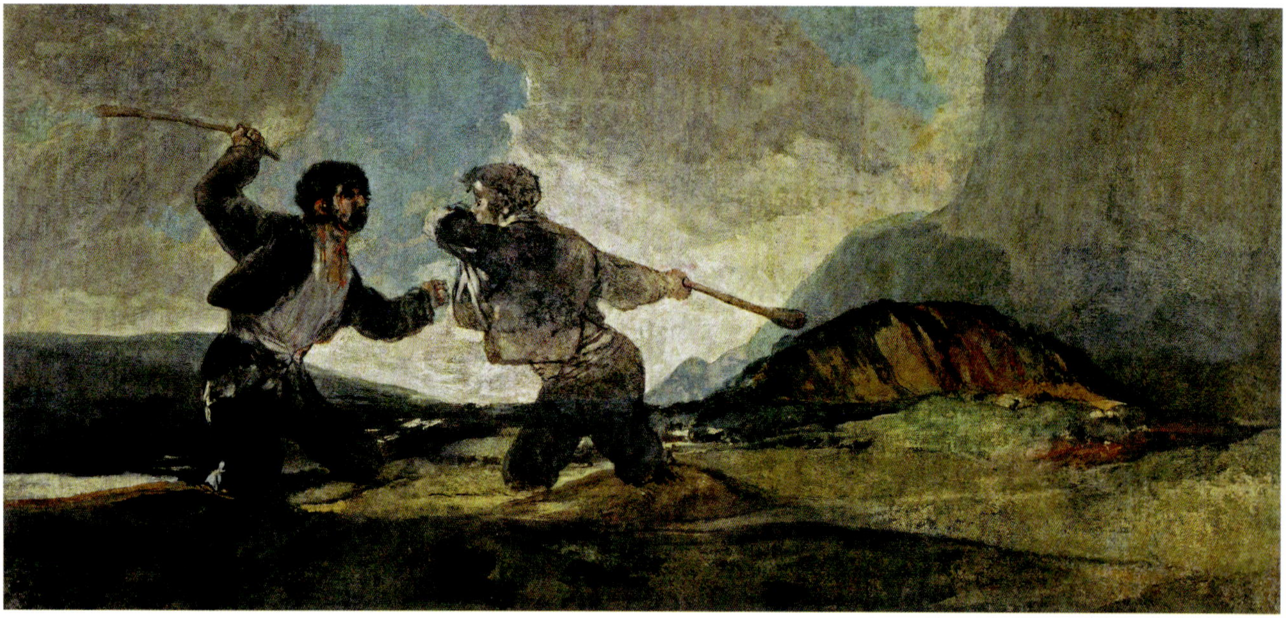

Duel with Cudgels, 1820–23

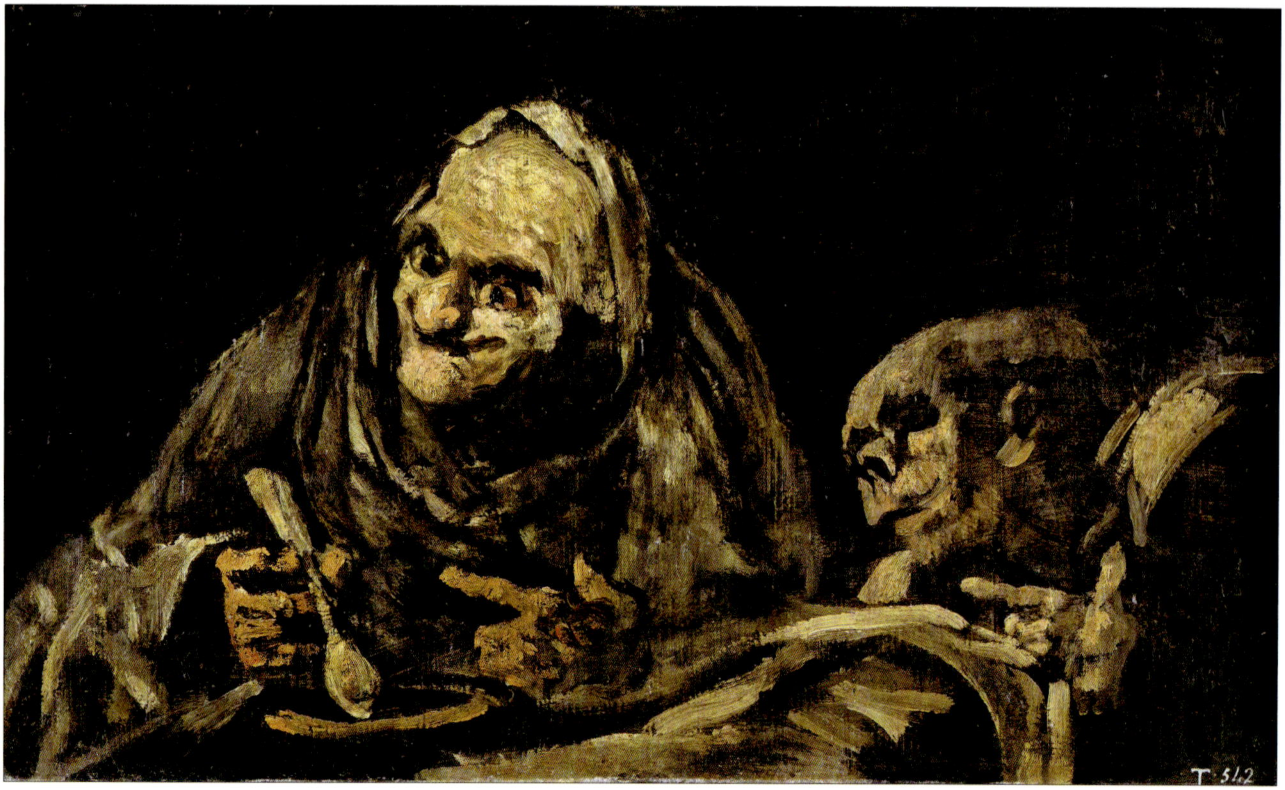

Two Old Men Eating, 1820–23

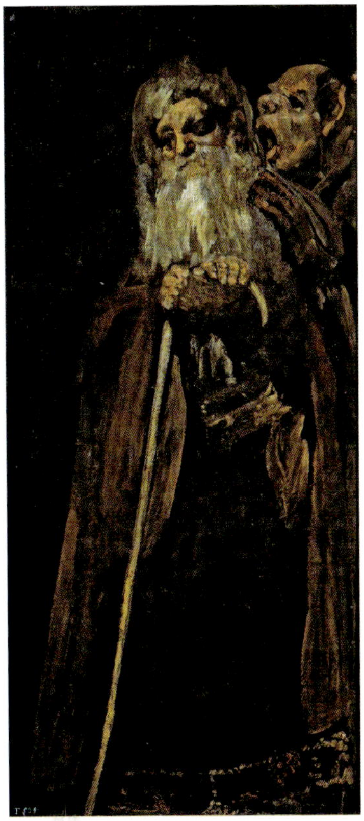

Two Old Men, 1820–23

The Dog, 1820–23

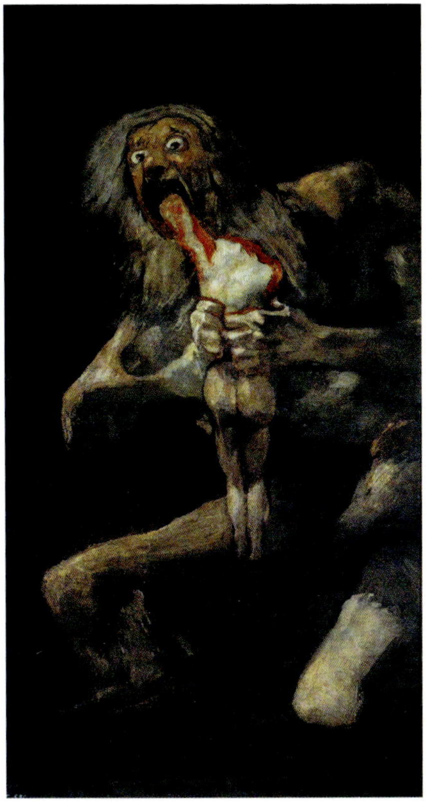

Saturn Devouring His Son, 1820–23

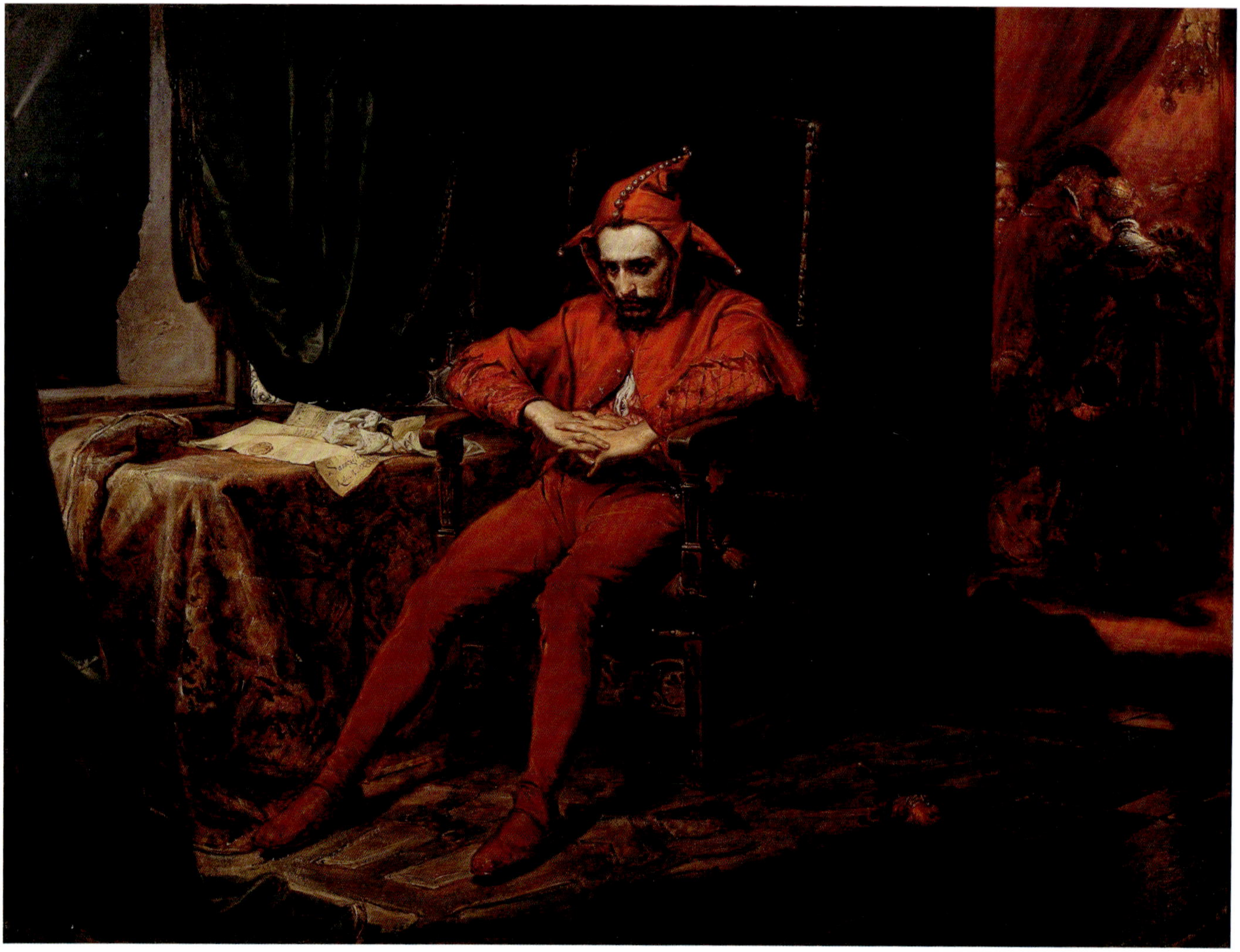

Stańczyk

Jan Matejko, 1862

As Francisco Goya shows us, the art of reading art is a practice where understanding political context can make the difference between a casual visual experience and a groundbreaking revelation: an idea that becomes apparent once again in Jan Matejko's *Stańczyk*.

So, what do we have here? Well, obviously we have Stańczyk, the famed Polish court jester, renowned for his wit and intelligence. And we have what looks like a party in the background on the right side of the painting, and on the left, a night sky.

"But, Matthew, what of the letter on the table?"

While it's hard to discern exactly what the letter is, with the right clue, we can deduce a devastating idea. Because this painting, though popularly known as just *Stańczyk*, is actually titled *Stańczyk During a Ball at the Court of Queen Bona in the Face of the Loss of Smolensk*.

"Holy tongue twister."

Quite. And in light of the political turmoil of our scene, it is here, my friends, that Jan Matejko takes this painting to new stratospheric heights.

Because we are not simply observing sadness but are instead experiencing an existential crisis on the eve of a political meltdown. And the only person who seems to give a damn about any of it is a helpless royal court jester. The irony of it is perplexing. In the place of those who hold real power, the court jester is the one contemplating the outcomes of a catastrophe: one that would have life-changing, world-shattering consequences for all those involved. And who is involved? Everyone partying away in the background. The red room of said partygoers ties directly to Stańczyk's red outfit, but the two are separated by a pillar of darkness: a clear disconnect of duties that works so well.

Stańczyk's contemplation becomes our own. He is delivered as a mirror of exactly how we're meant to respond to the predicament. He serves a role beyond the scope of a character, and in effect, narrates the audience's inner dialogue. Jan Matejko shows us here what is possible in great paintings, and it gives way to a fascinating question: *Is art a matter of relatability?*

It's difficult to imagine relating to a portrait of the Pope, for example, and yet, we can look at one and fantasize about great swathes of unchecked power. We can see an image of a grand military general, and without ever having gone to war, we might daydream of vast conquests of expansion and unrattled bravery. Our minds are spectacular machines, and they always seem to find a way. While we can't always connect to who, and what, and when, there is something about human nature that sees a little bit of itself in everything. And perhaps great art is a conduit for that. A tool for contemplation, but also a tool for conjuring what could have been, because why couldn't I be? A general, a king, a knight, a princess, a god. Anything.

It lends to the idea that the Church might have been onto something.

Now, we need to define a clear line here before we carry on, because it's very important to understand exactly where I'm going with this story. On one side of the line, we have the Catholic Church, and everything that it embodied before 31 October, 1517. On the other side, we have the Catholic Church and all the ways in which it braced for impact after Martin Luther shared his *95 Theses*.

So, who was doing the bracing? Before Luther, the Catholic Church was a single unified institution that held great amounts of influence in western Europe. They were headed by the Pope, who was believed to be the successor to Saint Peter. They were supported by an enormous hierarchy of cardinals, bishops, abbots, priests, and monks. They controlled vast amounts of wealth, held power over enormous plots of territory, influenced major legal systems, and mediated the cultural landscape.

"Sounds like an empire."

It kind of was. Religious and political.

The Church governed everything, from matters of spirituality to policy, economy, culture, all the way to how you felt: a form of psychological authoritarianism that defined sin, redemption, and everything in between. It dictated moral existence, and you didn't have much of a choice.

Of course, the Church was supposed to guide man to salvation through a life structured by Christ's teachings. But unfortunately, the men in charge of guiding the figurative blind often fell foul at the first hint of power. Forgiveness and retribution became a lever of control. Salvation was for the privileged, and the privileged alone.

The papacy gained enormous influence over who sat on thrones across Europe, and it also controlled the flow of knowledge. The sacred Book of God was out of reach because most people couldn't read Latin, let alone read at all. That was another practice reserved for those who could afford it. The Church ran most schools and had a vice grip on intellectual life. They exerted control at every level of society, from the very bottom to the top.

All empires eventually fall, however.

As the centuries progressed, humanism rose, the printing press arrived on the scene, and we slowly see the unravelling of one of the world's great powers.

Which takes us to 1517. Now, it's a hotly debated subject as to whether or not Martin Luther actually pinned his *95 Theses* onto the door of Wittenberg's Castle Church, but I am a sucker for a dramatic story, so we'll go with that version.

In his theses, Luther attacks the abuses of the Church and argues that true repentance is not something that can be purchased. He questions the legitimacy of the Pope's powers, and perhaps, most importantly of all, attacks the Church's history of financial exploitation.

Within weeks, printers produced copies that spread through Germany. Within months, these ideas spread across Europe in what felt like an overnight evolution. Luther would rise to the stars, and the Church would never be the same. In the years following, political shifts across Europe loosened the papacy's power over the continent's secular rulers.

The iron grip of the Church was over. At least, one would think.

True power lies with those who can manipulate culture. A very modern idea, perhaps, and rooted in my very modern experiences. But if I transport myself back to medieval Europe, I am ruled by a Church that channels God's authority. This conference of power is abstract, perhaps, but the Church's influence over my conversations with my friends, butcher, barber, and anyone else who I pass by is not. And neither are all those images I see, in stained glass windows and on frescoes that the Church paid for: images that the papacy, with its connections to the heavens, created to teach. To communicate. To influence. But why art?

Look at the bodies of power throughout history that gained influence—political, religious, or otherwise. Many shaped the way people thought by connecting to them through whatever means allowed them to exert influence. Often this effort has been, at least in part, visual. In my medieval past, the Pope is a figure of near mythical proportions who has little to do with my day-to-day, but in art, I can really feel his weight. I can see him, alongside the disciples of the God who grants him power. I can relate to them, and their messages. Which ties us back to Stańczyk and my initial question: *Is art a matter of relatability?* And if it is, in the right hands, is great art a device to manipulate those who view it for power? Maybe *the Church was onto something*.

Here is an institution that had everything, and in a matter of less than a century, lost it all. They were eroded by greed and corruption, but if they wanted to make it through this fall out of humanity's good graces, they would need to change fast.

And now here comes Michelangelo Merisi, who you likely know as Caravaggio, born in 1571. You could claim that he is the single greatest artist in history and I wouldn't argue, because to see his work in person is a transformative experience—a feeling you will never forget, whether or not you care about paintings. His genius is undeniable. Which is why, when Caravaggio landed in Rome in 1592, the fate of the Church, and the fate of art, would change forever.

This was a man with no money. He had fled Milan to survive legal troubles and was a complete outsider to Roman society, arriving in the city with nothing but raw talent. He would struggle, with minor work here and there, sort of living on the edges of poverty. It didn't help that he had a poor attitude to boot: Caravaggio refused to conform.

He didn't want to paint in the pretty Mannerist style that was fashionable at the time. Instead, he preferred painting *real* people—models, friends, prostitutes, it didn't matter who—in a way that highlighted their realest aspects. He set scenes how he wanted, to tell the stories that he wanted, and maybe he refused to give in to popular taste because this art was *his*. For a man with nothing, maybe the freedom to paint as he desired was all he had.

His work didn't catch on right away, with people perhaps dismissing him as a chronicler of normal life, marking him as unlikely to succeed. But Caravaggio came to Rome at exactly the right time, because he was what the Vatican needed. The Church was desperate to make themselves accessible to those regular people, and who better to help make this happen than one of the most spectacular "regular people" that the world has ever known.

The Cardsharps

Caravaggio, c. 1594–95

"I think you have a winning hand, young man."

But does he? It's hard to say because we don't know the game being played. However, it's almost certain he's got a three or some combination of it.

"How could you possibly know that?"

The mark has given it away. As he whispers into that man's ears, whatever it is that venomous snakes do, he peeks over his shoulder and signals the number three with his tattered glove to his accomplice. Yes, the rather young-looking fellow is his accomplice, who reaches into his belt at the signal to pluck the winning card. And just in case things go wrong, he'll have no problem sticking his opponent like a pig with that knife.

So, what is Caravaggio trying to tell us? The truth is, probably nothing, right? The painting is simply a display of raw artistic fundamentals, arranged to show us an everyday scene of everyday life in sixteenth-century Italy. But it does ignite a fascinating philosophical query, which is *who in this image is being screwed?* Have a closer look at their faces. The oblivious, hopeful gaze of someone who sincerely thinks they have a chance. The nervous look of someone who knows he doesn't and is ready to escalate, if need be, but certainly not willing, with a face that still maintains a childlike innocence. And then there's the face of a man at work—just another day. "If not him, then me." Three different characters bound together by Caravaggio in this theater, in a play on the precipice of its final act. And how will it end? Well, with one boy being duped for his innocence, while we watch the others vanish into the shadows, all thanks to the guy with the tattered gloves.

This painting marked a major milestone for Caravaggio, because he painted it in an attempt to establish himself as an independent artist after leaving the workshop of Cavaliere d'Arpino, also known as Giuseppe Cesari, for whom he had been painting "flowers and fruit." It was the right move. The painting caught the attention of a prominent art collector, diplomat, and highly influential Italian cardinal, Francesco Maria del Monte, who purchased *The Cardsharps* and became the artist's first important patron, and his first real introduction to Rome's powerful.

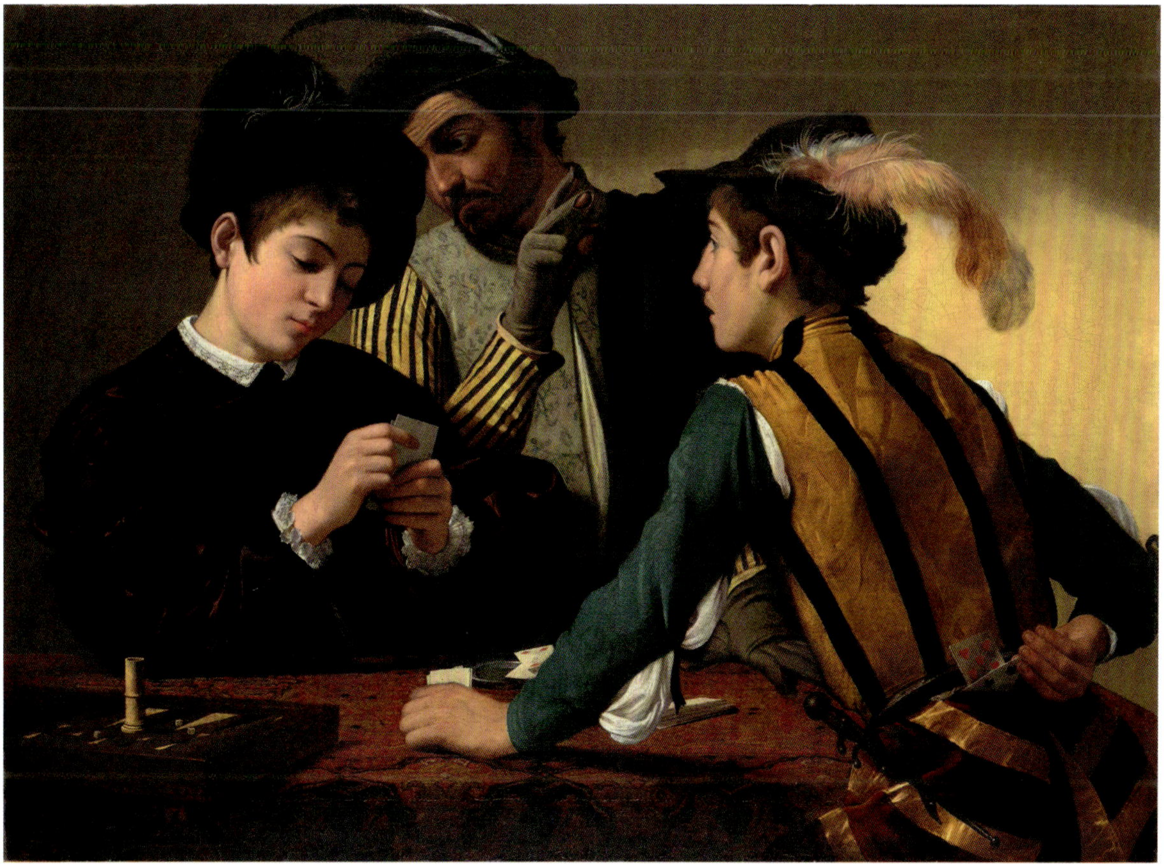

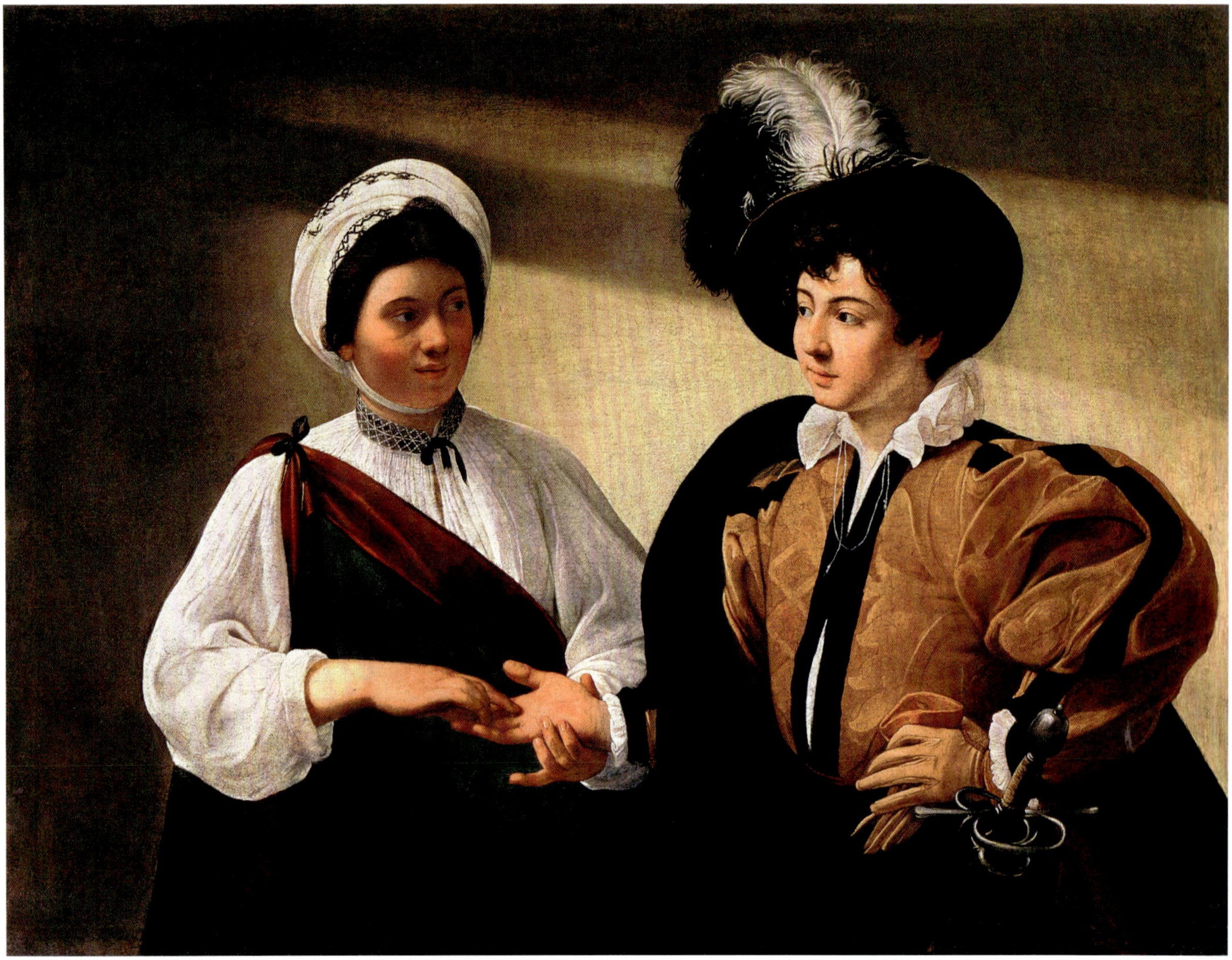

The Fortune Teller

Caravaggio, c. 1595

Shortly after *The Cardsharps*, Caravaggio does it again, commissioned by the same new-found patron.

Once again, something sinister is happening here, and you likely haven't noticed, just like the handsome young man. He is getting his palm read by the pretty Romani fortune teller, eyes glued to hers, while *she* is making off with his ring. It is a detail so subtle it's no wonder you didn't spot it. But what does it say about the man who painted it?

For most people, it really doesn't say much. But you? Well, you are no longer most people. And Caravaggio was not most painters. Just have a look at her eyes. Little beads of temptation hovering over a faux smile, all of which sit just outside of the direct light. His eyes, in contrast, are blind, drunk with flirtatious possibilities, and fully illuminated. This is because he is the subject of the painting, and she is not. At least, not her face.

If you follow her arm all the way down to her hand, you'll notice this is a well-practised routine: the pincer-like grip of her delicate touch, applying just the right amount of pressure to strike a balance between a devious act and coquettish intentions. And while he imagines an evening of whatever it is that young boys do, she pockets his ring and is off to seduce her next victim. But wait, because this painting is about to get so much better.

Caravaggio tells us this entire story at the split second that you laid your eyes on the picture, and just like the gullible young boy, you had no idea it was happening. He does it all with light. While the brightest items in the scene are clearly the feather in the hat, the fluffy shirt, and the baggy garment that seems to hover over the young lady's arm, the items that matter to the story hang somewhere in the middle, at the exact same value as one another; his face, his palm, her fingertips, and her hand are almost identical in luminosity. And when reverted back to color, we see them as a secret message whispered into our ears.

But unless you knew how to look, you wouldn't realize. And like the handsome young boy trapped in a seductive gaze, we too find ourselves seduced by a masterpiece.

This is a hallmark of Caravaggio's work—its seductive nature. His paintings draw you in, make you feel the urge to stay longer than you had planned. His art has that effect: You wouldn't be the first person to linger in front of one of his works. But it pays to be wary of seduction, as the soon-to-be ringless man is going to realize.

And Caravaggio, as well. In one of art's great instances of foreshadowing, his painting *Bacchus* offers us a glimpse of what would ultimately lead to his downfall.

Bacchus

Caravaggio, c. 1596–98

There is a very good chance you've seen this masterpiece before, as it is one of the most famous images ever produced. But as with many of the paintings we've discussed, I can almost guarantee you've missed its greatest secret. It is not plastered onto the soft details of the handsome Bacchus, or the ripples in his wine glass, or the delicate cloth wrapped around his anatomically perfect body, or even within the exquisitely lit fruits and foliage.

Rather, Caravaggio dangles this surprise under our noses in a place we are unlikely to look. You might not see it at first, so search carefully. Spotted it yet? It's impossibly faint, but hidden on the glass wine jug in the bottom left corner is the reflection of a man.

"Oh my God! Who is that?"

Only Bacchus will ever know. We know he does, because this reflection's placement tells us that someone is standing directly in his eyeline. In a van Eyck–like inclusion, perhaps it's Caravaggio himself. And now that you've spotted it, consider what this might mean.

Let's start with Bacchus, the Roman god of wine, inebriation, fertility, and theater. None of that sounds all that bad on any given night, but Bacchus is also the god of ritual madness. He is the god of insanity. And here he is, sitting in front of the artist, seductive gaze and all, pulling you into the universe within the frame. Pulling Caravaggio into his world.

I think about being in the painter's shoes: about being a man who came to Rome with nothing, and now, four years later, is finally finding succeeding in his dreams. In that position, what does one do? It's so tempting to spiral out of control when you don't have a care in the world and the guardrails have been taken off, because when everything seems perfect, nothing could ever go wrong. But maybe he knows about the dangerous game he's playing. He senses his own calling for self-destruction and, deep down, he knows that he can't help himself.

This is a man who is now painting commissions for cardinals in the day and drowning in jugs of wine at night, and he just can't stop himself.

And as you'll soon find out, he might have been onto something.

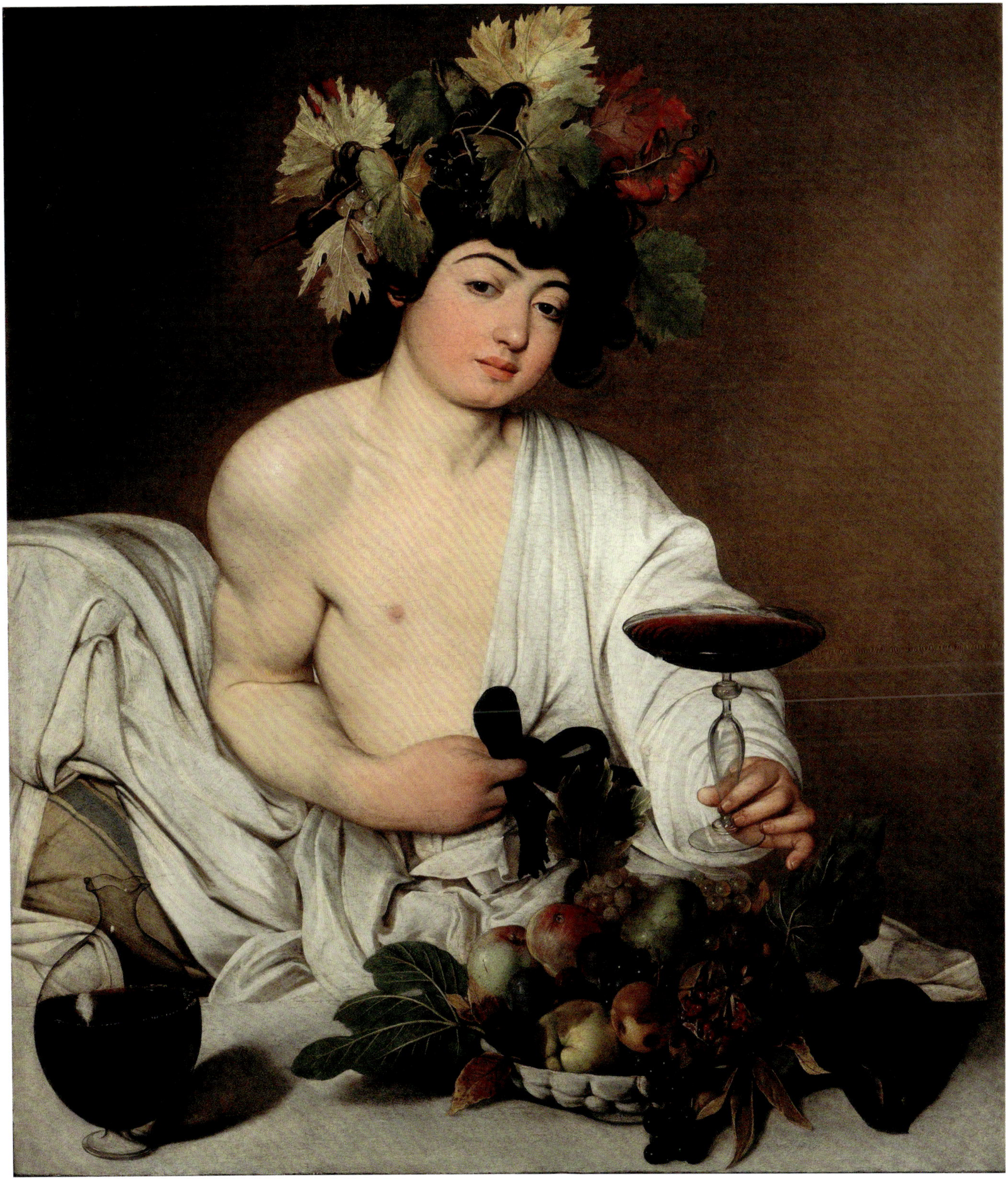

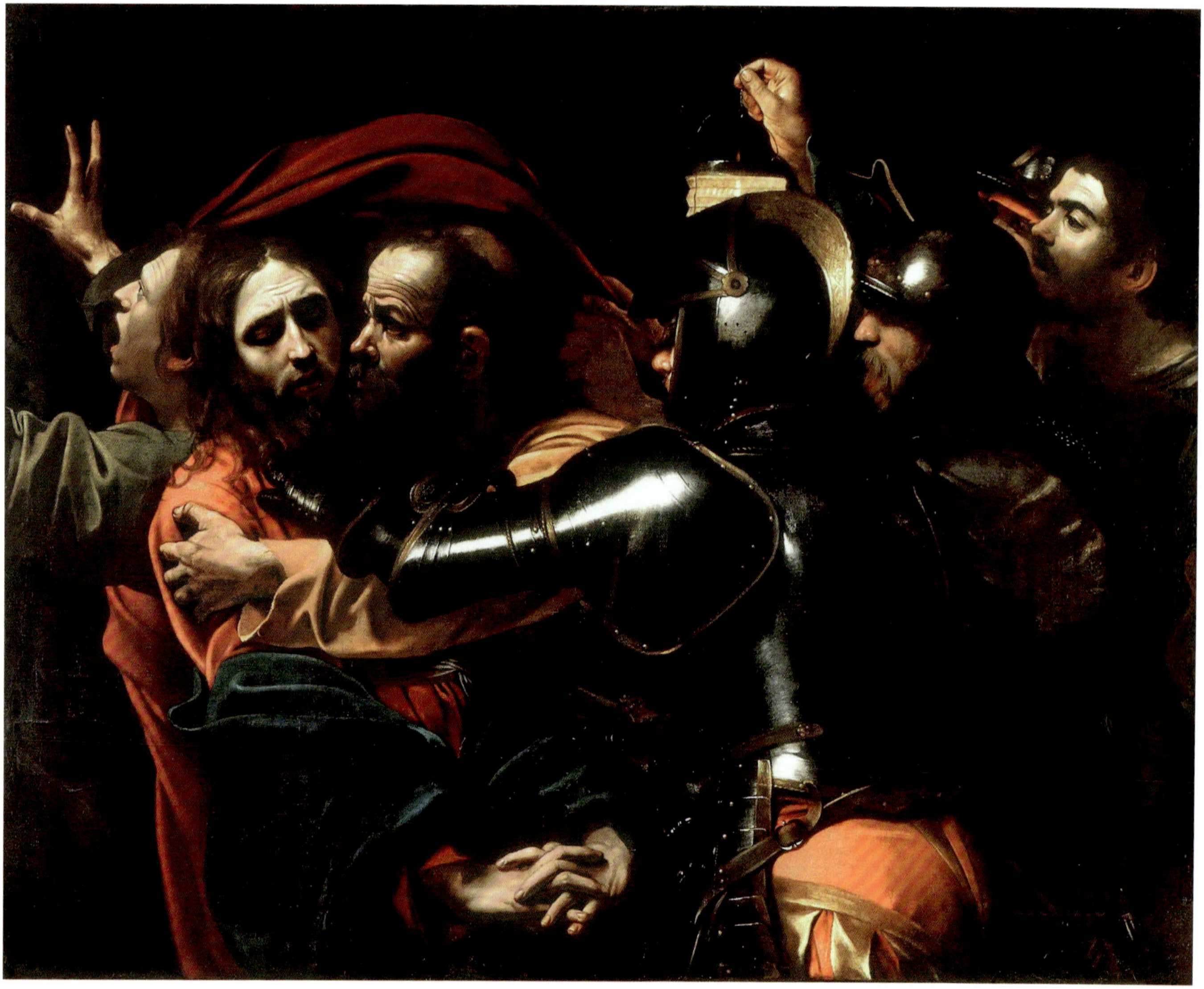

The Taking of Christ

Caravaggio, 1602

In the wake of the Reformation taking hold, the Catholic Church's power was dwindling, its congregations moving to alternative systems of faith. In response, it sought to reform its governance and image across many issues, including art.

Instead of the flourishes and excesses that marked pre-Reformation imagery, the Church decided they needed to tell the story of Christ directly. If they were going to win back public opinion, they needed to meet the public at eye level. And who better to tell biblical stories without any flourish than Caravaggio, whose ability to capture the fabric of real, everyday people gave his work an invaluable appeal. He could paint a scene that was so convincing, you felt as though you were an active participant in the drama. This meant, in theory, one might become an active participant in the bible's stories.

And so we arrive at *The Taking of Christ*.

There are few stories more famous than the crucifixion, and the events leading up to it. It has been retold countless times across writing and art. In Caravaggio's version, he frames it through the elements that tell us a story of living people.

Just outside the city of Jerusalem, Judas kisses Jesus on the cheek, as Roman soldiers charge forward to take him away. And while none of them know it, it is this final act—this kiss of death—that will lead to one of the most symbolic, controversial, and hotly debated moments in the history of theology.

Caravaggio suspends tension across the canvas in seven spectacular ways, and we, the audience, feel every ounce of it when reading the painting. What you might have noticed first is direction. Caravaggio paints seven figures who all seem to be tilted toward the left side of the painting, countered only by the pull of Judas's hand. A hand that grips Christ, I might add, with such intensity you can feel it on your own arm. But it is not only a tool for balance, you see, as Caravaggio is far too clever. The hand of Judas also unveils itself as a form of texture, like a rock plunging into still water, with Christ the only form of calm in the masterpiece, serenely coming to terms with fate. But Judas is only one point of tension. As we pull away from the source, chaos ensues.

The numbing reflection of hard steel juxtaposed by a sea of warm flesh: hot and cold as an effect of both bodily temperature and color. The bright clothes of Christ and his disciples are swallowed whole by a listless death. And you can hear it. Not only the clacking of steel plates, but the scream of uncertain times, and even louder still, the silence of contemplation as the curious bystander off to the right watches the event unfold. He holds a lamp: a source of light in a very dark place. A source of light in a world condemned to sin. And as the scene unfolds, what is likely missed is the greatest form of tension in the entire artwork, which lives directly at the source.

A kiss. An act of love twisted into an act with life-ending consequences, because this is the signal that gives Jesus away, and Judas knew he would do it.

And Christ knew he would too.

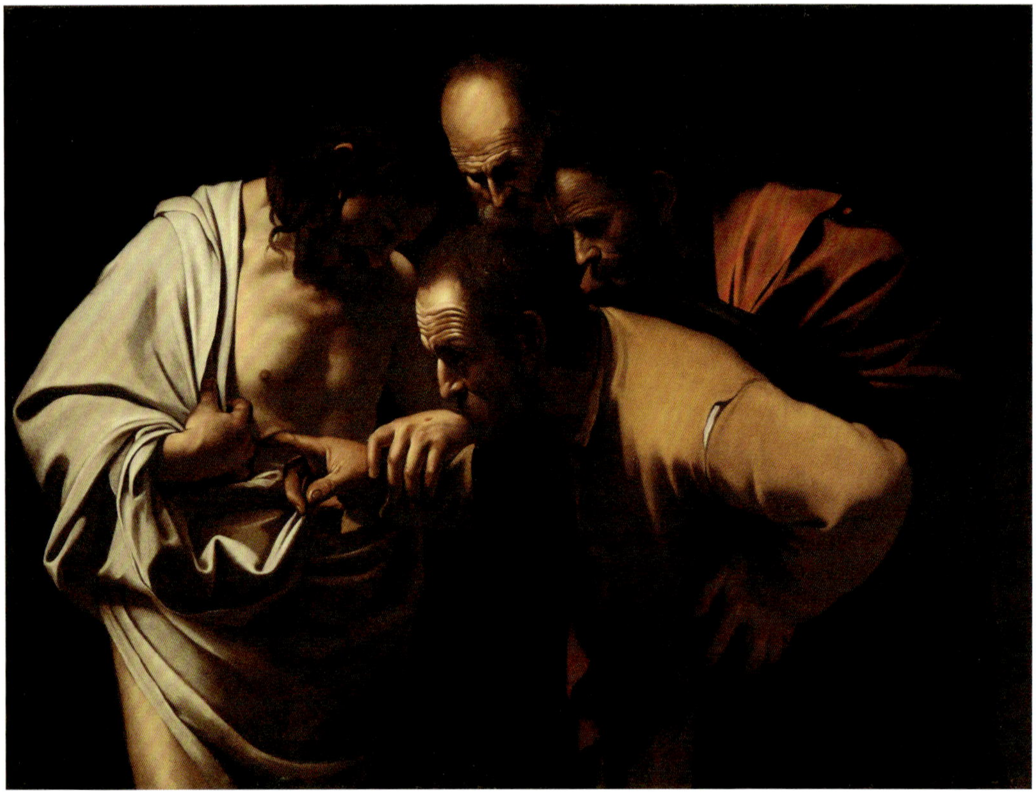

The Incredulity of Saint Thomas

Caravaggio, c. 1601–02

Christ dies on the cross and then rises from the dead, and this is where the man turns to myth.

"This is impossible." This reaction from Thomas seems rational. Because how could Christ resurrect from the dead, as the whispers rumored?

Thomas inspects the marks on Christ's hands, the wound at his midsection, and it is all a little overwhelming. And that is exactly the point. Where most would recount this miracle in a way that feels larger than life, Caravaggio leans into its strangeness. He doesn't need a grandiose setting and religious symbolism—just the natural response of a man in utter disbelief to suspend us in our own.

There are four figures in the painting, and to know where to look between them, simply follow the light. The picture is anchored on the furrowed forehead of Thomas in the front, but light also cascades off the heads of Peter and John behind him, which reveals Caravaggio's first motif: inner dialogue. This painting is not about the mystical, but rather the response it, and the conversion of doubt into faith through the accounts of real people who witnessed a real event. It's puzzling for Thomas especially, and Caravaggio lights his arm to reinforce the expedition of thinking through an impossible riddle.

His arm, as a device, leads us to a second motif, which is again revealed in the light. With one hand, Christ exposes his wounded torso, and with the other he guides the hand of Thomas. The flesh of the immortal touches the flesh of man, and Thomas no longer just sees the miracle: He touches it. It's all so intimate and suddenly, somehow, also possible. And in a way that only Caravaggio would, he underpins it all with a final gesture.

There is no halo over the head of Christ. There is no halo over these three saints. There is nothing supernatural about any of them. Caravaggio paints a real wound and real incredulity, and through this, he shows us a path toward faith. We, like Thomas, are left to use our instruments to decode the spectacular.

Saint Jerome Writing

Caravaggio, c. 1605–06

The story of faith often takes its shape through an understanding of one's own mortality. It is realized in moments of contemplation over the course of an entire life, not just through reading of the mythical.

This idea is a central claim in Caravaggio's work.

Death is an inevitability, as is fear of the void. But in his interpretation of *Saint Jerome Writing*, we can acknowledge that death, as it pertains to the living, is a necessity. It gives contrast to our existence: a realization which can offer moral guidance, and which Caravaggio captures here with his signature mastery.

An image can't speak. And yet, through a series of subtle signals, we observe the wisdom of Saint Jerome with an astonishing clarity. Revered for translating the Bible into Latin, he dedicated his soul to Scripture. Now, though, his age is undeniable. This very same man who, no doubt, was once sprightly and limber, is now reduced to flesh and bone.

And yet he continues to copy passages, which are akin to another breath, another day lived. It is survival in the most spiritual sense, and it's the exact motif required to parallel the fragility of life itself. On the left side of the picture, Caravaggio plays with contrasts again, right there with the skull. It's hard and cold, unlike the warm flesh of the saint who sits a foot away, foreshadowing the impending nature of nature. Jerome is both the flesh and the bone, the living and the dead in tandem, and while the skull might suggest the futility of his efforts, those very efforts adopt immortal qualities through the saint's acceptance of fate. In his limited time on Earth, alive and with free will, Saint Jerome gives it all to something greater than himself.

We can only wish that Caravaggio did the same. And maybe he did, in ways, give everything to his craft, but at what cost? Our beloved Caravaggio was a troubled man. He was imperfect in all of the ways that regular people are. He made art with a profound effect: paintings that challenged moral frameworks. And yet, for all the good that his art would do, for the Church and for the soul, it had little effect on guiding his own decisions. Decisions that would ultimately lead to his downfall, starting around the period he painted Saint Jerome. This image dates to the end of his time in Rome, from which he fled for his life.

For the beginning to Caravaggio's end, we look to one last story.

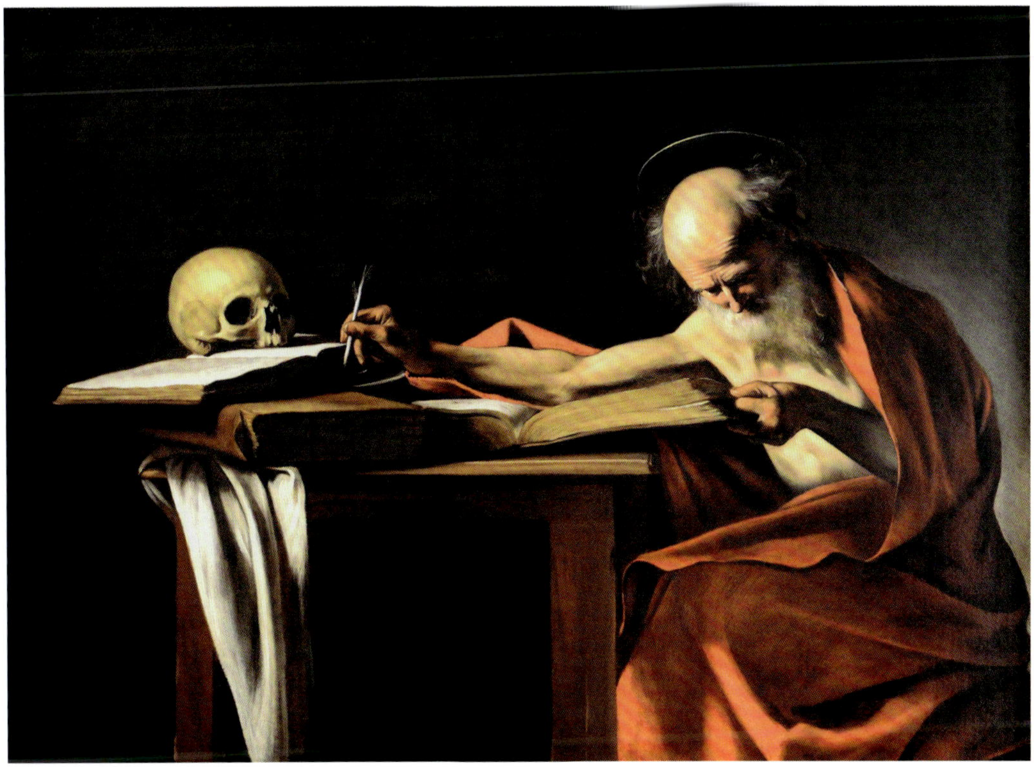

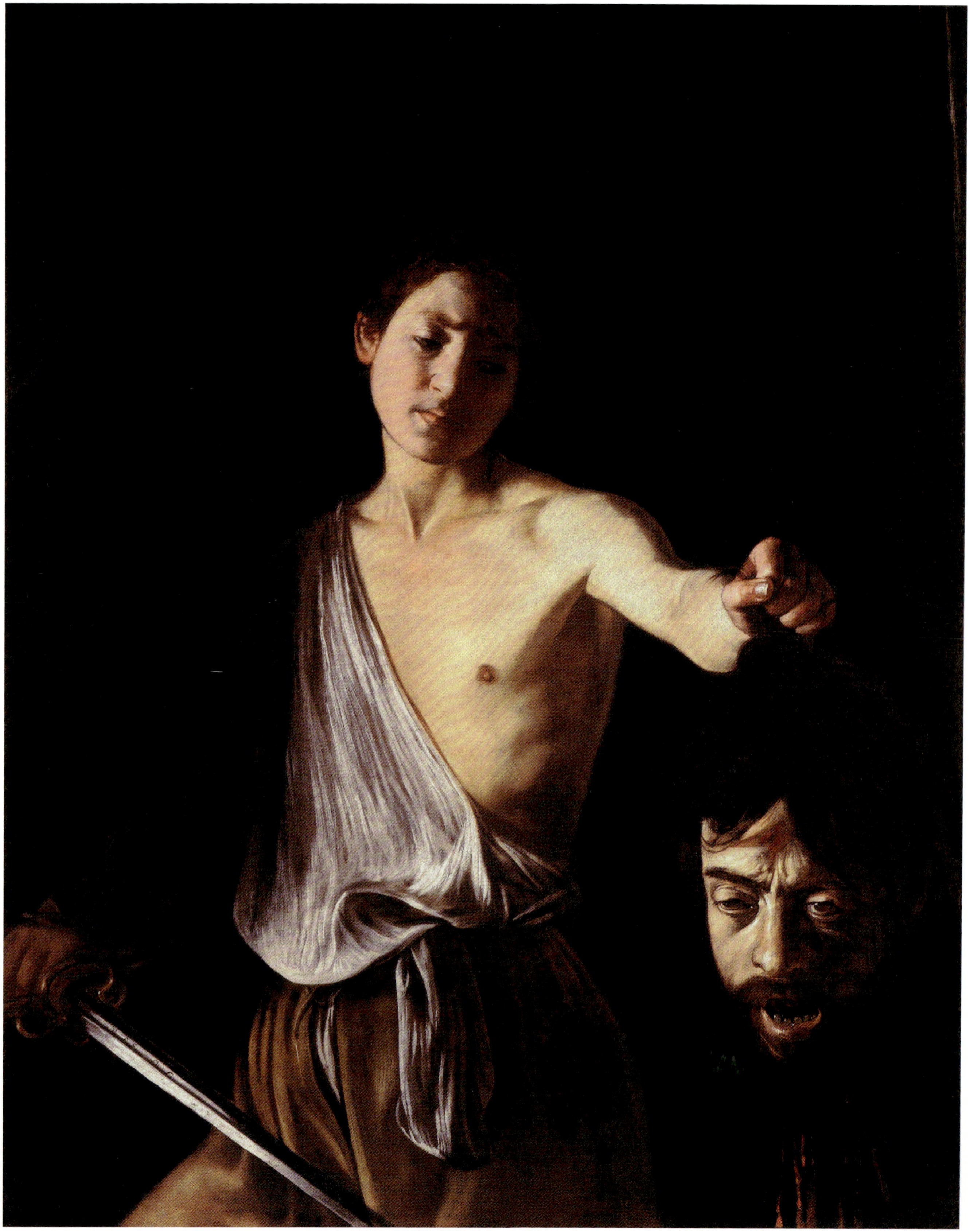

David with the Head of Goliath

Caravaggio, c. 1609–10

You probably know the reference immediately: the biblical telling of David and Goliath, executed through Caravaggio's dramatic signature style—fitting for such an important event.

There is so much happening in the picture, but the easy interpretation would be to say that the painting represents the triumph of good over evil. One glance at David's face, though, and we see everything but elation. In fact, his expression appears akin to pity—a moral dilemma of sorts—and on its own, this presents a fascinating question about good and evil. Where does one draw the line as it pertains to justice?

If we scan the painting further, we'll notice some markings on David's sword. *H-AS OS*, an abbreviation of *Humilitas occidit superbiam*. Humility kills pride. And in the wild world of overthinking, where we can plug that phrase into some historical context, this painting might actually be a plea for forgiveness, because it is widely held that this piece was created after Caravaggio was banished from Rome for murder.

The painter killed Ranuccio Tomassoni during a duel that escalated from a brawl, either over a tennis match bet or a woman. The exact disagreement doesn't really matter. Tomassoni's death would mark the beginning of the end for one of history's greatest painters. And who, in this incident's wake, did Caravaggio give this painting to? A cardinal, possibly as a bribe for a pardon.

This makes even more sense when you consider that the head of Goliath is portrayed as a self-portrait of Caravaggio himself.

As the records tell us, however, the artist's bribe didn't buy his return to Rome. Instead, Caravaggio traveled to Malta where he wounded Giovanni Rodomonte Roero, and again had to flee. What irony: He made a career of giving the Church back its political power, and in the end, that political power is useless to him. His art was a hand for rebuilding influence, but like the Church he helped, he was undone by his own human imperfections.

A conduit of scripture, and a conduit of humanity's worst impulses, recorded together on canvases that both reflected and shaped the world he lived in.

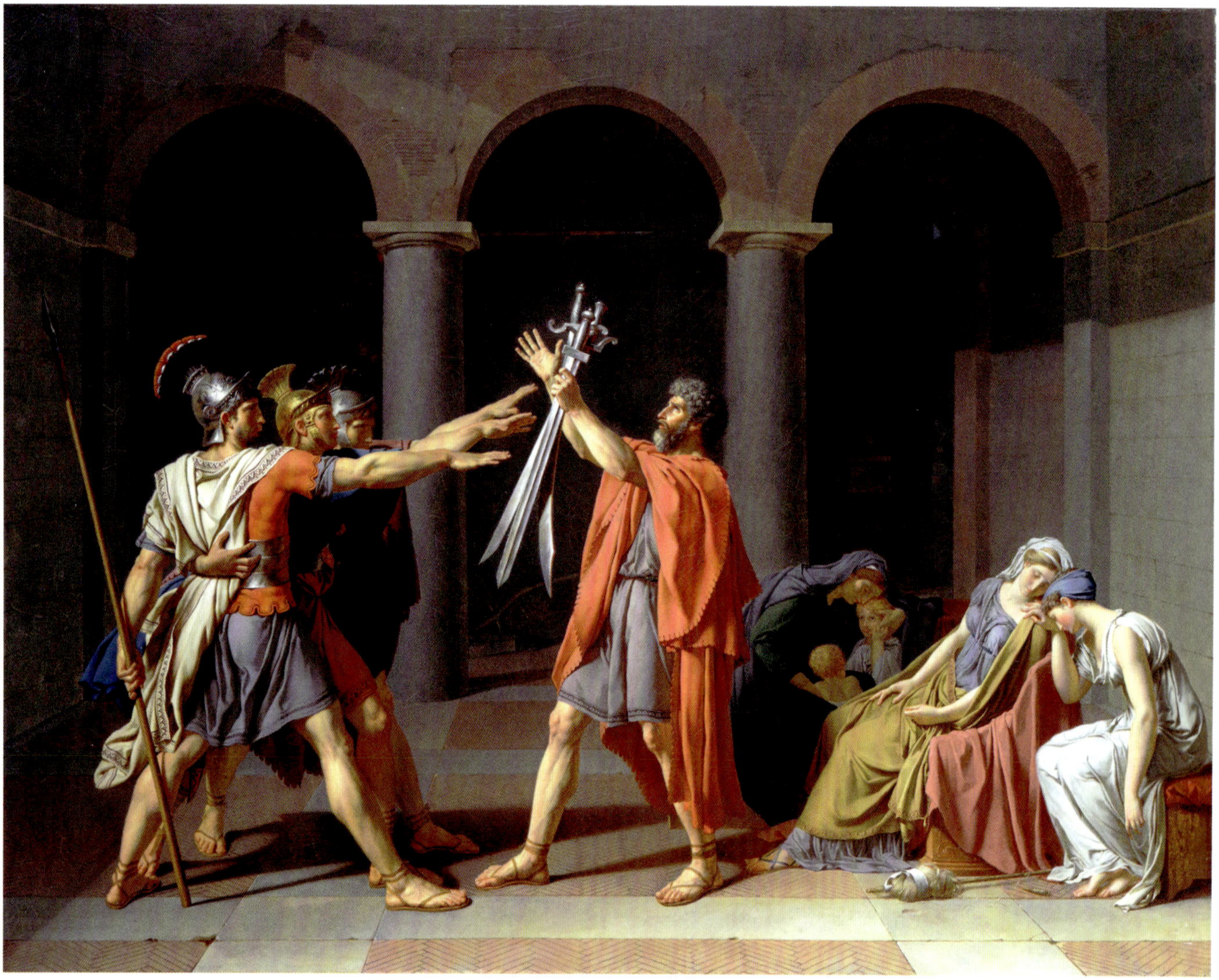

Oath of the Horatii

Jacques-Louis David, 1784

We've explored two strikingly different examples of how power across Europe drastically changed, and the fate of the artists within those currents: Goya's world, and its deterioration, as a result of war; Caravaggio's world, and its deterioration, by way of influence. The powers that painters help create and the worlds they build on and off the canvas do not destroy all great artists, however. Enter Jacques-Louis David. A man who, funnily enough, lived through almost the exact same years as Goya, to the north in France, where he painted at the helm of grand political powers and their shifts.

David was the defining painter of the French Revolution and the Napoleonic Era, and arguably the single most influential European artist of the late eighteenth and early nineteenth centuries. He engineered the visual language of modern political powers, and more than just a painter, he was an architect of ideology. His works served as a visual propaganda for an entire political revolution, crystalizing the heroic style that became the aesthetic backbone for a power shift in France.

Think about that: an entire nation persuaded by the brush of a single man. I know that it sounds bold, but it's true. He was the imperial painter to Napoleon. He sculpted the general's image to that of the ultimate modern ruler, and not through a documentation of events, but rather, through deliberate heroic fabrications. Through razor-sharp contours and an unmatched sculptural clarity. Through cold, moralistic lighting and arrangements of compositions that feel like stage sets. Jacques-Louis David reshaped how art and power interact, and his work would become the visual ancestor for every political propaganda image from the nineteenth century onward.

To appreciate his full impact, however, it helps to start with his early career.

In *Oath of the Horatii*, a pre-Revolution moral drama and prototype for propaganda, we are witnessing a death sentence. At least, for two of these three Horatii brothers, who've been elected to fight three Curiatii brothers in the name of Rome. A victory for the Horatii means a victory for the state: an honor of unprecedented measure. And yet, in a painting that appears to be about the bravery of duty, Jacques-Louis David tells us that instead, this might be a painting about its costs: the levy of sacrifice in the name of the greater good.

Three separate sections divide the picture into what feels like three separate phases, each with one distinct element of the same motif. On the left we have the brothers, stone cold, emotionless, and undeniably brave, demonstrating the traits required of selfless devotion to the greater good at any and all costs, including one's own life. In the center, we have a father whose contribution to the state is as great as any. He gives three swords to his three boys, offering up his blood to Rome. On the right we see weeping women: the human soul enduring the weight of sacrifice. Because these aren't just any women, but the sisters and the wives of warriors.

On the left, dressed in blue and yellow, is the wife of one of the Horatii. Beside her is Camilla, sister of the Horatii and the fiancée of one of the Curiatii brothers: her own brothers' enemies.

As fate would have it, out of the men who will fight, only one Horatii brother will survive, at the cost of the five other men. Five lives paid for a Roman victory. Five tributes given to the gods. A father left without his sons, all in the name of Rome.

"Cursed Rome," Camilla will weep upon her brother's return from battle. Because Publius, the sole survivor, will return draped with the bloodstained cloth of her beloved fiancé, woven by her own hands.

Her tears cost Camilla her life. Out of anger at this perceived betrayal, and for the crime of weeping for the enemy, Publius murders his sister on the spot. The cost of duty. The cost of war. A sacrifice for the greater good of Rome.

The Death of Socrates

Jacques-Louis David, 1787

In 1787, Jacques-Louis sentences another person to death. But this is *not* an execution.

It is instead the story of one of the most poetic deaths in the history of both painting and philosophy. Because in his final minutes of life, Socrates, who has been sentenced to death by poison, seizes an important opportunity to impart a very valuable lesson.

He was a man who practised what he preached, and through his challenges to the mortal world around him, he acquired very powerful enemies. Some of whom, when their beliefs were challenged, felt that a world without Socrates would be a far better place.

He was arrested, tried, and found guilty of impiety and corrupting Athens' youth. With such a verdict hanging over our own heads, many of us might plead for our innocence—or at the very least, beg for exile. For his part, Socrates simply accepted the verdict, because betraying his own philosophical being was the only cause worthy of death. When offered a chance to request his punishment, he responded so outlandishly that he sealed his fate, and when he was offered opportunities to bribe officials to escape, he cheerfully declined.

"But, Matthew, how does that make this painting any more poetic?"

Because, my friends, this is not just a painting, but a memory. Of course, not from the mind of Socrates, but from the man who recounted the entire event so that we know about it today. Plato was only a young man when his teacher took his final breath, but Jacques-Louis David depicts him, sitting at the foot of the bed, as someone old enough to reflect on the possibility that Socrates might have had it right when he chose to walk across that bridge, on toward the unknown. Among the perfect details and the exquisitely orchestrated composition of this masterpiece, which has inspired generations of artists, it is this idea that matters. Because it tells us that Socrates's conviction was a wisdom worth holding.

In his unwavering bravery in the last moments of his life, Socrates imparted the wisdom necessary for us to live our own lives fearlessly, right until the end.

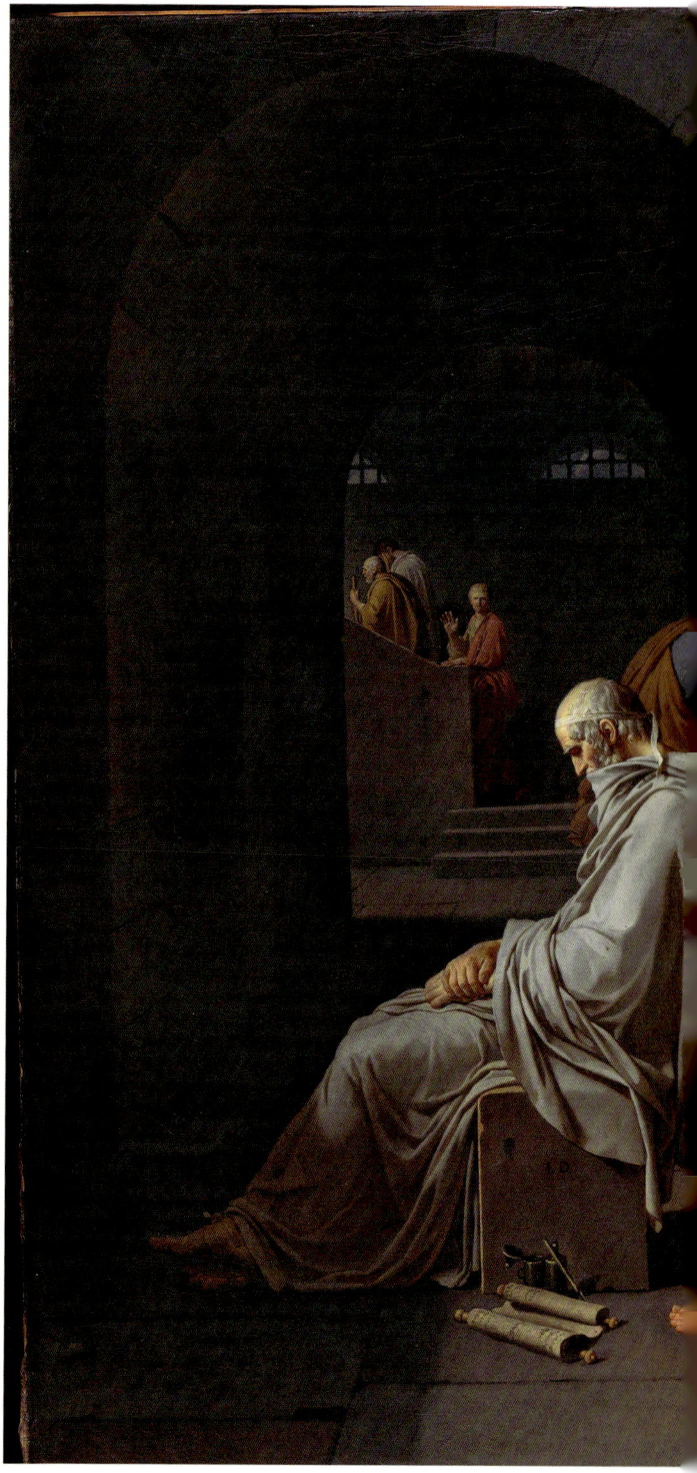

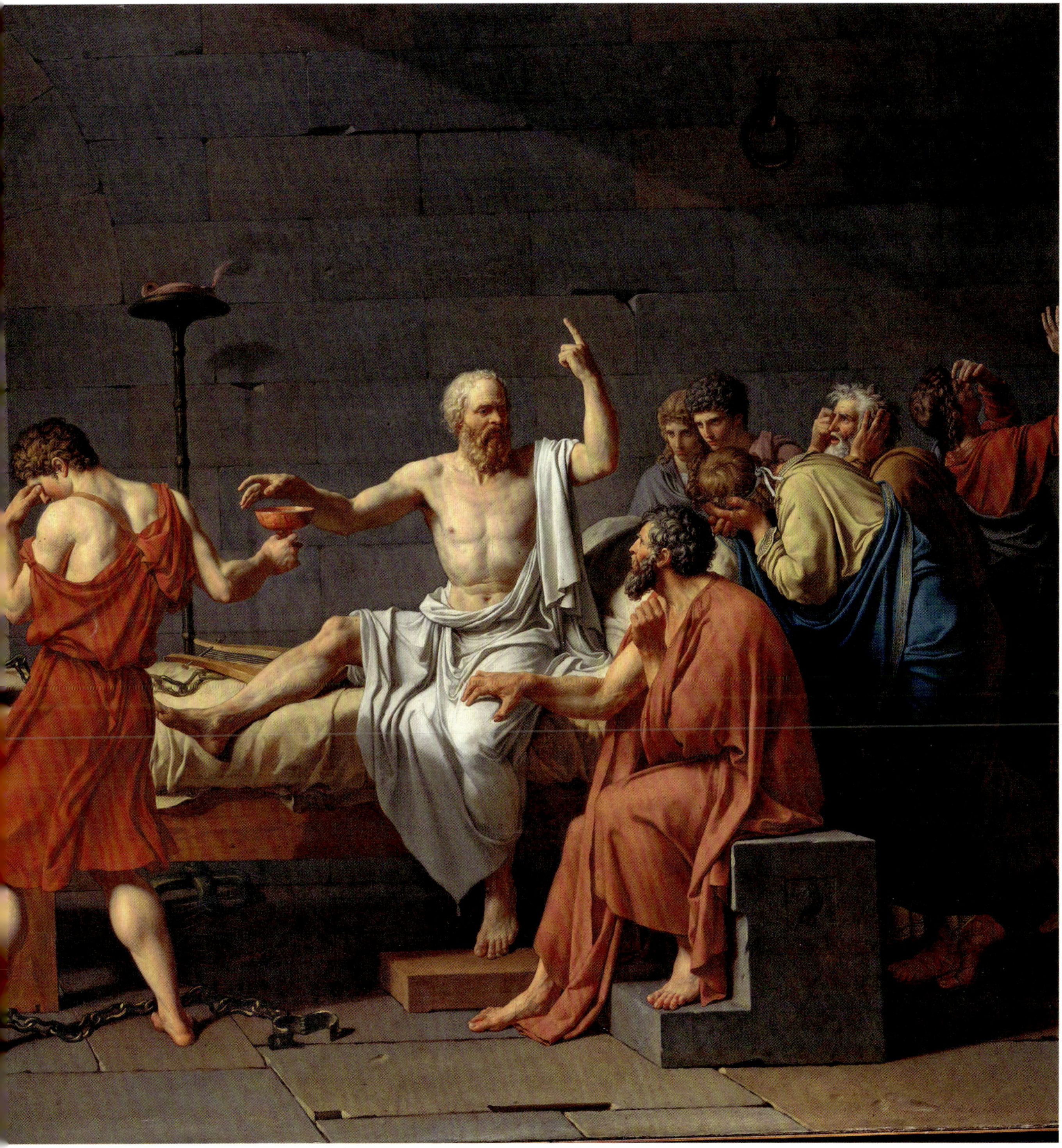

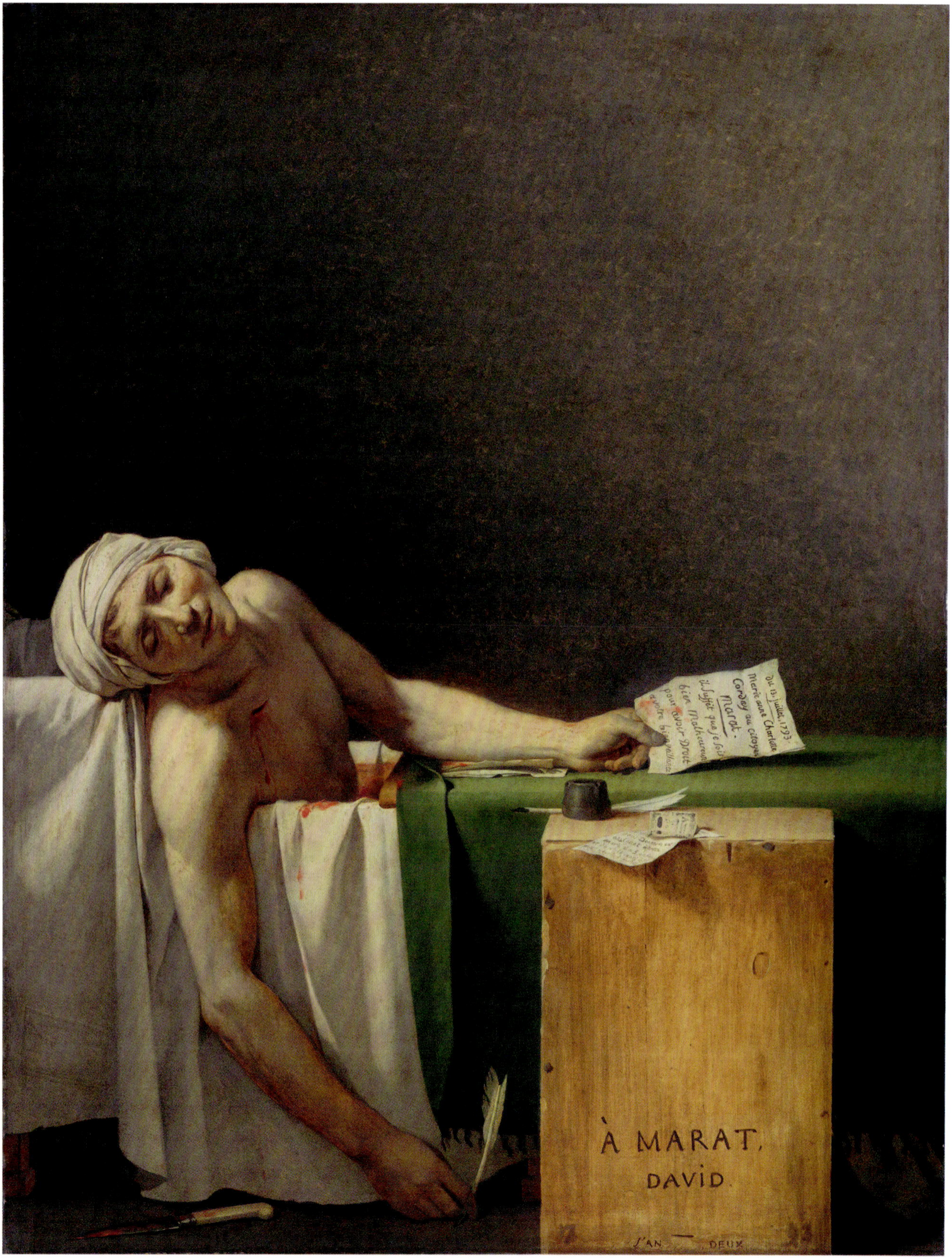
Du 13 juillet, 1793.
Marie anne Charlotte
Corday au citoyen
Marat.
il suffit que je soi
bien malheureu
pour avoir Droit
À MARAT,
DAVID
L'AN DEUX

The Death of Marat

Jacques-Louis David, 1793

Oath of the Horatii and *The Death of Socrates* are among history's greatest masterpieces, and yet, these two paintings only mark the beginning for Jacques-Louis David and his impact. *The Death of Marat*, while not his first "politically charged" painting, would be his first fully realized artwork that covered the French Revolution, and it would go down as one of the greatest political images ever produced.

To execute it, David took one of the most divisive political scandals in history and turned it into a religious symbol on the scale of Michelangelo's *Pietà* (1498). *The Death of Marat* captures the assassination of Jean-Paul Marat, a polarizing figure of the Revolution who was seen by many as a voice for the common people, and by others as a radical, bloodthirsty tyrant. Jacques-Louis capitalized on this moment of ideological martyrdom that sent shockwaves through France to send his own shockwaves through the annals of art history.

He takes a gruesome scene and plays on our instincts for sympathy. Pietà, Italian for pity or compassion, is exactly what you feel when you look at this painting in its entirety. The soft skin of Marat and the delicacy of his face force our hand: We feel remorse. The negative space used to capture a warm spotlight suggests the divine nature of the moment, reinforced by our figure's resemblance to Christ's body after being removed from the cross, a symbol for selfless sacrifice. The weight of the large, soft green cloth, which occupies a sizable portion of the composition, is perfectly visually balanced against the jarring red spatters of blood seen on the white cloth hanging from the side of the tub, on the chest of the central figure, in the water, and on the murder weapon, which lies on the ground.

It is a level of balance created entirely through well understood and well executed fundamentals, which David uses to challenge our own morality, and some of us are knocked off our feet.

For me, it is his most powerful work of art. It's not over complicated, and therefore, hits the nail on the head. It perfectly captures the gruesome nature of political strife without trying to over deliver on its promises. We sympathize with the man in the tub without any consideration for who the man is, or what he believes. Without any context, he's defenseless, and we don't judge. It's only after we learn about who he is that we might begin to formulate an opinion, but at that point, it's almost too late to matter. Wherever your beliefs lie, the image of a man murdered in a bathtub outweighs the nature of his beliefs, because no man deserves to be slain in cold blood. But I digress.

While I have always felt that this is David's greatest work of art, I can see why others might not agree. In fact, many may point to his coverage of Napoleon instead, on a brilliant white horse, crossing the Alps: a powerful piece of propaganda that masquerades as a portrait.

To understand its power, though, we'll need the slightest bit of context.

Napoleon Crossing the Alps

Jacques-Louis David, 1801

In May 1800, Napoleon crossed the Great St. Bernard Pass with his army to surprise the Austrian forces in Italy. However, unlike in this painting, Napoleon did *not* ride a rearing stallion, and instead, crossed the Alps on a mule while sporting a thick winter coat, accompanied by a guide.

David paints the exact opposite.

We see Napoleon as calm, composed, and under control. He wears a heroic uniform and mounts a powerful stallion, wind whipping his cloak in dramatic fashion. The nature that surrounds him is jagged, cold, and in turmoil, but he takes the shape of an immovable object. His horse is overly muscular, the white of its eye an exaggeration, highlighting that it's untamed, and yet Napoleon controls his mount with a single hand: the visual equivalent of commanding the entire world. He doesn't point forward, but to the sky: a statement of destiny and not direction, which aligns him with the divine and the historically inevitable. It is a pose David borrows from equestrian statues of Roman emperors.

At the bottom of the image, you might have noticed a few names carved into the rocks: Hannibal, Karolus Magnus, and Bonaparte. David places Napoleon beside ancient empire builders, and in doing so, declares him to be the next conqueror of the world. A man cut of the same cloth—and speaking of cloth, look at his cloak. It is so classically statuesque, as though it has been carved from stone, and it is pulled upward by a wind that is intentionally unreal. Nature is in full revolt, but Napoleon, on his steed, is unaffected. And this is where David takes a step into the halls of greatness, because he doesn't just subliminally influence our feelings about Napoleon through the painting's physical attributes. By arranging them as he does, he makes those suggestions undeniable.

The horse and cloak form a strong diagonal vortex within the composition, while Napoleon serves as a powerful vertical axis: a play on the geometric properties of the work that scream of heroism under pressure. He lights the scene theatrically, spotlighting Napoleon as a sort of stage actor, and we no longer see the work as a product of rational art-making, but instead, as a weaponization of art: as a part of the propaganda machinery—and it's executed so convincingly, it forever reshaped how Napoleon is viewed. This is the progenitor of every image of Napoleon that ever came after it, from coins, to statues, to prints, to Hollywood movies, and beyond.

But believe it or not, some would argue we still haven't seen David's best work…

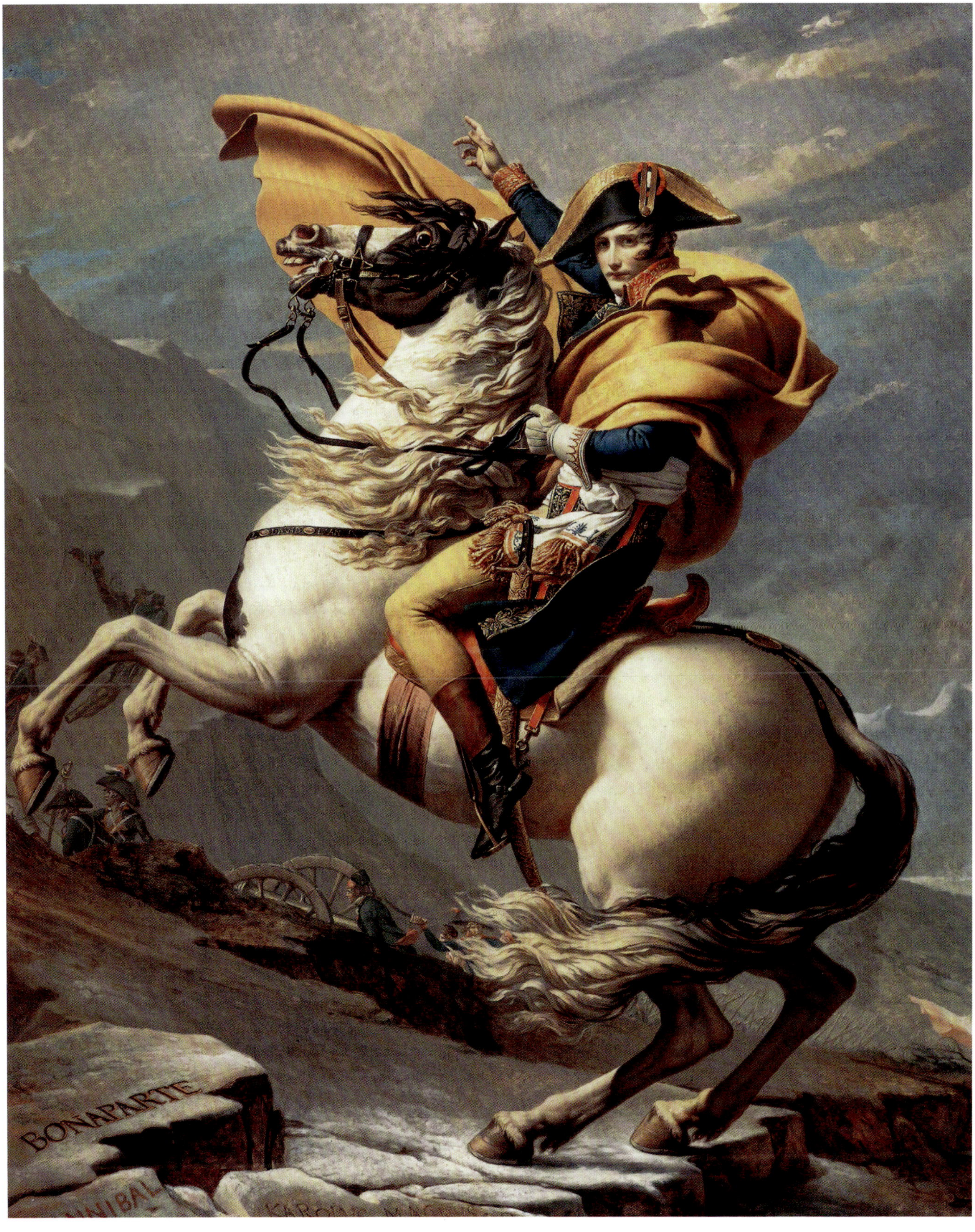
BONAPARTE

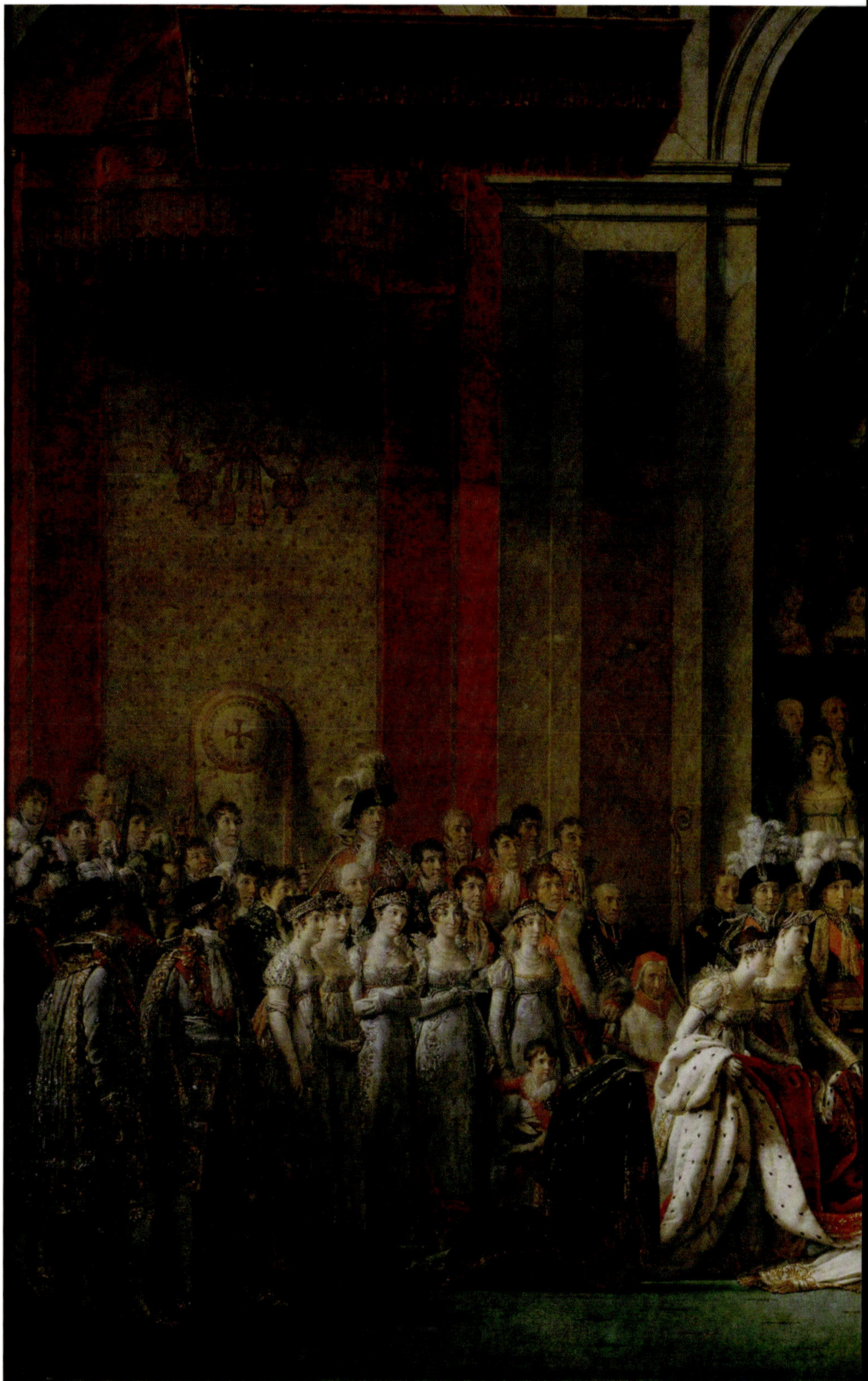

The Coronation of Napoleon, Jacques-Louis David, 1805–07

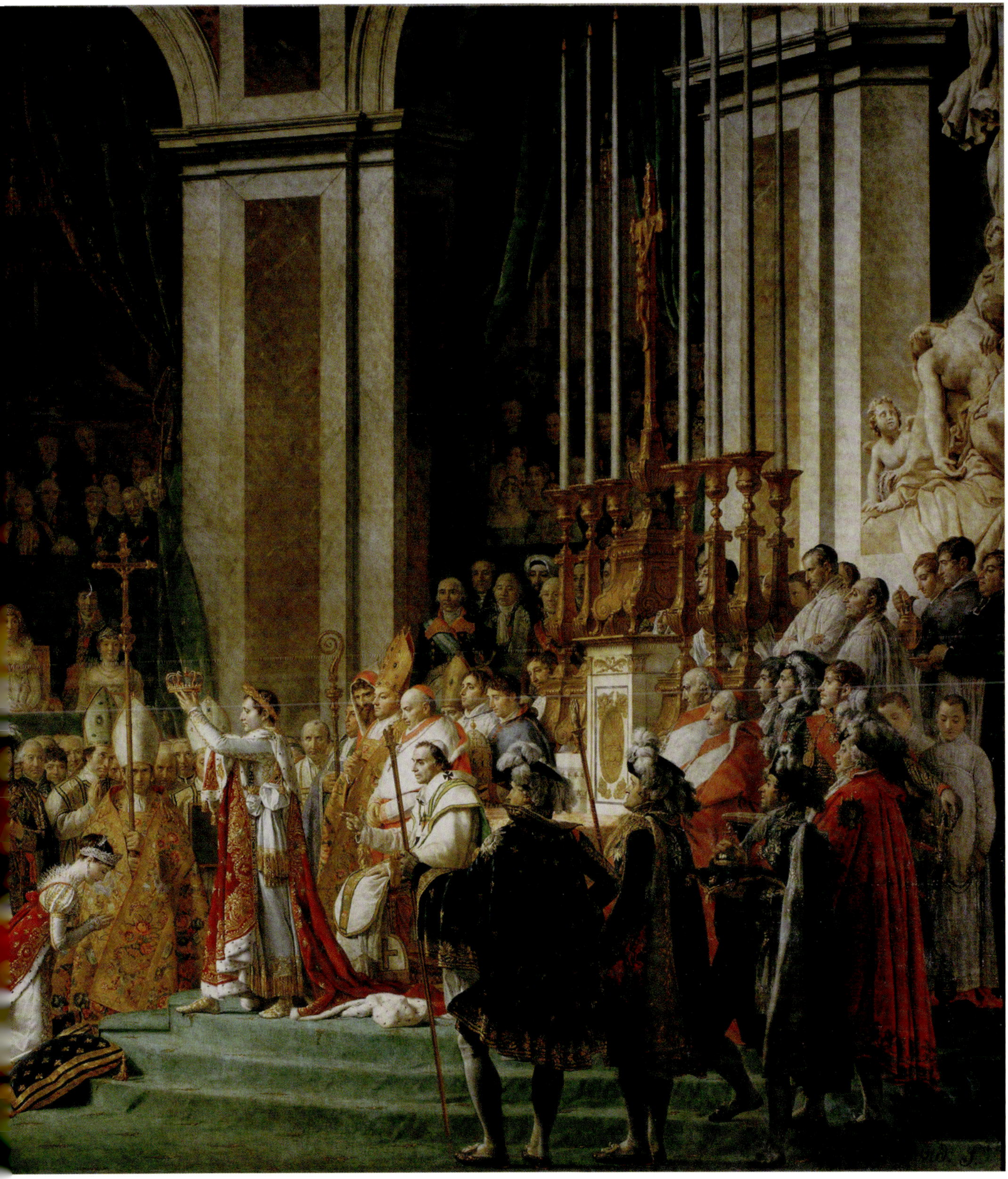

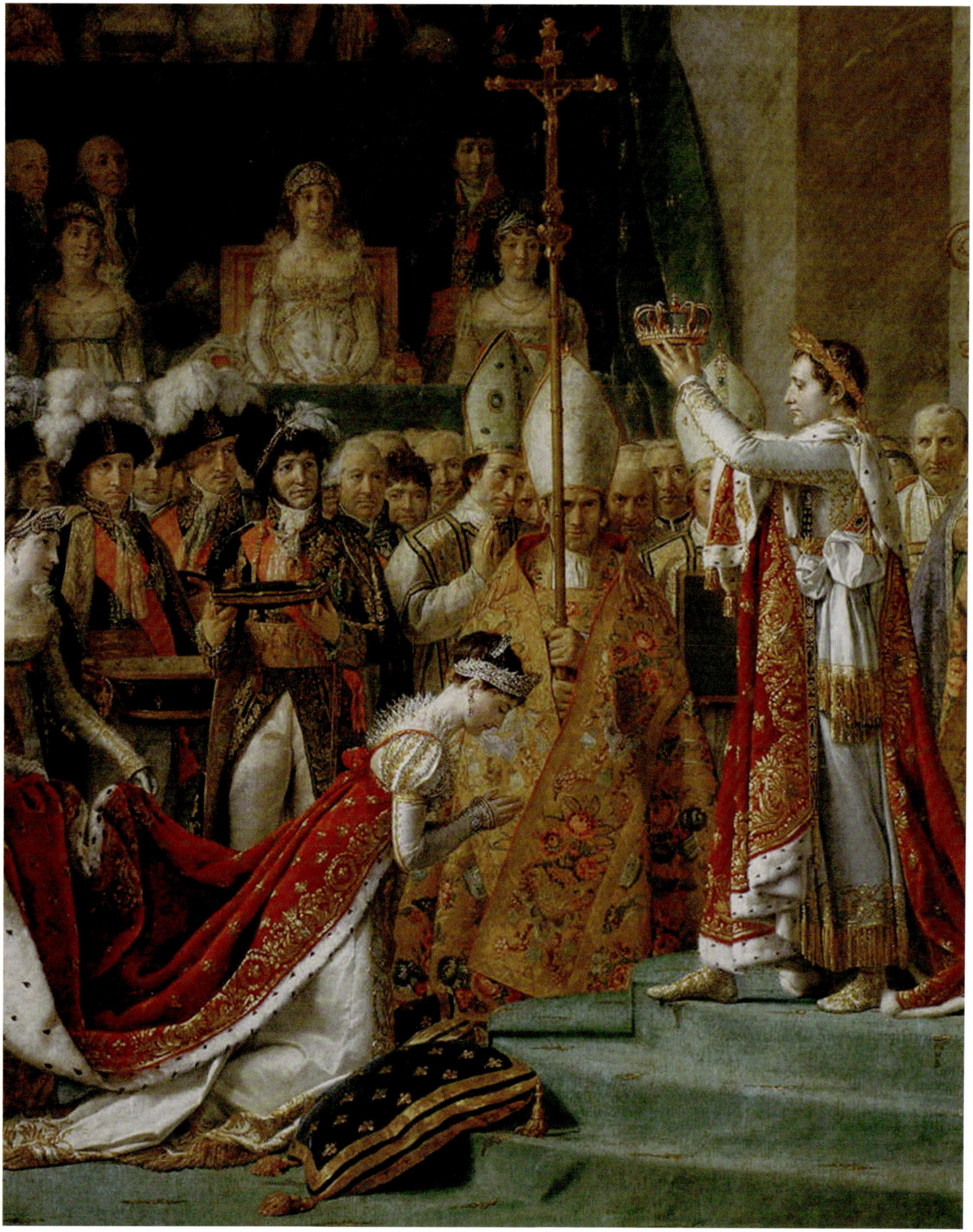

The Coronation of Napoleon

Jacques-Louis David, 1805–07

It is an artwork so big, it swallows you whole: an enormous 32 × 20 foot masterpiece, commissioned by Napoleon himself, which rewrote history in real time. The birth of a new imperial order.

On 2 December, 1804, Napoleon was crowned the Emperor of the French inside Paris's Notre-Dame. This painting of that day is not a snapshot of reality, though. It is a curated myth, crafted to legitimize Napoleon's rule, align him with the grandeur of ancient Rome, and to rewrite the power dynamics between Church and State. Now, what *is* true is that he did in fact crown himself. Pope Pius VII was present at the coronation, but Napoleon took the crown from the altar and placed it on his own head, and he did it intentionally to humiliate the Church. His power came from his own doings: It was not given to him by God or tradition.

In the painting, David modifies this: Napoleon isn't crowning himself, but is instead crowning his wife, Josephine. By choosing to highlight this moment instead, David does three things. Firstly, he softens Napoleon's arrogance. Where self-coronation looks tyrannical, by crowning Josephine, Napoleon looks noble and chivalric. Secondly, David highlights imperial stability. Josephine symbolizes continuity, grace, and a dynasty. Lastly, he centers Napoleon as a moral, orderly emperor. In this painting, he doesn't look like a usurper but instead an anointed ruler, conducting a solemn ritual. This is propaganda at its most intelligent.

Now let's have a closer look at individual characters in the artwork. First, Napoleon, at the center of it all. Dressed in imperial robes modeled after Roman emperors and Carolingian kings, he stands tall with arms raised in a gesture of controlled theatrical command. David idealizes him physically, and for a moment, we might even be tricked into believing we are looking at a Roman emperor, not a French one. Josephine kneels on a raised platform. Draped in white satin and gold, she is covered from neck to toe in embroidery. Her hands are gently folded, and she becomes the moral heart of the composition: a symbol of purity and legitimacy. To the right of them both, the Pope. See if you can spot him.

In the original drawings of the image, the Pope was pictured with his hands crossed in his lap, but Napoleon objected. Allegedly, he claimed that the Pope was not present to do nothing and instructed that he should anoint the proceedings, and it's almost what we get. In the final picture, Pope Pius VII is depicted as mentally present, visible, and passive. His hand is lifted, not necessarily as an act of blessing, but in a way that feels like a polite acknowledgement. What he is *not* doing is crowning Napoleon, controlling the ritual, or acting as a source of authority. In David's painting, the Church watches and does not dictate.

Napoleon's mother is also in the painting, but it's important to note that on the day of the coronation, she was not in attendance. She refused to come due to familial drama. Napoleon ordered that she appear in the work anyway, and David seats her in the place of highest honor. Try and guess which figure she is.

David surrounds the central scene with cardinals, marshals, court officials, Napoleon's siblings, and the grand society of the new empire, and each figure is its own miniature portrait: over 200 likenesses painted with a forensic accuracy, organized in a painting that's modeled like a Roman relief. A horizontal procession, a vertical power axis, and architectural arches, which frame authority. And all of this revolves around the central symbolic triangle of Napoleon, the Pope, and Josephine.

The painting served its purpose beautifully. It was meant to act as a visual constitution of Napoleon's empire, and it legitimized his crowning, diminished the Church's authority, aligned the new emperor with other great leaders, and presented France as the center of European civilization. It became another of Napoleon's defining images and influenced European court portraiture for the decades that followed.

THE LONELY WORLD OF EDWARD HOPPER

I was once told that to look at a painting by Edward Hopper is to look at the three states of living: alone, with someone, or working. It was one of the most striking ideas I've ever heard, because it highlighted, in that moment, that Hopper might have understood what it really is to be a person, better than any other artist. His works remind us that we always return to solitude, even when we're not alone.

Nighthawks

Edward Hopper, 1942

There is no painting on earth quite like Edward Hopper's *Nighthawks*.

And frankly, there has never been an artist quite like Edward Hopper. A man whose entire body of work can be ground down to the realization that in a world full of interaction, we are always alone. We can sit on a boat with friends, and at the exact same time, contemplate in complete isolation. We can entertain company at a restaurant and listlessly wander off in our thoughts. Hopper shows us the deafening power of silence in a moment of introspection, boredom, duty, curiosity, or doubt. He reminds us of the age-old tale of serving oneself, and oneself alone, in a world built through collaboration. And while we can turn to any one of Hopper's paintings to explore the themes of loneliness, it is only in *Nighthawks* that we, the audience, participate in it.

The painting depicts a diner, at the corner of an empty street, late into the night. Inside, we have four distinct characters: the couple, the barman, and the lonely patron. Four people, sitting in the same room, completely isolated from one another, living only within the confines of their own thoughts. But they are not the only ones who are alone.

The genius of *Nighthawks* is the insulation of its figures, within the confines of a doorless diner. It is us, the audience, who are left to our own devices, in the observation of the artwork, to wonder in silence. We are welcomed to participate in Edward Hopper's lonely universe, but not quite invited inside to disturb it.

It's a much different approach to what Hopper would do with *Automat*.

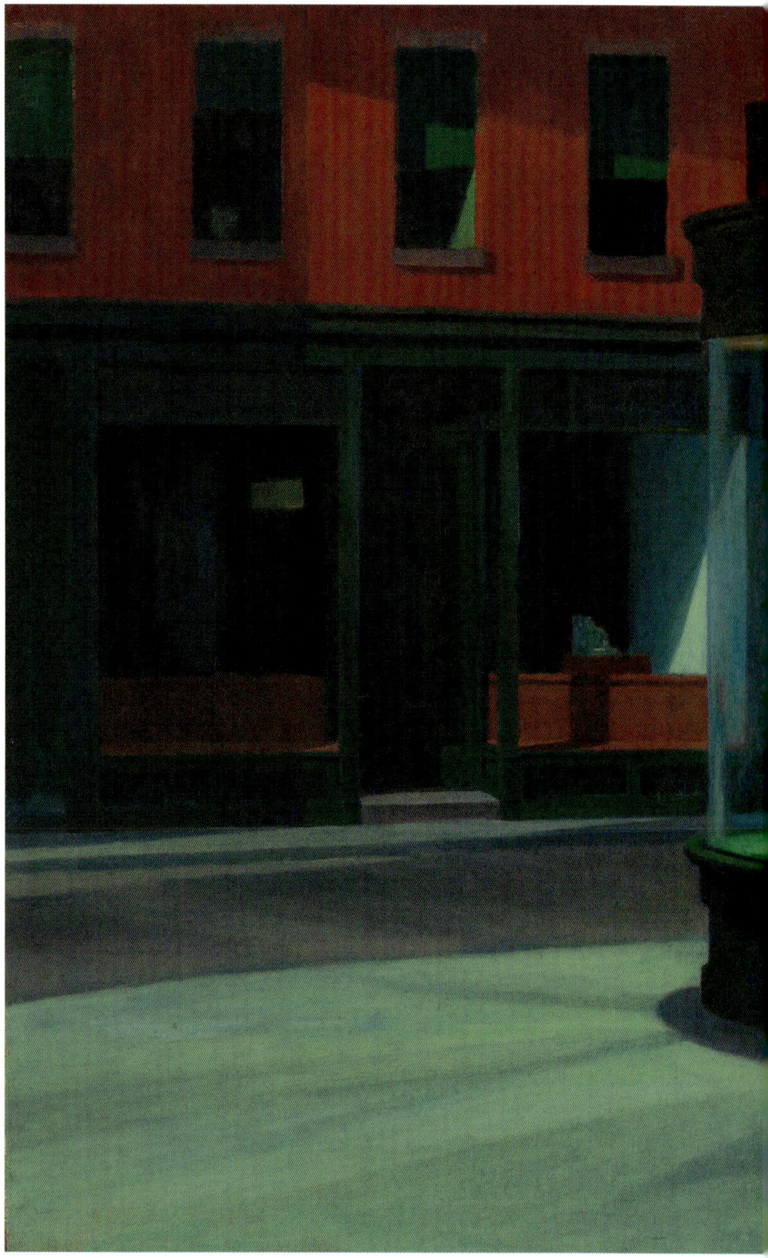

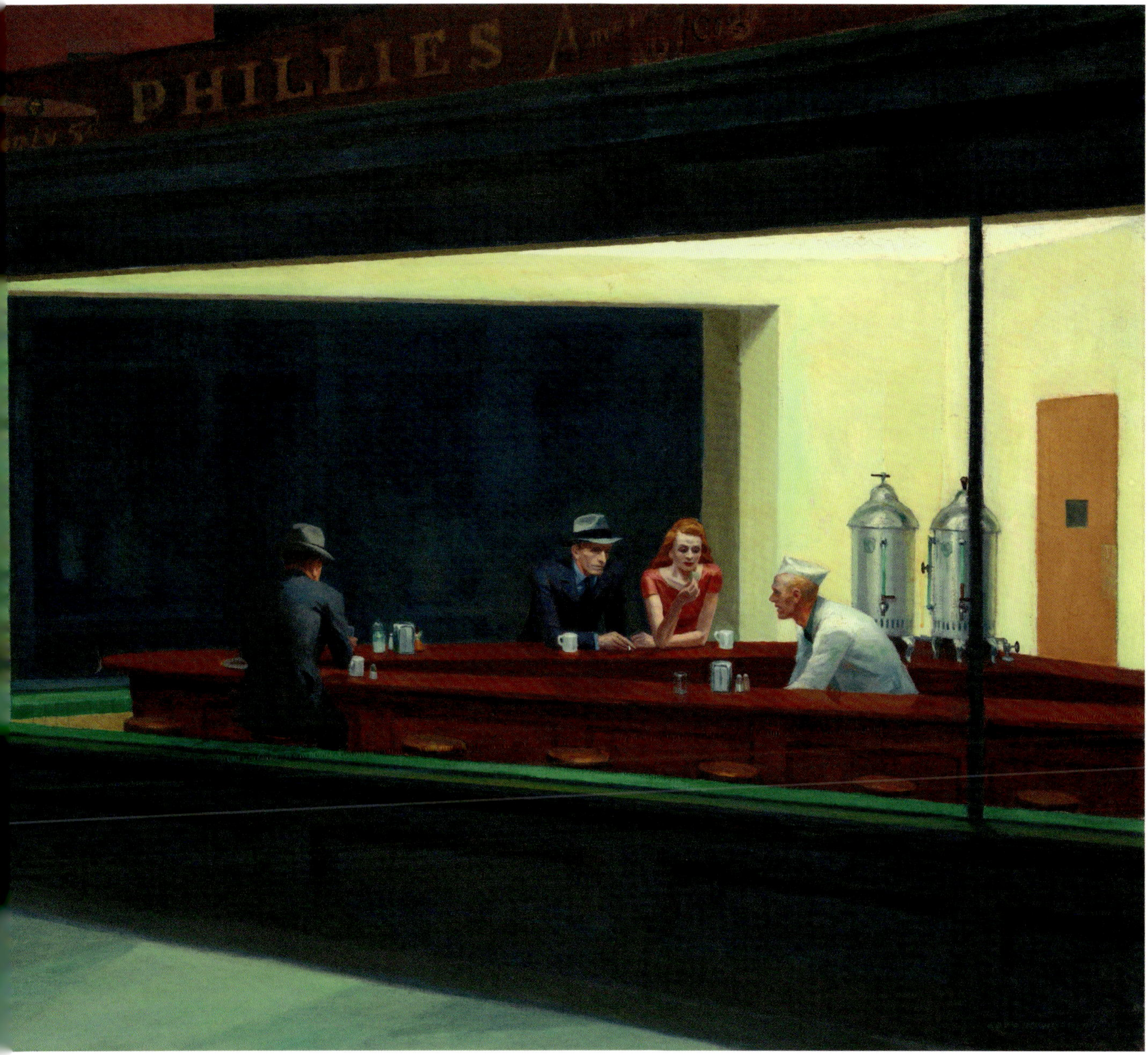
PHILLIES

Automat

Edward Hopper, 1927

In a body of work rooted in a need to look "in"—to a window, a person, a situation, or ourselves—it is in this painting, and this painting alone, that Hopper suspends us inside. We find ourselves no longer peeking in, but trapped instead. And unlike in his other works, this isn't a loneliness of deep contemplation or sadness. Not one of remorse, guilt, or self-reflection. It is, instead, a loneliness akin to that of an unmuffled silence, and an unprecedented observation.

We don't know much about her, the woman with the orangey–yellow hat. We can't tell if she's just arrived, or just about to leave. We don't know if she's been here for a while or only for just a minute. But what we can say for sure, is that she *is*, and we *are*. Hovering in the space, her presence is undeniable.

In other works by Hopper, our ability to interfere is guarded: by a window in *Nighthawks*, a desk in *Office at Night* (1940), an arrangement of seats and a balcony in *Two on the Aisle* (1927), and even a bright distraction in *Morning Sun* (1952). In the automat, however, we are left to our own intuitions.

And we do absolutely nothing, because why would we? Just like the woman, we find ourselves trapped. The giant window in the background, a cascade of fluid darkness, gives us no indication of a world outside. Only a reflection of what is within. And where our human dispositions leave us always wanting what we can't have—with the urge to break through the "figurative boundaries" of people and pry into what we're not privy to for a bit of escapism—it is here, in this automat, that we don't try.

We certainly can. We probably should. But we won't. Instead, we just watch.

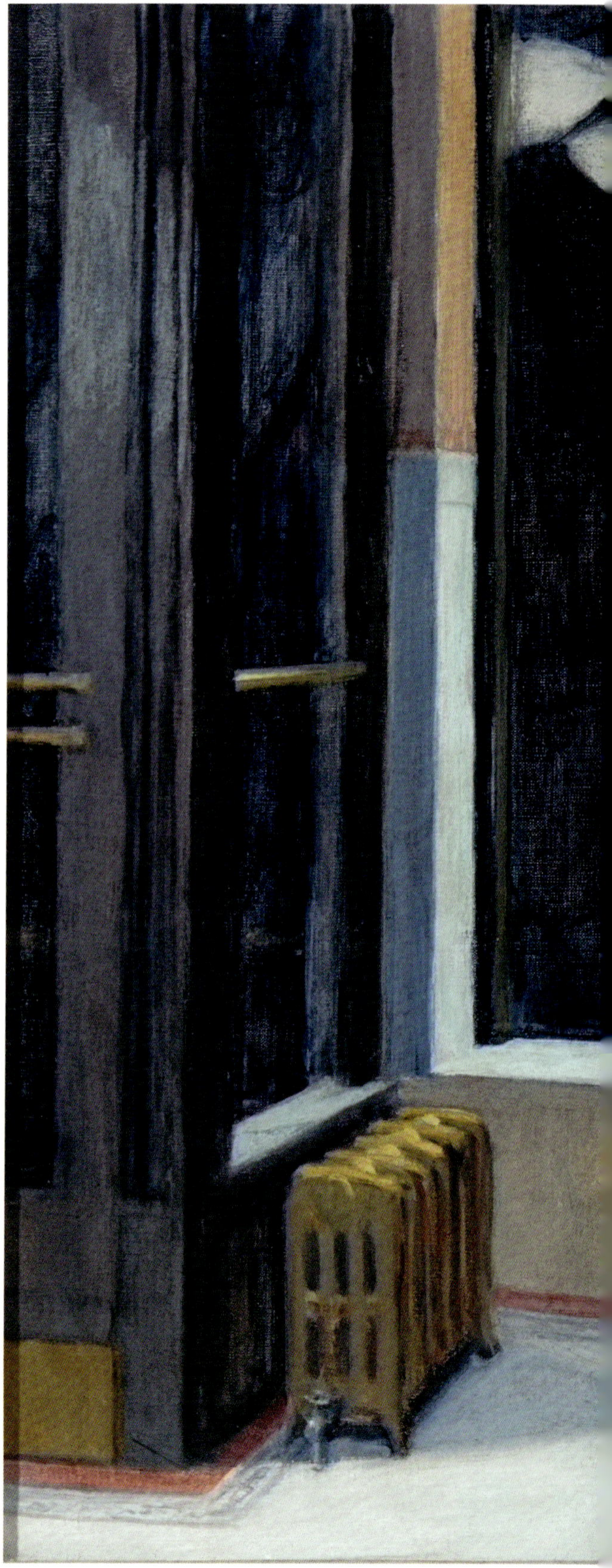

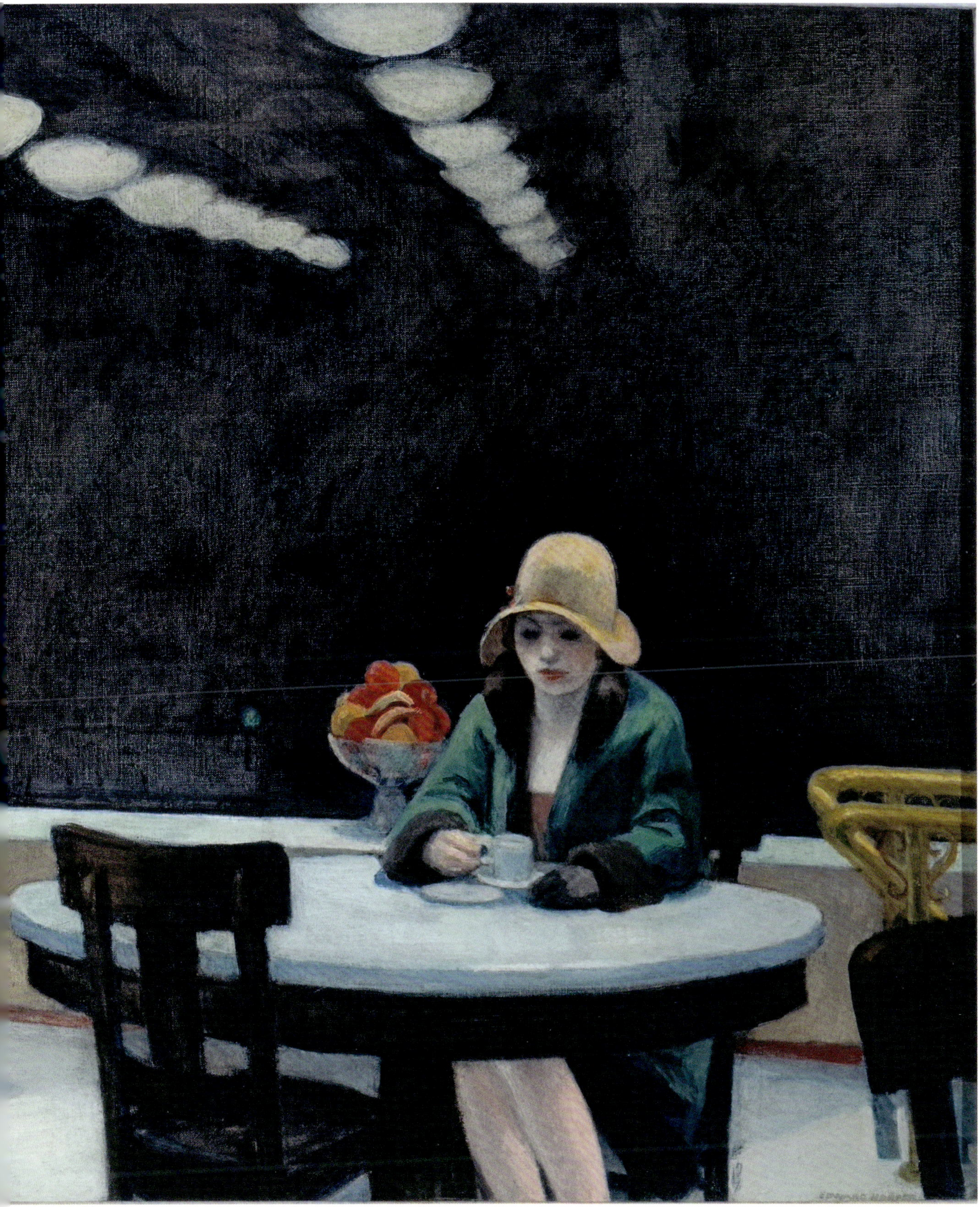

Chop Suey

Edward Hopper, 1929

Imagine sitting in a restaurant right across from a friend and not saying anything at all. We've all been there, right? Wandering off into the distance, on autopilot. You're listening, but not *actively*, instead actively pretending as you sift through a thousand thoughts.

In our world that is designed for spontaneity and interaction, Edward Hopper leads us to short bursts of introspection, and yet in this painting, unlike many of his others, there's *nothing quiet about it*.

Do you hear the atmosphere of a busy restaurant? The muffled sounds of cars passing by outside? The clattering of cutlery on plates and teacups touching coasters? Somehow, you can look at this painting and hear every sound *but* the sound of chatter. Not a single whisper from a fellow human being. You don't feel like you're eavesdropping into a conversation, but rather you're just sort of hovering around.

It's kind of genius, don't you think? Art is intentional, and Hopper uses the motif of atmosphere and sound to hammer home the message that in *this* restaurant, at *this* table with *this* friend, you're completely on your own.

You're in your head for a split second, and voilà! Here we are. He harmonizes the tangible with the philosophical, and we're suspended in time for eternity. Or at least what feels like an eternity before we snap out of it a second later and carry on.

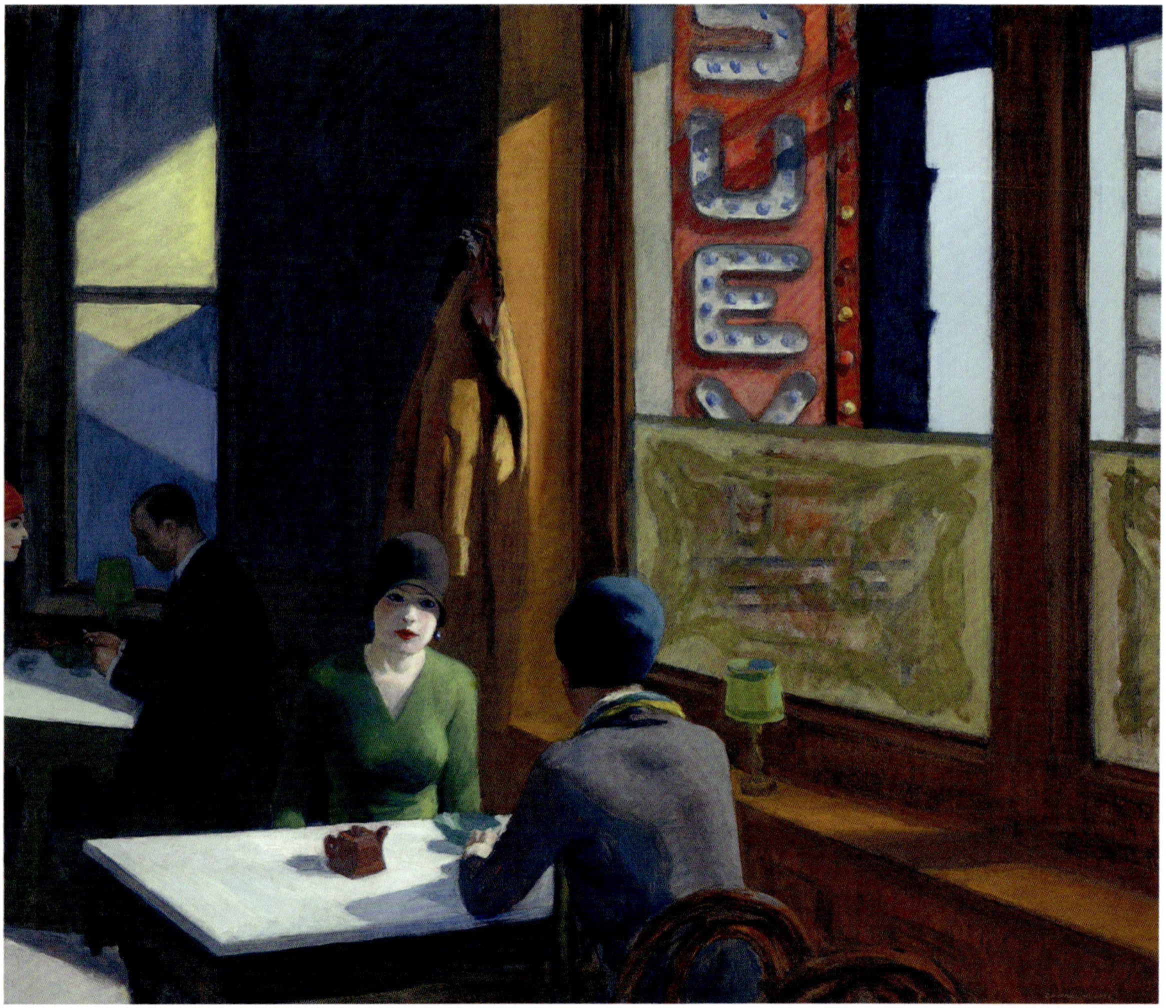

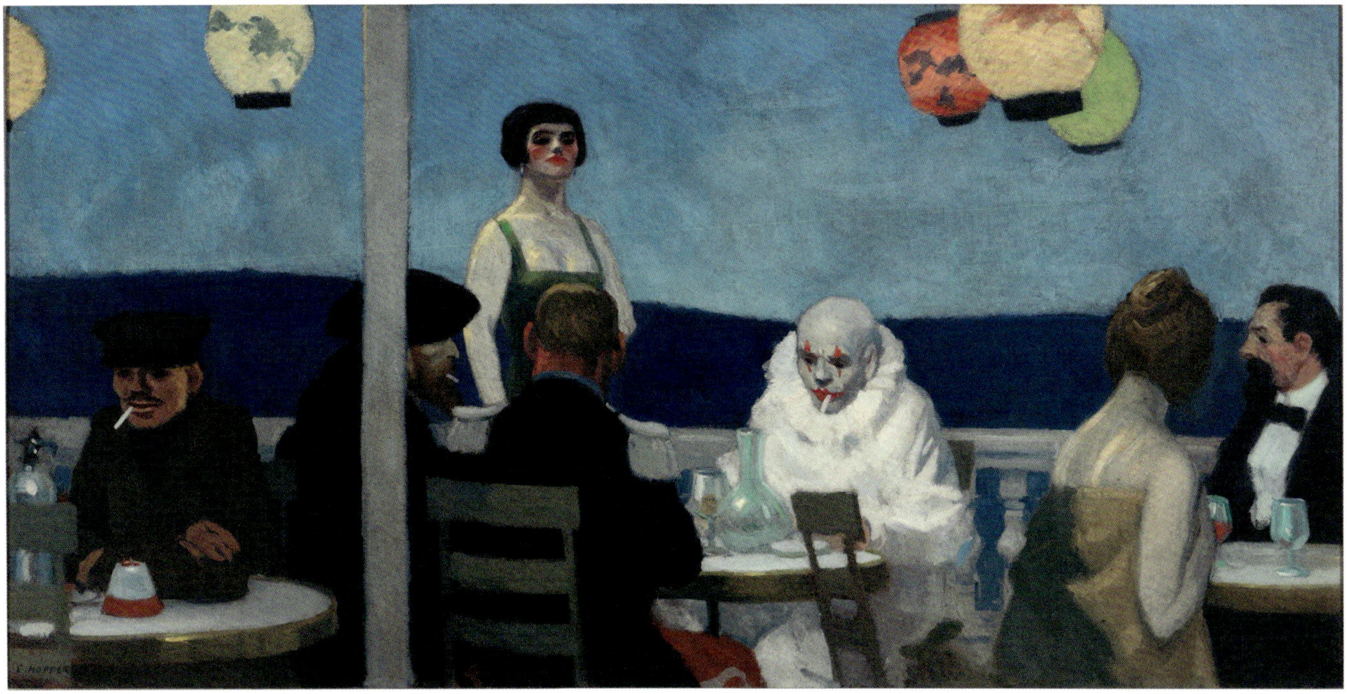

© Edward Hopper. ARS/Copyright Agency, 2026; Hopper, Edward, *Soir Bleu*, 1914, Oil on canvas. Overall: 36 1/8 x 71 15/16in. (91.8 x 182.7 cm), Josephine N. Hopper Bequest. Inv. N.: 70.1208, Whitney Museum of American Art, New York, USA

Soir Bleu

Edward Hopper, 1914

There is something to be said about the silence of a clown. A loneliness that feels like a black void in the back of your mind. In Hopper's world, seclusion is a right of passage, but it is only in this 1914 masterpiece that we really feel its consequences.

In what many could argue is his most potent painting, Edward Hopper does not simply create a scene, but instead, arranges tension. In the place of conversation, and the hustle and bustle of a Parisian café, he chooses to capture the limp hum of introspection. He doesn't show us glimmers of the familiar, but instead, focuses the light on a brilliant bright-white outfit at the center of a blue abyss. A clown without an audience, ground down into the dusts of his fundamental existence.

Just another person, hiding behind the façade that they project onto a world which they are left alone to navigate. And in a place designed for the sole purpose of connectivity, Hopper uses disconnection as the motif for his somber blue evening, leaving us, the audience, also feeling disconnected as we too stand on our own, to contemplate it all.

MASTERS OF GENRE

The art of the genre painting: my favorite creative pursuit by a long country mile, and it's because I think it's the closest we get to understanding people at any given point in history. These aren't pictures of saints, kings, mythic scenes, or grand historical events, but just everyday ordinary people engaged in ordinary day-to-day activities. They're intimate moments of real life that are no different than our own, and it's such a breath of fresh air. A great genre painting is like a window into another world. It's a time machine that lets us watch people walking around the streets, going about their business. We can peek into the private lives of a family. We can eavesdrop into a conversation, attend a wedding we weren't invited to, and catch a moment of intimacy.

Maybe I find it to be the most rewarding form of art because it's the most natural: These paintings show who we are at our core. The contemporary rituals of humankind, relative to the time of their creation, executed through a knowledge of classical ideals, relative to that same time, to produce something that feels entirely brand new.

The Conjurer

Hieronymus Bosch, 1502

While most of Hieronymus Bosch's paintings describe classical biblical stories through wild interpretations and even wilder characters, there is one painting that El Bosco created that tells a story so true to the human condition, and in a way that is so simple, you'll wonder if it is even his.

It's called *The Conjurer*, and in it there are 11 people, four animals—sort of—and one Flemish proverb to tie the piece together, all of which are centered around a table.

The conjurer plays his trick. The player, mesmerized by the ball, spits out a toad. The crowd watches in amazement, and unbeknownst to them all, the accomplice steals a purse.

"Okay, slow down Matthew. What does this mean?"

Let's go back. The conjurer holds an owl, a medieval symbol of wit and deceit, while he plays his trick on a man who, in utter bewilderment, vomits a toad: an amphibian symbol for mischief. Amongst the crowd, shocked by the sleight of hand, is a nun. Do you see her?

It probably wouldn't be that out of place for a nun to be in a crowd in medieval times, but we know that everything in a Bosch painting is meant to be. So what does her presence say? I suspect he's taking a jab at the Church, implying that even those bestowed with God's grace aren't immune to stupidity. So much stupidity that they risk losing their purses.

Now, about that Flemish proverb. It goes, *he who lets himself be fooled by conjuring tricks loses his money and becomes the laughingstock of children.*

I'm not entirely sure why a "scam" is such an enjoyable theme, but it's always so pleasing to see an artist execute it well in a painting. Bosch does it in such a unique way here, which feels so different to Caravaggio's *The Cardsharps* and *The Fortune Teller*.

Quentin Matsys, as we'll see, has his own fun way of capturing con artists, and it is equally as pleasing.

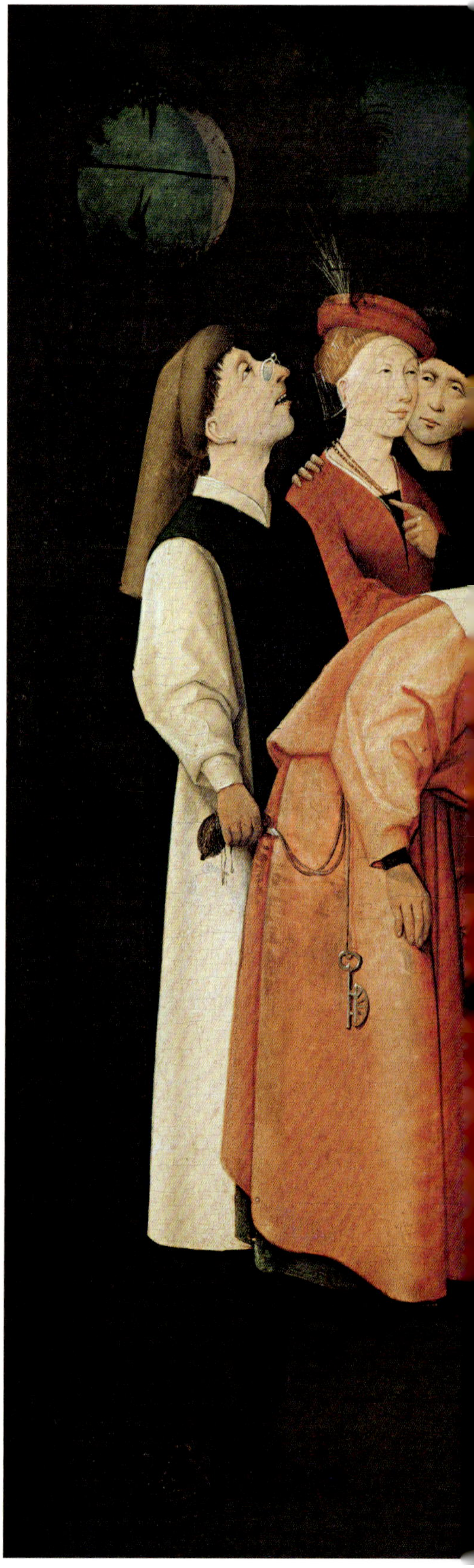

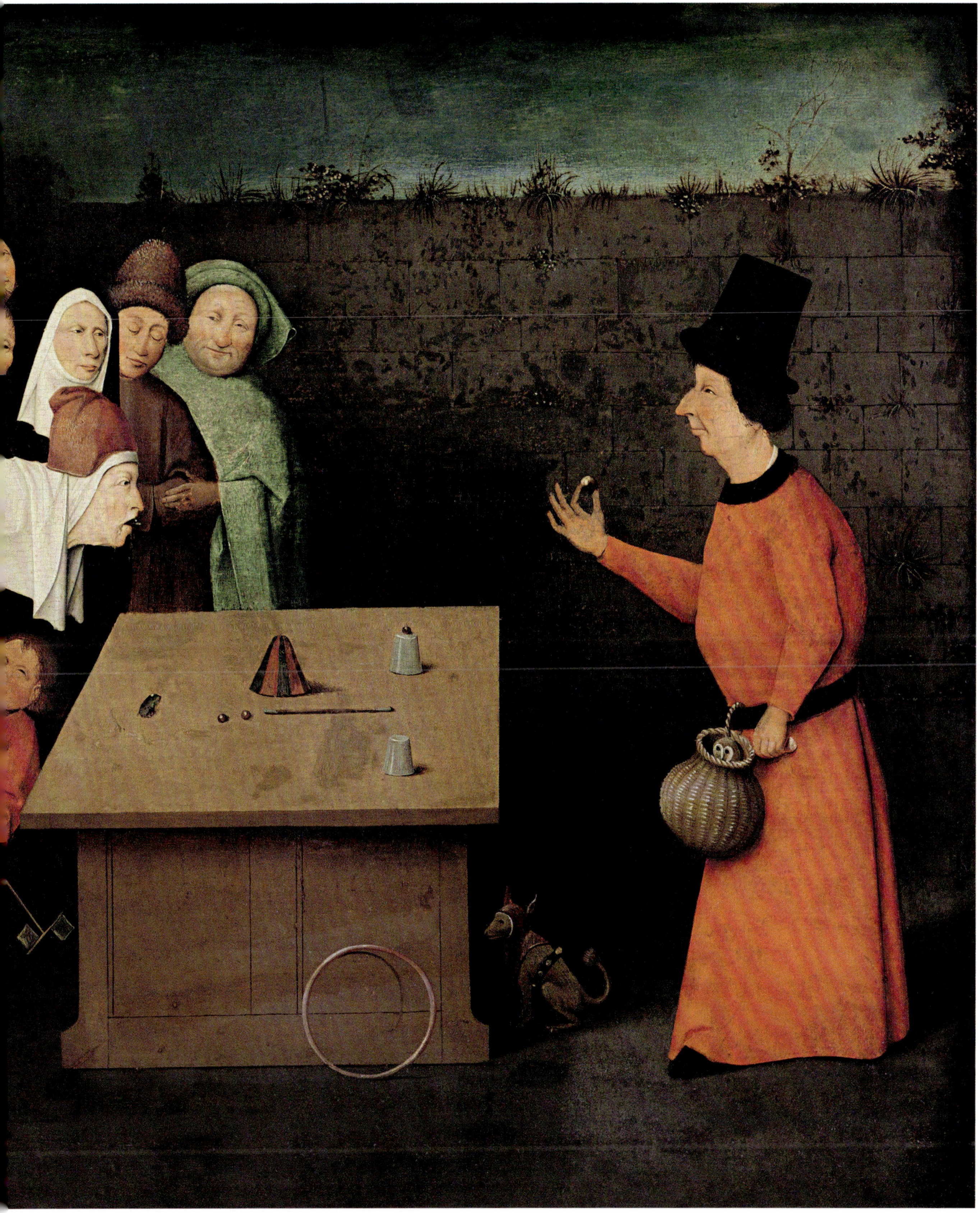

The Ill-Matched Lovers

Quentin Matsys, c. 1520–25

The guy on the left is *such* a weirdo. And what makes him even weirder is seeing what's happening right in front of him. Or does it? Because from the up-close perspective, what looks like a man creepily peeking at a flirtatious event between an ill-matched couple is actually far more sinister than you possibly expected. And it only becomes apparent when you pull yourself away from the painting.

Quentin Matsys, in his sneaky little picture, hides an even sneakier little detail and dangles it right under your nose. And by uncovering the truth of this troubling tale, we uncover a truth about the nature of people. This isn't a couple who love each other. Hell, it's not a couple that even *likes* each other. It's a scene of three people brought together under the *illusion* of togetherness, with some very clear ulterior motives. And yes, everyone here *clearly* has an ulterior motive.

This old man is not a dummy. Not very careful, I will admit. But he's in no way under any illusion that this woman loves him. He's in this little arrangement, for one thing and one thing only. Need I say more?

The woman isn't a dummy either. In fact, by the looks of it, she's done this before. The delicate brush of her fingertips across the elder man's face, a seductive, flirtatious gaze. You can almost smell the floral perfume radiating from her neckline. It all draws you in, and I probably wouldn't have noticed that my purse was being snatched from me either.

While it can certainly be poor manners to judge a real person, I think within the context of a fictional story, it's anybody's game. In its own quirky way, it's a practice that's good for the soul, judging others in the safe space of a painting. That being said, an excellent genre painting doesn't always show people's negative sides. In fact, most of the time, they show their best: the parts of people that are collaborative and fun. Take, for instance, *The Concert*, by Gerard van Honthorst.

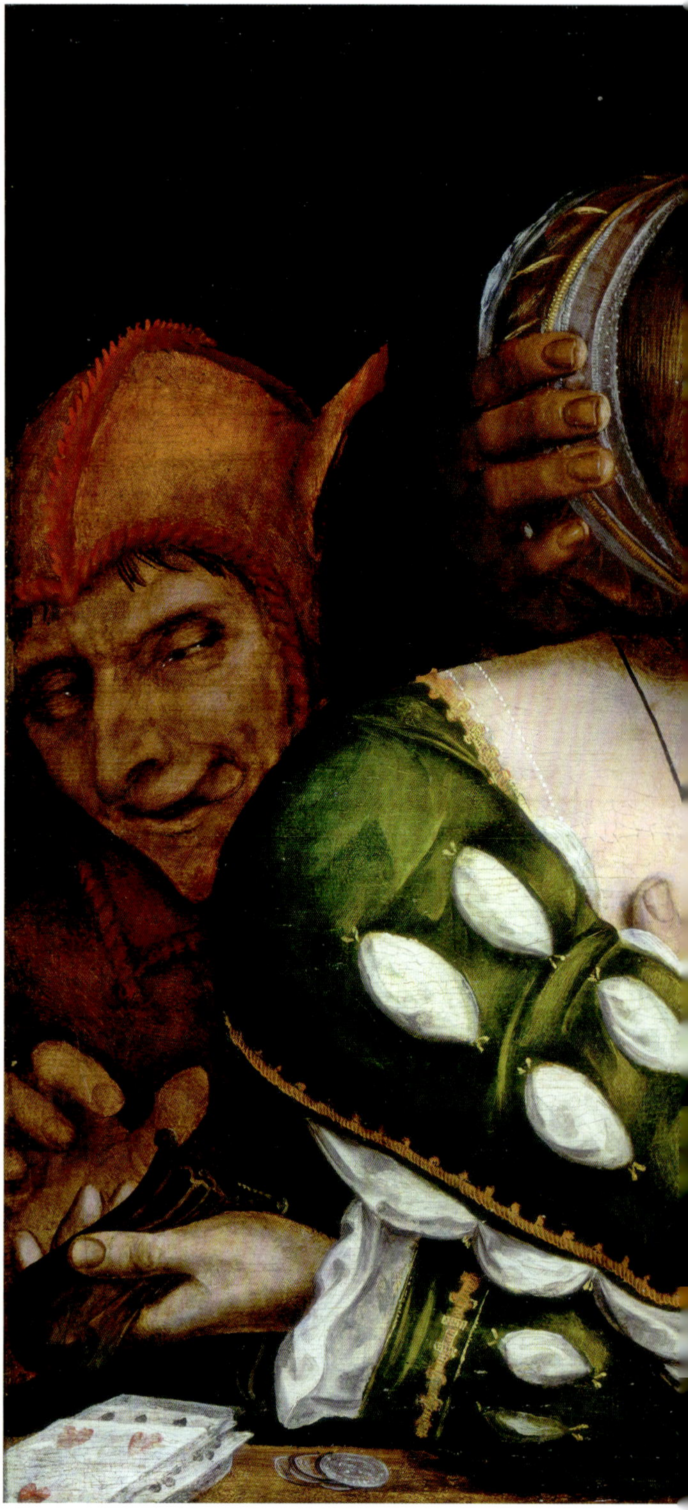

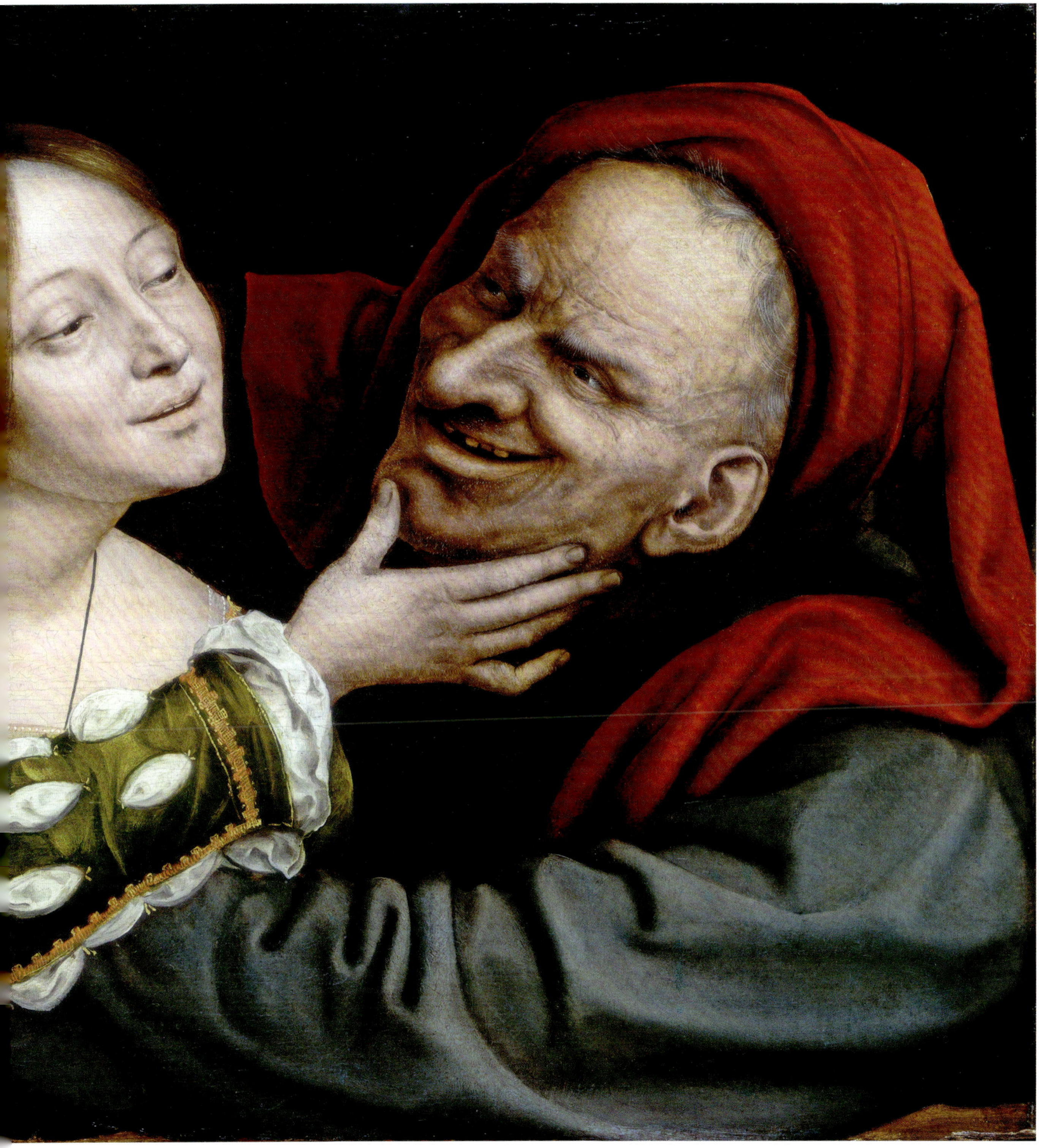

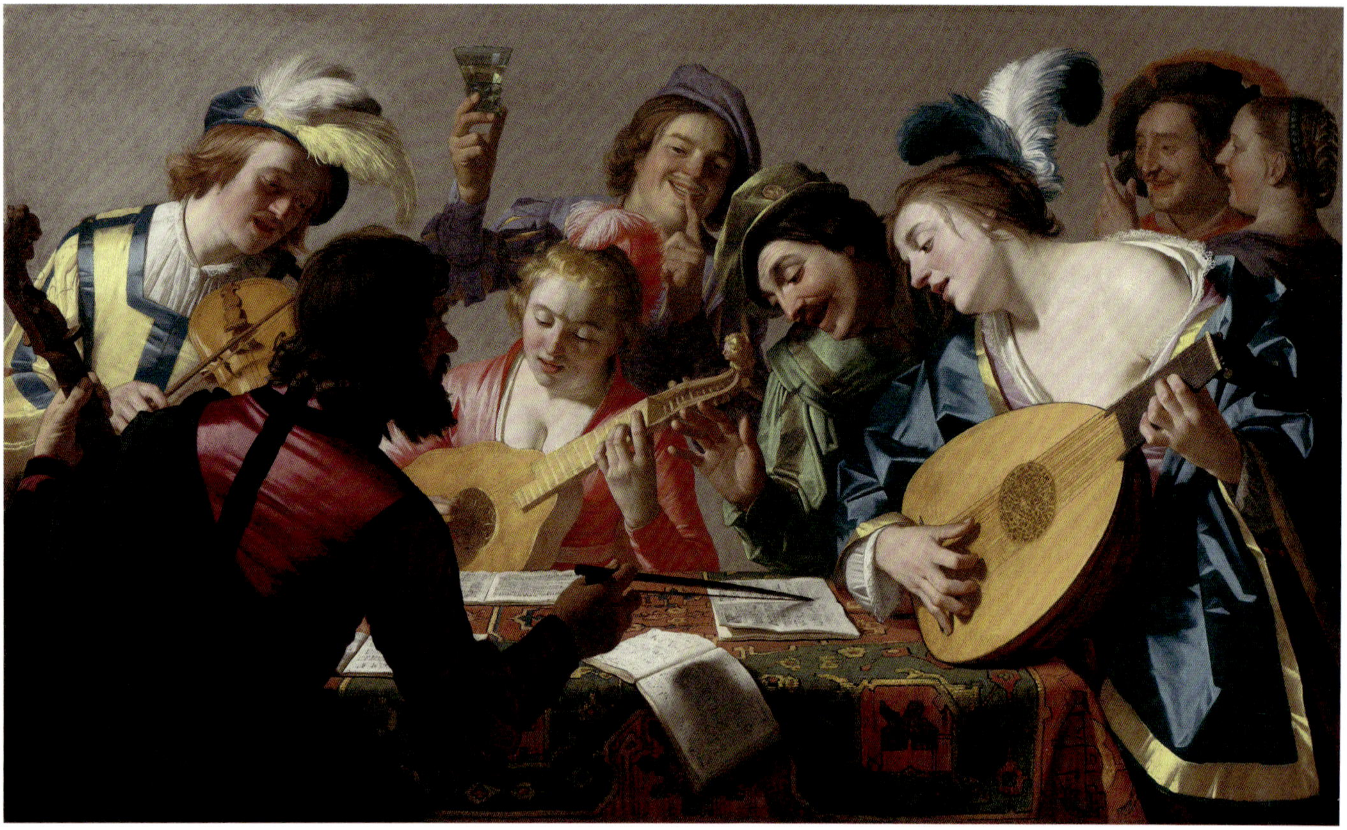

The Concert

Gerrit van Honthorst, 1623

At first glance you feel inclined to be quiet. Maybe it's the guy shushing you, and for good reason, because you're about to watch a concert, tableside. And while we wouldn't dare interrupt a party of happy musicians, it's kind of tempting, don't you find?

Honthorst invites us to come a little closer. He hangs a book off the end of the table, which serves as some sort of portal into another world. He dangles everyone's attention over the irresistible vortex of some infinitely interesting singularity. And damn it, wouldn't you love to know what the hell they're looking at? Everyone, except for the two looking at the man in purple, are suspended over something with such intent, you can't help but inch closer and closer. And then you see it.

The eyes tell us everything we want to know, whether they belong to the lady in pink or the guy with the green cap, or the concertmaster and his bow. What's revealed as we peek over a silky red shoulder, or under an arm, is that Honthorst, by design, made sheet music the glue. This band of happy musicians are all laser focused on the exact same music that made us stop to watch this tableside concert in the first place.

And it's at this point, exactly, when you hear it. And you realize you've gotten just a little too close for comfort.

"Shhh."

The Banjo Lesson

Henry Ossawa Tanner, 1893

Music is a fantastic art form, because it's so often a collaborative effort—but while we feel the pull to participate in Honthorst's work, we don't feel as inclined to interrupt Henry Ossawa Tanner's. In fact, stepping into the room feels like you might be doing something wrong.

At the intersecting line between two generations of one family, Tanner does something with a paintbrush that is so utterly mesmerizing. He shares a special private moment between a grandfather, who experienced the erosive nature of slavery in the United States, and contrasts those experiences with the innocence of a fresh generation who will only ever know it through stories. These are two entirely separate realities compressed into a singularity, and it feels unbelievable to think that they could have ever existed in the same world.

Tanner approaches the work in a style that feels like a mix between Impressionism and Academic Realism, and we're left feeling both visually stimulated and emotionally invested. It's not a work that is over complicated. There are no secrets hidden—it's about as straightforward as representative art can be—but it doesn't need anything more than these two as they are. Complexity is not a requirement for the privilege of observing the sacred, which is what this moment represents: two people who love one another unconditionally, from two completely different universes, creating a memory that will last forever. Unified by ritual, love, and a banjo lesson.

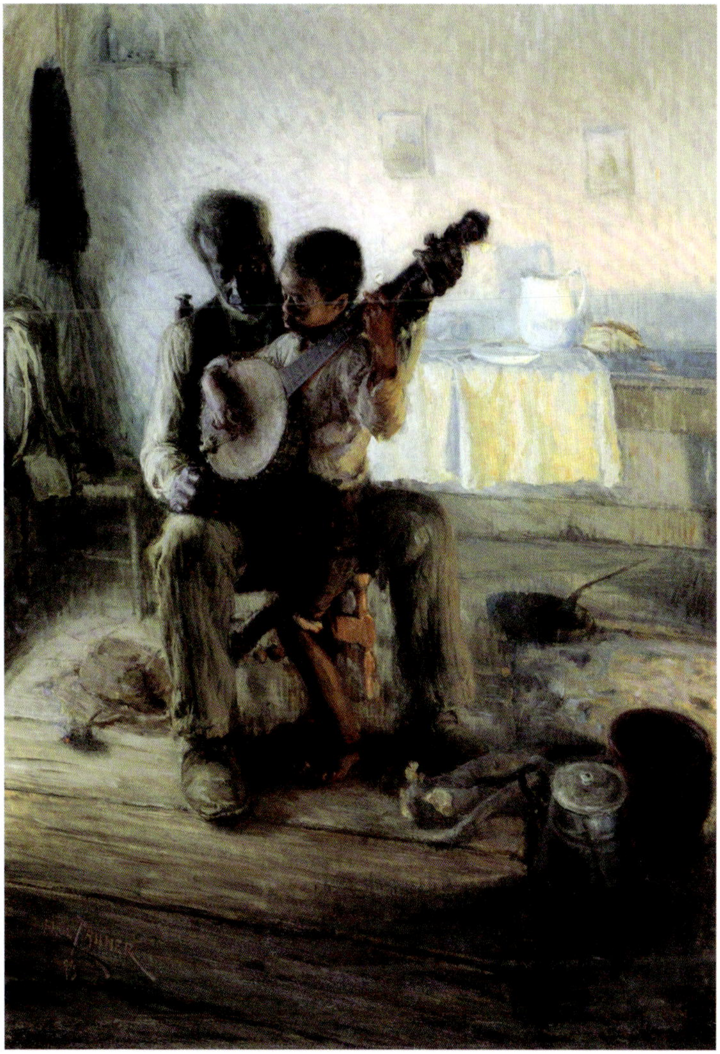

In a Roman Osteria

Carl Bloch, 1866

"Who the hell do you think you are?"

If you've found yourself verbally responding to a painting that couldn't possibly talk back, I don't blame you, because Carl Bloch really takes breaking the fourth wall to a whole new level. And it's all so startling, you'll find yourself looking at this work over and over and over again.

I mean, even the cat is telling you to bugger off. Just look at him: If eyes could kill, you'd be carved into a thousand little pieces. His glare is a far cry from the look that the woman on the left is giving you. You must be wearing something ridiculous, because she's clearly judging you, or maybe you're kind of beautiful? The woman in the yellow seems to think so.

"Whoa! Flirty."

Bloch paints her eyes with such vivid clarity, you can visualize her visualizing you taking it all off. And it's that exact attention to detail, that precision with a paintbrush, that makes the gaze of these patrons so potent. It's no wonder, then, that you missed all the other little details in the picture, like the wasp and fly circling the jug of wine. Or the flies feeding on breadcrumbs and whatever other residues are on the messy table. Who's judging who now, lady?

The texture of the bread is so perfectly delivered you can feel its crust, almost in the same way that you can feel the lace fabric that's draped over the red fabric of the woman's shirt. Scanning it over closely evokes the same sensation as rubbing it between your fingertips. And it's not the only detail that you can feel with your eyes. There's something about the tablecloth that feels vastly different to the gold embroidery on the cuff of that red shirt, or the yellow shawl on the other woman's shoulders, or the male figure's scarf belt looking thing. And I bet you never noticed his folding pocketknife. *It's no wonder you felt threatened.* An attack on the subconscious, which stole your attention away from the gentlemen in the back of the room.

Three well-dressed men sit there, sipping on a little wine of their own, not a single fly in sight. The two men whose faces we can see are deep in discussion with a third man, who just so happens to be the artist himself: a cameo of Carl Bloch, ever so slightly out of focus. He sits in the corner, face obscured, so that you, the audience, can focus on more pressing matters.

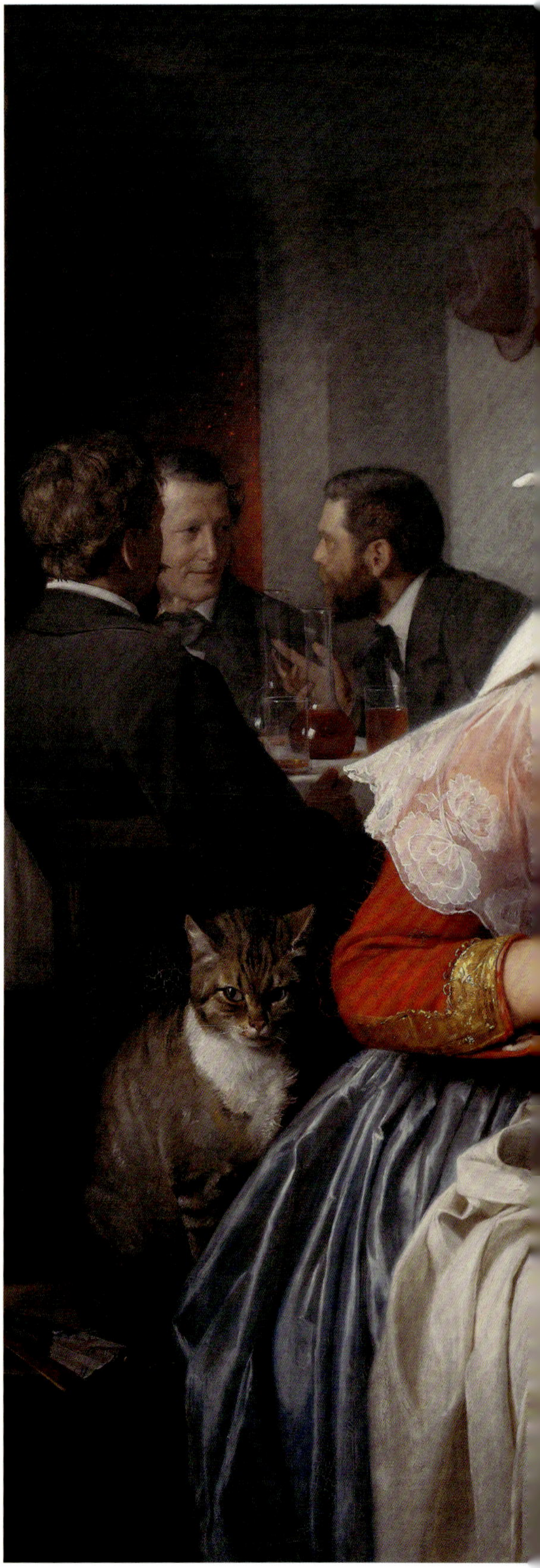

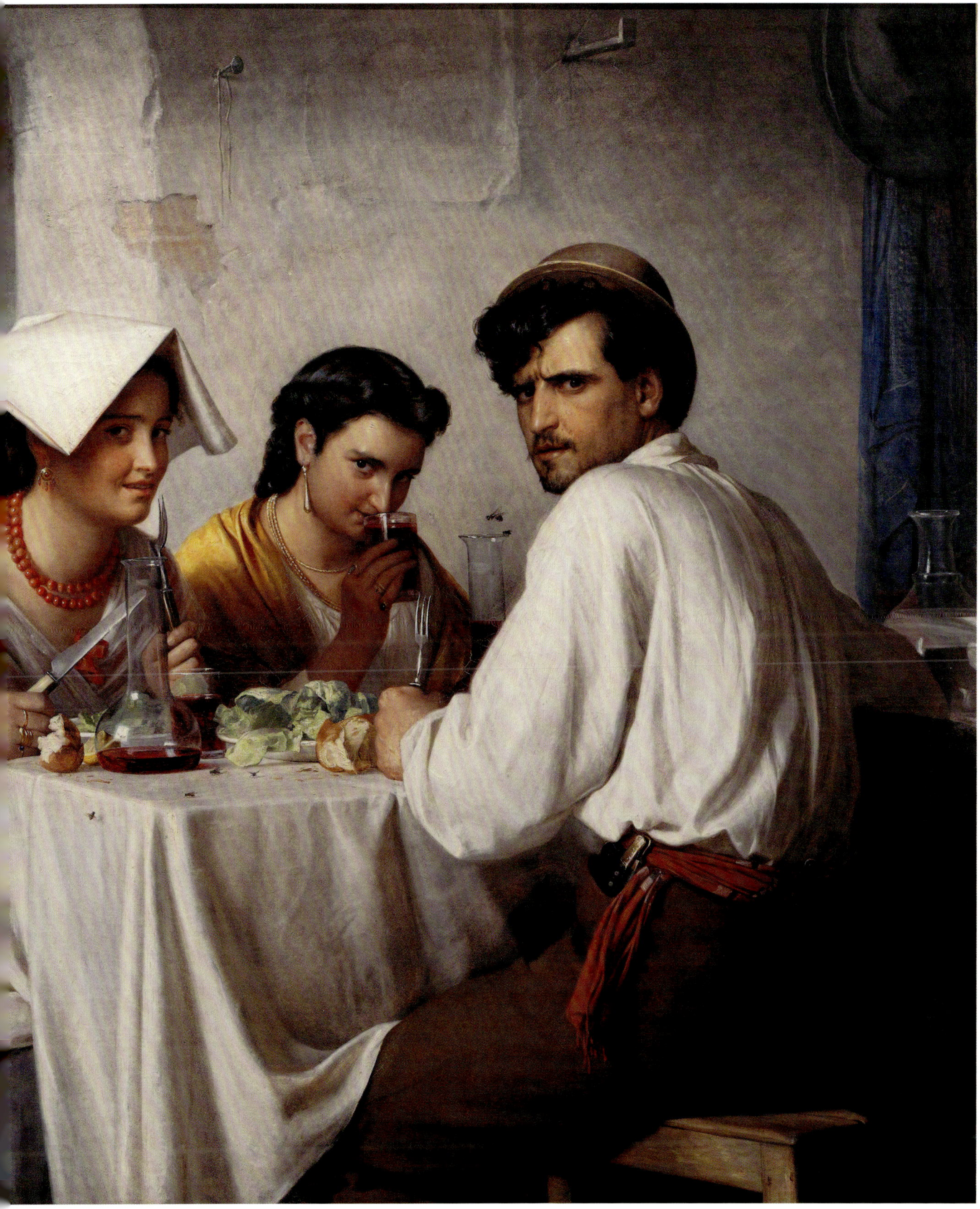

Peasant Wedding

Bruegel the Elder, c. 1568

Can you spot the bride? Should be relatively easy to find, but what about her husband? It's a reasonable question to ask at a wedding. Is it the guy on the back wall chomping down on a bowl of porridge? Or maybe it's the guy to the left of him, talking his ear off?

"Um. I hope it's not him."

It could be the guy sitting across from the bride in the black, who's so drunk he doesn't know where he is. Or the one pouring gallons of ale in the foreground, into large jugs from even larger jugs. Or maybe it's the man with the bagpipe? Unlikely. He doesn't seem interested in anyone, really. There are the men carrying the food, but they're obviously servers. And the fellow at the corner of the table, right side of the painting, seems to be plotting away, so he does feel rather doubtful. But knowing that we're looking at a painting by Pieter Bruegel, there must be a clue.

Over the head of the bride, we have what appears to be a paper crown, so we can be sure that it's her wedding day. But what might give away who she married? Not the dog, I assure you. And it's not the children, eating away. It's not the third foot (look under the porridge-laden planks the servers are carrying), because it feels like it's just a mistake. But wait, what about that weird-looking ornament on the wall? The one made of hay and a stick with what appear to be nails protruding from the sides. That does look awfully suspicious, doesn't it?

And it is pointed at *him*, the man serving plates of food to his guests, wearing a red cap. This lines up with medieval wedding traditions, so it's plausible. And this isn't the only phallic symbol we have in the artwork. Notice anything curious about his arm or the knife? Or what looks like a salt cellar? All of which are pointing toward the one ovular-shaped bowl in the entire piece, which he is passing down the table. Was Bruegel hinting at a post-wedding consummation? Maybe. Or maybe it's something else. Because while we hunt for clues about the groom, the painter hides another message and stuffs it right under our noses. But unless you know old Flemish proverbs, it's unlikely you would have caught it. Because, as the saying goes, *It is a poor man who is not able to be at his own wedding*. And perhaps the bride's first day as a married woman has been spoiled before it even started.

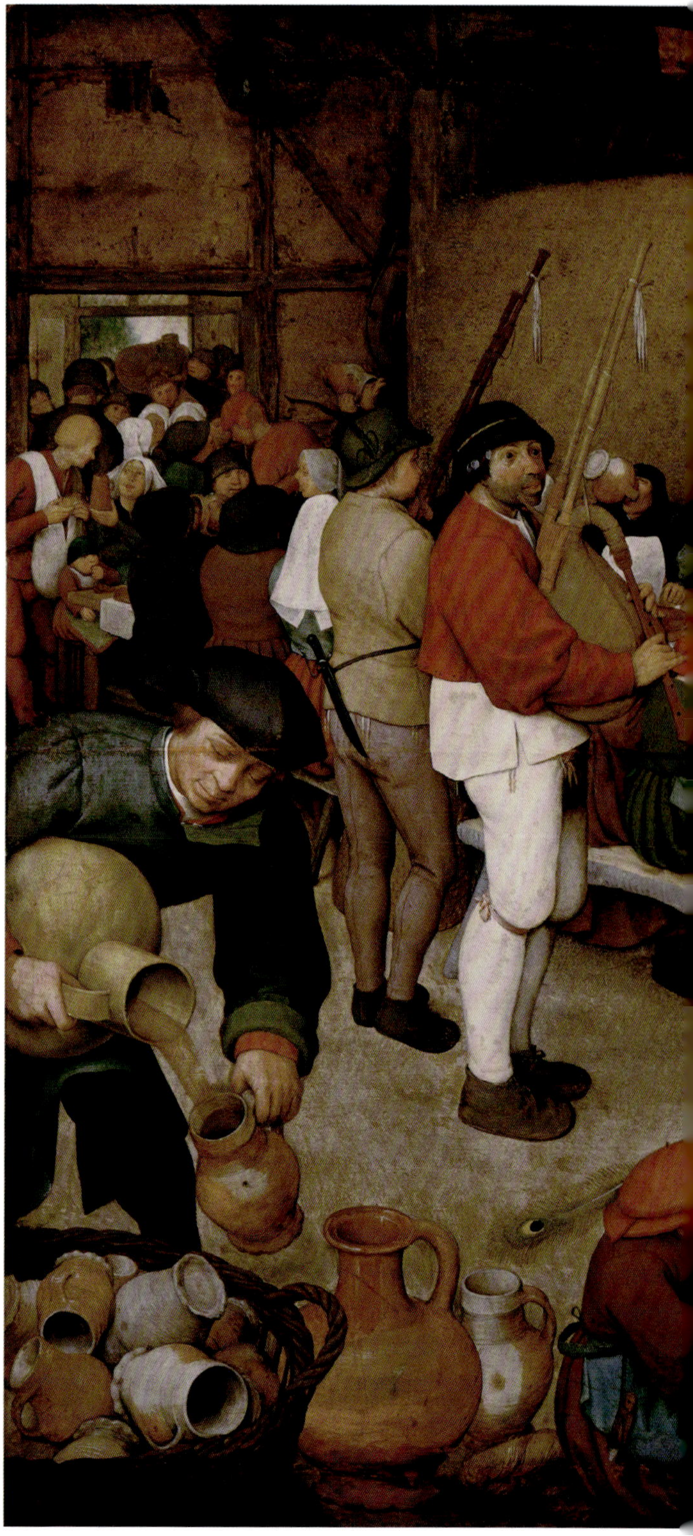

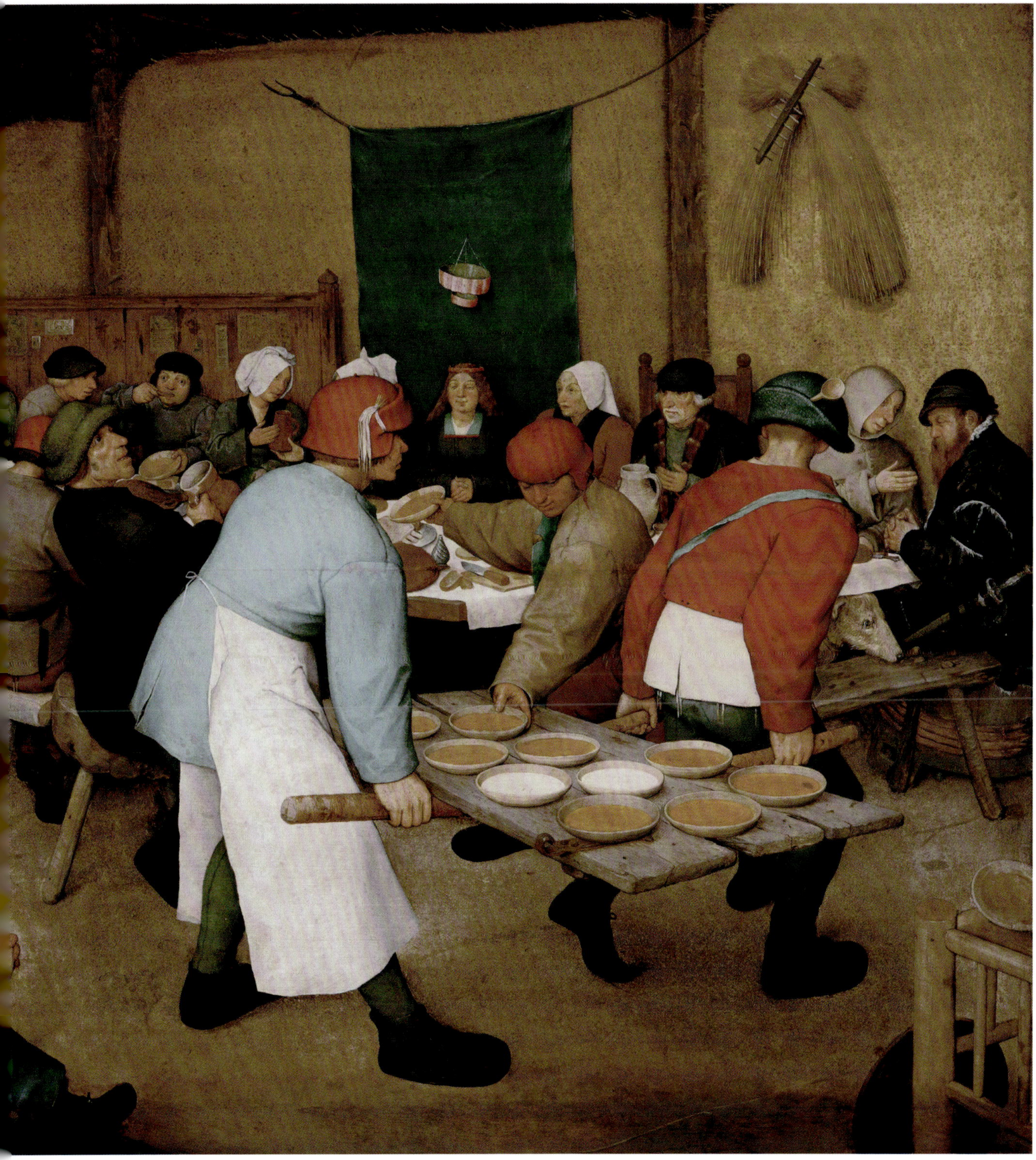

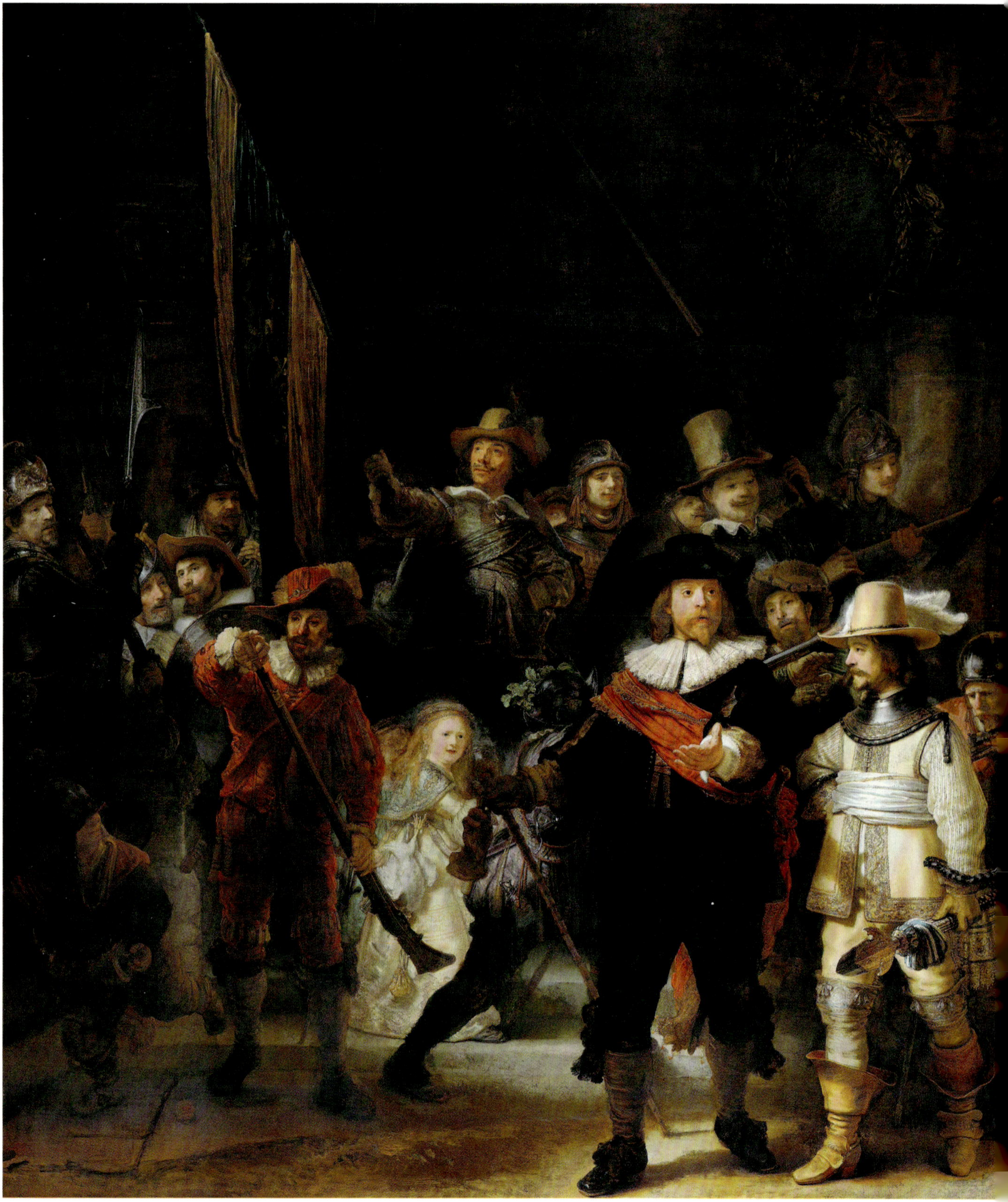

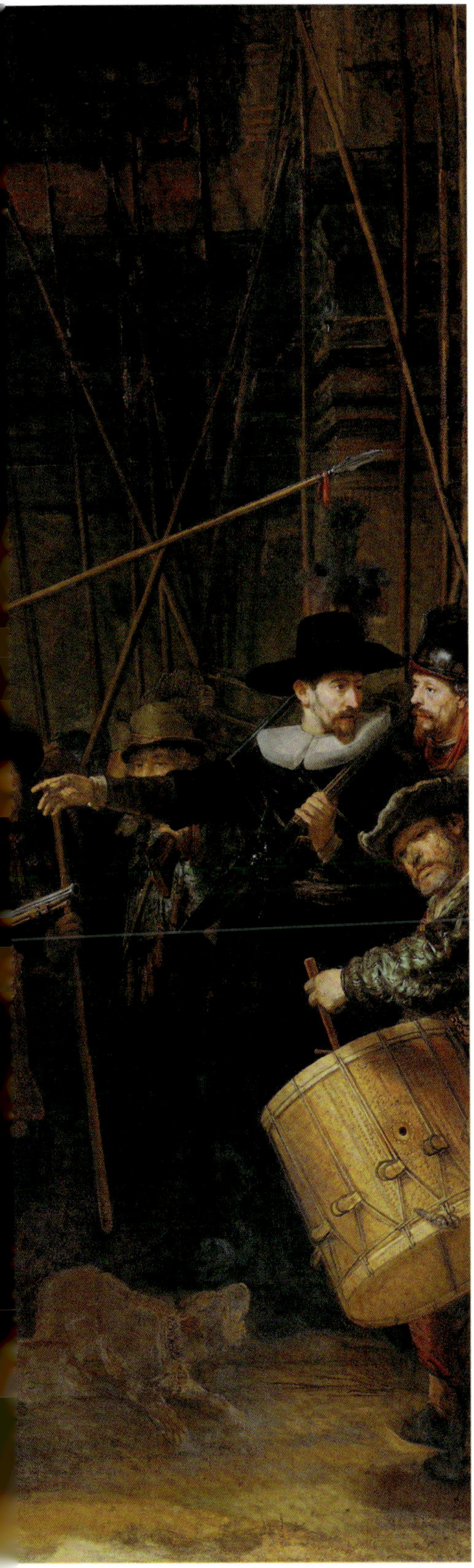

The Night Watch, Rembrandt, 1642

The Night Watch

Rembrandt, 1642

The Night Watch by Rembrandt van Rijn is not a genre painting, technically—generally, it is categorized as a group portrait. However, *The Night Watch* does possess some of the best qualities that genre paintings have to offer. Where, in a portrait, a group of people might traditionally strike a pose, in Rembrandt's masterpiece, we watch a company of the civil guard in motion, on the cusp of a march. It is dynamic and spontaneous. While beautifully detailed and grandiose, it doesn't feel formal. Rembrandt is depicting the reality of this life, in a style that isn't sanctimonious or beyond its own means. These are men of duty, so he gives us men of duty. And it's because of these decisions that *The Night Watch* transcends genre: You couldn't possibly slot it into a single category. It's one of the greatest accomplishments in the history of painting, and it's truly a marvel to uncover.

This work was commissioned for the Musketeers' Guild of Amsterdam, or more specifically, the Company of District II, which was a militia group under the leadership of Captain Frans Banning Cocq (as seen at the center of the painting dressed in black with a red sash) and Lieutenant Willem van Ruytenburch (next to Frans, dressed in a golden outfit). Surrounding them is a company of men: defenders of the Dutch Republic, even if only in a symbolic capacity. Their position in the guild was a badge of honor and an act of patriotism and civic duty. To have Rembrandt paint these men would have been an incredible experience for them all.

And Rembrandt executes something extraordinary. *The Night Watch* is by far his most complex multi-figure composition, and it really highlights his mastery of painting in so many ways. He litters the arrangement with strong vertical lines that reveal themselves through objects like muskets, spears, flags, and arms, and in doing so, he adds dynamic movement to the group. He then proceeds to anchor it all on the two central figures of the masterpiece: Captain Cocq holds the entire left side of the painting in check, and the Lieutenant secures the right. By setting the painting in this way, with motion in the rear and stability at the center, Rembrandt creates the feeling that it is falling toward us. The men are marching, and they break the stage. He adds to this effect by separating the composition into three planes: the foreground, the middle ground, and the background. The foreground is the brightest section, highlighting the work's central elements; the middle ground is caught outside the direct light, made of the officers and a drummer; and the background is almost entirely in the shadows. The effect is that this group of men is stepping toward us.

Speaking of lighting, this painting is a prime example of Rembrandt's chiaroscuro. He isolates characters of symbolic or psychological importance by illuminating them, and then counters that lighting with harsh shadows, to give the entire painting a sense of rhythm. But Rembrandt also chooses to do something else with light that's unique. Have a look at the little girl to the left of Captain Cocq, hiding in the middle ground. It feels odd that she's lit in the way that she is, as it doesn't quite fit the rest of the picture. But there is a reason.

That little girl isn't meant to represent a real person, but rather, she serves as a symbol. She is an unnatural element in the work, and therefore, is highlighted via an unnatural beam of light. This is not the light of the world around her, but a narrative light. She's a mascot: an allegory, and one of the most symbolically charged figures in the work, because she represents the militia itself. A dead chicken hangs from her belt, which was a civic guard tradition. Its claws (or talons) were also the emblem of the Musketeers' Guild. Her pistol is a firearm that the militia carried: an item that projects an authority, and even at some level, a unity between the group. But most important is the fact that she's highlighted at all, because the girl is also a spiritual emblem: She is all the people in the picture. She is the institution that is being represented. Rembrandt couldn't highlight every person with the same intensity, but by highlighting her, he highlights them all, because together, they represent something bigger than any one man.

This is Rembrandt at maximum power. Thick impasto highlights on fabrics, metal, and weapons. Loose gestural marks in the shadows that allow forms to dissolve, and where it matters the most, hyper-observed details. Every single mark that the artist made fought for its place on this canvas, which is giant: 12 x 14 feet, and this is after it was trimmed down for transportation.

And we've only just scratched the surface.

Let's look again at our central figures. Captain Cocq wears black and red, colors symbolizing authority. Lieutenant van Ruytenburch wears gold, symbolizing wealth and civic virtue. When viewed together, they take on an even greater meaning, which is the duality of leadership. And it doesn't stop there, because one must also look at what they are physically doing. The Captain extends his hand, which not only enhances the forward motion of the group, but is a motion of authority. He's issuing an order, and the Lieutenant listens, in a subtle yet powerful detail. He's attentive, responding to the command, which signals to the party that it is okay to move.

To the far right of the painting, we see a drummer reinforcing the mobilization. He captures the civic spirit, and we can hear it: the beat of every single step. Meanwhile, on the painting's left, you might have noticed a man in red who looks to be loading his musket. Now can you spot the man who's firing his? See if you can find him. He isn't easy to spot, but behind Captain Cocq is a man who appears to have his back turned away from us, and he's sporting a shiny helmet with leaves on the top. If you look at this musket, you can see the light haze of smoke, right behind the Lieutenant's head. And directly to the right of that, you'll notice a man clearing his gun's pan. Between these three men, Rembrandt turns the masterpiece into an instruction manual on musket operation, and I can guarantee you, 99 percent of people who have seen this painting missed that detail.

The same people, I might add, who probably missed the dog: bottom of the picture, sandwiched between the drummer and the Lieutenant. He's an important character too. A dog is a great way to symbolize loyalty and alertness, but it also has an amazing effect of humanizing the scene. Dogs were a humorous touch that were often added to paintings of militia gatherings.

Rembrandt shows us men in traditional plated armor, and men in modern clothes, and he shows us every weapon from spears, to pikes, to swords, to muskets, and everything in between. In doing so, he shares with us the history of the militia, including its weapons from the medieval ages all the way until the day the painting was made, highlighting that these men belong to an institution steeped in tradition. And in the background, right behind the man who holds the banner, Rembrandt even slips himself into the work, among his never-ending supply of motifs and little secrets.

But… could all of this have been a bit of a meme? A little bit of satire on the artist's behalf? Think about it. A group of men who take their roles so seriously, but they aren't painted to feel that serious at all. In fact, the whole image does feel a little theatrical. A "modern militia" with outdated weapons, and outdated armor, who don't actually serve a purpose, parading around the city out of tradition, not necessity. It's a great badge of honor to be a part of the group, or is it? Maybe only for those who are in it to begin with. We might never actually know.

The only thing that we can know for sure, is that this is one of Rembrandt's best.

COMPOSITION

The bones of a painting: They are not an option in great art, but a requirement. Composition is the framework that an artist uses to anchor their entire vision, and it's possibly the most important fundamental in art-making.

Imagine someone has hired you to do a portrait, and on the day that they sit for you, a million thoughts run through your head. Your eyes pick up on everything. An artist's peripheral vison is their worst enemy, because painting is not about capturing *everything*, but instead, everything that *counts*. Everything that forwards whatever it is that an artist is trying to project. Yes, painters consider light, texture, and more, but their main consideration is *how* to arrange their subject.

Once you understand what makes for a great composition, you can go back through this book, and you will find that every single artwork we've discussed is rooted in its structure. This is the basis of all art, and it will hit you in the face like a ton of bricks. It's one of those things that, once seen, appears everywhere.

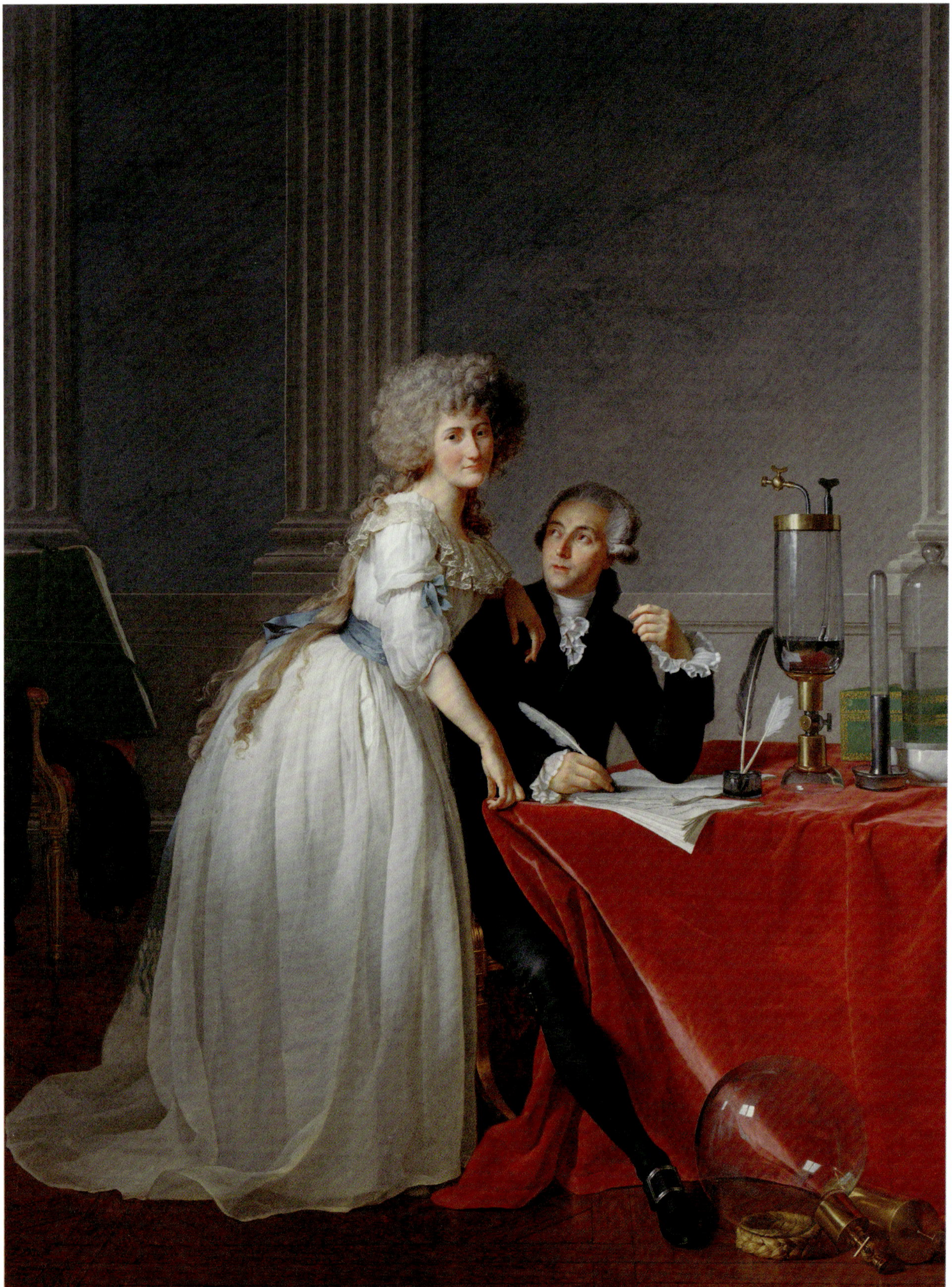

Antoine Laurent Lavoisier (1743–1794) and Marie Anne Lavoisier (Marie Anne Pierrette Paulze, 1758–1836)

Jacques-Louis David, 1788

Because of course we need to see Jacques-Louis David again.

To the untrained eye, this is a simple portrait of Mr. and Mrs. Lavoisier, a husband and wife, both of whom were renowned chemists, posing in an office decorated with classical pilasters and a false marble wall. David tells us everything we need to know about them. He stages laboratory instruments on the scarlet velvet tablecloth, quills and paper, and a couple hard at work as they were on any day, contributing to the sciences. And I know what you're thinking.

"Okay, Matthew, on with it, then. What did we miss?"

Well, have a look again, because you see, while David stages the painting to tell us about who this couple is, he also tells us exactly where to look, and in doing so, masterfully harmonizes their portrait. It starts with the ripple on the tablecloth: the one that shoots out from the round glass flask on the floor and continues straight through Madame Lavoisier's arm, reinforced by the leg of her husband. And these aren't the only lines that point in that direction. Have another look at the faux marble wall. The veins, in near perfect symmetry, are used to the exact same effect; however, this time they parallel only Marie Anne's backside. These lines converge at a point, guiding our attention to the dark side of the room—to tremendous effect, I might add, because this painting feels unbelievably balanced, doesn't it?

Even though this work highlights the table's instruments in the same light as its characters, it doesn't feel lopsided. David balances the physical with the technical to masterful effect. But there's even more method to the madness, because in the shadows lies another clue that serves as both a technical and physical gesture with a radical effect on our understanding of this portrait.

It is a document case—not for scientific papers, but for artistic pursuits. And not only does it serve as a tool for creating the portrait's left to right symmetry, but it tells us more about our female figure. A student, for a short time albeit, with artistic interests, who in 1788 was taught how to draw by David himself, and who in this painting, either by purpose or by the nature of the subconscious, is just a little brighter, even in a painting that is clearly about two people. You notice her first because, in all likelihood, he knew her just a little more. And it's spectacular to see.

The very foundation of David's composition is what makes the artwork feel cohesive. Everything works in tandem to support the painting's singular objective, which is to highlight *who* these people are.

Of course, this is only one example. We can look to Jacques-Louis David's pupil, Jean-Auguste-Dominique Ingres, and see an entirely different approach in *Grande Odalisque*.

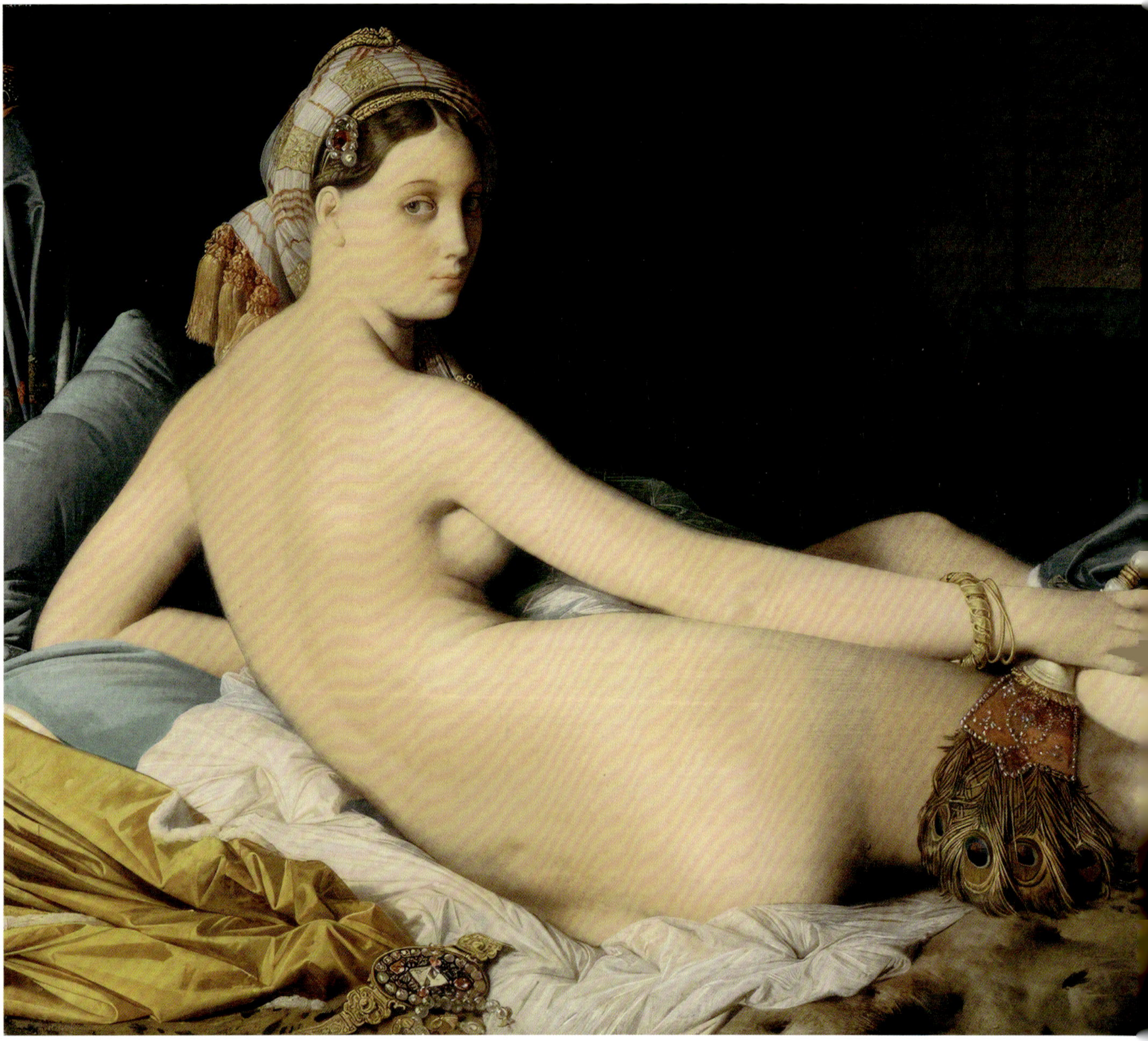

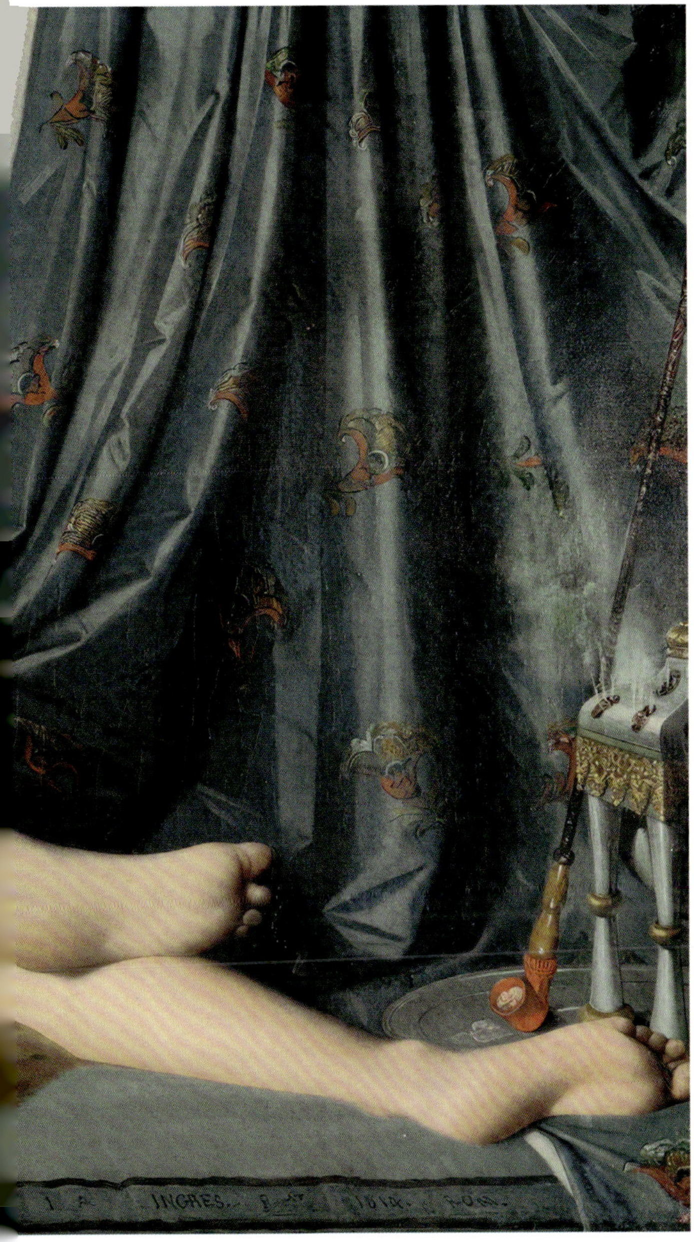

Grande Odalisque

Jean-Auguste-Dominique Ingres, 1814

An entire composition structured around a serpentine axis that runs from the sitter's head, through her spine, down toward her hip, and finishes in her foot. None of which is anatomically accurate, and instead, purely compositional. In fact, this was one of the great criticisms of this artwork upon its exhibition—its anatomical inaccuracies—but they serve a very real purpose. By pointing out issues with her extended back, her impossibly long arm, her hip, and her thigh that taper into a refined, almost porcelain smoothness, what's missed is that Ingres creates a continuous, unbroken visual flow that makes the figure feel like a single calligraphic stroke.

He also chooses to compress the space. The background details like the curtain, the bedding, the cushions, and the hookah are all squeezed into one tight visual plane, and by limiting the architectural space, the setting functions like a stage. It pushes the figure forward, as if she's been carved out from the background, and allows Ingres to emphasize her contour over her depth. That S-shaped line is Ingres's visual statement. It's his obsession. Everything in the image is arranged to frame it. The rich blue drapery and the white sheets, and even the shadow behind her body, are all softened to make her contour crisp and uninterrupted. It's a composition that is biomechanically challenging, but it works the moment you realize that Ingres isn't painting a woman, but rather a line. He's covering a subject in the abstract, and the rest becomes irrelevant.

It's this idea that makes Ingres a precursor to modernity. He is taking representative art and executing it in an impossible way: creating idealized beauty that can't be replicated in the real world, and yet it stays with you still because it is so striking.

Arrangement in Grey and Black No. 1

James McNeill Whistler, 1871

James McNeill Whistler had a similar idea, and his is even further abstracted in *Arrangement in Grey and Black No. 1*, or as most people might know it, *Whistler's Mother*.

Once again, we have a painting rooted entirely in its structure. Whistler approaches the canvas like a designer and prioritizes geometry, proportion, and tonal harmony over sentimentality. Everything is built around a strict, almost musical structure of verticals, horizontals, and muted greys. It's a painting of his mother, yes, but she isn't the point.

Whereas Ingres builds the entire structure of the *Grande Odalisque* around the serpentine curve, Whistler builds his painting around rectangles. The entire image feels like a never-ending series of right angles, and you should really take it in: the vertical line of the wall's skirting board, the horizontal line of the grey curtain panel to the left, the vertical black shape of her dress, and the rectangular picture frame. And his mother—at least her floating head and hands—sits somewhere at the intersection of all of them: an obelisk anchoring the entire visual field. There is nothing about this picture that screams "portrait," because it's not a portrait at all. It's abstract art decades before abstract art was a thing.

Whistler removes all notions of texture too. The dress isn't treated as a fabric but as a solid mass: an enormous block that dominates the picture's entire right side. But it's not overwhelming. Rather, it's really a perfect gesture. Her dress grounds the entire composition, functioning as its own visual well of gravity within which everything around it circulates. Whistler creates tension, but only subtly. He pits the strong horizontal lines that make up the bulk of the composition, like the line of the chair, or her lap, or the picture frame, against two very sharp verticals—her upright torso and the curtain—and when viewed together, they give the painting its power. Without them working together, the entire arrangement collapses underneath its own weight.

"But why do it this way?"

Because why not? Whistler makes a painting that is strictly about composition because he recognizes that composition is the basis of all great art. And in the process of doing so, he elevates art-making. He reduces a portrait to its most basic elements, because he understands that a painting—like all visual stimuli—is at its core a culmination of simpler, fundamental rules.

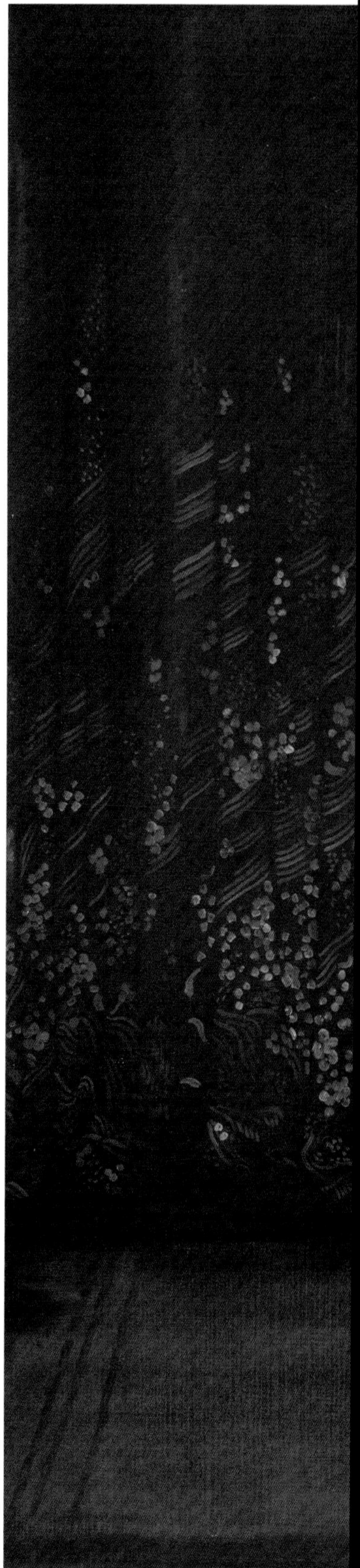

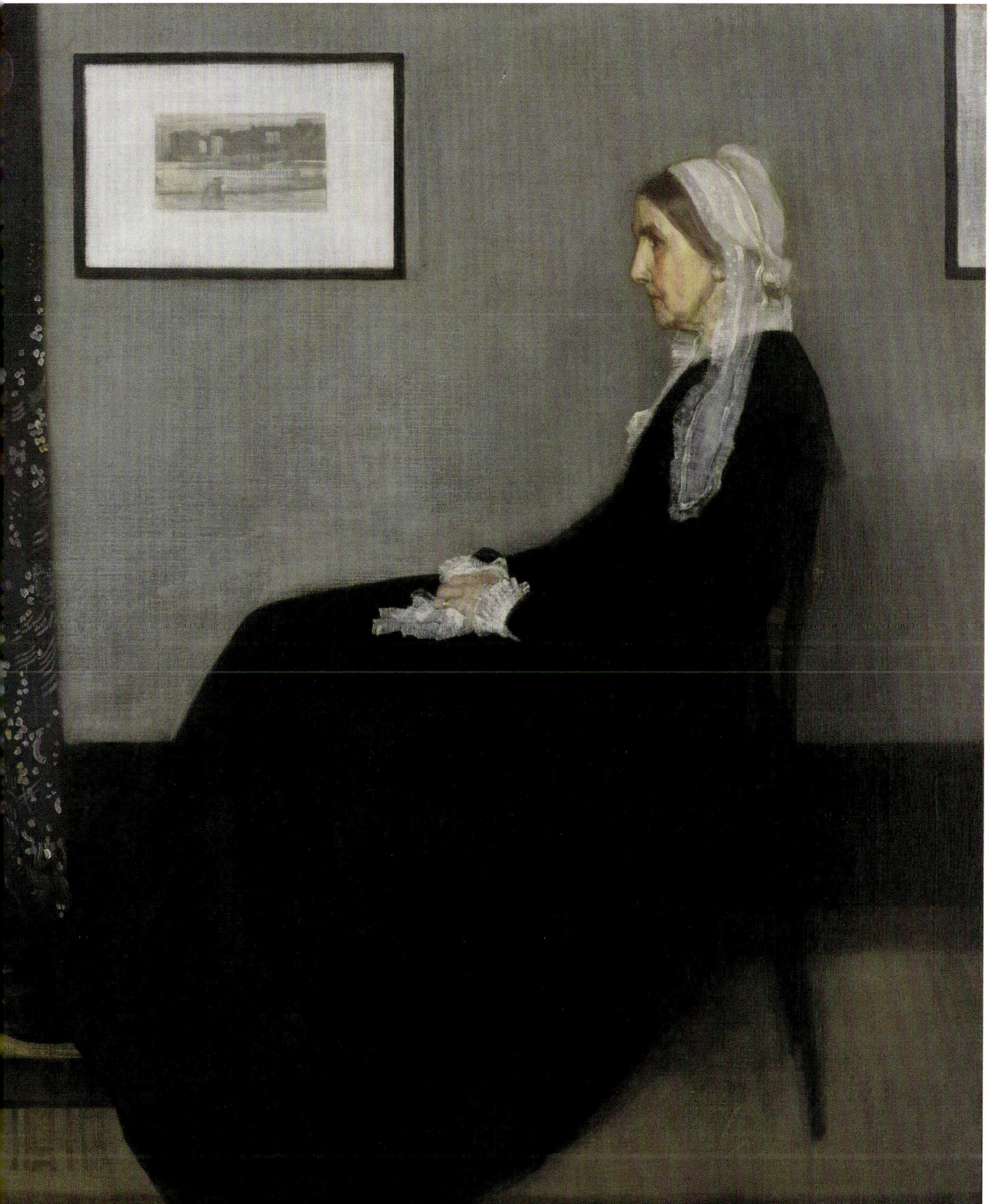

The Massacre of the Innocents

Peter Paul Rubens, c. 1611–12

Hundreds of years before both Whistler and Ingres, Peter Paul Rubens tells us a violent story that he constructs on a series of diagonal lines. Violent, unrelenting diagonal lines that intersect with one another, carrying force, motion, and emotional substance: a whirlpool of bodies spiraling into madness. In *The Massacre of the Innocents*, there is no horizontal stability, and no vertical calmness. It is chaos everywhere you look.

The center of the painting is a densely compressed torsion knot. A soldier bends forward, his muscles coiled. A mother pulls backward with an equalizing force. Limbs overlap in impossible angles, and infants lie between them as the fulcrum of the struggle. Rubens compresses the central action like a spring, and all the movement, tension, and emotional energy radiates outward. Baroque Dynamism at its very best.

Rubens manipulates his figures for a kinetic charge. He twists the anatomy of every character, transforming each body into an instrument of motion, as he lights the scene like an interrogation. He carves out the most violent actions from the shadows and highlights suffering. We are exposed to the horror in its most raw and immediate form, and he doesn't leave us with any room to breathe. The figures fill the frame from end to end. None of his diagonals resolve.

Not a single element of this painting is calm, and they shouldn't be, because the focus of Rubens's painting is an atrocity; it retells the biblical story in which King Herod the Great orders the execution of all the male children in Bethlehem, aged two and under, in an attempt to kill an infant Jesus.

Put yourself in the shoes of a parent with a little boy: Can you imagine what that would have been like? Now, ask yourself whether Rubens's composition supports the story. If the answer is yes, then we're getting somewhere.

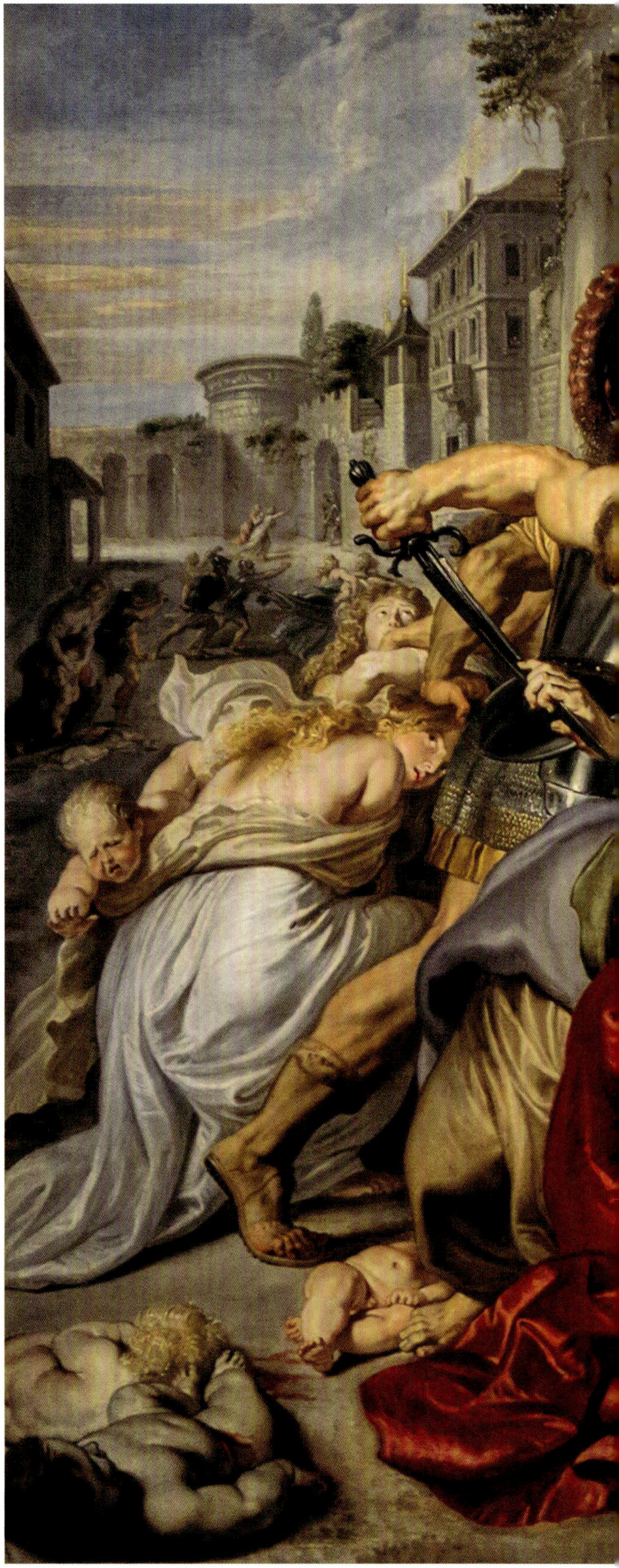

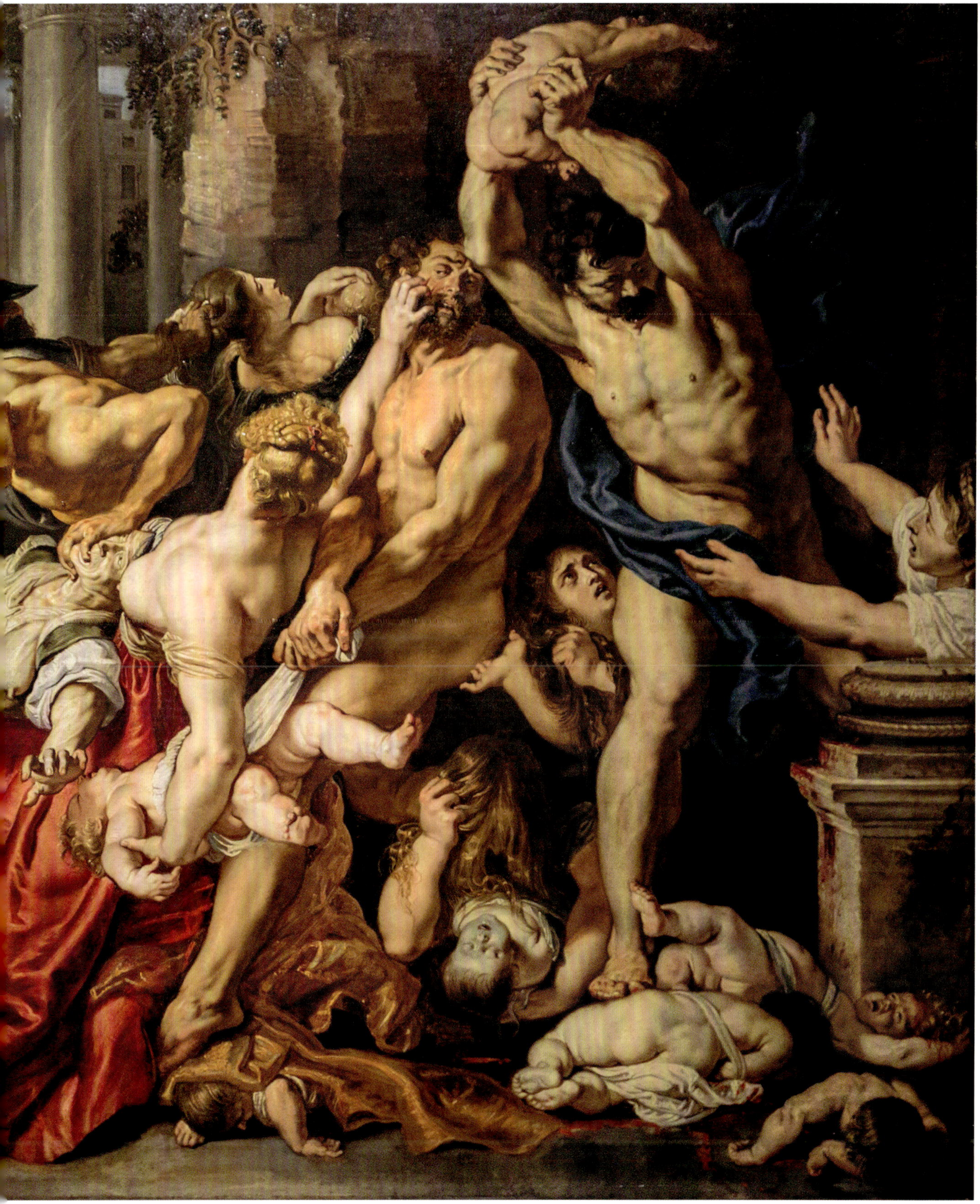

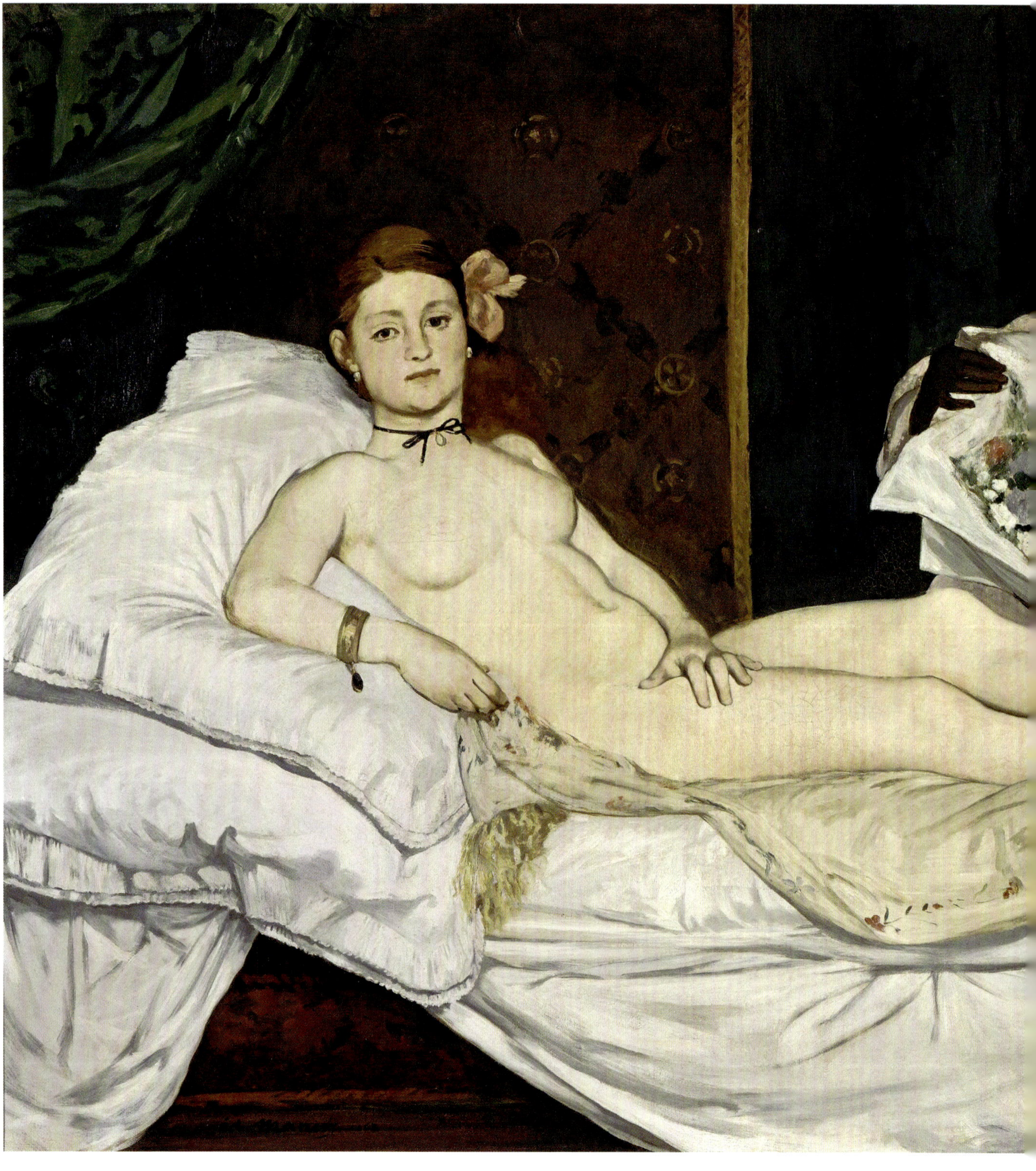

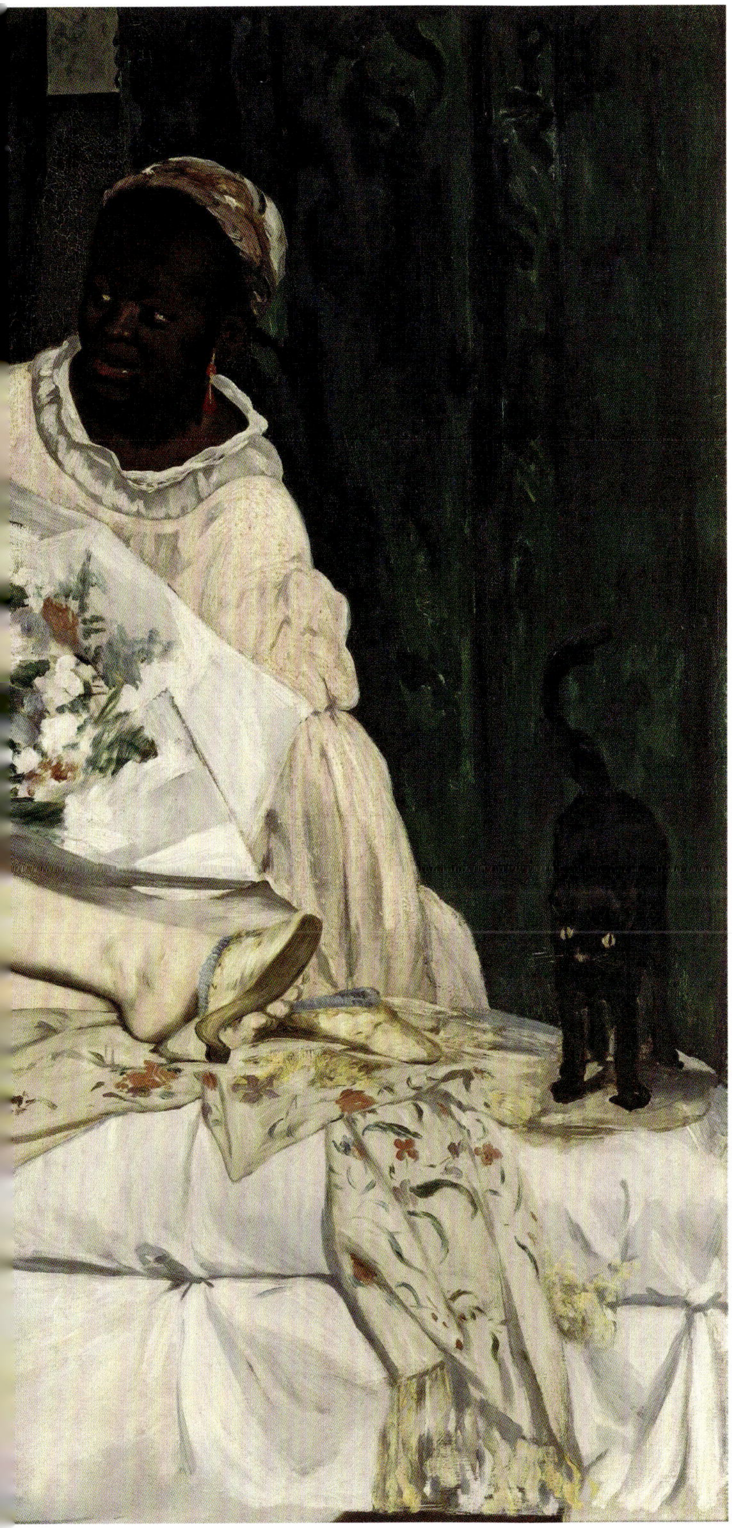

Olympia

Édouard Manet, 1863

You are not invited into the scene. Rather, you're accused of looking. At least, that's how it feels.

Every part of *Olympia* is arranged in a way that maximizes that unforgettable stare. It prints itself on your mind, even though Édouard Manet doesn't try to trick you. This isn't a painting that tries to tell you it's not one. Manet wants you to confront the work for what it is. It's not a *scene*.

He flattens the space. The background curtain is a vertical wall of muted brown and green. The bed is a thin, flat plane with almost no recession. Manet treats every element in the entire painting like a Japanese print would: one dimensional. Have a look at Olympia's body. It isn't rounded as you might expect but carries over some angular properties. It's made of abrupt transitions. It's modeled with minimal gradation and is positioned parallel to the canvas plane. Manet paints her as a shape.

All of this highlights her gaze, which is the work's central feature. Every element is designed to pull your gaze back toward it—the lines, the lighting, the forms. With a glance, she brings you right back home. And the maid? Stare at the painting and think about the consequences of her form in the image. She is a nearly vertical column, made up of the darkest tones, to offset Olympia and structurally support the work. The same goes for the cat. Both figures aren't meant to serve any narrative function and instead work exclusively to maintain the painting's strength. And because the gaze from Olympia is so well supported, and is so compelling, movement isn't required. The image is incredibly still, from every possible angle, all to support the single idea that you, the viewer, are not just viewing a painting—you are actively being viewed.

A Bar at the Folies-Bergère
Édouard Manet, 1882

Manet had an uncanny ability to include the viewer in the story. Let's have a look at his last major work, *A Bar at the Folies-Bergère*. It's one of the cleverest pieces of art, and unlocking it all comes down to answering the question of whether or not we are looking at a mirror in the background. And if we are, does that mean that we're the man in the hat?

Now I know what you're thinking.

"Who the *hell* is that guy?"

While it's fair to assume that we're one and the same, what if I told you it's all a bit of an optical illusion meant to distort reality when we look at the painting in its entirety? The very first thing you'll have noticed is the barmaid. She's looking directly at you, but it's not clear what she wants. She's sort of expressionless, as if she's waiting for you to place an order, or she's just asked you a question. Or maybe she's thinking about what you just asked her? She's got this blank look about her, and it adds a sort of mystery to the whole thing. And then you peek behind her, and it's chaos: an organized chaos of happy partygoers at a music hall chatting away, sipping on various spirits and champagne, as implied by the bottles on the bar. Hell, there's even a trapeze artist in the top left corner.

So why, then, does her reflection seem so odd? Shouldn't it be directly behind her? Well, not unless this mirror (and it is a mirror, have a look at the golden frame) is on an angle. And while this doesn't seem to be the case at first, the only feasible explanation for her reflection's placement is because you aren't looking at the mirror head-on, which means the guy in the hat probably isn't you.

"Thank God."

You, the viewer, are somewhere just out of the frame. And now you can kind of see it. It does seem like he's looking past her and she's looking past him. So why does any of this matter? It matters the moment you realize that this painting isn't meant to be a portrait. It's not about her, or you, or any one particular person. It's about the very place of the scene itself. By disorienting us, Manet tells us exactly what it was like to be there, scattered with others in the calculated madness of the Folies-Bergère, and we, and him, and her, are just the pawns necessary to make the entire effect work as he intended.

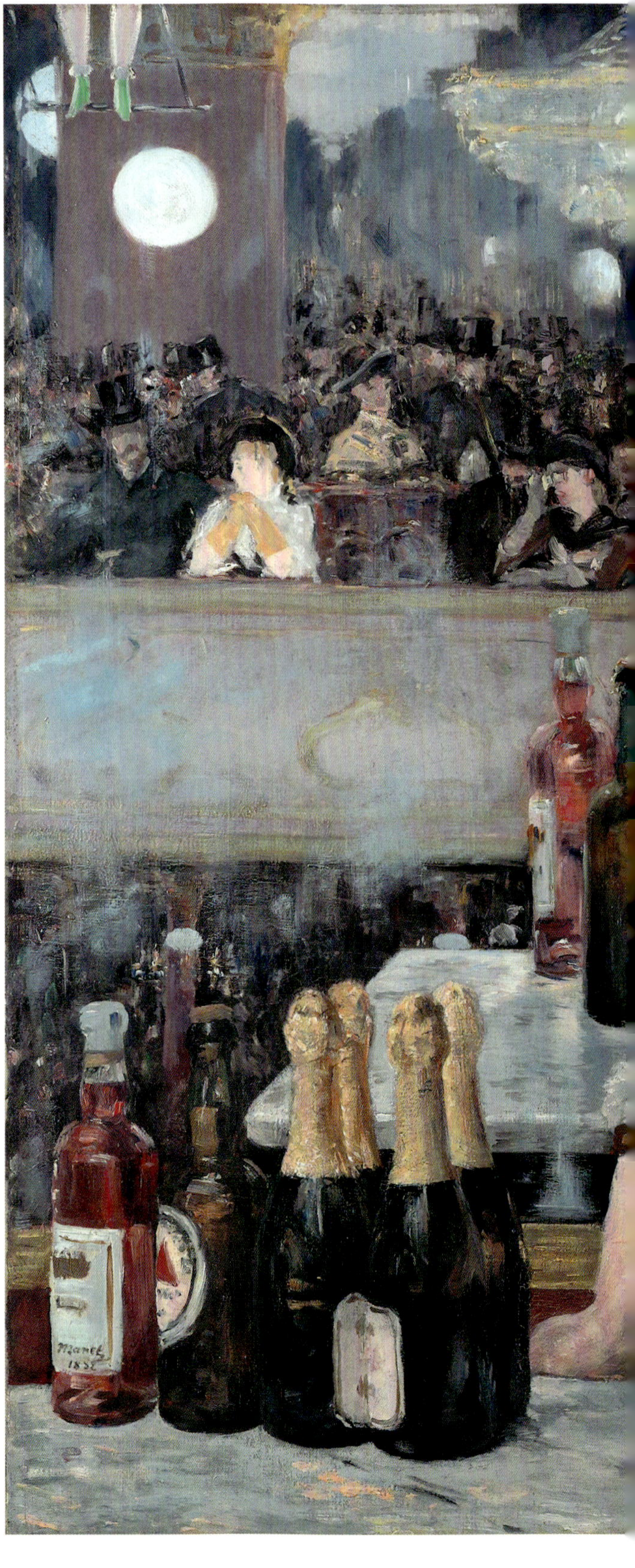

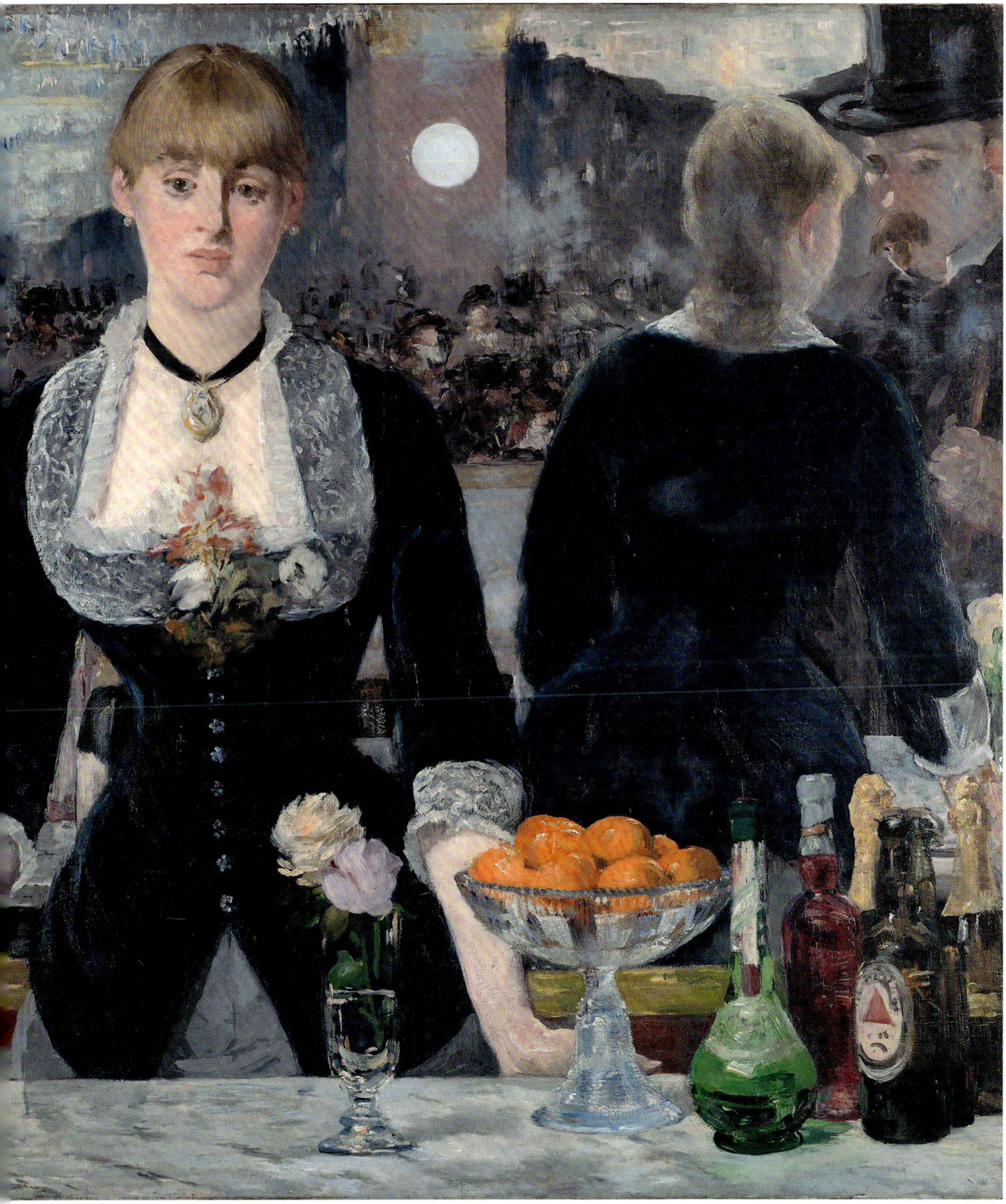

Little Girl in a Blue Armchair

Mary Cassatt, 1878

This painting marks one of the moments when Mary Cassatt fully steps into Impressionism: not as a product of theme, but of composition. Instead of presenting an idealized, refined portrait of a child, she shows a little girl collapsed, bored, and sprawled out on a blue chair in a painting that is purely observational.

The work revolves around the girl's slumped posture. She isn't centered, but instead, is sinking into the cushions of the blue armchair on the right side of the image. On the left side, to counter her presence, is a small dog. The girl's stillness is anchored against the strong diagonal line created by the grey rug, and it gives the painting both a sense of motion and depth. It's all very clever.

Where an artist of the nineteenth century would traditionally render the portrait of a child to be refined and symmetrical, to some degree, Cassatt breaks all the rules. She intentionally unbalances the entire work to throw us off tradition's scent. Again, this isn't an idealized artwork: It's supposed to capture the true nature of what Cassatt sees. And what is that? Well, in this instance, a little girl who has a personality and might be kind of bored. She'd rather be doing a million other things than pose for a painting, and Cassatt really nails it. And to hammer home that idea even further, the artist does something with the child's form. Consider this: The girl isn't unruly. Instead, the world around her is too formal. It's too large, it's too adult, and it's lame. It's rectangular, and angular, and made of solid masses, and here is this little girl and her dog, and they're anything but that. Cassatt paints them with soft arcs and curved limbs and with a looseness that feels organic. They represent the only *reality* in the painting, whereas everything else is a fabrication. It's quite a modern idea, and it's further accentuated by a modern framing. The way Cassatt crops the image, cutting off the edge of the chair in the foreground, and even just the tip of the little girl's foot, gives the entire piece the feeling of psychological immediacy, and I think that's the goal here. This is a painting about a little girl, so she captures what it is to encounter one.

So do Cassatt's composition choices serve her work's objective? The answer is yes: The composition does the heavy lifting, which should be the rule. Composition should do 90 percent of the work, and in reading any painting, it's the composition we should start with: the surest way to solve an image.

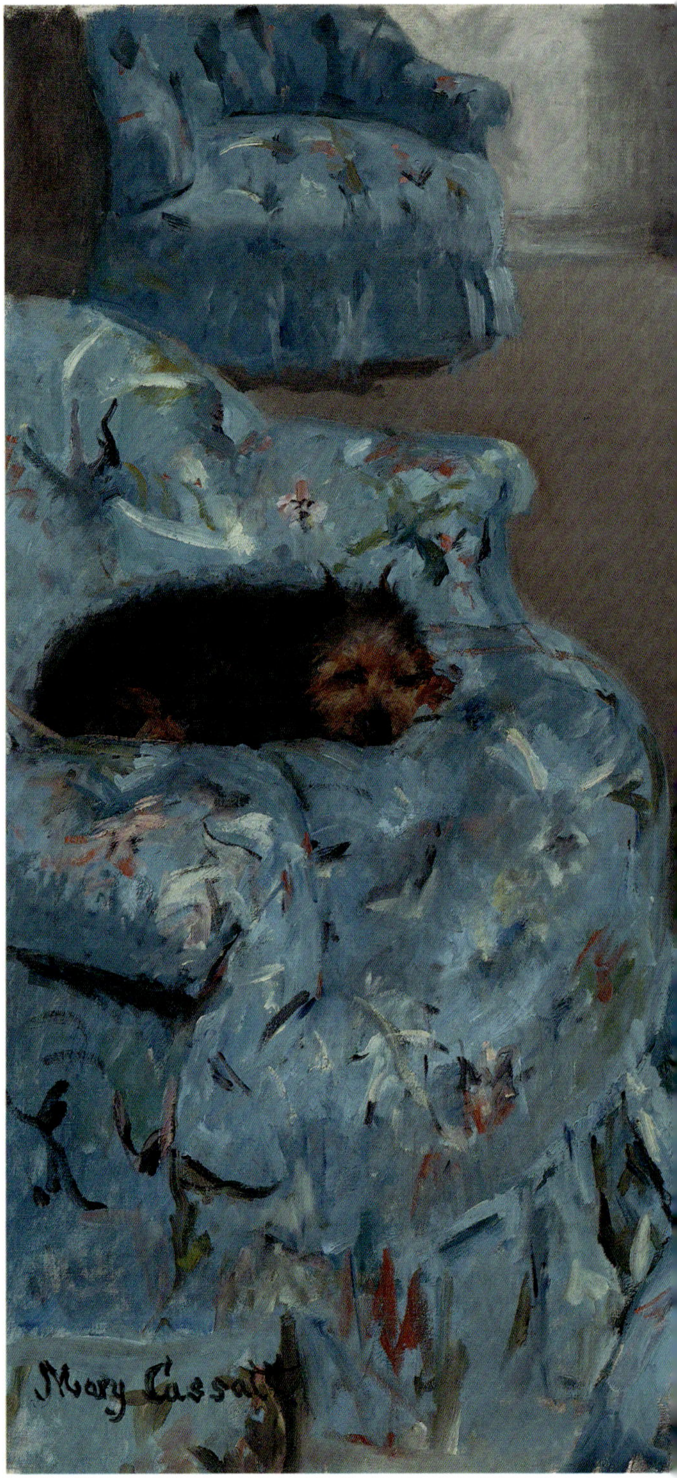

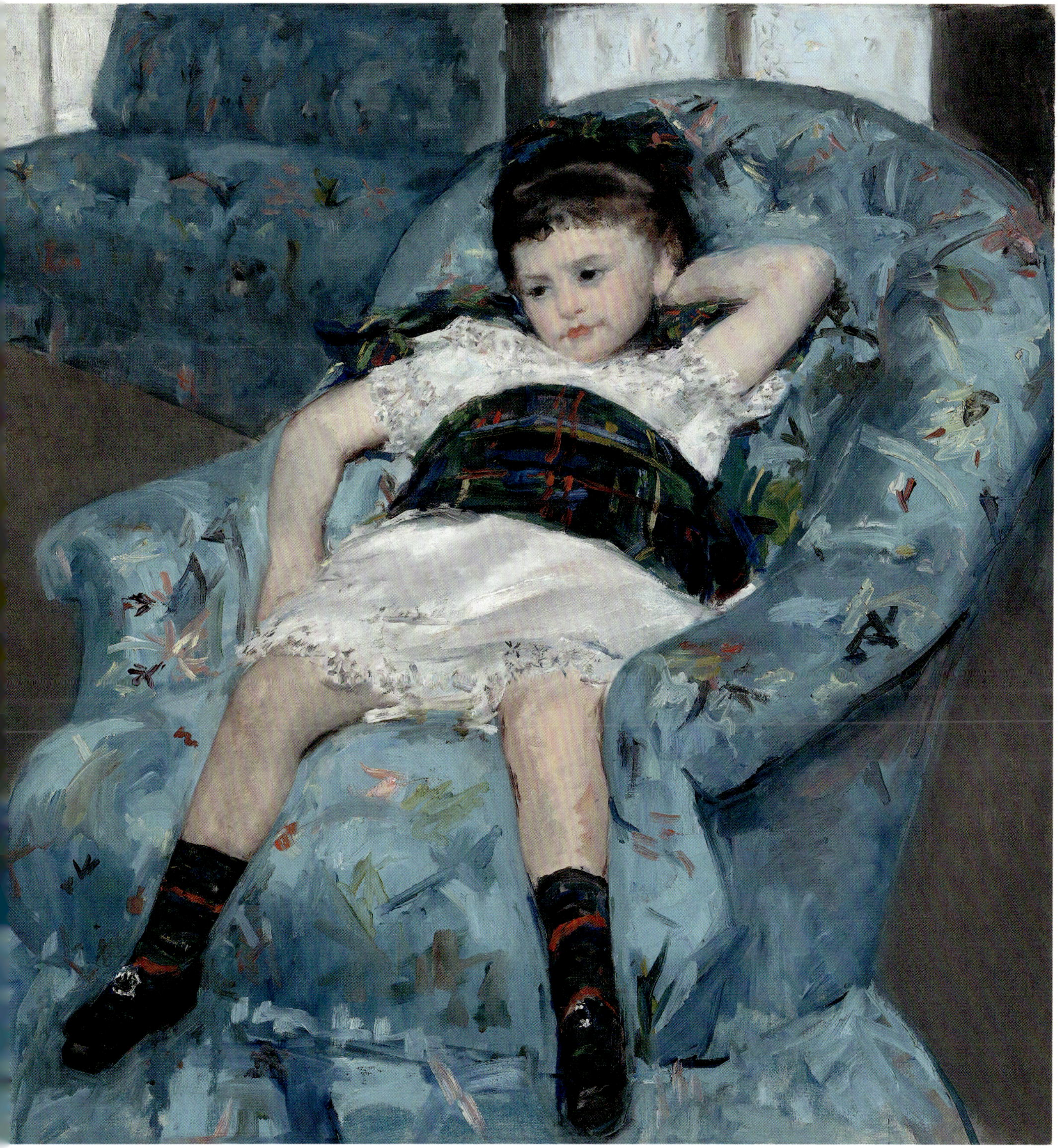

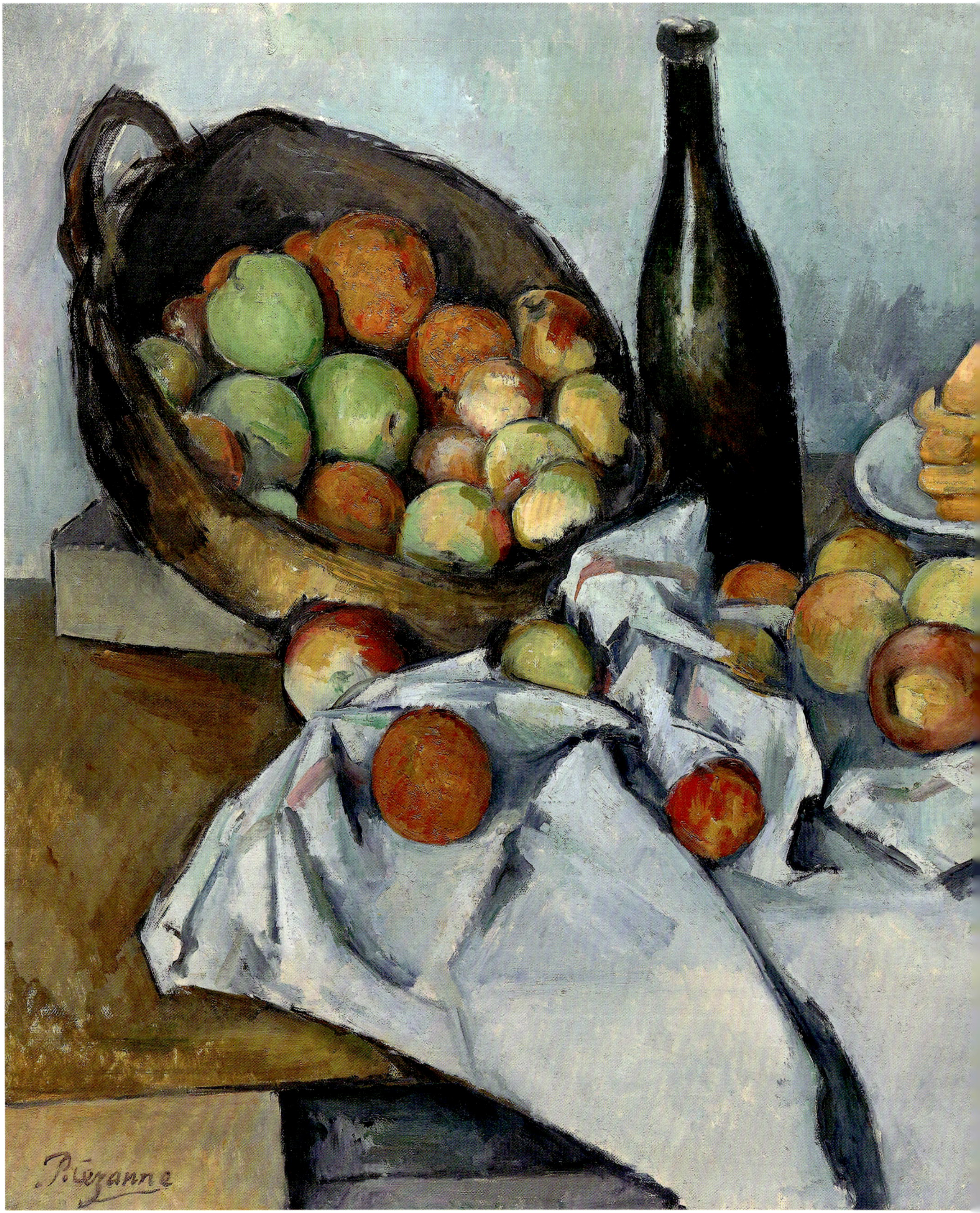

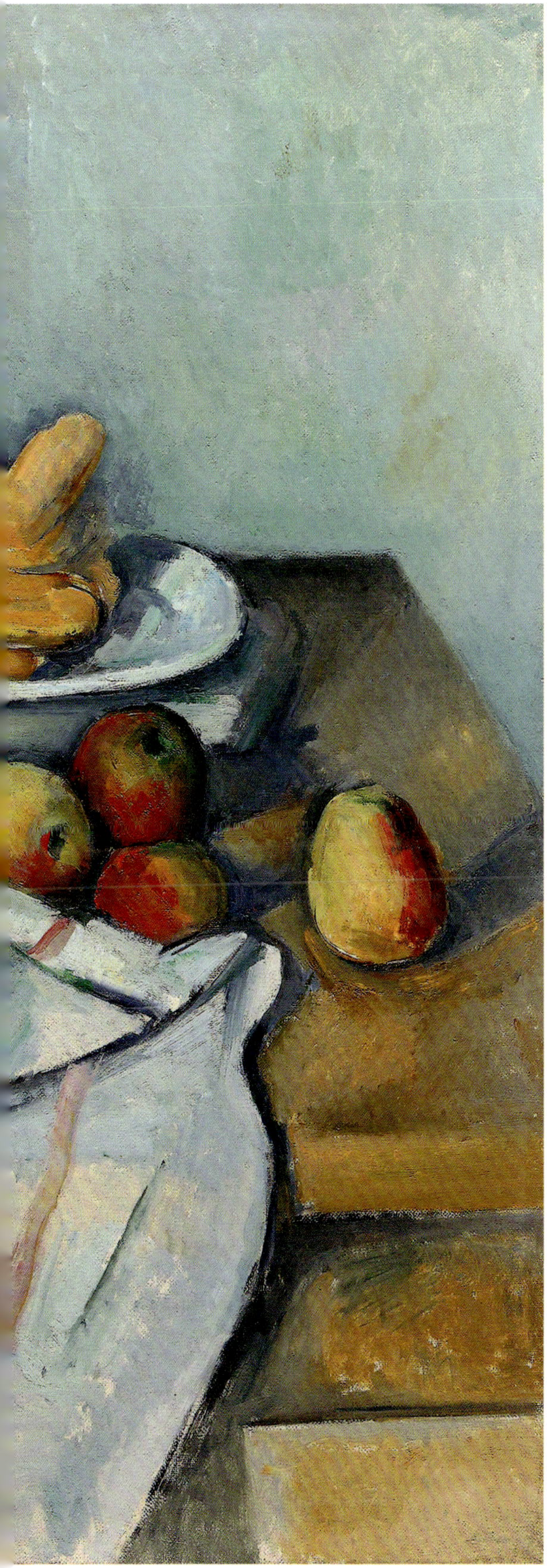

The Basket of Apples

Paul Cézanne, 1895

Speaking about solving images ... right away, there is something about this painting that feels wrong. The table feels like it slopes downward, the basket tilts forward as if it's about to spill over, the bottle leans left, and every part of the work appears like a distortion, but these aren't errors. This is the core of Paul Cézanne's approach.

None of Cézanne's compositions are decorative, or naturalistic. They are, instead, highly functional and efficient. His approach to art was architectural: a hallmark of his contributions. Cézanne created images that are constructed on tilted planes, utilizing multiple viewpoints, and treated all of the elements in his works like building blocks: a geometry to organize his vision. He reduced forms, and in doing so, gave his work stability, weight, balance, and most importantly, monumentality.

In this painting, he abandons single-point perspective in favor of something entirely new, because he recognizes that the eye wanders. He approaches the still life from multiple viewpoints, and by interlocking each, creates a spatial tension that makes the image feel alive. There is a musicality to it: a rhythm through a repetition of forms. The roundness of the apples repeats over and over again. The reds and yellows replay in your mind as you pan across the work. One echoing mass after the next, and it's harmonious.

Cézanne also builds depth through color, in planes that advance or recede items in the work. He doesn't need to dramatize any one idea, because he understands the effects of order and the collapse of order, and the world that exists in between. Through the rhythm of the apples, the structural diagonals, balanced color masses, warped perspective, and clear geometry pitted against a tilted table, Cézanne gives us a painting with perfect equilibrium. In a way, he is a compositional purist.

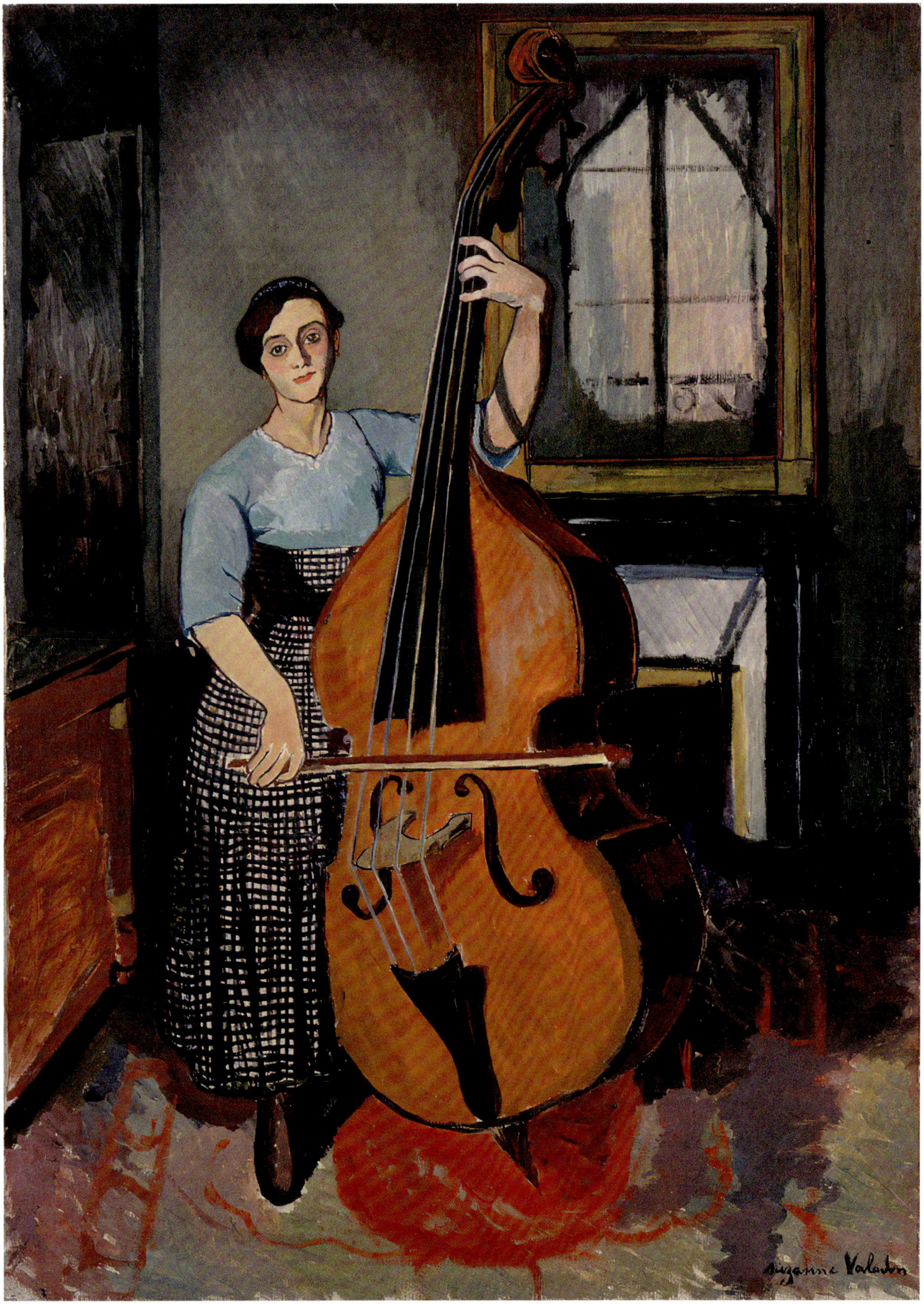
Suzanne Valadon

Woman with a Double Bass

Suzanne Valadon, 1908

Suzanne Valadon is another artist who arranges her compositions with an architectural edge, though in a much different way than Cézanne. In this example, she organizes her entire image on the back of two massive vertical anchors, the woman and the bass. They dominate the composition. Many artists might have approached the work in a way that made the instrument a prop, but here, Valadon makes the bass the partner to the woman. It's got its own life. It is the painting's central architectural form.

Valadon creates a dialogue between the work's two pillars. The woman is constructed as slightly angular, with linear arms and a straight posture, and is defined by clear edges, in comparison to the bass, which is curved, organic, bulbous, and sensual in its silhouette. This is the visual tension in the painting. Valadon does not blend, but rather, juxtaposes. And it's this harmony that makes for a pleasing visual experience. It's what makes Valadon a conductor of great ideas and gives her a unique visual identity, defined exclusively through her own philosophy and approach.

An artist's approach to their art is how we come to define them. It sounds obvious but it's something we often take for granted, I think. Picasso is undeniably Picasso, Cézanne is Cézanne, Monet is Monet, and so on. Everyone has a fingerprint, and everyone is different. And of all artists, maybe one of the most profound and unique approaches to composition is that of Diego Velázquez: one of the most important and influential painters of all time, and a pioneer who created his own visual language during a period that was dominated by so many rules.

Las Meninas

Diego Velázquez, 1656

There are paintings that show you something, and then there are paintings that pull you inside their machinery. Velázquez's *Las Meninas* is the latter: a composition so deliberately engineered that it feels less like a picture and more like a trapdoor into the seventeenth-century Spanish court. At first glance, it's a charming studio moment. The young Infanta Margaret Theresa flanked by her attendants, a couple of royal court dwarfs, a giant dog sprawled on the floor. But Velázquez has no interest in giving you a clean narrative. What he builds instead is an architectural puzzle in a space designed to confuse the hierarchy between viewer, artist, and subject.

Everything in the painting orbits around three anchors: the Infanta, Velázquez himself, and the faint reflection of the King and Queen in the mirror at the back of the room. These points form an invisible triangle of power. The child is illuminated like the future of the dynasty, Velázquez stands just taller than every other figure, and the monarchs exist only as a ghostly reflection. This triangle is the real skeleton of the composition. Velázquez wants you to feel the tension, which is that the painter and the royal couple share the same level of authority inside the picture. It's an outrageous claim for a court painter, and he makes it using pure structure.

Then there's the mirror, the painting's secret engine. It hangs in the background, glowing faintly, and it reflects the King and Queen standing exactly where we, the viewers, are. Suddenly the composition flips. The painting resolves itself, not as it depicts the royal family, but rather as it uses us to complete the image. We occupy the monarchs' physical space. We become the subject of Velázquez's gaze. The canvas he's working on, the one we see only from behind, is painting us back. Velázquez collapses the boundary between art and reality until you can't tell whose viewpoint you're occupying anymore.

He builds the room using multiple depth planes: foreground figures, midground shadows, the open doorway glowing in the back, and the mirror, which creates a fourth, metaphysical layer. The entire composition funnels your eye from the bright silhouette of the Infanta, to Velázquez's towering presence, to that flicker of reflected royalty. Light becomes a ranking system. The child blazing in center, the painter second in line, the monarchs the faintest whisper of power. Even the chamberlain in the doorway, frozen mid-step, becomes a piece of narrative architecture. He's the timekeeper, the reminder that everything here is suspended between entering and leaving, seeing and being seen.

And the best part? This whole elaborate structure is disguised as a casual moment. A dog snoozes. A menina curtsies. Quiet chatter floats around the room, and it all looks effortless, but it's a façade. Velázquez choreographs every inch, and his composition is a thesis on painting itself. One on authorship, on the construction of royal image-making, on the way a painter can control reality simply by deciding what to show and what to hide. Velázquez doesn't just ask you to look at his world: He makes you confront the fact that he's looking right back at you.

This is why *Las Meninas* is one of the greatest compositions ever made. A game of power disguised as a picture, and a painting that places the artist, not the king, at the center of the universe.

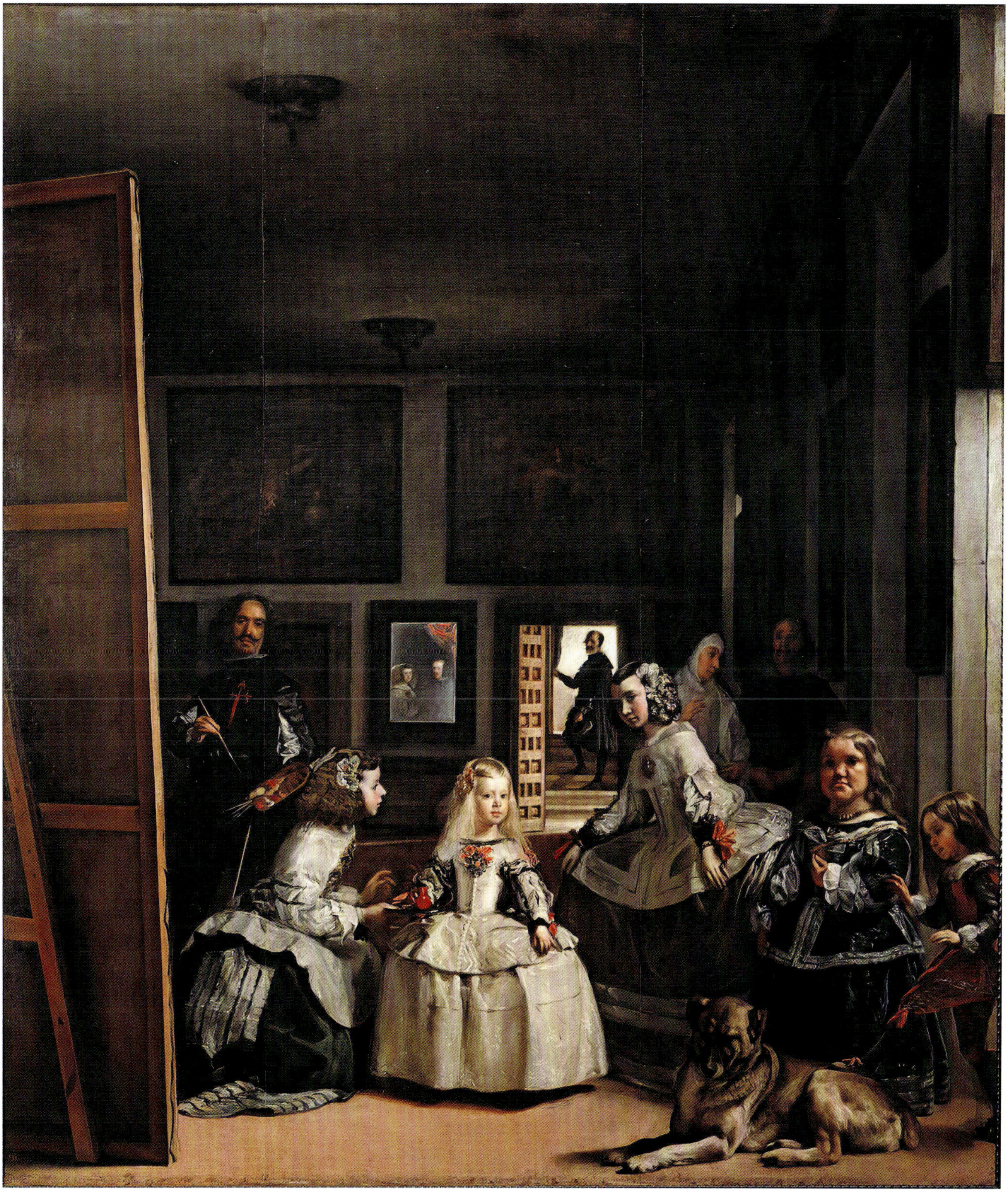

GREAT
IDEAS

Art has no true boundaries. A great idea has the ability to circumnavigate the world and, along the way, shape that same world in such spectacular ways, through one of the greatest gifts that people can bestow on other: the transfer of knowledge for the betterment of the collective. There is something truly extraordinary about watching ideas collide, and something even better about witnessing worlds meet on a canvas.

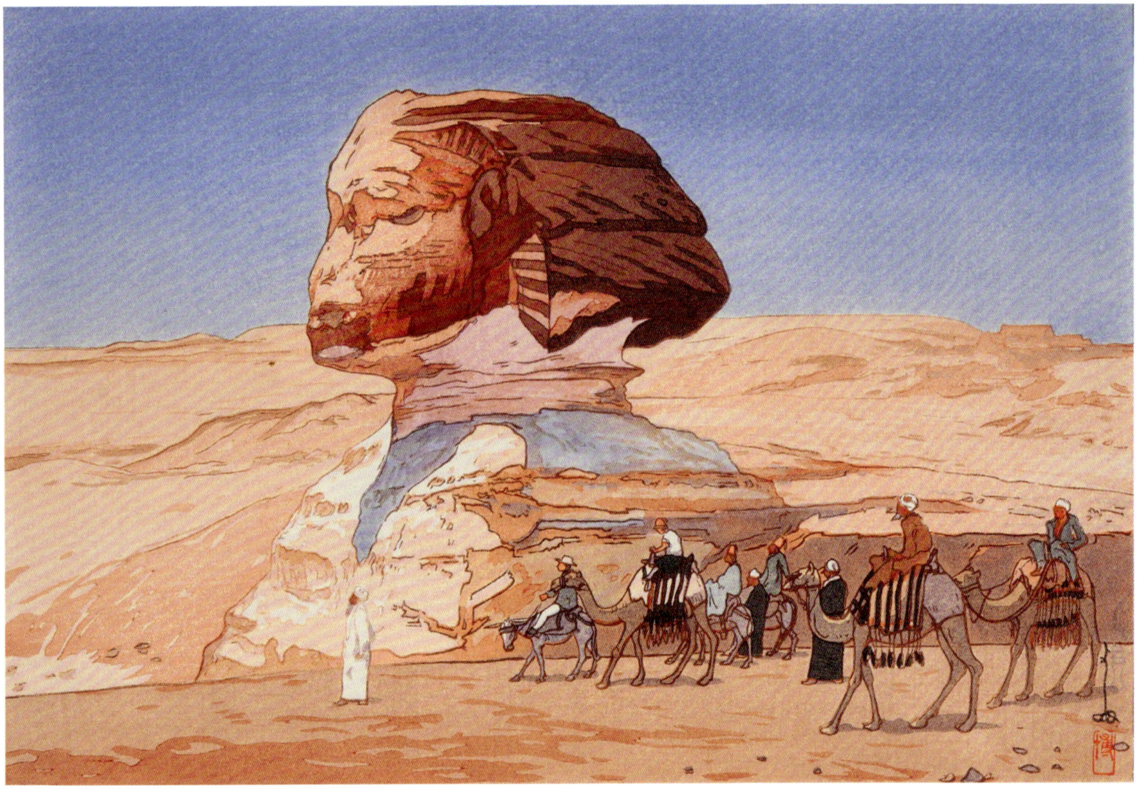

Sphinx, Day, Yoshida Hiroshi, 1925

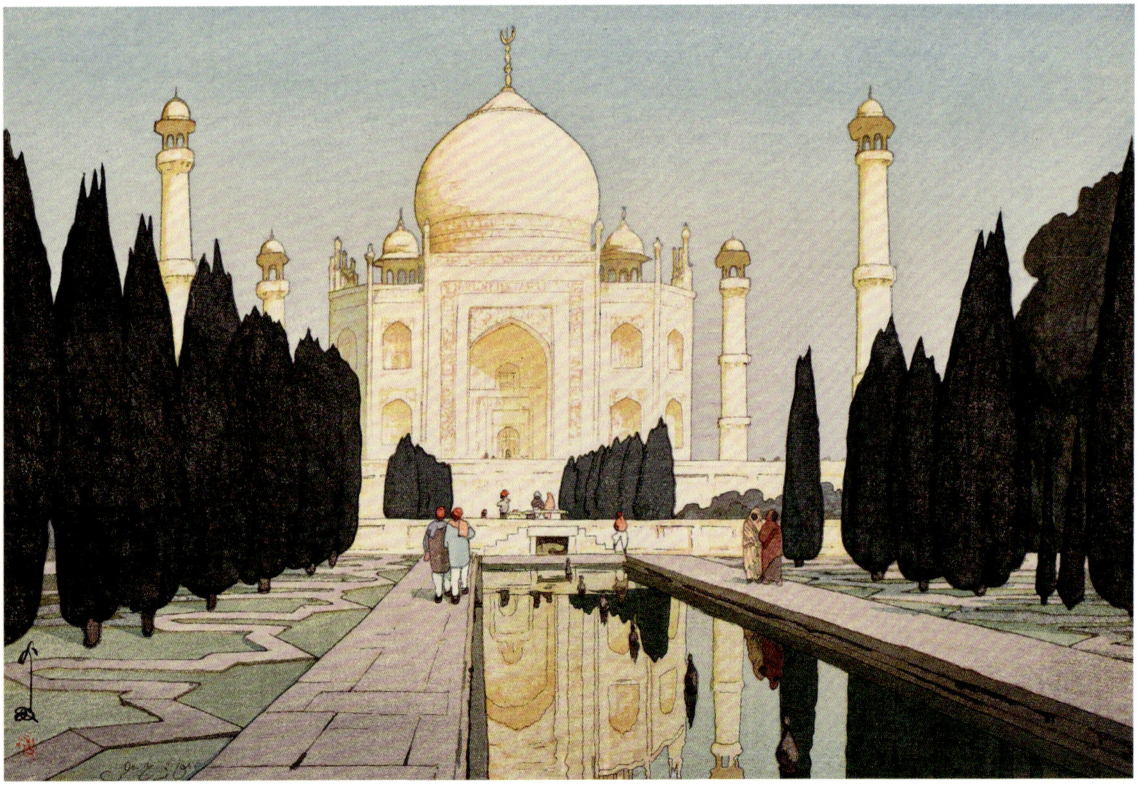

The Taj Mahal Gardens, Yoshida Hiroshi, 1931

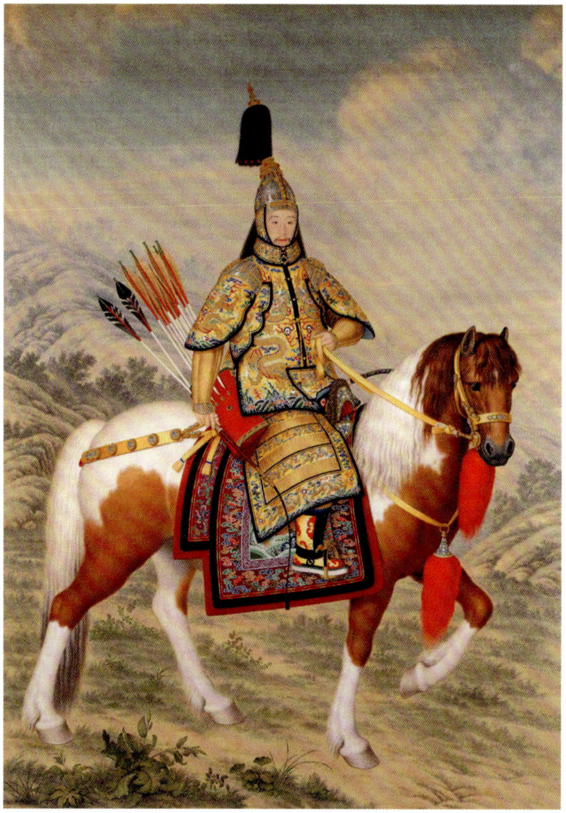

The Qianlong Emperor in Ceremonial Armour on Horseback, Giuseppe Castiglione, 1739 or 1758

Various works by Yoshida Hiroshi and Giuseppe Castiglione

1739–1931

Just have a look at the works to the left by twentieth-century Japanese artist Yoshida Hiroshi. Often lauded as one of the greatest woodblock printmakers, his work carries a near-mystical property as it pertains to his colorful depictions of Japan, but it's his coverage of life outside his home country that transcends the imagination. The familiarity of landmarks such as the Sphinx, the Acropolis, Venetian waterways, and the Taj Mahal transform into entirely different dreamscapes, as seen through an entirely different point of view.

And what of the painting above, created two centuries earlier, by of one of China's greatest artists? Of course, I should probably mention that he's not even Chinese—he's Italian.

Giuseppe Castiglione served not one, not two, but three emperors of China, blending European and Chinese traditions in a way that makes him one of art's most interesting figures. Not quite as jarring as an elephant roaming the streets of Jaipur with a Japanese twist, but still mesmerizing.

When it comes to the great ideas illuminating new ones, though, there may be no better example than Hokusai's *Great Wave*. It is one of the most important images in the history of art, made by one of history's most important artists. But, to fully appreciate it, we'll need to circle halfway around the world and rewind a few hundred years to meet Filippo Brunelleschi, a pioneering Italian architect, engineer, and sculptor who, through a series of mathematical experiments between the years 1415 to 1420, is credited with inventing a concept in art called linear perspective, which showed artists how to see in 3D. Perhaps the greatest example of that contribution to painting can be seen in this next work by Raphael.

School of Athens

Raphael, 1509–1511

Everything about this painting points to it being about the two figures at its center: Plato on the left, Aristotle on the right, and in between, that groundbreaking principle in art of perspective. And to be more specific, a single-point perspective where the architectural lines meet, sandwiched in between two giants of thought. Now have a look at their hands. In the subtlest of gestures, Raphael exposes the nature of three-dimensional space, because while gravity pulls us down, Plato's finger points to the heavens: a y-axis, in mathematical terms. Aristotle's foreshortened arm points forward, countered only by the depth of the building itself, and we have our z-axis. The giant horizon line stretches from left to right, and…

"We got the point, Matthew. But this isn't just a painting about perspective, is it?"

Well no, it's not. While the forms of these figures expose the spectacular nature of space in the artwork, they also reveal a critical philosophical crossroads: a divergence of ideas split between the ideal and the empirical.

Plato's finger points to the heavens. Aristotle's palm faces the floor. Plato wears colors associated with divinity, while Aristotle's colors are tied to the earth—one school of ideas rooted in innate knowledge, the other grounded in the principles of observation. Classical thought versus contemporary thought, the old world and the new.

And it's about to get way cooler. The Italian master paints a classical setting in a contemporary space, and in doing so blends antiquity with the Renaissance through modern architectural features inspired by the architect Bramante. He then fills this space with the greatest minds in human history: Plato, Aristotle, Anaximander, Pythagoras, Socrates, Heraclitus and Cleitus, Diogenes, Alcibiades, Xenophon, Zeno of Citium and Parmenides, Averroes, Epicurus, Carneades, and more. And well, you missed it, because Plato is painted in the likeness of Leonardo, while Heraclitus looks quite like Michelangelo. Raphael even paints himself as Apelles, and in doing so, once again blends the old world with the new to create a reality in which ideas form on the backs of intellectual interactions and knowledge is synthesized through art.

And Raphael isn't the only one glancing out toward us. In a move with so much depth, you'll be picking your jaw up off the floor, he paints *her*: Hypatia, a revered figure in the fields of mathematics, astronomy, and philosophy. And where in the world of antiquity,

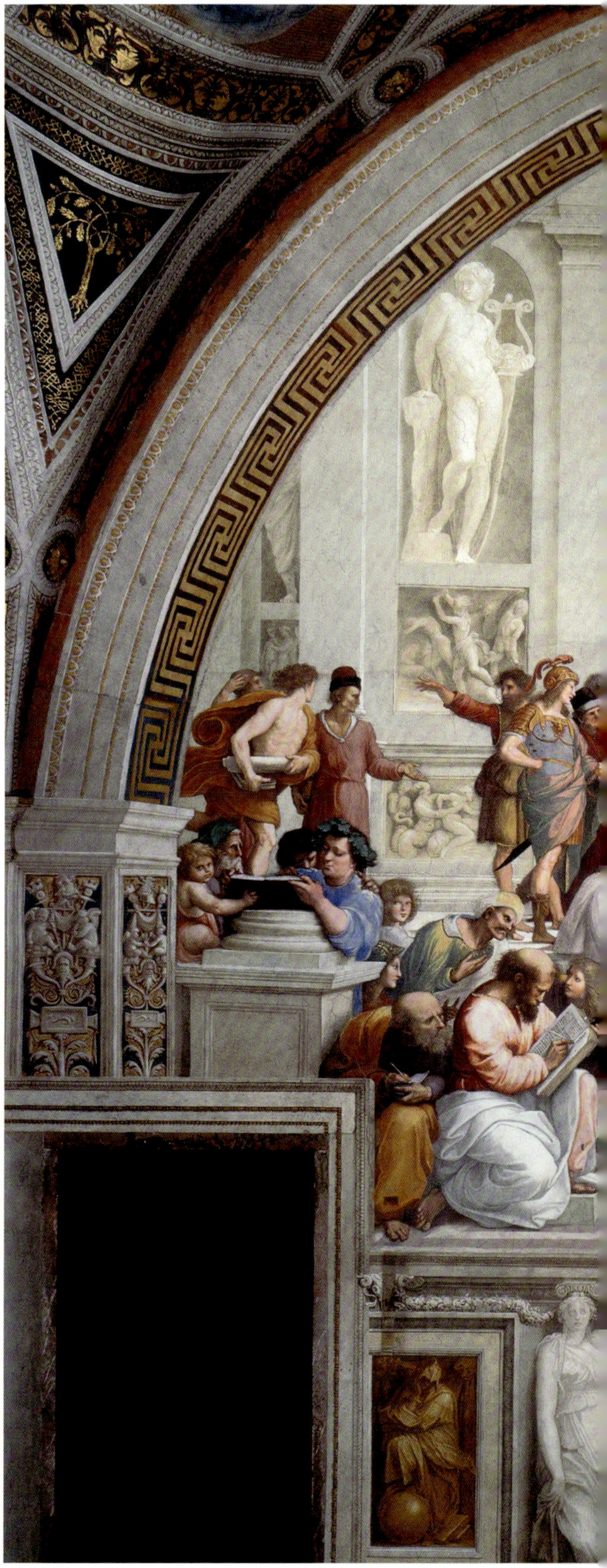

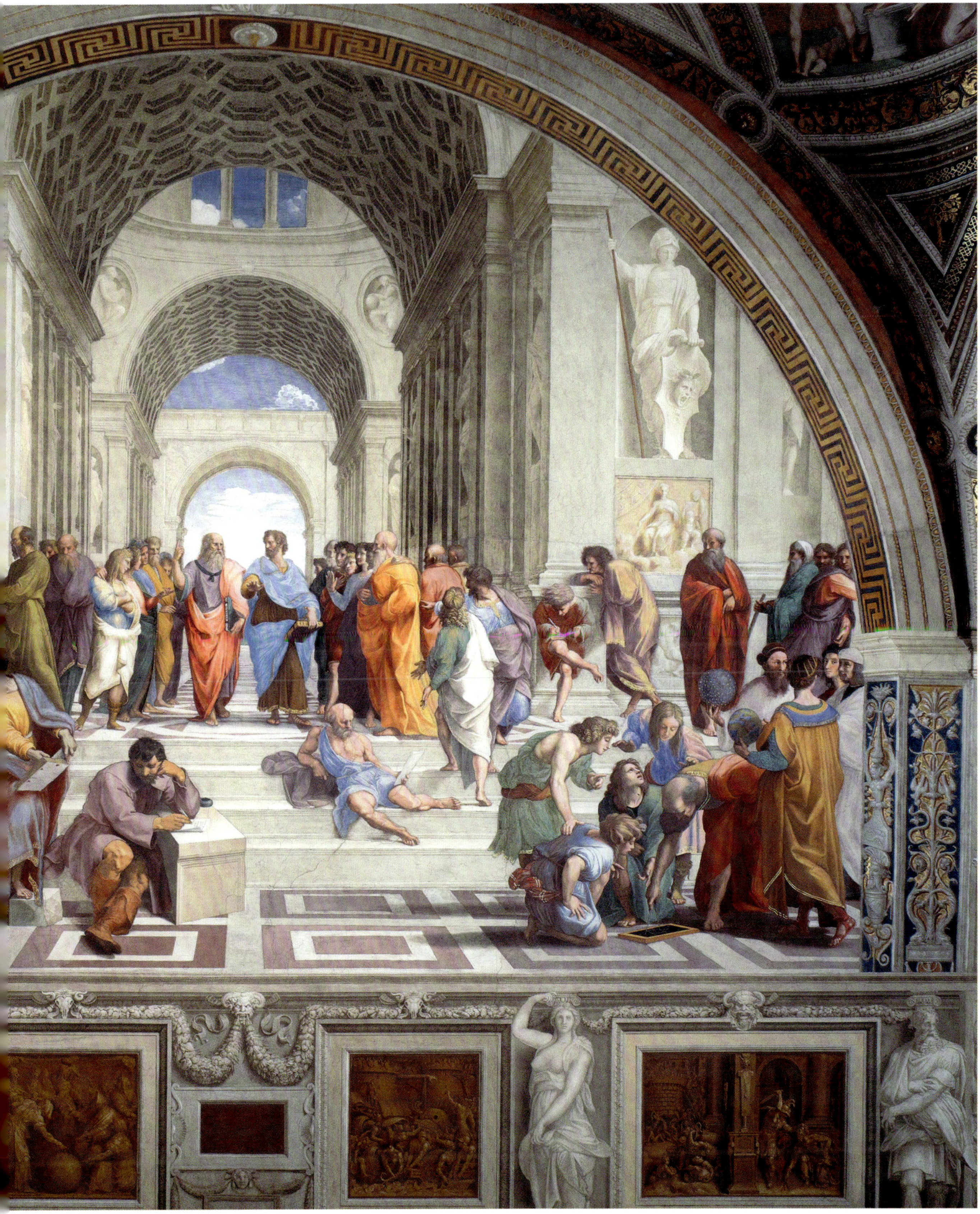

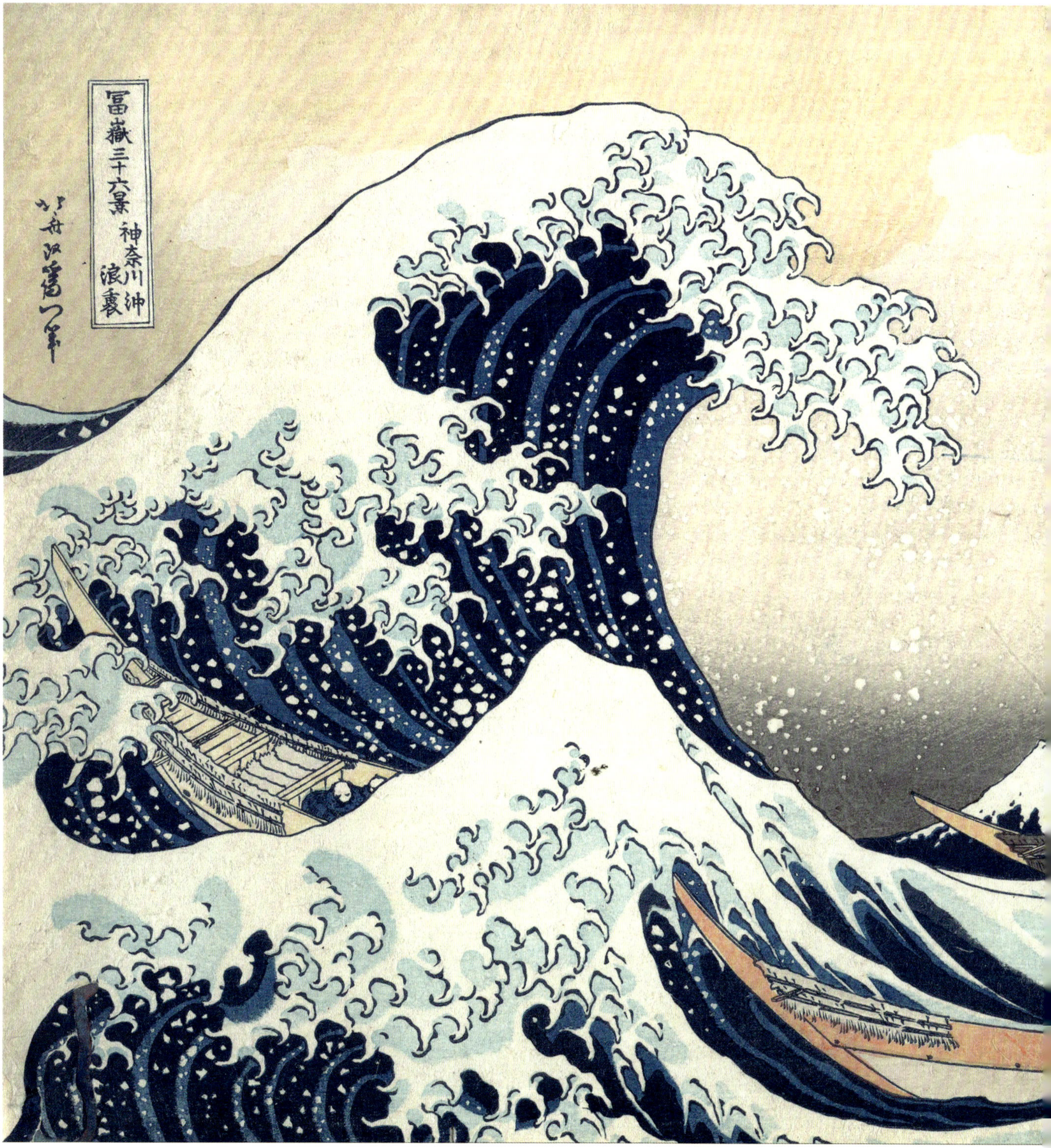
冨嶽三十六景
神奈川沖
浪裏

a woman's ideas would often have been silenced and held as passing thoughts, Hypatia was well regarded and respected by her peers. A taste of modern world, over a thousand years before it arrived, where all great ideas are met in the middle, moving us all a little further forward.

"Right. So, what does this have to do with Hokusai?"

Believe it or not, it kind of has everything to do with him. Like a piece of contraband smuggled across guarded borders, Brunelleschi's linear perspective would find its way around the globe and into the mind of the Japanese artist, where it would inspire a work so important, it would change the world.

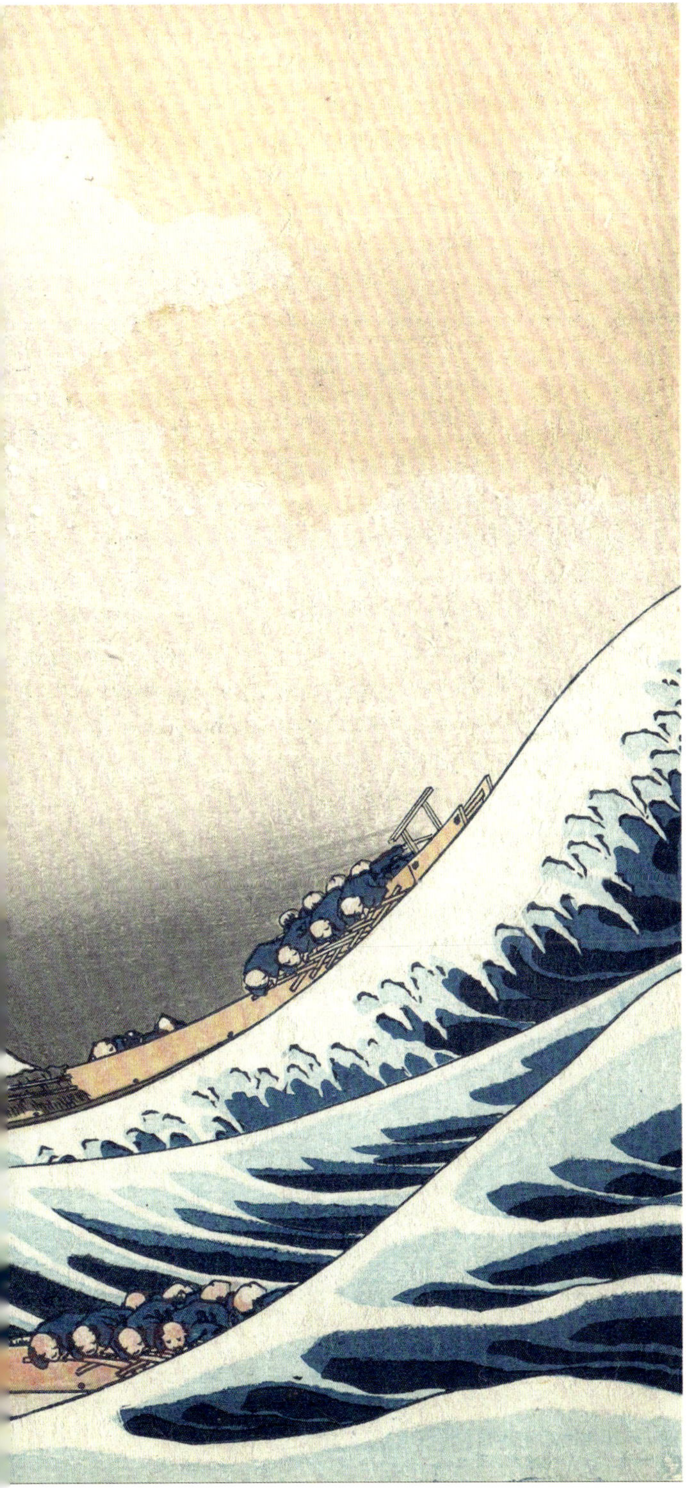

The Great Wave off Kanagawa

Katsushika Hokusai, 1830–31

Three boats caught in the chaos of a storm-tossed sea, anchored only to the immovable calmness of Mount Fuji off in the distance. The snowcapped peak is the only element of peace in an artwork designed to capture chaos and destruction, and it works perfectly.

The beautiful Prussian blue waves of the ocean are suspended in time, on the lines of a mathematical observation theorized on the other side of the world, and it creates an atmosphere so surreal that when Japan's self-imposed isolation ended in 1853, Hokusai's greatest contribution to art would make its way back around the world and land in a new set of hands.

From Claude Monet to Vincent van Gogh to Mary Cassatt to Georges Seurat, Hokusai's *Great Wave*, along with many other woodblock prints from Japan, would back academic art onto its heels and transform the Western landscape into an atmospheric wonderland. Brilliant bright color fields that cared little for the representation of what was, focusing almost exclusively on how the world felt. And from the corridors of academic rejection in France, a flame was lit once again that would spread across Europe like a wildfire.

The Grand Canal in Venice

Umberto Boccioni, 1907

Those embers carried things full circle back to Italy, and more specifically, Venice, where Umberto Boccioni shows us the intersecting line between full-blown modern abstraction and art rooted in tradition. By carefully dotting pigment onto the canvas, Boccioni distills every notion of reality into an impression in an artwork that is entirely about how it *feels* to look onto a scene of boats sailing the Venetian canal. It is an image in which every reflection and every glimmer of light are so familiar, even if we have never stood in this spot: an atmosphere that rejects the past while still connected to it.

And it is in this specific context that two paintings from two very different times are eternally bound. Hokusai's, rooted in the old world, and Boccioni's, propelled by the new one, are married by their ability to affect how we feel. Two drastically different approaches that are injected with radically atmospheric properties, both progressing the art world we know today. Ideas that would inspire generations of artists that came after, sailing around the world like the boats in this canal, or those that are caught in a storm.

But the influence of great ideas in art isn't limited to just museums. These ideas don't happen in a vacuum. They find their way into our daily lives, whether in the books and movies we read and watch, or in the halls of government. In turn, what happens in the world finds its way back onto paint palettes, which is how we end up with *Guernica* by Pablo Picasso.

In his largest ever commission, the Spanish Republican government tasked Picasso with capturing the devastating tragedy that befell his beloved Spain so the entire world could see it. However, to properly appreciate the genius of this painting, we'll need to rewind again, all the way back to the year 1889, when Henri de Toulouse-Lautrec, the legendary French painter and printmaker, created an artwork named *Moulin de la Galette*.

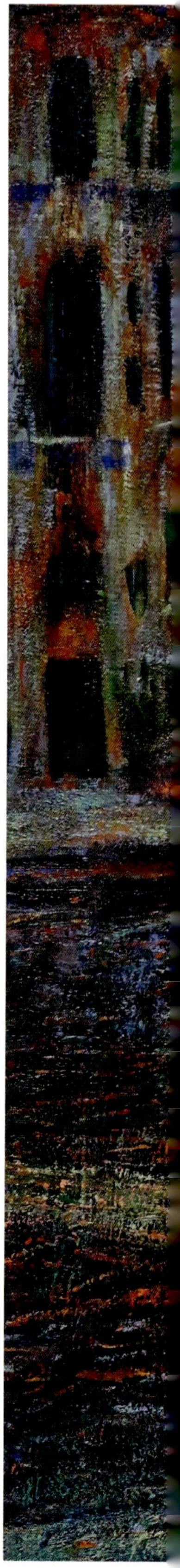

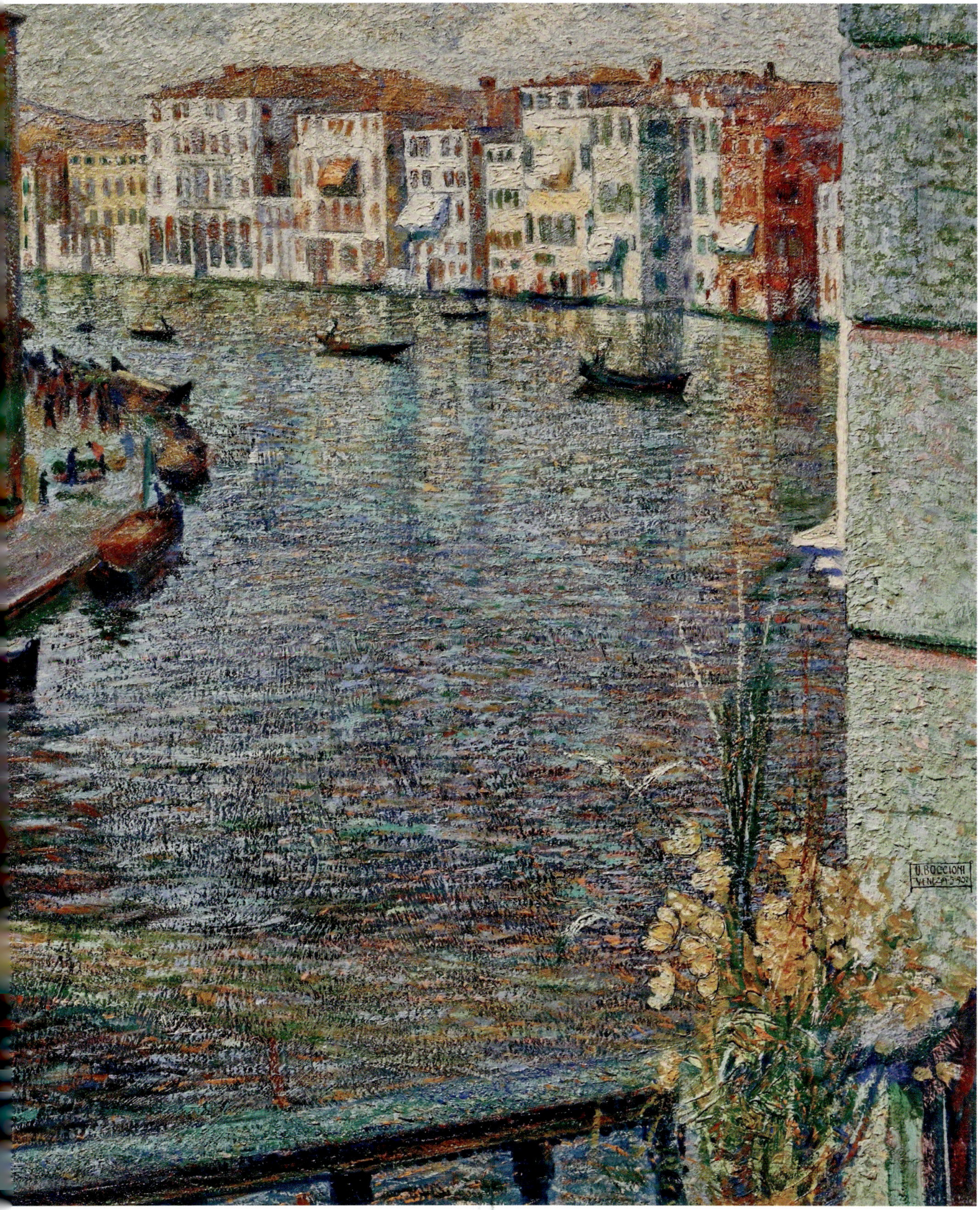
U.BOCCIONI

Moulin de la Galette

Henri de Toulouse-Lautrec, 1889

This picture depicts four individuals in the foreground and a crowd of happy partygoers off in the background. Toulouse-Lautrec employs sharpness in the details of his four main characters to evoke a sort of stillness, which is made more apparent when contrasted against the backdrop of rapidly sketched lines depicting motion. Picasso loved this idea so much that, in his own version of the painting, he employs a similar motif.

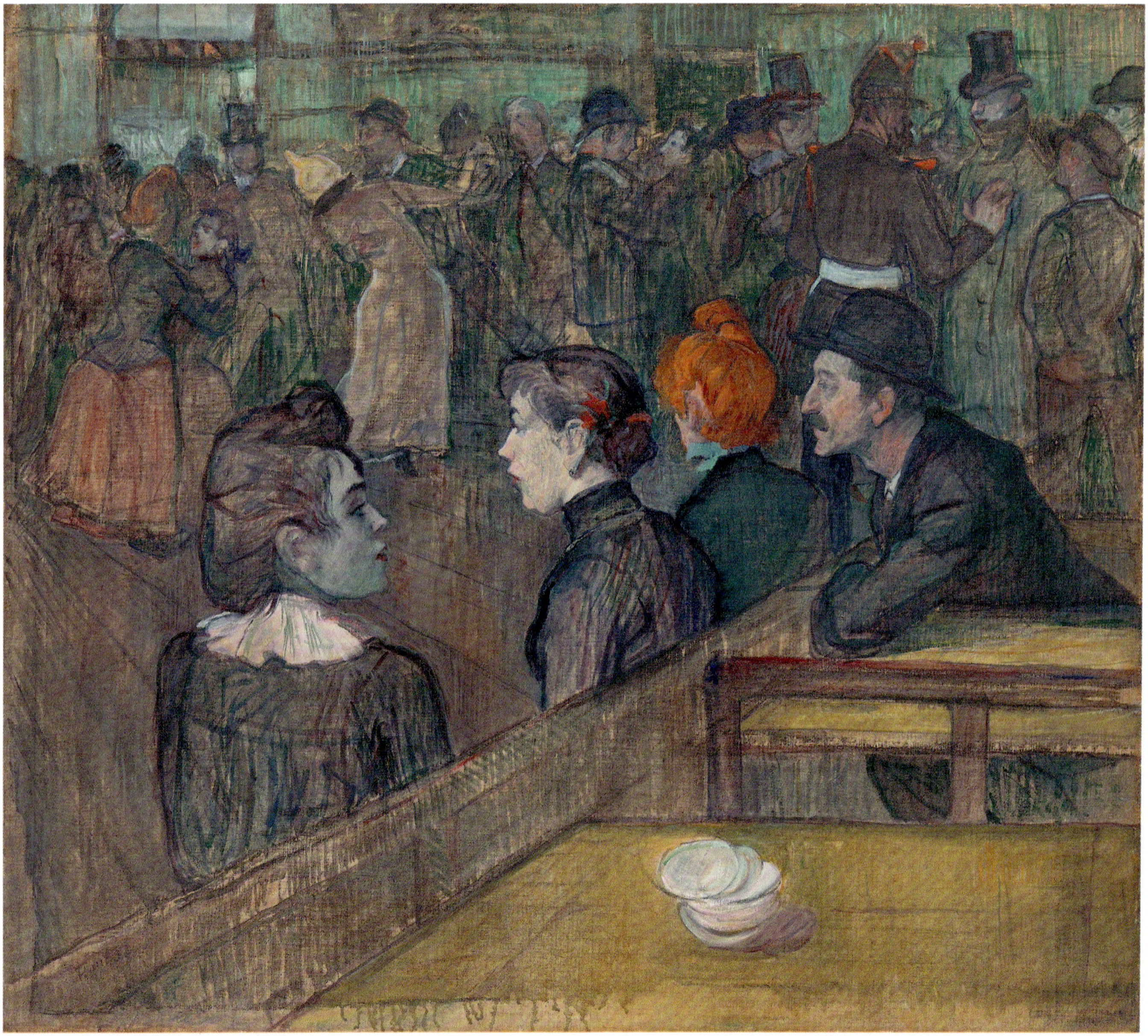

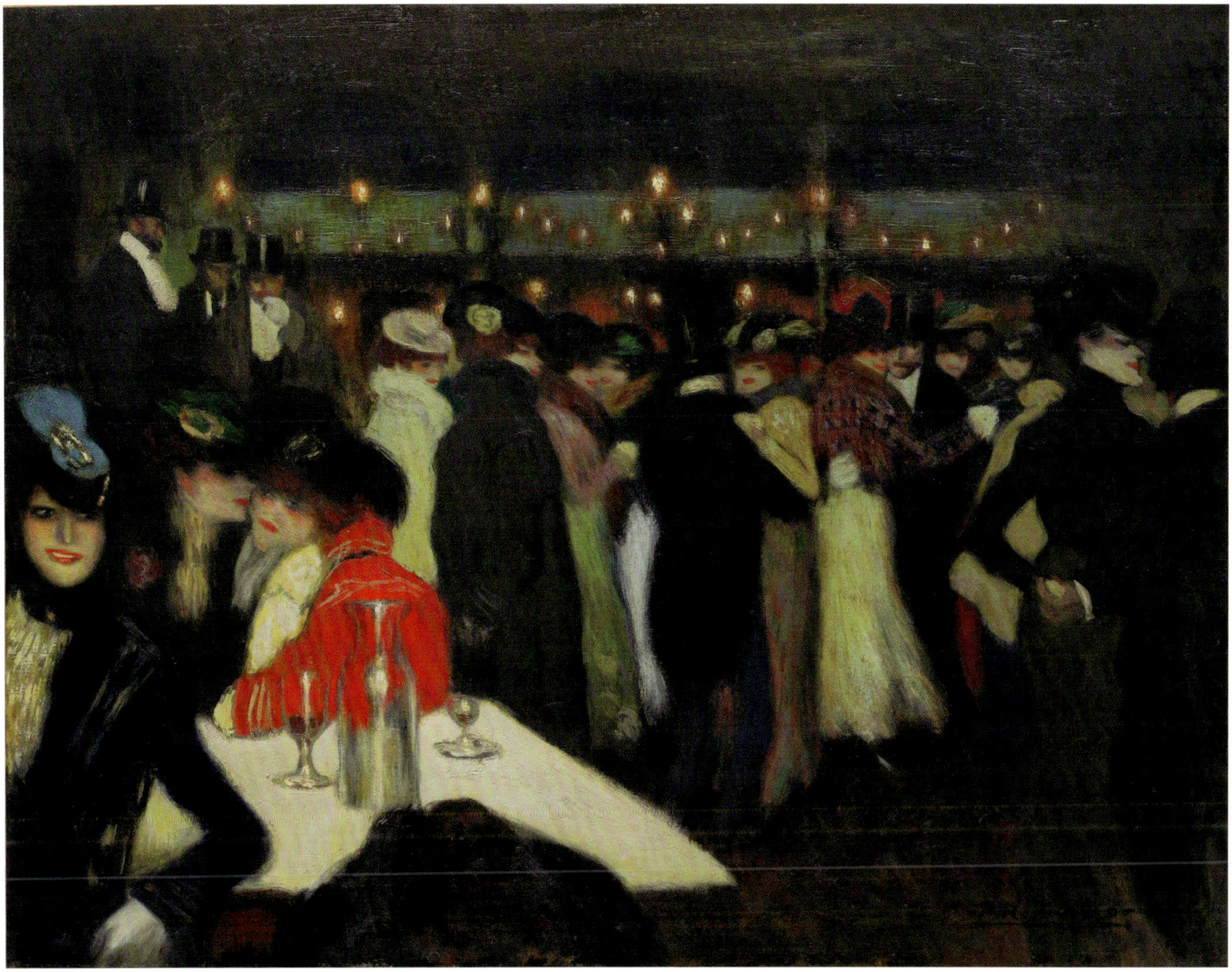

Le Moulin de la Galette

Pablo Picasso, 1900

Stillness in the front, movement in the back, and this isn't the only example of Picasso learning from his predecessors. Just look at any work from his Blue Period: frail, elongated forms, and the powerful push and pull of intense contrasts. It's impossible not to see the influences of El Greco. Or, consider his masterpiece *Les Demoiselles d'Avignon* (1907), with all its mystical, spiritual characteristics: no doubt an image inspired by the magical properties of African tribal art and a few other masterpieces, if you know where to look.

So in 1937, when Picasso was commissioned after the bombing of Guernica, he once again looked to sources of great inspiration to create what we could argue is his greatest ever painting.

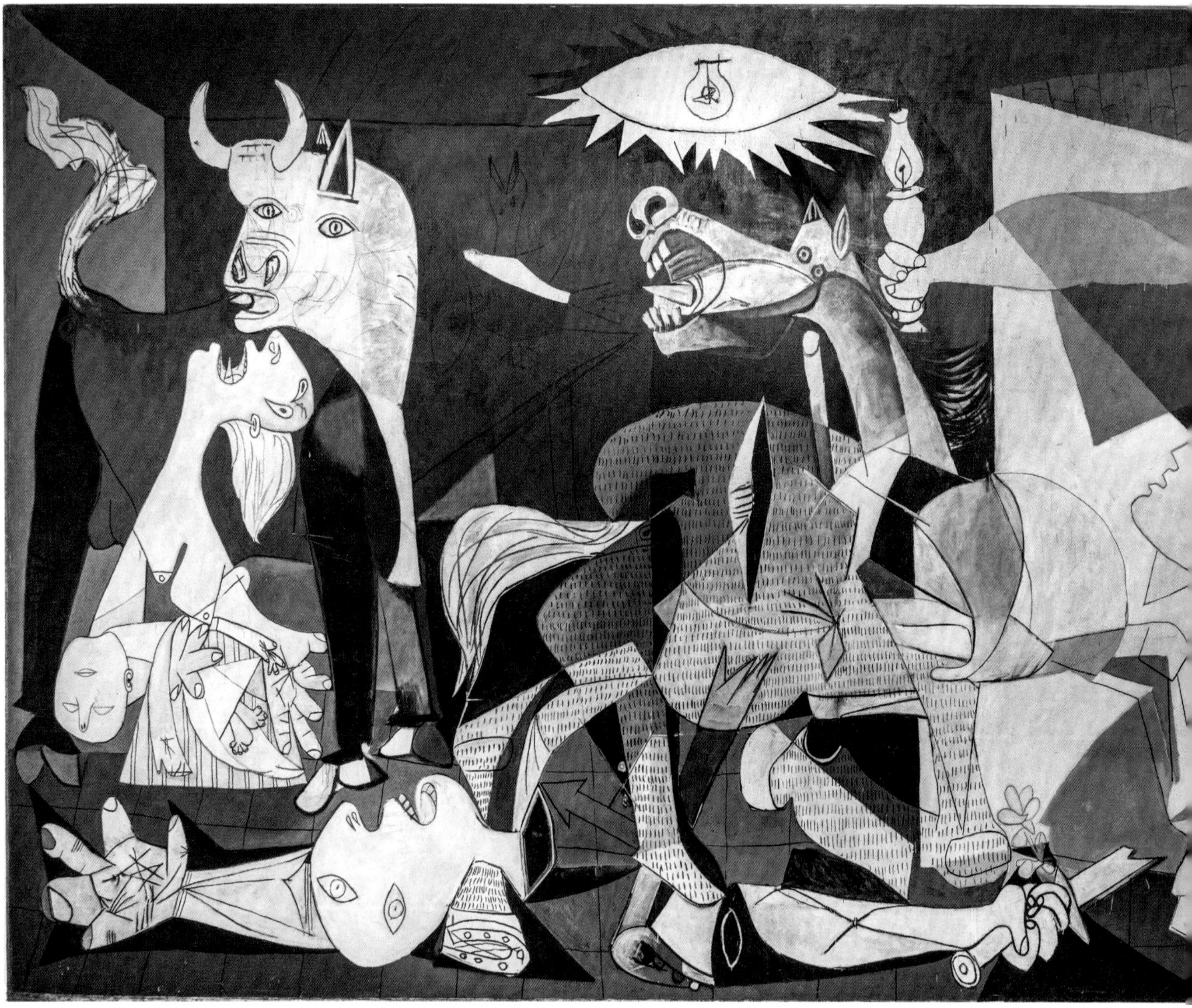

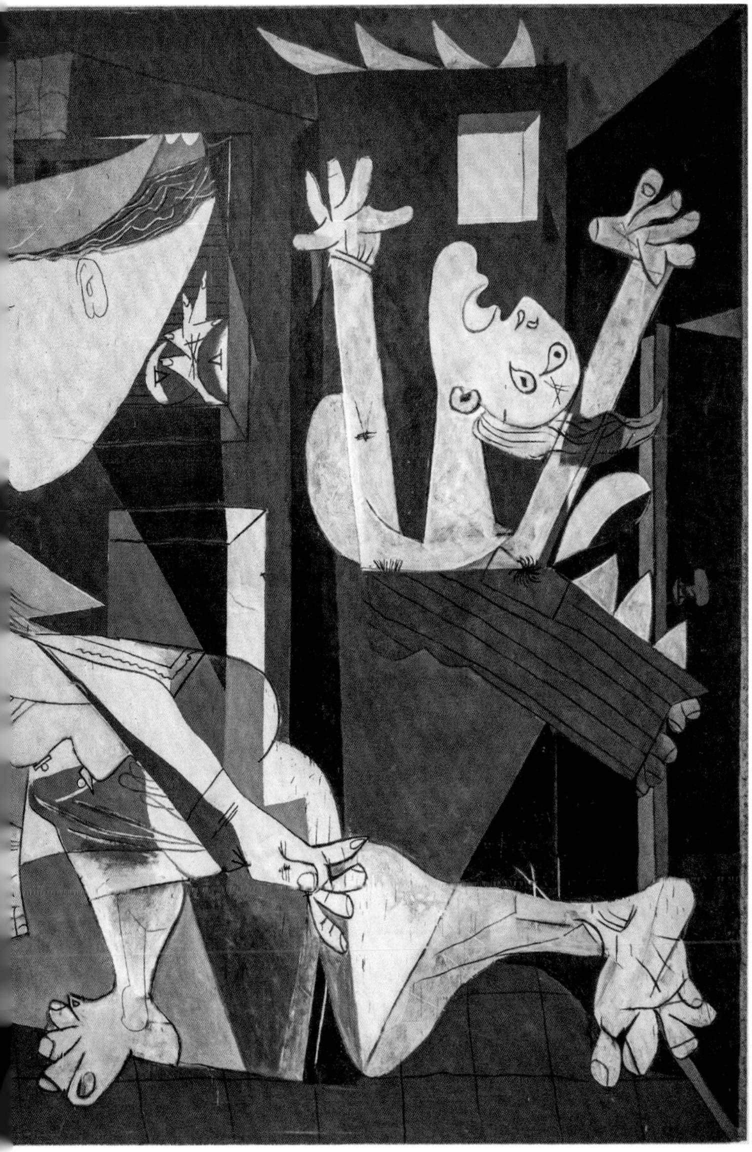

Guernica

Pablo Picasso, 1937

For this composition, Picasso studies Goya. He uses tragedy to show us tragedy. He depicts the scene in black and white, void of color, resembling the horrors and atrocities of death and destruction published in newspapers.

Picasso wasn't only a student of painting, however, but one of photography as well. On the right side of the painting, he references a 1936 Spanish Civil War photo by Robert Capa called *The Falling Soldier*. On the left side of the artwork, he references David Seymour's photo *Nursing Mother* (1936). When viewed altogether, he shows us the collective pitfall of humanity suspended in time through what we see and how we see it, reminding us to never make the same mistake again.

The painting was so effective in its mission that, in the decades that followed, *Guernica* would transcend the status of masterpiece and become an internationally recognized symbol for indiscriminate slaughter; a tapestry in its likeness still hangs in the UN Security Council chambers, which was allegedly once covered at the request of a sitting US president while Colin Powell attempted to persuade the council for an invasion of Iraq.

Despite its status, though, I wouldn't exactly say *Guernica* is the most influential idea in art history. As far as powerful ones go, it certainly has its place. But if we want to talk *really* influential ideas, we're going to need to chat about Eugène Delacroix.

Liberty Leading the People

Eugène Delacroix, 1830

There are few words uttered in any tongue created by man, woman, or god that can adequately describe the ferocity of Delacroix's 1830 masterpiece, *Liberty Leading the People*. It is a painting that imposes its will on you unlike any other, not only because of its immense scale, but through a brilliant series of unforgettable ideas.

Delacroix shows us a version of Lady Liberty as a goddess-like woman of revolution. On her head, she wears a Phrygian cap, a symbol of liberty from the first French Revolution. At her feet, a pile of rubble and death—Liberty triumphs through adversity. She does not simply stand at the center of the painting: She breaks through the boundaries of it. Delacroix's barefooted, bare-breasted figure, who burns into the imagination of all who see her, was created in the name of freedom. She was painted as a symbol to release those who were bound to oppression—the figures who surround her—and in the very same light, became a symbol of freedom on her own. She was born as the result of a once-radical idea, and through the genius of Delacroix, became a driver for more.

But *Liberty Leading the People* also had an unexpected effect. Through its untamed brushstrokes, its brilliant blues, and its break from the academic traditions of clean lines and invisible facture, another seed was planted in the mind of one Édouard Manet.

It is a seed that would reshape the world that was, transforming it into the one that we recognize today through the artistic revolution of the Impressionists, in whose art we see the convergence of great ideas across history, from medieval portraits to woodblocks to revolutionary images. A group of artists who, in the late nineteenth century in Paris, turned the conventional rules of art-making onto their figurative head. This was a group who painted for the sake of painting. They painted what they wanted, when they wanted: scenes of regular people, colorful depictions of landscapes, parties, life. They weren't lightning in a bottle: They were *freedom* in a bottle, and they would set the art world on fire.

We could attribute this period's influence on art history to any one of the brilliant artists who participated in the movement, but there is one painting in particular that started things off, changing the imaginations of humanity forever, and it's Manet's *Le Déjeuner sur l'Herbe.*

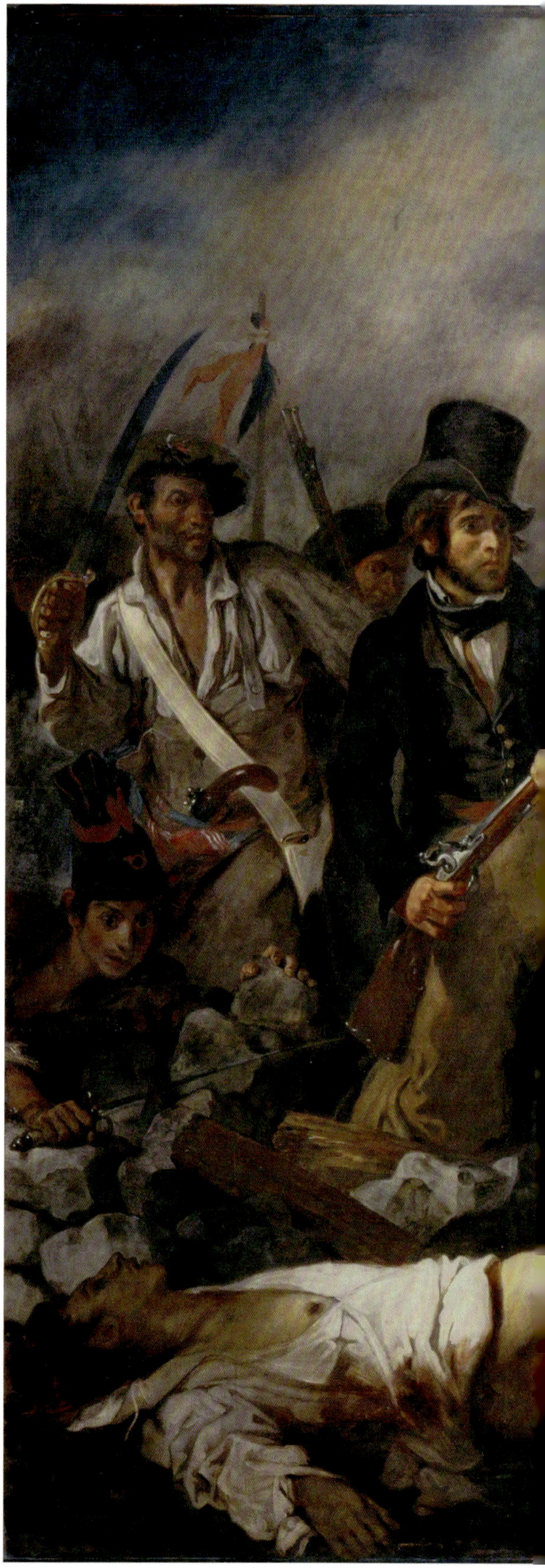

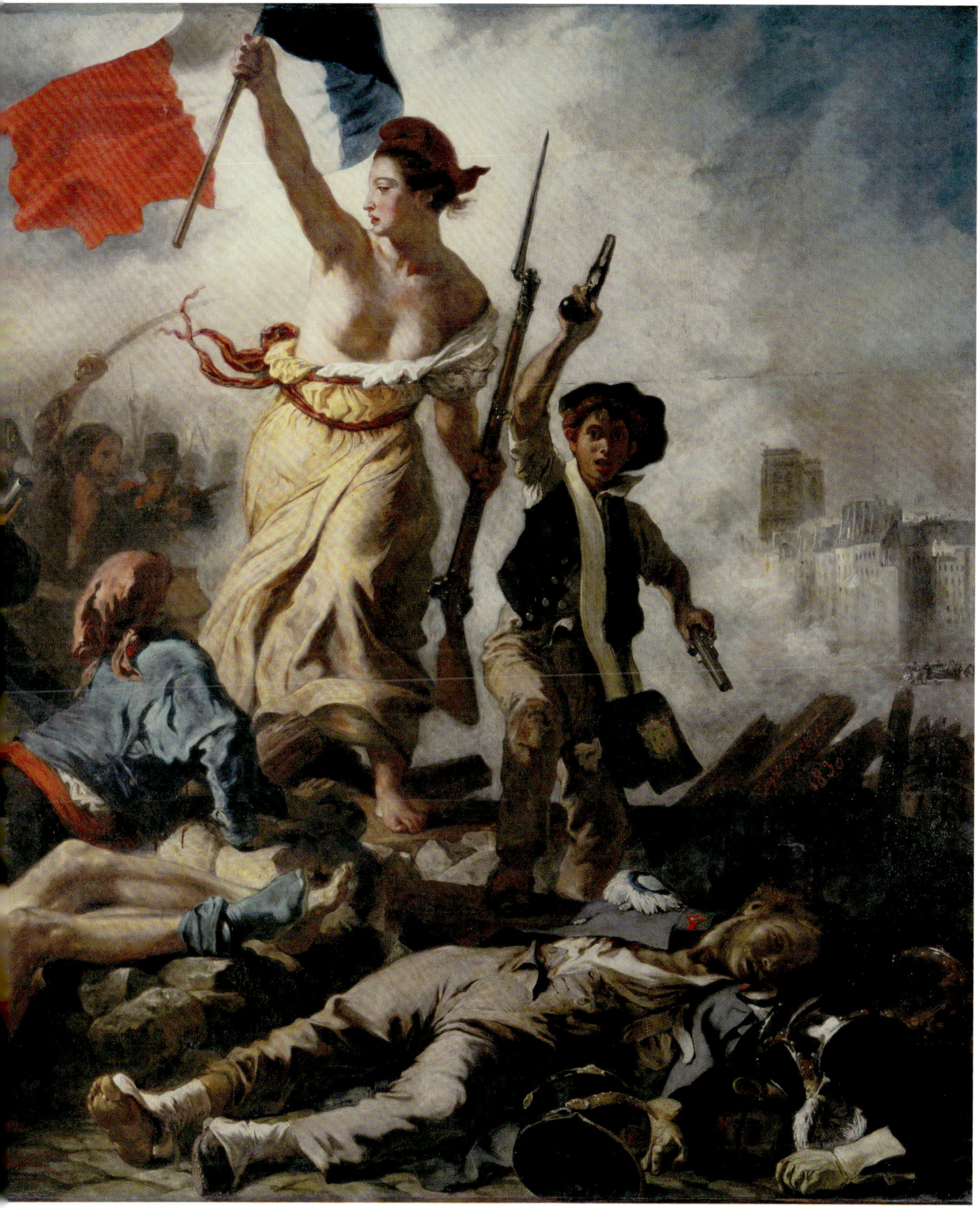

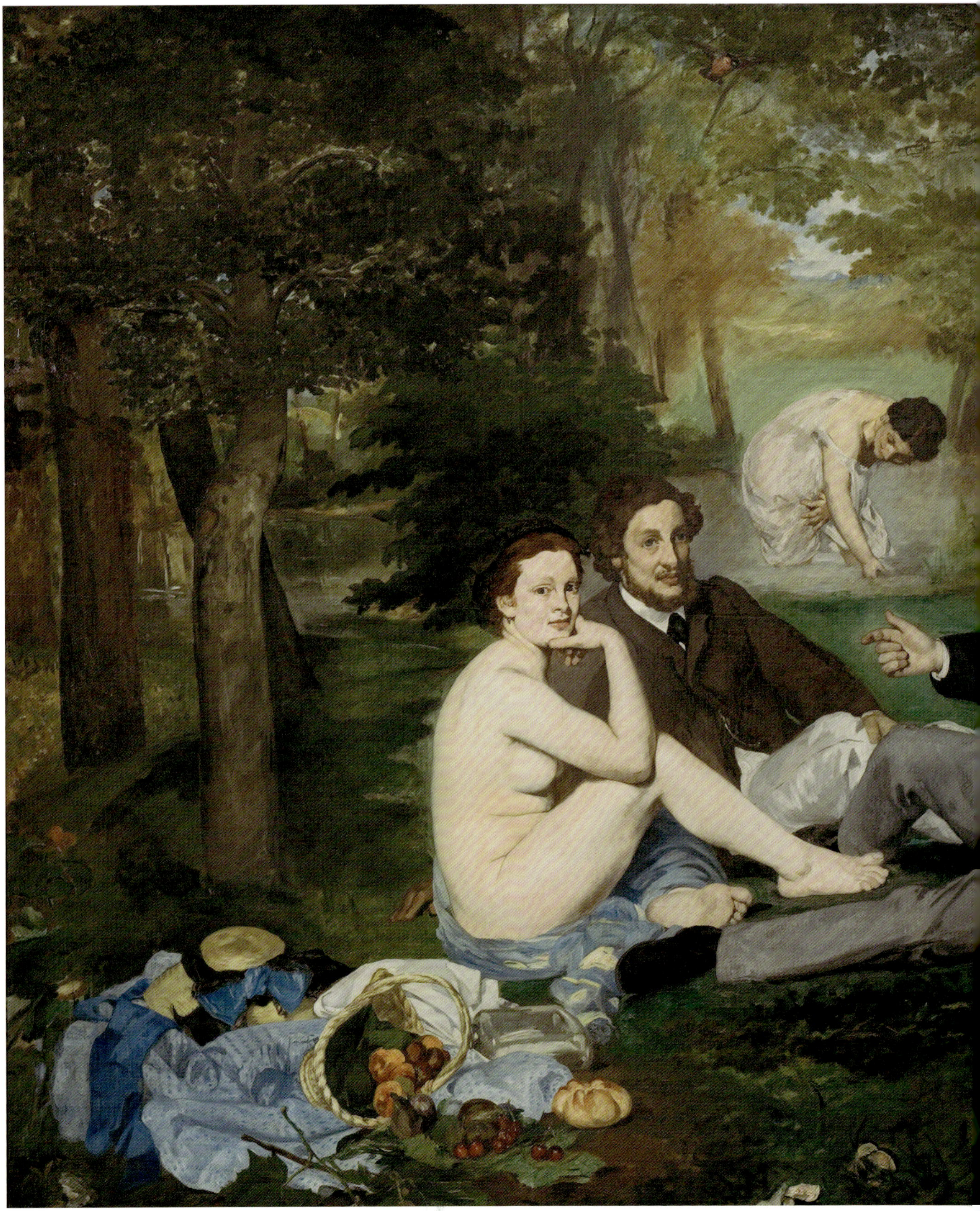

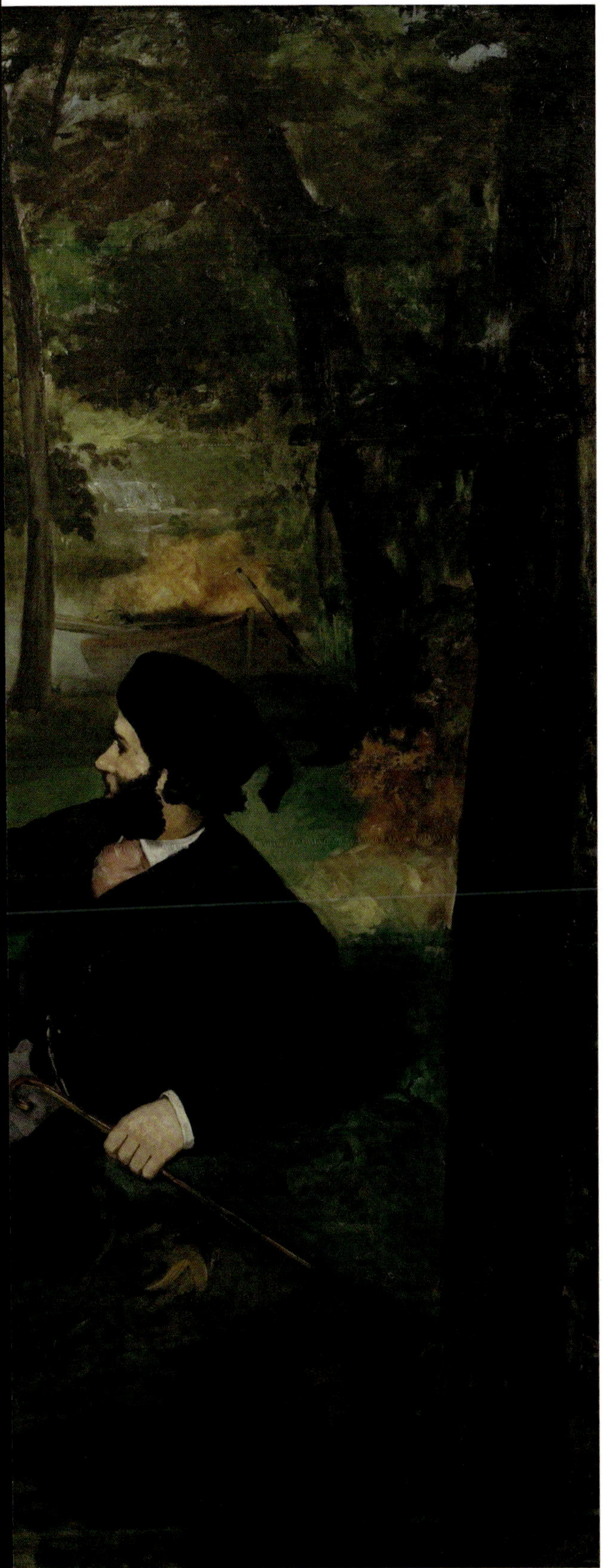

Le Déjeuner sur l'Herbe

Édouard Manet, 1863

The rules for the Académie des Beaux-Arts were simple. Art must meet certain criteria to be deemed worthy of appreciation: It must cover nobility, mythology, or theology; nudes are only permitted as narrative elements of legendary tales; the brushwork must be perfect, every detail prim and proper, and if you wanted to make it in this world, in any capacity, you'd need to play by the rules. No ifs, ands, or buts, got it?

I don't think Manet got the message, because *Le Déjeuner sur l'Herbe* is everything the Académie could never stand for.

In the place of gods and nobles, Manet paints four figures sitting in a park, having what looks to be some type of sexy picnic. Two men lying on the grass and two women, one rinsing herself off in a tiny pond, the other nude and gazing out toward us, maybe even inviting us over to participate.

But to be honest, the subject matter, the style of painting, the vibrant greens, expressive brushstrokes, the individual components standing on their own, and even the painting's rejection from the Salon in 1863 is all irrelevant, at least as far as this story goes, because this artwork is less about *what*, and almost entirely about *why*. The greatness of *Le Déjeuner sur l'Herbe* and the legacy that it created is rooted in the ideas that it instilled in Manet's contemporaries. The image tells a story of an artist who decided that his art should capture his reality, his experience, and come from his point of view.

Manet doesn't paint regular people in the place of gods and nobility because of a need to revolt, he does so because he is one of those regular people. He doesn't paint a palace, he paints a park because he goes to that park. He eats that food. He's sat under those trees. He is a man of desires, and possibly even a man of simple tastes. He doesn't know anything but his own existence, so why pretend?

In this painting, Manet puts himself first. And in doing so, he would radically capture the imaginations of generations of artists and free thinkers alike.

An idea that turned into countless other great ones, and a painting that would change the world forever.

VISUAL INDEX

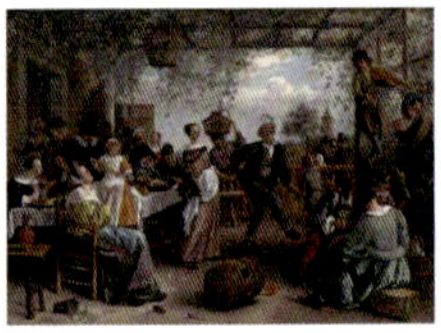

10 ***The Dancing Couple***
Jan Steen
National Gallery of Art, Washington, DC

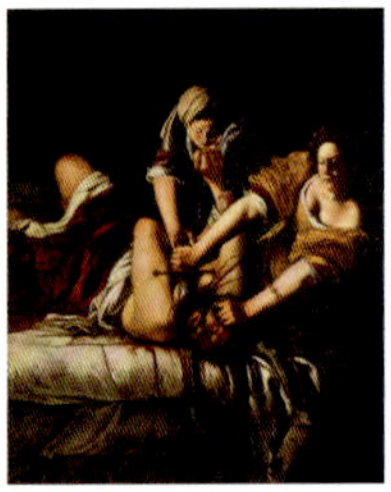

15 ***Judith Beheading Holofernes***
Artemisia Gentileschi
Uffizi Galleries, Florence

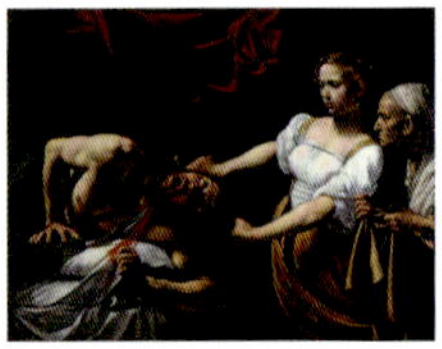

16 ***Judith Beheading Holofernes***
Caravaggio
Palazzo Barberini, Rome

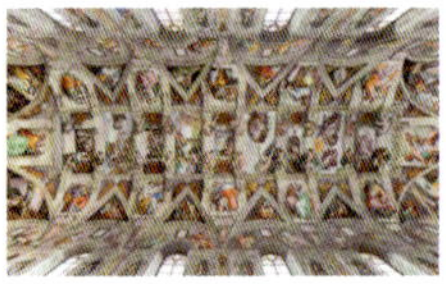

20 **The Sistine Chapel Ceiling**
Michelangelo
Sistine Chapel, Vatican City

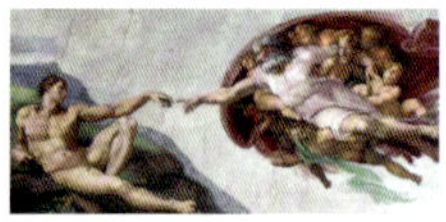

20 ***The Creation of Adam***
Michelangelo
Sistine Chapel, Vatican City

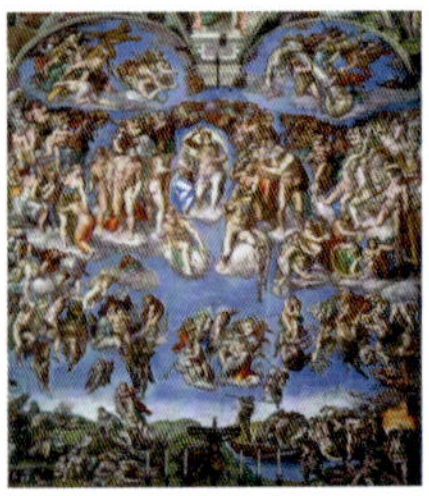

23 ***The Last Judgment***
Michelangelo
Sistine Chapel, Vatican City

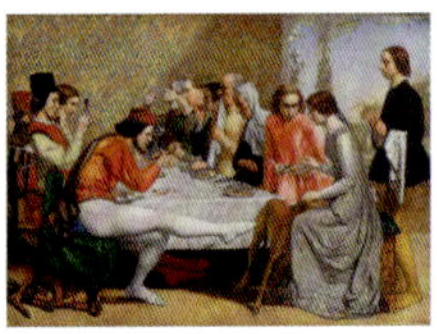

27 ***Isabella***
John Everett Millais
Walker Art Gallery, Liverpool

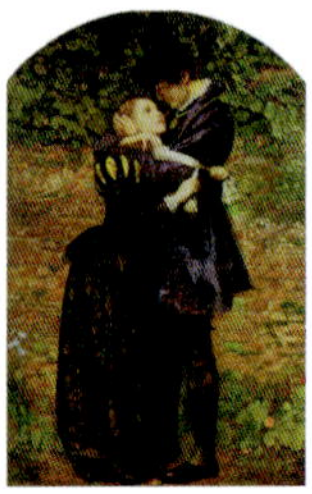

28 ***A Huguenot, on St. Bartholomew's Day***
John Everett Millais
Private collection

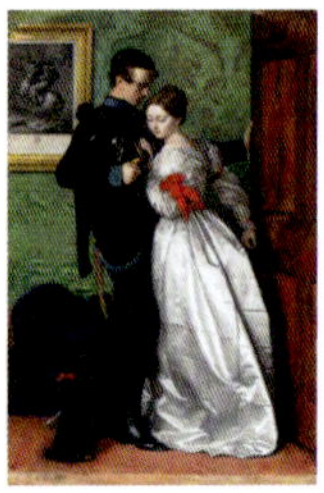

31 ***The Black Brunswicker***
John Everett Millais
Lady Lever Art Gallery, Liverpool

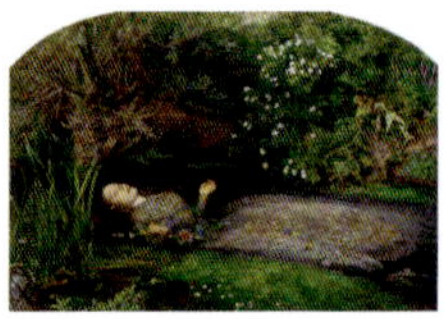

33 ***Ophelia***
John Everett Millais
Tate Britain, London

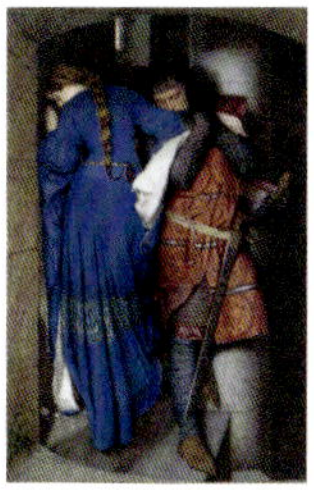

37 ***The Meeting on the Turret Stairs***
Frederic William Burton
National Gallery of Ireland, Dublin

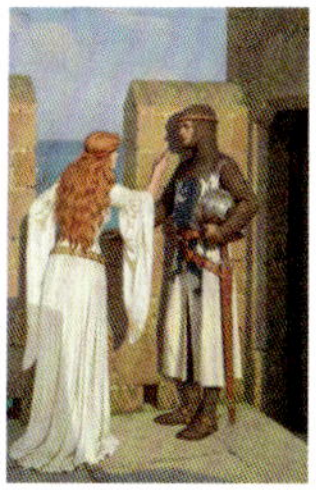

38 ***The Shadow***
Edmund Blair Leighton
Berman Museum, Anniston, and City Hall, Cardiff

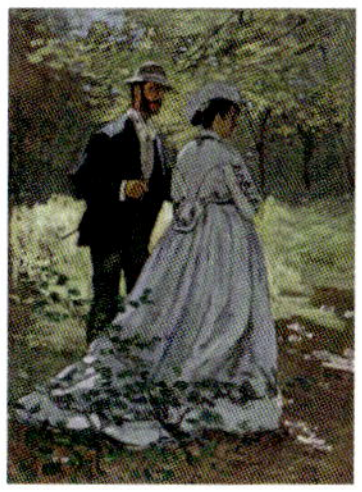

41 ***Bazille and Camille***
Claude Monet
National Gallery of Art, Washington DC

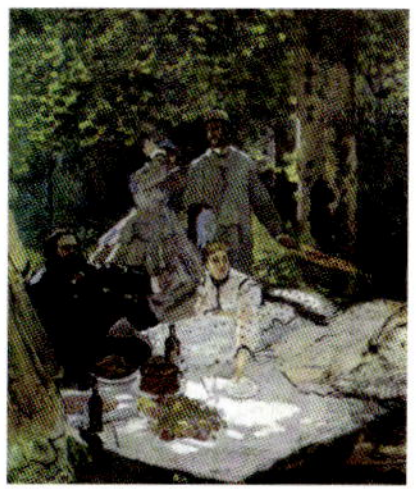

41 ***Le Déjeuner sur l'herbe***
Claude Monet
Musée d'Orsay, Paris

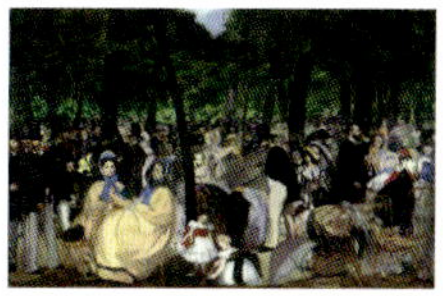

42 ***Music in the Tuileries Gardens***
Édouard Manet
The National Gallery, London

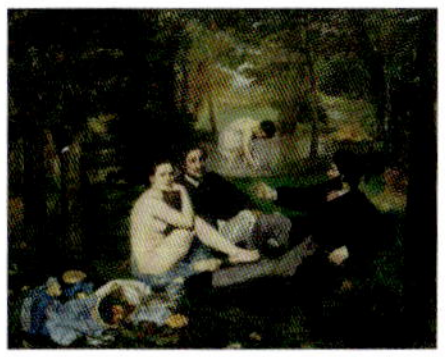

43, 265 ***Le Déjeuner sur l'Herbe***
Édouard Manet
Musée d'Orsay, Paris

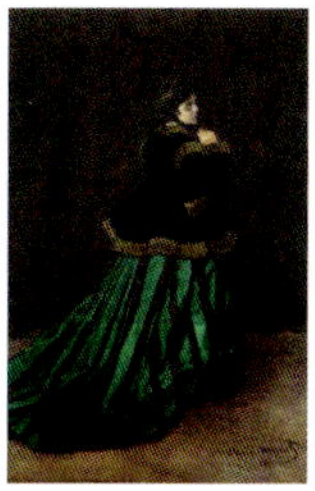

45 ***The Woman in a Green Dress***
Claude Monet
Kunsthalle Bremen, Bremen

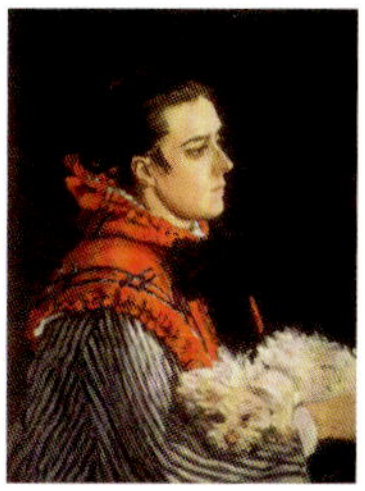

45 ***Camille with a Small Dog***
Claude Monet
Kunsthaus Zürich, Zürich

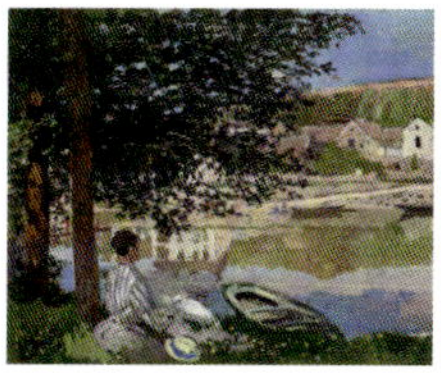

47 ***On the Bank of the Seine, Bennecourt***
Claude Monet
Art Institute of Chicago, Chicago

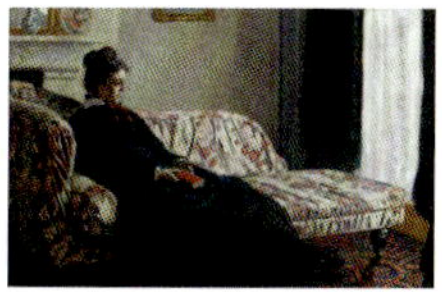

48 ***Meditation, Madame Monet on the Sofa***
Claude Monet
Musée d'Orsay, Paris

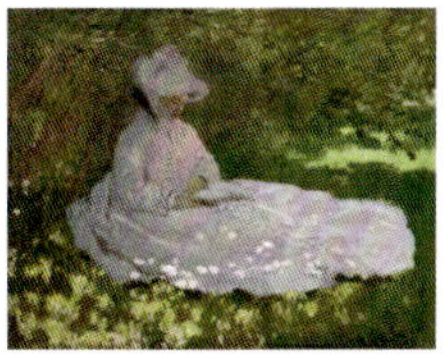

49 ***Springtime***
Claude Monet
The Walters Art Museum, Baltimore

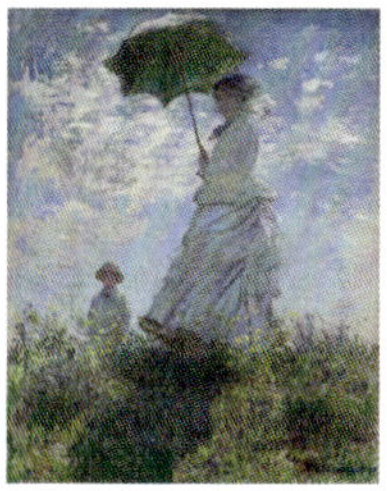

50 ***Woman with a Parasol — Madame Monet and Her Son***
Claude Monet
National Gallery of Art, Washington DC

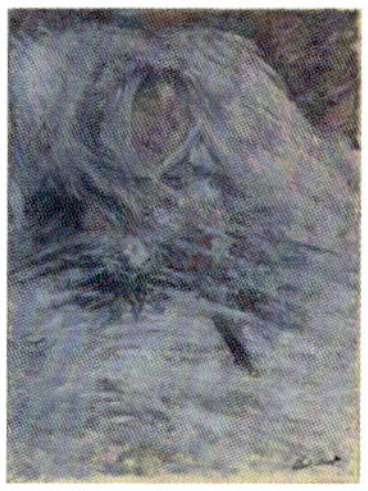

53 ***Camille Monet on Her Deathbed***
Claude Monet
Musée d'Orsay, Paris

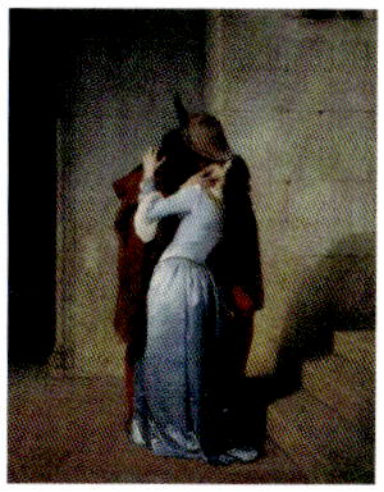

54 ***The Kiss***
Francesco Hayez
Pinacoteca di Brera, Milan

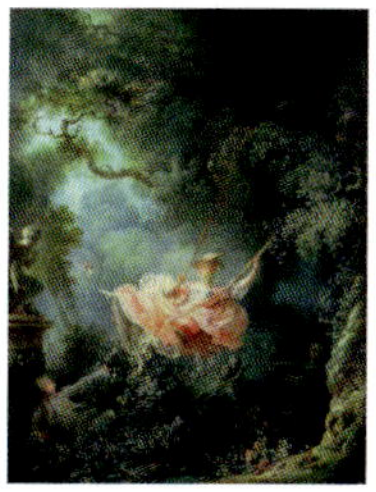

57 ***The Swing***
Jean-Honoré Fragonard
The Wallace Collection, London

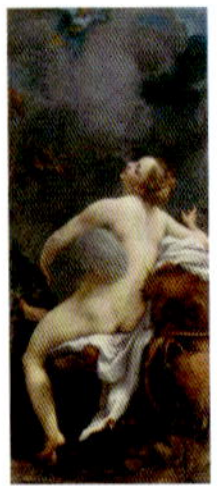

58 ***Jupiter and Io***
Antonio da Correggio
Kunsthistorisches Museum, Vienna

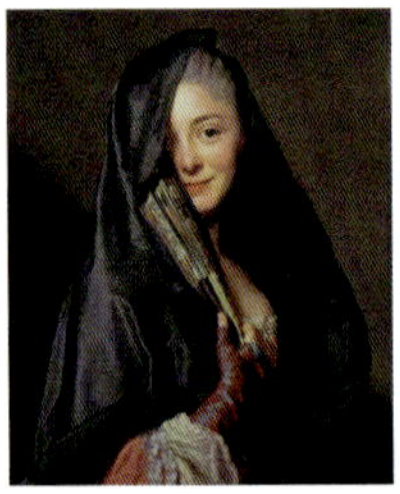

61 ***The Lady with the Veil***
Alexander Roslin
Nationalmuseum, Stockholm

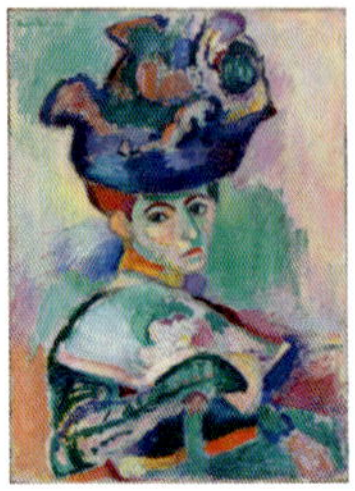

65 ***Woman with a Hat***
Henri Matisse
SFMOMA, San Francisco

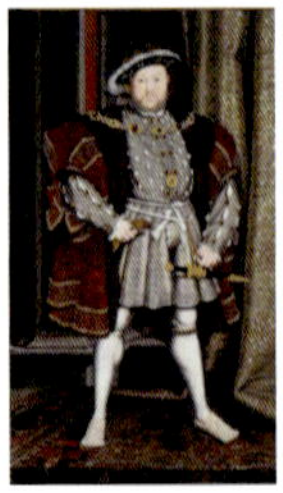

66 ***Portrait of Henry VIII***
Hans Holbein the Younger
Walker Art Gallery, Liverpool

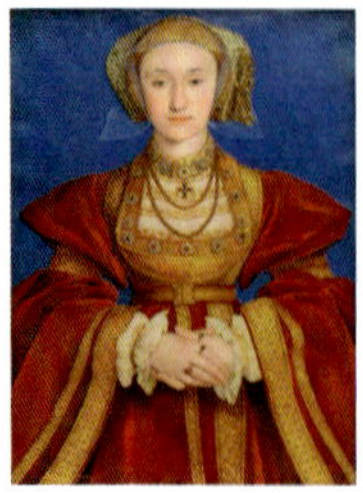

66 ***Portrait of Anne of Cleves***
Hans Holbein the Younger
Louvre, Paris

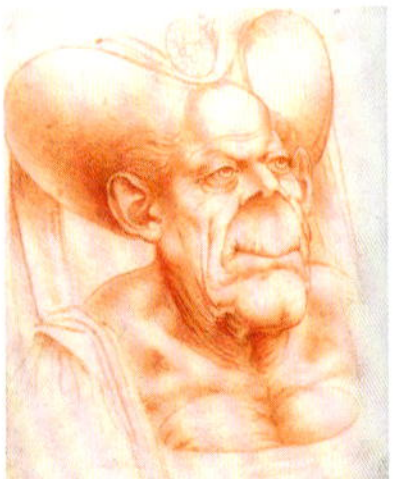

68 ***The Bust of a Grotesque Old Woman***
After Leonardo da Vinci
Royal Collection Trust, United Kingdom

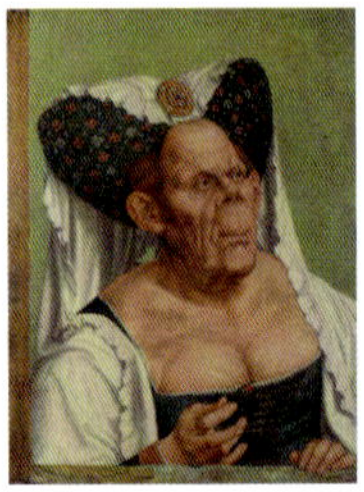

68 ***The Ugly Duchess***
Quentin Matsys
The National Gallery, London

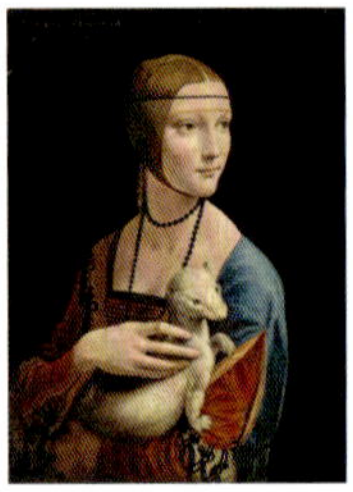

71 ***Lady with an Ermine***
Leonardo da Vinci
Czartoryski Museum, Kraków

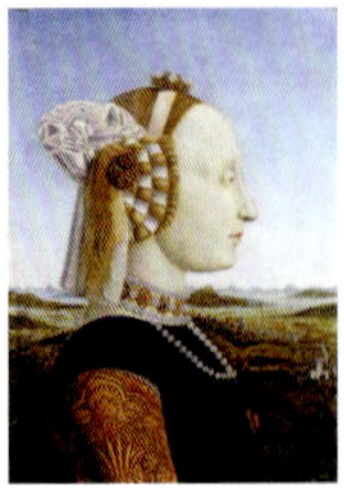

73 **Detail from *The Duke and Duchess of Urbino Federico da Montefeltro and Battista Sforza***
Battista Sforza
Uffizi Galleries, Florence

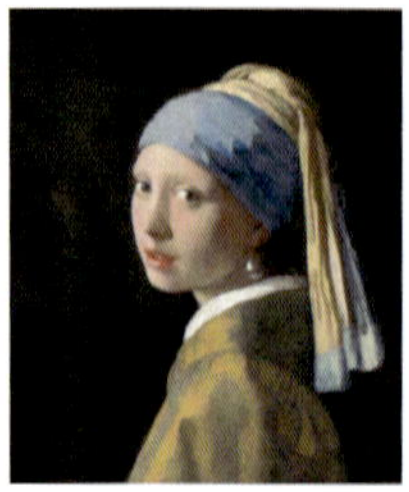

73 ***Girl with a Pearl Earring***
Johannes Vermeer
Mauritshuis, The Hague

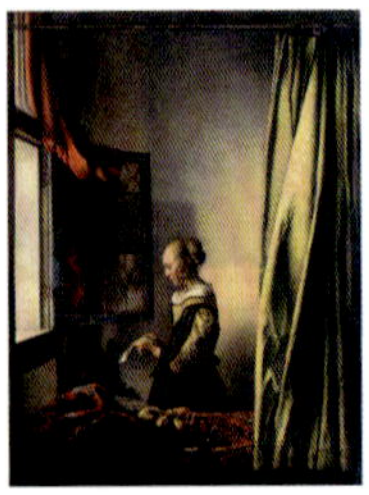

74 ***Girl Reading a Letter at an Open Window***
Johannes Vermeer
Gemäldegalerie Alte Meister, Dresden

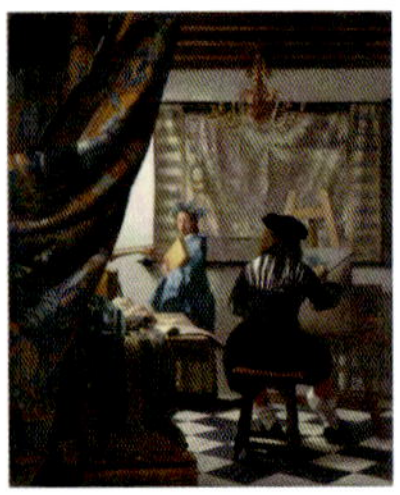

74 ***The Art of Painting***
Johannes Vermeer
Kunsthistorisches Museum, Vienna

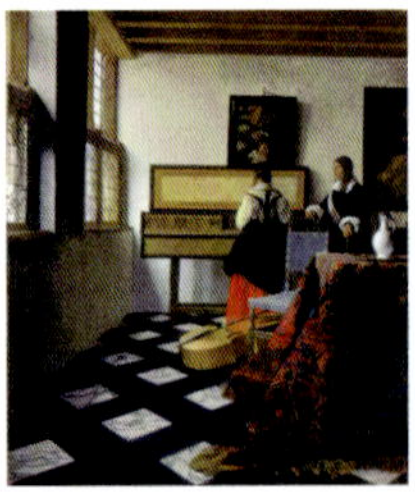

74 ***The Music Lesson***
Johannes Vermeer
Royal Collection Trust, United Kingdom

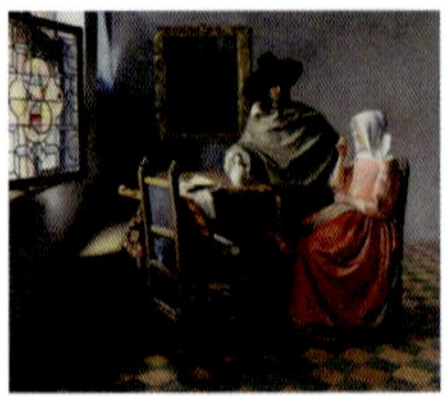

74 ***The Glass of Wine***
Johannes Vermeer
Gemäldegalerie, Berlin

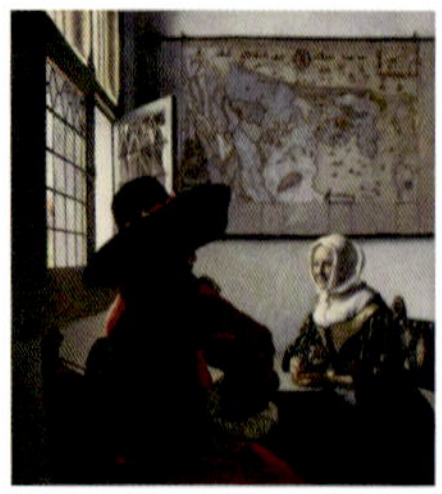

74 ***Officer and Laughing Girl***
Johannes Vermeer
The Frick Collection, New York

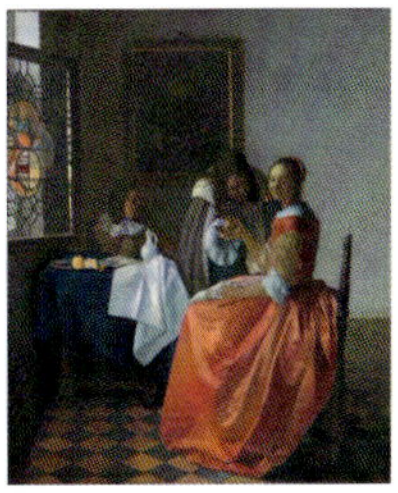

74 ***The Girl with the Wine Glass***
Johannes Vermeer
Herzog Anton Ulrich-Museum, Braunschweig

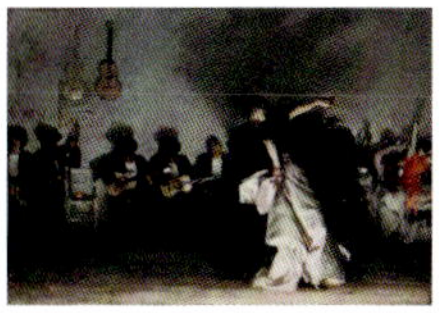

78 ***El Jaleo***
John Singer Sargent
Isabella Stewart Gardner Museum, Boston

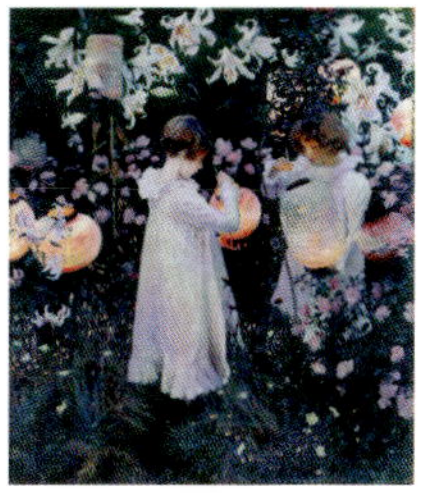

80 ***Carnation, Lily, Lily, Rose***
John Singer Sargent
Tate Britain, London

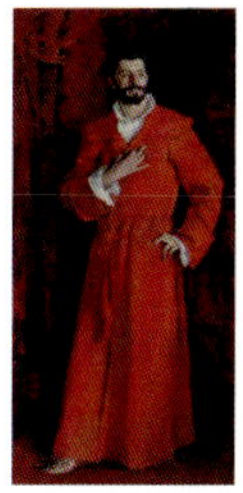

81 ***Dr. Pozzi at Home***
John Singer Sargent
Hammer Museum, Los Angeles

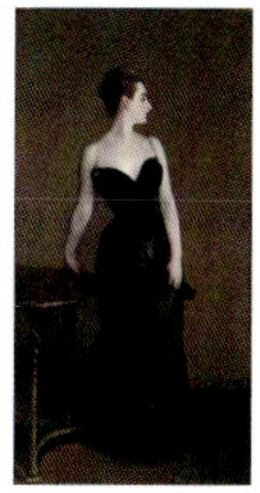

82 ***Madame X***
John Singer Sargent
The Metropolitan Museum of Art, New York

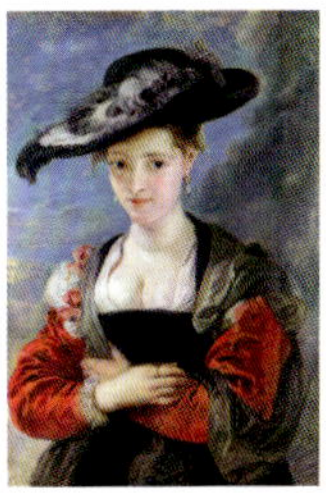

84 ***Portrait of Susanna Lunden***
Peter Paul Rubens
The National Gallery, London

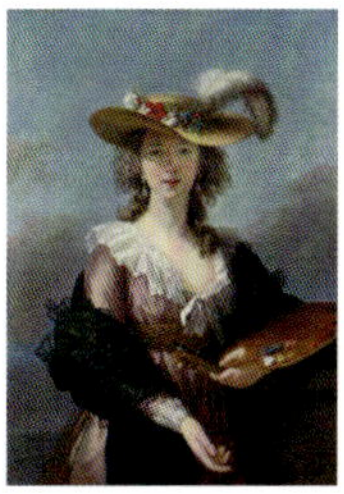

84 ***Self-Portrait in a Straw Hat***
Élisabeth Vigée Le Brun
The National Gallery, London

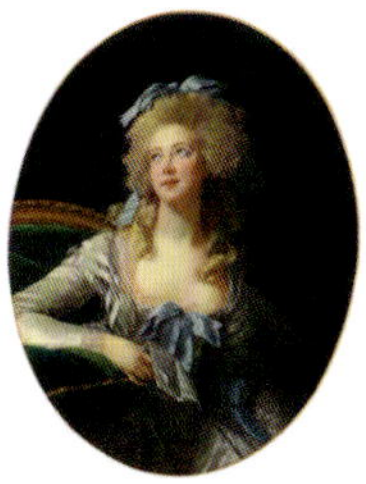

87 ***Madame Grand (Noël Catherine Vorlée, 1761–1835)***
Élisabeth Vigée Le Brun
The Metropolitan Museum of Art, New York

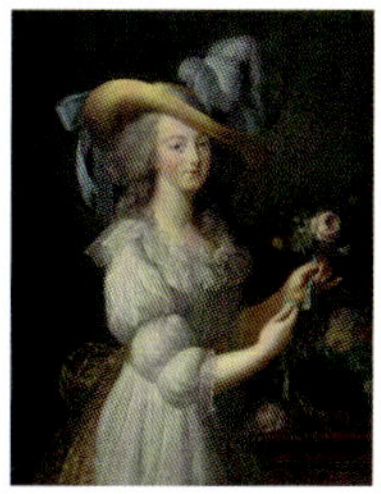

88 ***Marie Antoinette in a Chemise Dress***
Élisabeth Vigée Le Brun
Museum Schloss Fasanerie, Eichenzell

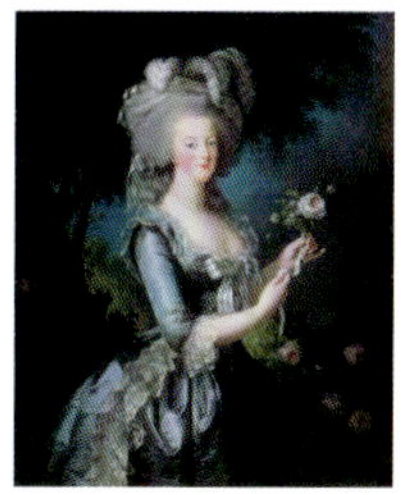

88 ***Marie Antoinette with a Rose***
Élisabeth Vigée Le Brun
Palace of Versailles, Versailles

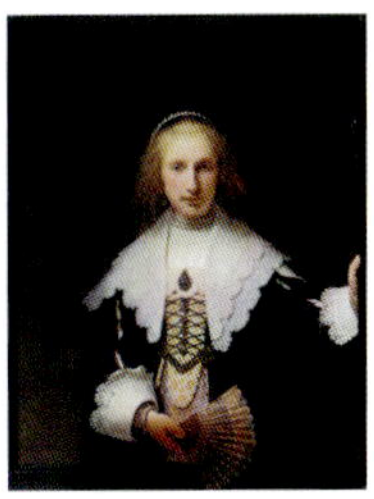

91 ***Agatha Bas***
Rembrandt
Royal Collection Trust, United Kingdom

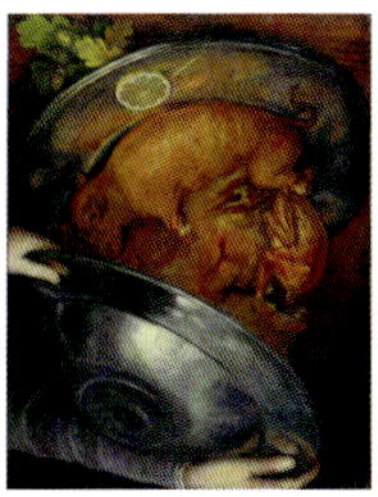

94 ***The Cook***
Giuseppe Arcimboldo
Nationalmuseum, Stockholm

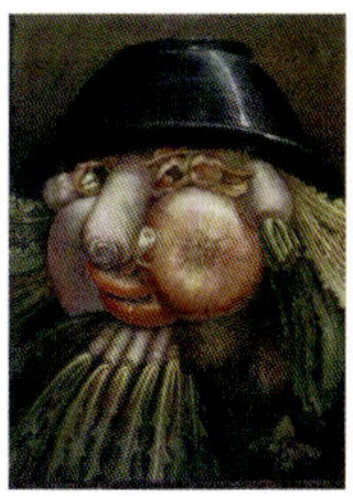

94 ***The Gardener***
Giuseppe Arcimboldo
Museo Civico Ala Ponzone, Cremona

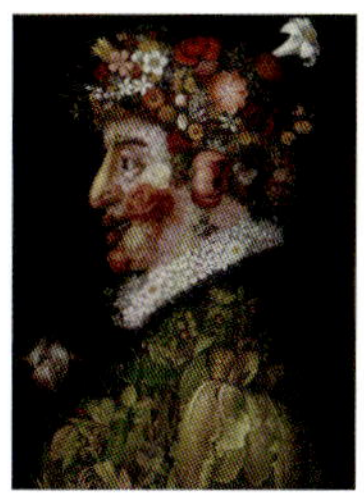

94 ***Spring***
Giuseppe Arcimboldo
Real Academia de Bellas Artes de San Fernando, Madrid, and Louvre, Paris

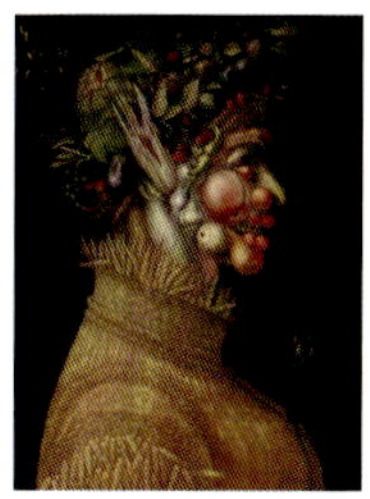

94 ***Summer***
Giuseppe Arcimboldo
Kunsthistorisches Museum, Vienna, and Louvre, Paris

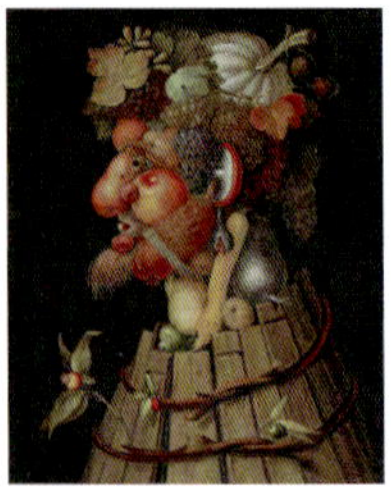

94 ***Autumn***
Giuseppe Arcimboldo
Louvre, Paris

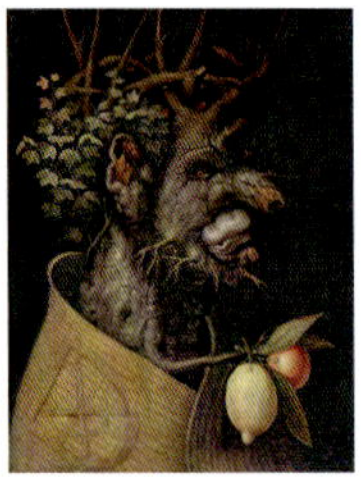

94 ***Winter***
Giuseppe Arcimboldo
Kunsthistorisches Museum, Vienna, and Louvre, Paris

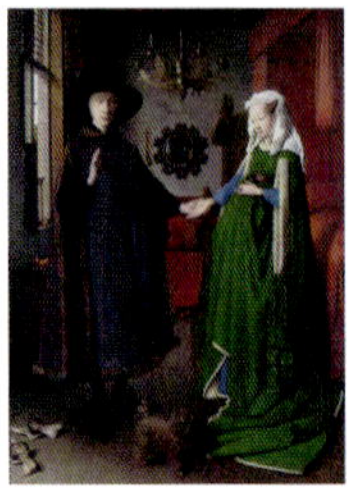

99 ***The Arnolfini Portrait***
Jan van Eyck
The National Gallery, London

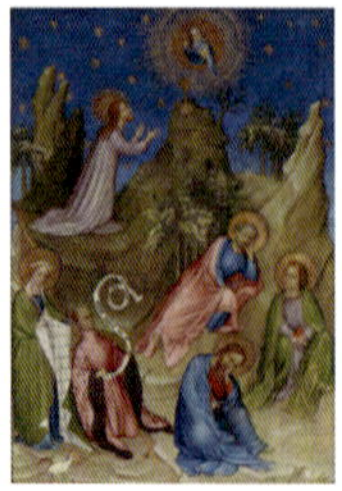

100 ***The Agony in the Garden with the Donor Louis I of Orléans***
Colart de Laon
Museo Nacional del Prado, Madrid

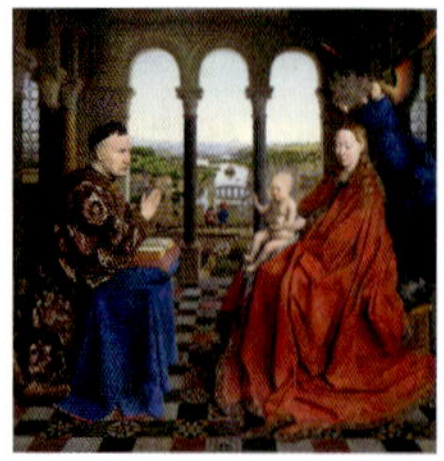

100 ***Madonna of Chancellor Rolin***
Jan van Eyck
Louvre, Paris

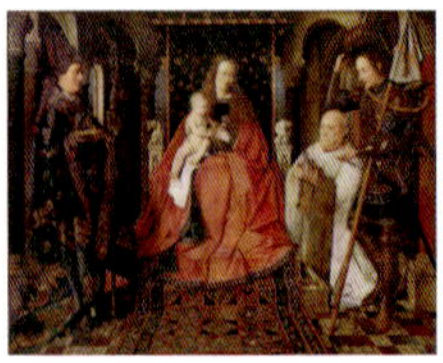

102 ***Virgin and Child with Canon Joris van der Paele***
Jan van Eyck
Groeningemuseum, Bruges

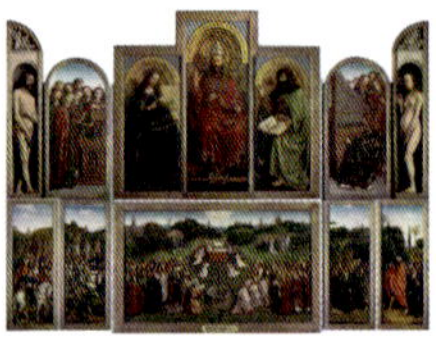

106 ***The Ghent Altarpiece***
Jan van Eyck
Saint Bavo's Cathedral, Ghent

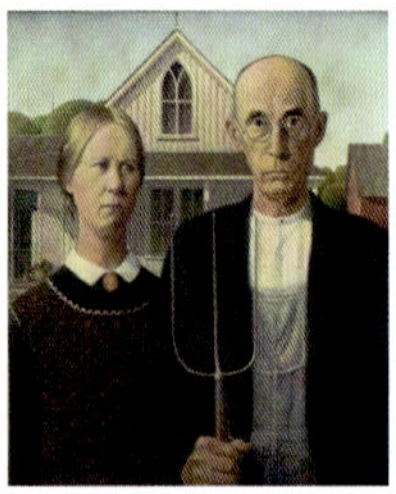

109 ***American Gothic***
Grant Wood
Art Institute of Chicago, Chicago

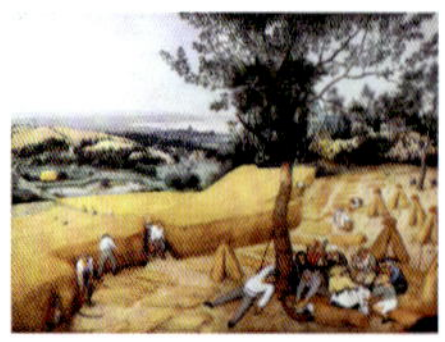

110 ***The Harvesters***
Pieter Bruegel the Elder
The Metropolitan Museum of Art, New York

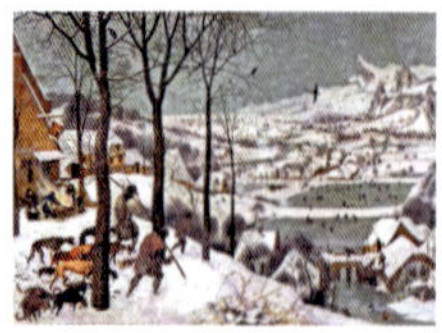

112 ***Hunters in the Snow***
Pieter Bruegel the Elder
Kunsthistorisches Museum, Vienna

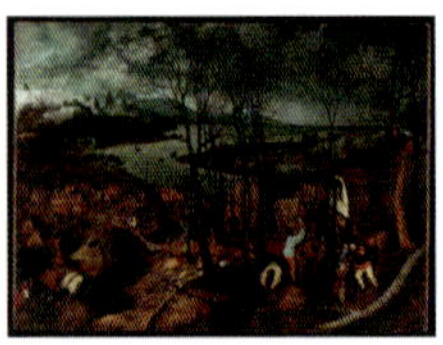

112 ***Gloomy Day***
Pieter Bruegel the Elder
Kunsthistorisches Museum, Vienna

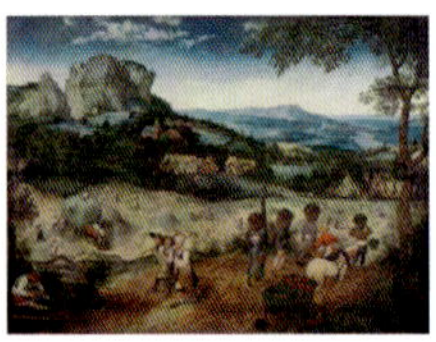

112 ***The Hay Harvest***
Pieter Bruegel the Elder
Lobkowicz Palace, Prague

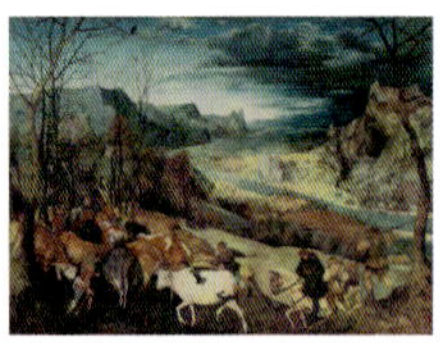

112 ***The Return of the Herd***
Pieter Bruegel the Elder
Kunsthistorisches Museum, Vienna

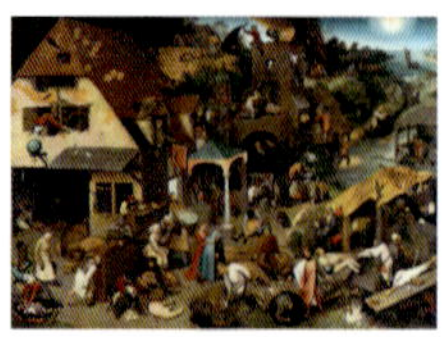

114 ***Netherlandish Proverbs***
Pieter Bruegel the Elder
Gemäldegalerie, Berlin

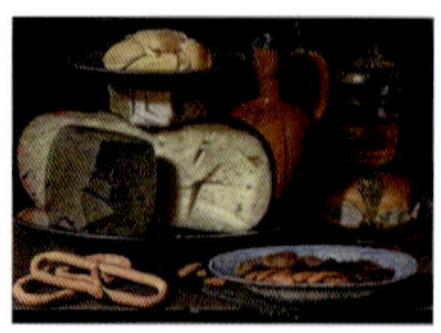

125 ***Still Life with Cheeses, Almonds and Pretzels***
Clara Peeters
Mauritshuis, The Hague

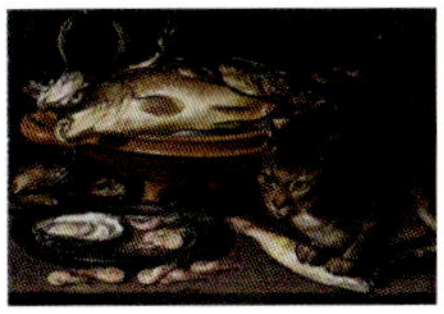

125 ***Still Life of Fish and Cat***
Clara Peeters
National Museum of Women in the Arts, Washington DC

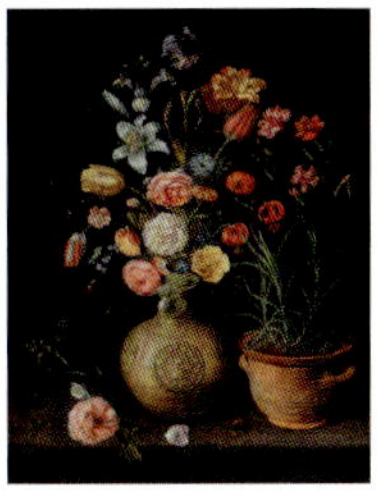

125 ***Roses, Lilies, an Iris and Other Flowers in an Earthenware Vase, With a Pot of Carnations and a Butterfly on a Ledge***
Clara Peeters
Private collection

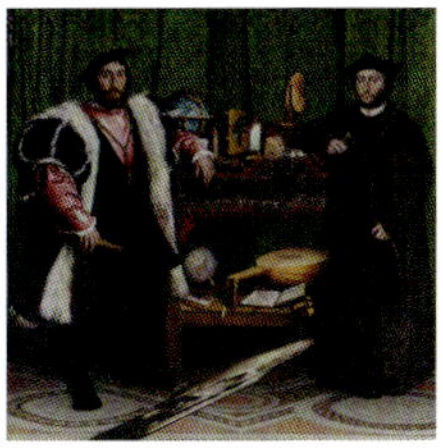

127 ***The Ambassadors***
Hans Holbein the Younger
The National Gallery, London

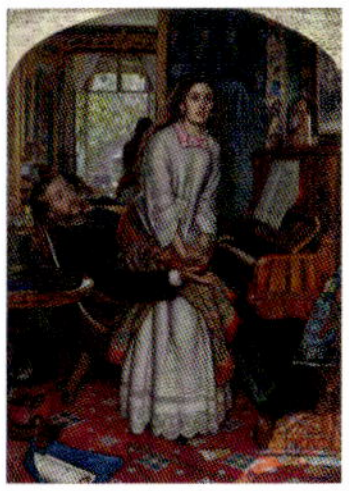

128 ***The Awakening Conscience***
William Holman Hunt
Tate Britain, London

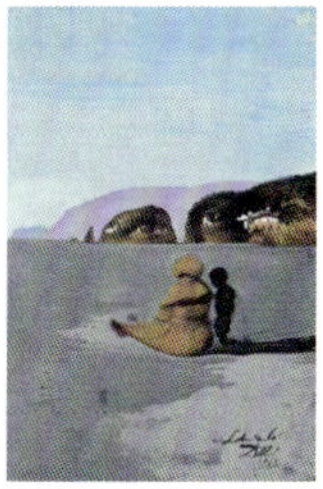

128 ***Adolescence***
Salvador Dalí
Private collection

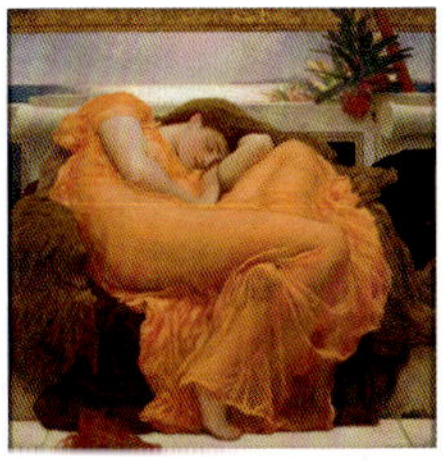

135 ***Flaming June***
Edmund Blair Leighton
Museo de Arte de Ponce, Ponce

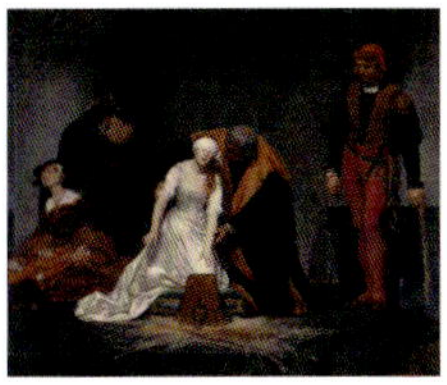

137 ***The Execution of Lady Jane Grey***
Paul Delaroche
The National Gallery, London

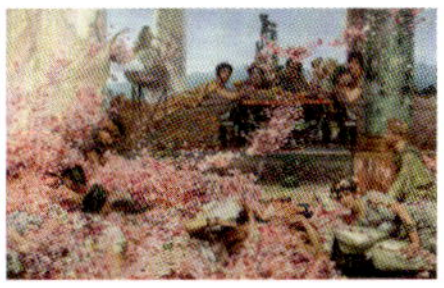

138 ***The Roses of Heliogabalus***
Lawrence Alma-Tadema
Private collection

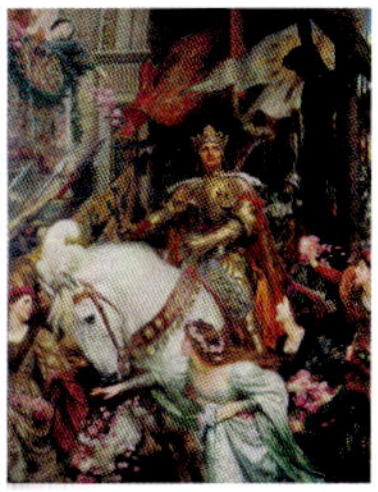

140 ***The Two Crowns***
Frank Dicksee
Tate, United Kingdom

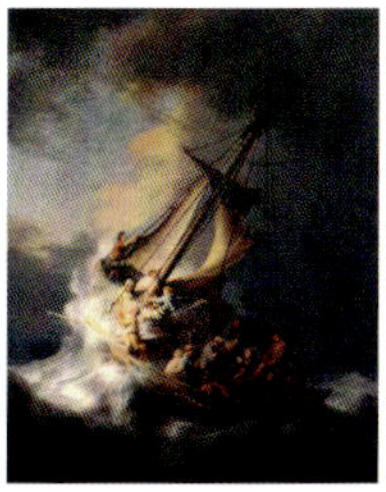

143 ***Christ in the Storm on the Sea of Galilee***
Rembrandt
Stolen from Isabella Stewart Gardner Museum

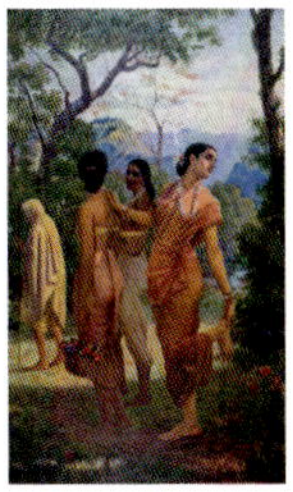

145 ***Shakuntala***
Ravi Varma
Sree Chitra Art Gallery, Thiruvananthapuram

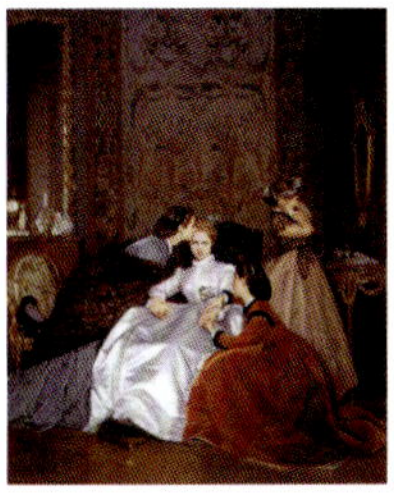

149 ***The Reluctant Bride***
Auguste Toulmouche
Private collection

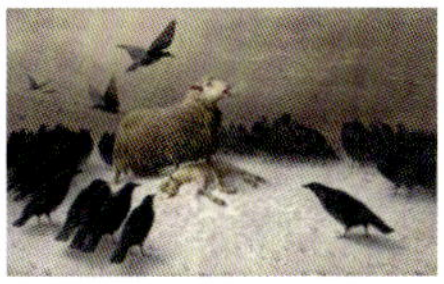

148 ***Anguish***
August Friedrich Schenck
National Gallery of Victoria, Melbourne

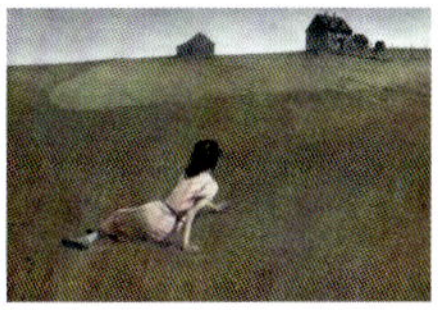

151 ***Christina's World***
Andrew Wyeth
MoMA, New York City

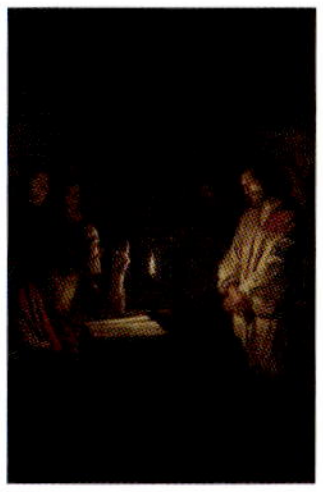

152 ***Christ Before the High Priest***
Gerrit van Honthorst
The National Gallery, London

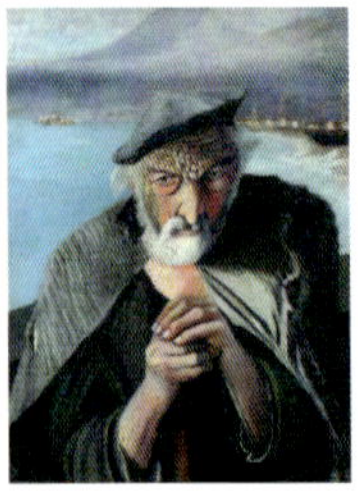

155 ***Old Fisherman***
Tivadar Csontváry Kosztka
Herman Ottó Museum, Miskolc

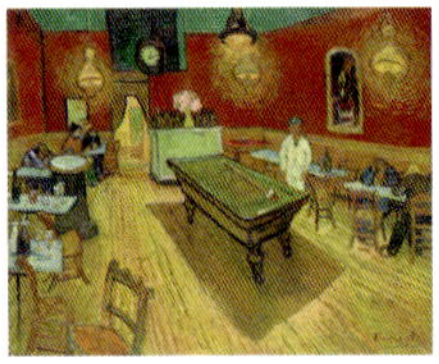

156 ***The Night Café***
Vincent van Gogh
Yale University Art Gallery, New Haven

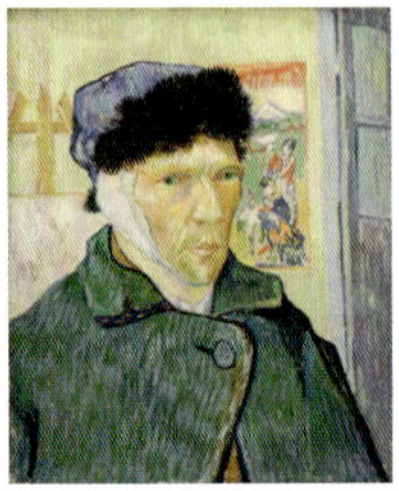

159 ***Self-Portrait with Bandaged Ear***
Vincent van Gogh
Courtauld Gallery, London

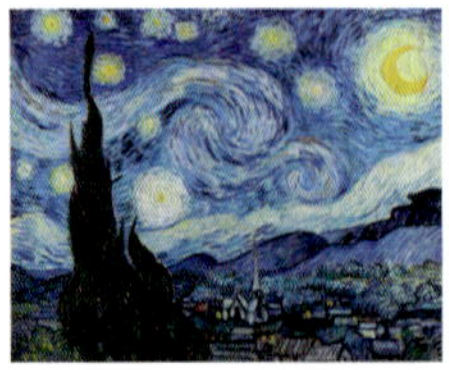

160 ***The Starry Night***
Vincent van Gogh
MoMA, New York City

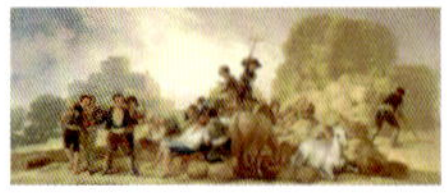

165 ***The Threshing Ground***
Francisco Goya
Museo Nacional del Prado, Madrid

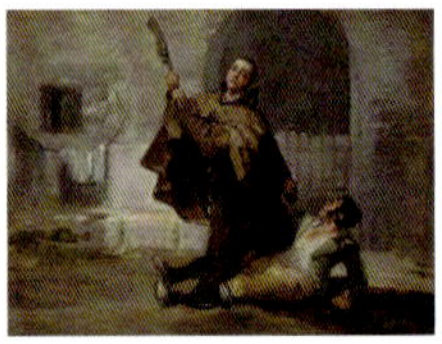

165 ***Friar Pedro Clubs El Maragato with the Butt of the Gun***
Francisco Goya
Museo Nacional del Prado, Madrid

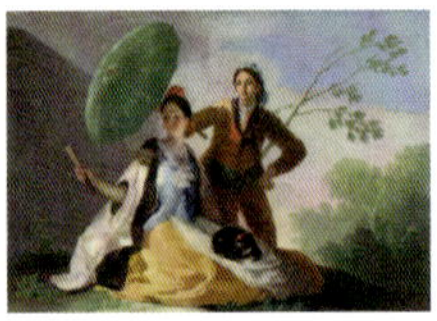

166 ***The Parasol***
Francisco Goya
Museo Nacional del Prado, Madrid

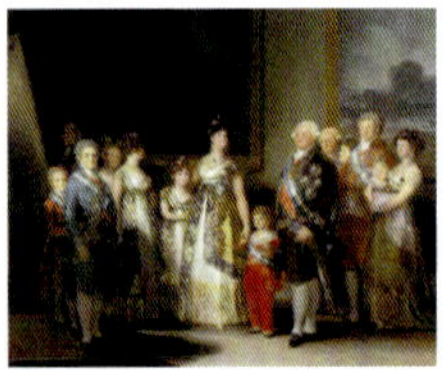

167 ***The Family of Carlos IV***
Francisco Goya
Museo Nacional del Prado, Madrid

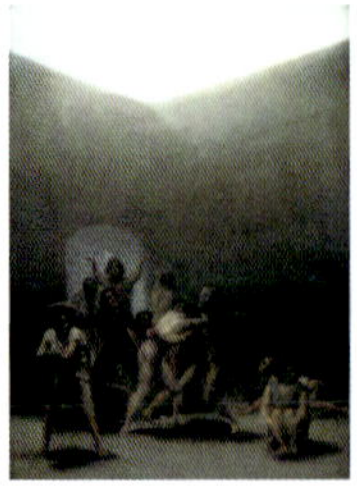

169 ***Yard with Lunatics***
Francisco Goya
Meadows Museum, University Park

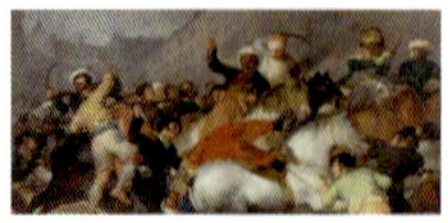

170 ***The Second of May 1808***
Francisco Goya
Museo Nacional del Prado, Madrid

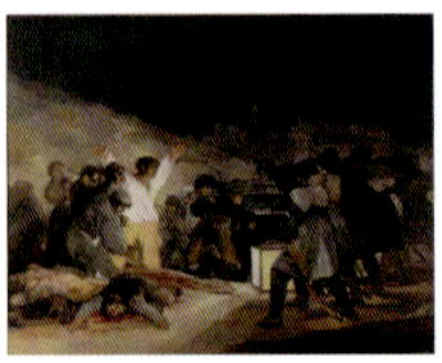

173 ***The Third of May 1808***
Francisco Goya
Museo Nacional del Prado, Madrid

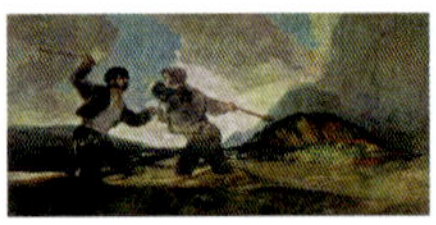

174 ***Duel with Cudgels***
Francisco Goya
Museo Nacional del Prado, Madrid

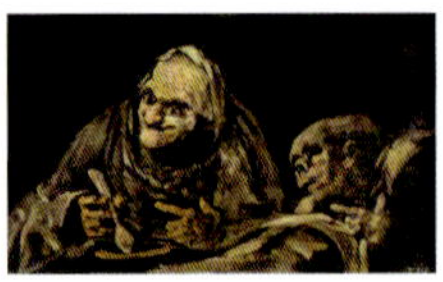

174 ***Two Old Men Eating***
Francisco Goya
Museo Nacional del Prado, Madrid

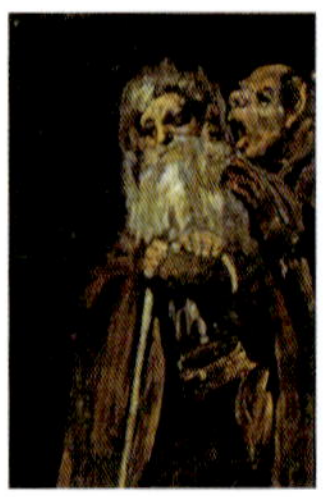

175 ***Two Old Men***
Francisco Goya
Museo Nacional del Prado, Madrid

175 ***The Dog***
Francisco Goya
Museo Nacional del Prado, Madrid

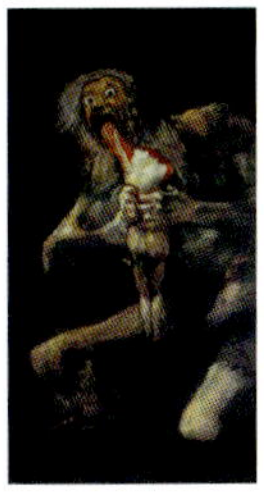

175 ***Saturn Devouring His Son***
Francisco Goya
Museo Nacional del Prado, Madrid

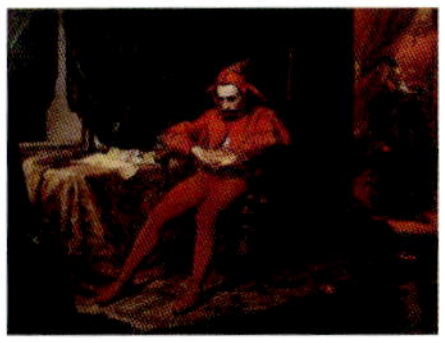

177 ***Stańczyk***
Jan Matejko
National Museum in Warsaw, Warsaw

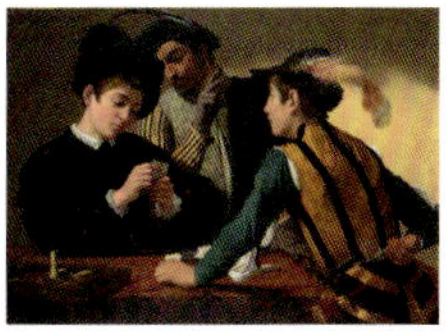

179 ***The Cardsharps***
Caravaggio
Kimball Art Museum, Fort Worth

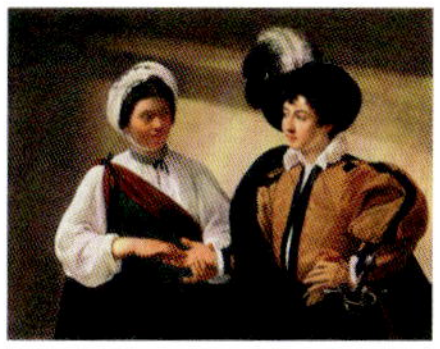

181 ***The Fortune Teller***
Caravaggio
Louvre, Paris

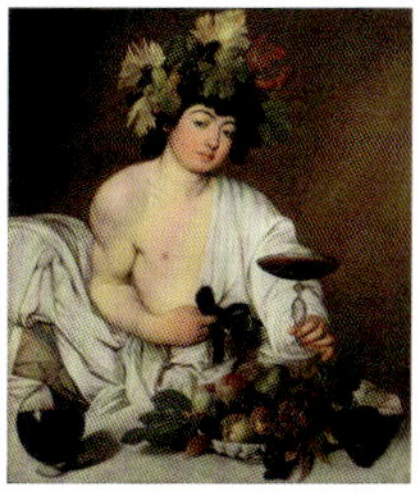

182 ***Bacchus***
Caravaggio
Uffizi Galleries, Florence

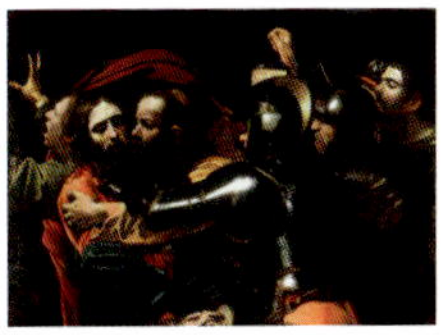

185 ***The Taking of Christ***
Caravaggio
National Gallery of Ireland, Dublin

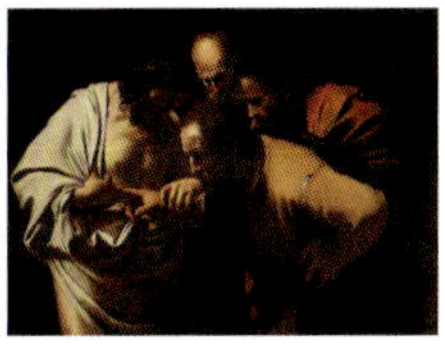

186 ***The Incredulity of Saint Thomas***
Caravaggio
Picture Gallery of Sanssouci, Potsdam

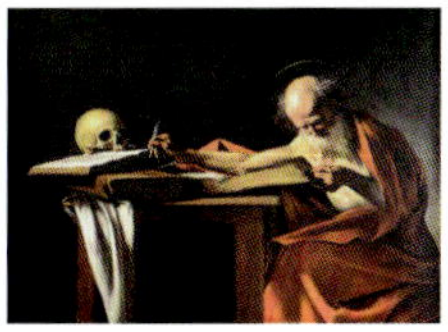

187 ***Saint Jerome Writing***
Caravaggio
Galleria Borghese, Rome

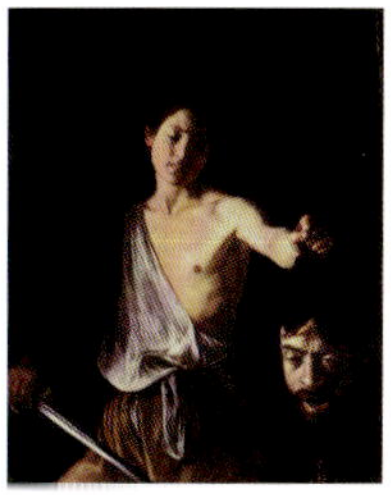

189 ***David with the Head of Goliath***
Caravaggio
Galleria Borghese, Rome

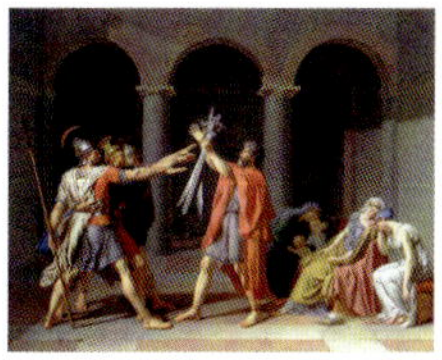

191 ***Oath of the Horatii***
Jacques-Louis David
Louvre, Paris

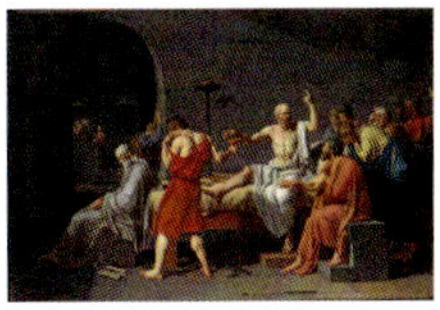

192 ***The Death of Socrates***
Jacques-Louis David
The Metropolitan Museum of Art, New York

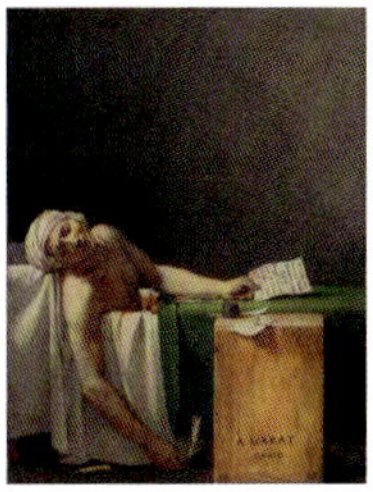

195 ***The Death of Marat***
Jacques-Louis David
Oldmasters Museum, Brussels

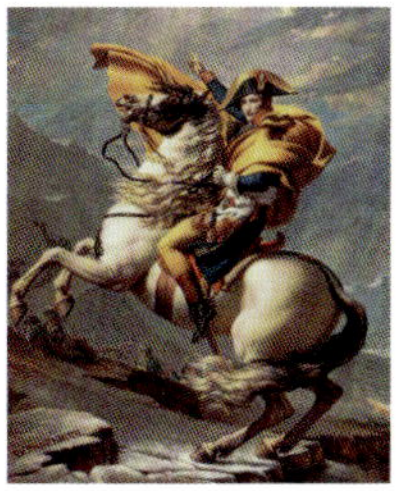

196 ***Napoleon Crossing the Alps***
Jacques-Louis David
Château de Malmaison, Rueil-Malmaison

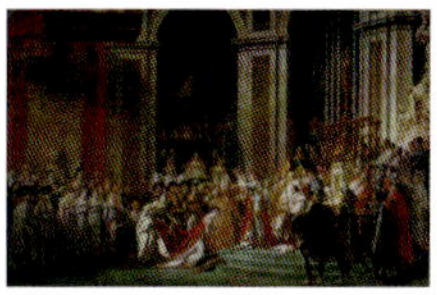

201 ***The Coronation of Napolean***
Vincent van Gogh
Louvre, Paris

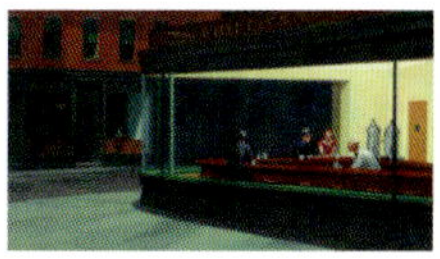

204 ***Nighthawks***
Edward Hopper
Art Institute of Chicago, Chicago

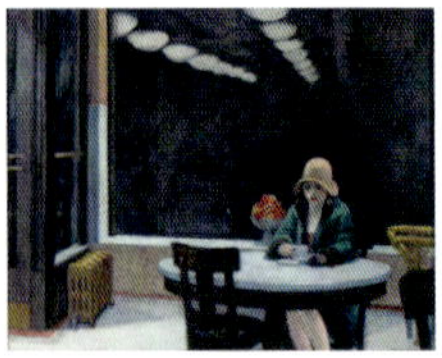

206 ***Automat***
Edward Hopper
Des Moines Art Center, Des Moines

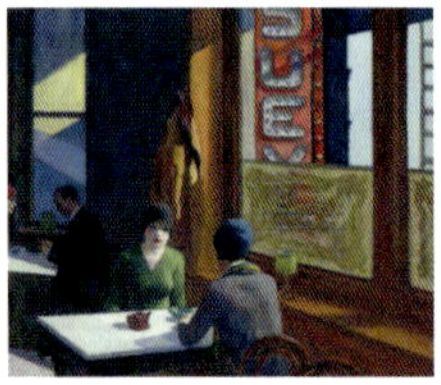

208 ***Chop Suey***
Edward Hopper
Private collection

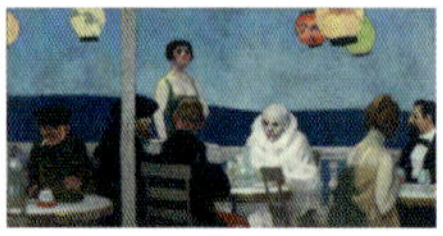

209 ***Soir Bleu***
Edward Hopper
Whitney Museum of American Art, New York

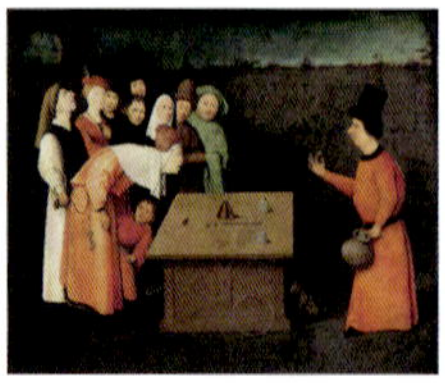

212 ***The Conjurer***
Hieronymus Bosch
Musée Municipal, Saint-Germain-en-Laye

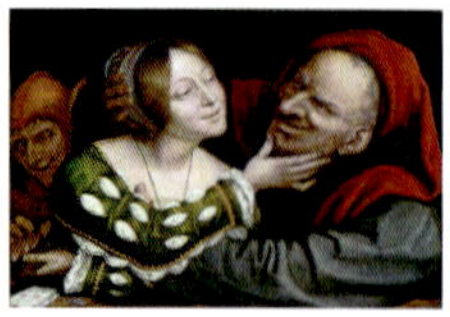

214 ***Ill-Matched Lovers***
Hieronymus Bosch
National Gallery of Art, Washington DC

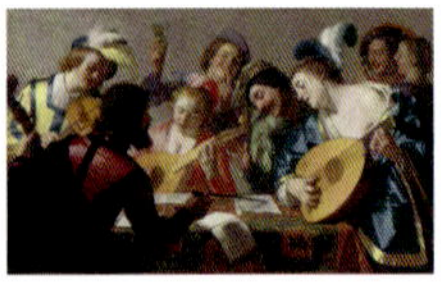

216 ***The Concert***
Gerrit van Honthorst
National Gallery of Art, Washington DC

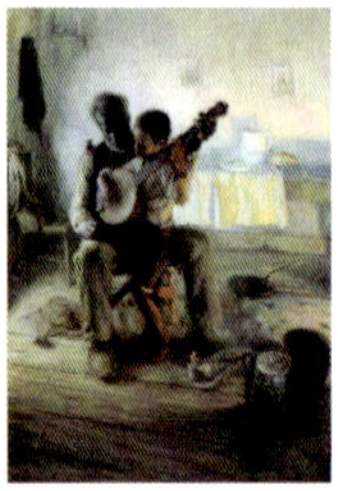

217 ***The Banjo Lesson***
Henry Ossawa Tanner
Hampton University Museum, Hampton

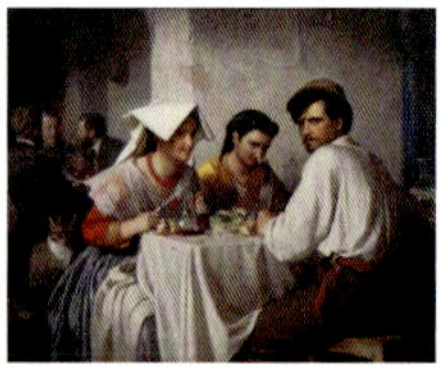

218 ***In a Roman Osteria***
Carl Bloch
Statens Museum for Kunst, Copenhagen

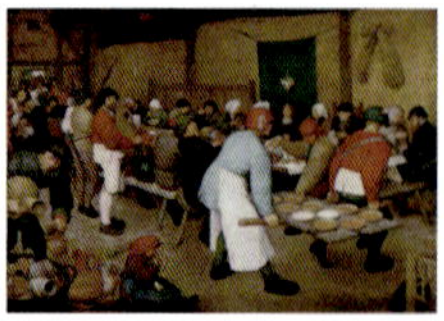

220 ***Peasant Wedding***
Pieter Bruegel the Elder
Kunsthistorisches Museum, Vienna

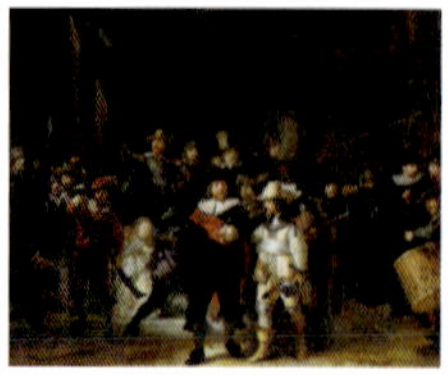

224 ***The Night Watch***
Rembrandt
Rijksmuseum, Amsterdam

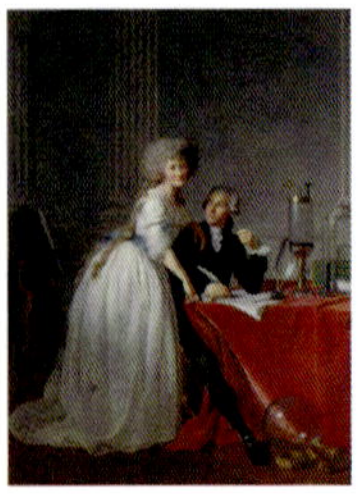

229 ***Antoine Laurent Lavoisier (1743–1794) and Marie Anne Lavoisier (Marie Anne Pierrette Paulze, 1758–1836)***
Jacques-Louis David
The Metropolitan Museum of Art, New York

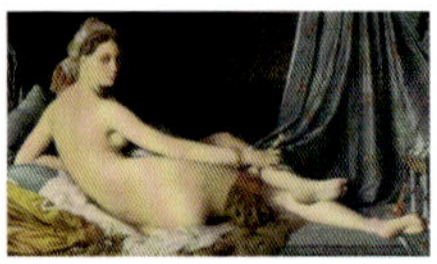

231 ***Grande Odalisque***
Jean Auguste Dominique Ingres
Louvre, Paris

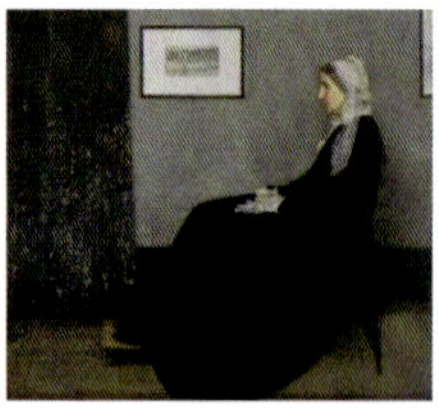

232 ***Arrangement in Grey and Black No. 1***
James McNeil Whistler
Musée d'Orsay, Paris

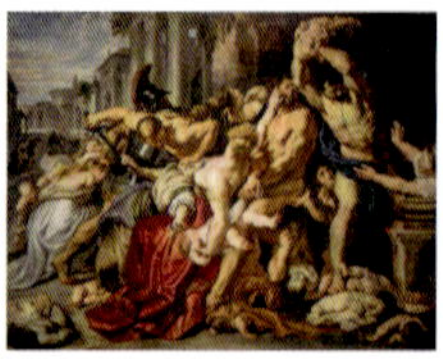

234 ***The Massacre of the Innocents***
Peter Paul Rubens
Art Gallery of Ontario, Toronto

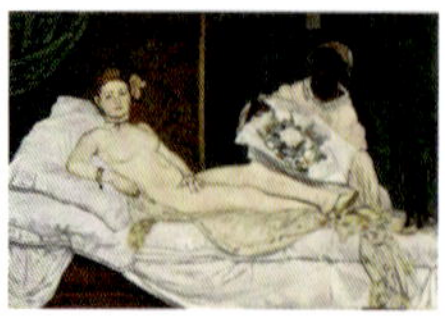

237 ***Olympia***
Édouard Manet
Musée d'Orsay, Paris

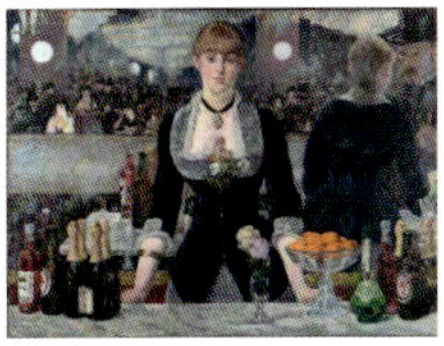

238 ***A Bar at the Folies-Bergère***
Édouard Manet
Courtauld Gallery, London

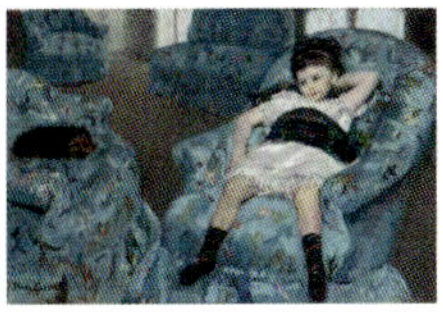

240 ***Little Girl in a Blue Armchair***
Mary Cassatt
National Gallery of Art, Washington DC

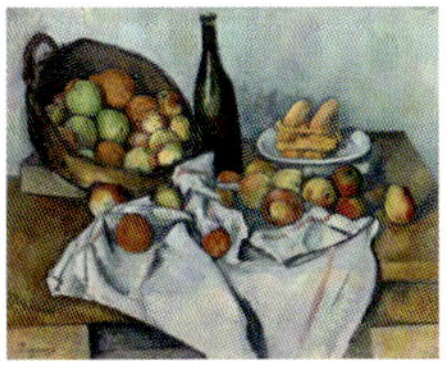

243 ***The Basket of Apples***
Paul Cézanne
Art Institute of Chicago, Chicago

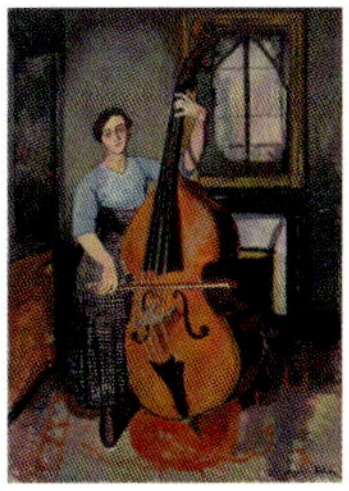

245 ***Woman with a Double Bass***
Suzanne Valadon
Private collection

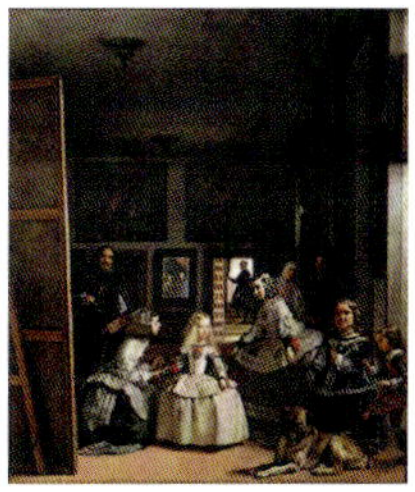

246 ***Las Meninas***
Diego Velázquez
Museo Nacional del Prado, Madrid

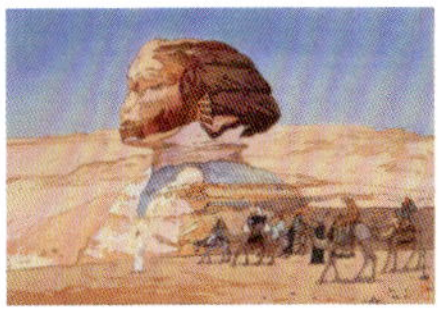

251 ***Sphinx, Day***
Yoshida Hiroshi
National Museum of Asian Art, Washington DC

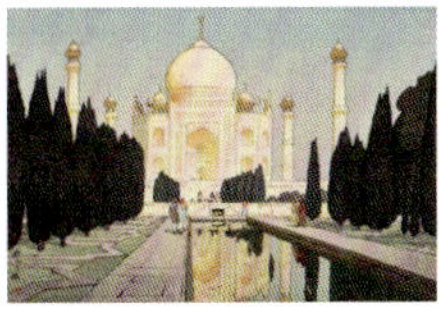

251 ***The Taj Mahal Gardens***
Yoshida Hiroshi
Various museums

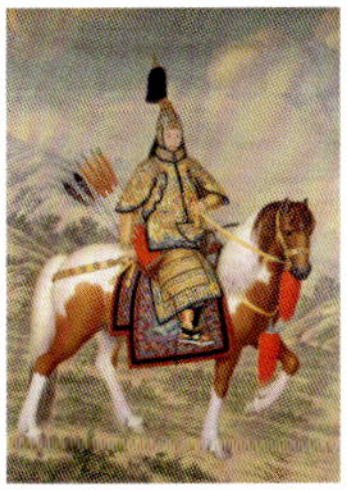

251 ***The Qianlong Emperor in Ceremonial Armor on Horseback***
Giuseppe Castiglione
Palace Museum, Beijing

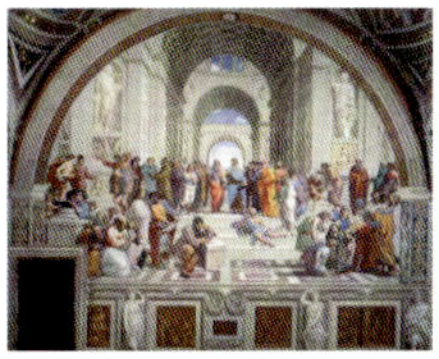

252 ***School of Athens***
Raphael
Stanza della Segnatura, Vatican City

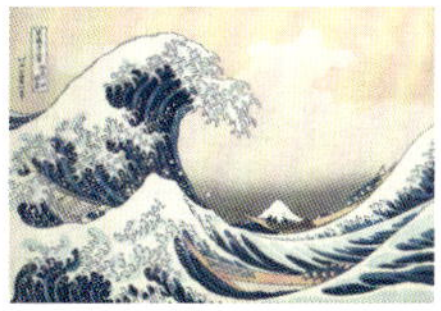

255 ***The Great Wave off Kanagawa***
Katsushika Hokusai
Various museums

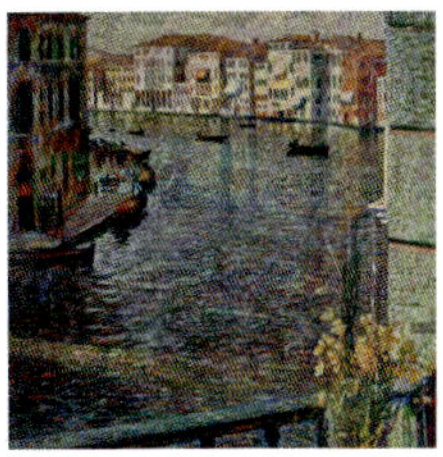

256 ***The Grand Canal in Venice***
Umberto Boccioni
Galleria Dello Scudo, Verona

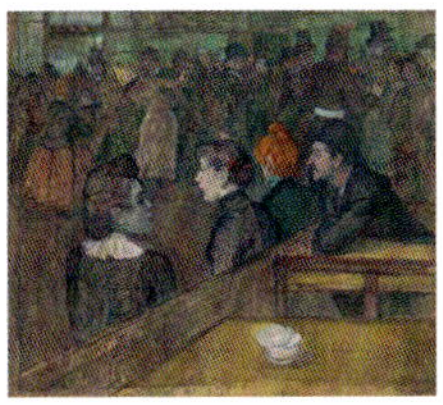

258 ***Moulin de la Galette***
Henri de Toulouse-Lautrec
Art Institute of Chicago, Chicago

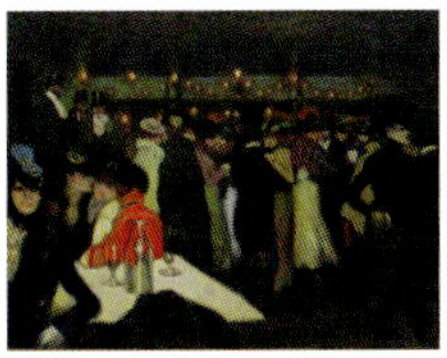

259 ***Le Moulin de la Galette***
Pablo Picasso
Solomon R. Guggenheim Museum, Thannhauser Collection, Gift, Justin K. Thannhauser, New York

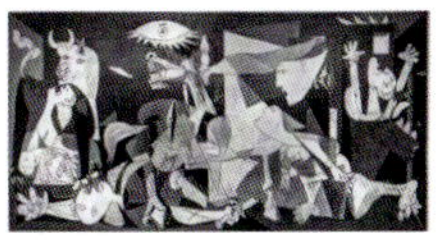

261 ***Guernica***
Pablo Picasso
Museo Nacional Centro de Arte Reina Sofía, Madrid

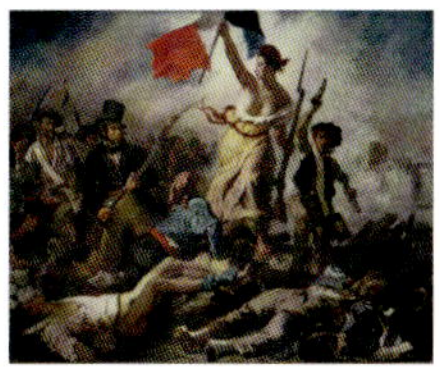

262 ***Liberty Leading the People***
Eugène Delacroix
Louvre, Paris

ABOUT THE AUTHOR

Matthew Olivier is an artist and author whose figurative paintings and essays on classical art draw on the discipline of the old masters to tell stories rooted in the present. Both his paintings and his writing are built slowly, layer by layer, and ask the same of the viewer: time, attention, and a willingness to look twice.

He is the creator of Codex Algorithm, an ongoing project that has grown into one of the most widely followed artworks in the world online, built on the conviction that great works of art still have urgent things to say to anyone willing to slow down and look. Through its digital presence, he has reached millions of people around the world who might never set foot in a museum, and has worked alongside many of the major institutions that shape how art is seen today.

The Art of Reading Art is his first book—a distillation of the project's central argument, and an invitation to learn the habits of attention that turn looking into seeing.

THE ART OF READING ART

This book is an artifact of Codex ALGORITHM

AUTHENTICATED · APRIL 2026

Smith Street Books

Published in 2026 by Smith Street Books
Naarm (Melbourne) | Australia
smithstreetbooks.com

Distributed outside of ANZ, North & Latin America by
Thames & Hudson Ltd., 6–24 Britannia Street, London, WC1X 9JD
thamesandhudson.com

EU Authorised Representative: Interart S.A.R.L.
19 rue Charles Auray, 93500 Pantin, Paris, France
productsafety@thameshudson.co.uk; www.interart.fr

ISBN: 978-1-9235-0333-5

Smith Street Books respectfully acknowledges the Wurundjeri People of the Kulin Nation, who are the Traditional Owners of the land on which we work, and we pay our respects to their Elders past and present.

Publisher: Paul McNally
Commissioning editor: Avery Hayes
Design concept: Daniel New
Design layout: Nikola Roberts
Proofreader: Katri Hilden
Production manager: Aisling Coughlan
Cover prepress: Megan Ellis
Text prepress: Splitting Image Colour Studio

Printed & bound in China by C&C Offset Printing Co., Ltd.

Book 481
10 9 8 7 6 5 4 3 2 1

FSC www.fsc.org MIX Paper | Supporting responsible forestry FSC® C008047